Tough Love: The European Union's Relations with the Western Balkans

To my parents

Tough Love:
The European Union's Relations with the Western Balkans

Steven Blockmans

T·M·C·Asser Press
The Hague

Published by T·M·C·ASSER PRESS
P.O.Box 16163, 2500 BD The Hague, The Netherlands
<www.asserpress.nl>

T·M·C·ASSER PRESS English language books are distributed exclusively by:

Cambridge University Press, The Edinburgh Building, Shaftesbury Road,
Cambridge CB2 2RU, UK,
or
for customers in the USA, Canada and Mexico:
Cambridge University Press, 100 Brook Hill Drive, West Nyack, NY 10994-2133, USA

<www.cambridge.org>

ISBN 978-90-6704-258-1

T.M.C. Asser Instituut - Institute for Private and Public International Law, International Commercial Arbitration and European Law
Institute Address: R.J. Schimmelpennincklaan 20-22, 2517 JN The Hague, The Netherlands; P.O. Box 30461, 2500 GL The Hague, The Netherlands; Tel.: (31-70)3420300; Fax: (31-70)3420359; URL: <www.asser.nl>.
Over forty years, the T.M.C. Asser Institute has developed into a leading scientific research institute in the field of international law. It covers private international law, public international law, including international humanitarian law, the law of the European Union, the law of international commercial arbitration and increasingly, also, international economic law, the law of international commerce and international sports law. Conducting scientific research either fundamental or applied, in the aforementioned domains, is the main activity of the Institute. In addition, the Institute organizes congresses and postgraduate courses, undertakes contract-research and operates its own publishing house, T.M.C.ASSER PRESS. Because of its inter-university background, the Institute often cooperates with Dutch law faculties as well as with various national and foreign institutions. The Institute organizes Asser College Europe, a project in cooperation with East and Central European countries whereby research and educational projects are organized and implemented.

PREFACE

The relations between the European Union and the Western Balkans form a theme with a deep historical background covered by many discussions and publications. It is striking to note that current legal and political academic literature has a tendency to deal with each Western Balkan country separately. In a region where all things seem related, this approach not only denies a more holistic understanding of the needs to effectively stabilise the Western Balkans but also obscures the international community's actions and ambitions in south-eastern Europe. It is my view that, pending the final status and constitutional settlements in the region, the European Union will have to take the lead in the international effort to see the defining processes through. It will have to adapt its policies and instruments to the new political, legal, economic and social environment and complement them with the expertise and tools of other international organisations in order to prevent the outbreak of fresh armed conflict and permanently stabilise the Western Balkans. Hence, it is useful to evaluate the international community's efforts at stabilisation, partnership and integration as applied to the Western Balkans. It is only by adopting a more interdisciplinary approach to studying the relations between the European security organisations and all the Western Balkan countries that one is able to offer insights into the linkages that exist between the different policies and the contractual relations that underpin them and to make suggestions how to better organise them. This book offers an academic analysis of the role and impact of the international community in the Western Balkans, primarily from an EU perspective.

This book is dedicated to all those who gave their time, insights and support during the production process. Much credit lies with my family and friends. The book is also a tribute to the memory of Professor Dr Hein Schermers, who was a fervent supporter of an all-encompassing approach to the theme. I benefited greatly from his advice in the preparatory stages of this study and thoroughly enjoyed discussing issues of 'South Slavia' with him. In the same vein, I would like to thank Professor Hanspeter Neuhold and Professor Christophe Hillion for their support. I would like to thank the colleagues at the T.M.C. Asser Institute for the opportunities to match my academic research with relevant project work in the Western Balkans. The research has greatly benefited from the insights gleaned from the commercial activities that I carried out in the region with people from the region. I would like to express my gratitude to the Director of the T.M.C. Asser Institute, Professor Frans Nelissen, for providing financial and logistical support for the production of this book. Special thanks go to Inge van Dun-van den Bosch and Daniel Stephens for editing and typesetting the manuscript.

Brussels, August 2007 Steven BLOCKMANS

TABLE OF CONTENTS

DETAILED TABLE OF CONTENTS

ABBREVIATIONS

AAK	Aleanca për Ardhmërinë e Kosovës (Alliance for the Future of Kosovo)
ACTORD	Activation Order
AFDI	Annuaire Français de Droit International
AII	Adriatic-Ionian Initiative
AJIL	American Journal of International Law
ASIL	American Society of International Law
AU	African Union
Australian YIL	Australian Yearbook of International Law
BBC	British Broadcasting Corporation
BiH	Bosnia-Herzegovina
BSEC	Black Sea Economic Cooperation
Bull. EC	Bulletin of the European Communities
Bull. EU	Bulletin of the European Union
BYIL	British Yearbook of International Law
CARDS	Community Assistance for Reconstruction, Development and Stabilisation
CBD	Center for Balkan Development
CDA	Christen Democratisch Appèl
CDDRL	Center on Democracy, Development and the Rule of Law
CDL	European Commission for Democracy through Law
CDU	Christlich Demokratische Union Deutschlands
CEE	Communauté économique européenne
CEEC	Central and Eastern European Countries
CEFTA	Central European Free Trade Agreement
CEI	Central European Initiative
CEPS	Centre for European Policy Studies
CFE	Conventional Armed Forces in Europe
CFI	Court of First Instance
CFSP	Common Foreign and Security Policy
CIA	Central Intelligence Agency
CiO	Chairman-in-Office
CIS	Commonwealth of Independent States
CMLR	Common Market Law Reports
CML Rev.	Common Market Law Review
CoE	Council of Europe
COM	European Commission document
COPS	Comité politique et de sécurité
Cornell ILJ	Cornell International Law Journal
COWEB	EU Council on the Western Balkans
CPC	Conflict Prevention Centre
CPE	Coopération politique européenne
CRS	Congressional Research Service
CSCE	Conference on Security and Cooperation in Europe

CSO	Committee of Senior Officials
CSU	Christlich Soziale Union in Bayern
DAV	Direktie Atlantische Samenwerking en Veiligheidheidszaken (Atlantic Cooperation and Security Affairs Department of the Netherlands Ministry of Foreign Affairs)
DG	Directorate General
DG ECFIN	Directorate General for Economic and Financial Affairs
DG ELARG	Directorate General for Enlargement
DG RELEX	Directorate General for External Relations
DOS	Democratic Opposition of Serbia
DPS	Democratic Party of Socialists
DRC	Democratic Republic of Congo
D-SACEUR	Deputy Supreme Allied Commander Europe
DSRSG	Deputy Special Representative of the Secretary-General
EA	Europe Agreement
EAEC	European Atomic Energy Community
EAPC	Euro-Atlantic Partnership Council
EAR	European Agency for Reconstruction
EBRD	European Bank for Reconstruction and Development
EC	European Community/Communities
ECAA	European Common Aviation Area
ECHO	European Community Humanitarian Aid Office
ECHR	European Convention for the Protection of Human Rights and Fundamental Freedoms
ECJ	European Court of Justice
ECMM	European Community Monitoring Mission
ECOSOC	Economic and Social Council
ECOWAS	Economic Community of West African States
ECR	European Court Reports
ECSC	European Coal and Steel Community
ECU	European Currency Unit
EEC	European Economic Community
EFA Rev.	European Foreign Affairs Review
EIB	European Investment Bank
EIDHR	European Initiative for Democracy and Human Rights
EIPA	European Institute of Public Administration
EJIL	European Journal of International Law
EL Rev.	European Law Review
ENP	European Neighbourhood Policy
ENPI	European Neighbourhood and Partnership Instrument
EP	European Parliament
EPC	European Political Cooperation
ESDP	European Security and Defence Policy
ESF	European Security Forum
ESI	European Stability Initiative
ESS	European Security Strategy
ETS	European Treaties Series
EU	European Union

EUAM	European Union Administration of Mostar
EUF	European Union-led Forces
EUFOR	European Union Force in Bosnia and Herzegovina
EU OHQ	EU Operation Headquarters
EUI	European University Institute, Florence
EUISS	European Union Institute for Security Studies
EUMC	European Union Military Committee
EUMM	European Union Monitoring Mission
EUPAT	EU Police Advisory Team
EUPM	European Union Police Mission
EUPOL	European Union Police Mission
EUPT	European Union Planning Team for Kosovo
EUSR	European Union Special Representative
EVRM	Europees Verdrag voor de Rechten van de Mens en Fundamentele Vrijheden
FAIFE	IFLA Committee on Free Access to Information and Freedom of Expression
FAO	Food and Agriculture Organisation
FBiH	Federacije Bosne i Hercegovine (Federation of Bosnia-Herzegovina)
FIDE	Fédération Internationale du Droit Européen
Finnish YIL	Finnish Yearbook of International Law
FRY	Federal Republic of Yugoslavia
FYROM	Former Yugoslav Republic of Macedonia
G-7	Canada, France, Germany, Italy, Japan, the United Kingdom and the United States of America
G-8	G-7 plus Russia
GA	General Assembly
GAERC	General Affairs and External Relations Council
GATT	General Agreement on Tariffs and Trade
GDP	gross domestic product
GIS	Geographic Information System
GMT	Greenwich Mean Time
GSP	Generalised System of Preferences
GSZ	Ground Safety Zone
HCNM	High Commissioner on National Minorities
HDZ	Hrvatska Demokratska Zajednica (Croatian Democratic Union)
HFUM	Helsinki Follow-Up Meeting
HLPM	High-Level Plenary Meeting
HQ	headquarters
HR	High Representative
HRW	Human Rights Watch
ICB	International Commission for the Balkans
ICFY	International Conference on the Former Yugoslavia
ICG	International Crisis Group
ICJ	International Court of Justice
ICLQ	International and Comparative Law Quarterly

ICM	International Civilian Mission
ICO	International Civilian Office
ICR	International Civilian Representative
ICRC	International Committee of the Red Cross
ICTY	International Criminal Tribunal for the former Yugoslavia
IFLA	International Federation of Library Associations and Institutions
IFOR	Implementation Force
IGC	Intergovernmental Conference
IHT	International Herald Tribune
ILF	International Law FORUM du droit international
ILM	International Legal Materials
IMF	International Monetary Fund
IMP	International Military Presence
IOLR	International organizations law review
IPA	Instrument for Pre-Accession Assistance
IPTF	International Police Task Force (UN)
ISPA	Instrument for Structural Policies for Pre-Accession
ISS	Institute for Security Studies
IWPR	Institute for War & Peace Reporting
JAT	Jugoslovensko Aviontransport
JCMS	Journal of Common Market Studies
JDW	Jane's Defence Weekly
JHA	Justice and Home Affairs (EU)
JNA	Jugoslovenska narodna armija (Yugoslav People's Army)
JT	Journal des tribunaux (Belgium)
KFOR	Kosovo Force
KLA	Kosovo Liberation Army
KPC	Kosovo Protection Corps
KPS	Kosovo Police Service
KSIP	Kosovo Standards Implementation Plan
KVAB	Koninklijke Vlaamse Academie van België voor Wetenschappen en Kunsten
KVM	Kosovo Verification Mission
LDK	Lidhja Demokratike e Kosovës (Democratic League of Kosovo)
LIEI	Legal Issues of European Integration
LJIL	Leiden Journal of International Law
LNTS	League of Nations Treaty Series
LSE	London School of Economics and Political Science
MAP	Membership Action Plan
MAPE	Multinational Advisory Police Element (UN - Albania)
MC	Ministerial Council
MEDA	Euro-Mediterranean Partnership
MEP	Member of the European Parliament
MINUK	Mission d'administration intérimaire des Nations Unies au Kosovo
MoU	Memorandum of Understanding
MTA	Military Technical Agreement

NAC	North Atlantic Council
NACC	North Atlantic Cooperation Council
NAT	North Atlantic Treaty
NATO	North Atlantic Treaty Organisation
NGO	non-governmental organisation
NHQSa	NATO Headquarters in Sarajevo
NJCM	Nederlands Juristen Comité voor de Mensenrechten
NLA	National Liberation Army
Nordic JIL	Nordic Journal of International Law
NPAA	National Programme for the Adoption of the *Acquis*
OAS	Organization of American States
OAU	Organization of African Unity
ODIHR	OSCE Office for Democratic Institutions and Human Rights
OECD	Organisation for Economic Cooperation and Development
OHR	Office of the High Representative
OJ	Official Journal of the European Communities/Union
OMIK	OSCE Mission in Kosovo
OMRI	Open Media Research Institute
OSCE	Organisation for Security and Cooperation in Europe
OSZE	Organisation für Sicherheit und Zusammenarbeit in Europa
OTAN	Organisation du Traité de l'Atlantique Nord
PACE	Parliamentary Assembly of the Council of Europe
PC	Permanent Council
PCA	Partnership and Cooperation Agreement
PDK	Partia Demokratike e Kosovës (Democratic Party of Kosovo)
PESC	Politique étrangère et de sécurité commune
PfP	Partnership for Peace
PHARE	Poland Hungary Assistance for the Reconstruction of the Economy
PIC	Peace Implementation Council
PISG	Provisional Institutions of Self-Government
PRST	presidential statement
PSC	Political and Security Committee
PSIO	Program for the study of international organization(s)
RBDI	Revue belge de droit international
RCC	Regional Cooperation Council
RdC	Recueil des cours
RGDIP	Revue Générale de Droit International Public
RNIS	Refugee Nutrition Information System
RRF	Rapid Reaction Force
RRM	Rapid Reaction Mechanism
RS	Republika Srpska
RSFY	République socialiste fédérale de Yougoslavie
RTDE	Revue Trimestrielle de Droit Européen
SAA	Stabilisation and Association Agreement
SAC	Stabilisation and Association Council
SaM	Serbia and Montenegro

SAO	Serbian Autonomous Oblast
SAP	Stabilisation and Association Process
SAPARD	Special Accession Programme for Agriculture and Rural Development
SC	Security Council
SDS	Serbian Democratic Party
SEC	European Commission documents which cannot be classified in any of the other series
SECI	Southeast European Cooperative Initiative
SEE	south-eastern Europe
SEECP	South-East Europe Cooperation Process
SEESP	South East European Studies Programme (Oxford University)
SEW	Sociaal Economische Wetgeving
SFOR	Stabilisation Force in Bosnia and Herzegovina
SFRY	Socialist Federal Republic of Yugoslavia
SG/HR	Secretary-General/High Representative
SHAPE	Supreme Headquarters Allied Powers Europe
SIPRI	Stockholm International Peace Research Institute
SNP	Socialist People's Party of Montenegro
SOFA	Status of Forces Agreement
SRSG	Special Representative of the Secretary-General
STM	SAP Tracking Mechanism
SWP	Stiftung Wissenschaft und Politik
TACIS	Technical Assistance to the Commonwealth of Independent States
TCE	Treaty establishing a Constitution for Europe
TEC	Treaty establishing the European Community
TEU	Treaty on European Union
UDHR	Universal Declaration of Human Rights
UK	United Kingdom
UN	United Nations
UNC	United Nations Charter
UNCRO	United Nations Confidence Restoration Operation
UNCTC	United Nations Centre on Transnational Corporations
UN Doc.	United Nations Documents
UNDP	United Nations Development Programme
UNDPI	United Nations Department of Public Information
UNESCO	United Nations Educational, Scientific and Cultural Organization
UNGA	United Nations General Assembly
UNHCR	United Nations High Commissioner for Refugees
UNMIBH	United Nations Mission in Bosnia and Herzegovina
UNMIK	United Nations Interim Administration Mission in Kosovo
UNMOP	United Nations Mission of Observers in Prevlaka
UNO	United Nations Organization
UNPA	United Nations Protected Area
UNPF	United Nations Peace Forces
UNPREDEP	United Nations Preventive Deployment Force
UNPROFOR	United Nations Protection Force
UNPSG	United Nations Police Support Group
UNSC	United Nations Security Council

UNSCR	United Nations Security Council Resolution
UNSG	United Nations Secretary-General
UNTAES	United Nations Transitional Authority in Eastern Slovenia
UNTS	United Nations Treaty Series
UPFM	Unified Police Force Mostar
US	United States
USD	US Dollar
VCLT	Vienna Convention on the Law of Treaties
Virginia JIL	Virginia Journal of International Law
WEU	Western European Union
WFP	World Food Programme
WIIW	Wiener Institut für Internationale Wirtschaftsvergleiche (Vienna Institute for International Economic Studies)
WTO	World Trade Organisation
ZaöRV	Zeitschrift für ausländisches öffentliches Recht und Völkerrecht
ZEI	Zentrum für Europäische Integrationsforschung

MAPS*

* Sources: Joint World Bank - European Commission Office for South East Europe (map of Western Balkans); University of Texas Libraries (all other maps).

Albania

Bosnia and Herzegovina

Croatia

Macedonia

Montenegro

Serbia

FACTS AND FIGURES

Croatia – Geographical and political profile

Official name	Republic of Croatia (Republika Hrvatska)
Independence	25 June 1991
Area	56,542 km²
Neighbouring countries	Bosnia and Herzegovina (932 km), Hungary (329 km), Serbia (241 km), Montenegro (25 km), Slovenia (670 km), coastline (5,835 km)
Population	4.5 million (2007, est.)
Density	78 inhabitants per km²
Distribution	53.3% urban population, 46.7% rural population (2002)
Population profile	Croat (89.6%), Serb (4.5%), Bosniak (0.47%), Hungarian (0.37%), Czech (0.34%), Slovene (0.3%), Roma (0.21%) (2001 census)
Languages	Croatian (96.1%), Serbian (1%), other, including Italian, Hungarian, Czech, Slovak and German (2.9%) (2001 census)
Religions	Roman Catholic (87.8%), Orthodox (4.4%), Muslim (1.3%), Protestant (0.3%), others (6.2%)
Life expectancy	Average: 74.9 years, male: 71.3 years, female: 78.8 years (2007 est.)
Main political parties in Parliament (152 seats)	HDZ - Croatian Democratic Union (63), SDP - Social Democratic Party (34), HNS - Croatian People's Party (11), HSS - Croatian Peasants' Party (9)
President	Stjepan (Stipe) MESIC (HNS, since 18 February 2000)
Prime Minister	Ivo SANADER (HDZ, since 9 December 2003)

Croatia – Economic profile

GDP	Approx. €27.6 billion (2004)
GDP per capita	€6,200 in purchasing power standards (48.86% of EU-25 average) (2004)
Economic growth	5.3% in 2003; 3.8% in 2004; 4.3% in 2005; 4.6% in 2006
Inflation rate	3.4% (2006 est.)
Unemployment rate	17.2% (2006 official)
Population below poverty line	11% (2003)
Currency	Kuna (HRK)
Government budget balance	-3.9% of GDP
Current account balance	-7.7% of GDP (second quarter of 2006, four quarter moving average)
Foreign debt	82.5% of GDP (end 2005)

Croatia – Economic profile (cont'd)

Natural resources	oil, some coal, bauxite, low-grade iron ore, calcium, gypsum, natural asphalt, silica, mica, clays, salt, hydropower
Agricultural products	wheat, sugar beets, sunflower seed, barley, alfalfa, clover, olives, citrus, grapes, soybeans, potatoes, livestock, dairy products
Industries	chemicals and plastics, machinery, fabricated metal, electronics, pig iron and rolled steel products, aluminium, paper, wood products, construction materials, textiles, shipbuilding, petroleum (refining), food and beverages, tourism
Export products	transport equipment, textiles, chemicals, foodstuffs, fuels
Import products	machinery, transport and electrical equipment, chemicals, fuels and lubricants, foodstuffs
Most prominent trading partners	Export: Italy 21.8%, Bosnia and Herzegovina 14.7%, Germany 10.7%, Slovenia 8.1%, Austria 7.3% (2005) Import: Italy 15.9%, Germany 14.9%, Russia 9.1%, Slovenia 6.8%, Austria 5.8%, China 4.7%, France 4.2% (2005)
Trade with the EU	Exports to the EU: 64% of total (€3.92 billion) (2005) Imports from the EU: 70% of total (€9.78 billion) (2005) Trade deficit = €5.86 billion

Macedonia – Geographical and political profile

Official name	The former Yugoslav Republic of Macedonia
Independence	8 September 1991
Area	25,333 km²
Neighbouring countries	Albania (151 km border), Serbia (221 km), Bulgaria (148 km), Greece (246 km), coastline (0 km)
Population	2.06 million (2007 est.)
Density	78.7 inhabitants per km²
Population profile	Macedonian (64.2%), Albanian (25.2%), Turkish (3.9%), Roma (2.7%), Serb (1.8%), Bosniak (0.8%), Vlach (0.5%), other (0.9%) (2002 census)
Languages	Macedonia (66.5%), Albania (25.1%), Turkish (3.5%), Serbia (1.2%), other (3.7%)
Religions	Orthodox (64.8%), Muslim (33.3%), other (1.9%) (2002 census)
Life expectancy	Average: 74.2 years, male: 71.7 years, female: 76.9 years (2007 est.)
Main political parties in Parliament (120 seats)	VMRO-DPMNE (VMRO-Democratic Party for Macedonia National Unity) (45), SDSM (Social Democratic Union of Macedonia) (32), BDI/DUI (Democratic Union of Integration) (17), PDSh-DPA (Democratic Party of Albanians) (11)
President	Branko CRVENKOVSKI (SDSM, since 12 May 2004)
Prime Minister	Nikola GRUEVSKI (VMRO-DPMNE, since 26 August 2006)

Macedonia – Economic profile

GDP	Approx. €4.3 billion (2004)
GDP per capita	€5,600 in purchasing power standards (25% of EU-25 average) (2004)
Economic growth	4.0% in 2005; 3.1% in 2006
Inflation rate	3% (2006 est.)
Unemployment rate	37.3% (2005 ILO definition)
Population below poverty line	30% (2005)
Currency	Macedonian Denar (MKD)
Government budget balance	2005 budget surplus: 0.3% of GDP (general government)
Current account balance	-1.4% of GDP (2005)
Foreign debt	38% of GDP (natura, August 2006)
Natural resources	low-grade iron ore, copper, lead, zinc, chromite, manganese, nickel, tungsten, gold, silver, asbestos, gypsum, timber, arable land
Agricultural products	grapes, wine, tobacco, vegetables, milk, eggs
Industries	food processing, beverages, textiles, chemicals, iron, steel, cement, energy, pharmaceuticals
Export products	food, beverages, tobacco, textiles, miscellaneous manufactures, iron and steel
Import products	machinery and equipment, automobiles, chemicals, fuels, food products
Most prominent trading partners	Export: Serbia and Montenegro 22.5%, Germany 17.8%, Greece 15.3%, Italy 8.3% (2005) Import: Russia 13.2%, Germany 10.4%, Greece 9.2%, Serbia and Montenegro 8.2%, Bulgaria 7.3%, Italy 6% (2005)
Trade with the EU	Exports to the EU: 52.3% of total (2004) Imports from the EU: 64.4% of total (2004)

Albania – Geographical and political profile

Official name	Republic of Albania
Independence	28 November 1912
Area	28,748 km²
Neighbouring countries	Greece (282 km), FYROM (151 km), Montenegro (172 km), Serbia (115 km), coastline (362 km)
Population	3.6 million (2007 est.)
Density	109 inhabitants per km²
Distribution	44% urban population, 56% in rural areas
Population profile	Albania (95%), Greek (3%), other (2%) (Vlach, Roma, Serb, Macedonian, Bulgarian) (1989 est.)

Albania – Geographical and political profile (cont'd)

Languages	Albanian, Greek, Vlach, Romani, Slavic dialects
Religions	Muslim (70%), Albanian Orthodox (20%), Roman Catholic (10%) (est.)
Life expectancy	Average: 77.6 years, male: 74.9 years, female: 80.5 years (2007 est.)
Main political parties in Parliament (140 seats)	Democratic Party (56), Socialist Party (42), Republican Party (11), Party of Social Democracy (7), Liberal Union Party (5), other (19)
President	Alfred MOISIU (DP, since 24 June 2002)
Prime Minister	Sali BERISHA (SP, since 10 September 2005)

Albania – Economic profile

GDP	Approx. €5.4 billion (2004)
GDP per capita	€3,983 in purchasing power standards (8% of EU-25 average) (2003 est.)
Economic growth	3.4% in 2002; 6.0% in 2003; 6.3% in 2004; 5% in 2006
Inflation rate	2.4% in 2003; 3.4% in 2004; 2.5% in 2006
Unemployment rate	13.8% (2006, official)
Population below poverty line	25%
Currency	Lek
Government budget balance	-4.9% of GDP (2004)
Current account balance	-6.0% of GDP (2004)
Foreign debt	20.2% of GDP (2003)
Natural resources	petroleum, natural gas, coal, bauxite, chromite, copper, iron ore, nickel, salt, timber, hydropower
Agricultural products	wheat, corn, potatoes, vegetables, fruits, sugar beets, grapes, meat, dairy products
Industries	food processing, textiles and clothing, lumber, oil, cement, chemicals, mining, basic metals, hydropower
Export products	textiles and footwear, asphalt, metals and metallic ores, crude oil, vegetables, fruits, tobacco
Import products	machinery and equipment, foodstuffs, textiles, chemicals
Most prominent trading partners	Export: Italy 72.4%, Greece 10.5%, Serbia and Montenegro 5% (2005) Import: Italy 29.3%, Greece 16.4%, Turkey 7.5%, China 6.6%, Germany 5.4%, Russia 4% (2005)
Trade with the EU	Exports to EU-25: €1.11 million (2003) Imports from EU-25: €368 million (90%) (2003) Trade deficit = €393 million

Bosnia-Herzegovina – Geographical and political profile

Official name	Bosnia and Herzegovina
Independence	1 March 1992
Entities	Federation of BiH, Republika Srpska, Brcko district
Area	51,129 km²
Neighbouring countries	Croatia (932 km), Montenegro (225 km), Serbia (302 km), coastline (20 km)
Population	4.5 million (2007 est.)
Density	71 inhabitants per km² (est.)
Distribution	43% urban population, 57% rural population (est.)
Population profile	Bosniak (48%), Serb (37.1%), Croat (14.3%), other 0.6% (2000 est.)
Languages	Bosnian, Croatian, Serbian
Religions	Muslim (40%), Orthodox (31%), Catholic (15%), Protestant (4%), other (10%) (est.)
Life expectancy	Average: 78.2 years, male: 74.6 years, female: 82.0 years (2007 est.)
Main political parties in the House of Representatives (42 seats)	Party for Democratic Action (SDA, Bosniak) (9), Party for Bosnia and Herzegovina (SBiH, Bosniak) (8), Party of Independent Social Democrats (SNSD, Serb) (7), Social Democratic Party of Bosnia and Herzegovina (SDP BiH, multi-ethnic) (5), Croatian Democratic Union of Bosnia and Herzegovina (HDZ, Croat) (3), Serb Democratic Party (SDS, Serb) (3), Croat Democratic Union 1990 (HDZ 1990, Croat) (2)
Presidency (rotating)	Nebojsa RADMANOVIC (Serb), Haris SILAJDZIC (Bosniak) and Zeljko KOMSIC (Croat) (since November 2006)
Prime Minister BiH	Nikola SPIRIC (since 11 January 2007)
Prime Minister RS	Milorad DODIK (since November 2006)
Prime Minister FBiH	Nedzad BRANKOVIC (since March 2007)

Bosnia-Herzegovina – Economic profile

GDP	Approx. €7.5 billion (2005)
GDP per capita	€933 (2005)
Economic growth	6% (2006 est.)
Inflation rate	8.2% (2006, following the introduction of VAT)
Unemployment rate	45.5% (2005, official); 25-30% (2005, ILO standards)
Population below poverty line	25%
Currency	Convertible Mark (KM)
Government budget balance	+0.9% of GDP (2005)
Current account balance	-21.7% of GDP (2005)

Bosnia-Herzegovina – Economic profile (cont'd)

Foreign debt	29% of GDP (2005)
Natural resources	coal, iron ore, bauxite, copper, lead, zinc, chromite, cobalt, manganese, nickel, clay, gypsum, salt, sand, forests, hydropower
Agricultural products	wheat, corn, fruits, vegetables, livestock
Industries	steel, coal, iron ore, lead, zinc, manganese, bauxite, vehicle assembly, textiles, tobacco products, wooden furniture, tank and aircraft assembly, domestic appliances, oil refining
Export products	metals, clothing, wood products
Import products	machinery and equipment, chemicals, fuels, foodstuffs
Most prominent trading partners	Exports: Croatia 18.4%, Italy 17.1%, Slovenia 14.7%, Germany 12.8%, Austria 6.5%, Hungary 5.2%, China 4.2% (2005) Imports: Croatia 24.7%, Germany 13.6%, Slovenia 13%, Italy 11%, Austria 6.9%, Hungary 5.5% (2005)
Trade with the EU	Exports to EU-25: €1.3 billion (2005) Imports from the EU-25: €2.7 billion (2005)

Montenegro – Geographical and political profile

Official name	Republic of Montenegro
Independence	3 June 2006
Area	14,026 km²
Neighbouring countries	Albania (172 km), Croatia (25 km), Bosnia-Herzegovina (225 km), Serbia (203 km), coastline (293.5 km)
Population	684,736 (July 2007 est.)
Density	44.9 inhabitants per km² (est.)
Distribution	60% urban population, 40% rural population
Population profile	Montenegrin (43%), Serb (32%), Bosniak (8%), Albanian (5%), Muslim (4%), Croat (1.1%), other (4.3%)
Languages	Serbian (official; Ijekavian dialect), Bosnian, Albanian, Croatian
Religions	Orthodox, Muslim, Catholic
Life expectancy	Average: 72.5 years, male: 71 years, female: 74 years
Main political parties in Parliament (81 seats)	Coalition for European Montenegro (DPS/SDP) (39), Serbian List (12), Coalition SNP/NS/DSS (11), Movement for Changes (PZP) (11), Liberals and Bosniaks (3), Albanian minority parties (5)
President	Filip VUJANOVIC (since 11 May 2003)
Prime Minister	Zeljko STURANOVIC (since 13 November 2006)

Montenegro – Economic profile

GDP	€1.67 billion (2006 est.)
GDP per capita	€2,950 in purchasing power standards (2006 est.)
Economic growth	6.5% in 2006

CHAPTER 1

THE EUROPEAN UNION'S ROUGHEST NEIGHBOURHOOD

1. INTRODUCTION

The decomposition of the Socialist Federal Republic of Yugoslavia (SFRY) has been one of the most tragic events in Europe since the end of World War II. After almost fifty years of peace, war returned to the south-eastern corner of Europe, exactly at a time when twelve Western European countries redefined their organised cooperation with the establishment of the European Union, characterised by prosperity, democracy and ever closer integration.

From the very beginning of the 'Yugoslav' crisis, after the outbreak of war in Slovenia and Croatia in 1991, the European Communities (EC), and later the European Union (EU), were at the forefront of international efforts to stop the escalation of the armed conflict. But even if some heralded that 'the hour of Europe ha[d] dawned',[1] the crisis arrived at the wrong moment for the European Communities.[2] While the EC had developed itself into a powerful trading bloc, foreign affairs, let alone international security issues, still remained largely outside the ambit of its competences. Although the Single European Act, in Article 30, had established the first legal basis for cooperation in the field of foreign and (non-military) security policy, the legal foundations for a more comprehensive Common Foreign and Security Policy (CFSP) were still being negotiated in the framework of the pre-Maastricht Intergovernmental Conference (IGC). After Maastricht and throughout the rest of the 1990s, the European Union remained what it was once famously compared to by Belgian Minister of State Mark Eijskens: 'an economic giant, political mouse and military worm'.[3] The instruments through which the European Union could wield real influence were largely economic, and only to a much lesser extent diplomatic and political, but

[1] Declaration by J. Poos, Luxembourg's Foreign Minister, to the international press, 29 June 1991.

[2] See T. de Wilde d'Estmael, *La dimension politique des relations économiques extérieures de la Communauté européenne: sanctions et incitants économiques comme moyens de politique étrangère* (Brussels, Émile Bruylant 1998) at pp. 282-283: 'Si l'heure de l'Europe avait en apparence sonné, les Douze furent bien incapables d'assumer toutes les obligations du rendez-vous, tant en raison de la faiblesse des moyens de persuasion de la CPE/PESC que les divergences entre Etats membres sur la politique à mener. D'où l'émergence de ce syndrome d'autant plus aigu que la faillite européenne eut de tragiques conséquences à Dubrovnik, Vukovar, Sarajevo, Srebrenica, [...] Ce n'était toutefois pas faute d'avoir essayé.'

[3] M. Eyskens, *Bron en horizon. Het avondland uit de impasse* (Leuven, Lannoo 1985) at p. 316.

by no means military in nature. The lack of a comprehensive set of instruments to address the violent conflicts in the former Yugoslavia may well explain why the autonomous efforts of the European Union were sometimes partially successful but failed miserably to attain their objectives.

Then again, the disintegrative violence which seems so characteristic of the Western Balkans – captured in the generic terms 'balkanisation' or 'balkanism'[4] – is hard to contain in either time or space. Up till now, no single country or universal or regional organisation has been capable of preventing or solving a conflict in the Balkans by itself. So far, this has only been achieved through cooperation between several functionally specialised organisations. The United Nations, the North Atlantic Treaty Organisation (NATO), the Western European Union (WEU), the European Union, the Organisation for Security and Cooperation in Europe (OSCE) and the Council of Europe (CoE), to name just a few, have all made mutually reinforcing contributions towards creating a stable and secure environment in the Balkans. But, sadly, cooperation between these international organisations has not prevented the outbreak of two of Europe's gravest conflicts since the end of World War II in Bosnia-Herzegovina and Kosovo.[5] And while NATO's single-handed armed intervention in Kosovo did bring a temporary conclusion to the ten-year ethnic-territorial decomposition of Yugoslavia, it did not eliminate any of the fundamental socio-economic and political threats to the stability of South-Eastern Europe.

Whether or not they have been directly involved in conflict during the last fifteen years, the post-Communist societies of the Western Balkans still face widespread organised crime, high levels of unemployment and the displacement of tens of thousands of persons. While the worst affected areas are Bosnia-Herzegovina and Kosovo, no part of the region is untouched by the social distortion that has accompanied the disintegrative violence of the Yugoslav wars of the 1990s. Bosnia-Herzegovina and Kosovo can be described as the epicentres. Their 'gangster economies' have radiated outwards through networks of refugees, arms smugglers, money launderers, black market traders and drug, organ and

---

[4] For a critique of the use of these generic terms, see M. Todorova, *Imagining the Balkans* (Oxford, Oxford University Press 1997); J. Stilhoff Sörensen, 'Balkanism and the New Radical Interventionism: A Structural Critique', 9 *International Peacekeeping* (2002) pp. 1-22. For a nuanced analysis, see I. Kadare, 'The Balkans: Truths and Untruths', in D. Triantaphyllou, ed., 'The Southern Balkans: Perspectives from the Region', 46 *Chaillot Papers* (2001) pp. 5-16.

[5] For an analysis of the effectiveness of the European security architecture in these crises and proposals to improve the functioning of the system, see, e.g., J. Wouters and F. Naert, 'How Effective is the European Security Architecture? Lessons from Bosnia and Kosovo', 50 *ICLQ* (2001) pp. 540-576; and H. Neuhold, 'Collective Security After "Operation Allied Force"', in J. Frowein and R. Wolfrum, eds., *Max Planck Yearbook of United Nations Law* (2000) pp. 73-106. More generally, see N.M. Blokker and H.G. Schermers, eds., *Proliferation of International Organizations: Legal Issues* (The Hague, Kluwer Law International 2001).

people traffickers.[6] Both territories are surrounded by (largely overlapping) concentric circles of more or less war-affected societies. Hence, there is an inner ring of Croatia, Serbia, Montenegro and Macedonia, which are similarly affected; then Slovenia, where after 'only' ten days of war transition by peaceful means and political consolidation has gone further; then Albania, Romania and Bulgaria, where the consequences of the wars only became visible later; and, finally, there is an outer ring consisting of Member States of the European Union (most notably Greece, Austria, Hungary, Italy and Germany) and Turkey, which have not been able to prevent the influx of refugees and the spread of organised crime.

Fuelled by the above-mentioned socio-economic and political threats to stability, the recurring ethnically motivated violence in Kosovo[7] and the repeated calls for independence by political leaders of the Republika Srpska in Bosnia-Herzegovina[8] are reminders that further changes to parts of the region's composition should not be excluded. Any stable, long-term settlement in the Western Balkans will not be possible until all ethnic-territorial and constitutional disputes are resolved. In an attempt to reach agreement between Belgrade and Priština on the final status of Kosovo, the international community has opened what is potentially the most explosive of Pandora's many Balkan boxes.[9] If mismanaged, the outcome of the final status talks could spark Serbian irredentism, have a ruinous impact on the weak state of Bosnia-Herzegovina and push Albanian nationalists across the region to create a 'Greater Albania', thereby also threatening the precarious stability in Macedonia.[10] In short, an imposed solution on the

---

6 See M. Kaldor, V. Bojičić and I. Vejvoda, 'Reconstruction in the Balkans: A Challenge for Europe?', 2 *EFA Rev.* (1997) pp. 329-350 at pp. 330 and 333. See also V. Gligorov, M. Kaldor and L. Tsoukalis, 'Balkan Reconstruction and European Integration', *WIIW Policy Paper* (October 1999); M. Emerson, 'Perspectives for the Balkans and a Wider European Order', paper presented at the WIIW/LSE Conference on 'Reconstruction and Integration in South-Eastern Europe: Economic Aspects', Vienna, 12-13 November 1999; and M. Pugh, 'Postwar Political Economy in Bosnia and Herzegovina: The Spoils of Peace', 8 *Global Governance* (2002) pp. 467-482.

7 In March 2004, nineteen died in anti-Serb riots in Kosovo. Since then there have been several highly publicised security incidents that affected Kosovo Serbs but were 'not necessarily' of an inter-ethnic nature, although they were denounced as such by some Kosovo Serb leaders and the Serbian authorities. See the briefing of the UN Secretary-General's Special Representative for Kosovo to the Security Council, UN Doc. SC/8827, 13 September 2006, and the Report of the Secretary-General on the United Nations Interim Administration Mission in Kosovo, UN Doc. S/2006/906, 20 November 2006.

8 In the wake of the pro-independence referendum results in Montenegro of 21 May 2006, Bosnian Serb leaders renewed calls for the independence of Republika Srpska. They did so again in the run-up to the general elections of 1 October 2006 and in view of a possible declaration of independence by Kosovo. See 'Fragmented Bosnia urged to restart pro-EU reforms', *BBC News*, 24 October 2006, and 'Ivanic: independence of Kosovo could cause a chain reaction', *seeurope.net*, 14 November 2006.

9 On the final status talks, see chapter 4, section 3.3.

10 The notion of irredentism refers to cross-border nationalist agitation, based on historical, ethnic, and other reasons, for the incorporation of land. See, e.g., T. Musgrave, *Self-Determination and National Minorities* (Oxford, Oxford University Press 2000) ch. 9.

status of Kosovo that is not supported by the main parties to the dispute could create a potentially violent domino effect in the whole region. Hence, the critical mass for security stabilisation in the Western Balkans lies at the junction of Serbian-Albanian interests.[11]

To fill the relative 'black hole' on the map of South-Eastern Europe[12] with conflict-controlling and resolving mechanisms, and to create a belt of security, stability and prosperity stretching from Ireland in the west to Greece in the south-east, the European Union has, for some years now, committed itself to a strategy designed to favour a progressive process of socio-economic stabilisation and association of Albania, Bosnia-Herzegovina, Croatia, Macedonia, Montenegro and Serbia (including Kosovo). Add to this the recent establishment of a real and credible Common Foreign and Security Policy towards the Western Balkans and the launching of the first-ever EU missions in the framework of the European Security and Defence Policy (ESDP), and every self-respecting Europhile would be tempted to conclude that what we are witnessing is nothing less than the emergence of the first international organisation that is able to adopt, all by itself, a comprehensive strategy for the stabilisation of the Western Balkans. If this were really the case, then this would of course be a welcome development in the improvement of the European security architecture, especially in cases where other international players, such as the United Nations, NATO, the OSCE and the United States are unwilling or unable to act.

2. THESIS

Mismanagement of the remaining ethnic-territorial and constitutional issues in the Western Balkans could have severe and destabilising consequences, including a greater likelihood of political extremism, an increase in organised crime and other illegal economic activities, terrorism, armed conflict and further human displacement. New headline-grabbing violence will bring home to the international community what has been common knowledge in the region for some time: the ethnic-territorial status quo is unsustainable in parts of the Western Balkans.[13] Another episode of war, however limited, would be devastating for the region and beyond. It would also amount to a policy failure with damaging implications for

---

[11] See M. Hadzić, 'Kosovo and the Security Stabilization of South-East Europe', 7 *International Peacekeeping* (2000) pp. 83-94; D. Triantaphyllou, ed., *What Status for Kosovo?* (Paris, ISS 2001); and P. Jureković, ed., *Building Stability in Weak States: The Western Balkans* (Vienna, National Defence Academy 2002).

[12] See the map on p. xxiii.

[13] See, *inter alia*, International Commission on the Balkans, *The Balkans in Europe's Future* (Sofia, Centre for Liberal Strategies 2005) at p. 10.

the international organisations active in the region, in particular the European Union. Relapsing into violence can be avoided when sustainable solutions are found for the remaining status and constitutional issues and the region as a whole is moved from the stage of international protectorates and weak states to the stage of accession to NATO and the European Union. This scenario not only presupposes a reinvigorated drive for reform by the countries concerned but also presumes a continued, albeit reconfigured and rebalanced, engagement by the Euro-Atlantic security organisations.

The chief argument of this study is that, of all the international organisations that are active in the Western Balkans, the European Union possesses most of the mechanisms and the requisite political skills to face up to the challenges that the region will present over the next couple of years. The European Union does not only sport a unique combination of competences in the fields of policy, law, economics and security; it also has the money, interest and political will to stabilise the roughest of its neighbourhoods. Moreover, the European Union has the power of attraction. In the region, it is often criticised but never rejected, unlike other international organisations, as the countries of the Western Balkans all want to attain membership of this Union characterised by prosperity, democracy and peace. The prospect of future EU membership offers them a strategic objective and acts as the most powerful incentive for reform. Because the Union is best placed and has the greatest moral obligation to stabilise the Western Balkans, it carries the heaviest responsibility to see the process of stabilisation, association and integration through. It is in its own interest. The European Union admitted as much in its European Security Strategy (ESS): 'the credibility of our foreign policy depends on the consolidation of our achievements [in the Western Balkans].'[14] In other words, if the Union fails to 'brusselise' the Western Balkans, then 'Brussels' risks being 'balkanised'. Hence, the Union should put its (wo)men and money where its mouth is, because success in the Western Balkans is not guaranteed. In the absence of a panacea, a policy of 'tough love' is probably best to secure a positive outcome of the process. As much as the European Union

[14] *A Secure Europe in a Better World – European Security Strategy*, Brussels, 12 December 2003, at p. 8: 'Our task is to promote a ring of well-governed countries to the east of the European Union and on the borders of the Mediterranean with whom we can enjoy close and cooperative relations. The importance of this is best illustrated in the Balkans. Through our concerted efforts with the US, Russia, NATO and other international partners, the stability of the region is no longer threatened by the outbreak of major conflict.' The European Council adopted the European Security Strategy (ESS) on 12 December 2003. See *Bull. EU* 12-2003, point I.32.83. On the ESS in more general terms, see, e.g., R. Kissack, 'The European Security Strategy: A First Appraisal', 2 *CFSP Forum* (2004) pp. 19-20; S. Duke, 'The European Security Strategy in a Comparative Framework: Does it Make for Secure Alliances in a Better World?', 9 *EFA Rev.* (2004) pp. 459-481; A. Bailes, *The European Security Strategy. An Evolutionary History* (Stockholm, SIPRI 2005); and S. Biscop, *The European Security Strategy – A Global Agenda for Positive Power* (Aldershot, Ashgate Publishing 2005).

needs to enhance its presence in the Western Balkans, it ought to be firm but fair in monitoring the transition process in each country of the region. Consistency, as well as coherence, is crucial.[15] The Union should make it clear that countries will gain rewards if they meet tough conditions and that rewards will be denied or withdrawn if they lapse back into bad habits. In fact, this is what the Union is doing in the Western Balkans: with a special brand of conditionality, it provides the 'carrots and sticks' to ensure that the countries of the region continue on the path of progress and reform.

That is not to say that the European Union's record is flawless or, even less, that the Union should go it alone in the Western Balkans. The European Union does not have the same level of expertise and experience in fields in which other international organisations have specialised. Moreover, it cannot afford to devote most of its resources to the Western Balkans, to the detriment of other foreign policy goals. And it cannot risk falling prey to the negative consequences of being the sole security institution in the region. The Western Balkans would be better helped if the European Union were to take the lead in a revamped international effort to stabilise the region, in particular in Bosnia-Herzegovina and Kosovo. The Union should act under the authority of the United Nations and in harmony with NATO, the OSCE, the Council of Europe and other international players to increase the effectiveness of its civilian and military presence on the ground. Also, the European Union should devise a bolder accession strategy that could encompass all Western Balkan countries as new members within the next decade.[16] Failure to do so could result in a costlier and more dangerous intervention down the line and act as an unnecessary irritant in international relations.

---

[15] Art. 3 TEU states: 'The Union shall in particular ensure the consistency of its external activities as a whole in the context of its external relations, security, economic and development policies. The Council and the Commission shall be responsible for ensuring such consistency and shall cooperate to this end. They shall ensure the implementation of these policies, each in accordance with its respective powers.' More specifically, the ESS calls for a more coherent security policy regionally, especially when dealing with conflict. ESS, at p. 13.

[16] The third International Commission on the Balkans (ICB) has called on the European Union to demonstrate that a new European century will have arrived in Sarajevo on 28 June 2014, one hundred years to the day after Europe entered a century of madness and self-destruction. See ICB, op cit. n. 13, at p. 6. The Carnegie Endowment for International Peace sent a first international commission composed of six respected and influential individuals from different countries to the Balkans to report on the causes and conduct of the 1912 and 1913 wars. It was in much the same spirit that the second ICB was created in response to the violent break-up of the former Yugoslavia and the ferocity of the wars. For the background, composition and objectives of the ICB, see ibid., at pp. 3-4.

3. AIMS, METHODOLOGY, STRUCTURE

Legal and political issues arising out of any approach adopted to deal with the dissolution of states, the emergence of new ones and the stabilisation of relations within and between them require a thorough understanding of the relevant facts. While it is obvious that any academic discourse must proceed from firm factual foundations, it is necessary to emphasise the importance of the circumstantial dimensions of the issues at stake, given that the views on the pertinent facts usually diverge, especially during the policy-making stage. The assessment of facts is much easier from an historical distance.[17] Nobody today questions the wisdom of recognising the dissolution of the Spanish colonial empire in Latin America, or the independence of Greece from Ottoman rule. These events belong to history and have a comfortable place in contemporary textbooks on international relations. At the time, however, they were highly controversial political issues and contributed considerably to the collapse of the prevailing international system. Therefore, it seems necessary to recognise that the 'facts' and 'policy matters' concerning the dissolution and creation of states contain an important contextual – historical, geographical, religious, cultural, legal and even linguistic – dimension. Hence the importance of including maps (pp. xxiii-xxvi), essential statistical data (pp. xxvii-xxxvi), a chronology of crucial events (pp. 337-366) and an attempt to define key terminology (sections 4 and 5 below).

This study is an attempt to assess the role and impact of the international community's legal and political instruments and actions in stabilising the Western Balkans. As such, it deals with a series of topics and countries which, more often than not, are discussed in isolation in both time and space. In doing so, the analysis takes a 'tough love' attitude towards conflict prevention, crisis management and peacebuilding, paying particular attention to measures that strengthen those who pursue moderation and modernisation, while weakening those who espouse stagnation and extremism. The aim of this book is to craft realistic recommendations targeted at making the stabilisation efforts of the international community in the Western Balkans more effective. While trying not to resort to a series of moralising 'musts', the recommendations focus on a wise use of the resources in the interest of both the Western Balkans and the international community: preventing the region from becoming a vacuum in which organised crime and terrorism prevail and poverty and violence fuel migration to the

---

17 Although, as Rebecca West (the British-Irish author who wrote an epic 1,181-page travelogue, largely pro-Serb in its point of view, giving an account of Balkan history and ethnography, and the significance of Nazism, structured around her trip through Yugoslavia in 1937) has pointed out: '[i]t is sometimes very hard to tell the difference between history and the smell of skunk.' See R. West, *Black Lamb and Grey Falcon: A Journey through Yugoslavia*, 4th edn. (Edinburgh, Canongate Books 2001) at p. 127.

European Union and beyond. As such, this study aims to make a practical contribution to an assessment of the international community's policies and actions in the Western Balkans rather than to provide new theoretical or conceptual constructs for understanding such policies and actions. Of course, this study builds upon such existing edifices and may offer new insights into them.

To support the thesis that the European Union should take the leading role in the international effort geared towards bringing lasting peace and stability to the Western Balkans, and to answer the main question how the Union's strategies and actions should be reinforced accordingly, a short description and evaluation of the roles and impact of the other external players in attaining that goal is required. Such an inductive, bottom-up and comprehensive approach to the subtle linkages between and existing overlaps in the actions and strategies of the international organisations that are active in the region will be instrumental in the formulation of a more coherent and effective strategy aimed at bringing lasting peace and stability to the Western Balkans. It should be pointed out that, with an abundance of international stakeholders, it is impossible within the scope of this study to review all of them. Therefore, the current research is restricted to the past and present strategies and activities of the main universal and regional organisations active in the Western Balkans, namely the United Nations, NATO, the OSCE and the Council of Europe (chapter 2). The activities of some of the other international stakeholders (e.g., the WEU, the Contact Group, the G-8, the International Monetary Fund, the World Bank, etc.) are only briefly mentioned along the way.[18] To support the central argument of this study, and reflecting the organisation's front-row position in addressing the situation in the Western Balkans, most attention is devoted to the European Union. In three chapters, the Union's love-hate relationship with the Western Balkans is assessed from the moment the former Yugoslavia started falling apart: first through an overview of the European Union's foreign policy actions (in particular its sanctions policies) towards the SFRY and (the leaders of) its successor states in the period 1991-2001 (chapter 3); then via an analysis of the Union's emerging Common Foreign and Security Policy towards the region, roughly from 2001 onwards (chapter 4); and, finally, by means of an evaluation of the Union's application of the conditionality principle towards the Western Balkans, which will be of increasing importance in the near future (chapter 5). On the basis of the conclusions drawn from each of these analyses, recommendations are made to reinforce the role and impact of the international community – the European Union in particular – towards the Western Balkans (chapter 6).

---

[18] On the WEU, see chapter 2, section 1, and chapter 4, section 1. On the Contact Group, see, *inter alia*, C. Schwegmann, 'The Contact Group and its Impact on the European Institutional Structure', 16 *EUISS Occasional Papers* (2000).

In search of the right policy mix for the stabilisation of the Western Balkans, and as a result of the aim to strike a balance between taking a broad view of international relations with the Western Balkans as a whole and examining certain events, actions and policies in greater detail, this study does not dwell on specific legal questions relating to the nature of the European Union and/or the international legal order. Rather, its aim is primarily to assess the extent to which the international community, and in particular the European Union, is supplied with adequate legal instruments in the light of the policy objectives. The result of this approach is that the more specifically legal dimension of this study is rather dispersed. Two other points of caution should be raised. Firstly, measuring the success, failure and effectiveness of policy making and concrete actions targeted at creating lasting peace and stability in countries or regions is fraught with difficulties. It is near to impossible to determine to what extent single efforts and approaches have led to positive or negative results. Nevertheless, a number of activities and approaches may be ascribed a positive (or negative) influence on developments that have the potential to (de)stabilise a situation. It is on the basis of such general perceptions that general conclusions in this book are drawn and recommendations are formulated. Secondly, due to the fast-moving dynamics of both the European Union and the Western Balkans, any book, article or report on the relationship between the two is bound to be outdated before it is even published. While this study tries to take a contextual approach to problem solving in the Western Balkans, its recommendations are best understood when viewed in combination with the snapshot picture of the regional and international state of play at the time of writing. Research for this book was concluded on 31 May 2007.

4. THE BALKANS: CAUGHT BETWEEN HISTORY AND GEOGRAPHY

Although geographically speaking the Western Balkans is unquestionably part of the European continent, its turbulent history has left a mark – in the form of deep ethnic, religious, cultural, economic and political divisions – and blurred its European credentials. The geographical name of the entire region, 'the Balkan Peninsula' (*Balkan Halbinsel*), is a fictitious name introduced at the beginning of the nineteenth century by the German geographer August Zeune, in an attempt to avoid what were at the time politically incorrect names such as 'the European part of Turkey' or 'Turkey in Europe'.[19] Zeune made the erroneous assumption that

[19] See A. Zeune, *Gäa: Versuch einer wissenschaftlichen Erdbeschreibung* (Berlin 1811), quoted in P. Simić, 'Do the Balkans Exist?', in D. Triantaphyllou, ed., *The Southern Balkans: Perspectives from the Region* (Paris, ISS 2001) at p. 20.

the Balkan Mountains in Bulgaria (*Stara Planina*) ran right across the peninsula of South-Eastern Europe and thereby formed the northern geographical border of the region, much as the Pyrenees demarcate the top of the Iberian Peninsula.[20]

Nineteenth century sensitivities explain the fact that 'the Balkans', like 'Europe', has always been more than a geographical concept.[21] For the better part of the history of mankind, the Balkans formed the border between empires, religions and civilisations, while its peoples often clashed in their role as guardians of that border.[22] Among the consequences of imperial wars in the Balkans were large population migrations, which left the ethnic patterns of the peninsula 'spotted like a leopard's pelt', while various religious and cultural influences resulted in the mixing of Catholic and Orthodox Christianity with Islam.[23] Ethnic and religious animosities also belong to the consequences. The fiercest conflicts in the wars over Yugoslavia's succession, from 1991 to 2001, took place precisely in the areas of former boundaries between empires, such as Krajina in Croatia, where the Habsburg Empire had settled Serbian refugees from the Ottoman Empire since the seventeenth century to guard against Turkish incursions.[24] On the other side of the border, Bosnia-Herzegovina, which was under military administration of the Ottoman Empire, played a similar role. The most problematic source of current ethnic-territorial conflict in the Western Balkans – Kosovo – is the consequence of differences between Albanians, who converted to Islam in the sixteenth century and became the instrument of Ottoman rule, and neighbouring Christian nations, in particular the Serbs.[25]

---

20 See *infra* section 5.1. See also P. Liotta, 'The Geopolitics of the Balkans: Outcomes and Possibilities', 7/8 *New Balkan Politics* (2003). 'Balkans' means (forested) 'mountains' in Turkish.

21 It is striking that, in the context of the European Union's pre-accession process, there has not been any serious political debate about the question whether the Western Balkans are 'European' in the sense of Article 49 TEU. This observation reinforces the argument that, in terms of EU membership conditionality, geography *is* more important than identity. This conclusion shows the hypocrisy of the claim that Turkey should not be allowed to join the European Union because of its Muslim culture. Albania, Bosnia-Herzegovina and Macedonia all have substantial Muslim populations and the European Union has put them all on the integration track. On the idea and identity of Europe, see E. Bussière, M. Dumoulin and G. Trausch, eds., *Europa: The European Idea and Identity from Greek Antiquity to the 21st Century* (Antwerp, Yuste 2001). For more on EU membership conditionality, see chapter 5.

22 See W. Blockmans, *A History of Power in Europe* (Antwerp, Mercatorfonds 1997); and R. Detrez, *De Balkan: van burenruzie tot burgeroorlog*, 4th edn. (Antwerp, Hadewijch 1993).

23 See Simić, loc. cit. n. 19.

24 See A. Gerolymatos, *The Balkan Wars: Conquest, Revolution, and Retribution from the Ottoman Era to the Twentieth Century and Beyond* (New York, Basic Books 2002). 'Krajina' means 'frontier' in the language formerly known as Serbo-Croat and is derived from the original name 'Vojna krajina', the 'military frontier' during the Habsburg Empire.

25 See T. Judah, *Kosovo: War and Revenge*, 2nd edn. (New Haven, Yale University Press 2002). See also the references mentioned *supra* n. 11.

Wars of liberation and national revolutions in the Balkans at the beginning of the nineteenth century brought into conflict the national projects of the Balkan peoples, while interventions by great powers prevented any of them from establishing ethnic borders or attaining hegemony in the region. As a consequence, the twentieth century in the Balkans began and ended with ethnic wars, giving it a reputation as Europe's 'powder keg' and other negative stereotypes.[26] This reputation was reinforced in the West by the wars of Yugoslavia's succession throughout the 1990s.[27] Frequent motives for the wars in the Balkans were ethnic-territorial issues, with a goal to create nation-states, i.e., ethnically homogenous states that extend to the entire territory of one nation. The national programmes of most Balkan peoples emphasised the idea of an ethnic or 'greater' nation-state, with borders reflecting the nation-state's size at the apex of its historical development.[28] Attempts at achieving these ambitions in the geographically limited and ethnically and culturally very heterogeneous area of the Balkans inevitably led to conflicts and mass migrations. In addition to ethnic conflicts, the quest for nation-states created economically non-viable mini-states which sooner or later became strongholds of authoritarian regimes.[29]

After World War I, the United States, France and Britain drew a new political map of the Balkans in an attempt to stop ethnic and territorial conflicts and include the region in the new international order in Europe. There were a total of six states on this map, five of which were essentially nation-states (Albania, Bulgaria, Romania, Greece and Hungary), while the fifth – the Kingdom of Serbs, Croats and Slovenes[30] – was a multi-ethnic state of South ('Yugo') Slavs.[31] The pre-World War II borders between Bulgaria, Greece and Yugoslavia were forcibly restored and diplomatically sealed at the end of World War II, this time with the participation of the Soviet Union.[32] The Cold War and bloc discipline froze national conflicts in South-Eastern Europe and borders remained in place until the violent implosion of the SFRY in 1991.

---

26 See F. Larrabee, ed., *The Volatile Powder Keg: Balkan Security after the Cold War* (Washington, American University Press 1994); and R. Kaplan, *Balkan Ghosts: A Journey Through History* (New York, Vintage Books 1994).

27 See Todorova, op. cit. n. 4.

28 See M. Mazower, *The Balkans: From the End of Byzantium to the Present Day*, 4th ed. (London, Phoenix 2003) at pp. 101-151; and K. Mulaj, 'A Recurrent Tragedy: Ethnic Cleansing as a Tool of State Building in the Yugoslav Multinational Setting', 34 *Nationalities Papers* (2006) pp. 21-50.

29 Ibid.

30 Renamed 'Yugoslavia' in 1929.

31 On the Versailles Treaty of 28 June 1919, see M. MacMillan, *Peacemakers – The Paris Conference of 1919 and Its Attempt to End War* (London, John Murray 2003).

32 On the Yalta Conference, see A. Beevor, *The Fall of Berlin 1945* (New York, Viking Penguin 2002).

This study will not repeat what has been exhaustively dealt with elsewhere concerning the history of the 'Yugoslav crises' of the 1990s.[33] Instead, it will make use of a chronology of key events which took place on the Western Balkans and the international scene.[34] This Balkan timeline provides a historical background for the analysis of actions, operations and strategies of the main international and regional organisations in the Western Balkans.

5. TERMINOLOGY

5.1 **Western Balkans**

Geographically speaking, what is currently perceived as the Balkan Peninsula ('the Balkans') is roughly the region within the natural boundaries formed by the Sava and Danube rivers in the north, the Adriatic, Ionian and Aegean Seas in the west and the south, and the Black Sea and the Bosporus in the east. With the Balkan Mountains running along 43 degrees latitude north, one would logically expect any division of the peninsula to result in the creation of a northern and a southern sphere. But such notions have never been coined. Instead, the phrase 'Western Balkans' is widely used by policy-makers, journalists and other observers from the European Union to denote the group of republics consisting of Albania, Bosnia-Herzegovina, Croatia, Macedonia, Montenegro and Serbia (including Kosovo). Less frequently, the term 'Eastern Balkans' is used for Bulgaria and Romania.[35] Greece does not fall within the scope of either phrase because of its integration with the European Union. The same applies to Slovenia. Although Slovenia is a successor state of the SFRY, its EU integration trajectory differs dramatically from that of the other republics of the former Yugoslavia. After 'only' ten days of war in the summer of 1991, Slovenia managed to escape from the spiral of violence which dragged Bosnia-Herzegovina, Croatia, Serbia and Montenegro further down. The EC officially recognised Slovenia as an

---

[33] See, e.g., D. Owen, *Balkan Odyssey* (New York, Harcourt, Brace & Co. 1995); S. Woodward, *Balkan Tragedy: Chaos and Dissolution after the Cold War* (Washington, Brookings Institution 1995); L. Silber and A. Little, *The Death of Yugoslavia*, rev. edn. (London, Penguin Books 1996); M. Glenny, *The Fall of Yugoslavia*, 3rd edn. (London, Penguin Books 1996); R. Hayden, *Blueprints for a House Divided: The Constitutional Logic of the Yugoslav Conflicts* (Ann Arbor, The University of Michigan Press 2000); M. Glenny, *The Balkans: Nationalism, War, and the Great Powers, 1804-1999* (Penguin Books, London 2001); and R. Bideleux and I. Jeffries, *The Balkans: A Post-Communist History* (London, Routledge 2007).

[34] See pp. 337-366.

[35] As the term 'Eastern Balkans' has been said to denote the region of the Lower Danube, together with the Carpathians in the north and the Thracian highlands to the south, Moldova is sometimes also understood to be covered by this notion.

independent state in January 1992 and quickly hammered out a Cooperation Agreement, which already entered into force in September 1993.[36] As a reward for the country's consistent efforts to reform its economy, administration and legal order, the European Union concluded a Europe Agreement with Slovenia in June 1996 and granted it candidate country status at the European Council summit of Luxembourg in December 1997.[37] On 1 May 2004, Slovenia acceded to the Union, that is to say, even before any other successor state of the former Yugoslavia was granted candidate country status.

In essence, the concept of the 'Western Balkans' is a political invention by the European Union designed for those countries in the south-eastern corner of Europe which, at the end of the war in Bosnia-Herzegovina, did not qualify for the conclusion of Europe Agreements.[38] As Europe Agreements had already been signed with Romania and Bulgaria,[39] and as a Europe Agreement with Slovenia was in the process of being negotiated, Albania remained the only country outside the borders of the former Yugoslavia that could be integrated into a regional approach aimed at economic, administrative and legal reforms and the development of good neighbourly relations. Bilateral relations between these countries and the European Union would be based on a different kind of association agreement: the Stabilisation and Association Agreement.[40]

The categorisation of the 'Western Balkans' is thus not coterminous with either 'the Balkans' (as it excludes Romania, Bulgaria and Greece) or with the territory occupied by the successor states of the SFRY (as it excludes Slovenia but includes Albania). As in the policy documents of the European Union, the terms 'Western Balkans' and 'South-Eastern Europe' will be used interchangeably throughout this study to designate the following countries: the Republic of Albania, the Republic of Bosnia-Herzegovina (BiH), the Republic of Croatia, the Former Yugoslav Republic of Macedonia (FYROM, alternatively Macedonia), the Republic of Serbia (including Kosovo, following UN Security Council resolution 1244) and the Republic of Montenegro. The name 'Kosovo' is used in this study for ease of reference, not out of political conviction. The Albanian and Serb appellations for the region are

---

[36] Cooperation Agreement between the European Economic Community and the Republic of Slovenia, *OJ* 1993 L 189/2.

[37] Negotiations on the Europe Agreement with Slovenia started in March 1995. The Agreement was signed on 10 June 1996 and entered into force in January 1997. See Europe Agreement establishing an association between the European Communities and their Member States, acting within the framework of the European Union, of the one part, and the Republic of Slovenia, of the other part, *OJ* 1996 L 51/3. On the decision to open accession negotiations with Slovenia, see *Bull. EU* 12-1997, point I.5.27.

[38] See Council Conclusions and Declaration on former Yugoslavia, *Bull. EU* 1/2-1996, point 1.4.108.

[39] The Europe Agreements with Romania and Bulgaria were signed on 8 March 1993 and published in *OJ* 1994 L 357/2 and *OJ* 1994 L 358/3 respectively.

[40] See chapter 5.

'Kosova' and 'Kosovo-Metohija' respectively. Similarly, the term 'Macedonia' is used here as an informal name. Greece believes that the name Macedonia should properly be applied to its own northern region with origins dating from the time of Alexander the Great.[41] The United States and Turkey, however, recognise the Republic of Macedonia with its constitutional name. Poland recently rendered a decision to use the Macedonian constitutional name in official communication between the countries, thus adopting the practice of several other EU Member States, including France, Germany, the United Kingdom, Bulgaria and Romania.[42] The terms 'former Yugoslavia', 'ex-Yugoslavia' and 'Yugoslavia' should not be confused with the name 'Federal Republic of Yugoslavia' (FRY). The former are used here to refer to the Socialist Federal Republic of Yugoslavia (SFRY), which was established under that name in 1974 and dissolved in the period of 1991-1992; the latter refers to the previous name of the state union of Serbia and Montenegro, which itself ceased to exist with the declarations of independence of Montenegro and Serbia in June 2006.

5.2 European security architecture

This notion is borrowed from doctrine.[43] The maintenance of peace and security on the European continent is the realm of several international organisations,[44] mainly the United Nations, the European Union, NATO, the OSCE and, to a lesser extent, the Council of Europe. The founding documents of each of these universal and regional organisations refer, directly or indirectly, to the maintenance of peace and security on the European continent.[45] Together, these collective security institutions

---

41 See UNSC resolution 817 (1993) para. 2 on the admission of FYROM to the United Nations and UNGA resolution 225 (1993) para. 2: the 'Former Yugoslav Republic of Macedonia' is a temporary name 'pending settlement of the difference that has arisen over the name of that State'. For a legal analysis, see M. Craven, 'What's in a Name? The Former Yugoslav Republic of Macedonia and Issues of Statehood', 16 *Australian YIL* (1995) pp. 199-239.

42 As reported in 'Several European Countries Use Constitutional Name of Macedonia', *seeurope.net*, 30 August 2005. See further chapter 3, section 2.6.4, and chapter 5, section 5.4.

43 See, e.g., A. Williams, *Reorganizing Eastern Europe: European Institutions and the Refashioning of Europe's Security Architecture* (Aldershot, Dartmouth Publishing Group 1994); G. Aybet, *A European Security Architecture After the Cold War: Questions of Legitimacy* (New York, St. Martin's Press 2000); and Wouters and Naert, loc. cit. n. 5.

44 On the difficulty of defining international organisations, see J. Klabbers, *An Introduction to International Institutional Law* (Cambridge, Cambridge University Press 2002) at pp. 7-13. A helpful definition is offered by H.G. Schermers and N.M. Blokker, *International Institutional Law – Unity within Diversity*, 4th edn. (Boston, Martinus Nijhoff Publishers 2003) at p. 26, para. 33: '[I]nternational organizations are defined as forms of cooperation founded on an international agreement usually creating a new legal person having at least one organ with a will of its own, established under international law.'

45 See Preamble, Arts. 1 and 2, and chapters VI, VII, and VIII of the 1945 UN Charter; Preamble, Art. 2, and Title V of the 1992 TEU (as amended); Preamble, Arts. 1, 2, 5, and 10 of the 1949 North

create a patchwork, the geographical density of which is unique in the world. These organisations interact in many ways and claim to be mutually reinforcing.[46] The question is whether that is really the case.

The above-mentioned international organisations are just a few of the many foreign actors in the Western Balkans. Others are drawn from three different groups: governments, non-governmental organisations and the commercial sector. From this assortment, too, certain key players emerge: stakeholders that possess the political, economic, social and/or military means to influence, persuade or compel the Western Balkan governments to act in ways consistent with the development of democratic governance, market economies, civil societies and ethnically integrated militaries under civilian democratic control. Among the governments, the key stakeholders are the United States, certain Member States of the European Union (particularly Austria, Bulgaria, France, Germany, Greece, Hungary, Italy, Romania, Slovenia and the United Kingdom) and Russia and Turkey as regional heavyweights. Within the non-governmental sector, a considerable international presence comprised of Western grant-making foundations, advocacy groups and service providers – such as the Carnegie Endowment for International Peace, the Soros Foundations Network, the International Crisis Group and the National Endowment for Democracy – operate at the grassroots level to promote democracy, transparency and civil society development, train local partners and provide humanitarian relief. Finally, the business community in the Western Balkans, though nascent in many parts, is attracting – mainly European – investors through the opening of markets and the privatisation of state-owned industries. For the purposes of this study, the stakeholders belonging to these three strands of the international presence in the Western Balkans will not be considered as belonging to the European security architecture. The definition of the concept 'European security architecture' is restricted here to the main international organisations with a mandate given to them by governments to secure peace and stability on the European continent.

5.3 Stabilisation and other international security concepts

Neuhold has noted that the discourse on international security, which is traditionally littered with large quantities of ill-defined terms, has suffered even more

Atlantic Treaty; Preamble and various principles laid down in the sections on 'Questions relating to Security in Europe' and 'Questions relating to Security and Co-operation in the Mediterranean' of the 1975 Helsinki Final Act; Preamble and Art. 1 of the 1949 Statute of the Council of Europe.

46 See, e.g., K. Smith, 'Western Actors and the Promotion of Democracy', and R. Vukadinović, 'Former Yugoslavia: International Efforts to Link Peace, Stability and Democracy', in J. Zielonka and A. Pravda, eds., *Democratic Consolidation in Eastern Europe, Vol. 2: International and Transnational Factors* (Oxford, Oxford University Press 2001) pp. 31-57 and 437-454.

from 'terminological inflation' at the hands of the European Union.[47] In the rapid build-up of a CFSP/ESDP, the European Union has committed itself to develop capabilities to conduct a whole series of so-called 'Petersberg tasks', ranging from humanitarian and rescue tasks, via peacekeeping and crisis management, to peacemaking, while refraining from specifying its understanding of such operations.[48] Confusion arises when international organisations give different explanations to the same terms. The term 'peacemaking', for instance, is understood in the context of the United Nations as the pacific settlement of disputes, in particular in accordance with Article 33 of the UN Charter.[49] In the EU context, however, there is little doubt that the use of military troops to enforce a solution on a party to a conflict exceeds the settlement methods covered by chapter VI and includes a resort to armed force. While terminological confusion in security policy may serve strategic, diplomatic or political interests, it creates legal uncertainty. In the absence of internationally agreed definitions of such fluid concepts as 'conflict prevention', 'crisis management' and 'conflict resolution', an attempt should be made at clarifying these terms. It is beyond the scope of this study to attempt a thorough substantive interpretation of the key security concepts listed below. Suffice it to state that the meaning of these concepts has been distilled from a wide variety of policy papers, legal documents, handbooks and academic texts.[50]

The term 'stabilisation' is used here as a conceptual umbrella to cover all efforts geared towards removing the determinants of conflicts and crises. The notion of 'crisis' is widely understood as an acute situation in which armed force

---

47 H. Neuhold, 'Terminological Ambiguity in the Field of International Security', in K. Dicke, et al, eds., *Weltinnenrecht: Liber Amicorum Jost Delbrück* (Berlin, Duncker & Humblot 2005) pp. 473-486 at p. 475. NATO is also to be blamed for creating confusion, with terms like 'peace support operations' and 'crisis response operations'.

48 Art. 17 TEU. On the gradual development of CFSP/ESDP, see chapter 4, section 1.

49 See H. Neuhold, 'The United Nations System for the Peaceful Settlement of International Disputes', in F. Cede and L. Sucharipa-Behrmann, eds., *The United Nations: Law and Practice* (The Hague, Kluwer Law International 2001) at p. 59 et seq.

50 See, *inter alia*, *An Agenda for Peace*, UN Doc. A/47/277-S/24111, 17 June 1992, paras. 20-59; *Supplement to An Agenda for Peace*, UN Doc. A/50/60-S/1995/1, 3 January 1995, paras. 23-80; *Report of the Panel on United Nations Peace Operations*, UN Doc. A/55/305-S/2000/809, 21 August 2000; *NATO Handbook* (Brussels, NATO Office of Information and Press 2001); *OSCE Handbook*, 3rd edn. (Vienna, OSCE Secretariat 2000); *A Secure Europe in a Better World – European Security Strategy*, Brussels, 12 December 2003; *EU Security and Defence: Core Documents 2004. Vol. V* (Paris, ISS 2005); A. Schmid, *Thesaurus and Glossary of Early Warning and Conflict Prevention Terms* (Rotterdam, Erasmus University 1998); P. van Tongeren, H. van de Veen and J. Verhoeven, *Searching for Peace in Europe and Eurasia: An Overview of Conflict Prevention and Peace-building Activities* (Boulder, Lynne Rienner 2002); V. Kronenberger and J. Wouters, eds., *The European Union and Conflict Prevention: Policy and Legal Aspects* (The Hague, T.M.C. Asser Press 2004); and N. Gnesotto, ed., *EU Security and Defence Policy: The First Five Years (1999-2004)* (Paris, ISS 2004).

is (likely to be) used. The much broader 'conflict' is intended to denote every national or international situation where there is a threat or breach to priority values, interests and goals. The catch-all phrase 'conflict prevention' is understood here as the adoption and implementation of measures that aim to impede the escalation of a non-violent dispute into a crisis. 'Crisis management' refers to the organisation, procedures and arrangements to contain a crisis and shape its future course while resolution is sought. 'Conflict resolution' refers to efforts to impose a (partial) settlement in the case of a crisis and consolidate the cessation of violence. Actions meant to address the root causes of crises which have been resolved are dubbed post-conflict reconstruction and rehabilitation measures (or 'peacebuilding').

These are by no means hard distinctions. The lines between the different categories are often blurred. For instance, the strategies and actions aimed at inducing the stabilisation and association of the countries of the Western Balkans are adopted in the wake of crises and are intended to prevent the resurgence of armed violence in both the short and the longer term. As such, these strategies fall within the realm of both conflict resolution and peacebuilding.

CHAPTER 2

ROLE AND IMPACT OF THE UN, NATO, THE OSCE AND THE COE: THE WESTERN BALKANS LOST IN THE ALPHABET SOUP?

1. INTRODUCTION

As observed in the previous chapter, the disintegrative violence on the territory of the former Yugoslavia has been – and could again be – hard to contain. Up to the present, no international organisation concerned with the maintenance of peace and security in Europe has been able to single-handedly prevent and suppress outbursts of armed conflict in the Western Balkans and to take the necessary measures to prevent them from re-erupting. This chapter will analyse the role of the main international organisations that make up the European security architecture and assess their effectiveness in suppressing violent conflicts in the Western Balkans and weeding out their root causes. To that end, it has been broadly divided into two parts. In the first part (sections 2-5), the conflict prevention, crisis management and post-conflict rehabilitation tools that are at the disposal of each of the organisations are discussed. In the second part (sections 6-10), the practices of these organisations with respect to the Western Balkans are described and their effectiveness analysed. As explained in the previous chapter, the main actors on the European security stage are the United Nations (sections 2 and 6), NATO (sections 3 and 7), the OSCE (sections 4 and 8), the Council of Europe (sections 5 and 9) and the European Union (chapters 3-5). While the Western European Union (WEU) also mounted operations in the Western Balkans, it only did so in support and in the framework of the United Nations, NATO, the OSCE and the European Union. Its operations are briefly discussed in chapter 4 of this book. On the basis of the overviews and impact assessments of the main organisations' activities in and strategies for the Western Balkans, some recurring barriers to success will be discussed (section 10).

2. UNITED NATIONS

The United Nations occupies a central place in the constellation of international organisations dealing with the maintenance and restoration of international peace and security. Under its umbrella, policies and actions in the field of conflict prevention, peacekeeping, peacemaking and post-conflict peacebuilding have gradually been developed. But in spite of its unique expertise in each of these areas, the United Nations still faces a significant 'expectations-capabilities' gap in its role as guarantor of international peace and security.[1]

2.1 Legal and operational framework

In the preamble of the UN Charter (UNC), 'the peoples of the United Nations' declare themselves 'determined to save succeeding generations from the scourge of war' and to that end state, *inter alia*, their resolve to combine their efforts 'to ensure, by the acceptance of principles and the institution of methods, that armed force shall not be used, save in the common interest'. Article 1(1) UNC states as the very first objective of the organisation to

> maintain international peace and security, and to that end: to take effective collective measures for the prevention and removal of threats to the peace, and for the suppression of acts of aggression or other breaches of the peace, and to bring about by peaceful means, and in conformity with the principles of justice and international law, adjustment or settlement of international disputes or situations which might lead to a breach of the peace.

Two obligations are aimed at contributing to this objective and thus to the prevention and resolution of international conflicts: all UN Member States must 'settle their international disputes by peaceful means in such a manner that international peace and security, and justice, are not endangered' (Art. 2(3) UNC) and they must 'refrain in their international relations from the threat or use of force against the territorial integrity or political independence of any state, or in any other manner inconsistent with the Purposes of the United Nations' (Art. 2(4) UNC). These cornerstone provisions state that states ought to strive to settle their disputes peacefully and not use force except in self-defence (Art. 51 UNC)[2] or when authorised to do so by the UN Security Council.[3]

The methods provided for in chapter VI of the UN Charter geared towards the peaceful settlement of disputes follow the same logic: Article 33(1) obliges

> [t]he parties to any dispute, the continuance of which is likely to endanger the maintenance of international peace and security, [to], first of all, seek a solution by negotiation, enquiry, mediation, conciliation, arbitration, judicial settlement, resort to regional agencies or arrangements, or other peaceful means of their own choice.

---

[1] A variation to the famous phrase first coined by C. Hill, 'The Capability-Expectations Gap, or Conceptualising Europe's International Role', 31 *JCMS* (1993) pp. 305-328.

[2] The UNC sets a number of limitations on the use of the right of self-defence enshrined in Art. 51. See A. Randelzhofer, 'Article 51', in B. Simma, ed., *The Charter of the United Nations: A Commentary*, 2nd edn. (Oxford, Oxford University Press 2002) pp. 788-806, including references for further reading.

[3] Formally speaking, Art. 106 UNC is a third ground of exception, but this is a transitory provision and has now become obsolete.

Pursuant to Article 34, 'any dispute, or any situation [...] likely to endanger the maintenance of international peace and security' can be investigated by the Security Council,[4] which 'may, at any stage of [such] a dispute [...], recommend appropriate procedures or methods of adjustment' (Art. 36(1)). Any UN Member State may bring such a dispute or situation to the attention of the Security Council or of the General Assembly (Art. 35(1)). Should the parties to a dispute of the nature referred to above fail to settle it by the means indicated in Article 33, they must refer it to the Security Council (Art. 37(1)). If the latter considers that 'the continuance of the dispute is in fact likely to endanger the maintenance of international peace and security, it shall decide whether to take action under Article 36 or to recommend such terms of settlement as it may consider appropriate' (Art. 37(2)).

The enforcement mechanisms provided for under chapter VII of the Charter endow the Security Council with broad powers of forcible intervention. Once the Security Council has determined the existence of a threat to the peace, a breach of the peace or an act of aggression (Art. 39), it can decide upon sanctions not involving the use of armed force (Art. 41)[5] or take armed action against the aggressor or the state threatening the peace if it considers that the measures provided for in Article 41 would be inadequate or have proved to be inadequate (Art. 42).[6] However, the 'army' that should have been put at the disposal of the Security Council by the Members through special arrangements (Art. 43) was never established.[7]

---

[4] However, this article fell into oblivion in the early years of the United Nations. See T. Schweisfurth, 'Article 34', in Simma, op. cit. n. 2, at pp. 594-608.

[5] Art. 41 UNC gives the following examples: 'These may include complete or partial interruption of economic relations and of rail, sea, air, postal, telegraphic, radio, and other means of communication, and the severance of diplomatic relations.' See, e.g., N. Schrijver, 'The Use of Economic Sanctions by the UN Security Council: An International Law Perspective', in H. Post, ed., *International Economic Law and Armed Conflict* (Dordrecht, Martinus Nijhoff 1994) pp. 123-161; L. Damrosch, 'Enforcing International Law through Non-forcible Measures', 269 *RdC* (1997) pp. 13-250; F. Alabrune, 'La pratique des comités des sanctions du Conseil de sécurité depuis 1990', 45 *AFDI* (1999) pp. 226-279; and J. Frowein and N. Kirsch, 'Article 41', in Simma, op. cit. n. 2, at pp. 735-749 and the literature referred to therein.

[6] Art. 42 UNC grants the Security Council the power to 'take such action by air, sea, or land forces as may be necessary to maintain or restore international peace and security. Such action may include demonstrations, blockade, and any other operations by air, sea, or land forces of Members of the United Nations.' See, e.g., G. Gaja, 'Use of Force Made or Authorized by the United Nations', in C. Tomuschat, ed., *The United Nations at Age Fifty; A Legal Perspective* (The Hague, Kluwer Law International 1995) pp. 39-58; N. Blokker, 'Is the Authorization Authorized? Powers and Practice of the UN Security Council to Authorize the Use of Force by "Coalitions of the Able and Willing"', 11 *EJIL* (2000) pp. 541-568; J. Frowein and N. Kirsch, 'Article 42', in Simma, op. cit. n. 2, at pp. 749-759; N. White, 'The Will and Authority of the Security Council After Iraq', 17 *LJIL* (2004) pp. 645-672; E. de Wet, *The Chapter VII Powers of the United Nations Security Council* (Oxford, Hart Publishing 2004); and N.M. Blokker and N.J. Schrijver, eds., *The Security Council and the Use of Force: Theory and Reality – A Need for Change?* (Leiden, Koninklijke Brill 2005).

[7] See J. Frowein and N. Kirsch, 'Article 43', in Simma, op. cit. n. 2, at pp. 760-763.

In chapter VIII, the UN Charter recognises that 'regional arrangements or agencies' are appropriate means for maintaining peace and security, provided that their activities are consistent with the purposes and principles of the Charter (Arts. 52-54 UNC). Regional peacekeeping and subcontracting of enforcement action have led to the question which specific institutions meet the criteria to be considered 'regional' in the sense of chapter VIII.[8] The Charter itself does not provide a definition of 'regional arrangements or agencies', but merely indicates that such institutions have the task of taking care of the peaceful settlement of disputes within their own region (Art. 52 UNC). A small number of international organisations have explicitly identified themselves as 'regional', either in their constituent charter (e.g., the OAS) or in later declarations (e.g., the OSCE, the CIS and the Arab League). Others, like NATO and the European Union, have avoided qualifying themselves as such, and this has led to doctrinal debates.[9] The Security Council, however, has adopted a rather pragmatic, flexible approach to the matter and has linked up with regional organisations that were 'able and willing' to promote the peaceful settlement of disputes and maintain or restore international peace and security (e.g., ECOWAS, the (O)AU, the OSCE and so forth).[10] It is likely that the UN Security Council will increasingly direct itself towards combined action with regional organisations. With the gradual development of the European Union into a full-fledged international 'crisis manager', one may expect the Security Council to call on the Union more frequently in the

[8] See W. Hummer and M. Schweitzer, 'Article 52', in Simma, op. cit. n. 2, at pp. 807-853; G. Ress and J. Bröhmer, 'Article 53', in Simma, op. cit. n. 2, at pp. 854-890; and W. Hummer and M. Schweitzer, 'Article 54', in Simma, op. cit. n. 2, at pp. 890-895, and the literature referred to in these three contributions.

[9] For a discussion on and references to literature about NATO's perceived character as a 'regional' organisation in the sense of chapter VIII UNC, see M. Reichard, *The EU-NATO Relationship: A Legal and Political Perspective* (Aldershot, Ashgate 2006) at pp. 99 and 105-106. Frowein has argued that the European Union, especially after integrating the WEU, could also be regarded as a regional agency under chapter VIII. See J. Frowein, 'Die Europäische Union mit WEU als Sicherheitssystem', in O. Due, M. Lutter and J. Schwarze, eds., *Festschrift für Ulrich Everling* (Baden-Baden, Nomos Verlag 1995) pp. 315-326. Wessel, on the other hand, has pointed out that, in its current legal constellation, neither the European Union, nor the WEU for that matter, can be regarded as a full-fledged regional arrangement. Practice, however, has demonstrated that the European Union and WEU function as a regional arm of the United Nations. See R. Wessel, 'The EU as a Black Widow: Devouring the WEU to Give Birth to a European Security and Defence Policy', in V. Kronenberger, ed., *The European Union and the International Legal Order: Discord or Harmony?* (The Hague, T.M.C. Asser Press 2001) pp. 405-434 at pp. 428-429.

[10] See C. Walter, *Vereinte Nationen und Regionalorganisationen. Eine Untersuchung zu Kapitel VIII der Satzung der Vereinten Nationen* (Heidelberg, Springer 1996); Z. Deen-Racsmány, 'A Redistribution of Authority between the UN and Regional Organizations in the Field of Maintenance of Peace and Security', 13 *LJIL* (2000) pp. 297-312; and M. Zwanenburg, 'Regional Organisations and Maintenance of International Peace and Security: Three Recent Regional African Peace Operations', 11 *Journal of Conflict and Security Law* (2006) pp. 483-508.

future.[11] As long as it respects the primary role of the Security Council in the maintenance of international peace and security, and the need for an authorisation for enforcement action, this evolution should be welcomed.

To a large extent, the UN Charter tends to uphold a concept of 'negative peace' (i.e., the absence of war) rather than 'positive peace' (i.e., the introduction of justice for the purpose of preventing political tensions from degenerating into armed conflicts as much as possible). This is not to say that the United Nations closes its eyes to political reality and refrains from suggesting political solutions calculated to prevent armed conflicts. Indeed, universal respect for human rights (Art. 55c) and cooperation in the economic, social and political fields are promoted (Arts. 13(1)b, 62, 55a and b), and a role for the United Nations was also envisaged in regard to furthering cooperation in respect of disarmament (Art. 11(1)). Here again, as in many other provisions of the UN Charter, a link was established with the maintenance of international peace and security. Stability is considered an essential condition for the development and maintenance of peaceful relations among states. Through some of its specialised agencies and organs (e.g., ECOSOC, the UNDP, etc.), the United Nations has promoted human rights, disarmament and economic and social cooperation in various fields (both through technical assistance and via the conclusion of treaties).

2.2 The evolution of UN conflict prevention, crisis management and post-conflict peacebuilding

The United Nations's record of preventive and enforcement action has been rather mixed. Faced with a more or less constant stalemate in the Security Council during the Cold War, an alternative UN policy has been developed since the 1950s for which the UN Charter did not make any provision and which has been referred to – in the words of the UN's second Secretary-General Dag Hammarskjöld – as 'chapter six and a half' action: peacekeeping operations.[12] Such operations have evolved over time, from so-called 'first generation' (monitoring ceasefires), via 'second generation' (interpositioning troops between adversarial

[11] See S. Blockmans, 'A New Crisis Manager at the Horizon – The Case of the European Union', 13 *LJIL* (2000) pp. 255-263; S. Duke, *The EU and Crisis Management: Development and Prospects* (Maastricht, EIPA 2001); J. Wouters and T. Ruys, 'UN-EU Cooperation in Crisis Management', in J. Wouters, F. Hoffmeister and T. Ruys, eds., *The United Nations and the European Union: An Ever Stronger Partnership* (The Hague, T.M.C. Asser Press 2006) pp. 229-258; M. Trybus and N.D. White, eds., *European Security Law* (Oxford, Oxford University Press 2007); S. Blockmans, ed., *The European Union and International Crisis Management: Legal and Policy Aspects* (The Hague, T.M.C. Asser Press 2008, forthcoming); and chapter 4 of this book.

[12] See UN Department of Peacekeeping Operations, *United Nations Peacekeeping: In the Service of Peace. An Evolving Technique*, available at: <http://www.un.org/Depts/dpko/dpko/intro/1.htm>.

parties), to 'third generation' (multi-dimensional operations including political, military, humanitarian, police, economic, social, reconstruction and judicial activities) and even 'fourth generation' operations (whereby the United Nations becomes the authority that actually governs during a transitional period until a new, democratic state can be established).[13] Incrementally, and spurred by the rebirth of the Security Council after the end of the Cold War, the United Nations has sought to put peacekeeping operations into use not only for the preservation of (a sometimes fragile) peace, but also for the resolution and prevention of conflicts. The Yugoslav crises in the 1990s provide a string of examples which show this developing nature of peacekeeping operations.[14]

At the request of the special Security Council summit of 31 January 1992, UN Secretary-General Boutros Boutros-Ghali produced a landmark report entitled 'An Agenda for Peace' (1992).[15] The report contains an ambitious agenda for a more peaceful world and offers 'a coherent contribution towards securing peace in the spirit of the Charter.'[16] It stresses the need for an integrated approach, whereby the UN's aims should be:

- To seek to identify at the earliest possible stage situations that could produce conflict, and to try through diplomacy to remove the sources of danger before violence results;
- Where conflict erupts, to engage in peacemaking aimed at resolving the issues that have led to conflict;
- Through peace-keeping, to work to preserve peace, however fragile, where fighting has been halted and to assist in implementing agreements achieved by peacemakers;
- To stand ready to assist in peace-building in its differing contexts: rebuilding the institutions and infrastructures of nations torn by civil war and strife; and building bonds of peaceful mutual benefit among nations formerly at war;
- And in the largest sense, to address the deepest causes of conflict: economic despair, social injustice and political oppression [...].[17]

In his report, the Secretary-General sought to intertwine the old and the new. For example, some of the classical instruments for the peaceful settlement of disputes, such as good offices, mediation and fact-finding were put at the disposal of (the

---

[13] The literature on the evolution of peacekeeping operations is voluminous. For overviews and analyses of operations, as well as further references to the literature, see UN Department of Public Information, *The Blue Helmets: A Review of United Nations Peace-keeping*, 3rd edn. (New York, UNDPI 1996); and M. Bothe, 'Peace-keeping', in Simma, op. cit. n. 2, at pp. 648-700.

[14] See *infra* section 6.

[15] Report of the Secretary-General pursuant to the statement adopted by the Summit Meeting of the Security Council on 31 January 1992, *An Agenda for Peace. Preventive Diplomacy, Peacemaking and Peacekeeping*, UN Doc. A/47/277 – S/24111 (17 June 1992).

[16] Ibid., at para. 22.

[17] Ibid., at para. 15.

newly defined concept of) preventive diplomacy.[18] In turn, preventive diplomacy was tied to other key concepts such as peacekeeping and post-conflict peacebuilding. 'An Agenda for Peace' also devotes a whole chapter to cooperation between the United Nations and regional arrangements, which has given an extra impetus to the process of regionalisation of security arrangements and organisations under the authority of the Security Council.[19] Although Boutros-Ghali undertook various initiatives to make the United Nations more suited to its tasks,[20] there were a number of practical difficulties in implementing the objectives set out in 1992. In his 1995 'Supplement to an Agenda for Peace',[21] the Secretary-General noted that it was not the lack of information, analytical capacity or ideas that constituted the greatest practical obstacle to UN actions but often the reluctance of one party or another to accept the UN's assistance, due to strong sentiments of sovereignty and non-interference.[22] The Secretary-General did not see an immediate solution to this problem.[23] Instead, he hoped for a long-term solution in which 'a climate of opinion, or ethos, within the international community' would emerge in which Member States would be more inclined to accept an offer of UN good offices.[24]

Events in the 1990s forced the UN Secretariat to reconsider its position and to embrace a more comprehensive approach to conflict prevention, crisis management and post-conflict rehabilitation.[25] The humanitarian tragedies of Somalia, Rwanda and Srebrenica, and the UN's failures in these crises, painfully exposed the inadequacy of the UN's peacekeeping operations. Faced with the reluctance of its members to commit resources and risk lives when no vital interests are at stake, the argument for more structural prevention policies carried the day.[26] Increasingly, attention at UN level has been devoted to what the organisation is better at: promoting incremental change and reform. A whole series of official reports has been devoted to the topic. In Kofi Annan's 1999 report 'Preventing

---

18 For definitions of the key terms used in 'An Agenda for Peace', see ibid., at para. 20.

19 See J. Wouters, 'The United Nations, the EU and Conflict Prevention: Interconnecting the Global and Regional Levels', in V. Kronenberger and J. Wouters, eds., *The European Union and Conflict Prevention: Policy and Legal Aspects* (The Hague, T.M.C. Asser Press 2004) pp. 369-392 at pp. 374-375.

20 The creation of the Department of Political Affairs is a case in point.

21 B. Boutros-Ghali, *Supplement to An Agenda for Peace: Position Paper of the Secretary General on the Occasion of the Fiftieth Anniversary of the United Nations*, UN Doc. A/50/60 – S/1995/1 (3 January 1995).

22 Ibid., at para. 27.

23 Ibid., at para. 28.

24 Ibid.

25 See, e.g., K. Zemanek, 'Peace-keeping or Peace-making?', in N. Blokker and S. Muller, eds., *Towards More Effective Supervision by International Organizations – Essays in Honour of Henry G. Schermers*, Vol. I (Dordrecht, Martinus Nijhoff Publishers 1994) pp. 29-47.

26 See J. Wouters, loc. cit. n. 19, at p. 377.

War and Disaster: A Growing Global Challenge', the Secretary-General stressed that 'the United Nations has long argued that prevention is better than cure; that we must address the root causes, not merely their symptoms' and that '[o]ur aspiration has yet to be matched by effective action.'[27] In his well-received 'Millennium Report' (2000), Annan noted that 'strategies of prevention must address the root causes of conflicts, not simply their violent symptoms.'[28] The Secretary-General's recommendations were endorsed in the 'Report of the Panel on UN Peace Operations' of August 2000, better known as the 'Brahimi Report', named after the panel's chairman.[29] In the 'Millennium Declaration', the UN General Assembly resolved '[t]o make the United Nations more effective in maintaining peace and security by giving it the resources and tools it needs for conflict prevention, peaceful resolution of disputes, peacekeeping, post-conflict peace-building and reconstruction.'[30] While announcing a comprehensive report for the General Assembly in which he intended to present recommendations on how to strengthen the UN's capacity in order to ensure that conflict prevention is made the cornerstone of the UN's collective security system in the twenty-first century, the Secretary-General identified integrating conflict prevention further into its activities as the key task for the UN system in the coming years.[31] Meanwhile, the Security Council held a number of open debates on a series of issues relating to comprehensive conflict prevention, including cooperation of the United Nations with regional organisations in stabilisation processes.[32]

On 2 December 2004, the High-level Panel on Threats, Challenges and Change presented its report 'A more secure world: our shared responsibility', proposing ways of strengthening collective security and urging the adoption of new, far-reaching ground rules to help the world face new and evolving threats in the twenty-first century and to strengthen the United Nations.[33] Besides reaffirming the right of states to defend themselves – including pre-emptively, i.e., when an attack

---

[27] Report of the Secretary-General on the Work of the Organisation, GA Official Records, Suppl. No. 1, UN Doc. A/54/1, para. 1.

[28] K. Annan, *We the Peoples. The Role of the United Nations in the 21st Century*, UN Doc. A/54/2000. In July 2000, the Security Council invited the Secretary-General to submit a report with recommendations on the prevention of armed conflict. This request led to the detailed report of 7 June 2001 'Prevention of Armed Conflict', UN Doc. A/55/985 – S/2001/574. The ten principles which should enable the United Nations to move 'from a culture of reaction to a culture of prevention' were expressly recognised by the Security Council in resolution 1366 (2001) on 'the role of the Security Council in the prevention of armed conflicts'. The General Assembly did so too in resolution 57/337.

[29] UN Doc. A/55/305 – S/2000/809 (21 August 2000).

[30] UNGA resolution 55/2, 8 September 2000, point 9.

[31] Interim report of the Secretary-General on the prevention of armed conflict, UN Doc. A/58/365 – S/2003/888, para. 33.

[32] See S.PV.5007 as well as the Presidential Statement S/PRST/2004/27 of 20 July 2004.

[33] UN Doc. A/59/565.

is imminent – and warning that 'nightmare scenarios' – for instance those combining terrorists and weapons of mass destruction – may call for more proactive and decisive measures by the UN Security Council, the High-level Panel endorsed the idea of a collective responsibility to protect civilians from genocide, ethnic cleansing and other comparable atrocities. In case sovereign states are unable or unwilling to fulfil this responsibility, the wider international community should intervene – acting preventively where possible, responding to violence if need be and working to rebuild shattered societies after the event. 'Force, if it needs to be used, should be deployed as a last resort' and should be authorised by the Security Council, according to the Panel.[34] It also recommended the creation of a new UN body, the Peacebuilding Commission, which would identify countries at risk of violent conflict, organise prevention efforts and 'marshal and sustain the efforts of the international community in post-conflict peacebuilding.'[35]

Five years after the adoption of Millennium Declaration, in his report 'In larger freedom: towards development, security and human rights for all' to the General Assembly, the Secretary-General urged UN members to adopt a package of specific, concrete proposals to tackle global problems and enable the United Nations to respond better to current challenges.[36] The report formed the launch pad for the 14-16 September 2005 World Summit, which reiterated the world's commitment to the so-called 'Millennium Development Goals' and addressed the possible reform of the United Nations.[37] Unfortunately, much of this was eventually postponed to a later date. Notable exceptions concerned the agreement on the creation of a new Human Rights Council,[38] the establishment of the Peacebuilding Commission[39] and the endorsement of the so-called 'Responsibility to Protect', a

---

34 Ibid., at paras. 201-203. In para. 207, the panel proposed five criteria to guide the Council in deciding whether to authorise use of force: seriousness of threat, proper purpose, last resort, proportional means and balance of consequences (i.e., whether military action is likely to have better or worse results than inaction).

35 Ibid., at para. 83.

36 UN Doc. A/59/2005 (21 March 2005).

37 Revised draft outcome document of the High-level Plenary Meeting of the General Assembly of September 2005 submitted by the President of the General Assembly, UN Doc. A/59/HLPM/CRP.1/Rev.2 (5 August 2005).

38 Ibid., at paras. 138-140. The Human Rights Council was established by UNGA resolution 60/251, 3 April 2006. Documents and background information are available at: <http://www.ohchr.org/english/bodies/hrcouncil>.

39 Ibid., at paras. 76-87. The Security Council, in resolution 1645 (2005) of 20 December 2005, acting concurrently with the General Assembly, in resolution 60/180 of 30 December 2005, formally decided on the establishment of the Peacebuilding Commission as an intergovernmental advisory body geared at assisting and mobilising support for countries emerging from conflict. To that end, the Peacebuilding Commission, which started its activities on 1 January 2006, will provide necessary information in the immediate aftermath of war and focus attention on development and institution-building efforts necessary for recovery and will support the development of integrated strategies for countries emerging from conflict, in order to prevent them from relapsing into conflict. In addition, it

formulation of a right of humanitarian intervention developed by the International Commission on Intervention and State Sovereignty (ICISS) and proposed by Kofi Annan as part of his 'In Larger Freedom' reform package.[40] The 'Responsibility to Protect' obliges the international community, through the United Nations, to intervene, including under chapters VI and VIII of the Charter, 'should peaceful means be inadequate and national authorities be unwilling or unable to protect their populations' from 'genocide, war crimes, ethnic cleansing and crimes against humanity.'[41]

In spite of the proliferation of these initiatives, reports and institutional innovations,[42] there are a number of practical obstacles to more effective UN policies on conflict prevention, crisis management and post-conflict peacebuilding.[43] Firstly, the sovereignty and non-interference concerns of various of its members continue to make the UN's efforts on each of these issues a delicate balancing act. Secondly, the lack of political will on the members' part often leads to non-compliance with their commitments, especially with regard to financing. And, thirdly, as opposed to richer regional organisations, the United Nations suffers from a comparative disadvantage with respect to the limited resources it has at its disposal. These and other limits to UN action in the field will be illustrated by a case-study of the role and impact of the United Nations in the Western Balkans since 1991 (section 6).

3. NATO

3.1 **Legal and operational framework**[44]

Based on the North Atlantic Treaty (NAT) adopted in Washington on 4 April 1949,[45] NATO was established as a collective defence organisation. Nonetheless,

---

will provide recommendations and information to improve coordination of all stakeholders inside and outside the United Nations, develop best practices, help to ensure predictable financing for early recovery activities, and extend the period of attention by the international community to post-conflict recovery. Documents and background information are available at: <http://www.un.org/peace/peacebuilding>. See further C. Stahn, 'Institutionalizing Brahimi's "Light Footprint": A Comment on the Role and Mandate of the Peacebuilding Commission', 2 *IOLR* (2005) pp. 403-415.

40 Ibid., at paras. 118-120.

41 Ibid., at para. 118.

42 See N. Schrijver, 'UN Reform: A Once-in-a-Generation Opportunity', 2 *IOLR* (2005) pp. 271-275.

43 See J. Wouters, loc. cit. n. 19, at pp. 381-382.

44 For a detailed guide to the history, structures and work of the organisation, see *NATO Handbook* (Brussels, NATO Office of Information and Press 2001) and <http://www.nato.int>.

45 The Treaty is reproduced in 34 *UNTS* 243. It came into force on 24 August 1949, after the deposition of the ratifications of all signatory states.

NATO has been in the conflict prevention and crisis management business since its inception. Although the terminology was not used at the time, the commitment to consult when any Ally perceives a threat to its security, sovereignty or territorial integrity (Art. 4 NAT) and to regard an attack on one or more Allies as an attack on all and to respond (Art. 5 NAT) were later referred to as the basis for NATO crisis management. The language of Article 4 is mirrored in the invitation given to states to join the Partnership for Peace (PfP) programme, which aims to enhance stability and security throughout Europe: 'NATO will consult with any active participant in the Partnership if that Partner perceives a direct threat to its territorial integrity, political independence or security.'[46] A number of PfP members have perceived such threats and have requested consultations, during which Allies have agreed to take action to address the problems raised.[47] Article 5 of the Washington Treaty, no doubt the most pivotal element of NATO crisis management, consists of two elements: the commitment to view an armed attack against one as an attack against all and the commitment to assist in concert by such action that each member deems necessary, including the use of armed force. Article 5 NAT can best be understood as a statement of deterrence to would-be attackers, a statement made credible, despite its less than categorical nature, by the existence of the necessary capabilities (reflected in the integrated military structure, force commitments and readiness levels) and the evident political will to respond to any attack.[48]

In spite of the belligerent undertone of Article 5, the parties to the Washington Treaty have recognised the primary responsibility of the UN Security Council for the maintenance of international peace and security (Art. 7 NAT). Consequently, they agreed that nothing in the Washington Treaty can affect or shall be interpreted to affect the rights and obligations arising from the UN Charter. They have undertaken 'to settle any international dispute in which they may be involved by peaceful means in such a manner that international peace and security and justice are not endangered, and to refrain in their international relations from the threat or use of force in any manner inconsistent with the purposes of the United Nations' (Art. 1 NAT).

---

[46] NATO, *Partnership for Peace: Framework Document*, adopted by the Ministerial Meeting of the North Atlantic Council (NAC) and the North Atlantic Cooperation Council (NACC), Brussels, 10-11 January 1994. NAC is NATO's principal decision-making organ and is composed of the permanent representatives of the members of the Alliance. For more on NACC, see *infra* n. 71.

[47] For example, in response to Albania's request following the 1997 collapse of the pyramid savings schemes, NATO Allies agreed to a variety of measures, including assistance in developing Albania's national crisis management organisation and procedures.

[48] See P. Duignan, *NATO: Its Past, Present, and Future* (Stanford, Hoover Press 2000); B. Simma, 'NATO, the UN and the Use of Force', 10 *EJIL* (1999) pp. 1-22; and P. Gallis, 'NATO: Article V and Collective Defense', *CRS Report for Congress*, 17 July 1997.

3.2 Adaptations to the operational framework

During the Cold War, the kinds of crises that the Alliance faced were largely, but not exclusively, military and so – to a large extent – were its tools. In the post-Cold War era, the focus shifted to 'out of area' crises resulting from tensions generated by ethnic conflicts, extreme nationalism, intra-state political strife, failed or inadequate political change, severe economic problems and, since 11 September 2001, international terrorism and the threat posed by weapons of mass destruction. Against the backdrop of this radical evolution of the security environment since the end of the Cold War, the Allies reinterpreted the provisions of the Washington Treaty and agreed to new tools so as to enable 'their' Alliance to prevent and manage the 'new' kinds of conflicts and/or crises.[49] The nature and modalities of NATO's cooperation with other international organisations which contribute to international peace and security, in particular the United Nations, the European Union and the OSCE, were also remodelled.[50] In this transformation process, three stages stand out: the Strategic Concepts of Rome (1991), Washington (1999) and Prague (2002). As political declarations, the Strategic Concepts lack any legally binding force, even if the crisis management and conflict prevention functions contained therein clearly go beyond the original scope of the Washington Treaty.[51]

On 9 November 1991, NATO's members agreed to a new Strategic Concept, which encompassed a broader approach to security and greater opportunities to achieve long-standing objectives through political means.[52] Key aspects of the new approach included: (a) more active use of political and diplomatic means; (b) close interaction and cooperation with other international organisations; and (c) significant changes in NATO's command and force structures. Crisis management and conflict prevention, including non-Article 5 crisis response operations, were major themes in the adaptation of the Alliance to the post-Cold War security environment.[53] The 1991 Strategic Concept also called for dialogue and cooperation

---

[49] See H. Tromp, 'NATO and the New World Order: Anarchy?', in S. Trifunovska, ed., *The Transatlantic Alliance on the Eve of the New Millennium* (The Hague, Kluwer Law International 1996) pp. 43-55.

[50] See Reichard, op. cit. n. 9, at pp. 99-119 (ch. 4: 'NATO Today'), with references to further literature.

[51] See T. Gazzini, 'NATO's Role in the Collective Security System', 8 *Journal of Conflict and Security Law* (2003) pp. 231-263 at pp. 244-245; and U. Schürr, *Der Aufbau einer europäischen Sicherheits- und Verteidigungsidentität im Beziehungsgeflecht von EU, WEU, OSZE und NATO* (Frankfurt am Main, Lang 2003) at p. 107, referred to by Reichard, op. cit. n. 9, at p. 104.

[52] NATO, *The Alliance's New Strategic Concept*, adopted by Heads of State and Government, Rome, 9 November 1991, reproduced in *NATO Handbook* (Brussels, NATO Office of Information and Press 2001).

[53] Ibid., at paras. 31 and 32: 'In the new political and strategic environment in Europe, the success of the Alliance's policy of preserving peace and preventing war depends even more than in the

with the Conference for Security and Cooperation in Europe (CSCE) and other institutions 'to prevent conflict since the Allies' security is inseparably linked to that of all other states in Europe.'[54]

Further significant changes to the Alliance's mission statement were agreed to at the Washington Summit of 24 April 1999. In general terms, the Strategic Concept and Washington Summit Declaration delineated a broad approach to security, encompassing complementary political and military means and emphasising cooperation with states and international organisations that share NATO's objectives.[55] Allies noted that 'a coherent approach to crisis management, as in any use of force by the Alliance, will require the Alliance's political authorities to choose and coordinate appropriate responses from a range of both political and military measures and to exercise close political control at all stages.'[56] NATO members also stated that, in the light of the demanding nature of conflict prevention and crisis management operations and the requirement for the same qualities of cohesion, multinational training and extensive prior planning needed for Article 5 situations, such operations would be handled through the same structures and procedures used for Article 5 operations.[57] Allies agreed to a number of measures to ensure that NATO would have the necessary military capabilities for all NATO missions, including contributing to conflict prevention and crisis management.

The new Strategic Concept listed crisis management and conflict prevention under the section 'fundamental security tasks' of the Alliance. It stated:

> [...] in order to enhance the security and stability of the Euro-Atlantic area:
> - Crisis Management: To stand ready, case-by-case and by consensus, in conformity with Article 7 of the Washington Treaty, to contribute to effective conflict prevention and to engage actively in crisis management, including crisis response operations.[58]

The Strategic Concept of 1999 also recognised the need for 'military capabilities effective under the full range of foreseeable circumstances' as 'the basis of the Alliance's ability to contribute to conflict prevention and crisis management

past on the effectiveness of preventive diplomacy and successful management of crises affecting the security of its members [...]. In these new circumstances there are increased opportunities for the successful resolution of crises at an early stage. [...] The success of the Alliance policy will require a coherent approach determined by the Alliance's political authorities choosing and coordinating appropriate crisis management measures as required from a range of political and other measures, including those in the military field.'

54 Ibid., at para. 33.

55 NATO, 'The Alliance's Strategic Concept', Press Release NAC-S(99)65, 24 April 1999.

56 Ibid., at para. 32.

57 Ibid., at para. 29.

58 Ibid., at para. 10.

through non-Article 5 crisis response operations.'[59] The Allies noted that NATO's preparedness to carry out such operations supported the broader objective of reinforcing and extending stability and would often involve the participation of NATO's PfP countries. The latter would be done by making full use of partnership, cooperation, dialogue and NATO's links to other organisations to contribute to preventing crises and, should they arise, defusing them at an early stage.[60] The Heads of State and Government thereby highlighted the importance of consultations pursuant to Article 4 of the Washington Treaty. In fact, the 1999 Strategic Concept identified consultations as the second of the Alliance's 'fundamental security tasks.'[61]

Measures agreed upon at the Prague summit of 21-22 November 2002, including enlargement of NATO, the Prague Capabilities Commitment, the NATO Response Force and the new command arrangements, all contributed to the Alliance's conflict prevention and crisis management capabilities.[62] Allies also gave additional impetus to cooperation with the European Union in crisis management (the so-called 'Berlin Plus' arrangements),[63] as well as in other areas, stating that

> [e]vents on and since 11 September 2001 have underlined further the importance of greater transparency and cooperation between our two organisations on questions of common interest relating to security, defence and crisis management, so that crises can be met with the most appropriate military response and effective crisis management ensured.[64]

In conclusion, while maintaining collective defence as it primary task, the greatest and most visible change in NATO's activities since the end of the Cold War is its involvement in ending conflict, restoring peace and building stability in crisis regions in both Europe and other parts of the world. On paper, NATO now attaches great importance to cooperation with non-members and other international organisations: '[i]n every instance, NATO is deploying in support of the wider interest of the international community and working closer together with other organisations to help resolve deep-rooted problems and create conditions in which the various peace processes can become self-sustaining.'[65]

---

59 Ibid., at para. 29.

60 Ibid., at para. 32.

61 Ibid., at para. 10.

62 NATO Prague Summit Declaration issued by the Heads of State and Government participating in the meeting of the NAC in Prague on 21 November 2002, NATO Press release (2002)127, 21 November 2002.

63 See Reichard, op. cit. n. 9, at pp. 273-310 (ch. 8: 'The Berlin Plus Agreement'); and chapter 4 of this book, section 4.2.1.

64 NATO Prague Summit Declaration, loc. cit. n. 62, at para. 11.

65 NATO Briefing, *Crisis Management*, October 2003.

3.3 Enlargement as a means to extend security and stability

The end of the Cold War provided a unique opportunity to build improved security in the entire Euro-Atlantic area.[66] Since NATO's creation in 1949, the Alliance has taken in new members on five separate occasions: in 1952 (Greece and Turkey), 1955 (Germany), 1982 (Spain), 1999 (Czech Republic, Hungary and Poland) and 2004 (Bulgaria, Estonia, Latvia, Lithuania, Romania, Slovakia and Slovenia).[67] In this way, the twelve founding members[68] have grown to twenty-six, thereby bringing in nine former members of the Warsaw Pact. The fifth (and largest) round of NATO enlargement may not be the last. At present, three Western Balkan states (Albania, Croatia and Macedonia) are parties to NATO's Membership Action Plan (MAP), designed to assist aspiring partner countries in meeting NATO standards and preparing for possible future membership (see below).

Enlargement of NATO is based upon Article 10 of the Washington Treaty, which states that membership is open to any 'European State in a position to further the principles of this Treaty and to contribute to the security of the North Atlantic area.' In addition, countries seeking NATO membership are also expected to meet certain political, economic and military requirements, which are laid down in the 1995 'Study on NATO Enlargement'.[69] No fixed list of membership conditions exists, but the 'Study on NATO Enlargement' points out in chapter 5 (paras. 68-78) that aspirant countries should provide evidence, *inter alia*, that they:

- represent a functioning democratic political system based on a market economy;
- conform to the basic principles embodied in the Washington Treaty: democracy, individual liberty and the rule of law;
- treat minority populations in accordance with the guidelines of the OSCE;
- have resolved outstanding disputes with neighbours and have made an overall commitment to the peaceful settlement of disputes;
- accept the *acquis* of the Alliance;[70]

---

[66] See V. Krivokhizha, 'The NATO Enlargement: Implications and Perspectives for Transatlantic Relations', in Trifunovska, op. cit. n. 49, at pp. 57-67.

[67] See S. Larrabee, *NATO Enlargement: Prague and Beyond* (Brussels, CEPS 2001); and D. Abenheim, 'The Big Bang of NATO Enlargement', *Hoover Digest* (2003), available at: <http://www.hoover.org/publications/digest/3063166.html>.

[68] Belgium, Canada, Denmark, France, Iceland, Italy, Luxembourg, Netherlands, Norway, Portugal, United Kingdom and United States.

[69] Available at: <http://www.nato.int/docu/basictxt/enl-9501.htm>.

[70] These include, in particular, the Agreement on the Status of the North Atlantic Treaty Organisation, National Representatives and International Staff (Ottawa Convention, 1951); the NATO

- apply security rules and procedures;
- undertake to participate fully in the Alliance consultation and decision-making process on political and security issues of concern to NATO;
- have the ability and willingness to make a military contribution to the Alliance and to achieve interoperability with other members' forces; and
- are committed to democratic civil-military relations and institutional structures.

Aspirant countries are expected to participate in the MAP, which presupposes participation in the PfP programme. At its Brussels Summit of 10-11 January 1994, NATO addressed the PfP invitation to all states participating in the North Atlantic Cooperation Council[71] and the CSCE who were 'able and willing to contribute to the programme'.[72] Thus, participation in the PfP comes with its own conditionality:

> Protection and promotion of fundamental freedoms and human rights, and safeguarding of freedom, justice, and peace through democracy are shared values fundamental to the Partnership. In joining the [PfP, states] recall that they are committed to the preservation of democratic societies, their freedom from coercion and intimidation, and the maintenance of the principles of international law. They reaffirm their commitment to fulfil in good faith the obligations of the Charter of the United Nations and the principles of the Universal Declaration on Human Rights, specifically, to refrain from the threat or use of force against the territorial integrity or political independence of any State, to respect existing borders and to

Agreement on the Mutual Safeguarding of Secrecy of Inventions relating to Defence, and for which Applications for Patents Have Been Made (Paris, 1960); the Agreement between the Parties to the North Atlantic Treaty regarding the Status of their Forces (London, 1951); the NATO Agreement on the Communication of Technical Information for Defence Purposes (Brussels, 1970); as well as the Strategic Concepts; Summit Declarations and NAC Decisions in ministerial and permanent session as reflected in NAC Communiqués, including those issued in Oslo in June 1992 and Brussels in December 1992 in which the Alliance undertook to support, on a case-by-case basis in accordance with its own procedures, peacekeeping activities under the responsibility of the OSCE and peacekeeping operations under the authority of the UN Security Council, including by making available Alliance resources and expertise; documents on cooperation between NATO and any partner state already agreed when new member(s) join the Alliance (recognising that NATO's policies are dynamic instruments).

71 The establishment of the NACC in December 1991 brought together the Member States of NATO and, initially, nine Central and Eastern European countries (Bulgaria, the Czech Republic, Estonia, Hungary, Latvia, Lithuania, Poland, Romania and Slovakia) in a new consultative forum. In March 1992, participation in the NACC was expanded to include all members of the Commonwealth of Independent States and by June 1992, Georgia and Albania had also become members. In 1997, the NACC was replaced by the Euro-Atlantic Partnership Council (EAPC). In this consultative body, the forty-six NATO Member States and partners meet regularly to consider cooperation activities and political and security questions.

72 The 1994 PfP Invitation is available at: <http://www.nato.int/docu/comm/49-95/c940110a.htm>, and as NATO Mini. Comm. M-1(94)2, Brussels, 10-11 January 1994.

> settle disputes by peaceful means. They also reaffirm their commitment to the Helsinki Final Act and all subsequent CSCE documents and to the fulfilment of the commitments and obligations they have undertaken in the field of disarmament and arms control.[73]

The invitation has since been accepted by a total of thirty-three countries. Most recently, Bosnia Herzegovina, Montenegro and Serbia joined the PfP programme and the Euro-Atlantic Partnership Council.[74] There are currently twenty-three countries participating in the PfP programme.[75]

The Membership Action Plan was launched in April 1999 at NATO's Washington Summit as a programme of advice, assistance and practical support tailored to the individual needs of countries wishing to join the Alliance.[76] The MAP's main features are:

- the submission by aspiring members of individual annual national programmes on their preparations for possible future membership, covering political, economic, defence, resource, security and legal aspects;
- a feedback mechanism on aspirant countries' progress on their programmes that includes both political and technical advice, as well as annual meetings between all NATO members and individual aspirants at the level of the North Atlantic Council to assess progress;[77] and
- a defence planning approach for aspirants which includes the elaboration and review of agreed planning targets.

Participation in the MAP does not prejudge any decision by the Alliance on future membership. Aspirants must be officially invited by the North Atlantic Council to begin membership negotiations. The aim of these negotiations is to obtain formal confirmation from the invitees of their willingness and ability to meet the political, legal and military obligations and commitments of NATO membership, as laid out in the Washington Treaty and in the 'Study on NATO Enlargement'. The end product of these discussions is a timetable to be submitted by each invitee for the completion of necessary reforms, which may continue even after

---

73 See Partnership for Peace Framework Document, para. 2, annexed to the 1994 PfP Invitation and available at: <http://www.nato.int/docu/comm/49-95/c940110b.htm>.

74 See Riga Summit Declaration, Press Release (2006)150, 29 November 2006, para. 36 for the invitation to join the PfP and the EAPC; and NATO Update, 'Bosnia and Herzegovina, Montenegro and Serbia join NATO Partnership for Peace', 14 December 2006, for the effectuation thereof.

75 Albania, Armenia, Austria, Azerbaijan, Belarus, Bosnia-Herzegovina, Croatia, Finland, Georgia, Ireland, Kazakhstan, Kyrgyzstan, Macedonia, Moldova, Montenegro, Russia, Serbia, Sweden, Switzerland, Tajikistan, Turkmenistan, Ukraine and Uzbekistan.

76 NATO, 'Membership Action Plan (MAP)', Press Release NAC-S(99)66, 24 April 1999.

77 An annual consolidated progress report on activities under the MAP is presented to the Ministers of Foreign Affairs and Defence at their annual NAC meetings in spring.

these countries have become NATO members. While undertaking these reforms, countries can also become involved alongside NATO members in some of the Alliance's operations. Participation in these operations enables candidate countries to demonstrate that, in addition to being consumers of security – benefiting in particular from NATO's collective defence guarantee – they are also able to contribute to security and to help increase stability in and beyond the Euro-Atlantic area. The ability to contribute militarily to collective defence, peacekeeping and other new missions of the Alliance could be a factor in deciding whether to invite a candidate to join NATO.[78] Ultimately, Allies decide by consensus whether to invite a candidate country to join NATO, basing their decision on their judgement of whether membership of a specific country would contribute to security and stability in the North Atlantic area. Once admitted, new members enjoy all the rights and assume all the obligations of membership. These include acceptance of all the principles, policies and procedures previously adopted by the other Alliance members – i.e., NATO's *acquis*.[79] As such, NATO enlargement serves as a vehicle to take away some of the root causes of conflicts on the European continent.

For some time now, the three countries that are currently participating in the MAP (Albania, Croatia and Macedonia) have been preparing themselves for the responsibilities and obligations of membership. But despite these aspirant states' hopes for an invitation for membership at the end of 2006, NATO Heads of State and Government at the Riga Summit declared that the Alliance intends to extend new invitations to those countries that meet 'NATO's performance-based standards and are able to contribute to Euro-Atlantic security and stability' only at the next summit, in the spring of 2008.[80] In short, obtaining NATO membership represents the culmination of a long preparatory process. The seven countries that joined NATO in 2004 already started participating in the PfP shortly after it was created in 1994. Since 1999, all of these countries have benefited from intensified cooperation under the MAP, pushing comprehensive reforms well beyond defence and security issues and military structures. Similar timeframes will apply to the first three Western Balkan states to join NATO as full members.[81]

---

78 The seven new Member States have become involved alongside NATO partners in some of the Alliance's operations, including NATO-led peacekeeping missions in the Balkans. See *infra* section 7.

79 See *supra* n. 70.

80 See Riga Summit Declaration, Press Release (2006)150, 29 November 2006, para. 30.

81 Croatia joined the PfP in 2000 and the MAP in 2002. Albania joined the PfP in 1994 and the MAP in 1999. Macedonia joined the PfP in 1995 and the MAP in 1999. See also chapter 6.

4. OSCE

4.1 Legal and operational framework

On 1 August 1975, the participating states to the Conference on Security and Cooperation in Europe (CSCE) adopted the Helsinki Final Act.[82] The Final Act, a political document which was not meant to be legally binding, contained the principles for East-West dialogue and coexistence. It was also one of the first official documents that recognised and integrated a broad security concept: the so-called 'human dimension.'[83] Further, it was the start of a process which increasingly led from coexistence to cooperation and to a gradual institutionalisation.[84] This process led to the transformation of the *Conference* on Security and Cooperation in Europe into the *Organisation* for Security and Cooperation in Europe in 1994.[85]

With its fifty-six participating states, the OSCE is the world's largest regional security arrangement.[86] All European states, including Belarus, take part in the organisation. But the geographical scope of the OSCE is not restricted to the European continent. With the participation of non-European states like the United States, Canada and the Caucasian and Central Asian states that gained independence after the dissolution of the Soviet Union, the OSCE encompasses the region of the northern hemisphere, from Vancouver to Vladivostok. Within this region, the OSCE sees important duties for itself in the fields of conflict prevention and post-conflict rehabilitation. In particular, the OSCE is engaged in activities such as arms control, cooperation in the economic and environmental fields, supervision of compliance with human and minority rights and the observation and organisation of elections.[87]

The OSCE's activities are based on the principles that security is indivisible and requires mutual cooperation. Politico-military issues, the protection and promotion of human rights and fundamental freedoms, economic and environmental issues are interconnected elements of a wider security dimension; stagnation in one dimension

---

[82] Reproduced in 14 *ILM* 1307 (1975).

[83] See Principle VII and the 'basket' entitled 'Cooperation in Humanitarian and Other Fields'. See E. Decaux and L.-A. Sicilianos, eds., *La CSCE: Dimension humaine et règlement des différends* (Paris, Montchrestien 1993).

[84] See E. Suy, 'The Development of Supervisory Mechanisms Within the CSCE Framework', in Blokker and Muller, op. cit. n. 25, at pp. 83-92.

[85] See I. Dekker and R. Wessel, 'Van CVSE naar OVSE: de sluipende institutionalisering en onvermijdelijke juridisering van een internationale conferentie', 31 *Vrede en Veiligheid* (2002) pp. 425-438.

[86] The Republic of Montenegro joined the OSCE most recently, on 21 June 2006. See MC.DEC/2/06, Decision No. 2/06 'Accession of Montenegro to the OSCE' of 21 June 2006.

[87] For a detailed guide to the history, structures and work of the organisation, see Secretariat of the OSCE, *OSCE Handbook*, 3rd edn. (Vienna, OSCE 2000) and <http://www.osce.org>.

has a negative effect on the other security dimensions. Similarly, the security of one state cannot and may not be considered separately from that of another state. Security can never be achieved at the expense of or in competition with other states, only by cooperation with others.[88]

The principles of indivisibility and mutual cooperation are reflected in the decision-making process of the OSCE. All participants have the same status and therefore the same voice in the decision-making process. The down-side of this is that the principle of having to reach consensus on political decisions (not the operational ones) can easily block decision-making between the fifty-six participating states.[89] Exceptionally, unanimity 'minus one' (the 'one' being a state grossly violating its OSCE commitments) or 'minus two' (the parties to a conflict) is possible.[90] OSCE decisions and documents have a political rather than a legally enforceable nature (e.g., the 1990 Charter of Paris for a New Europe[91]), with some notable exceptions (e.g., the 1990 CFE Treaty[92]). Although some legal academics argue the contrary, the OSCE does not formally have international legal personality, despite the fact that the CSCE was rechristened as the OSCE in 1994 in order to reflect its character as a permanent international organisation with its own responsibilities.[93] In the mid-1990s, the OSCE acquired the status of a UN 'regional arrangement' under the terms of chapter VIII of the UN Charter.[94]

The OSCE has a number of permanent institutions, of which the Secretariat, the Conflict Prevention Centre,[95] the High Commissioner on National Minorities

---

[88] For background and analysis, see, e.g., L. Nyholm, ed., *OSCE – A Need for Co-operation* (Copenhagen, The Danish United Nations Association 1998); and M. Bothe, N. Ronzitti and A. Rosas, eds., *The OSCE in the Maintenance of Peace and Security: Conflict Prevention, Crisis Management, and Peaceful Settlement of Disputes* (The Hague, Kluwer Law International 1998).

[89] See AIV, *The Netherlands and the Organisation for Security and Cooperation in Europe in 2003: Role and Direction* (The Hague, AIV 2002) at p. 22.

[90] Ibid.

[91] Reprinted in 30 *ILM* 190 (1991).

[92] Treaty on Conventional Armed Forces in Europe, reprinted in 30 *ILM* 1 (1991), entered into force on 9 November 1992. The Treaty was amended in Istanbul on 19 November 1999. The amendment has not yet entered into force.

[93] On the discussion, see N. Blokker, 'Internationale organisaties en hun leden. Van oude vragen, de dingen die voorbij gaan?', Inaugural Lecture, Leiden University, 2001, at pp. 15-16, with reference to a proponent of legal personality, I. Seidl-Hohenveldern, 'Internationale Organisationen aufgrund von soft law', in U. Beyerlin, et al., eds., *Recht zwischen Umbruch und Bewahrung – Festschrift für Rudolf Bernhardt* (Berlin, Springer Verlag 1995) pp. 229-239.

[94] See Secretary General Jan Kubis' remarks to the Second UNCTC Special Meeting with International, Regional and Sub-Regional Organisations, 7 October 2003, Washington D.C.

[95] Under the guidance of the Secretary General, the CPC provides support to the Chairman-in-Office and other OSCE negotiating and decision-making bodies in the fields of early warning, conflict prevention, crisis management, and post-conflict rehabilitation. To assist in this, it maintains an Operations Centre to identify potential crisis areas and to plan for future missions and operations. The Forum for Security and Cooperation Support Unit in the CPC covers politico-military aspects of security in the OSCE area. For an evaluation of the CPC's activities, see H. Vetschera, 'Ten Years of

and the Office for Democratic Institutions and Human Rights are the most important ones for this study. The latter two will be briefly discussed below. In addition, the Permanent Council[96] and the Chairman-in-Office (CiO) play a pivotal role in day-to-day management. The CiO acts primarily as an honest broker in the process of building consensus between the participating states. This chairmanship rotates annually among the participating states.

As a security organisation with a strong focus on conflict prevention, the OSCE has developed a whole range of tools to identify situations and developments that have the potential to escalate into violent conflicts and to react rapidly.[97] They include fact-finding and rapporteur missions,[98] personal representatives of the CiO[99] and *ad hoc* steering groups.[100] It is interesting to note that, over the years, the OSCE has developed a number of measures for (*ad hoc*) use in times of crisis or increasing tension that are intended to promote direct contacts between the parties to a dispute, as well as the other parties involved. For example, pursuant to the so-called 'Vienna Mechanism' – established in the Vienna Concluding Document of 1989,[101] participating states are allowed, through an established set of procedures, to raise questions relating to the human dimension

---

the Conflict Prevention Centre – Origins and Development', in Institute for Peace Research and Security Policy at the University of Hamburg, ed., *OSCE Yearbook 2001* (Baden-Baden, Nomos Verlag 2002) pp. 401-420.

96 In addition to being responsible for the day-to-day business and decision making of the organisation, the Permanent Council also holds informal committee meetings, enabling representatives to exchange views on various issues pertaining to the OSCE and raise concerns regarding developments in the OSCE area. As a permanent forum for multilateral dialogue and political consultations, the Permanent Council can be regarded as 'the king-spider in the OSCE's web of conflict prevention' or 'an ongoing security council without privilege'. See A. Bloed, 'The OSCE Main Political Bodies and Their Role in Conflict Prevention and Crisis Management', in Bothe et al., op. cit. n. 88, at p. 35.

97 See, e.g., M. van der Stoel, 'The Role of the OSCE in Conflict Prevention', *Studia Diplomatica* (1996) pp. 33-39; J. Grussendorf, 'Conflict Prevention in the OSCE', in Nyholm, op. cit. n. 88, at pp. 43-56, J. Cohen, *Conflict Prevention in the OSCE: An Assessment of Capacities* (The Hague, Netherlands Institute of International Relations 'Clingendael' 1999); E. Bakker, 'A Culture of Conflict Prevention: OSCE Experience and Cooperation with the EU', in Kronenberger and Wouters, op. cit. n. 19, at pp. 393-413.

98 These are usually comprised of short-term visits by experts and/or leading politicians or diplomats; the objective is to become acquainted with the facts during an on-the-spot visit. These missions report to the OSCE bodies. They are also employed to assess whether – and, if so, the extent to which – the OSCE should initiate missions and field operations.

99 Leading diplomats or (former) politicians may be requested by the CiO to carry out a specific short-term task in connection with the prevention of conflicts or crisis management. In 1997, for example, the former Austrian Chancellor Vranitzky played an important role in the restoration of stability and the prevention of the re-escalation of the conflict in Albania.

100 Steering groups comprised of a limited number of members assist the CiO as the need arises. The three members of the Troika – the past, present and future CiO – are always members of these steering groups, supplemented with representatives from states which the CiO believes may be able to make a contribution to the resolution of the specific problem.

101 Available at: <http://www.legislationline.org/legislation.php?tid=160&lid=5431>.

situation in other OSCE states. The latter are under the obligation to furnish information when so requested by other participating states.[102] The so-called 'Moscow Mechanism' (established at the last meeting of the CSCE on the Human Dimension in Moscow in 1991) builds on this and provides for the additional possibility for a minimum of six participating states (consequently, in this instance, a consensus is not required) to establish *ad hoc* missions of independent experts to assist in the resolution of a specific human dimension problem either on their own territory or in other OSCE participating states.[103] In addition to issues of relevance to the human rights dimension, consultation and cooperation mechanisms and procedures have been developed for emergency situations (the so-called 'Berlin Mechanism'). From 1991 to 1994, this mechanism for emergency situations was used four times altogether, in connection with the conflicts in the former Yugoslavia and Nagorno-Karabakh. A corresponding request from Russia in the context of the 1999 Kosovo crisis was rejected.[104]

As becomes clear from this overview, the OSCE is primarily geared towards conflict prevention and post-conflict rehabilitation. It has a minor role to play in crisis management and 'peacemaking'.[105] Of all OSCE conflict prevention and post-conflict rehabilitation instruments, the (long-term) missions (including election observation) and the High Commissioner on National Minorities contribute most directly to dispute resolution and therefore merit closer attention.

4.2 OSCE field presence

The decision to establish, extend and conclude field operations is usually taken by the Permanent Council, the principal decision-making body of the OSCE. The Permanent Council decides on the mandate, the number of staff and the budget of such operations. Field operations vary in duration of deployment. Short-term missions (i.e., fact-finding and expert or election observation missions) investigate

---

[102] This consultation mechanism was activated extensively prior to the first phase of the Yugoslav crisis (1989-1990). See Bakker, loc. cit. n. 97, at p. 399.

[103] The Moscow Mechanism is an instrument which provides for the deployment of expert missions to examine human rights concerns in OSCE countries. It has been activated on five occasions. For instance, it was activated in 1992 by the then twelve states of the European Community and the United States on the issue of reports of atrocities and attacks on unarmed civilians in Croatia and Bosnia-Herzegovina and in June 1993 by the CSCE Committee of Senior Officials *vis-à-vis* Serbia and Montenegro to investigate reports of human rights violations (this mission was unable to fulfil its task because of the Federal Republic of Yugoslavia's lack of cooperation). See: <http://www.osce.org/odihr/13483.html>.

[104] See R. Zaagman, 'OSCE Conflict Prevention and the Economic and Environmental Dimension', 10 *Helsinki Monitor* (1999) pp. 40-48.

[105] See, e.g., OSCE and Swiss Institute for World Affairs, 'Report of the Colloquium on "The Future of the OSCE"', Washington, 5-6 June 2005, available at: <http://www1.osce.org/cio/15467.html>.

specific situations and/or establish the local contacts which are required to respond quickly to potential threats to stability and security. Long-term missions fill the gap between short-term missions and traditional peacekeeping.[106] Their ongoing presence enables them to perform an early warning role and act in specific ways to address (potential) tensions. The OSCE's missions and field operations are the 'eyes and ears' of the organisation.[107] They monitor compliance with the OSCE's principles and obligations – in particular with regard to respect for human rights, democracy and the rule of law – and submit reports to the OSCE concerning political and other developments in the host state. In addition, they promote and provide support to political processes designed to prevent conflicts and to foster conflict management. The OSCE began its first (long-term) mission in September 1992 in Kosovo, Sandjak and Vojvodina (since concluded). Fifteen years later, the organisation has missions or offices at almost twenty locations in Eastern Europe and Central Asia. In many ways, this field presence constitutes the OSCE's core business to which no less than 80 per cent of its total budget is allocated.[108]

Election observation is one of the most – some say the only – politically relevant aspects of the organisation.[109] The OSCE's reputation as Europe's leading agency in the field of election observation is built upon its systematic, comprehensive and verifiable election observation methodology.[110] Through its Office for Democratic Institutions and Human Rights (ODIHR), the OSCE observes elections in all fifty-six participating states to assess the implementation of OSCE commitments relating to elections.[111] Where necessary, the ODIHR offers recommendations to bring electoral processes into line with those commitments. The ODIHR also conducts technical-assistance projects to improve the legislative and administrative framework for elections in specific countries.[112]

Other OSCE missions, for example the ones in Bosnia-Herzegovina and Kosovo, are focused on the reconstruction of the state and/or society in the phase

106 See Cohen, op. cit. n. 97, at p. 86.

107 E. Bakker and B. Bomert, *The OSCE and the Netherlands as Chairman-in-Office* (The Hague, Netherlands Helsinki Committee 2003) at p. 22.

108 See OSCE CPC Secretariat, 'Survey of OSCE Long-Term Missions and Other OSCE Field Activities', SEC.INF/115/04, 2 June 2004.

109 See OSCE and Swiss Institute for World Affairs, loc. cit. n. 105.

110 Based on the premise that an election is more than a one-day event, this methodology provides insights into all elements necessary for a democratic electoral process: the legal and regulatory framework, the election administration, the election campaign (including the media environment), the complaints and appeals process, voting, counting and tabulation, and the announcement of results.

111 See the Document of the Copenhagen Meeting of the Conference on the Human Dimension of the CSCE of 29 June 1990, 'International Standards of Elections'. The commitments agreed upon emphasise fundamental principles that are central to a democratic tradition and can be summed up in seven key words: universal, equal, fair, secret, free, transparent and accountable.

112 Information about these projects is available at: <http://www.osce.org/odihr-elections>.

subsequent to the resolution of a conflict. In Bosnia-Herzegovina, Kosovo and elsewhere, the missions work closely together with other organisations that are active in the field. These missions will be described in further detail below.[113]

4.3 High Commissioner on National Minorities

In reaction to the eruption of ethnic violence and the disintegration of Yugoslavia and the Soviet Union, the CSCE in 1992 adopted a proposal tabled by the Netherlands to appoint a High Commissioner on National Minorities (HCNM).[114] The Dutch diplomat and politician Max van der Stoel was appointed as the first HCNM, with an office in The Hague. His mandate was extended on several occasions. In July 2001, he was succeeded by the present incumbent, the Swedish diplomat Rolf Ekéus.

The High Commissioner is an instrument for the prevention of conflicts at the earliest possible stage.[115] His mandate is based on the principle that action on minorities issues should be taken as quickly as possible, that is to say, when they risk escalating into a conflict, thereby threatening stability and peaceful relations between participating states of the OSCE. The mandate bestows two main duties on the HCNM. Firstly, he must detect threats to peace and stability. Secondly, he must try to reduce tensions in crises involving minorities. In addition, he is required to warn the OSCE in the event that he cannot control a specific situation with the resources at his disposal. The political bodies of the OSCE can then exercise their discretion in deciding whether to take action.[116]

---

[113] See *infra* section 8.

[114] A reference to the original proposal is given by O. Brenninkmeijer, 'The OSCE High Commissioner on National Minorities: Negotiating the 1992 Conflict Prevention Mandate', PSIO Occasional Paper 5/2005, at p. 15, n. 3; Archive of the Netherlands Ministry of Foreign Affairs. 'Officiële Indiening Nederlands Voorstel Inzake HCM Commentaar: Tekst zoals werkelijk uitgesproken op de laatste plenaire voor het paasreces, woensdag 15 april 's avonds' (Official submission of the Netherlands proposal concerning HCM commentary. Statement as actually delivered on the last plenary before the Easter break, Wednesday evening, 15 April), Fax report from the CSCE Helsinki delegation, to DAV, The Hague, fax no. 333, 16 April 1992. The process of negotiation ended with the acceptance of the original mandate by all participating states at the closure of the CSCE's Helsinki Follow-up Meeting (HFUM) on 10 July 1992. See CSCE Helsinki Document 1992, 'The Challenges of Change', section on Helsinki Decisions, 8-14, available at: <http://www.osce.org/mc/13018.html>.

[115] See the literature referred to in n. 97. In addition, see M. Amor and M. Estebanez, 'The High Commissioner on National Minorities: Development of the Mandate', in Bothe et al., op. cit. n. 88, at pp. 123-165; H.-J. Heintze, 'Minority Issues in Western Europe and the OSCE High Commissioner on National Minorities', 7 *International Journal on Minority and Group Rights* (2000) pp. 381-392; and A. Inder Singh, 'Minorities, Justice and Security in Post-Communist Europe', *Journal of Ethnopolitics and Minority Issues in Europe* (2002), available at: <http://ecmi.de/jemie>.

[116] A description of the HCNM's current mandate and the tools at his disposal is available at: <http://www.osce.org/hcnm/13022.html>.

The HCNM has a number of tools available for the performance of his mandate. The most important of these are the collection of information (from OSCE missions, NGOs representing specific minorities and local partners – both governments and minorities), on-site consultations (for which the HCNM does not require special permission to visit the relevant country), the formulation of reports (some of which have contributed to the necessary amendment of national legislation, as well as the implementation of consultation mechanisms – or at least dialogue – between governments and the representatives of minorities) and the issuing of recommendations to governments (often as a result of a visit). The latter constituted perhaps the most important instrument of the first HCNM because they did not denounce the relevant government but instead tried to convince it that the country's stability would benefit most by granting specific rights or freedoms to members of the national minorities.

5. COUNCIL OF EUROPE

5.1 Legal and operational framework

The Council of Europe (CoE), established in 1949, is regarded as a security organisation for the purposes of this study.[117] With its wide membership (forty-seven members),[118] the organisation was given a mission to promote and defend pluralist democracy, human rights and the rule of law for the purpose of realising the ideals and principles that are their common heritage and facilitating their economic and social progress (Art. 1 Statute).[119] The only area specifically excluded from the Council of Europe's mandate is national defence (Art. 1(d)). But this does not mean that the CoE has no impact on security and stability in Europe. Quite the contrary: since the fall of the Berlin Wall, the CoE's main job

117 See chapter 1 for the rationale to adopt a broad notion of security. See also J. Wouters and F. Naert, 'How Effective is the European Security Architecture? Lessons from Bosnia and Kosovo', 50 *ICLQ* (2001) pp. 540-576 at p. 546.

118 The Republic on Montenegro was the last country to join the CoE, on 11 May 2007. In addition to the forty-seven members, the EC and several non-CoE members participate in this cooperation, notably by being party to CoE treaties which contain wider membership clauses. For example, Canada, Chile, Costa Rica, Israel, Tonga and the United States are parties to the Convention on the Transfer of Sentenced Persons (ETS No. 112, 1983). The EC is a contracting party, for example, to the Convention on the Conservation of European Wildlife and Natural Habitats (ETS No. 104, 1979). On the basis of Art. I-7(2) TCE, the European Union could become a party to the European Convention for the Protection of Human Rights and Fundamental Freedoms (i) if the TCE enters into force (see chapter 5, section 6.2) and (ii) if the other parties to the Convention agree to the European Union becoming a contracting party.

119 Statute of the Council of Europe, London, 5 May 1949, ETS Nos. 1/6/7/8/11. The texts of all CoE treaties are available on the website of the CoE Treaty Office, at: <http://conventions.coe.int>.

has become to act as a political anchor and human rights watchdog for Europe's post-Communist democracies. It assists the Central and Eastern European countries (CEECs) in carrying out and consolidating political, legal and constitutional reform, especially by providing know-how. In this way, the CoE helps to build 'democratic security, an essential complement to military security and a prerequisite for the continent's stability'.[120]

The main component parts of the CoE are the Committee of Ministers (the organisation's decision-making body composed of ministers of foreign affairs or their representatives), the Parliamentary Assembly (bringing together 630 members from all national parliaments), the Congress of Local and Regional Authorities (composed of a Chamber of Local Authorities and a Chamber of Regions), the Secretariat (headed since September 2004 by Secretary-General Terry Davis) and the European Court of Human Rights (which falls under the budget of the organisation and is composed of forty-seven judges). The CoE's European Commission for Democracy through Law, better known as the 'Venice Commission', has provided constitutional advice in a number of conflict areas, notably in South-Eastern Europe.[121] This Commission is composed of independent experts from the forty-seven Member States and takes its name from the place where it has its seat.

5.2 Tools to create and enhance democratic security

The Council of Europe's ability to promote political dialogue and to ensure practical cooperation on the basis of fundamental values is the key to its role in conflict prevention and peacebuilding.[122] Political dialogue is particularly intense within the Parliamentary Assembly, much more so than in the Committee of Ministers. Apart from expressing the whole range of political opinions, the CoE has consistently – and often effectively – put pressure on governments and proposed innovative solutions. The CoE's biggest achievement, however, is the initiation of 198 legally binding European treaties or conventions on topics ranging from human rights and fundamental freedoms to the fight against organised crime. But the Council of Europe distinguishes itself from other international organisations not only by the large number of binding obligations that Member States have entered into but also by the sophisticated mechanisms ensuring the compliance of Member States with these obligations, especially in

---

[120] The CoE's Vienna Summit in October 1993 set out new political aims. The Heads of State and Government cast the CoE as a guardian of democratic security – founded on human rights, democracy and the rule of law.

[121] See: <http://www.venice.coe.int/site/dynamics/N_calendar_ef.asp?L=E> and further section 9.

[122] See J. Kleijssen, 'No Peace without Human Rights: The Council of Europe and Conflict Prevention', in Kronenberger and Wouters, op cit. n. 19, pp. 439-449 at p. 440.

the field of human and minority rights. Violations of human rights are an important cause of armed conflict. By ensuring the observance of these rights, the CoE is therefore addressing an important root cause of conflict. The unique feature of the European Convention on Human Rights (ECHR) of 1950 is exactly its control mechanism.[123] The protection of fundamental rights is entrusted to a permanent European Court of Human Rights. The Court can be seized by both states and individuals. Its judgments are legally binding upon CoE Member States. Even in politically highly sensitive cases, its judgments are implemented – even if not always immediately.[124] The Convention for the Prevention of Torture and Inhuman or Degrading Treatment or Punishment complements the protection available under the ECHR by establishing a European Committee for the Prevention of Torture, composed of independent and impartial experts from a variety of backgrounds.[125] The Framework Convention for the Protection of National Minorities[126] is the first-ever legally binding multilateral instrument devoted to the protection of national minorities. As a counterpart to the Framework Convention, the European Charter for Regional or Minority Languages came into force in March 1998.[127]

In addition to these legal instruments, the long-term institutional cooperation activities of the Council of Europe are important tools. Following the fall of the Berlin Wall, the Council of Europe embarked on a programme of cooperation and assistance with the CEECs, aimed at helping them carry out democratic reforms and integrating them into European structures. These programmes focus on democratic institution building, constitutional reform, harmonisation of legislation with European standards, in particular the ECHR, reform of the judiciary, electoral reform, media legislation, reform of education curricula, minority rights and protection, training of law officers, development of local democracy and the promotion of civil society. These programmes are being adapted on a case-by-case basis to help prevent the (re-)emergence of particular conflict situations.[128]

5.3 Enlargement as a means to extend security and stability

Direct negotiation and the use of political leverage in the context of obligations linked to the membership perspective are also amongst the CoE's specific tools to

---

123 ETS No. 5, 1950.

124 See R.A. Lawson and H.G. Schermers, *Leading Cases of the European Court of Human Rights*, 2nd edn. (Nijmegen, Ars Aequi Libri 1999). For an evaluation of the ECHR at 55, see T. Barkhuysen, M. Kuijer and R.A. Lawson, eds., *55 jaar EVRM* (Leiden, NJCM 2006).

125 ETS No. 126, 1987.

126 ETS No. 157, 1995.

127 ETS No. 148, 1992.

128 See information on legal cooperation, at: <http://www.coe.int/T/E/Com/About_Coe/legal.asp>.

take away the root causes of conflict and extend the zone of security and stability in Europe. During the Cold War period, the CoE already demonstrated its capacity to integrate countries that had freed themselves from totalitarian regimes. Thus, in 1977, Greece was readmitted (under the Colonels' regime it had withdrawn from the organisation when it was about to be excluded) and Portugal and Spain were admitted in 1976 and 1977 respectively, following the restoration of democracy. The fall of the Berlin Wall finally enabled the CoE to achieve what it had been set up to do from the beginning: to unite the whole of Europe on the basis of common values. Following the accession of Montenegro on 11 May 2007, the CoE now has forty-seven Member States and represents over 800 million Europeans. Only Belarus is absent from the 'European democratic family'. Its application for membership of 12 March 1993 has been put on ice in view of the repressive regime's poor record on the protection of human rights, democratic principles and the rule of law.

According to Article 4 of the Statute of the CoE '[a]ny European State which is deemed to be able and willing to fulfil the provisions of Article 3 may be invited to become a member of the Council of Europe by the Committee of Ministers'.[129] Article 3 lays down the essential membership criteria. This provision obliges every Member State to 'accept the principles of the rule of law and of the enjoyment by all persons within its jurisdiction of human rights and fundamental freedoms' and to work together in the realisation of the aims for which the CoE was set up. The latter is an indirect reference to Article 1. In this respect, the signature and subsequent ratification of the ECHR has become an additional admission criterion.[130] In fact, the Parliamentary Assembly, whose opinion the Committee of Ministers seeks before making a decision on the invitation of a state to accede to the organisation, has in recent years established a comprehensive list of political commitments which have to be accepted by the authorities of the countries applying for membership.[131] These commitments are tailored to each candidate country's situation and concern, *inter alia*, endeavours (i) to prevent or overcome conflict situations with political means, in line with democratic principles and respect for human rights;[132] (ii) to sign and ratify a whole array of the CoE's treaties and

---

[129] Article 5 lays down that, '[i]n special circumstances, a European country which is deemed to be able and willing to fulfil the provisions of Article 3, may be invited by the Committee of Ministers to become an associate member of the Council of Europe'.

[130] This is the case since 1976. Since 1993, a time limit for the ratification of the ECHR (normally within a year from accession) has been established. See Resolution No. 1031 (1994).

[131] See R. Lawson, 'Extending the European Family of Nations – The Response of the Council of Europe to Growing Membership', in N. Blokker and H. Schermers, eds., *Proliferation of International Organizations* (The Hague, Kluwer Law International 2001) pp. 415-432.

[132] In the case of the countries of the Western Balkans that applied for membership after 1995, the commitments include sections on cooperation with the ICTY. See Opinion No. 234 (2002) on Bosnia-Herzegovina's application for membership of the CoE and Opinion No. 195 (1996) on

protocols in the field of human and minority rights, local democracy and criminal law;[133] and (iii) to ensure the proper functioning of the state's institutions.[134] The Committee of Ministers takes these commitments as the basis of its decision to invite a state to the organisation.

The verification procedure which has been established over the years consists of an examination of the compatibility of the legal order of the candidate country with CoE's standards. The Parliamentary Assembly, mainly through its Political Affairs Committee and Committee on Legal Affairs and Human Rights, makes an evaluation of legislation and other formal domestic acts by means of questionnaires, interviews and other contacts with national authorities and various representatives of the civil society (NGOs, press, etc.). Such an examination particularly concerns conformity with the basic conditions of a democratic state relating to the separation of powers, free elections, existence of political parties, freedom of the press and media and independence of the judiciary. The Assembly may decide to interrupt the examination of a request to accede[135] or include in its opinion on membership a suspension clause relating to the time of accession.[136]

Croatia's request for membership of the CoE, para. 9. Opinion No. 239 (2002) on the application for membership of the Federal Republic of Yugoslavia, in para. 12, also demands cooperation in establishing the facts concerning the fate of missing people and handing over all information concerning mass graves. The commitments in the Opinion on Croatia's application for membership reflect the fact that the opinion was adopted shortly after the end of the war: 'The Assembly further expects Croatia: (i) to observe strictly the provisions of international humanitarian law, including in the event of armed conflict within its territory; [...] (iv) to grant, without delay, a general amnesty for all former combatants not suspected of war crimes, in order to encourage the return of Croatian Serbs; [...] (ix) to solve, in accordance with the standards and principles of the Council of Europe, the problems relating to the confiscation of property during the fascist and communist regimes.' In Opinion No. 191 (1996) on FYROM's application for CoE membership, in para. 10, the Assembly notes that Macedonia intends 'to abide by the Geneva Convention of 1951 on the Status of Refugees and its 1967 New York Protocol, and to ensure that asylum-seekers and refugees are not deported to countries where they would be at risk of human rights violations or to any other country without ensuring that they would be given effective and durable protection against return to a country where they might be at risk.'

133 Apart from those referred to in section 5.2 and n. 119 in this chapter, mention should be made of the European Charter of Local Self-Government (ETS No. 122, 1985); the European Outline Convention on Trans-Frontier Cooperation between Territorial Communities or Authorities (ETS No. 106, 1980) and its protocols; the Conventions on Extradition (ETS No. 24, 1957), Mutual Assistance in Criminal Matters (ETS No. 30, 1959), Laundering, Search, Seizure and Confiscation of the Proceeds from Crime (ETS No. 141, 1990) and the Transfer of Sentenced Persons (ETS No. 112, 1983); and the European Social Charter (ETS No. 35, 1961).

134 See, e.g., Opinion No. 239 (2002) on the application for membership of the Federal Republic of Yugoslavia, para. 12, on the drafting of the Constitutional Charter of the state union of Serbia and Montenegro; the organisation of referenda on independence at the end of the three-year trial period mentioned in the Belgrade Agreement – see chapter 6, section 4.3.3; and the peaceful dispute settlement concerning the future status of Kosovo.

135 This is what happened with the membership application of Belarus. See, e.g., PACE Recommendation 1441 (2000) and Resolution No. 1306 (2002) on the situation in Belarus.

136 See, e.g., Opinion No. 154 (1990) on Poland's application for membership of the CoE.

In the case of a positive opinion of the Parliamentary Assembly, the Committee of Ministers decides whether or not to invite the candidate country to become a member. Membership of a country becomes effective upon the deposit on its behalf with the Secretary General of an instrument of accession to the present Statute. Both the Assembly and the Committee of Ministers have each created a special monitoring procedure to verify compliance with the above-mentioned membership commitments.[137] Sanctions are possible when the political will to cooperate is found to be lacking.[138]

6. EFFORTS TO BRING PEACE AND STABILITY TO THE WESTERN BALKANS: UNITED NATIONS[139]

6.1 Introduction

The United Nations became actively involved in the situation in the former Yugoslavia on 25 September 1991, when the Security Council unanimously adopted resolution 713, expressing deep concern at the fighting and calling on all states to implement immediately a 'general and complete embargo on all deliveries of weapons and military equipment to Yugoslavia.'[140] This resolution supported EC

137 The Assembly follows a country-by-country approach. See complementary texts to the Rules of Procedure of the Assembly, Honouring of Obligations and Commitments by Member States of the Council of Europe, Resolution 1115 (1997) on the setting up of an Assembly committee on the honouring of obligations and commitments by Member States of the Council of Europe (Monitoring Committee), available at: <http://assembly.coe.int>. The Committee of Ministers follows a thematic approach (freedom of information, local democracy, independence of the judiciary, etc.) towards all Member States.

138 Art. 8 of the Statute states: 'Any member of the Council of Europe which has seriously violated Article 3 may be suspended from its rights of representation and requested by the Committee of Ministers to withdraw under Article 7. If such member does not comply with this request, the Committee may decide that it has ceased to be a member of the Council as from such date as the Committee may determine.' For example, the Parliamentary Assembly suspended the voting rights of the Russian delegation in April 2000 (and restored them in January 2001) because of the human rights situation there. Persistent failure to comply with the organisation's principles could result in expulsion from the organisation.

139 The historical facts in the following paragraphs are largely drawn from L. Silber and D. Little, *The Death of Yugoslavia*, rev. edn. (London, Penguin Books 1996); and B. Marković, *Yugoslav Crisis and the World: Chronology of Events January 1990 – December 1995* (Belgrade, Institute of International Politics and Economics 1995).

140 On additional sanctions, see UNSC resolutions 724, 757, 787 and 820, the latter two authorising enforcement under the Security Council's authority. UNSC resolution 942 ordered an embargo against the Bosnian Serbs. The sanctions were suspended and terminated by UNSC resolutions 943, 1021, 1022 and 1074 (1 October 1996). For a legal analysis, see E. Kalpyris, R. Vork and A. Napolitano, *Les sanctions des Nations Unies dans le conflit de l'ex-Yougoslavie* (Brussels, Bruylant 1995) pp. 3-73.

initiatives already undertaken to restore peace and dialogue in ex-Yugoslavia.[141] On 8 October 1991, UN Secretary-General Pérez de Cuéllar appointed Cyrus Vance, former US Secretary of State, as his Personal Envoy for Yugoslavia. Thereafter, the Secretary-General and his Personal Envoy maintained constant contact with all the parties to the conflict, the Presidency of the European Community, the Chairman of the CSCE, Lord Carrington, then Chairman of the EC's Peace Conference on Yugoslavia, and other interested parties in their efforts to find a solution to the crisis.

It soon became clear that the most valuable contribution the United Nations could make at that stage was a 'peacekeeping' operation to create the necessary conditions for the pursuit of political negotiations for a peaceful settlement. With little peace to keep at the time, the United Nations would embark on activities that were very different from any that the organisation had undertaken elsewhere.[142] As part of the collective effort to stop the fighting and to find a peaceful solution to the conflict, Cyrus Vance undertook several missions to Yugoslavia and discussed with all parties concerned, among other things, the feasibility of deploying a UN peacekeeping operation. On 23 November 1991, he convened a meeting in Geneva at which the presidents of Serbia and Croatia signed a ceasefire agreement and requested the speedy establishment of a UN peacekeeping force.[143] The Security Council decided, however, that the conditions for the deployment of such a force had not been met because the ceasefire had broken down almost immediately.[144] Subsequently, on 2 January 1992, an implementing accord on an unconditional ceasefire was signed at Sarajevo, and a small UN mission, composed of fifty liaison officers, was sent to supervise the newly negotiated ceasefire.[145] Notwithstanding the fact that certain political groups in Yugoslavia were still expressing objections to the UN plan, the Secretary-General recommended to the Security Council the establishment of the United Nations Protection Force (UNPROFOR).[146] In making this recommendation, he stressed that, in his view, the danger that a UN peacekeeping operation would fail for lack of cooperation from the parties was less grievous than the danger that delay in its dispatch would lead to a breakdown of the ceasefire and to a new conflagration.

---

141 See chapter 3, section 2.

142 See M. Bothe, 'Peace-keeping', in Simma, op. cit. n. 2, at pp. 648-700.

143 UN Doc. S/23239, Annex.

144 See UNSC resolutions 721 and 724, both at para. 2.

145 See UNSC resolution 727, paras. 2 and 3. The accord (UN Doc. S/23363, Annex III) is reprinted in D. Bethlehem and M. Weller, eds., *The 'Yugoslav' Crisis in International Law: General Issues (Part I)* (Cambridge, Cambridge University Press 1997) at p. 487.

146 UN Doc. S/23592 (15 February 1992), reprinted in Bethlehem and Weller, ibid., at p. 492.

6.2 UNPROFOR (1): too little, too late

6.2.1 *Establishment and rapid expansion of mandate and territory*

UNPROFOR was established by the Security Council by resolution 743 of 21 February 1992 'to create the conditions of peace and security required for the negotiation of an overall settlement of the Yugoslav crisis'.[147] For an initial period of twelve months, this peacekeeping operation was established in Croatia only, as an interim arrangement to ensure that the three 'United Nations Protected Areas' (UNPAs) in Croatia were demilitarised and that all persons residing in them were protected from fear of armed attack. It was only meant to start working in Bosnia after the primary task of disarmament in parts of Croatia had been completed.[148] However, due to the outbreak of hostilities in Bosnia, this was pushed forward: on 30 April 1992, the Secretary-General sent observers to Bosnia.[149] Unfortunately, by that time, the conflict had already erupted.

On 8 June 1992, as the conflict in Bosnia-Herzegovina intensified, UNPROFOR's mandate and strength were enlarged in order to ensure the security and functioning of the airport at Sarajevo and the delivery of humanitarian assistance to the city and its surroundings.[150] In September 1992, UNPROFOR's mandate was further enlarged to enable it to support efforts by the United Nations High Commissioner for Refugees (UNHCR) to deliver humanitarian relief throughout Bosnia-Herzegovina and to protect convoys of released civilian detainees if the International Committee of the Red Cross (ICRC) so requested.[151] In the wake of continuing reports of 'ethnic cleansing' in the second half of 1992, UNPROFOR's mandate was enlarged to include monitoring functions in certain other areas of Croatia ('pink zones'); to enable the force to control the entry of civilians into the UNPAs and to perform immigration and customs functions at the UNPA borders and at international frontiers (to enforce the sanctions and to prevent the infiltration into the country of irregular units); and to include monitoring of the demilitarisation of the Prevlaka Peninsula, a strategic area just south of

---

[147] UNSC resolution 743 (21 February 1992) para. 5. UNSC resolution 749 (7 April 1992) authorised the earliest possible full deployment of UNPROFOR. The force's mandate changed (see UNSC resolutions 769, 770, 776, 815 and 836), was extended and then terminated by the Dayton Agreement, Annex 1-A, Art. VII and UNSC resolution 1031 (15 December 1995). See also UNDPI, op. cit. n. 13, at pp. 488-491, 513-538 and 556-563.

[148] UNPROFOR's mandate is contained in UN Doc. S/23280 (11 December 1991) Annex 3, reprinted in Bethlehem and Weller, op. cit. n. 145, at p. 478.

[149] UN Doc. S/23836 (24 April 1992) para. 20, reprinted in Bethlehem and Weller, op. cit. n. 145, at p. 502.

[150] UNSC resolution 758.

[151] UNSC resolution 776.

Dubrovnik disputed by Croatia and the Federal Republic of Yugoslavia, and to ensure control of the Peruca dam, situated in one of the pink zones.[152]

In November 1992, the government of Macedonia officially requested the deployment of UN observers to prevent possible developments across its borders to undermine the stability in the country.[153] On 11 December 1992, the Security Council authorised the establishment of UNPROFOR's presence in the former Yugoslav Republic of Macedonia as 'UNPROFOR's Macedonia Command'. Its mandate was to monitor the border areas with Albania and the Federal Republic of Yugoslavia (Serbia and Montenegro), strengthen, by its presence, the country's security and stability and report on any developments that could threaten the country.[154]

As the initial twelve-month mandate was about to expire at the end of February 1993, the Security Council, on three consecutive occasions, temporarily extended UNPROFOR's mandate until 30 September so that the Secretary-General was given enough time to take appropriate measures to strengthen the security of the force, in particular by providing it with the necessary defensive means.[155] In 1992 and throughout 1993, the force, the UNPAs and the pink zones had regularly come under attack. By March 1993, the so-called 'no-fly' zone which UNPROFOR monitored pursuant to Security Council resolution 781 of 9 October 1992 had already been violated on more than 500 occasions. Acting under chapter VII of the UN Charter, the Security Council, by its resolution 816 of 31 March 1993, authorised Member States to use 'all necessary means' to enforce the flight ban. Subsequently, NATO adopted the necessary arrangements to ensure compliance with the ban on military flights.[156]

6.2.2 *'Safe areas'*

Almost simultaneously, the fighting in eastern Bosnia-Herzegovina intensified, with Bosnian Serb paramilitary units attacking several cities in the area. The attacks resulted in a heavy loss of life among the civilian population and severely impeded humanitarian relief efforts in the area. The UNHCR reported that thousands of Muslims were seeking refuge in Srebrenica from surrounding areas which were being attacked by Serb forces, and that thirty or forty persons were dying daily from military action, starvation, exposure to cold or lack of medical

---

152 UNSC resolutions 762, 769 and 779.

153 See UN Doc. S/24923 (9 December 1992), reprinted in Bethlehem and Weller, op. cit. n. 145, at p. 570.

154 UNSC resolution 795.

155 UNSC resolutions 807, 815, 847.

156 On Operation *Deny Flight*, see *infra* section 7.1, n. 293.

treatment.[157] Despite strong political pressure from the international community and the Security Council,[158] and the efforts by UNPROFOR and the UNHCR in the field, the fighting persisted and the humanitarian situation in the area continued to deteriorate. On 16 April, the Security Council, acting under chapter VII of the Charter, adopted resolution 819, in which it demanded that all parties treat Srebrenica and its surroundings as a 'safe area which should be free from any armed attack or any other hostile act' (para. 1). The Council requested the Secretary-General to take steps to increase the presence of UNPROFOR in Srebrenica (para. 4) and arrange for the safe transfer of the ill and wounded (para. 11) and demanded the unimpeded delivery of humanitarian assistance to all parts of Bosnia-Herzegovina, in particular to the civilian population of Srebrenica (para. 8). By other provisions of the resolution, the Council condemned and rejected the deliberate actions of the Bosnian Serb party to force the evacuation of civilians from Srebrenica and other parts of Bosnia-Herzegovina in its campaign of ethnic cleansing (paras. 2, 5, 6 and 7). On 6 May 1993, the Security Council adopted resolution 824, in which it declared that, in addition to Srebrenica, 'Sarajevo and other such threatened areas, in particular the towns of Tuzla, Žepa, Goražde, Bihać and their surroundings [...] should be treated as safe areas by all the parties concerned'. The Council further declared that in those areas armed attacks must cease, all Bosnian Serb military or paramilitary units must withdraw and all parties must allow UNPROFOR and the international humanitarian agencies free and unimpeded access to all safe areas. It authorised the strengthening of UNPROFOR's mandate by an additional fifty military observers to monitor the humanitarian situation in those areas.

On 4 June, the Security Council, by its resolution 836, again acting under chapter VII, further expanded the mandate of UNPROFOR to enable it to protect the safe areas, including deterring attacks against them, monitoring the ceasefire, promoting the withdrawal of military or paramilitary units other than those of the Bosnian government and occupying some key points on the ground. The Council authorised UNPROFOR, 'acting in self-defence, to take the necessary measures, including the use of force, in reply to bombardments against the safe areas by any of the parties or to armed incursion into them or in the event of any deliberate obstruction in or around those areas to the freedom of movement of the Force or of protected humanitarian convoys' (para. 9). The Council also decided that Member States, acting nationally or through regional organisations or arrangements, might take, under its authority, 'all necessary measures, through the use of air power, in and around the safe areas', to support UNPROFOR (para. 10). In

157 UN Doc. S/25519 (2 April 1993).

158 See, *inter alia*, Statement by the President of the Security Council, UN Doc. S/25520 (3 April 1993).

response to the Council's invitation to report to it on the requirements for implementing resolution 836, the Secretary-General indicated that it would be necessary to deploy additional troops on the ground and to provide air support.[159] While the UNPROFOR Force Commander had estimated an additional troop requirement of approximately 34,000 to obtain deterrence through strength, the Secretary-General stated that it was possible to start implementing the resolution under a 'light option', with a minimal troop reinforcement of around 7,600.[160] In adopting resolution 844 of 18 June 1993, the Security Council authorised an additional reinforcement of UNPROFOR by 7,600 troops as an initial approach and reaffirmed the use of air power in and around the declared safe areas to support the force in the performance of its mandate.

On 4 October 1993, after intensive consultations and two interim extensions of UNPROFOR's mandate – for a twenty-four-hour period on 30 September, and for another four days on 1 October – the Security Council, by its resolution 871, extended the mandate of the force for a period of six months, through 31 March 1994. The Council took this action under chapter VII of the Charter, reiterating its determination to ensure the security of UNPROFOR and its freedom of movement.

6.2.3 *The question of air strikes*

In the meantime, talks aimed at achieving a comprehensive ceasefire were continuing within the framework of the International Conference on the Former Yugoslavia (ICFY).[161] In fact, UNPROFOR monitored the implementation of a whole series of ephemeral ceasefire agreements, while all parties in Bosnia-Herzegovina were trying to take tactical advantage of its presence and were increasingly questioning its impartiality. At the same time, the military and humanitarian situation continued to worsen, especially in Bosnia. Fighting in and around Sarajevo continued unabated, including lethal mortar attacks against

---

159 See UN Doc. S/25939 (14 June 1993), reprinted in Bethlehem and Weller, op. cit. n. 145, at p. 625.

160 Ibid., at para. 6.

161 The follow-up conference to the EC-sponsored Conference on Yugoslavia; see chapter 3, section 2.5. The ICFY first convened in London on 26-27 August 1992, where David Owen (EC) and Cyrus Vance (UN) were appointed to co-chair the conference. Vance was replaced by former Norwegian Minister of Foreign Affairs Thorvald Stoltenberg in May 1993, Owen by former Swedish Prime Minister Carl Bildt in May 1995. The ICFY had a broad mandate for conflict settlement and prevention but focused chiefly on the Bosnian war, producing a series of proposals to end the fighting, including, in January 1993, the Vance-Owen Plan for keeping Bosnia-Herzegovina together with ten provinces in a decentralised, demilitarised state. The ICFY continued to operate until the end of the Bosnian war but gradually the focus began to shift towards great power mediation through the Contact Group (established on 26 April 1994), which included representatives from the United States, Russia, the United Kingdom, France and Germany.

civilian targets. On 5 February 1994, a mortar round fired at the central market killed at least fifty-eight civilians and wounded 142 others in the worst single incident of the twenty-two-month war. This followed a similar attack on one of the suburbs of Sarajevo on 4 February 1994 in which ten civilians were killed and eighteen injured. These acts were immediately strongly condemned by the international community, but the Security Council did not take any action. The Secretary-General instructed his Special Representative (since 3 January 1994, Yasushi Akashi) and the Force Commander of UNPROFOR to travel to Sarajevo in order to supervise the investigation of the incidents and to prevent further atrocities. UNPROFOR established that the round fired on 4 February had come from a Bosnian Serb position, but that it had not been possible to locate the source of the attack against the central market on 5 February. In a series of letters to the president of the Security Council, the Secretary-General stated that those two incidents made it necessary, in accordance with resolution 836 (1993), to prepare urgently for the use of air strikes to deter further attacks.[162] The Secretary-General also informed the Council that he had requested the Secretary-General of NATO to obtain 'a decision by the North Atlantic Council to authorise the Commander-in-Chief of NATO's Southern Command to launch air strikes, at the request of the United Nations, against artillery or mortar positions in and around Sarajevo which are determined by UNPROFOR to be responsible for attacks against civilian targets in that city.'[163]

The North Atlantic Council (NAC) accepted the request of the UN Secretary-General. On 9 February, moving to end the strangulation of Sarajevo, it issued a statement calling for 'the withdrawal, or regrouping and placing under UNPROFOR control, within ten days, of heavy weapons (including tanks, artillery pieces, mortars, multiple rocket launchers, missiles and anti-aircraft weapons) of the Bosnian Serb forces located in the area within 20 kilometres of the centre of Sarajevo, and excluding the area within 2 kilometres of the centre of Pale.'[164] It also called upon the Muslim-led government of Bosnia-Herzegovina, within the same period, 'to place the heavy weapons in its possession within the Sarajevo exclusion zone described above under UNPROFOR control, and to refrain from attacks launched from within the current confrontation lines in the city.'[165] The NAC decided that, ten days from 10 February 1994, heavy weapons of any of the parties found within the Sarajevo exclusion zone, unless controlled

---

[162] See UN Docs. S/1994/159 (11 February 1994), S/1994/182 (16 February 1994) and S/1994/217 (25 February 1994), all reprinted in Bethlehem and Weller, op. cit. n. 145, at pp. 672-675.

[163] UN Doc. S/1994/131 (6 February 1994).

[164] Decisions taken at the meeting of the North Atlantic Council on 9 February 1994, Press release (94)15, 9 February 1994, para. 6.

[165] Ibid., at para. 7.

by UNPROFOR, would, along with their direct and essential military support facilities, be subject to NATO air strikes.[166]

The Security Council eventually met on 14-15 February 1994 at the request of the governments of Russia, Bosnia-Herzegovina and Pakistan. Over the course of four meetings, it heard from a total of fifty-eight speakers. Member States generally welcomed the decision by NATO and the steps taken by the Secretary-General to prepare for the use of force, adding that those actions had been fully authorised by existing Council resolutions. They emphasised that force was designed to underpin efforts by the United Nations and the European Union to achieve a negotiated settlement of the conflict and that air strikes had to be carried out with caution and precision. Although the NATO ultimatum was widely supported, several Member States either opposed it or expressed concern that, as a result of air strikes, UNPROFOR might become a target for retaliatory measures. No Security Council resolution or statement was put forward during the meetings.[167]

On 17 February 1994, following a meeting with Russian officials in Bosnia, the Bosnian Serbs agreed to withdraw within two days all their heavy weapons to the distance set by NATO. On 20 February 1994, the Security Council met in informal consultations at the request of the Russian Federation, with the NATO deadline for withdrawal of heavy weapons scheduled for midnight that night. The Council was briefed by Kofi Annan, then still Under-Secretary-General for Peacekeeping Operations, who reported that according to the Secretary-General's Special Representative for the former Yugoslavia, the UNPROFOR Force Commander and NATO, Serbian compliance with the ultimatum had been effective. Certain weapons on both the Serb and Muslim sides, which had not been removed from the exclusion zone, would be monitored in place by UNPROFOR. As a result, the Council decided, in coordination with NATO, not to recommend that air strikes be carried out.[168]

6.2.4 *Air strikes and consequences*

A repetition of the horrible scenario described above took place when, at the end of March 1994, the Bosnian Serb forces launched a big offensive against the safe area of Goražde. Despite the Council's demand and UNPROFOR's efforts to arrange for a ceasefire, attacks against Goražde continued unabated.[169] After UN

166 Ibid., at para. 10.

167 See UNDPI, op. cit. n. 13, at pp. 529-530.

168 Ibid., at p. 530. A few days later, on 28 February 1994, NATO fighters shot down four Serb aircraft violating the UN's 'no-fly' zone over central Bosnia. This was the Alliance's first use of force since it was founded in 1949.

169 UN Doc. S/PRST/1994/14 (6 April 1994).

military observers in the city were endangered by Serb shelling, UNPROFOR's Command requested NATO to use its air support for the self-defence of UN personnel. Consequently, on 10 and 11 April 1994, aircraft belonging to NATO states bombed Bosnian Serb positions.[170] Notwithstanding the Bosnian Serbs' repeated commitments to a ceasefire, the heavy shelling of the city did not cease. On 18 April, after the situation in and around Goražde became extremely dire, the Secretary-General asked NATO to authorise the use of air strikes, at the request of the United Nations, against artillery, mortar positions or tanks attacking civilians in Goražde, as well as in four other safe areas, namely the towns of Tuzla, Žepa, Bihać and Srebrenica.[171] On 22 April 1994, the NAC authorised the use of air strikes against Bosnian Serb military targets around Goražde if the Bosnian Serbs did not end their attacks against the safe area immediately, pull their forces back three kilometres from the city centre by 24 April, and allow UN forces and humanitarian relief convoys freedom of movement there.[172] Although the Bosnian Serbs had not yet fully complied when the 24 April deadline expired, the Force Commander of UNPROFOR decided against the immediate use of air strikes. On 26 April 1994, the Secretary-General announced that Bosnian Serb forces had complied with the demands.

In August and September 1994, the security situation in Bosnia-Herzegovina again deteriorated. Continued fighting persisted in several regions of the Republic and there were numerous interferences with humanitarian aid. In the safe area of Sarajevo, attacks, especially by snipers, escalated in frequency and deadly effect. The extent of heavy weapons attacks also increased. Attacks occurred in both the city centre and the suburbs and on many occasions were directed at residences, pedestrians and moving vehicles, such as trams packed with people. UN personnel were also targeted and suffered fatalities. Twice, on 5 August and 22 September, UNPROFOR called in NATO warplanes to hit Serbian heavy weapons violating the exclusion zone around Sarajevo.[173]

In the wake of a Krajina Serb assault on the safe area of Bihać in November, the Security Council decided that the authorisation given to Member States under resolution 836 (1993) to use force in support of UNPROFOR also applied to such measures taken in the Republic of Croatia.[174] On 21 November, NATO launched an air strike on the airstrip used by Krajina Serbs in Croatia to attack the Bihać

---

170 See UNDPI, op. cit. n. 13, at p. 531.

171 UN Doc. S/1994/466, Annex.

172 See Decisions taken at the meeting of the North Atlantic Council on 22 April 1994, Press release (94)31, 22 April 1994, paras. 6-7; and UN Doc. S/1994/495, Annex.

173 See NATO Press release (94)64, 'NATO aircraft conduct air strikes at request of UNPROFOR', 5 August 1994; and NATO Press release (94)90, 'NATO aircraft attack Bosnian-Serb tank', 22 September 1994.

174 UNSC resolution 958 (19 November 1994).

enclave across the border into Bosnia-Herzegovina.[175] On 23 November, after the Bosnian Serb forces fired missiles at two British Harrier jets patrolling the Bihać area, NATO conducted air strikes against surface-to-air missile sites in the area.[176] When the Bosnian Serbs started shelling the town of Bihać again on 25 November, NATO planes were again called in by UNPROFOR to protect UN troops. The planes flew for sixty minutes but could not initiate any attack without endangering both UNPROFOR troops and civilians.[177] Despite all efforts and warnings, the Bosnian Serbs continued their attack, eventually capturing some high ground within the Bihać safe area. Also, in an apparent retaliation for NATO air strikes, throughout Bosnia-Herzegovina, the Bosnian Serbs detained a number of blue helmets, restricted their movement, subjected some to humiliation and stopped most humanitarian and supply convoys in territories under Bosnian Serb control. The Security Council, in a statement by its president, condemned in the strongest possible terms all violations, in particular, the 'flagrant and blatant' entry of Bosnian Serb forces into the safe area.[178] It demanded that all parties agree to an immediate and unconditional ceasefire in the Bihać region, particularly in and around the safe area. The call for a ceasefire was not accepted.

6.2.5 *Reorganisation of UNPROFOR*

Despite a lull in the fighting in December and January, largely thanks to strong international diplomatic pressure on all parties to agree to a ceasefire, offensives around Travnik and Tuzla in February 1995 caused the war to continue. The Bosnian Serbs again began restricting UNPROFOR's freedom of movement in the areas controlled by them and also increased their obstruction of humanitarian assistance. The security situation in Sarajevo deteriorated with increasing sniping and targeting of UNPROFOR and UNHCR aircraft.

In view of the expiration of UNPROFOR's mandate on 31 March 1995, the Secretary-General drew up a report in which he sketched the situation.[179] In Croatia, the retention of UNPROFOR in its existing form no longer enjoyed the consent of the government. However, the total withdrawal of all UN peacekeeping forces would have resulted in a grave threat to peace and security extending beyond Croatia's borders. The maintenance of a reduced force under a new mandate seemed the only way to reduce the risks of a renewed major war. With

---

175 See NATO Press release (94)110, 'NATO aircraft attack Udbina airfield', 21 November 1994.

176 See NATO Press releases (94)111 and 112, 'NATO airstrike' and 'NATO airstrike II', 23 November 1994.

177 See UNDPI, op. cit. n. 13, at p. 536.

178 S/PRST/1994/71 (26 November 1994).

179 UN Doc. S/1995/222 (22 March 1995).

regard to Bosnia-Herzegovina, the Secretary-General viewed UNPROFOR's performance as a mixture of achievements and setbacks. The force's presence on the ground had not been matched by political progress on a negotiated settlement and therefore operated in a sort of vacuum. While UNPROFOR continued to perform humanitarian and confidence-building tasks, the lack of progress at the negotiation table had created a situation in which it could do little but to delay rather than prevent a renewed outbreak of hostilities. Understandably, the Bosnian government had expressed its wish for possible changes in the existing arrangements. The Secretary-General reported that although the military situation in Macedonia remained relatively calm and stable, there had been regular skirmishes with border patrols from the Federal Republic of Yugoslavia (FRY). UNPROFOR, in close coordination with the ICFY and the CSCE, had acted as a successful mediator in several such encounters, achieving the withdrawal of soldiers on both sides. The Secretary-General noted further that the most serious difficulties experienced by Macedonia were economic. Social stability was endangered by rising unemployment and a declining economy resulting, among other things, from the effects of the economic blockade imposed by Greece on 17 February 1994 and the UN sanctions against the FRY, formerly the country's primary trading partners. Internal political tensions between Macedonians and ethnic Albanians had also increased. Against this background, the government of Macedonia had expressed the wish that the UN forces in the country should be separated from UNPROFOR. With regard to UNPROFOR's presence in the FRY (a liaison office and a mission monitoring the demilitarisation of the Prevlaka peninsula), the Secretary-General simply noted that the cooperation the force had received from Belgrade had proved vital to the effective functioning of all three of the operation's commands.

On 31 March 1995, the Security Council decided, at the suggestion of the Secretary-General, to restructure UNPROFOR, replacing it with three separate but interlinked peacekeeping operations collectively known as the United Nations Peace Forces (UNPF). By its resolutions 981, 982 and 983, the Council established the United Nations Confidence Restoration Operation in Croatia (UNCRO), extended the mandate of UNPROFOR in Bosnia-Herzegovina and decided that UNPROFOR in Macedonia would be known as the United Nations Preventive Deployment Force (UNPREDEP). All operations were given mandates until 30 November 1995. The administrative and logistic activities of all three operations were coordinated at the UNPF headquarters in Zagreb.

6.3 Bosnia-Herzegovina: UNPROFOR (2), IPTF and UNMIBH

From March to November 1995, the situation in Bosnia-Herzegovina was dominated by three main developments. Firstly, there was an unprecedented level of military activity, including offensives by all sides, accompanied by major movements of refugees and displaced persons and violations of international humanitarian law, particularly by the Bosnian Serb forces. Secondly, both UNPROFOR and NATO used force against the Bosnian Serbs. And thirdly, the US-led peace initiative, together with a country-wide decrease in fighting in October and November, provided a solid opportunity for a political solution to the conflict.

6.3.1 *UNPROFOR becomes part of the problem*

Fighting in and around Sarajevo intensified after 1 May 1995. The use of heavy weapons by the two sides and sustained shelling resulted in numerous civilian and UNPROFOR casualties and mounting calls for stricter enforcement of the weapons exclusion zone. After the failure of the Bosnian Serbs to respect UNPROFOR's deadline for the return of heavy weapons, two NATO air strikes, on 25 and 26 May, were conducted against an ammunition dump near Pale.[180] Bosnian Serb forces reacted by surrounding additional UN weapons collection points. They took 300 UNPROFOR soldiers as hostages, using some of them as human shields to deter further air attacks on potential targets. They also cut electricity to the city. Fighting between UNPROFOR troops and Bosnian Serb forces erupted on 27 May 1995, when the latter seized an observation post at the Vrbanja bridge in Sarajevo and detained some blue helmets. The position was recaptured by UNPROFOR at the cost of two dead and fourteen wounded.[181]

Reporting to the Security Council on 30 May, the Secretary-General stated that UNPROFOR's role had become untenable and had to be changed.[182] He put forward a number of options for consideration by the Council,[183] including a revision of the mandate so that it included only those tasks that a peacekeeping operation could realistically be expected to perform in the prevailing circumstances (good offices; liaison; negotiation; border monitoring and monitoring ceasefires as long as the parties were willing to implement them; a presence in the safe areas; supporting humanitarian activities; and the use of force only in self-defence). Any option which would involve the continuation of UNPROFOR in

---

180 See NATO Press release (95)53, 'NATO airstrikes again in Bosnia-Herzegovina', 26 May 1995.

181 See UNDPI, op. cit. n. 13.

182 Report of the Secretary-General containing analysis of UNPROFOR's mandate in Bosnia and Herzegovina, UN Doc. S/1995/444 (30 May 1995).

183 Ibid., at para. 72: 'Option A: To withdraw UNPROFOR, leaving at the most a small political mission, if that was the wish of the parties; Option B: To retain UNPROFOR's existing tasks and the methods currently used to implement them; Option C: To change the existing mandate to permit UNPROFOR to make greater use of force; Option D: To revise the mandate so that it includes only those tasks that a peace-keeping operation can realistically be expected to perform in the circumstances currently prevailing in Bosnia and Herzegovina.'

Bosnia-Herzegovina would, however, need to be accompanied by measures, including the possible deployment of additional forces, to provide better security both for UNPROFOR personnel and that of the UNHCR and other civilian agencies.[184]

6.3.2 *Rapid Reaction Force*

A group of countries (France, the Netherlands and the United Kingdom) expressed their readiness to provide military reinforcements for UNPROFOR in order to reduce the vulnerability of its personnel and to enhance its capacity to carry out its mandate.[185] The Secretary-General recommended that the Security Council accept the proposal.[186] The troops proposed for the Rapid Reaction Force amounted to about 15,000, of whom 2,500 were already in Bosnia. The Security Council, by its resolution 998 of 16 June 1995, welcomed the establishment of the force and accordingly decided to authorise an increase in UNPROFOR by up to 12,500 additional troops.[187]

6.3.3 *The Srebrenica and Žepa massacres*

After the adoption of resolution 998, the situation on the ground further deteriorated. Intense fighting resumed, and the humanitarian situation consequently became a major concern, because it deeply affected the UNHCR's ability to continue providing assistance. UNPROFOR and the UNHCR warned of developing humanitarian disasters in Sarajevo, Bihać, Goražde, Srebrenica and Žepa. Due to obstructive actions by Bosnian Serb forces, humanitarian supplies and relief workers had great difficulties in reaching those areas.

On 6 July 1995, the Bosnian Serb forces, under the command of General Ratko Mladić, launched a full-scale assault against the 'safe area' of Srebrenica. Despite the presence of a Dutch battalion of UN peacekeepers and an urgent demand by the Security Council for the Bosnian Serbs to cease their offensive and withdraw from the area,[188] the thousands of people who had sought refuge under the flag of the United Nations were swept from Srebrenica. It was not until after the fall of Srebrenica on 11 July that, in response to a request from

---

184 Ibid.

185 Letter dated 9 June 1995 from the Secretary-General addressed to the President of the Security Council, UN Doc. S/1995/470, 9 June 1995, Annex.

186 Ibid.

187 The Rapid Reaction Force (RRF) was expected to become operational by 15 July 1995. However, because the governments of Croatia and Bosnia-Herzegovina took the position that RRF troops were not covered by the Status of Forces Agreement (SOFA) covering other UNPROFOR troop deployments, the deployment of major RRF elements was significantly delayed.

188 See UN Doc. S/PRST/1995/32 and the rather late UNSC resolution 1004 (12 July 1995).

UNPROFOR, NATO aircraft provided 'close air support' in the Srebrenica area, attacking ground targets identified by the UN forces.[189] This belated action did not prevent the Serbs from beginning an attack on the nearby safe area of Žepa, which – despite an international threat that further violations of the safe areas would be met with decisive force, including the use of NATO air strikes[190] – fell to their forces on 25 July. Deeply concerned at the plight of the civilian population in both safe areas, the Security Council demanded that the Bosnian Serbs give immediate access to the UNHCR, the ICRC and other international agencies to persons displaced from those areas and permit representatives of the ICRC to visit and register any persons detained.[191] The Council reiterated that all those who committed violations of international humanitarian law would be held individually responsible in respect of such acts.[192]

---

189 See NATO Press release (95)68, 'NATO aircraft provide close air support in the Srebrenica area', 11 July 1995.

190 Declaration of the 21 July 1995 London Conference of representatives of the Contact Group, NATO, and UNPROFOR troop-contributing nations, as reported by P. Moore, 'Display of air power "not seen since the Gulf War"', *OMRI Daily Digest II*, No. 141, 21 July 1995.

191 UNSC resolution 1010 (10 August 1995).

192 On 27 November 1995, at the request of the Security Council in resolution 1019 (9 November 1995), the Secretary-General submitted a report according to which there was undeniable evidence that summary executions, rape, mass expulsions and large-scale disappearances had occurred around Srebrenica, Žepa, Banja Luka and Sanski Most. The full horror of atrocities had yet to be revealed, the Secretary-General reported, adding that the international community should insist that the Bosnian Serb leadership cooperate fully with all relevant international mechanisms (including the ICTY), so that the events might be thoroughly investigated and the truth established. 'The moral responsibility of the international community is heavy indeed,' the UNSG concluded. In an effort to get closer to the truth, the General Assembly, in resolution 53/35 of 30 November 1998, requested 'a comprehensive report, including an assessment, on the events dating from the establishment of the safe area of Srebrenica on 16 April 1993 under Security Council resolution 819 (1993) of 16 April 1993, which was followed by the establishment of other safe areas, until the endorsement of the Peace Agreement by the Security Council under resolution 1031 (1995) of 15 December 1995, bearing in mind the relevant decisions of the Security Council and the proceedings of the International Tribunal in this respect' (para. 18). The result was the publication of the detailed Report of the Secretary-General pursuant to General Assembly resolution 53/35, *The fall of Srebrenica*, UN Doc. A/54/549, 15 November 1999. The lessons drawn from the Srebrenica tragedy are hard: '501. The international community as a whole must accept its share of responsibility for allowing this tragic course of events by its prolonged refusal to use force in the early stages of the war. This responsibility is shared by the Security Council, the Contact Group and other Governments which contributed to the delay in the use of force, as well as by the United Nations Secretariat and the mission in the field. Clearly the primary and most direct responsibility lies however with the architects and implementers of the attempted genocide in Bosnia. Radovan Karadić and Ratko Mladić, together with their major collaborators, have been indicted by the International Tribunal for the Former Yugoslavia. To this day, they remain free men. They must be made to answer for the barbaric crimes with which they have been charged. 502. The cardinal lesson of Srebrenica is that a deliberate and systematic attempt to terrorize, expel or murder an entire people must be met decisively with all necessary means, and with the political will to carry the policy through to its logical conclusion. In the Balkans, in this decade, this lesson has had to be learned not once, but twice. In both instances, in Bosnia and in Kosovo, the international community tried to reach a

6.3.4 *Cease-fire and peace agreements*

On 28 August, five mortar rounds landed in the vicinity of Sarajevo's Markale market, one of which killed thirty-seven people and wounded more than eighty others. In order to restore the heavy weapons exclusion zone around Sarajevo and to deter any further attacks on safe areas, multiple NATO air strikes were conducted against ammunition supply depots and other military facilities throughout Eastern Bosnia.[193] Soon after NATO had launched its twelve-day Operation *Deliberate Force*,[194] Bosnian government and Bosnian Croat forces began to advance in the western part of the country. As a result of the offensive, an estimated 50,000 Bosnian Serbs were displaced to Banja Luka, a city which had already received large numbers of refugees from the Krajina region in August (see below). At the same time, the eviction of Muslim and Croat minorities from the area around Banja Luka continued. NATO suspended its air strikes on 14 September for three days, following an agreement signed in Belgrade by Bosnian Serb military and political leaders, in which they committed themselves to withdrawing their heavy weapons from the twenty-kilometre exclusion zone around Sarajevo. After the Bosnian Serbs fulfilled those commitments and allowed the reopening of Sarajevo airport, NATO and UNPROFOR agreed not to resume the air strikes.

The peace initiative undertaken by the United States with the support of the Security Council, the Contact Group and the Co-Chairmen of the ICFY Steering Committee, resulted on 5 October 1995 in a country-wide ceasefire agreement. UNPROFOR military and civilian personnel immediately undertook various measures to ensure the successful implementation of the agreement, including

negotiated settlement with an unscrupulous and murderous regime. In both instances it required the use of force to bring a halt to the planned and systematic killing and expulsion of civilians. 503. The United Nations experience in Bosnia was one of the most difficult and painful in our history. It is with the deepest regret and remorse that we have reviewed our own actions and decisions in the face of the assault on Srebrenica. Through error, misjudgement and an inability to recognize the scope of the evil confronting us, we failed to do our part to help save the people of Srebrenica from the Serb campaign of mass murder. No one regrets more than we the opportunities for achieving peace and justice that were missed. No one laments more than we the failure of the international community to take decisive action to halt the suffering and end a war that had produced so many victims. Srebrenica crystallized a truth understood only too late by the United Nations and the world at large: that Bosnia was as much a moral cause as a military conflict. The tragedy of Srebrenica will haunt our history forever.' This message was repeated by the UNSG and many political leaders at the tenth commemoration of the Srebrenica massacre. See, *inter alia*, Press Release SG/SM/9993, 11 July 2005, and Center for Balkan Development, 'Tenth Anniversary of Srebrenica massacre brings Tributes, Solidarity', 11 *CBD Briefs* (2005) No. 1.

193 See NATO Press release (95)73, 'Statement by the Secretary General of NATO', 30 August 1995.

194 See NATO Press release (95)79, 'Statement by the Secretary General of NATO', 5 September 1995; and section 7.1, n. 294.

demining activities that were necessary for the repair and reopening of utilities in Sarajevo.

The diplomatic initiative to end the Bosnian war culminated in the talks held in Dayton, Ohio in November 1995.[195] On 21 November, the Peace Agreement was initialled and, on 14 December, formally signed at a ceremony in Paris.[196]

6.3.5 *IFOR, IPTF and UNMIBH*

Along with plans for the withdrawal of UNPROFOR, the Dayton Agreement included a request by the parties – the Republic of Bosnia-Herzegovina, the Republic of Croatia, the Federal Republic of Yugoslavia, the Federation of Bosnia-Herzegovina and the Republika Srpska – to the Security Council to adopt a resolution authorising Member States or regional organisations and arrangements to establish a multinational military Implementation Force (IFOR) to help ensure compliance with the military provisions of the peace agreement.[197] IFOR would be composed of ground, air and maritime units from the members of NATO and from non-NATO states.[198] The parties also requested the establishment of a United Nations International Police Task Force (IPTF).[199]

The Secretary-General subsequently recommended that the IPTF's central and regional headquarters should, where possible, be co-located with IFOR headquarters.[200] In his view, UNPROFOR's existing mandate had to be extended for two months, or until an appropriate transfer of authority to IFOR had taken place. The Security Council, by its resolution 1026 of 30 November 1995, extended the mandate of UNPROFOR until 31 January 1996.

Acting under chapter VII of the UN Charter, the Security Council, by its resolution 1031 of 15 December 1995, authorised Member States to establish IFOR, under unified control and command and composed of ground, air and maritime units from NATO and non-NATO countries. The Council decided to review the situation one year after the transfer of authority from UNPROFOR to IFOR, in order to determine whether to end the authorisations granted by the resolution. It further decided to terminate UNPROFOR's mandate with effect from the day the Secretary-General reported to it that the transfer of authority to IFOR had taken place. In a separate resolution, the Security Council decided to establish the IPTF

195 For a brilliant account of the negotiations leading up to Dayton, see R. Holbrooke, *To End a War* (New York, Random House 1998).

196 35 *ILM* (1996) p. 75 et seq.

197 Ibid., Annex 1A, Art. I(1)a.

198 For more on IFOR, see *infra* section 7.1.

199 Ibid., Annex 11, Art. I(2).

200 Report of the Secretary-General regarding the arrangements for eventual transfer of responsibility from UNPROFOR to IFOR, UN Doc. S/1995/987 (23 November 1995).

and a United Nations Civilian Office for a period of one year from the date of transfer of authority.[201] Subsequently, this operation became known as the United Nations Mission in Bosnia and Herzegovina (UNMIBH). On 20 December 1995, the transfer of authority from UNPROFOR to IFOR took place.[202]

UNMIBH exercised a wide range of functions related to law enforcement activities and police reform in Bosnia-Herzegovina.[203] The mission also coordinated other UN activities in the country relating to humanitarian relief and refugees (UNHCR), demining, human rights (UNHCHR), elections and the rehabilitation of infrastructure and economic reconstruction.[204] It consisted of the UN Civilian Office and the IPTF. In addition, a UN coordinator was appointed to coordinate all activities in Bosnia.[205] A 'Commissioner' was in charge of the IPTF, a force which was not mandated to maintain law and order. Its task consisted mainly of supervising the police and the justice system and advising the parties on matters concerning police and justice.[206] Investigating human rights violations was later added to this.[207] The IPTF had an authorised strength of 2,057 police officers.[208]

Following the successful conclusion of its mandate, UNMIBH was terminated on 31 December 2002. Through UNMIBH, the United Nations demonstrated its ability to complete a complex mandate in accordance with a strategic plan and within a realistic and finite timeframe. UNMIBH completed the most extensive police reform and restructuring project ever undertaken by the United Nations.[209] A follow-on mission was provided for by the European Union (EUPM).[210]

6.4 Bosnia-Herzegovina: Office of the High Representative

The High Representative for Bosnia-Herzegovina was appointed in 1995 to oversee the civilian implementation of the Dayton Agreement. The High Representative and the Office of the High Representative (OHR) represent the international community

---

201 UNSC resolution 1035 (21 December 1995).

202 Letter dated 20 December 1995 from the Secretary-General addressed to the President of the Security Council, UN Doc. S/1995/1050 (20 December 1995).

203 Documents and background information are available at: <http://www.un.org/Depts/dpko/missions/unmibh/>.

204 UNSC resolution 1035 (21 December 1995) para. 2; and Report of the Secretary-General relating to the UN role in implementation of the peace agreement for Bosnia and Herzegovina, UN Doc. S/1995/1031 (13 December 1995) paras. 13-35.

205 UNSC resolution 1035 (21 December 1995) paras. 2-3.

206 Dayton Agreement, Annex 11, Arts. I, II, III and V.

207 UNSC resolution 1088 (30 July 1998) para. 27.

208 UNSC resolution 1168 (21 May 1998) para. 1.

209 Report of the Secretary-General on the United Nations Mission in Bosnia and Herzegovina, UN Doc. S/2002/1314 (2 December 2002).

210 See chapter 4, section 4.1.1.

through the United Nations. The High Representative is not only the UN Secretary-General's Special Representative (SRSG) but also functions as the European Union's Special Representative (EUSR).[211] The *de facto* governor of Bosnia-Herzegovina is thus a multi-hatted personality. So far, all five incumbents have come from EU Member States: Carl Bildt (1995-1997, Sweden), Carlos Westendorp (1997-1999, Spain), Wolfgang Petrisch (1999-2002, Austria), Paddy Ashdown (2002-2006, United Kingdom) and Christian Schwarz-Schilling (since 2006, Germany).[212]

The civilian aspects of the challenges facing the authorities of Bosnia-Herzegovina at the end of the war in 1995 were daunting and required a wide range of activities, including continuation of the humanitarian aid effort for as long as necessary, rehabilitation of infrastructure and economic reconstruction, the establishment of political and constitutional institutions in Bosnia-Herzegovina, promotion of respect for human rights and the return of displaced persons and refugees and the holding of free and fair elections. In view of the complexities facing them, the parties to the Dayton Agreement – the Republic of Bosnia-Herzegovina, the Republic of Croatia, the Federal Republic of Yugoslavia, the Federation of Bosnia and Herzegovina (FBiH) and the Republika Srpska (RS) – requested in Annex 10 ('Agreement on Civilian Implementation') the designation of a High Representative 'to facilitate the Parties' own efforts and to mobilise and, as appropriate, coordinate the activities of the organisations and agencies involved in the civilian aspects of the peace settlement by carrying out, as entrusted by a U.N. Security Council resolution, the tasks' set out in Article II (Mandate and Methods of Coordination and Liaison):

- Monitor the implementation of the peace settlement;
- Maintain close contact with the Parties to promote their full compliance with all civilian aspects of the peace settlement and a high level of cooperation between them and the organizations and agencies participating in those aspects;
- Coordinate the activities of the civilian organizations and agencies in Bosnia and Herzegovina to ensure the efficient implementation of the civilian aspects of the peace settlement. The High Representative shall respect their autonomy within their spheres of operation while as necessary giving general guidance to them about the impact of their activities on the implementation of the peace settlement. The civilian organizations and agencies are requested to assist the

211 Council Joint Action 2002/211/CFSP of 11 March 2002 on the appointment of the EU Special Representative in Bosnia and Herzegovina, *OJ* 2002 L 70/7, repealed by Council Joint Action 2004/569/CFSP of 12 July 2004 on the mandate of the European Union Special Representative in Bosnia and Herzegovina and repealing Council Joint Action 2002/211/CFSP, *OJ* 2004 L 252/7, last amended by Council Joint Action 2006/49/CFSP of 30 January 2006 appointing the European Union Special Representative in Bosnia and Herzegovina, *OJ* 2006 L 26/21.

212 See the OHR's portal at: <http://www.ohr.int>.

High Representative in the execution of his or her responsibilities by providing all information relevant to their operations in Bosnia-Herzegovina;
- Facilitate, as the High Representative judges necessary, the resolution of any difficulties arising in connection with civilian implementation;
- Participate in meetings of donor organizations, particularly on issues of rehabilitation and reconstruction;
- Report periodically on progress in implementation of the peace agreement concerning the tasks set forth in this Agreement to the United Nations, European Union, United States, Russian Federation, and other interested governments, parties, and organizations;
- Provide guidance to, and receive reports from, the Commissioner of the International Police Task Force [...];

In the pursuit of his mandate, the High Representative convenes and chairs the Joint Civilian Commission, comprised of senior political representatives of the parties to the Dayton Agreement, the IFOR Commander or his representative and representatives of civilian organisations. The High Representative does not, however, have authority over IFOR and is not allowed to interfere in any way in the conduct of military operations or the IFOR chain of command. It is further interesting to note that, according to Article III(4) of Annex 10 to the Dayton Agreement, the OHR and its premises, archives and other property enjoy the same privileges and immunities as enjoyed by a diplomatic mission and its premises, archives and other property under the Vienna Convention on Diplomatic Relations. The same applies to the privileges and immunities enjoyed by the High Representative, professional and other members of his staff and their families. According to Article V of the same Annex 10, the High Representative is the final authority ('in theatre') regarding the interpretation of the Agreement on Civilian Implementation.

From the foregoing overview, the picture emerges that the Dayton Agreement has established a foreign civil presence with important functions. But going by the black letter law, it would be going too far to conclude that these functions are comprehensive or that the foreign civil presence is the sole authority within the territory of Bosnia-Herzegovina. Instead, Dayton foresaw the parallel existence of two authorities: the international presence (the OHR) and the institutions of the state of Bosnia-Herzegovina, including its political subdivisions.[213] However, in response to massive obstructionism of the political process in the first two years of the implementation of the Dayton Agreement, the Peace Implementation

[213] Under the Dayton Agreement, Bosnia-Herzegovina is recognised as a state. See Art. I of Annex 4 to the Agreement (Constitution of Bosnia and Herzegovina). On the difficulty of coming to terms with such a parallel constitutional order, see T. Grant, 'Internationally Guaranteed Constitutive Order: Cyprus and Bosnia as Predicates for a New Nontraditional Actor in the Society of States', 8 *Journal of Transnational Law and Policy* (1998) pp. 1-55 at pp. 19-25 and 51-55.

Council (PIC), a group of fifty-five countries and international organisations that sponsor and direct the peace implementation process, drastically increased the mandate and powers of the High Representative at a meeting in Bonn on 10 December 1997, enabling him to dismiss officials and impose laws if this was deemed necessary.[214] Westendorp, Petrisch and Ashdown all made use of these so-called 'Bonn powers'. During their years in office, locally-elected leaders were routinely overruled and sometimes sacked by international fiat.[215] While the High Representative s 'hired and fired' to embolden EU-friendly reformers and establish the institutions necessary for a viable, modern democracy in Bosnia-Herzegovina, they also undermined popular faith in the democracy the sought to achieve.[216] Many commentators have suggested that the transition to Bosnian ownership has been held back by the Dayton framework (especially the Bonn Powers), which created a weak central state and a country divided into two separate entities, the Republika Srpska and the Muslim-Croat Federation of Bosnia and Herzegovina, with ten cantonal governments, as well as an autonomous region, Brcko.[217]

Eleven years on, the idea that the post-war transition has been frustrated by an excess of Bosnian governing institutions, protected by their Dayton status, could not be further from the truth.[218] While it is true that the international powers of administration, under the OHR, have been vastly increased, thereby reducing the Bosnian institutions established by Dayton to administrative shells, there has recently been a transition away from Dayton: from the *ad hoc* regulatory controls of the self-selected 'coalition of the willing' assembled in the PIC towards an expanded framework of European Union regulation (SAP), covering all aspects of the post-Dayton process.[219] Thus, the Dayton solution has proved highly flexible,

---

214 See Peace Implementation Council, Summary of Conclusions, 10 December 1997, available at: <http://www.ohr.int/pic/default.asp?content_id=5183>.

215 As recently as on 16 December 2004, Paddy Ashdown, the international community's envoy in Bosnia-Herzegovina, sacked senior Bosnian Serb security officials. Lord Ashdown accused the officials of harbouring war crimes suspects including Ratko Mladić. The decision, in line with the Dayton Peace Agreement, was supported by the European Union's SG/HR, which underlines that Ashdown acted on behalf of the European Union. Reported in *Agence Europe*, 18 December 2004, at p. 11.

216 Many Bosnian Serbs, for instance, still worry that the international community seeks ultimately to dissolve Republika Srpska, the ethnic Serb half of Bosnia-Herzegovina. See International Crisis Group, 'Bosnia's Nationalist Governments: Paddy Ashdown and the Paradoxes of State Building', 146 *Europe Reports* (2003).

217 See, *inter alia*, G. Knaus and F. Martin, 'Travails of the European Raj', 14 *Journal of Democracy* (2003) pp. 60-74; R. Caplan, 'International Authority and State Building: The Case of Bosnia and Herzegovina', 10 *Global Governance* (2004); M. Logan, 'Examining the High Rep's Mantle', *Transitions Online* (2004); and M. Skrbić, 'Bosnia: Ban the Bonn Powers?', *Transitions Online* (2005).

218 D. Chandler, 'From Dayton to Europe', 12 *International Peacekeeping* (2005) pp. 336-349.

219 On the Stabilisation and Association Process (SAP), see chapter 5, in particular section 3.2.3.

with external institutions rewriting their mandates and powers. As such, the international community in Bosnia-Herzegovina has succeeded in taking the peace process forward and preparing the country for its 'European' future. Bosnia-Herzegovina has travelled a long way in the past decade as the country has sought to rebuild itself with international support in the wake of Europe's most devastating conflict since World War II. But progress will only be irreversible when Bosnians take responsibility for the peace process. In this context, the extraordinary powers of the High Representative are no longer an appropriate tool of international assistance to Bosnia-Herzegovina and must be terminated. This was recognised by the PIC, which decided in June 2006 that the OHR should immediately begin preparations with a view to closing down on – the provisional date of – 30 June 2007.[220]

It is the task of Christian Schwarz-Schilling, as Bosnia-Herzegovina's last High Representative, to phase out the Bonn Powers and oversee the smooth transition from today's quasi-protectorate to local ownership. It is his task to put Bosnia-Herzegovina on the rails of a process of 'guided sovereignty', on the way to future integration into the Euro-Atlantic structures.[221] This guidance towards NATO and EU membership is a *conditio sine qua non* for a country where local antagonisms and the enduring threat of crime and corruption can still undermine a political system caught in relatively shaky institutions. While the risk of slipping back into armed conflict is slim, the end of the protectorate would not have to mean the end of the international military presence, which has played a very important role in stabilising society,[222] nor would it have to mean the departure of Schwarz-Schilling. After all, he would remain the EUSR. Elections in October 2007 should provide Bosnians with an opportunity to debate the way forward and choose leaders who are best equipped to secure their country's European future. For they – not the High Representative – will be responsible for negotiating the terms and speed of their country's entry into NATO and the European Union.[223]

6.5 Croatia: UNCRO, UNTAES, UNMOP and UNPSG

By its resolutions 981 of 31 March 1995, the Security Council established the United Nations Confidence Restoration Operation in Croatia (UNCRO) as a follow-on of UNPROFOR in Croatia. On the basis of consultations conducted by

220 See Communiqué of the PIC Steering Board, 'Towards Ownership: From Peace Implementation to Euro-Atlantic Integration', Sarajevo, 23 June 2006.

221 See chapter 6, section 3.3.2.

222 See H. Vetschera and M. Damian, 'Security Sector Reform in Bosnia and Herzegovina: The Role of the International Community', 13 *International Peacekeeping* (2006) pp. 28-42. See also the previous section, *infra* section 7.1 and chapter 4, section 4.1.

223 See C. Schwarz-Schilling, 'How to Move Bosnia Forward', *IHT*, 1 February 2006.

his Special Envoy, Thorvald Stoltenberg, the UN Secretary-General reported on 18 April 1995 to the Security Council on the detailed implementation of the new UN mandate in Croatia.[224] On 28 April, the Security Council approved the proposed arrangements and decided to authorise the deployment of UNCRO.[225] The force's troops and observers were deployed in Serb-controlled Western Slavonia, Krajina, Eastern Slavonia and Baranja. Observers were also stationed on the Prevlaka peninsula. The new mandate included: (a) performing the functions envisaged in the ceasefire agreement of 29 March 1994,[226] that is to say, the inter-positioning of UN forces in a zone of separation and the establishment of additional control points, observation posts and patrols, as well the monitoring of the withdrawal of heavy weapons out of range of the contact line; (b) facilitating implementation of the economic agreement of 2 December 1994;[227] (c) facilitating implementation of all relevant Security Council resolutions; (d) assisting in controlling, by monitoring and reporting, the crossing of military personnel, equipment, supplies and weapons over the international borders between Croatia and Bosnia-Herzegovina and between Croatia and the FRY at the border crossings; (e) facilitating the delivery of international humanitarian assistance to Bosnia-Herzegovina through the territory of Croatia; and (f) monitoring the demilitarisation of the Prevlaka peninsula. It was decided that UNCRO should be an interim arrangement to create the conditions that would facilitate a negotiated settlement consistent with the territorial integrity of Croatia and guarantee the security and rights of all communities living in Croatia.

The reintegration of Western Slavonia in May 1995 and Croatia's big offensive against the Serbs (Operation Storm), which led to the 'liberation' of the Krajina region in August, effectively eliminated the need for UN troops in those areas. In fact, during the offensive, the Croatian army had imposed total restrictions on the movement of UNCRO. This precluded normal patrolling and hindered access to places that might have needed prompt humanitarian assistance. UN observation posts were overrun and destroyed. Croatian soldiers used peacekeepers as human shields, arrested and disarmed them, took their equipment and even killed some. The mass exodus of the Krajina Serb population created a humanitarian crisis of significant proportions. Despite repeated demands by the

224 Report of the Secretary-General submitted pursuant to paragraph 4 of Security Council Resolution 981 (1995), UN Doc. S/1995/320 (18 April 1995).

225 UNSC resolution 990 (1995). Facts and figures on this operation are available at: <http://www.un.org/Depts/dpko/dpko/co_mission/uncro.htm>.

226 The agreement was concluded in Zagreb by representatives of the government of Croatia and the local Serb authorities in the UNPAs. See UN Doc. S/1994/367, Annex.

227 The 29 March 1994 ceasefire agreement helped to create a climate conducive to the conclusion of an agreement on economic issues. See UN Doc. S/1994/1375, Annex.

Security Council,[228] the hostilities continued. This underlined the reality that, without the cooperation of the parties, peacekeeping forces could not keep the peace. As a result, UNCRO's overall troop strength was reduced to 8,750. In some sectors, troops were withdrawn altogether.[229]

On 6 August, the Secretary-General's Special Representative concluded a nine-point agreement with the head of the Croatian Commission for Relations with UNCRO to allow the United Nations, together with other international organisations, to cope with the humanitarian problem, monitor the human rights situation and permit the safe return of displaced person.[230] The Special Representative established a humanitarian crisis cell to collate information and coordinate responses. Numerous violations of human rights of the Serb population were recorded.[231] However, in Eastern Slavonia – the last Serb-controlled territory in Croatia – the mandate of UNCRO remained essentially unchanged. The government of Croatia and the Croatian Serb leadership agreed to resolve the issue of Eastern Slavonia through negotiation. Following the signing of the Basic Agreement on the Region of Eastern Slavonia, Baranja and Western Sirmium on 12 November 1995,[232] the Security Council expressed its readiness to consider the request to establish a transitional administration to govern the region and authorise an appropriate international force.[233] Following the establishment of the United Nations Transitional Administration in Eastern Slavonia, Baranja and Western Sirmium (UNTAES),[234] the mandate of UNCRO was terminated on 15 January 1996. By its resolution 1038 (1996), the Council authorised twenty-eight UN military observers to take over the task of monitoring the demilitarisation of the Prevlaka peninsula from UNCRO. The mission would be known as the United Nations Mission of Observers in Prevlaka (UNMOP). Following the successful completion of its mandate, UNMOP was terminated on 15 December 2002.[235]

UNTAES was established to govern the region for an initial period of twelve months and help it reintegrate into Croatia's legal and constitutional system. The mission came with both military and civilian components. By its resolution 1037 (1996), the Security Council decided that Member States, acting nationally or through regional organisations, might take all necessary measures, including close

---

228 See, *inter alia*, UN Docs. S/PRST/1995/23, 26, 37 and UNSC resolutions 994 (17 May 1994) and 1009 (4 August 1994).

229 See UN Doc. S/1995/370 (9 May 1995).

230 See UN Doc. S/1995/666 (6 August 1995) Annex III.

231 See UN Doc. S/PRST/1995/44 (7 September 1995).

232 See UN Doc. S/1995/27 (12 November 1995) Annex.

233 UNSC resolutions 1023 (1995) and 1025 (1995).

234 UNSC resolution 1037 (1996).

235 UNSC resolution 1437 (2002). See also the positive evaluation of this mini-mission in Report of the Secretary-General on the United Nations Mission of Observers in Prevlaka, UN Doc. S/2002/1341 (10 December 2002).

air support, to defend UNTAES or help it withdraw and that such actions would be based on the request of UNTAES.[236] In line with its mandate, the military component supervised and facilitated the demilitarisation of the region, as provided in the Basic Agreement, monitored the voluntary and safe return of refugees and displaced persons to their homes of origin in cooperation with the UNHCR and contributed, by its presence, to the maintenance of peace and security in the region. The civilian component established a temporary police force, defined its structure and size, developed a training programme and oversaw its implementation. In addition, it monitored the treatment of offenders and the prison system, undertook tasks relating to civil administration and the functioning of public services, and organised elections, assisted in their conduct and certified the results. The civilian component also undertook other activities relevant to the Basic Agreement, including monitoring and facilitating the demining of territory within the region, assisting in the coordination of plans for the development and economic reconstruction of the region and monitoring the parties' compliance with their commitments to respect the highest standards of human rights and fundamental freedoms.

The mandate of UNTAES was extended twice for a period of six months.[237] By the end of the prescribed two-year period, UNTAES claimed the successful accomplishment of its key objective under the November 1995 Basic Agreement: peacefully reintegrating the ethnically mixed Danube region into Croatia. The Council endorsed the plan for restructuring UNTAES and the withdrawal of its military component by 15 October 1997. By adopting resolution 1145 on 19 December 1997, the Security Council decided to establish, with effect from 16 January 1998, a United Nations Police Support Group (UNPSG) of 180 civilian police monitors for a single period of up to nine months in the post-UNTAES period, so as to continue the monitoring of the performance of the Croatian police in the region, particularly in connection with the return of displaced persons. In the same resolution, the Council noted the termination of UNTAES on 15 January 1998. The Council reiterated the continuing obligation, under the Basic Agreement, of the government of Croatia to respect the highest standards of human rights and fundamental freedoms and reaffirmed the right of all refugees and displaced persons originating from Croatia to return to their homes of origin. The Council welcomed the progress made in the peaceful two-way return of displaced persons and the return of refugees in the region. It encouraged liaison between the UNPSG and the OSCE to facilitate a smooth transition of responsibility to that organisation. The Police Support Group helped to prevent the return of instability

236 UNTAES and NATO's Implementation Force (IFOR) in Bosnia-Herzegovina were requested to cooperate with each other and with the High Representative (see below).

237 UNSC resolutions 1079 (15 November 1996) and 1120 (14 July 1997).

to the region. It proved to be a cost-effective instrument in helping to maintain conditions conducive to an orderly handover to the OSCE, pending the ultimate transfer of full responsibilities to the Croatian authorities.[238] After the successful completion of its mandate, the UNPSG came to an end on 15 October 1998. The OSCE took over the police monitoring responsibilities on the following day.[239]

6.6 Macedonia: UNPREDEP

Established on 31 March 1995 to replace UNPROFOR in Macedonia, the composition and strength of the United Nations Preventive Deployment Force (UNPREDEP) were maintained. The mandate of the mission also remained the same: to monitor and report any developments in the border areas with Albania and the FRY that could undermine confidence and stability in Macedonia.[240] The mission continued to serve as an early-warning source for the Security Council, helped to strengthen mutual dialogue among political parties and assisted in monitoring respect for human rights as well as inter-ethnic relations in the country. UNPREDEP also assisted in the country's social and economic development along with other agencies and organisations of the UN family.[241]

Despite the fact that inter-ethnic tensions continued to pose a threat to the country's social fabric and its long-term stability, as the incident over the Albanian-language 'Tetovo University' had shown,[242] the security situation in Macedonia and bilateral relations between FYROM and its neighbours continued to improve.[243] Consequently, UNPREDEP's mandate was extended for relatively short periods of time,[244] the third time with a view to reducing the mission's military component by 300 personnel.[245] However, in response to the crisis in neighbouring Albania, where the collapse of investment schemes robbed thousands of their lifetime savings, the Council extended the mission and suspended

---

[238] See Final Report of the Secretary-General on United Nations Police Support Group, UN Doc. S/1998/1004 (27 October 1998).

[239] See *infra* section 8.

[240] UNSC resolution 983 (1995).

[241] See H. Sokalski, *An Ounce of Prevention: Macedonia and the UN Experience in Preventive Diplomacy* (Washington, Endowment of the US Institute of Peace 2003); A. Ackerman, 'International Intervention in Macedonia: From Preventive Engagement to Peace Implementation', in P. Siani-Davies, ed., *International Intervention in the Balkans Since 1995* (London, Routledge 2003) pp. 105-119.

[242] Tensions had been generated by the ethnic Albanians' insistence upon and the government's consistent refusal to recognise as legal the 'Tetovo University'. This situation had been further aggravated by the imprisonment of some of the university's organisers and the high political profile of the issue on both sides. See further chapter 4, section 3.1.1.

[243] See Report of the Secretary-General pursuant to Security Council Resolution 1058 (1996), UN Doc. S/1996/819 (30 September 1996).

[244] UNSC resolutions 1027 (1995) and 1058 (1996).

[245] UNSC resolution 1082 (1996).

its reduction until after 1 October 1997.[246] The Albanian-Macedonian border was closed during curfew hours as the authorities feared an influx of refugees that might disrupt Macedonia's already fragile inter-ethnic balance. The start of the withdrawal of UNPREDEP, which began in the first week of March 1997, had thus begun at the most inappropriate time and clearly showed a lack of foresight. During May and June of 1997, UNPREDEP was active in preventing the further escalation of tension along the Albanian-Macedonian border and stayed in close contact with the military leadership of the Italian-led *Operazione Alba*.[247]

In spite of the evident social unrest and the collapse of state institutions in Albania, as well as a tense situation in Kosovo, the Security Council, by its resolution 1142 of 4 December 1997, decided to extend the mandate of UNPREDEP for a final period until 31 August 1998, with the withdrawal of the military component immediately thereafter.[248] However, the situation in Kosovo deteriorated, with violent ethnic clashes during the summer and autumn of 1998.[249] Worried that the unfolding crisis in Kosovo might disturb the fragile balance maintained in Macedonia, the Security Council, by adopting resolution 1186 on 21 July 1998, reaffirmed its commitment to the independence, sovereignty and territorial integrity of Macedonia and decided to extend the mandate of UNPREDEP for another period of six months until 28 February 1999 and to authorise an increase in troop strength up to 1,050. The force was also charged with the new responsibilities of monitoring and reporting on illicit arms flows and other activities prohibited under resolution 1160 of 4 December 1997.

Peace and stability in Macedonia continued to depend largely on developments in other parts of the region, in particular in Kosovo. The potential repercussions of continued violence in Kosovo on the external and internal security of Macedonia were serious given the large proportion of ethnic Albanians in the country's population. UNPREDEP maintained close cooperation with

---

[246] UNSC resolutions 1105 (9 April 1997) and 1110 (28 May 1997).

[247] See *infra* section 8.7.

[248] In the Report of the Secretary-General on the United Nations Preventive Deployment Force pursuant to Security Council resolution 1142 (1997) (UNPREDEP), UN Doc. S/1998/454 (1 June 1998), the UNSG stated that the Macedonian Minister of Foreign Affairs, in a letter of 15 May 1998 (UN Doc. S/1998/401), had referred to the changed circumstances in the region which spoke against weakening the international presence in the country. Concern was expressed as to the negative developments north of the border, especially in Kosovo, the yet unmarked border between Macedonia and the FRY, and tensions along the border between Albania and the FRY. Thus, peace and security in Macedonia could be endangered and a security gap would arise should UNPREDEP's military's component be withdrawn after 31 August 1998. Against this background, the UNSG noted that one possible option the UNSC might wish to consider was to extend the mission with its mandate unchanged for a further period of six months until 28 February 1999.

[249] On 15 June 1998, some eighty-five NATO planes carrying live ammunition participated in the air exercise *Determined Falcon* over Macedonia and Albania. Arguably, NATO's demonstration of its firm stand on the ongoing crisis in Kosovo did not really have an impact on the situation on the ground.

the OSCE Spillover Monitor Mission to Skopje and the European Community Monitoring Mission (ECMM, later EUMM).[250] It also established a working relationship with NATO, the Kosovo Verification Coordination Centre and the NATO Extraction Force deployed in the host country.[251]

The functions of UNPREDEP came to an abrupt end on 28 February 1999, after the Security Council failed to adopt draft resolution S/1999/201 due to the veto of China on 25 February 1999.[252] Speaking after the vote, the representative of China said that peace and stability in Macedonia had not been adversely affected by regional developments.[253] On the contrary, in China's view, the situation in Macedonia had stabilised in the previous years and its relations with neighbouring countries had improved. Moreover, the Secretary-General had reported that the original goals of the Security Council in establishing UNPREDEP had been met. In that context, China saw no need to further extend the mandate of the mission, especially when the United Nations' scarce resources could be put to better use in tackling conflicts in Africa and other regions. Several other UN members argued that there could be a spillover of the tensions in Kosovo across the border with Macedonia. In hindsight, China's assessment – largely coloured by Macedonia's decision to recognise Taiwan – proved entirely wrong. In 2001, fighting broke out which brought the country to the brink of civil war.[254]

In any event, UNPREDEP demonstrated that preventive deployment is an effective form of peacekeeping and that results can be achieved even with a small, almost symbolic deployment of peacekeepers if it is done at the right time and with a clear mandate. Until February 1999, the fundamental objective of the operation, namely to prevent the conflicts in the former Yugoslavia from spreading, had indeed been achieved. After the termination of UNPREDEP, the mission was renamed UN SKOPJE.

6.7 Kosovo: UNMIK

A lot has been written about the Kosovo crisis of 1999 and its aftermath.[255] This section will only deal with the role and impact of the United Nations Mission in

---

250 On the ECMM/EUMM, see chapter 3, section 2.4.

251 See Report of the Secretary-General on the United Nations Preventive Deployment Force pursuant to Security Council resolution 1186 (1998), UN Doc. S/1999/161 (12 February 1999).

252 See UN Doc. S/PV.3982 (25 February 1999).

253 See Press release SC/6648, 'Security Council fails to extend mandate of United Nations Preventive Deployment Force in Former Yugoslav Republic of Macedonia', 25 February 1999.

254 See chapter 4, section 3.1.1.

255 See, *inter alia*, H. Krieger, ed., *The Kosovo Conflict and International Law: An Analytical Documentation 1974-1999* (Cambridge, Cambridge University Press 2001); T. Judah, *Kosovo: War and Revenge*, 2nd edn. (New Haven, Yale University Press 2002); J. Kokott, 'The Development of

Kosovo (UNMIK) in stabilising the province. A chronicle of events leading up to this mission is presented in section 7.3.1 below.[256]

The undeclared war between NATO and the Federal Republic of Yugoslavia, initiated by NATO on 24 March 1999, was formally ended on 9 June 1999, with the signing of a Military Technical Agreement (MTA) between the International Security Force (KFOR) and the government of the Federal Republic of Yugoslavia.[257] One day later, on 10 June 1999, the UN Security Council adopted resolution 1244 (1999), which reaffirmed 'the commitment of all Member States to the sovereignty and territorial integrity of the Federal Republic of Yugoslavia', even while pledging to secure 'substantial autonomy and meaningful self-administration for Kosovo'. The Security Council decided on the establishment, 'under the auspices of the United Nations', of international civil *and* security presences. NATO agreed to deploy KFOR as the international security presence under the terms of resolution 1244 (1999), thus 'until the international civil presence can take responsibility for this task'.[258] From this passage flows the conclusion that, formally speaking, the United Nations is the sole 'trustee' administering the tasks on the territory of the trustor, that is to say, the rightful sovereign.[259] This conclusion is reinforced when considering the comprehensive list of legislative and executive powers with which resolution 1244 (1999) endowed the international civil presence in Kosovo:[260]

---

the Human Rights Situation in Kosovo 1989-1999', in C. Tomuschat, ed., *Kosovo and the International Community: A Legal Assessment* (The Hague, Kluwer Law International 2002) pp. 1-35; I. King and W. Mason, *Peace at Any Price: How the World Failed Kosovo* (Ithaca, Cornell University Press 2006); and T. Knudsen and C. Laustsen, *Kosovo Between War and Peace: Nationalism, Peacebuilding and International Trusteeship* (London, Routledge 2006).

256 A chronology of events between 10 June 1999 and March 2002 is available at: <http://www.unmikonline.org/chrono.htm#jun99>.

257 The MTA is available at: <http://www.nato.int/kfor/kfor/documents/mta.htm>.

258 UNSC resolution 1244 (1999) para. 9(c). On KFOR, see further *infra* section 7.3.1.

259 Nevertheless, the relationship between UNMIK (the 'civil presence') and KFOR (the 'security presence') is characterised by cooperation, not subordination.

260 For a debate on the concept, legality and limitations of such UN involvement in internal conflicts, see, *inter alia*, T. Garcia, 'La mission d'administration intérimaire des Nations Unies au Kosovo (MINUK)', 14 *RGDIP* (2000) pp. 61-71; M. Ruffert, 'The Administration of Kosovo and East-Timor by the International Community', 50 *ICLQ* (2001) pp. 555-573; C. Stahn, 'International Territorial Administration in the Former Yugoslavia: Origins, Developments and Challenges Ahead', 61 *ZaöRV* (2001) p. 105 et seq.; C. Tomuschat, 'Yugoslavia's Damaged Sovereignty over the Province of Kosovo', in G. Kreijen, ed., *State, Sovereignty, and International Governance* (Oxford, Oxford University Press 2002) pp. 323-348; M. Bothe and T. Marauhn, 'UN Administration of Kosovo and East Timor: Concept, Legality and Limitations of Security Council-Mandated Trusteeship Administration', in Tomuschat, op. cit. n. 255, at pp. 217-325; and more recently C. Stahn, 'Governance Beyond the State: Issues of Legitimacy in International Territorial Administration', 2 *IOLR* (2005) pp. 9-56.

(a) Promoting the establishment, pending a final settlement, of substantial autonomy and self-government in Kosovo [...];
(b) Performing basic civilian administrative functions where and as long as required;
(c) Organizing and overseeing the development of provisional institutions for democratic and autonomous self-government pending a political settlement, including the holding of elections;
(d) Transferring, as these institutions are established, its administrative responsibilities while overseeing and supporting the consolidation of Kosovo's local provisional institutions and other peacebuilding activities;
(e) Facilitating a political process designed to determine Kosovo's future status [...];
(f) In a final stage, overseeing the transfer of authority from Kosovo's provisional institutions to institutions established under a political settlement;
(g) Supporting the reconstruction of key infrastructure and other economic reconstruction;
(h) Supporting, in coordination with international humanitarian organizations, humanitarian and disaster relief aid;
(i) Maintaining civil law and order, including establishing local police forces and meanwhile through the deployment of international police personnel to serve in Kosovo;
(j) Protecting and promoting human rights; [and]
(k) Assuring the safe and unimpeded return of all refugees and displaced persons to their homes in Kosovo.[261]

At the request of the Security Council, the UN Secretary-General appointed Bernard Kouchner, founder and president of *Médecins sans Frontières* and former Minister of Health of France, as his Special Representative (SRSG) to head the United Nations Mission in Kosovo (UNMIK).[262] At the same time, Kofi Annan appointed four other internationals to head the major components – or 'pillars' – of the mission: Dennis McNamara (New Zealand) for the UNHCR-led first pillar concerning 'Humanitarian Assistance';[263] Dominique Vian (France) for the UN-led second pillar focusing on 'Interim Civil Administration'; Daan Everts (Netherlands) for the OSCE-led third pillar aimed at 'Democratization and Institution Building'; and Joly Dixon (United Kingdom) for the EU-led fourth pillar on 'Reconstruction and Economic Development'.[264] With NATO providing

---

261 UNSCR 1244 (1999) para. 11.

262 See UN Docs. S/1999/748 and 749 (6 July 1999) and UN Press release SG/SM/7057, 'Secretary-General appoints Bernard Kouchner (France) as his Special Representative for United Mission in Kosovo', 2 July 1999.

263 In June 2000, at the end of the emergency stage, the UNHCR-led Pillar I (Humanitarian Assistance) was phased out. In May 2001, a new Pillar I (Police and Justice) was established under the leadership of the United Nations.

264 See UN Press release SG/SM/7057, 'Secretary-General appoints Bernard Kouchner (France) as his Special Representative for United Mission in Kosovo', 2 July 1999. On the European Union's role in UNMIK, see chapter 4, section 3.3.1.

the international security presence in Kosovo, an unprecedented UN operation was set up, encompassing the activities of three non-UN organisations under the United Nation's overall jurisdiction. As the most senior international civilian official in Kosovo, Bernard Kouchner – and his successors in the job[265] – preside(d) over the work of the pillars and facilitate(d) the political process designed to determine Kosovo's final status.[266]

In the wake of what Kouchner described as 'forty years of Communism, ten years of apartheid and a year of ethnic cleansing',[267] peacebuilding in Kosovo has proved to be an exceptionally difficult and long-term task. Military victory was but the first step on a long road to building a durable, multi-ethnic society free from the threat of renewed conflict. The challenges for Kosovo's interim protectors have been staggering. In the year preceding NATO's armed intervention, Belgrade's security forces had scorched the province, while NATO's bombardment had caused further damage. According to the UN food agencies, Kosovo lost 65 per cent of its agricultural produce and livestock as a result of the war in the spring of 1999, with the wheat production in 1999 was able to meet only 30 per cent of the province's needs.[268] In addition, some 120,000 houses had been destroyed or damaged. Estimates of the cost to rebuild the province's economy have ranged from $2 billion to $5 billion.[269]

A second challenge, quite apart from the confirmed deaths of some 12,000 Kosovar Albanians between February 1998 and June 1999, was the displacement and disappearance of persons. By early August 1999, nearly 90 per cent of the Albanians who had fled the province between 1998 and 1999 had returned (700,000 from neighbouring countries and 30,000 from countries outside the

---

265 Kouchner served as head of UNMIK from July 1999 to January 2001. He was succeeded by Hans Haekkerup (Denmark), who served from February 2001 to December 2001. Michael Steiner (Germany) served as the third SRSG from January 2002 to July 2003. The fourth head of UNMIK was Harri Holkeri (Finland), who served from August 2003 to June 2004. He was succeeded by Søren Jenssen-Petersen (Denmark), who served from August 2004 to June 2006. The current Special Representative of the Secretary-General for Kosovo is Joachim Rücker (Germany).

266 The SRSG reports up to four times a year to the Security Council. These reports include a technical assessment of the implementation of the so-called 'Standards for Kosovo' programme, which covers a range of activities designed to promote good governance and multi-ethnicity (see below).

267 Cited by Lord Robertson, Secretary General of NATO, in a speech at the Los Angeles World Affairs Council, 'Kosovo: The Real Story', 6 April 2000.

268 See FAO/WFP Crop and Food Supply Assessment Mission to the Kosovo Province of the Federal Republic of Yugoslavia, 'Special report', UN Doc. X2901/E (30 August 1999), available at: <http://www.fao.org/docrep/004/x2901e/x2901e00.htm>; UN Sub-Committee on Nutrition, 'Refugee Nutrition Information System (RNIS), No. 28 – Report on the Nutrition Situation of Refugees and Displaced Populations', 28 September 1999, ch. 15; and FAO Conference, 30th Session, 12-13 November 1999, UN Doc. C/99/INF/5.

269 In addition to the references above, see IMF, 'The Economic Consequences of the Kosovo Crisis: An Updated Assessment', 25 May 1999, available at: <http://www.imf.org/external/pubs/ft/kosovo/052599.htm>. See also chapter 4, section 3.3.1.

region).[270] On the other hand, roughly 2,000 Kosovar Albanians remained incarcerated in Serbian prisons, having been taken hostage by Serbian forces in the spring of 1999, while more than 80,000 of the roughly 200,000 Serbs living in the province had fled Kosovo under Albanian pressure by the end of July.[271]

A third challenge had to do with infrastructure, particularly education and the legal system. For a decade, Kosovo's Albanians had relied on an underground educational system operating out of people's homes, in conditions of extreme scarcity. In addition, in the mid-1990s, the Serbian authorities had pulped Albanian language books from the Priština National Library in an effort to erase the province's cultural memory. But that was just the tip of the iceberg. About two-thirds of Kosovo's 180 libraries were said to have been destroyed between 1990 and 1999, during which time the Serbian authorities destroyed more than 900,000 books, almost half of all library books in Kosovo. An additional 263,000 books were destroyed by fire during NATO's aerial campaign in the spring of 1999.[272] With the legal system also in disarray, UNMIK set about drafting a penal code, setting up forty-seven courts, training judges and establishing a detention system. The Kosovo Law Centre, established by the OSCE in June 2000 as a centre for legal research and publisher of all laws, regulations and decrees, is regarded as a building block for establishing the rule of law in the province.[273] UNMIK also undertook to train local recruits to serve in a new Kosovo Police Service (KPS). The first 200 graduates – Serbian and Albanian women and men – received their diplomas in ceremonies on 7 September 1999. As of 30 October 2000, there were 4,130 UNMIK police officers stationed in Kosovo, alongside 2,549 KPS officers.[274]

The fourth challenge, criminality, is closely associated with the aforementioned need to develop respected legal institutions and enforcement agencies. Although crime rates remain high, there are at least some positive trends. The murder rate, for example, has dropped from 291 in 2000 to 205 in 2001, 143 in 2002, 131 in 2003, 111 in 2004 and 101 in 2005.[275]

Fifth, there was the most immediate challenge of confiscating the weapons held by paramilitaries in the province and establishing KFOR's unchallenged ability to assure a secure environment. Although paramilitaries were not permitted under the MTA, the Albanians were quick to point out that they had not been

---

270 See UNMIK's chronology, available at: <http://www.unmikonline.org/chrono.htm#jun99>.

271 Ibid.

272 See C. Frederiksen and F. Bakken 'Libraries in Kosova/Kosovo: A general assessment and a short and medium-term development plan', IFLA/FAIFE report of Joint UNESCO, CoE and Kosova Library Mission, April 2000, available at: <http://www.ifla.org/faife/faife/kosova/kosorepo.htm>.

273 See: <http://www.kosovolawcentre.org>.

274 See: <http://www.kosovopolice.com/english/index_english.html>.

275 See UNMIK, 'Factsheet: Kosovo in October 2006', available at: <http://www.unmikonline.org/docs/2006/Fact_Sheet_Oct_2006.pdf>.

signatories to the agreement and for a few days there was some uncertainty as to the willingness of the leadership of the KLA to comply with this requirement. By 19 June 1999, however, NATO commanders had reached a tentative agreement with KLA leaders that the rebel force would be disbanded and that it would surrender its arms.[276]

In practical terms, the United Nations could not have met the challenges and performed the functions described above without possessing full governmental powers in the territory of Kosovo. That is why, on 25 July 1999, the SRSG signed Regulation No. 1999/1, vesting all legislative and executive authority in the territory in UNMIK.[277] Section 1 of the Regulation states that:

> 1. All legislative and executive authority with respect to Kosovo, including the administration of the judiciary, is vested in UNMIK and is exercised by the Special Representative of the Secretary-General.
> 2. The Special Representative of the Secretary-General may appoint any person to perform functions in the civil administration in Kosovo, including the judiciary, or remove such person. Such functions shall be exercised in accordance with the existing laws, as specified in section 3, and any regulations issued by UNMIK.

Working closely together with Kosovo's would-be leaders, UNMIK initially performed the whole spectrum of administrative functions and services of a quasi-sovereign entity, covering such fields as health and education, banking and finance, post and telecommunications, and law and order.[278] Gradually, however, UNMIK has started sharing the performance of these tasks with locally appointed and – as of June 2002 – elected – leaders in the so-called 'Provisional Institutions of Self-Government' (PISG).[279] This trend was put in motion by the adoption of the 'Constitutional Framework for Provisional Self-Government', signed by the SRSG on 15 May 2001.[280] The Constitutional Framework's purpose was to define

---

276 Although most of these confiscations have involved Albanian-held weaponry, KFOR peace-keeping troops reported that they had found assault rifles, light anti-tank weapons and various other armaments in a search of two Serbian villages in Kosovo on 1 November 1999. More on KFOR's activities in section 7.3.3.

277 UNMIK/REG/1999/1 on the Authority of the Interim Administration in Kosovo, 25 July 1999, later amended.

278 For an evaluation of UNMIK's performance during this first stage, see E. Chevallier, 'L'ONU au Kosovo: leçons de la première MINUK', 35 *EUISS Occasional Paper* (2002).

279 In December 1999, three Kosovar Albanian political leaders signed a landmark agreement to share the provisional management of Kosovo with UNMIK until elections. See Press release UNMIK/PR/115, 'Kosovo Political Leaders Agree to Share Administration of Kosovo with UNMIK', 15 December 1999. The agreement established a Kosovo-UNMIK joint Interim Administrative Council. Municipal elections took place in October 2000. In the long aftermath of the November 2001 general elections – LDK (Democratic League of Kosovo) won 47 seats, PDK (Democratic Party of Kosovo) 26, the (ethnic Serb) Coalition Povratak 22 and (Alliance for the Future of Kosovo) AAK 8 – Ibrahim Rugova (LDK) was elected President of Kosovo in March 2002. A multi-ethnic provisional self-government was installed on 13 June 2002.

280 See UNMIK/PR/581, 'SRSG Signs Constitutional Framework', 15 May 2001.

the shape and power of the interim institutions to which UNMIK could transfer further power and responsibility until the determination of Kosovo's final status. In this document, the PISG were granted greater autonomy, in order to share provisional interim management of Kosovo with UNMIK, while respecting resolution 1244 (1999) and the legislative and executive authority retained by the SRSG.[281] Thus, the bottom line is that the full range of governmental powers remains vested in UNMIK until such time as the Security Council agrees upon Kosovo's final status.[282]

In its activities, UNMIK has been guided by its 'Standards for Kosovo', set out in a document published in Priština on 10 December 2003 and subsequently endorsed by the Security Council.[283] The 'Standards for Kosovo' document set a target for Kosovo as a truly multi-ethnic, stable and democratic entity that approaches European standards. In essence, Kosovo was expected to make progress on eight standards: functioning democratic institutions; the rule of law; freedom of movement; return and reintegration; the economy; property rights; dialogue with Belgrade; and the Kosovo Protection Corps, a civilian emergency services organisation set up a part of the transformation of the KLA.[284] The Kosovo Standards Implementation Plan (KSIP) of 31 March 2004 listed the concrete actions needed to meet the 'standards' and defined who was responsible for each of the actions and the timeframe in which they should be performed.[285] As such, the standards process was in harmony with the European Union's parallel Stabilisation and Association Process Tracking Mechanism (STM) for Kosovo,[286] but the 'Standards for Kosovo' document remained the target, and progress concerning the latter was the basis for the decision to begin the political process concerning Kosovo's final status. Despite the fact that UNMIK gradually transferred a large number of competences to Kosovo's PISG and that many of the 'standards' were achieved, poverty and unemployment remained widespread.[287]

---

281 As UNSC resolution 1244 (1999) is rather elusive on the latter point, all regulations adopted by the SRSG, in their preamble, take account of UNMIK Regulation 1999/1 on the Authority of the Interim Administration in Kosovo.

282 On the final status process, see chapter 4, section 3.3, and chapter 6, section 4.3.

283 The 'Standards for Kosovo' were agreed between the PISG and UNMIK and subsequently launched by the Special Representative of the Secretary-General (SRSG) Harry Holkeri and Kosovo's Prime Minister Bajram Rexhepi on 10 December 2003. See Press release UNMIK/PR/1078 of that date. The 'Standards' were endorsed by the Security Council on 12 December 2003. See Presidential Statement S/PRST/2003/26.

284 See UNMIK/REG/1999/8 on the Establishment of the Kosovo Protection Force, 20 September 1999. More information on the KPC is available at: <http://www.unmikonline.org/1styear/kpcorps.htm>.

285 The KSIP is available at: <http://www.unmikonline.org/pub/misc/ksip_eng.pdf>.

286 See chapter 5, section 3.2.5.

287 In 2004, over half of Kosovo's two million inhabitants were living on or below the poverty line. The average daily income was €3 and the official unemployment rate was 39.7 per cent. There were daily debilitating power cuts. See Statistical Office of Kosovo, *Series 1: Kosovo in Figures*

Bitterness and resentment grew over the 'corrupt' and 'colonial' ways of UNMIK's international staff.[288] Local frustrations connected to the ambiguity regarding the final status spilled over into organised inter-ethnic violence, as witnessed in March 2004.[289] The status quo – that is, 'standards before status' – had become unsustainable and forced the international community to develop a fresh approach to promoting reforms and development in Kosovo. It was eventually acknowledged that working on the standards in the context of the future status was a better strategy than insisting on the complying with standards before discussing status issues.[290] Following the comprehensive review of the situation in Kosovo by UNSG Special Envoy Kai Eide in the summer of 2005, the UN Security Council on 24 October 2005 endorsed final status talks.[291] This decision had been facilitated by the *rapprochement* between Priština and Belgrade after the resignation of Ramush Haradinaj as Kosovo's Prime Minister on 9 March 2005 and his surrender to the ICTY to face charges of persecuting Serbs, gypsies and suspected collaborators among the ethnic Albanians.[292]

7. EFFORTS TO BRING PEACE AND STABILITY TO THE WESTERN BALKANS: NATO

7.1 Bosnia-Herzegovina

Bosnia-Herzegovina has been the scene of many 'firsts' for NATO, and decisions taken in response to events in Bosnia have helped shape NATO's evolution since

2005, January 2006, available at: <http://www.ks-gov.net/esk/index_english.htm>. See also chapter 6, section 4.3.1. For an evaluation of UNMIK's state-builing activities, see R. Everly, 'Reviewing Governmental Acts of the United Nations in Kosovo', 8 *German Law Journal* (2007) pp. 21-37.

288 See H. Smith, 'Angry Kosovars call on "colonial" UN occupying force to leave', *The Observer*, 19 October 2003; and Press release UNMIK/PR/1053, 4 November 2003. For an academic analysis, see B. Knoll, 'Legitimacy and UN-Administration of Territory', 8 *German Law Journal* (2007) pp. 39-56; and, more generally, O. Korhonen, 'International Governance in Post-Conflict Situations', 14 *LJIL* (2001) pp. 495-526.

289 See chapter 1, n. 7.

290 See B. Knoll, 'From Benchmarking to Final status? Kosovo and the Problem of an International Administration's Open-ended Mandate', 16 *EJIL* (2005) pp. 637-660.

291 See UN Doc. S/PRST/2005/51. See also chapter 4, section 3.3, and chapter 6, section 4.3.1.

292 As a result of the October 2004 general elections, a government coalition had formed between LDK and AAK, and AAK leader Ramush Haradinaj had become Prime Minister. Haradinaj decided to resign and depart to The Hague when he was indicted by the ICTY on 8 March 2005. Two weeks later, a new government led by Bajram Kosumi (AAK) was formed on the basis of the same coalition. On 21 January 2006, President Ibrahim Rugova (LDK) died of lung cancer. In February, the Assembly elected Fatmir Sejdiu (LDK) as the new President. A subsequent change of government took place in March 2006, when former KLA Commander Agim Çeku (AAK) replaced Bajram Kosumi as Prime Minister.

the end of the Cold War. Under the cloak of Operation *Deny Flight*, the Alliance first used armed force on 28 February 1994 when it shot down four of six Bosnian Serb jets that were violating the UN-imposed flight ban.[293] NATO also launched its first air campaign (Operation *Deliberate Force*) in Bosnia-Herzegovina in August and September 1995.[294] NATO's operations against Bosnian Serb positions in August and September 1995 helped pave the way for the Dayton Peace Agreement. In line with UN Security Council resolution 1031 (1995), which authorised Member States to establish a multinational military force to implement the Dayton Peace Agreement, NATO launched Operation *Joint Endeavour*, its inaugural peacekeeping force (IFOR) and largest military operation ever, to put in place the military aspects of the Dayton Agreement.[295] On 16 December 1995, the deployment of 60,000 troops (50,000 NATO and 10,000 non-NATO) and equipment from thirty-two states began.[296] Adopted on the basis of chapter VII of the UN Charter, resolution 1031 and the rules of engagement allowed for the robust use of force by IFOR, if necessary, to carry out its mission and protect itself. IFOR's tasks were to ensure compliance with Annex 1A of the Dayton Agreement, which constituted the military portion of the agreement. Summarised, these clauses instructed IFOR to (i) maintain the cessation of

---

[293] Operation *Deny Flight* was conducted from 12 April 1993 to 20 December 1995. The mission of the NATO Operation was (i) to conduct aerial monitoring and enforce compliance with UNSC resolution 816 in the airspace of Bosnia-Herzegovina in the 'no-fly' zone; (ii) to provide close air support to UN troops on the ground at the request of, and controlled by, UNPROFOR under the provisions of UNSC resolutions 836, 958 and 981; and (iii) to conduct, at the request of and in coordination with the United Nations, approved ('dual-key') air strikes against designated targets threatening the security of the UN-declared safe areas. Almost 4,500 personnel from twelve NATO countries were deployed for this NATO operation. For other occasions on which NATO conducted air strikes in the framework of this operation, see *supra* section 6.2.4.

[294] Although initiated in response to the Bosnian Serb army's shelling of the Sarajevo market place on 28 August 1995, Operation *Deliberate Force* was the culmination of events and related planning over a long period. The air attack plan, triggered by a 'dual-key' decision, was intended to reduce military capability to threaten or attack safe areas and UN forces. Targets included fielded forces and heavy weapons; command and control facilities; direct and essential military support facilities; and supporting infrastructure and lines of communication A twenty-four-hour suspension of air strikes beginning on 1 September was requested by UNPROFOR in support of negotiation efforts. The suspension was extended until 5 September, when it turned out that negotiations had been unsuccessful. That day, in coordination with the United Nations, NATO resumed its air strikes. On 14 September, offensive operations were suspended in response to the warring factions' agreement to the conditions set out in the UN-brokered Framework Agreement: (i) cease all offensive operations within the Sarajevo exclusion zone; (ii) remove heavy weapons from the zone within 144 hours; (iii) unimpeded road access to Sarajevo; (iv) Sarajevo Airport opened for unrestricted use; (v) Bosnia-Herzegovina and Bosnian Serb army commanders meet to formalise a cessation of hostilities agreement. Compliance with all conditions left the United Nations and NATO to agree on 20 September that the mission of Operation *Deliberate Force* had been accomplished. See also *supra* section 6.2.4.

[295] See *supra* section 6.3.5.

[296] See IFOR fact sheet, available at: <http://www.nato.int/sfor>.

hostilities; (ii) separate the armed forces of the Bosnian-Croat Federation and the Republika Srpska; (iii) transfer territory between the two entities; (iv) move the forces and heavy weapons into authorised cantonment sites; (v) create a secure environment for civil aspects of the agreement; and (vi) control the airspace over Bosnia-Herzegovina.

Within one year, IFOR made substantial progress in carrying out its tasks in Bosnia-Herzegovina.[297] No significant military activity occurred after its arrival. By February 1996, all forces were withdrawn from the zone of separation on either side of the agreed ceasefire line and in March a new zone of separation was established along a so-called inter-entity boundary line. By April, the final stages in the military agreement concerning cantonment of heavy weapons were completed, and the peace plan was in full operation. Joint Military Commissions were developed, air defence radar was shut down, hostile forces withdrew from the zone of separation and most heavy weapons and non-demobilised forces were moved to barracks or designated areas. All in all, and certainly in comparison to the civilian responsibilities of the Dayton Peace Agreement, IFOR was immensely successful in its primary functions. By securing a relatively peaceful environment, it enabled the High Representative of the international community and other international organisations to start their work with regard to the implementation of the civil aspects of the peace agreement. It is here that significant difficulties remained, especially in the field of freedom of movement for regular citizens and prisoner release. Even more ominous were the political, social and economic problems that remained unresolved and still led to violent inter-ethnic attacks. The biggest problem left after IFOR completed its activities on 20 December 1996 concerned the organisation of democratic elections. While nation-wide 'entity' elections took place on 14 September 1996, the planned municipal elections were postponed for one year.

To support the ongoing international activities in the civil field, the UN Security Council appointed NATO's Stabilisation Force (SFOR) in resolution 1088 (1996).[298] As a follow-on to its Operation *Joint Endeavour*, NATO launched Operation *Joint Guard* for an initial period of eighteen months. Despite a contingent roughly half the size of its predecessor, SFOR essentially had the same peacekeeping mandate and mission.[299] It consisted of thirty-four participating countries (sixteen NATO and eighteen non-NATO, of which fourteen PfP

297 Ibid.

298 Para. 18.

299 Even though the role of IFOR was to implement the peace and the role of SFOR was to stabilise the peace. The difference in tasks is reflected in the name of the missions. SFOR's specific tasks were to (i) deter or prevent a resumption of hostilities or new threats to peace; (ii) promote a climate in which the peace process could continue to move forward; and (iii) provide selective support to civilian organisations within its capabilities.

partners) and was authorised to use 'all necessary means' to carry out its mission and protect itself.[300] Low-level violence continued throughout Bosnia-Herzegovina, especially in Mostar and in the villages in and around the zone of separation. In the first year of SFOR's deployment, there were several violent incidents involving displaced persons trying to return to their homes, and houses were destroyed by arson and explosion. Demining was not complete, and both Bosniak and Bosnian Serb parties were still non-compliant in relation to the mandatory return of prisoners. Despite the efforts of SFOR, the IPTF and the UNHCR, resettlement did not go smoothly, largely because freedom of movement remained a major problem. SFOR was active in helping the OSCE with its preparations for the municipal elections of 13-14 September 1997, but these proved to be a 'fake' show of democracy.[301] For all these reasons, the UN Security Council prolonged NATO's mandate in Bosnia-Herzegovina.[302] Operation *Joint Guard* (21 December 1996-19 June 1998) was succeeded by Operation *Joint Forge*, which ran until 2 December 2004, when the European Union took over responsibility for the international community's military presence in Bosnia-Herzegovina.[303] Whereas SFOR's initial size was around 32,000 troops, the North Atlantic Council decided on 25 October 1999, having taken into account the improved security situation in Bosnia-Herzegovina, to restructure the force and reduce it to about 12,000 troops by the beginning of 2003. After the handover of authority to the European Union, NATO maintained (and still maintains) a military headquarters in Sarajevo to carry out a number of specific tasks related, in particular, to assisting the government in reforming its defence structures to meet the requirements to join NATO's PfP programme.[304]

One of the internationally most visible tasks of SFOR was supporting the International Criminal Tribunal for the former Yugoslavia (ICTY) in carrying out its mandate.[305] In order to create a 'safe and secure environment' in Bosnia-

---

300 Paras. 19-21. Facts, figures and documents about SFOR are available at: <http://www.nato.int/sfor>.

301 See CSCE, *The 1997 Municipal Elections in Bosnia-Herzegovina* (October 1997); and D. Chandler, *Bosnia: Faking Democracy after Dayton*, 2nd edn. (London, Pluto Press 2000) at pp. 122-125.

302 It did so on six occasions for an additional period of twelve months, see S/RES/1174 (1998), S/RES/1247 (1999), S/RES/1305 (2000), S/RES/1357 (2001), S/RES/1423 (2002), S/RES/1491 (2003) and, for a final period of six months, S/RES/1551 (2004).

303 See chapter 4, section 4.1.2.

304 For the mission statement of the NATO Headquarters Sarajevo Mission (NHQSa), see: <http://www.afsouth.nato.int/NHQSA/index.htm>.

305 See, *inter alia*, N. Figa-Talamanca, 'The Role of NATO in the Peace Agreement for Bosnia and Herzegovina', 7 *EJIL* (1996) pp. 164-175; and P. Gaeta, 'Is NATO Authorized or Obliged to Arrest Persons Indicted by the International Criminal Tribunal for the Former Yugoslavia', 9 *EJIL* (1998) pp. 174-181. The author of the second paper concludes that the NATO-led force is entitled but not obliged to arrest persons indicted by the ICTY, nor that such an obligation is incumbent upon individual troop-contributing states.

Herzegovina, SFOR detained and transferred to the ICTY twenty-seven persons indicted for war crimes when it came across them in the course of its normal duties. Another three were killed during attempts to arrest them. On 28 February and 1 March 2002, SFOR soldiers moved to detain Radovan Karadžić, but for reasons that are still not entirely clear Karadžić was not arrested.[306] This incident and the ongoing failure to catch both him and Ratko Mladić (despite a 300-strong presence in NHQSa tasked with, *inter alia*, the capture of the remaining ICTY indictees) have tarnished the shining armour of NATO's white knights.[307]

Nevertheless, the history of NATO's first deployment of ground forces outside its traditional area of operations has been extremely significant in the metamorphosis of NATO as an international peacekeeper. The results in Bosnia-Herzegovina clearly indicate major accomplishments for NATO in carrying out its specific military goals and objectives. Without the presence of IFOR and SFOR, the chances of achieving peacebuilding, reconstruction and civilian transformation would have been extremely unlikely in Bosnia-Herzegovina. NATO has shown that it can be employed 'out of area' and operate successfully under the authority of the UN Security Council. With the employment of NATO as its military arm, the Security Council – indeed the international community at large – finally came to understand what was needed in the Balkans, namely a consensus on political purpose and objectives, unity of diplomatic and military action and a clear mission for military engagement linked to the political purpose.

7.2 Macedonia

In 2001, NATO, in close cooperation with the European Union and the OSCE, helped stave off civil war in Macedonia through timely and coordinated intervention.[308] At the request of the Macedonian government, then NATO Secretary General Lord Robertson despatched a crisis management team to negotiate a ceasefire with the so-called 'National Liberation Army' (NLA), an armed group of ethnic Albanian rebels who had taken control of large swathes of territory in the western part of the country. At the time, the very survival of the Macedonia was at stake. A factor contributing to the unrest in Macedonia in 2001 was instability in neighbouring Kosovo. The NATO team succeeded in helping the European Union to persuade the NLA to agree to a ceasefire and to support the ongoing political negotiation process which culminated in the Ohrid Framework Agreement of 13 August 2001.

306 See 'NATO Comments by SecGen on SFOR Operations to Detain Radovan Karadzic', 1 March 2002, available at: <http://listserv.cc.kuleuven.ac.be/cgi-bin/wa?A1=ind0203&L=natodata>.

307 A variation of the title of the famous book by C. Bellamy, *Knights in White Armour: The New Art of War and Peace* (London, Hutchinson 1996).

308 For the background to the crisis, see chapter 4, section 3.1.

In the wake of this agreement, NATO deployed a force of only 4,000 troops in Operation *Essential Harvest* to oversee the NLA's disarmament.[309] During its thirty-day mission (27 August-26 September 2001), NATO collected close to 4,000 voluntarily surrendered weapons at several designated points. At the end of September, NATO declared that the task was complete and that the NLA had ceased to exist as a structured armed organisation. This step was a key precondition for a peace process to get underway as set out in the Ohrid Framework Agreement. After completing Operation *Essential Harvest*, NATO retained, at Skopje's request, a follow-on force of several hundred military personnel in the country to protect civilian observers tasked with monitoring the re-entry of the state security forces into former crisis areas – first in Operation *Amber Fox* (27 September 2001-15 December 2002)[310] and then in the further reduced Operation *Allied Harmony* (16 December 2002-31 March 2003).[311] On 31 March 2003, NATO handed over the responsibility for this operation to the European Union, which launched its first-ever military mission, *Concordia*.[312]

7.3 Kosovo

As noted earlier, a lot has already been written about the Kosovo crisis of 1999 and its aftermath.[313] This study is not concerned with what has been exhaustively dealt with elsewhere concerning the legitimacy and legality of NATO's 'humanitarian intervention' in Kosovo,[314] nor with the legal accountability of NATO

---

309 Documents and background information are available at: <http://www.nato.int/fyrom/tfh/home.htm>.

310 Documents and background information are available at: <http://www.nato.int/fyrom/tff/home.htm>.

311 Documents and background information are available at: <http://www.nato.int/fyrom/ah/home.htm>.

312 See chapter 4, section 4.2.

313 See *supra* n. 255.

314 See, *inter alia*, N. Chomsky, *The New Military Humanism: Lessons from Kosovo* (Monroe, Courage 1999); L. Henkin, 'Kosovo and the Law of "Humanitarian Intervention"', 93 *AJIL* (1999) at p. 824; R. Wedgwood, 'NATO's Campaign in Yugoslavia', ibid., at p. 828; R. Falk, 'Kosovo, World Order, and the Future of International Law', ibid., at p. 847; T. Franck, 'Lessons of Kosovo', ibid., at p. 857; B. Simma, 'NATO, the UN and the Use of Force: Legal Aspects', 10 *EJIL* (1999) pp. 1-22; A. Cassese, 'Ex Iniuria Ius Oritur: Are We Moving towards International Legitimation of Forcible Humanitarian Countermeasures in the World Community?', ibid., at pp. 23-30; N. Schrijver, 'NATO in Kosovo: Humanitarian Intervention Turns into Von Clausewitz War', *ILF* (1999) p. 155; S. Blockmans, 'Moving into UNchartered Waters: An Emerging Right of Unilateral Humanitarian Intervention', 12 *LJIL* (1999) pp. 759-786; I. Daalder and M. O'Hanlon, *Winning Ugly: NATO's War to Save Kosovo* (Washington, Brookings Institution 2000); S. Chesterman, *Just War or Just Peace? Humanitarian Intervention and International Law* (Oxford, Oxford University Press 2001); G. Seidel, 'A New Dimension of the Right of Self-Determination in Kosovo?', in Tomuschat, op. cit. n. 255, at pp. 203-215; M. Guillaume, 'Le cadre juridique de l'action de la KFOR au Kosovo', ibid., at

(members) and its (their) forces for inflicting 'collateral' damage.[315] Like previous paragraphs, this section will restrict itself to an examination of the role and impact of NATO's actions in Kosovo.

7.3.1 *Chronicle of an intervention foretold*

During 1998, open conflict between Serbian military and police forces and the Kosovo Liberation Army (KLA) resulted in the deaths of over 1,500 Kosovar Albanians and forced 400,000 people from their homes.[316] The international community became gravely concerned about the escalating conflict, its humanitarian consequences and the risk of it spreading to other countries, notably Macedonia and Albania. President Slobodan Milošević's disregard for diplomatic efforts aimed at peacefully resolving the crisis and the destabilising role of the militant KLA were also of concern. UN Security Council resolution 1199 (1998), among other things, expressed deep concern about the excessive use of force by the Serbian security forces and the Yugoslav army and called for a ceasefire by both parties to the conflict. On 13 October 1998, following a deterioration of the situation, the North Atlantic Council decided to issue activation orders for both limited air strikes and a phased air campaign in Yugoslavia, the execution of which was to begin approximately ninety-six hours later.[317] This move was designed to support US-led diplomatic efforts to make the Milošević regime withdraw its forces from Kosovo, cooperate in bringing an end to the violence and facilitate the return of refugees to their homes. At the last moment, following further diplomatic initiatives, including visits to Belgrade by NATO's Secretary General Javier Solana, US envoys Richard Holbrooke and Christopher Hill and

---

pp. 243-286; and A. Orford, *Reading Humanitarian Intervention: Human Rights and the Use of Force in International Law* (Cambridge, Cambridge University Press 2003).

315 See, *inter alia*, J. Cerone, 'Minding the Gap: Outlining KFOR Accountability in Post-Conflict Kosovo', 12 *EJIL* (2001) pp. 469-488; T. Stein, 'Kosovo and the International Community. The Attribution of Possible Internationally Wrongful Acts: Responsibility of NATO or of its Member States', in Tomuschat, op. cit. n. 255, at pp. 181-192; A. Pellet, 'L'imputabilité d'éventuels actes illicites – Responsabilité de l'OTAN ou des Etats members', ibid., at pp. 193-202; R. Lawson, 'Life After Banković: On the Extraterritorial Application of the European Convention on Human Rights', in F. Coomans and M. Kamminga, eds., *Extraterritorial Application of Human Rights Treaties* (Antwerp, Intersentia 2004) pp. 83-123. More generally, see M. Zwanenburg, *Accountability of Peace Support Operations* (Leiden, Martinus Nijhoff 2005).

316 Due to Serbian oppression, many Kosovar Albanians fled the province. The plight of those staying has been described by refugees leaving Kosovo. All indications pointed to organised persecution involving mass executions, exploitation as human shields, rape, mass expulsions, burning and looting of homes and villages, destruction of crops and livestock, suppression of identity, origins and property ownership by confiscation of documents, hunger, starvation and exhaustion and many other abuses of human rights and fundamental freedoms. See Kokott, loc. cit. n. 255.

317 See NATO Press release, 'Statement to the Press by the Secretary General Following Decision on the ACTORD', 13 October 1998.

the Supreme Allied Commander Europe, General Wesley Clark, President Milošević agreed to international demands and the air strikes were called off.[318] In the spirit of Security Council resolution 1199, limits were set on the number of Serbian forces in Kosovo and on the scope of their operations, following a separate agreement with NATO Generals Naumann and Clark.[319] It was agreed, in addition, that the OSCE would establish a Kosovo Verification Mission (KVM) to observe compliance on the ground and that NATO would establish an aerial surveillance mission.[320] The establishment of the two missions was endorsed by UN Security Council resolution 1203 (1998).

Despite these steps, the violence in Kosovo flared up again at the beginning of 1999, following a number of acts of provocation on both sides and the use of excessive and disproportionate force by the Serbian army and special police. Some of these incidents were defused through the mediation efforts of the OSCE verifiers, but the one at Račak was the proverbial straw that broke the international community's back. It concerned a clash in a small village by that name on 15 January 1999 between Yugoslav security forces and KLA fighters in which forty-five Kosovar Albanians died. Internationally, the deaths were widely blamed on the actions of the Yugoslav security forces, which were accused of having committed a deliberate massacre, but the government of the FRY consistently claimed that it was a legitimate police operation where no crime was committed by the state forces.[321] The Račak incident was one of the bloodiest incidents to have occurred in the conflict in Kosovo up to that point and later featured among the war crimes charges for which Milošević was eventually indicted and put on trial by the ICTY.[322] Renewed international efforts were made to give new political impetus to finding a peaceful solution to the conflict. The Contact Group met on 29 January 1999. It was agreed to convene urgent negotiations between the parties to the conflict, under international mediation. NATO supported and reinforced the Contact Group efforts by agreeing on 30 January to the use of air strikes, if required, and by issuing a warning to both sides in the

---

318 See NATO Press release, 'Statement by the NATO Spokesman on the NAC of 16 October 1998', 16 October 1998.

319 That agreement was signed with the government of the FRY. See NATO Press release, 'Press points by the Secretary General Dr Javier Solana', 15 October 1998.

320 On the KVM, see *infra* section 8.4. In support of the OSCE, the Alliance established a special military task force to assist with the emergency evacuation of members of the KVM, if renewed conflict should put them at risk. This 'extraction' force was deployed in Macedonia. In support of both NATO and OSCE operations in Kosovo, the WEU Satellite Centre embarked on a mission of general security surveillance of the Kosovo region in November 1998. See chapter 4, section 2.2.2.

321 See J. Silverman, 'Racak massacre haunts Milosevic trial', *BBC.com*, 14 February 2002; and Human Rights Watch, 'Yugoslav Government War Crimes in Racak', available at: <http://www.hrw.org/press/1999/jan/yugo0129.htm>.

322 Case No. IT-99-37, The Prosecutor of the Tribunal Against Slobodan Milosevic, Milan Milutinovic, Nikola Sainovic, Dragoljub Ojdanic, Vlajko Stojilkovic, Indictment, 22 May 1999.

conflict.[323] These concerted initiatives culminated in initial negotiations in Rambouillet (near Paris), from 6 to 23 February, followed by a second round in Paris, from 15 to 18 March. At the end of the second round of talks, the Kosovar Albanian delegation signed the proposed peace agreement but the talks broke down without a signature from the Serbian delegation.[324] Immediately afterwards, Serbian military and police forces stepped up the intensity of their operations against the ethnic Albanians in Kosovo, moving extra troops and tanks into the province in a clear breach of compliance with the October agreement. Tens of thousands of people began to flee their homes in the face of this systematic offensive.

On 20 March 1999, KVM was withdrawn from the region, having faced obstruction from Serbian forces to the extent that the OSCE verifiers could no longer continue to fulfil their task. Holbrooke then flew to Belgrade, in a final attempt to persuade President Milošević to stop attacks on the Kosovar Albanians or face imminent NATO air strikes. Milošević refused to comply and on 23 March, in the absence of a clear mandate from the UN Security Council, NATO launched its air campaign under the banner of Operation *Allied Force*.[325]

7.3.2 *Operation* Allied Force

NATO's objectives in relation to Operation *Allied Force* were set out in the statement issued at the Extraordinary Meeting of the North Atlantic Council held on 12 April 1999 and were reaffirmed by the Heads of State and Government at the NATO Summit in Washington on 23 April 1999:

- a verifiable stop to all military action and the immediate ending of violence and repression;
- the withdrawal from Kosovo of the military, police and paramilitary forces;
- the stationing in Kosovo of an international military presence;
- the unconditional and safe return of all refugees and displaced persons and unhindered access to them by humanitarian aid organisations;
- the establishment of a political framework agreement for Kosovo on the basis of the Rambouillet accords, in conformity with international law and the Charter of the United Nations.[326]

---

323 NATO Press release 99(12), 'Statement by the North Atlantic Council on Kosovo', 30 January 1999.

324 For an excellent analysis, see M. Weller, 'The Rambouillet Conference on Kosovo', 75 *International Affairs* (1999) pp. 211-252. See also E. Decaux, 'La Conférence de Rambouillet. Négociation de la dernière chance ou contrainte illicite?', in Tomuschat, op. cit. n. 255, at pp. 45-64.

325 For the debate on the legality of this move under public international law, see the references in n. 314.

326 NATO Press release M-NAC-1(99)51, 'The Situation in and around Kosovo. Statement Issued at the Extraordinary Ministerial Meeting of the North Atlantic Council held at NATO

Throughout the conflict, the achievement of these objectives, accompanied by measures to ensure their full implementation, was regarded by the Alliance as the prerequisite for bringing to an end the violence and human suffering in Kosovo.

NATO chose to counter violence with violence. After first targeting the FRY's air defences, NATO gradually expanded the campaign. Despite using 'precision-guided' weapons and avoiding civilian casualties to the greatest extent possible (by reviewing target selection at multiple levels of command to ensure that it complied with international law, was militarily justified and minimised the risk to civilian lives and property), Human Rights Watch estimated that between 488 and 527 civilians lost their lives due to NATO's attacks.[327] TV broadcasts of the 'collateral damage' caused by NATO bombs led to a public outcry and caused strains between the Allies. But the Alliance managed to hold together during an air campaign that lasted for seventy-eight days and in which more than 38,000 sorties (10,484 of them strike sorties) were flown, without a single Allied fatality.[328]

After consultations with the North Atlantic Council and confirmation from General Clark that the full withdrawal of Yugoslav forces from Kosovo had begun, NATO Secretary General Javier Solana on 10 June 1999 announced that he had instructed General Clark to temporarily suspend air operations against the FRY.[329] The withdrawal was in accordance with both the Military Technical Agreement, concluded between NATO and the FRY on the evening of 9 June,[330] and the diplomatic agreement between the FRY and the EU and Russian special envoys Martti Ahtisaari and Viktor Chernomyrdin, reached on 3 June.[331] On 10 June, the UN Security Council passed resolution 1244 (1999) welcoming the acceptance by the FRY of the principles for a political solution to the Kosovo crisis, including an immediate end to violence and a rapid withdrawal of its military, police and paramilitary forces. Resolution 1244 announced the Security Council's decision to establish international civil and security presences in Kosovo under UN auspices.[332] Acting under chapter VII of the UN Charter, the Security Council decided that the political solution to the crisis would be based on

---

Headquarters, Brussels, on 12th April 1999', 12 April 1999; and NATO Press release S-1(99)62, 'Statement on Kosovo. Issued by the Heads of State and Government participating in the meeting of the North Atlantic Council in Washington, D.C. on 23rd and 24th April 1999', 23 April 1999.

327 See Human Rights Watch, 'Civilian Deaths in the NATO Air Campaign', 12 *HRW Reports* (2000). For a debate on the legal accountability of NATO (members) and its (their) troops under international human rights and humanitarian law, see the references in n. 315.

328 Facts, figures and documents about the operation are available at: <http://www.nato.int/kosovo/all-frce.htm>.

329 Press release (1999) 093, 'Statement by NATO Secretary General Dr Javier Solana on suspension of air operations', 10 June 1999.

330 The MTA is available at: <http://www.nato.int/kfor/kfor/documents/mta.htm>.

331 See J. Vesikansa, 'Operation Balkans', *Suomen Kuvalehti*, 18 June 1999.

332 On the civil component, see *supra* section 6.7.

the general principles adopted on 6 May by the G-8 and the principles contained in the agreement of 3 June.[333] These documents were included, respectively, as Annex 1 and Annex 2 to the resolution. Apart from an end to all hostilities and the withdrawal of FRY forces, the principles contained therein included, among other things, the deployment of an effective international security presence, with substantial NATO participation, aimed at deterring renewed hostilities, demilitarising the KLA and establishing a secure environment for the return of refugees and in which the international civil presence could operate.

7.3.3 *KFOR*

Following the adoption of resolution 1244 (1999), General Michael Jackson, designated as the Commander of the International Security Force (or 'Kosovo Force' – KFOR) and acting on the instructions of the North Atlantic Council, made immediate preparations for the rapid deployment of the Security Council-mandated force. As agreed in the Military Technical Agreement of 9 June 1999, the deployment of KFOR was synchronised with the departure of Serb security forces from Kosovo. By 20 June, the Serb withdrawal was complete and KFOR was well-established in Kosovo. At its height, KFOR comprised approximately 50,000 personnel from thirty-nine troop-contributing countries. Nowadays, the force consists of approximately 16,000 personnel from thirty-seven countries, including nine PfP partners.[334]

In accordance with resolution 1244 (1999), KFOR has a mandate to secure public safety and enforce law and order until the UN Mission in Kosovo can fully assume this responsibility. To this end, NATO conducts air surveillance, patrols and search operations, operates checkpoints, confiscates weapons and ammunition, responds to emergency calls, controls the borders, investigates criminal activities and arrests or detains suspected criminals. Since the start of KFOR's deployment on the ground, the KLA was disbanded and is in the process of being transformed through resettlement programmes, the creation of the Kosovo Police Service and the establishment of the Kosovo Protection Corps – an unarmed civil relief organisation involved in the rebuilding of Kosovo's infrastructure.[335] KFOR itself has also been active in the reconstruction effort, transportation, railway

---

333 Statement by the Chairman on the conclusion of the meeting of the G-8 Foreign Ministers held at the Petersberg Centre on 6 May 1999, contained in a Letter dated 6 May 1999 from the Permanent Representative of Germany to the United Nations addressed to the President of the Security Council, UN Doc. S/1999/516 (6 May 1999).

334 Facts, figures and documents about the operation are available at: <http://www.nato.int/kfor>.

335 For an analysis of the achievements and shortcomings, see A. Heinemann-Grüder and I. Grebenschikov, 'Security Governance by Internationals: The Case of Kosovo', 13 *International Peacekeeping* (2006) pp. 43-59.

operations, mine clearance, fire services, protection of international workers, food distribution, removal of unexploded ordnance, mine awareness education, medical services and so forth. Since mid-June 1999, more than 775,000 refugees and displaced people have returned. A dramatic drop in the rate of murder, arson and looting has also confirmed the stabilisation of the situation. But despite its presence, ethnically-motivated violence continues. The recurring violence in and around the divided town of Mitrovica and the March 2004 riots that left nineteen Kosovar Serbs dead have exposed NATO's inability to fully control the security situation and have drawn special attention to the protection of Kosovo's minorities, who are often the victims of ethnic tensions and hatred.[336]

8. EFFORTS TO BRING PEACE AND STABILITY TO THE WESTERN BALKANS: OSCE

The OSCE used to claim an important role in the European security architecture, its strength being its wide membership.[337] But for the very same reason, the mechanism of the OSCE was never efficient, as the various interests and positions of the participating states often lay too far apart. Although the OSCE was involved in the 'Yugoslav' crises from the very beginning,[338] it did not achieve any major successes. Despite a long-standing presence on the ground, countless unpublicised missions by the High Commissioner on National Minorities and a series of mini-successes, the remaining pictures that capture the OSCE's ineffectiveness in the Balkans are the ones showing a convoy of orange OSCE jeeps, obstructed in their path by Serbian troops and the subsequent departure of OSCE verifiers from Kosovo. As can be seen from the descriptive overview of activities in the Balkans in this section,[339] the CSCE/OSCE did make and continues to make important efforts to prevent deadly conflict and rehabilitate war-torn societies. Election monitoring is the prime example.[340] However, it is clear that the instruments at the disposal of the OSCE are very weak, especially in situations when the parties to a conflict are not interested in any form of international mediation or intervention. During the different episodes of the crises in the Balkans, boundary

---

336 See International Crisis Group, 'Collapse in Kosovo', 155 *Europe Reports* (2004); and ibid., 'Bridging Kosovo's Mitrovica Divide', 165 *Europe Reports* (2005). See further chapter 4, section 3.3.

337 See *supra* section 4.

338 See, e.g., E. Remacle, 'The Yugoslav Crisis as a Test Case for CSCE's Role in Conflict Prevention and Crisis Management', in M. Lucas, ed., *The CSCE in the 1990s: Constructing European Security and Cooperation* (Baden-Baden, Nomos Verlag 1993) pp. 109-123.

339 Facts and figures in this section are drawn from OSCE, *Survey of OSCE Long-Term Missions and other OSCE Field Activities*, SEC.IN F/48/06/Corr.1, 2 October 2006.

340 The Stability Pact for South Eastern Europe less so. See chapter 4, section 3.3.1, and chapter 5, section 2.2.

and verification missions were deprived of efficient tools to combat mutual hate. Traditional instruments of international diplomacy have proved insufficient and inefficient, in particular since the OSCE was neither able, nor entitled, to propose unorthodox solutions and remained within the framework of classical international law (e.g., maintenance of territorial integrity of SFRY although ex-administrative units were entitled by other international actors to claim sovereignty). The OSCE's failures in the Balkans have caused some to deplore the death of the organisation's dispute management mechanisms,[341] while others have stressed the necessity of strengthening the competence of the organisation,[342] including the OSCE itself.[343]

8.1 OSCE Spillover Monitor Mission to Skopje

The decision to establish a CSCE monitoring mission in Macedonia was taken in mid-1992 in the context of the efforts to extend the European Community Monitoring Mission (ECMM) to other successor states of the SFRY to help avoid the spread of tension to their territories.[344] The CSCE Spillover Monitoring Mission to Skopje started its work with a fact-finding visit to Skopje on 10-14 September 1992. It continues its activities until today.[345] The objectives of the mission are to monitor developments along the Macedonian-Serb border and in other areas of Macedonia which may suffer from the spillover of the conflict in the former Yugoslavia 'in order to promote respect for territorial integrity and the maintenance of peace, stability and security and to help prevent possible conflict in the region'.[346] To this end, the tasks of the Spillover Monitor Mission consist, *inter alia*, of conducting dialogue with Macedonian governmental authorities,

---

341 See M. Kohen, 'L'emploi de la force et la crise du Kosovo: vers un nouveau désordre juridique international', 32 *RBDI* (1999) pp. 122-148 at p. 146.

342 See, e.g., R. Barry, 'After the Bombing – the OSCE in the Aftermath of the Kosovo Crisis', Institute for Peace Research and Security Policy at the University of Hamburg, ed., *OSCE Yearbook 1999* (Baden-Baden, Nomos Verlag 2000) pp. 49-57; L. Volmer, 'Crisis Prevention in Europe and the Strengthening of the OSCE: Lessons from the Kosovo Conflict', ibid., at pp. 41-48; and V.-Y. Ghébali and D. Warner, eds., *The Operational Role of the OSCE in South-Eastern Europe: Contributing to Regional Stability in the Balkans* (Aldershot, Ashgate 2001).

343 See OSCE and Swiss Institute for World Affairs, loc. cit. n. 105; and N. Afanasievsky, V. Shustov, et al., *Common Purpose: Towards a More Effective OSCE*, 27 June 2005.

344 See 15th CSO Meeting, 14 August 1992, Journal No. 2, Annex 1; 16th CSO Meeting, 18 September 1992, Journal No. 3, Annex 1; 17th CSO Meeting, 6 November 1992, Journal No. 2, Annex 3: 'Articles of Understanding concerning the CSCE Spillover Monitor Mission', 7 November 1992. On the ECMM, see chapter 3, section 2.4.

345 Currently, the mission consists of four members. The most recent renewal of its mandate, until 31 December 2006, was decided upon at the 614th PC Meeting, PC.DEC/727 of 22 June 2006. The Articles of Understanding remain in force until notification of termination by either party, fifteen days in advance.

346 17th CSO Meeting, see *supra* n. 344.

political parties, NGOs and ordinary citizens, assessing the level of stability and the possibility of conflict and unrest, maintaining a high profile in the country and, in the case of incidents, assisting in establishing the facts.

According to the modalities and the financial implications, the authorised strength of the mission is eight members, to be supplemented as required. On a number of occasions, the size and mandate of the mission were adjusted in view of developments in the region. In a special session on the Kosovo crisis on 11 March 1998, the Permanent Council decided to temporarily enhance the monitoring capabilities of the Spillover Monitor Mission in order to allow for 'adequate observation of the borders with Kosovo, FRY, and prevention of possible crisis spillover effects'.[347] In the first half of 2001, the Permanent Council, noting the reports of the mission indicating an upsurge of violent actions by ethnic Albanian armed groups in the area of the northern border regions in Macedonia, decided to increase the size of the mission to better monitor developments along the border.[348] In the wake of the August 2001 Ohrid Peace Agreement, the mission reached its peak size, with a further increase of seventy-two international confidence-building monitors, sixty police advisers and seventeen police trainers, as well as ten internationals to deal with administrative and support matters, for a total of 210 internationals.[349] In addition to police matters and confidence-building activities, the mission has been particularly active in media issues, decentralisation and support to the national ombudsman.

8.2 OSCE Mission to Bosnia and Herzegovina

At its December 1995 meeting in Budapest, the OSCE Ministerial Council decided to establish a Mission to Bosnia and Herzegovina to carry out its tasks as requested by the parties to the Dayton Agreement:[350]

---

347 Permanent Council Decision No. 218, 11 March 1998 (PC.DEC/218).

348 Permanent Council Decision No. 405, 22 March 2001 (PC.DEC/405); Permanent Council Decision No. 414, 7 June 2001 (PC.DEC/414).

349 Permanent Council Decision No. 437, 6 September 2001 (PC.DEC/437/Corr.1); and Permanent Council Decision No. 439, 28 September 2001 (PC.DEC/439): 'They will monitor and report regularly on the security situation in the host State, including: the situation in the northern border areas, including illicit arms trafficking; the humanitarian situation, including the return of refugees and internally displaced persons and trafficking in human beings; the situation in sensitive places with communities not in the majority; and cases of incidents and recurrence of hostilities. They will not monitor the arms collection process or conduct operations aimed exclusively at observing compliance with the ceasefire.' See also chapter 4, section 3.1.3.

350 See Dayton Agreement, Annexes 3 and 6. For the establishment and terms of reference, see Fifth Meeting of the Ministerial Council, Budapest, 8 December 1995 (MC(5).DEC/1). See further M. Sica, 'The Role of the OSCE in the Former Yugoslavia after the Dayton Peace Agreement', 7 *Helsinki Monitor* (1996) pp. 5-12.

- taking into consideration the role of the High Representative as defined in the Peace Agreement and in the conclusions of the Paris Meeting as well as the need to co-operate with other international actors, the Mission concentrated on providing assistance for the preparation and conduct of municipal elections in 1997 and on providing assistance in the establishment of a permanent election commission, in accordance with Annex 3 of the Peace Agreement, with respect to the elections scheduled to close the consolidation period;
- to assist in democracy building and be active in human rights promotion and monitoring, in particular in support of the Ombudspersons throughout Bosnia and Herzegovina;
- to continue assisting the Parties in implementation of regional stabilization measures;
- the Head of Mission will co-ordinate closely with the Chairman-in-Office and report to the Permanent Council regularly, at least every two months.

The Head of Mission started to work in Sarajevo on 29 December 1995, relying initially on the infrastructure of the existing OSCE mission in Sarajevo.[351] Since its date of inception, the mission has been prolonged each year for a further period of twelve months.[352] The mission, which currently totals 114 internationally seconded members, has four regional centres in Banja Luka, Mostar, Sarajevo and Tuzla. In addition, it has twenty-one field offices in the two entities of Bosnia-Herzegovina and an additional office in Brcko. The mission works in close cooperation with all other international stakeholders in Bosnia-Herzegovina.

8.3 OSCE Mission to Croatia

In its Decision of 18 April 1996, the Permanent Council noted the reports of the Fact-Finding Mission of the OSCE to Croatia (6-10 October 1995) and of the Personal Representative of the CiO on his visit to Croatia (20-23 February 1996), reaffirmed the OSCE's principles and commitments and its full support for the independence, sovereignty and territorial integrity of Croatia and welcomed the invitation of the government for an OSCE mission.[353] The Permanent Council decided that:

- The Mission will provide assistance and expertise to the Croatian authorities at all levels, as well as to interested individuals, groups and organizations, in the field of the protection of human rights and of the rights of persons belonging to national minorities. In this context and in order to promote reconciliation, the

---

351 See C. Giersch, *Konfliktregulierung in Jugoslawien 1991-1995: Die Rolle von OSZE, EU, UNO und NATO* (Baden-Baden, Nomos Verlag 1998).

352 Most recently until 31 December 2006 by the 580th PC Meeting, PC.DEC/694, 17 November 2005. The OSCE Unified Budget for 2006, adopted on 20 December 2005, PC.DEC/712, established the mission's budget at €18.4 million.

353 Permanent Council, 18 April 1996, PC.DEC/112.

rule of law and conformity with the highest internationally recognized standards, the Mission will also assist and advise on the full implementation of legislation and monitor the proper functioning and development of democratic institutions, processes and mechanisms.
- In carrying out its tasks, the Mission will co-operate with and use the expertise of the OSCE High Commissioner on National Minorities and of the Office for Democratic Institutions and Human Rights. It will also co-operate with other international organizations and institutions, notably the Council of Europe, the ECMM, the Special Envoy for Regional Issues, UNHCR, the ICRC and relevant NGOs.
- The Mission will offer close co-operation to UNTAES, in particular as regards confidence-building and reconciliation, as well as the development of democratic institutions, processes and mechanisms at the municipal and district/county level.[354]

The mission started working in Zagreb on 4 July 1996.[355] It has coordination centres in Knin, Vukovar, Sisak and Daruvar and a Zagreb area office co-located with the headquarters. In June 1997, the Permanent Council authorised the mission to assist with and monitor the implementation of Croatian legislation and agreements and commitments entered into by the Croatian government on the two-way return of all refugees and displaced persons and the protection of persons belonging to national minorities.[356] One year later, the OSCE expressed its readiness to deploy a maximum of 120 civilian police monitors to assume the responsibilities of the United Nations Police Support Group deployed in the Croatian Danubian region, in anticipation of the end of the UNPSG's mandate on 15 October 1998.[357] For two full years, the OSCE Police Monitoring Group contributed to the peaceful integration of the Danube Region. The OSCE ceased the operations of this distinct unit on 31 October 2000 by integrating the international civilian police officers into the structures of the mission.[358]

8.4 OSCE Mission in Kosovo

In Kosovo, the OSCE contributes to the implementation of UN Security Council resolution 1244 (1999), in particular the relevant parts of operative paragraph 11.

---

354 Ibid.

355 The mission's original mandate lasted until 31 December 1996. The most recent prolongation, until 31 December 2006, was decided at the 580th PC Meeting, PC.DEC/695, 17 November 2005. The PC authorised the mission to build up mission personnel to a ceiling of 250 expatriates with a view to full deployment by October 1998. The current number of mission members is sixty-four. The OSCE Unified Budget for 2006, adopted on 20 December 2005, PC.DEC/712, established the mission's budget at €8.7 million.

356 Permanent Council, 26 June 1997, PC.DEC/176.

357 Permanent Council, 25 June 1998, PC.DEC/239.

358 Permanent Council, 21 September 2000, PC.DEC/373.

The present OSCE Mission in Kosovo (OMIK) was established on 1 July 1999 as a follow-up to the Kosovo Verification Mission (KVM) and the Task Force for Kosovo.[359] After heavy international pressure over its human rights record in Kosovo,[360] the FRY agreed with the CiO of the OSCE on the terms of the establishment of the Kosovo Verification Mission.[361] The KVM was established on 25 October 1998 with the aim of verifying the compliance of the authorities of the FRY (and the KLA) in Kosovo with the requirements set forth by the international community in UN Security Council resolution 1199 (1998), in anticipation of a political solution to the crisis in the province.[362] Approximately 1,500 international staff were deployed by February 1999.[363] But these unarmed verifiers were unable to carry out the full scope of the tasks allocated under the FRY-

---

359 On the KVM, see also *supra* section 7.3.

360 See Kokott, loc. cit. n. 255.

361 See Agreement on the OSCE Kosovo Verification Missions, signed in Belgrade on 16 October 1998, by the CiO of the OSCE and the Minister of Foreign Affairs of the FRY (CIO.GAL/65/98/Corr.1).

362 See Permanent Council, 15 October 1998, PC.DEC/259; and Permanent Council, 25 October 1998, PC.DEC/263. The KVM's responsibilities are specified in chapter III of the Agreement. The KVM was tasked to:

' - verify the maintenance of the cease-fire by all elements. [...] investigate reports of cease-fire violations;
  receive weekly information from relevant FRY/Serbian military/police headquarters in Kosovo regarding movements of forces [...]. Upon request of the Verification Mission Director, Mission personnel may he invited to accompany police within Kosovo;
- look for and report on roadblocks and other emplacements which influence lines of communications erected for purposes other than traffic or crime control;
- maintain liaison with FRY authorities about border control activity and movement units with border control responsibilities [...]. The Verification Mission, when invited by the FRY authorities or upon its request, will visit border control units and accompany them as they perform their normal border control roles;
- when invited or upon request, the Verification Mission will accompany police units in Kosovo as they perform their normal policing roles;
- assist UNHCR, ICRC and other international organizations in facilitating the return of displaced persons to their homes [...]. The Mission will verify the level of co-operation and support provided by the FRY and its entities to the humanitarian organizations and accredited NGOs [...];
- as the political settlement defining Kosovo's self-government is achieved and implementation begins, the Mission Director will assist, both with his own resources and with augmented OSCE implementation support, in areas such as elections supervision, assistance in the establishment of Kosovo institutions and police force development in Kosovo;
- the Mission Director will receive periodic updates from the relevant authorities concerning eventual allegations of abusive actions by military or police personnel and status of disciplinary or legal actions against individuals implicated in such abuses;
- maintain liaison with FRY, Serbian and, as appropriate, Kosovo authorities and with ICRC regarding ICRC access to detained persons;
- convene representatives of national communities and authorities to exchange information and provide guidance on implementation of the agreement establishing the Verification Mission;
- report instances of progress and/or non-compliance or lack of full co-operation from any side to the OSCE and other organizations.'

363 Under the terms of part IV of the Agreement of 16 October 1998, a maximum of 2,000 unarmed verifiers from OSCE Member States would be permitted. The HQ (in Priština) and support staff (including a small liaison office in Belgrade) are included in this total.

OSCE Agreement.[364] They were hindered in the performance of their duties by both Yugoslav troops and members of the KLA. Following a steady deterioration in the security situation in the province and the global broadcast of TV images of orange KVM vehicles being refused access to some of the hotspots, the OSCE CiO decided to withdraw the mission on 20 March 1999. With the bulk of its members repatriated, the core of the KVM was temporarily based in Skopje, *inter alia,* to plan the re-entry of an OSCE Mission to Kosovo. The KVM was later dissolved and the Task Force for Kosovo created in its stead was primarily tasked with preparing for redeployment to Kosovo and continuing to assist the United Nations and other international organisations.[365] The Task Force for Kosovo was dissolved on 1 July 1999 and replaced by OMIK.

Since 1 July 1999, OMIK constitutes a distinct component, or 'pillar', within the overall framework of UNMIK. Within this overall framework, OMIK takes the lead role in matters relating to Human Resources Capacity and Institution Building and Human Rights. As such, it cooperates closely with other relevant organisations – intergovernmental and, as appropriate, non-governmental – in the planning and implementation of its tasks. According to its constituent document, OMIK concentrates its work in the following interrelated areas:

1. Human resources capacity-building, including the training of a new Kosovo police service within a Kosovo Police School which it will establish and operate, the training of judicial personnel and the training of civil administrators at various levels, in co-operation, *inter alia,* with the Council of Europe;
2. Democratization and governance, including the development of a civil society, non-governmental organizations, political parties and local media;
3. Organization and supervision of elections;
4. Monitoring, protection and promotion of human rights, including, *inter alia,* the establishment of an Ombudsman institution, in co-operation, *inter alia,* with the UNHCR;
5. Such tasks which may be requested by the Secretary-General of the United Nations or his Special Representative, which are consistent with the UNSC Resolution 1244 and approved by the Permanent Council.[366]

According to the same document, OMIK is guided by the importance of bringing about mutual respect and reconciliation among all ethnic groups in Kosovo and establishing a viable multi-ethnic society where the rights of each citizen are fully

---

364 See W. Czaplinski, 'The Activities of the OSCE in Kosovo', in Tomuschat, op. cit. n. 255, at pp. 37-44.

365 Permanent Council, 8 June 1999, PC.DEC/296.

366 Permanent Council, 1 July 1999, PC/DEC/305. The mission was prolonged until 31 December 2006 by 580th PC Meeting, PC.DEC/693, 17 November 2005. The OSCE Unified Budget for 2006, adopted on 20 December 2005, PC.DEC/712, established the mission's budget at €35.2 million.

and equally respected. The mission's headquarters are located in Priština. OMIK totals 296 international staff and has a strong field presence with eight OSCE offices, which allows it to cover all thirty municipalities effectively. Like the other UNMIK Pillar Heads, the Head of OMIK (since April 2005, Werner Wnendt of Germany) also serves as Deputy Special Representative of the Secretary General of the United Nations (DSRSG).

8.5 OSCE Mission to Serbia[367]

The OSCE Mission to Serbia was originally established as the OSCE Mission to the Federal Republic of Yugoslavia,[368] later renamed the OSCE Mission to Serbia and Montenegro,[369] and most recently the OSCE Mission to Serbia.[370] As stipulated in its original mandate, the mission, acting in close cooperation with the host government, will provide assistance and expertise to the authorities at all levels, as well as to interested individuals, groups and organisations, in the fields of democratisation and the protection of human rights, including the rights of persons belonging to national minorities. In this context, and in order to promote democratisation, tolerance, the rule of law and conformity with OSCE principles, standards and commitments, the mission has been tasked to:

- assist and advise on the full implementation of legislation in areas covered by the mandate;
- monitor the proper functioning and development of democratic institutions, processes and mechanisms;

---

367 Long before the OSCE mission described in this section, the OSCE had missions in three autonomous regions in Serbia: Kosovo, Sandjak and Vojvodina. The mandate of the missions, contained in the 15th CSO Meeting, 14 August 1992, Journal No. 2, Annex 1 and reiterated in the Memorandum of Understanding (MoU) signed on 28 October 1992 in Belgrade, was to (i) promote dialogue between the authorities concerned and representatives of the populations and communities in the three regions; (ii) collect information on all aspects relevant to violations of human rights and fundamental freedoms and promote solutions to such problems; (iii) establish contact points for solving problems that might be identified; and (iv) assist in providing information on relevant legislation on human rights, protection of minorities, free media and democratic elections. The missions started their work on 8 September 1992. According to the MoU, the duration of the missions was limited to an initial period of six months. Extension of this period was subject to mutual agreement by the parties. In a protocol signed by the government of the FRY and the Head of Mission on 29 April 1993, the period was extended until 28 June 1993. The missions were withdrawn in July 1993 after expiration of the MoU, since the FRY authorities refused the CSCE's request to prolong it. In the modalities and financial implications, the size of the missions was limited to twelve members, to be supplemented as required, but the missions never exceeded a total of twenty members.

368 Permanent Council, 11 January 2001, PC/DEC/401.

369 Permanent Council, 13 February 2003, PC/DEC/533.

370 Permanent Council, 29 June 2006, PC/DEC/733.

- assist in the restructuring and training of law enforcement agencies and the judiciary;
- provide assistance and advice in the field of the media;
- in close co-operation with the Office of the United Nations High Commissioner for Refugees, provide advice and support in order to facilitate the return of refugees to and from neighbouring countries and from other countries of residence as well as of internally displaced persons to their homes within the territory of Serbia.

In carrying out its tasks, the mission cooperates with and uses the expertise of the HCNM, ODIHR, the Representative on Freedom of the Media and the Coordinator of OSCE Economic and Environmental Activities. The Conflict Prevention Centre assists, *inter alia*, by organising training workshops and seminars in the field of confidence and security-building measures and other issues in the politico-military field. The mission closely cooperates with the representation of the Council of Europe in Serbia in order to coordinate programmes and efficiently plan joint projects. It also coordinates its activities with representatives of other international organisations and institutions in the host country, notably the European Commission, the Stability Pact for South Eastern Europe,[371] UN agencies, the ICRC and NGOs. The mission has its headquarters in Belgrade and is currently staffed by fifty-one internationals and 123 locals.[372] It has a multi-ethnic police training facility in Mitrovo Polje, operated in close cooperation with the Serbian authorities.[373]

8.6 OSCE Mission to Montenegro

The OSCE Mission to Montenegro was established shortly after Montenegro declared its independence.[374] As stipulated in its mandate of 29 June 2006, the tasks of the mission are to:

- assist and promote the implementation of OSCE principles and commitments as well as the cooperation of the Republic of Montenegro with the OSCE, in all dimensions, including the politico-military, economic and environmental and human aspects of security and stability;

---

371 See chapter 4, section 3.3.1, and chapter 5, section 2.2.

372 The mission's mandate has been extended annually and is currently valid until 31 December 2006. PC Decision 741 of 27 July 2006 established the budget of the mission at €8.6 million. On the day of the establishment of the OSCE Mission to Montenegro, the former OSCE field office in Podgorica was closed down.

373 For an evaluation of the OSCE's activities in the field of police reform, see M. Trivunovic, 'Police Reform – Introduction', 15 *Helsinki Monitor* (2004) p. 171; and M. Trivunovic, 'Status of Police Reform After Four Years of Democratic Transition in Serbia', 15 *Helsinki Monitor* (2004) pp. 172-186.

374 Permanent Council, 29 June 2006, PC/DEC/732. The mission has a mandate until 31 December 2006. PC Decision 742 of 27 July 2006 established the budget of the mission at €951,800.

- facilitate contacts, coordinate activities and promote information exchange with the CiO, OSCE institutions and, as appropriate, OSCE field operations, as well as cooperation with international organisations and institutions;
- establish and maintain contacts with local authorities, universities, research institutions and NGOs and assist in arranging events with OSCE participation.

The mission is headquartered in Podgorica and currently consists of fifteen international and thirty local staff.

8.7 OSCE Presence in Albania

On the basis of the reports by the Personal Representative of the CiO, Franz Vranitzky, on his visits to Albania on 8 and 14 March 1997, the Permanent Council decided to establish an OSCE Presence in Albania.[375] It started working in Tirana on 3 April 1997, under the wings of the Italian-led *Operazione Alba*, which was deployed almost simultaneously to help create a safe environment for the international organisations operating in Albania.[376] The total number of international staff is currently thirty, with international staff at the headquarters in Tirana and at four field stations in Gjirokaster, Kukes, Shkoder and Vlora.[377] In cooperation with the Albanian authorities, the OSCE has since provided the coordinating framework within which other international organisations have played their part in their respective areas of competence. As such, the OSCE has tried to support a coherent international strategy and facilitate improvements in the protection of human rights and basic elements of civil society. In particular, the OSCE has provided advice and assistance to the Council of Europe in the fields of democratisation, the media and human rights, election preparation and monitoring. Furthermore, it has supported NATO by monitoring the collection of weapons.

The OSCE Presence's mandate was substantially changed on two occasions. In a special session devoted to the aggravating humanitarian crisis in Kosovo, the Permanent Council decided to temporarily enhance the monitoring capabilities of

---

375 See Permanent Council, 20 March 1997, PC/DEC/158; and Permanent Council, 27 March 1997, PC/DEC/160.

376 Italy's early deployment of troops prevented the crisis in Albania over the collapse of the pyramid savings schemes from spiralling out of control. *Operazione Alba* was authorised by Permanent Council Decision 160 of 27 March 1997 and endorsed by UN Security Council resolution 1101 (1997). For background and analyses of the operation, see G. Kostakos and D. Bourantonis, 'Innovations in Peace-keeping: The Case of Albania', 29 *Security Dialogue* (1998) pp. 49-58; E. Foster, 'Ad hoc in Albania: Did Europe Fail? A Rejoinder', 29 *Security Dialogue* (1998) pp. 213-219; and P. Tripodi, 'Operation *Alba*: A Necessary and Successful Preventive Deployment', 9 *International Peacekeeping* (2002) pp. 89-104.

377 The OSCE Unified Budget for 2006, adopted on 20 December 2005, PC.DEC/712, established the budget of the OSCE Presence in Albania at €3.8 million.

the OSCE Presence in Albania in order to allow for adequate observation of the borders with Kosovo, the FRY and the prevention of possible crisis spillover effects.[378] With the end of the Kosovo crisis in 1999, the border monitoring activities of the OSCE Presence were progressively downscaled and the border monitoring field stations were transformed into normal field stations. At the end of 2003, the Permanent Council decided to bring the mandate in line with the overall progress achieved in Albania in the preceding years, as well as the increased central position that the country's institutions had taken.[379] Working in close consultation and cooperation with the government of Albania, the OSCE Presence now provides assistance and expertise in the following areas: legislative and judicial reform, including property law reform; regional administrative reform; electoral reform; parliamentary capacity building; anti-trafficking and anti-corruption, including supporting the implementation of relevant national strategies; development of effective laws and regulations on the independent media and its Code of Conduct; promotion of good governance and targeted projects for strengthening of civil society; and police assistance, in particular training for border police, within a coordinated framework with other international actors in the field.

9. EFFORTS TO BRING PEACE AND STABILITY TO THE WESTERN BALKANS: COUNCIL OF EUROPE

The Council of Europe has always been firmly committed to supporting the social and political stability of multi-ethnic societies in the Western Balkans. The organisation's actions have been concentrated on the creation of democratic institutions, the protection of human rights and respect for the rule of law in line with CoE norms and standards. When discussing the Council of Europe's role in the Western Balkans *in concreto*, two sorts of useful activities stand out: technical and legal assistance through the implementation of programmes and advice on constitutional matters.

As far as the former is concerned, the Council of Europe has, since the fall of the Berlin Wall, conducted programmes on fulfilling post-accession commitments, especially with regard to the functioning of judicial systems, judicial training and law faculty reform (all Western Balkan countries); the strengthening of (higher) education (e.g., Macedonia), court administration (e.g., Albania) and

---

378 Permanent Council, 11 March 1998, PC/DEC/218.

379 Permanent Council, 18 December 2003, PC/DEC/588. See also C. Jaenicke, 'The OSCE Presence in Albania – Raison d'Etre and Future Plans', Institute for Peace Research and Security Policy at the University of Hamburg, ed., *OSCE Yearbook 2003* (Baden-Baden, Nomos Verlag 2004) pp. 125-138.

self-government (e.g., Montenegro and Serbia); support for parliamentary institutions (e.g., Serbia); reform of prison systems (e.g., Macedonia); reconstruction of religious monuments and sites (Kosovo); and support for the freedom of the media (e.g., Serbia). All these programmes are designed to help (new) Member States forward with their institutional, legislative and administrative reforms. Since 1993, most of these programmes have been jointly funded by the European Commission – mostly by way of its special EuropeAid programme: 'European Initiative for Democracy and Human Rights' (EIDHR)[380] – and the Council of Europe. By combining forces in this way, the complementarity of the relevant activities of the European Union and the Council of Europe has been enhanced, as there is considerable overlap in the membership requirements for aspirant countries from, *inter alia*, the Western Balkans. To underline the importance of such joint programmes and offer more systematic means of programming and priority setting, both organisations signed a Joint Declaration on Cooperation and Partnership on 3 April 2001.[381] Most joint programmes are country-specific. They cover, *inter alia*, Albania (since 1993), Serbia and Montenegro (since 2001), Bosnia-Herzegovina (since 2003) and Macedonia (since 1996). Other Joint Programmes, for instance for Croatia, have also been implemented in the past. In addition, there have been multilateral thematic joint programmes, for example, on national minorities and the fight against organised crime and corruption.[382]

With regard to assistance offered by the Council of Europe on constitutional issues, the work of the European Commission for Democracy through Law, better known as the 'Venice Commission', occupies a central place.[383] The primary task of the Venice Commission is to assist and advise individual countries in constitutional matters at the request of those countries. Such assistance goes from providing assistance in the drafting of constitutional texts to the writing of an

---

380 See: <http://ec.europa.eu/europeaid/projects/eidhr/index_en.htm>. Programmes have also been concluded with the European Commission's CARDS programme. In 2001, two joint programmes were established with the European Agency for Reconstruction (EAR). On CARDS and EAR, see chapter 5, section 3.4. The Directorate General for External Relations of the European Commission and the Council of Europe's Directorate of Strategic Planning (as well as other services as applicable) set and match priorities for the purpose of Joint Programmes. Sometimes, the Council of Europe makes proposals to the European Commission for urgent joint undertakings. EuropeAid is the structure within the European Commission involved in the final selection and administrative follow-up of programmes. The Council of Europe counterpart throughout the project cycle is the Directorate of Strategic Planning, in close consultation with the different Council of Europe Directorates General responsible for the implementation of the activities. In recent years, the European Commission Delegations in the beneficiary countries have increasingly been implied in the Joint Programmes. Equally, Council of Europe Secretariat Offices in the field support planning and implementation.

381 Available at: <http://www.jp.coe.int/programmes/general/JointDeclaration_EF.asp>.

382 A list of joint programmes, with logframes and activities, is available at: <http://www.jp.coe.int/CEAD/JP/default.asp>.

383 See *supra* section 5.1.

opinion on whether a draft legislative text meets European standards and how to improve the draft accordingly. The Commission tends to pay particular attention to countries which have experienced or are experiencing ethno-political conflicts. In this respect, the continued assistance of the Venice Commission in drafting the electoral legislation in Albania (1997, 2000 and 2003) and Bosnia-Herzegovina (1997), both in close cooperation with ODIHR,[384] and developing and interpreting the constitutional law of Albania and Bosnia-Herzegovina stand out.[385] More recently, its opinions on the human rights situation in Kosovo,[386] the new Constitution of Serbia[387] and its assistance in the constitutional reform activities in the newly independent Republic of Montenegro[388] are worth noting. Thanks to its independent character and high level of expertise, the non-legally binding opinions of the Venice Commission carry a lot of weight and are usually reflected in the final result of legislative texts. As such, the Venice Commission plays a highly specific but important role in the stabilisation of the Western Balkans.

10. CONCLUDING REMARKS

10.1 European security architecture: lessons learned from the Western Balkans

The wars of Yugoslavia's dissolution, in particular the war in Bosnia-Herzegovina, caught the international community largely unprepared. The early responses to these crises highlighted the shortcomings of the European security architecture following the end of the Cold War. After the European Communities' actions ran into quicksand,[389] the United Nations was the principal institution attempting to broker an end to hostilities. But except for the fleeting ceasefires, there was hardly any peace to keep. The UN's task in Bosnia-Herzegovina was to try to make peace while attempting to mitigate the cruel effects of war. UNPROFOR proved largely ineffective. The United Nations was more successful

---

384 See *supra* section 4.2. More information on the Venice Commission's work in the electoral field is available at: <http://www.venice.coe.int/site/main/Elections_Referendums_E.asp>.

385 For a list of opinions, comments and recommendations on constitutional matters per (Western Balkan) country, see: <http://www.venice.coe.int/site/dynamics/N_Country_ef.asp?L=E>.

386 See 'Opinion on Human Rights in Kosovo: possible establishment of review mechanisms adopted by the Venice Commission at its 60th Plenary Session (Venice, 8-9 October 2004)', CDL-AD(2004)033, 11 October 2004.

387 See 'Constitution of Serbia as approved by the National Assembly on 30 September 2006', CDL(2006)089, 1 December 2006.

388 See speeches by K. Tuori, A. Bradley, A. Eide and G. Neppi Modona, at the Expert Meeting on the Constitutional Reform of the Republic of Montenegro (Podgorica, 28 November 2006), CDL(2006)106, 7 December 2006.

389 See chapter 3, section 2.

in Macedonia, where a real peacekeeping force prevented the armed conflict in Bosnia-Herzegovina and Croatia from spreading.

Over the years, NATO (and the WEU)[390] became involved in support of the United Nations through various air and sea-based support operations – enforcing economic sanctions, an arms embargo and a 'no-fly' zone – and the implementation of a peace plan.[391] These measures helped to contain the conflict and save lives, but in the end proved inadequate to bring an end to the war. The turning point in the war in Bosnia-Herzegovina came in the summer of 1995, with the murder of thousands of men and boys at Srebrenica, Europe's first genocide since World War II.[392] The Srebrenica massacre prompted the involvement of the United States on both the diplomatic and the military front. American engagement proved decisive for breaking the vicious cycle of war. The UN Security Council gave a mandate for NATO to launch a two-week air campaign against Bosnian Serb forces. This paved the way for the Dayton Agreement, the peace accord which ended the war in Bosnia-Herzegovina and under which a 60,000-strong NATO-led Implementation Force took military responsibility for the peace process.

The deployment of IFOR was the Alliance's first military engagement on land and has contributed greatly to reshaping its post-Cold War identity. Indeed, in only a few years, NATO transformed itself into an increasingly effective instrument for military and political crisis management. The adaptation and learning process was evident in the way in which peacekeeping in Bosnia-Herzegovina under IFOR and its successor SFOR has evolved and fed into the approach adopted for KFOR since June 1999. NATO deployed in Kosovo after a seventy-eight-day air campaign launched to halt a humanitarian catastrophe among Kosovar Albanians at the hands of Belgrade. The decision to intervene, which was

---

390 See chapter 4, section 1.

391 See also chapter 4, section 2.2.

392 See Case No. IT-98-33, *Prosecutor* v. *Krstić*, *Judgment*, Appeals Chamber, 19 April 2004. The Application of the Convention on the Prevention and Punishment of the Crime of Genocide (*Bosnia and Herzegovina* v. *Serbia and Montenegro*) is another landmark court case where, for the first time in the sixty-year history of the International Court of Justice, one state, Bosnia-Herzegovina, accused another state, Serbia and Montenegro, of genocide. The ICJ handed down its judgment on 26 February 2007. Accepting the ICTY's findings that the Srebrenica massacre was genocide, the ICJ ruled that Serbia could not be held financially liable for acts of genocide committed by Bosnian Serb forces in the 1992-1995 Bosnian war because the Serbian state did not aim to 'destroy in whole or in part' the Bosnian Muslim population. The ruling thus relieved Serbia from having to pay billions of euros in potential reparation claims to Bosnia-Herzegovina. The Court did conclude, however, that Belgrade financed and supplied weapons to local perpetrators and that Milošević's regime should have used its 'known influence' to restrain the Bosnian Serbs to 'try and prevent the tragic events then taking shape'. Judge Rosalyn Higgins, the ICJ's president, said the onus remained on Belgrade to arrest and extradite Ratko Mladić. For comments on the ruling of the ICJ, see T.D. Gill, 'The "Genocide" Case: Reflections on the ICJ's Decision in Bosnia and Herzegovina v. Serbia', 2 *Hague Justice Journal* (2007) pp. 43-47.

controversial under international law because of the lack of a mandate from the UN Security Council, followed after more than a year of fighting within Kosovo, the failure of the United Nations and other international efforts to resolve the conflict by diplomatic means and a strong determination on the part of the NATO Allies to prevent the kind of ethnic-cleansing campaigns seen earlier in Bosnia-Herzegovina and Croatia. Military victory over Serbia was but the first step towards post-conflict peacebuilding in both Bosnia-Herzegovina and Kosovo. The international community established international protectorates in Bosnia-Herzegovina (under the powers of the Office of the High Representative) and in Kosovo (under the authority of the UN Interim Administration Mission in Kosovo). Today, in addition to helping to preserve a secure environment, the United Nations, NATO, the OSCE and the CoE (and, as will be shown in the following chapters, the European Union) are actively involved in helping refugees and displaced persons return to their homes, seeking out and arresting individuals indicted for war crimes and helping to reform domestic structures in such a way as to prevent a return to violence – all tasks that require a long-term commitment. The international organisations that make up the European security architecture have learned that they cannot successfully engage in conflict prevention, crisis management and post-conflict rehabilitation in isolation. The key to long-term conflict resolution is cooperation between different functionally specialised institutions. Another important lesson that has been drawn from the violent collapse of the former Yugoslavia can be captured in the age-old adage that 'prevention is better than cure'. Whereas it took close to three-and-a-half years of bloodshed in Bosnia-Herzegovina and a year of fighting in Kosovo before the international community intervened to bring these armed conflicts to an end, NATO and the European Union became engaged in the spring of 2001, at the request of the government in Skopje, in what turned out to be a successful effort to prevent an escalating conflict in Macedonia from degenerating into full-scale civil war. In 2003, the European Union, in cooperation with NATO and the OSCE, took over the responsibility to further a process of reconstruction, reconciliation and reform.

What then are the determinants for effective conflict prevention, crisis management and post-conflict rehabilitation? In the sections below, some ideas are offered for overcoming some recurring barriers to success.

10.2 Lack of consent; sovereignty and non-interference

To be effectively implemented, conflict prevention, crisis management and post-conflict peacebuilding need to be based on the explicit or tacit consent of at least one of the parties involved. All OSCE missions are based on the prior consent of the host country. This is particularly true as one moves further through the conflict life cycle: peacekeeping, to be effective, must be seen as being impartial.

The successful deployment, in Macedonia, of the first-ever UN preventive peacekeeping operation was made possible by the invitation and cooperation of Macedonia's president. More often than not, however, protagonists in conflicts do not wish and/or cannot be forced to accept external preventive action. Despotic leaders have a direct interest in creating and sustaining the conditions of conflict (notably by demonising adversaries, terrorising target populations, promoting hostile and/or divisive messages, etc.) and, thus, in refusing any external mediation or intervention.[393]

The issue of consent is intertwined with that of the inviolability of state sovereignty. In the case mentioned above, the fact that Macedonia was already recognised by the international community as a sovereign state also helped in the decision to deploy UNPREDEP. In contrast, as demonstrated in Kosovo with regard to NATO's Operation *Allied Force*, there is traditionally major reluctance on the part of members of international organisations to intervene in an internationally recognised territory without the consent of the parties concerned. Thus, generally speaking, the principles of state sovereignty and non-interference in domestic affairs continue to prevail over humanitarian considerations in the post-Cold War era.

10.3 Lack of political will within international organisations

In the slipstream of what was discussed in the previous section, it should be noted that international organisations are member-driven. They are only as effective as their members allow them to be. In crisis situations requiring operational action, decisions must be taken in a speedy manner. Even though some international organisations now allow some exceptions to the unanimity rule, in practice action is taken by consensus. The ever-present possibility of a veto from one of the members (a permanent member of the UN Security Council, participants in the OSCE, etc.) acts as a major brake on international intervention, especially in cases where sovereignty is an issue. In the case of the United Nations and, to a lesser extent, NATO and the OSCE, divisions in international organisations are often symptomatic of diverging patterns of interest and culture. Cultural sensitivity, in particular, is crucial in conflict prevention. The dilemma for democracies concerning the use of force in crisis management (beyond humanitarian-oriented deployment) is especially acute in the case of the European Union, whose foundations are based on non-coercive (economic and functionalist) pacification of antagonist actors (originally France and Germany). However, not all powers

[393] For example, Milošević's non-cooperative stance in the Rambouillet negotiations. See R. Väyrinen, 'Challenges to Preventive Action', in K. Spillmann, et al., eds., *Peace Support Operations: Lessons Learned and Future Perspectives* (Bern, Peter Lang 2001) at p. 59.

and cultures take the same approach to military intervention. Public opinion in the United States, for example, is traditionally much more supportive of the use of force (including ground troops, in spite of possible casualties) than EU public opinion.[394]

10.4 Competing international organisations

The implementation of coordinated international prevention actions is complicated by competing international organisations. Of course, not all international organisations are involved in every conflict situation, but, in the course of a conflict's life cycle on the European continent, the United Nations, NATO, the OSCE and the CoE (and of course the European Union) can all claim to have a role to play in the stabilisation effort. The OSCE, for instance, shares with the CoE (and the European Union) the role of promoting democratic values and structures in Central and Eastern European countries, including the countries of the Western Balkans. Practice has shown that these organisations embark on similar missions (fact-finding, election monitoring, etc.), which creates overlap. The problem of such a lack of synergies is that local actors can become involved in an uncoordinated manner and work at cross-purposes. This was the case, *inter alia*, in Bosnia-Herzegovina, where NATO advocated resorting to air power while the United Nations feared that military force would jeopardise its UNPROFOR peacekeeping mission on the ground. But the often cited lack of synergy should not overshadow cases of good cooperation between international organisations. This is particularly apparent in the international community's post-conflict rehabilitation efforts, where there is a plethora of examples of fruitful coordination between international organisations. There are, however, also problems of diffusion of responsibility between international actors, whereby each international organisation abdicates responsibility to another.

It would of course be best if all participating states could agree to let one of 'their' organisations take the lead in a particular field. However, in the world of power politics, it is not always the most efficient and effective solution which

[394] This study is undertaken at a time when the United States still seems prone to reject multilateral organisations as venues for the effective promotion of US foreign policy, especially in so far as unilateral 'preventive wars' are concerned. While it is difficult to contradict this stance in the case of Operation *Iraqi Freedom*, it is also apparent that the United States has always had a different approach to conflict management *lato sensu*. Yet, in many policy areas, the United States still considers that multilateralism can help achieve its goal, especially in so far as burden-sharing is concerned. Apart from the international fight against terrorism, an excellent example of this is provided by Operation *Concordia* in Macedonia, where the United States agreed to the dispensing of its assets in the multilateral framework of NATO so as to enable EU-led operations (see chapter 4, section 3). The US stance on the use of force can thus be complementary to that of 'soft security' oriented institutions.

prevails. Major powers naturally favour the action of the international organisations where their weight is greatest. Hence the insistence of the United States, for example, on OSCE intervention in the Balkans instead of intervention by way of the Council of Europe, where it is not a full member.

At the other end of the spectrum, membership of different international organisations offers important inducements to prospective members to achieve the principles of good governance. The prospect of membership creates momentum for reform in aspirant countries. Enlargement of the European security organisations is seen as the best way to entrench peace, stability and democracy on the European continent. Parallel enlargements of the Council of Europe, NATO and the European Union catalyse compliance with a set of structural standards within the realm of peacebuilding. More poignantly, it converts the economic power of the European Union and the hard security clout of NATO into driving forces for the adoption of norms of good governance.

10.5 Lack of resources

A lack of resources has to be seen in relation to the mandate. For instance, UNPROFOR in Bosnia-Herzegovina clearly lacked the necessary means to act in self-defence, let alone prevent massacres and deportations. As a result of its limited resources, UNPROFOR personnel were made hostage to Bosnian Serb forces, and this aggravated the situation on the ground. Limited resources aggravate the dilemma between *ex ante* prevention and *ex post* management. As international organisations' resources are strained, the tendency to focus on problems that have reached the stage of open conflict (and public opinion) at the expense of preventive action is exacerbated. Although lack of funding is particularly acute in the case of the United Nations, in view of its wide-ranging commitments, it is a feature that is common to all international organisations. The 'expectations-capabilities' gap will only be bridged with appropriate resource commitments on the part of the Member States of international organisations. As international organisations exist by the grace of their members' willingness to pay for the fulfilment of the organisations' tasks, Member States of the European security architecture should put their money where their (organisation's) mouth is in order to see a return on their common desire to stabilise the Western Balkans.

CHAPTER 3

THE EUROPEAN UNION'S ACTIONS TOWARDS THE SOCIALIST FEDERAL REPUBLIC OF YUGOSLAVIA AND ITS SUCCESSOR STATES (1991-2001)*

1. INTRODUCTION

At the very beginning of the 'Yugoslav' crises, the European Communities, and later the European Union, were at the forefront of the international effort to stop the escalation of armed conflict. Despite Jacques Poos' optimistic claim that 'the hour of Europe ha[d] dawned,'[1] the crisis arrived at the 'wrong' moment for the European Communities.[2] The instruments through which the EC/EU could wield influence were primarily economic (e.g., suspension of trade and aid relations and sanctions), to a much lesser extent diplomatic and political (e.g., peace conferences and shuttle diplomacy), but by no means military in nature.[3] The lack of a comprehensive set of instruments to address the violent conflicts in the former Yugoslavia may well explain why the autonomous efforts of the EC/EU were sometimes partially successful but generally failed miserably to attain their objectives.[4]

The analysis in this chapter is devoted to the autonomous actions of the EC/EU during four successive stages of the Yugoslav wars. After the outbreak of war in Slovenia and Croatia in 1991, the EC spearheaded international efforts to find a peaceful solution to the conflict (section 2). This first stage is characterised by the adoption of a wide range of economic and political instruments. The

---

* This chapter is a revised and extended version of my contribution 'The European Union's Troubled Relations with the Federal Republic of Yugoslavia (1991-2001)', in J.W. de Zwaan, et al., eds., *The European Union, an Ongoing Process of Integration: Liber Amicorum Alfred E. Kellermann* (The Hague, T.M.C. Asser Press 2004) pp. 337-356.

1 Declaration of J. Poos, Luxembourg's Foreign Minister, to the international press, 29 June 1991.

2 See T. de Wilde d'Estmael, *La dimension politique des relations économiques extérieures de la Communauté européenne: sanctions et incitants économiques comme moyens de politique étrangère* (Brussels, Émile Bruylant 1998) at pp. 282-283.

3 The lopsided, unfinished structure of the European Union was a point of major criticism at the time. See, e.g., the legal analysis of D. Curtin, 'The Constitutional Structure of the Union: A Europe of Bits and Pieces', 30 *CML Rev.* (1993) pp. 17-69.

4 The literature on the European Union's handling of the Yugoslav wars between 1991 and 1995 is voluminous. Two of the more focused studies worth noting are S. Lucarelli, *Europe and the Breakup of Yugoslavia. A Political Failure in Search of a Scholarly Explanation* (The Hague, Kluwer Law International 2000); and R. Ginsberg, *The European Union in International Politics – Baptism by Fire* (Lanham, Rowman & Littlefield Publishers 2001).

escalation of war in Bosnia-Herzegovina (1992-1995) led the United Nations to take over from the EC in trying to coax the belligerent parties into a peace agreement. During the Bosnian war and in its aftermath, European involvement in the Yugoslav crises consisted primarily of supporting UN-adopted initiatives, instruments and activities. Nevertheless, some autonomous action towards the end of this second stage is worth pointing out (section 3). The third stage of EU action in the wars in the former Yugoslavia concerns the array of unilateral sanctions adopted against the Federal Republic of Yugoslavia over the crisis in Kosovo. These sanctions ran parallel to those adopted by the UN Security Council (section 4). The ethnic conflict in Macedonia (2001) forms the last stage during which the European Union adopted new punitive measures to prevent the conflict from spreading and force the warring parties back to the negotiating table (section 5). The chapter closes with some concluding remarks (section 6).

As most of the European Union's (re)actions during the Yugoslav wars involved the adoption and implementation of sanctions, a few preliminary remarks are appropriate. The legal debate on EC/EU sanctions has so far mostly revolved around the implementation of UN Security Council resolutions, with a focus on the European Union's decision-making powers and procedures in the field of economic and financial sanctions, in particular the separate roles of the Community and its Member States.[5] However, these aspects have more or less been settled with the incorporation of Articles 60 and 301 into the EC Treaty.[6] The

---

[5] For an analysis of the problems encountered by the European Union and its Member States in this context, see, *inter alia*, S. Bohr, 'Sanctions by the United Nations Security Council and the European Community', 4 *EJIL* (1993) pp. 256-268; K. Lenaerts and E. De Smijter, 'The United Nations and the European Union: Living Apart Together', in K. Wellens, ed., *International Law: Theory and Practice. Essays in Honour of E. Suy* (The Hague, Kluwer Law International 1998) pp. 439-458; D. Bethlehem, 'Regional Interface between Security Council Decisions and Member States Implementation: The Example of the European Union', in V. Gowlland-Debbas, ed., *United Nations Sanctions and International Law* (The Hague, Kluwer Law International 2001) pp. 291-305; and the literature referred to in the next note.

[6] Art. 301 TEC reads: 'Where it is provided, in a common position or in a joint action adopted according to the provisions of the Treaty on European Union relating to the common foreign and security policy, for an action by the Community to interrupt or to reduce, in part or completely, economic relations with one or more third countries, the Council shall take the necessary urgent measures. The Council shall act by a qualified majority on a proposal from the Commission.' The article refers to CFSP measures adopted on the basis of Arts. 14 and 15 TEU. Art. 60(1) TEC reads: 'If, in the cases envisaged in Article 301, action by the Community is deemed necessary, the Council may, in accordance with the procedure provided for in Article 301, take the necessary urgent measures on the movement of capital and on payments as regards the third countries concerned.' See P. Eeckhout, *The External Relations of the European Union: Legal and Constitutional Foundations* (Oxford, Oxford University Press 2004) pp. 422-464. More recently, in the wake of a new wave of judgments of the European Court of Justice in a series of sanctions cases, see, *inter alia*, R. van Ooik and R. Wessel, 'De Yusuf en Kadi-uitspraken in perspectief. Nieuwe verhoudingen in de interne en externe bevoegdheden van de Europese Unie', 54 *SEW* (2006) pp. 230-241; M. Bulterman, 'Fundamental Rights and the United Nations Financial Sanction Regime: The *Kadi* and *Yusuf*

analysis in this chapter is limited to sanctions imposed autonomously by the European Union, that is to say, not as a derivative of the obligations resting upon the Member States to implement sanctions adopted at the level of the UN Security Council. The European Union's own sanctions policies in dealing with the SFRY and its successor states since 1991 will be analysed and evaluated. The decisions to adopt sanctions will be briefly presented against their specific political backgrounds. After a legal analysis of the sanctions, their impact will be evaluated. Sanctions imposed by EU Member State governments (individually or collectively) outside the framework of the European Union fall outside the scope of this study.[7]

2. LEADING THE INTERNATIONAL PEACE EFFORTS (1991)

2.1 Political objectives

The first episode of the wars in the former Yugoslavia (between 27 June 1991 and 11 January 1992) saw the lighting of the fuse in the wake of the declarations of independence by Slovenia and Croatia (both on 25 June 1991) and the escalation of hostilities after Bosnia-Herzegovina seceded from the SFRY (on 20 December 1991).[8] In the absence of direct initiatives or involvement from the United Nations, NATO, the CSCE, the CoE and the United States at the outset of the

---

Judgments of the Court of First Instance of the European Communities', 19 *LJIL* (2006) pp. 753-772; P. Eeckhout, 'External Relations of the EU and the Member States: Competence, Mixed Agreements, International Responsibility, and Effects of International Law – General Report', presented at FIDE 2006, at pp. 10-12 and 26-29, available at: <http://www.fide2006.org>; and by the Community Rapporteur at FIDE 2006, M. Cremona, 'External Relations of the EU and the Member States: Competence, Mixed Agreements, International Responsibility, and Effects of International Law', EUI Working Papers (2006/22) at pp. 12-13 and 33-36.

[7] Examples of such individual sanctions are various orders enacted by the United Kingdom to prohibit exports to Serbia and Montenegro, including the *Serbia and Montenegro (United Nations Sanctions) Order 1992*, which broadly covered the same ground as Council Regulation (EEC) No. 1432/92 of 1 June 1992 prohibiting trade between the European Economic Community and the Republics of Serbia and Montenegro, *OJ* 1992 L 205/2; and Council Regulation (EEC) No. 3534/92 of 7 December 1992 amending Regulation (EEC) No. 1432/92 prohibiting trade between the European Economic Community and the Republics of Serbia and Montenegro, *OJ* 1992 L 358/16. For a judicial consideration of the issues that arose as a result of the overlapping nature of these measures, the respective obligations to act in implementation of sanctions by the Community and its Member States and the relationship between the two sets of measures in the event that both apply, see the judgments of the English Court of Appeal in *R.* v. *Searle and Others*, 3 *CMLR* (1995) p. 196; of the English High Court in *R.* v. *HM Treasury and Bank of England*, ex parte Centro-Com Srl, 1 *CMLR* (1994) p. 109; and of the ECJ in Cases C-124/95 *R.* v. *HM Treasury and Bank of England*, ex parte Centro-Com Srl [1997] *ECR* I-81; and C-177/95 *Ebony Maritime SA* v. *Prefetto Della Provincia di Brindisi* [1997] *ECR* I-1111.

[8] For references to the literature, see chapter 1.

war, the EC found itself sitting alone in the front row to address this new situation, a problem of considerable political magnitude and complexity.[9] The EC assumed leadership and responsibility and tried to call a halt to the conflict by imposing a comprehensive solution on the warring parties. It sent a troika to Belgrade and Zagreb that secured a ceasefire accord by threatening the belligerents to block trade and withdraw the economic aid of which the SFRY was a major beneficiary.[10] It was the success of this first European intervention in the Slovenian crisis which led Jacques Poos to make the boast that would haunt him forever, for it soon proved that the assurances that the troika had received in Belgrade and Zagreb were the first of a long series of (dis)illusions. The fighting in Slovenia and Croatia continued and forced the Community to follow up on its threat.

On 5 July 1991 the European Communities suspended the second and third protocols to the 1980 Cooperation Agreement between the EEC and the SFRY.[11] The Member States also imposed an arms embargo against Yugoslavia and appealed to others (the CSCE, the United States and the United Nations) to follow suit, which they did.[12] The adoption of these sanctions and intensive diplomatic

---

9 In a certain way, it seems that the international community had delegated the task of bringing peace to the Balkans to the Europeans. Javier Pérez de Cuéllar, then Secretary-General of the United Nations, did not want to put the matter to the Security Council, fearing that an intervention of the United Nations would be perceived as 'une sorte d'ingérence dans les efforts européens.' Reported in *Agence Europe*, No. 5527, 4 July 1991. See a similar comment made by Thomas Pickering, the US ambassador to the United Nations at the time, reported in *Le Monde* of 5 July 1991: 'Les Etats-Unis n'ont aucun rôle à jouer en Yougoslavie, sauf si les efforts des Européens échouaient.' More generally, see O. Rehn, 'The European Community and the Challenge of a Wider Europe', *Sussex Working Papers in Contemporary European Studies*, No. 6 (July 1994).

10 A declaration of the European Council, which was strangely enough only published in *Agence Europe*, No. 5523, 29 June 1991, served as the mandate for the troika. The content of the declaration was supposed to have been presented to the Yugoslav authorities to make it absolutely clear what the European stance towards the crisis was. The text closed with the statement that 'in anticipation of an improvement of the situation, the European Council suspends all Community and national aid (assistance) to Yugoslavia.' Despite the affirmative tone of the declaration, the text should not be interpreted in too positivistic a manner. It did not suggest an immediate executorial title but constituted a threat that, if the troika's mission would fail, financial cooperation with Yugoslavia would be suspended. Hanging as a sword of Damocles above the federal authorities' heads, economic coercion was applied to force the Yugoslavs to accept three European demands: respect for a ceasefire accompanied by the return of all militaries to their barracks; a moratorium of three months on rendering effect to the declarations of independence by Slovenia and Croatia to facilitate dialogue between all the parties to the conflict; and the lifting of the Serbian reservation against the election of a Croat (Stipe Mesić) to the Presidency of the Federation.

11 See *infra* section 2.2.1.

12 Ibid. The United States endorsed the EC arms embargo on 8 July 1991. At its meeting in Prague on 3-4 September 1991, the CSCE also called for an embargo on weapons and military equipment against all parties to the conflict. It was only on 25 September that the UN Security Council adopted resolution 713 (1991) imposing an arms embargo on Yugoslavia and calling for the immediate cessation of hostilities.

pressure led the parties to sign an effective ceasefire agreement for Slovenia on the island of Brioni, Tito's idyllic retreat in the Adriatic. The Brioni Accord of 7 July was hailed as a triumph of European diplomacy, but it left every important item of contention unresolved, pending a three-month cooling-off period.[13] By turning its offensive against Croatia, and later Bosnia-Herzegovina, Yugoslavia's 'federal' army (JNA) tore the heart right out of the proud, confident, new Europe. A pattern of negotiated ceasefires facilitated by EC mediation – and mostly broken by the Serb-dominated JNA – was accompanied by a series of threats by the European Communities to impose economic sanctions on Serbia and recognise the other republics seeking independence.[14] In response to the factions' failure to honour the ceasefires and accept the comprehensive peace plan tabled by the European Communities at the Conference on Yugoslavia, which was held at The Hague in October 1991,[15] the twelve Ministers of Foreign Affairs on 8 November decided to unilaterally suspend all coordinated assistance to and relations with Yugoslavia, including the 1980 Cooperation Agreement between the EEC and the SFRY.[16]

It was obvious that, with the latter, the aim of the European Communities was not merely to economically sanction the country, or rather those parts of the Federation supporting the war, but to take account of the factual dissolution of Yugoslavia as a state. This observation is confirmed by a tangible demonstration of

---

13 For the text of the Brioni Accord, see 30 *ILM* (1991).

14 See EPC Statements of 6 August 1991 (EPC, No. P 73/91) and 27 August 1991 (EPC, No. P 82/91), followed by some sort of ultimatum on 6 October 1991 (EPC, No. P 98/91) and the final ultimatum on 28 October 1991 (EPC, No. P 106/91).

15 See *infra* section 2.5.

16 See EPC Statement of 8 November 1991, *Bull. EC* 11-1991, point 1.4.4. For the punitive measures, see *infra* nn. 27-29. The Cooperation Agreement between the EEC and the SFRY was signed in Belgrade on 2 April 1980 and approved on behalf of the Community by Council Regulation (EEC) No. 341/83 of 24 January 1983 on the conclusion of the Cooperation Agreement between the European Economic Community and the Socialist Federal Republic of Yugoslavia, *OJ* 1983 L 41/1. See Cooperation Agreement between the European Economic Community and the Socialist Federal Republic of Yugoslavia, *OJ* 1983 L 41/2; Protocol 1 on the products referred to in Article 15 of the Cooperation Agreement between the European Economic Community and the Socialist Federal Republic of Yugoslavia, *OJ* 1983 L 41/28; Protocol 2 on financial cooperation between the Socialist Federal Republic of Yugoslavia and the European Economic Community, *OJ* 1983 L 41/37; Protocol 3 of the Cooperation Agreement between the European Economic Community and the Socialist Federal Republic of Yugoslavia concerning the definition of the concept of 'originating products' and methods of administrative cooperation, *OJ* 1983 L 41/39. The Cooperation Agreement had already been given effect in 1980 thanks to the entry into force of an Interim Agreement between the European Economic Community and the Socialist Federal Republic of Yugoslavia on trade and trade cooperation, *OJ* 1980 L 130/2. Related instruments concerned sectoral agreements entered into by the EEC and the SFRY for sheep meat, goat meat and textiles. Finally, relations were defined by the mixed Agreement between the Member States of the European Coal and Steel Community and the European Coal and Steel Community, of the one part, and the Socialist Federal Republic of Yugoslavia, of the other part, *OJ* 1983 L 41/113.

support for those republics in favour of the EC peace initiative. Firstly, in their statement of 6 October 1991, the twelve Foreign Ministers expressed their intention to apply a differentiated treatment to the different parties to the conflict, which 'inevitably' led to the recognition of those republics wishing to be independent and the adoption of restrictive measures against those parties that continued to flout the desire of the other Yugoslav parties for a successful outcome of the Conference on Yugoslavia.[17] Secondly, on 2 December 1991, the EC restored trade links, the Generalised System of Preferences (GSP) and economic and financial aid terms *vis-à-vis* all Yugoslav republics, except Serbia and Montenegro.[18] And thirdly, on the morning of 17 December, eleven Ministers of Foreign Affairs succumbed to what amounted to an ultimatum by their German colleague Hans-Dietrich Genscher and agreed to invite those republics seeking diplomatic recognition to submit applications by 24 December or else lose the opportunity.[19] Four republics (Bosnia-Herzegovina, Croatia, Macedonia and Slovenia) rose to the occasion and requested to be recognised as sovereign states. On 11 January 1992, the EC's Arbitration Commission, charged with the task of deciding on these applications, opined that two out of the four republics (Macedonia and Slovenia) met all the criteria to be recognised as new states.[20] The political impact of these measures on the dissolution of and the war in the former Yugoslavia was significant, because EC action isolated and punished the Serb/Montenegrin-dominated federal authorities in Belgrade. It also ended the sole European stewardship of the international efforts to negotiate a peaceful settlement to the conflict in Croatia, because the EC had to acknowledge the collapse of the peace talks in The Hague as well as Serbia's distrust of the EC as a mediator.

---

[17] EPC Statement of 6 October 1991 (EPC, No. P 98/91), *Bull. EC* 10-1991, point 1.4.7. This view is supported by H.-D. Genscher, *Erinnerungen* (Berlin, Siedler Verlag 1995) at p. 954: 'unvermeidlichen Konsequenz.' See also European Parliament, *Rapport de la commission politique sur la proposition relative à une décision concernant la dénonciation de l'accord de coopération entre la CEE et la RSFY*, Rapporteur: Cassanmagnago Ceretti, Doc. A3-0323/91, 18 November 1991, at p. 6: 'Le Parlement estime par ailleurs que le raisonnement qui est à la base de la décision du Conseil, à savoir la dissolution de la Yougoslavie en tant que telle [...].' One has to point out, however, that at the moment of the Community's decision to suspend all coordinated assistance and cooperation, no Yugoslav republic had been recognised by third states. This means that the Council's attitude has pushed forward the dissolution of the SFRY.

[18] Council Regulation (EEC) No. 3567/91 of 2 December 1991 concerning the arrangements applicable to the import of products originating in the Republics of Bosnia-Herzegovina, Croatia, Macedonia and Slovenia, *OJ* 1991 L 342/1.

[19] While some states – notably Britain and the United States – argued that premature recognition could derail the peace process, political opinion in Germany was contemptuous. Bonn argued that the peace process had been derailed already – by Belgrade. Genscher made it clear that if the EC did not move towards recognition, then Germany would break ranks and recognise some of the republics (especially Croatia and Slovenia) unilaterally. Needless to say that this was a bitter blow to the spirit of common purpose which had prevailed during the pre-Maastricht IGC.

[20] See *infra* section 2.6.

2.2 Economic and financial instruments

2.2.1 *Arms embargo, suspension and termination of aid and trade relations*

Very soon after the conflict broke out in Slovenia on 27 June 1991, the EC decided on a first set of economic measures designed to influence the Yugoslav parties. At their meeting of 5 July 1991, the twelve Ministers of Foreign Affairs decided upon an embargo on armaments and military equipment applicable to the whole of Yugoslavia.[21] The arms embargo was not the EC's but the Member States' competence.[22] What did fall into the shared competence of the Communities and the Member States was the suspension of the second financial protocol with Yugoslavia.[23] The EC and the Member States expressed the hope that a normalisation of the situation would permit them to resuscitate the financial protocols 'so as to contribute to the indispensable recovery of the country.'[24]

Despite the fact that the war in Slovenia lasted for 'only' ten days, the political problems at the federal level remained unresolved. In fact, the JNA, which had intervened in Slovenia on the pretext that it was defending the unity of the SFRY against secessionist forces, was now openly and indisputably fighting for territory for the Serbs outside Serbia. In Croatia, it stood behind the Serb paramilitary forces that were engaged in a land grab to extend the territory of the self-proclaimed 'Serb Autonomous Oblast of Krajina'. In this situation, PHARE cooperation was stopped, *ipso facto* in the summer and formally in the autumn of 1991.[25] Belgrade tried to prevent the suspension of financial aid under the PHARE programme. In a *note verbale* sent to the European Commission on 22 August 1991, it stated that

---

21 See EPC Statement of 5 July 1991 (EPC, No. P 61/90), *Bull. EC* 7/8-1991, point 1.4.3.

22 See C.-D. Ehlermann, 'The Scope of Article 113 of the EEC Treaty', in P. Manin, et al., eds., *Mélanges offerts à Pierre-Henri Teitgen* (Paris, Editions Pédone 1984).

23 The application of the Second Financial Protocol (the engagement of remaining amounts worth 100 million ECU) was suspended, while the Council never transmitted the proposal for a Council decision on the conclusion of the Third Financial Protocol for the years 1991 to 1995, published as SEC/91/796 final in *OJ* 1991 C 134/5, to the European Parliament to obtain its opinion. For the financial consequences, see *Agence Europe*, No. 5523, 29 June 1991.

24 EPC Statement of 5 July 1991, *Bull. EC* 7/8-1991, point 1.4.3.

25 XXVth General Report, 1991, point 818. The PHARE programme, which provided 35 million ECU in grants for technical assistance in the financial sector and for an enterprise reform programme in Yugoslavia, was suspended by an internal decision of the Community, despite the fact that Yugoslavia was still included in the regime laid down in Regulation (EEC) No. 2698/90 of 17 September 1990 amending Regulation (EEC) No. 3906/89 in order to extend the economic aid to other countries of Central and Eastern Europe, *OJ* 1990 L 257/1. In the end, this money was never used for the above-mentioned purposes; some of it was spent for humanitarian purposes (8.5 million ECU) and environmental projects (6 million ECU).

> PHARE carries sizeable political importance as it brings benefits to all parts of Yugoslavia. It also enhances the stature of the Federal Government at the presently delicate moment.[26]

In response to the parties' failure to respect the ceasefires and accept the peace plan tabled by the EC in October 1991, the European Communities on 11 November unilaterally suspended the trade concessions provided for by the 1980 Cooperation Agreement between the EEC and the SFRY, the application of the agreement and related protocols and instruments, as well as the trade concessions provided for by and the application of the Agreement on ECSC Products between the Communities, their Member States and the SFRY.[27] It removed Yugoslavia from the lists of beneficiaries of the Community's GSP for 1991 for both EEC and ECSC products[28] and restored quantitative restrictions on imports of Yugoslav textiles.[29] The representatives of the governments of the Member States, meeting within the Council of 11 November 1991, also denounced the Agreement between the Member States of the ECSC and the SFRY, on the basis of Article 15

---

[26] Cited in D. Lopandić, 'The European Community and the Yugoslav Crisis (1989-1992) – Some Issues of International Law', 41 *Jugoslovenska Revija za Medunarodno Pravo* (1994) pp. 311-349 at p. 316.

[27] Council Regulation (EEC) No. 3300/91 of 11 November 1991 suspending the trade concessions provided for by the Cooperation Agreement between the European Economic Community and the Socialist Federal Republic of Yugoslavia, *OJ* 1991 L 315/1 (based on Art. 113 TEEC; now Art. 133 TEC); Decision No. 91/588/ECSC of the Representatives of the Governments of the Member States, meeting within the Council of 11 November 1991 suspending the trade concessions provided for by the Agreement between the Member States of the European Coal and Steel Community and the Socialist Federal Republic of Yugoslavia, *OJ* 1991 L 315/49; and Decision No. 91/586/ECSC, EEC of the Council and the Representatives of the Governments of the Member States, meeting within the Council of 11 November 1991 suspending the application of the Agreements between the European Community, its Member States and the Socialist Federal Republic of Yugoslavia, *OJ* 1991 L 315/47. This decision *sui generis* does not mention a legal basis but refers to the EPC Statements of 5, 6, and 28 October 1991 in which the EPC states the existence of a 'crisis in Yugoslavia.' For the legality of this decision under public international law, see *infra* section 2.2.4.

[28] Decision No. 91/589/ECSC of the Representatives of the Governments of the Member States, meeting within the Council of 11 November 1991 withdrawing Yugoslavia from the list of beneficiaries of the Community generalized tariff preferences scheme for 1991, *OJ* 1991 L 315/50; and Council Regulation (EEC) No. 3302/91 of 11 November 1991 withdrawing Yugoslavia from the lists of beneficiaries of the Community generalized tariff preferences scheme for 1991, *OJ* 1991 L 315/46.

[29] Council Regulation (EEC) No. 3301/91 of 11 November 1991 on the arrangements for imports of certain textile products originating in Yugoslavia, *OJ* 1991 L 315/3. This regulation replaced the supplementary protocol covering the trade in textile products, negotiated in 1986 and published in the wake of Council Decision 90/649/EEC of 24 September 1990 concerning the conclusion of a supplementary protocol to the cooperation Agreement between the European Economic Community and the Socialist Federal Republic of Yugoslavia on trade in textile products, *OJ* 1990 L 352/120. The adoption of the replacement regulation was necessary to unilaterally reimpose quantitative quotas on imports.

of this agreement.[30] One-and-a-half weeks later, after having received the assent of the European Parliament,[31] the Council finally formally denounced the Cooperation Agreement between the EEC and Yugoslavia, on the basis of Article 60 of this agreement.[32] The agreement ceased to be applicable only six months later, on 26 May 1992. Diplomatic relations were maintained.

In more than one respect, the sanctions represented a precedent in the EC's practice:

- for the first time in the Community's history, a Cooperation Agreement with a third country (based on Art. 238 TEEC; new Art. 310 TEC) was denounced;
- it was the first time that the EC opted to suspend, almost immediately (within twenty-four hours), all aspects of its relations with a third country, including the trade regime; and
- the peculiar situation developed whereby different trade or financial sanctions were applied *vis-à-vis* different parts of the same state.

Each of these points will now be dealt with in more detail.

2.2.2 *Re-establishing trade relations with those republics supporting peace*

In a move to single out those whom it regarded as the instigators of the armed aggression against Slovenia and Croatia, as well as the opponents to its peace plans, the European Communities on 2 December 1991 – retroactively[33] – re-established the trade concessions granted by the former Cooperation Agreement

---

30 Decision No. 91/587/ECSC of the Representatives of the Governments of the Member States, meeting within the Council of 11 November 1991 denouncing the Agreement between the Member States of the European Coal and Steel Community and the Socialist Federal Republic of Yugoslavia, *OJ* 1991 L 315/48.

31 The decision was delayed because the legal basis of the agreement (Art. 238 TEEC; new Art. 310 TEC) required the assent of the European Parliament, which was delivered on 20 November 1991 after a discussion of the Cassanmagnago Ceretti Report (see *supra* n. 17). On the legal basis of the EEC-SFRY Cooperation Agreement, see C. Flaesch-Mougin in his chronicles on the external accords of the EEC, 20 *Revue Trimestrielle de Droit Européen* (1984) p. 467 and 26 *RTDE* (1990) at pp. 89 and 92.

32 Council Decision 91/602/EEC of 25 November 1991 denouncing the Cooperation Agreement between the European Economic Community and the Socialist Federal Republic of Yugoslavia, *OJ* 1991 L 325/23. See *infra* section 2.2.4.

33 As of 15 November 1991, the date on which the restrictive measures against the whole of Yugoslavia entered into force. A reasoning is given by D. Lopandić, 'Un exemple de sanctions économiques de la CEE: Suspension/dénonciation de l'accord de coopération entre la CEE et la Yougoslavie', *Revue des Affaires Européennes* (1992) pp. 67-72 at n. 12: 'L'application rétroactive des préférences a cet avantage de rendre d'avance sans intérêt une éventuelle action en justice des entreprises touchées (dans la Communauté) sur la question de la légalité des sanctions communautaires.'

in favour of all Yugoslav republics except Serbia and Montenegro.[34] The basic provision of Regulation (EEC) No. 3567/91 was that the imports from Bosnia-Herzegovina, Croatia, Macedonia, and Slovenia into the Communities were admitted without quantitative restrictions or measures having equivalent effect and exempt from customs duties and taxes having equivalent effect.[35] The exceptions to this rule were provided in the annexes to the Regulation.[36] The regulation was in a way incomplete, because it was adopted at the end of the year and only concerned the trade regime for 1991. At the same time, the Council called on the Commission to restore the PHARE programme and to use the remaining 100 million ECU from the Second Financial Protocol to finance projects in the four republics.[37] However, due to technical reasons, those last measures were not applied in practice.[38]

Despite the fact that the Council stated that the adoption of Regulation (EEC) No. 3567/91 was without prejudice to the question of the recognition of the recipient republics, it was clear that the European Communities had *de facto* accepted the final dismemberment of the SFRY and the recognition of its successor states. It was a unique case in EC practice to grant specific trade treatment to products originating from different parts of the same country. In fact, this constituted a flagrant violation, *inter alia*, of the non-discrimination principle laid down in Article 57 of the Cooperation Agreement between the EEC and SFRY.[39] Regulation (EEC) No. 3567/91 was soon thereafter replaced by another set of regulations and decisions covering 1992, adding tariff ceilings and Community surveillance for imports of certain agricultural and industrial products originating in the republics of Croatia, Slovenia, Bosnia-Herzegovina, Macedonia *and* Montenegro.[40] The inclusion of Montenegro in the list of republics 'contribut[ing] [...] to the furtherance of a peaceful solution to the conflict' served to further isolate Serbia.[41]

At the beginning of 1992, it was possible, for a while, to believe that international mediation and the measures spearheaded by the EC were actually producing

---

34 Council Regulation (EEC) No. 3567/91 of 2 December 1991 concerning the arrangements applicable to the import of products originating in the Republics of Bosnia-Herzegovina, Croatia, Macedonia and Slovenia, *OJ* 1992 L 342/1.

35 Art. 1, equivalent to Art. 15 of the Cooperation Agreement.

36 Excluded from the re-establishment of concessions were certain agricultural and industrial products. These became subject to new tariff ceilings.

37 See Council Communication No. 9558/91 (Presse 220-G), 2 December 1991.

38 See Lopandić, loc. cit. n. 26, at p. 319.

39 This is a reason why the whole Cooperation Agreement was suspended.

40 Council Regulations (EEC) Nos. 545-548/92 of 3 February 1992, *OJ* 1992 L 63/1-49; and Decisions Nos. 92/150-151/ECSC of 3 February 1992, *OJ* 1992 L 63/50-66.

41 EPC Declaration of 10 January 1992, *Bull. EC* 1-1992, point 1.5.8.

positive effects and that the conflict was heading towards appeasement: the ceasefire was holding in Croatia. On 7 April 1992, in the same declaration recognising Bosnia-Herzegovina as a state, the European Communities even decided to extend to Serbia the benefits of the 'positive measures' granted to the other republics.[42] However, this decision was never implemented because the war escalated in Bosnia-Herzegovina.

While the arms embargo of 5 July 1991 remained in place against all successor states of the former Yugoslavia, no further sanctions were adopted against Slovenia, Croatia, Macedonia and Bosnia-Herzegovina. In the years to follow, the Federal Republic of Yugoslavia, that is to say, the federation of Serbia and Montenegro (including Kosovo), was the main target for international sanctions, as it was seen as the main instigator for armed conflict on the territory of the former SFRY.

2.2.3 *Effects of the measures*

The immediate effect of the measures adopted on and soon after 5 July 1991 was that Yugoslavia lost all tariff and other preferences applied to imports into the EC. The suspension of the Cooperation Agreement had automatically produced the suspension of all activities of cooperation, protocols or other actions undertaken on the basis of the agreement. Apart from its economic impact, the decisions dealt a heavy political blow to the international position of Yugoslavia and in particular Serbia, which by then had commandeered the emptied shell of the federal Yugoslav government.[43] As mentioned before, it was obvious that the aim of the EC was not only to economically sanction a country – as was the case in some earlier examples of EC sanctions[44] – but to take account of the factual dissolution of Yugoslavia as a state.

2.2.4 *Legality under public international law*

The Federal Government of Yugoslavia reacted twice to the measures adopted by the EC, asking it to 'reconsider' its decisions. By a *note verbale* of 28 November 1991, the Yugoslav government stated that the termination of the agreements constituted 'a unilateral implementation of economic sanctions in violation of the

---

42 *Bull. EC* 4-1992, point 1.5.4.

43 Apart from Serbia, only Montenegro and Bosnia were represented in the Federal Government. See V. Bojičić and D. Dyker, 'Sanctions on Serbia: Sledgehammer or Scalpel', *Sussex Working Papers in Contemporary European Studies*, No. 1 (June 1993).

44 Cf., the sanction regimes against Greece (1967) and Turkey (1980). See J. Pertek, 'Les sanctions politiques à objet économique prises par la CEE à l'encontre des Etats tiers', 26 *Revue du Marché Commun* (1983) p. 205.

universally recognized norms of international law [...]. [These measures] will lead to the weakening of Yugoslavia, internally and internationally [...].'[45] In a second *note verbale* of 23 December 1991, the Federal Government asked the EEC to convene an extraordinary meeting of the EEC-Yugoslavia Cooperation Council in order to examine the economic and political consequences of the measures adopted by the Community.[46] The Community did not reply to either of these notes, as it did not consider itself, at that stage, bound by the Cooperation Agreement.[47] But was the Community's decision to combine the immediate suspension of the entire Cooperation Agreement (the political objective) and its termination in a period of six months (the contractual clause in the agreement) justified under international law?

While the termination of the Cooperation Agreement was foreseen in Article 60, nothing in the agreement permitted its immediate and total suspension.[48] Such suspension could therefore be justified only by general rules of international law allowing a deviation from the traditional canon of *pacta sunt servanda*. Of course, the 1969 Vienna Convention on the Law of Treaties provides for some exceptional means for the suspension and termination of treaties: Article 61 mentions 'the impossibility to execute the treaty', Article 62 talks about a 'fundamental change of circumstances' (*rebus sic stantibus*) and Article 65 sets up a procedure concerning the termination or suspension of a treaty.[49]

The European Communities and their Member States based their decision of 11 November 1991 to immediately suspend the EEC-SFRY Cooperation Agreement (and related protocols and instruments), as well as the Agreement on ECSC Products, on two international legal elements. First, they invoked UN Security Council resolution 713 (1991), which expressed the concern that the continuation of the situation in Yugoslavia would constitute 'a threat to international peace and security'. While this is a somewhat ambiguous reference to Article 39 of the UN Charter, the resolution in no way mentioned the possibility of economic or legal sanctions (Art. 41 UN Charter), at least not in the way envisaged by the European Communities and their Member States. The only explicit reference to the provisions of chapter VII relates to the imposition of an arms embargo in paragraph 6 of the resolution. However, had the Security

---

45 Cited in Lopandić, loc. cit. n. 26, at p. 319.

46 Ibid.

47 This was the main reason why the EEC suspended not just the commercial parts but the Cooperation Agreement as a whole.

48 Art. 60 reads as follows: 'This agreement is concluded for an unlimited period. Either Contracting Party may denounce this Agreement by notifying the other Contracting Party. This Agreement shall cease to apply six months after the date of such notification.'

49 8 *ILM* (1969) p. 679.

Council wanted to rupture the economic and financial relations of states with the SFRY in September 1991, it would have sufficed to add a few simple words to that paragraph. Secondly, Decision No. 91/586/ECSC, EEC stated in its preamble that 'the pursuit of hostilities and their consequences on their economic and trade relations, both between the Republics of Yugoslavia and with the European Community, constitute a radical change in the conditions under which the Cooperation Agreement [...] and its Protocols, as well as the Agreement concerning the European Coal and Steel Community, were concluded,' which 'call into question the application of such Agreements and Protocols.'[50] The only further justification for the denunciation of the Cooperation Agreement, mentioned in Council Decision No. 91/602/EEC of 25 November 1991, was that 'the situation prevailing in Yugoslavia no longer permits the above-mentioned Agreement and the related instruments to be upheld.'[51] While the Communities and their Member States did not explicitly mention the provisions of the Vienna Convention, the language used leaves no doubt that the clauses on 'change of circumstances' (Art. 62) and 'impossibility of execution' (Art. 61) of the Vienna Convention were implicitly invoked.

The EEC-SFRY Cooperation Agreement was a typical example of a mixed agreement, concluded between the SFRY, on the one hand, and the EEC and its Member States, on the other. While the 1969 Vienna Convention was concluded to govern treaties agreed to between states, it does not apply to treaties concluded between states and international organisations. The latter are the subject of the 1986 Vienna Convention on the Law of Treaties between States and International Organisations or between International Organisations.[52] Although the 1986 Convention is not yet in force, there can be little doubt that its provisions, which are only slight modifications to the rules of the 1969 Convention to take into account the different nature of international organisations,[53] are generally accepted as applicable law.[54] Moreover, it flows from Article 3(b) of the 1969 Convention that, in so far as the rules of the Convention reflect the

---

50 Preamble to Decision No. 91/586/ECSC, EEC of the Council and the Representatives of the Governments of the Member States meeting within the Council of 11 November 1991 suspending the application of the Agreements between the European Community, its Member States and the Socialist Federal Republic of Yugoslavia, *OJ* 1991 L 315/47.

51 Preamble to Council Decision (EEC) No. 91/602 of 25 November 1991 denouncing the Cooperation Agreement between the European Economic Community and the Socialist Federal Republic of Yugoslavia, *OJ* 1991 L 325/23.

52 25 *ILM* (1986) p. 543.

53 The first seventy-two articles deal with the same subjects as Arts. 1-72 of the 1969 Vienna Convention.

54 See P. Manin, 'The EC and the Vienna Convention on the Law of Treaties between States and International Organisations or between International Organisations', 24 *CML Rev.* (1987) p. 457 et seq.

rules of customary international law applicable to treaties with international organisations, they will apply.[55]

The principle, recognised by domestic law, that a person may no longer be bound by a contract if there has been a fundamental change in circumstances which existed at the time it was signed, has been frequently abused in the past, particularly between the two World Wars. The use of the conditions under which the *rebus sic stantibus* clause could be invoked in international relations has thus always raised strong arguments, both in practice and in legal doctrine.[56] The most widely accepted mode of terminating treaties was denunciation by one of the contracting parties. However, in this field it was questionable if and under what circumstances a state could denounce a treaty when the right of denunciation was not provided for in the treaty itself. One of the major advances made in the 1969 Vienna Convention were the strictly defined (cumulative) conditions under which the principle of *rebus sic stantibus* may be invoked. In particular, it was clarified in Article 62(1) that to warrant recourse to the clause,

> [a] fundamental change of circumstances which has occurred with regard to those existing at the time of the conclusion of a treaty, and which was not foreseen by the parties, may not be invoked as a ground for terminating or withdrawing from the treaty unless:
> (a) the existence of those circumstances constituted an essential basis of the consent of the parties to be bound by the treaty; and
> (b) the effect of the change is radically to transform the extent of obligations still to be performed under the treaty.

The concept has been invoked many times, has been recognised by treaties and has been applied by an international tribunal. In its 1997 *Gabčíkovo* judgment (in which the principal treaty at issue predated the entry into force of the 1969 Convention for the parties to the case), the International Court of Justice (ICJ) brushed aside the question of possible non-applicability of the Convention's rules to questions of termination and suspension of treaties and applied Articles 60-62 as reflecting customary international law, even though they had been considered rather controversial.[57]

---

[55] See A. Aust, *Modern Treaty Law and Practice* (Cambridge, Cambridge University Press 2003) at p. 8.

[56] See O. Lissitzyn, 'Treaties and Changed Circumstances (*Rebus Sic Stantibus*)', 61 *AJIL* (1967) p. 895 et seq.

[57] *Gabčíkovo-Nagymaros* case (*Hungary* v. *Slovakia*), *ICJ Reports* 1997, at 7, paras. 42-46 and 99. See also the judgment of the ICJ in *Fisheries Jurisdiction* case (*United Kingdom* v. *Iceland*), *ICJ Reports* 1973, at 3, para. 36: '[t]his principle, and the conditions and exceptions to which it is subject, have been embodied in Article 62 of the Vienna Convention on the Law of Treaties, which may in many respects be considered as a codification of existing customary law on the subject of the termination of a treaty relationship on account of change of circumstances.'

In the case at hand – the suspension and denunciation of the EEC-SFRY Co-operation Agreement – it is hard to shake off a serious suspicion of the arbitrary application of the clause. Was there truly a radical change in the nature of the obligations of the Community towards Yugoslavia? The fact that the EEC, soon after the suspension, unilaterally – and retroactively – re-established the essence of trade concessions towards four of the Yugoslav republics suggests that it was possible to execute the (trade) obligations of the Cooperation Agreement and that the nature of the obligations had not changed.[58] Moreover, it is difficult to accept that only a change in political circumstances would be sufficient to invoke the clause without a simultaneous change in international legal conditions. At the time of the suspension of the Cooperation Agreement, the SFRY was still the only international subject of its territory, and the so-called 'Badinter Arbitration Commission'[59] had not yet opined that the SFRY was in a state of dissolution. Even in the case of a very serious disturbance of the political and constitutional order of a country, it is doubtful that this single fact opens up the possibility to other states and international organisations to suspend or immediately repudiate their international obligations. After all, the ICJ has made it clear in its *Gabčíkovo* judgment that the stability of treaty relations requires that Article 62 VCLT be applied only in the most exceptional of circumstances.[60] Otherwise it could be used as an excuse to evade all sorts of inconvenient treaty obligations. Another question is whether the *rebus sic stantibus* clause could be used together with the denunciation clause of Article 60 of the Cooperation Agreement. It seems that, in this case, the changed circumstances doctrine would be acceptable only if there was absolute material or legal impossibility for a party to execute some of the obligations of the agreement. It would be unacceptable to use Article 62 only in order to hasten the termination of a treaty or indeed the situation on the ground.

In spite of the above-mentioned suspicions, the European Court of Justice (ECJ) in its *Racke* judgment of 16 June 1998 upheld Council Decision No. 91/586/ECSC, EEC.[61] The ECJ accepted that, since the changed conditions in Yugoslavia could amount to a fundamental change of circumstances, in adopting the decision, the Council of Ministers had not made 'a manifest error of assessment.'[62] However, the Court approached the matter as one of judicial review, and the Article 62 point was not dealt with in much depth. The ECJ said, in effect,

58 It should be noted that, apart from trade obligations, the rights of Yugoslav workers living in the EEC were also directly based on the Cooperation Agreement and therefore suspended.

59 See *infra* section 2.6.

60 *Gabčíkovo-Nagymaros* case, *ICJ Reports* 1997, at 7, para. 104.

61 ECJ, Case C-162/96 *Racke* [1998] *ECR* I-3655.

62 Ibid., at para. 56.

that the Council had not been clearly wrong; it also did not say that the Council had been right to apply to principle.[63]

Whatever the case may be, a serious problem was that the suspension covered not only trade parts of the Cooperation Agreement but also the articles concerning the settlement of disputes, that is to say, the procedural requirements for the suspension and termination of the agreement.[64] The European Communities ignored Yugoslavia's requests for consultations under the provisions of the bilateral agreement as well as under Article 65 VCLT.[65] Instead, a political compromise was struck because certain Member States preferred to keep six months' room for manoeuvre through the application of the denunciation clause.[66] This led to a contradiction of legal solutions, whereby Regulation (EEC) No. 3300/91 and Decision No. 91/586/ECSC, EEC did not sit easily with the Council decisions denouncing the agreements (91/602/EEC and 91/597/ECSC) even if they were adopted simultaneously: the suspension of the agreements should logically lead towards the non-application of the denunciation (or revocation) clause; conversely, the denunciation of the agreements, which would take effect after six months, would be contrary to the logic and the justification of the decisions to immediately suspend the same agreements.

The logic adopted by the EC, if generalised, was dangerous because it could have produced anarchy in international (treaty) relations and could have harmed the successor states of the former Yugoslavia.[67] It is, however, possible to imagine that from the point of view of the European Communities and their Member States, the October 1991 Hague Conference on Yugoslavia was already the appropriate conciliatory forum. By the same logic, the delay given to the parties to accept the conference proposals could be considered as the appropriate delay of the notice of the suspension of the Cooperation Agreement. But all this is not very convincing. Posterior international practice implicitly acknowledges the doubtful method used by the Communities and their Member States in the case of the immediate suspension of the EEC-SFRY agreements. In agreements concluded with the new democracies from Central and Eastern Europe, an

---

[63] See J. Kokott and F. Hoffmeister, 'ECJ, Case C-162/96, *A. Racke & Co.* v. *Hauptzollamt Mainz*', 93 *AJIL* (1999) pp. 205-209.

[64] Art. 56 foresees consultations in the framework of the Cooperation Council and an arbitration procedure.

[65] See Lopandić, loc. cit. n. 26, at p. 338. Art. 65 excludes the right to an absolutely unlimited right to unilateral termination of a treaty and provides for (i) the notification of the other parties to the treaty of the intent to suspend the treaty; (ii) a three-month period for reply of the other parties; (iii) a settlement procedure; and (iv) a compulsory conciliation procedure.

[66] See Lopandić, loc. cit. n. 33, at p. 67, n. 35.

[67] Ibid., at n. 42: 'La logique appliquée par la Communauté conduirait en effet à permettre à tout État tiers de se délier immédiatement de toute obligation envers la Yougoslavie qui est pourtant restée l'État universellement reconnu. Ceci introduirait un élément d'anarchie juridique dans les relations entre les États et porterait préjudice même aux successeurs éventuels de l'État yougoslave.'

explicit provision was included concerning the possibility of immediate suspension of the agreement if there would be a breach of its 'essential elements'.[68]

2.3 Joint statements

European Political Cooperation (EPC) has been the principal institutional framework in which the twelve Member States tried to coordinate their positions and actions.[69] They used all existing instruments to exert influence over the parties to the conflicts, namely EPC declarations and troika visits. As the crisis continued, the Twelve progressively brought into play more specific instruments, such as a monitoring mission, an international peace conference and an arbitration commission.

Article 30 of the Single European Act had codified the practice of joint diplomatic actions of the Twelve. During the crises over the dissolution of Yugoslavia, the EPC produced a considerable number of joint statements during the 1991-1992 period (twenty-one statements in 1991 and twenty-four in 1992). Despite this activity, the positions of the Member States were often different and even opposed. While the majority of Member States favoured a cautious and well-balanced approach, Germany pressed hard in order to satisfy Slovenia's and Croatia's desire to be internationally recognised. These differences are reflected in the changing positions within the EPC during 1991.[70] In a few important statements, one can see the evolution of the positions adopted by the EC:

(a) *United Yugoslavia:* The EPC Joint Statement of 26 March 1991 said that '[i]n the view of the Twelve, a united and democratic Yugoslavia stands the best chance to integrate itself in the new Europe.'[71] The same formula was repeated in several declarations, but as of July 1991, the Twelve dropped the concept of 'unity' and started talking about the future organisation of Yugoslavia.

(b) *New situation:* Following the outbreak of war in Slovenia, the Hague Joint Statement of 5 July 1991 stated that 'in Yugoslavia all parties concerned accept the reality that a new situation has arisen' and that the future of Yugoslavia

---

[68] See, e.g., Arts. 2 and 127 of the 1996 Europe Agreement with the Republic of Slovenia, *OJ* 1999 L 51/3. For essential elements clauses in the new contractual relations with the states of the Western Balkans, see chapter 5.

[69] On the EPC, see A. Pijpers, E. Regelsberger and W. Wessels, eds., *European Political Cooperation in the 1980s – A Common Foreign Policy for Western Europe?* (Dordrecht, Martinus Nijhoff Publishers 1988); S. Nutall, *European Political Cooperation* (Oxford, Clarendon Press 1992); and T. Jürgens, *Die gemeinsame Europäische Aussen- und Sicherheitspolitik* (Cologne, Carl Heymanns Verlag 1994).

[70] For more details, see M. Weller, 'The International Response to the Dissolution of the Socialist Federal Republic of Yugoslavia', 86 *AJIL* (1992) pp. 569-607.

[71] *Bull. EC* 3-1991, point 1.4.6.

> should be based on the principles enshrined in the Helsinki Final Act and the Paris Charter for a new Europe, in particular respect for human rights, including rights of minorities and the right of peoples to self-determination in conformity with the Charter of the UN and with the relevant norms of international law, including those relating to territorial integrity of states (Charter of Paris).[72]

The EPC Joint Statement of 19 September clearly expressed the basic principles of the EC in the crisis:

> (i) the unacceptability of the use of force;
> (ii) the unacceptability of any change of borders by force;
> (iii) respect for the rights of all who live in Yugoslavia, including minorities;
> (iv) the need to take account of all legitimate concerns and aspirations.[73]

(c) *Recognition of independence:* The recognition of the Yugoslav republics was, for the first time, publicly envisaged in a Joint Statement of 6 October 1991, which linked recognition to the end of a negotiating process and to the question of minorities:

> At the meeting of 4 October, it was agreed that a political solution should be sought in the perspective of recognition of the independence of those republics wishing it, at the end of a negotiating process conducted in good faith and involving all parties. The right to self-determination of all the peoples of Yugoslavia cannot be exercised in isolation from the interests and rights of ethnic minorities within the individual republics.[74]

(d) *Immediate recognition:* Two-and-a-half months later, the EC decided to recognise any Yugoslav republic that requested recognition, after the accomplishment of some preliminary procedures for arbitration. Two declarations adopted on 16 December 1991 – one concerning the 'Guidelines on the Recognition of New States in Eastern Europe and in the Soviet Union' and the other on Yugoslavia more in particular – were of tremendous importance, in particular in view of the armed conflict which erupted in Bosnia-Herzegovina the following year.[75]

---

[72] *Bull. EC* 7/8-1991, point 1.4.3.

[73] *Bull. EC* 9-1991, point 1.4.7.

[74] *Bull. EC* 10-1991, point 1.4.7.

[75] 'Declaration on the "Guidelines on the Recognition of New States in Eastern Europe and in the Soviet Union"' and 'Declaration on Yugoslavia', Extraordinary EPC Ministerial Meeting (Brussels), EPC Press Releases P. 128/91 and P. 129/91, 16 December 1991; reproduced in *Bull. EC* 12-1991, points 1.4.5. and 1.4.6; and 31 *ILM* (1992) p. 1486. See *infra* section 2.6.2.

2.4 European Community Monitoring Mission (later EUMM)

Another type of EPC action was the troika missions. They were frequent in the first period of the crisis, under the Luxembourg and Dutch Presidencies. After the EC set up its Conference on Yugoslavia in September 1991, this type of action was abandoned. The troika missions in June and July 1991 paved the way for an effective ceasefire agreement in Slovenia, agreed to at Brioni.[76] This arrangement was supposed to create the framework for negotiations on the future of Yugoslavia and contained the seeds for a series of memoranda of understanding on the dispatch of a mission with the objective of monitoring the ceasefires in Slovenia and Croatia: the EC Monitoring Mission (ECMM). The first Memorandum of Understanding (MoU) on the Monitor Mission to Yugoslavia concerned Slovenia and Croatia and was signed in Belgrade on 13 July 1991 by a representative of the Dutch Presidency for the EC and its Member States, a representative of the federal authorities of Yugoslavia, the Minister of Foreign Affairs of Croatia and a representative of the government of Slovenia. In line with the CSCE's recommendations, it was agreed that the EC should send a delegation of up to fifty members to stabilise the ceasefire. A second MoU was signed in Belgrade on 1 September 1991 to allow for an extension of monitoring activities until 13 October of that year. It was signed by Hans van den Broek, European Commissioner for External Relations, the presidents of the six constituent republics, as well as the Presidency and the Federal Executive Council of the SFRY. The second MoU was one of the last arrangements concluded between the EC and the SFRY. A third MoU of 1 October 1991 concerned the extension of the activities of the Monitor Mission in Bosnia-Herzegovina. The text of ECMM's mandate is to be found in these MoUs.[77]

In fact, it was the CSCE Committee of Senior Officials, during its first-ever emergency meeting, that recommended the dispatch of an EC-based mission to supervise the ceasefire and a CSCE 'good offices' mission to assist in political dialogue because the new Conflict Prevention Centre of the CSCE had failed to reach the necessary unanimity on sending a CSCE observer mission.[78] On the basis of the three above-mentioned MoUs, a multinational mission of approximately 200 EC monitors (plus 400 support staff) was deployed, first in Slovenia and Croatia, and later in Bosnia-Herzegovina.[79] Initially, its duration was three months, but the mandate of ECMM was extended indefinitely at The Hague on 14 October 1991.[80]

---

76 See *supra* section 2.1.

77 On file with the author.

78 See M. Weller, *The 'Yugoslav' Crisis in International Law: General Issues (Part I)* (Cambridge, Cambridge University Press 1997) at p. xxviii.

79 Sanctioned by the UN Security Council in resolution 713 (1991).

80 Agreement on Prolongation and Extension of Activities of the Monitor Mission to Yugoslavia, signed by representatives of the EC and its Member States, SFRY, BiH, Croatia, Macedonia, Montenegro and Serbia. Slovenia was not a party to this agreement. On file with the author.

The ECMM's mandate encompassed: (i) rendering assistance in the stabilisation of the ceasefires; (ii) monitoring the suspension of the implementation of the declarations of independence; and (iii) monitoring the release and return of prisoners of war. With regard to the latter, in particular, the ECMM was to have unrestricted freedom of movement in the mission area. The EC Monitoring Mission was not a military operation, although some of its members had a military background. The duties of the EC monitors were of an impartial nature. They enjoyed diplomatic immunities (Art. X MoU 13 July 1991) and did not carry arms or wear uniforms (Art. VI MoU 13 July 1991). Only the EC flag was displayed on the premises and vehicles of the ECMM (Art. IV MoU 13 July 1991). The Head of the ECMM was a national of the Member State holding the EC Presidency and was required to report, through the Presidency, to all participating states on the activities and findings of the mission (Art. VII(1) and (2) MoU 13 July 1991). It is interesting to note that the Presidency was under an obligation to promptly inform the CSCE (Art. VII(3) MoU 13 July 1991). This is only logical, as nationals of CSCE countries other than the EC Member States were included in the activities of the ECMM.[81]

At the outset of its deployment, the warring parties were willing to let the ECMM play its role. The protection of minorities against gross human rights abuses became one of the fields in which the ECMM was able to reach isolated successes. This was done by organising meetings, overt patrolling, political pressure, attending to local requests and investigations. But as the conflicts increased in scope and cruelty, the ECMM was increasingly frustrated in carrying out its mandated activities. Access to a growing number of areas was denied, and the ECMM's movements were otherwise restricted by the parties (especially in the Serb Autonomous Oblast of Krajina and Bosnian Serb-controlled areas in Bosnia-Herzegovina). There was also a dramatic increase in incidents against monitoring officers that resulted in infringements of their immunity. The ECMM lost a great deal of its credibility with the parties to the conflicts and was eventually only approached for minor tasks, like prisoner or body exchanges.[82]

Despite the fact that the ECMM did not manage to decrease the tensions in the region overall, EC monitors did play a positive role at a more grass-roots level. Their mere presence reduced the level of fighting. In addition, some channels of indirect communications were established between the belligerents. But for the conclusion of ultimate ceasefires in Croatia and Bosnia-Herzegovina, more was needed than just a monitoring mission.

---

81 Canada, Poland, Sweden and the Czech and Slovak Federal Republic. In 2000, the fifteen EU Member States, Norway, and Slovakia had observers serving the mission.

82 See the bitter address by Jacques de Baenst, Head of Mission of ECMM, to a meeting of the HRC on 16 September 1993. On file with the author.

The ECMM was maintained throughout the later stages of the Yugoslav crises to supervise the Dayton Peace Agreement and assist in confidence building throughout the region. The ECMM implemented a restructuring of its organisation only in 2000. On 22 December 2000, the Council adopted Joint Action 2000/811/CFSP, whereby the ECMM became the European Union Monitoring Mission (EUMM).[83] The EUMM's mandate has since been amended and extended on a number of occasions.[84] The primary objective of the EUMM is to contribute by its activities (information gathering and analysis), in line with directions from – and appointments by – the Secretary General/High Representative and the Council, to the effective formulation of EU policy towards the Western Balkans. The particular focus of the EUMM is to monitor political and security developments as well as borders, inter-ethnic issues and refugee returns. The EUMM also contributes to early warning and confidence-building measures. By its nature, the EUMM is very flexible and adaptable to the particular needs of the developments in the region, so further organisational changes could occur. The mission is no longer instructed by the Presidency, but primarily by the SG/HR. Equally, the common costs of the mission are no longer financed by the Presidency and later refunded by the Member States on the basis of an agreed formula. The EUMM is now financed by a budget decided in Brussels and funded by the European Commission. As such, the ECMM could be regarded as an instrument of the Member States, whereas the EUMM can be described as a true instrument of the European Union's Common Foreign and Security Policy. The EUMM currently has approximately 120 monitors and seventy-five locally employed support staff. It operates in Bosnia-Herzegovina,[85] Macedonia,[86] Serbia, Kosovo and Montenegro.[87] Previously, the EUMM also operated in Croatia and Albania.

---

83 Council Joint Action of 22 December 2000 on the European Union Monitoring Mission, *OJ* 2000 L 328/53.

84 See Council Joint Action 2006/867/CFSP of 30 November 2006 extending and amending the mandate of the European Union Monitoring Mission (EUMM), *OJ* 2006 L 335/48 (until 31 December 2007); and Council Joint Action 2007/40/CFSP of 22 January 2007 amending Joint Action 2002/921/CFSP extending the mandate of the European Union Monitoring Mission, *OJ* 2007 L 17/22.

85 The operation of EUMM in Bosnia-Herzegovina is still governed by the MoU concluded in 1991. The same was the case for Albania and Croatia, which agreed to a MoU on the monitoring of their borders with the former Yugoslavia by the ECMM on 21 December 1992. On file with the author.

86 Council Decision 2001/682/CFSP of 30 August 2001 concerning the conclusion of the Agreement between the European Union and the Former Yugoslav Republic of Macedonia (FYROM) on the activities of the European Union Monitoring Mission (EUMM) in FYROM, *OJ* 2001 L 241/1.

87 Council Decision 2001/352/CFSP of 9 April 2001 concerning the conclusion of the Agreement between the European Union and the Federal Republic of Yugoslavia (FRY) on the activities of the European Union Monitoring Mission (EUMM) in the FRY, *OJ* 2001 L 125/1.

2.5 Conference on Yugoslavia

The idea to start negotiations on the future of Yugoslavia with EC assistance was already included in the Brioni Declaration. After it became clear that the Yugoslav parties themselves were unable and/or unwilling to organise such negotiations, the EC decided to convene a peace conference, for it could not 'stand idly by as the bloodshed [...] increases day by day [...].'[88] The Joint Statement of 3 September 1991 provided for several issues concerning the organisation of the conference.[89] Participants were to include the Federal Presidency and the Federal Government of the SFRY, the presidents of the constituent republics, the president of the EC Council and representatives of the Member States and the Commission. The EC proposed Lord Carrington, the former British Foreign Secretary, as chairman of the conference. The mandate of the Conference on Yugoslavia was formulated as follows:

> The Conference will adopt arrangements to ensure the peaceful accommodation of the conflicting aspirations of the Yugoslav peoples, on the basis of the following principles: no unilateral change of borders by force, protection of the rights of all in Yugoslavia and full account to be taken of all legitimate concerns and legitimate aspirations.[90]

An arbitration procedure was also envisaged.

The conference opened in the Peace Palace in The Hague on 7 September 1991. It lasted until August 1992, without producing any significant achievements. After the first phase (September-October 1991), during which a plan for a global solution of the Yugoslav crisis was proposed, the conference was politically 'killed' by the early recognition of Slovenia and Croatia (December 1991-January 1992).[91] Those two republics basically lost interest in the project and succeeded in limiting further negotiations to the issue of succession of the SFRY and the question of constitutional arrangements for Bosnia-Herzegovina. Unfortunately, the peace proposals developed in the second phase of the conference remained unsuccessful. Following the outbreak of war in Bosnia-Herzegovina in April 1992, Muslim representatives blocked further negotiations. At the same time, the Serbian representatives proclaimed the 'Republika Srpska' in Bosnia-Herzegovina, while Croats established the 'Croat Community of Herzeg-Bosnia'.

As far as the composition of the participants is concerned, two remarks are important. First, the 'autonomous provinces' of Vojvodina and Kosovo were, as

---

88 See EPC Joint Statement of 28 August 1991, *Bull. EC* 7/8-1991, point 1.4.25.
89 See EPC Joint Statement of 3 September 1991, *Bull. EC* 9-1991, point 1.4.2.
90 Ibid.
91 For more details, see *infra* section 2.7.

such, not represented at the conference. In this way, the EC seems to have implicitly recognised that these provinces were the internal problem of Serbia and not of the Yugoslav Federation.[92] Second, as of January 1992, the representatives of the federal organs were no longer invited to participate in the conference. Despite the protests of the remaining federal representatives, the chairman of the conference in this way implemented the Badinter Arbitration Commission's Opinion No. 1 on the dissolution of the SFRY and the EC decision on the recognition of two out of the six Yugoslav republics.[93]

In light of the perceived failure of the EC-sponsored Conference on Yugoslavia, the United Kingdom, as holder of the EC Presidency, announced on 25 July 1992 that an International Conference on the Former Yugoslavia (ICFY) would be held in August, involving the EC, the United Nations, the CSCE and the principal governments and parties to the conflict.[94] The ICFY convened in London on 26-27 August 1992. At this conference, the resignation of Lord Carrington as chairman of the EC-led peace process was announced. David Owen, like Carrington a former British Foreign Secretary, was named as his successor. With Cyrus Vance, the UN Special Envoy for Yugoslavia, Lord Owen was to co-chair the ICFY.[95]

2.6 Badinter Arbitration Commission

2.6.1 *Institutional aspects*

Following a French proposal,[96] an Arbitration Commission was established at the same time as the EC Conference on Yugoslavia in The Hague. The EPC Joint Statement of 28 August 1991 announced the creation of an Arbitration Commission

---

92 The constitutional position of the two provinces was specific in the SFRY, as they were part of Serbia and, at the same time, were directly represented in the federal organs. At the Conference on Yugoslavia, the question of minorities living in those provinces was treated as a question of minorities living in Serbia.

93 On the interrelationship between the Conference on Yugoslavia as the primary political vehicle through which the disputing parties would meet and the Badinter Arbitration Commission as the legal organ within the Community's framework to stabilise the region, see S. Terrett, *The Dissolution of Yugoslavia and the Badinter Arbitration Commission: A Contextual Study of Peace-making Efforts in the Post-Cold War World* (Aldershot, Ashgate 2000) at pp. 119-198.

94 See Weller, op. cit. n. 78, at p. xxxvii.

95 For further details, see chapter 2, sections 6.2.3, 6.2.5 and 6.3.4.

96 The idea of creating a 'European Court of Conciliation and Arbitration' in the framework of the CSCE had already been floated by Robert Badinter, President of the French Constitutional Court, in the spring of 1991. See R. Badinter, 'L'Europe du droit', 4 *EJIL* (1993) pp. 15-23 at p. 20. As Steve Terrett explains, the EC's motives for creating an arbitration procedure highlight the unusual situation it faced in Yugoslavia. In the absence of established mechanisms (ICJ, ECJ and CSCE 'Valetta Mechanism') for dealing with such intra-state conflicts, the EC was compelled to create an ad hoc organ for these purposes. See Terrett, op. cit. n. 93, at p. 121.

of five members chosen from the presidents of the constitutional courts of EC Member States.[97] Three members were to be appointed by the European Community and two members were to be appointed unanimously by the Presidency of the SFRY.[98] The 'relevant authorities' would submit their differences to arbitration and the Arbitration Commission would give its decision within two months. In the EPC Joint Statement of 3 September 1991, it was added that:

> In the framework of the Conference, the Chairman will transmit to the Arbitration Commission the issues submitted for arbitration, and the results of the Commission's deliberations will be put back to the Conference through the Chairman. The rules of procedure for arbitration will be established by the Arbitration Commission [...].[99]

There was no mention of the law to be applied by the Arbitration Commission, but in its jurisprudence, the Badinter Arbitration Commission, as it became known, mentioned the principles of public international law and referred to the peremptory norms of general international law. Thus, the Commission decided that the parties' differences had become international law issues and that this was the applicable law.[100] However, the choice of constitutional experts as members of the Arbitration Commission indicates the presumption of the EC, at least at the beginning of the Conference on Yugoslavia, that the questions to be dealt with would be more of an internal (constitutional) than of an international nature.[101] The Arbitration Commission never publicly established its rules of procedure. They always remained 'extremely flexible, informal, and discrete.'[102] On each 'difference', a *rapporteur* was appointed and the views of the parties were given in written form and collected by fax. There were no hearings, in spite of requests. Decisions could have been taken by a simple majority of the Commission's members, but it seems that all the arbitral opinions were adopted unanimously.[103]

---

97 See *Bull. EC* 7/8-1991, point 1.4.2.1.

98 The Presidency of the SFRY did not appoint any members, so it was the EC that appointed all five members: Robert Badinter (President, French), Aldo Corasaniti (Italian), Roman Herzog (German), Irène Petry (Belgian) and Francisco Tomas y Valiente (Spaniard). For a background to the creation, composition, procedure and jurisdiction of the Badinter Arbitration Commission, see Terrett, op. cit. n. 93, at pp. 120-141; and M. Craven, 'The European Community Arbitration Commission on Yugoslavia', 66 *BYIL* (1996) pp. 333-413.

99 *Bull. EC* 9-1991, point 1.4.2.

100 See the introductory note by M. Ragazzi, 'Conference on Yugoslavia Arbitration Commission', 31 *ILM* (1992) pp. 1488-1493; and A. Pellet, 'Note sur la Commission d'arbitrage de la Conférence européenne pour la Paix en Yougoslavie', 37 *Annuaire Français de Droit International* (1991) pp. 329-348. See also Terrett, op. cit. n. 93, at p. 138.

101 See Terrett, op. cit. n. 93, at p. 123.

102 Pellet, loc. cit. n. 100, at p. 332.

103 Ibid.

One of the main characteristics of the procedure was its speed. According to the EPC Joint Statement of 28 August, the Arbitration Commission had to give its decision within two months from the start of the procedure. In practice, the opinions were issued even faster: nine days to note that the SFRY was in a process of dissolution; about twenty days, including Christmas holidays, to propose which republics should be recognised; and about a month and a half for the other opinions. While this speed corresponded well with the overall atmosphere of the Conference on Yugoslavia and the need to find fast political solutions, it is extremely fast when compared to the usual length of proceedings in international judicial bodies.

Considering the above, one would be tempted to conclude that, even if the Commission itself ruled otherwise,[104] the Badinter Arbitration Commission neither constituted nor acted as an arbitration body within the meaning of international law.[105] After all, the Commission was not constituted by the parties to the dispute, that is to say, the SFRY and the constituent republics, but by a third party (the EC),[106] and it did not adopt binding awards but issued non-legally binding 'opinions'. It therefore seems more appropriate to conclude that it acted merely as a fact-finding and consultative body of the Conference on Yugoslavia and of the EC, which were given opinions which they chose to follow, or not.[107] Ragazzi points out that, in fact, there was a 'complex interaction between the deliberations of the Arbitration Commission and the political decisions of the EC institutions and the Member States.'[108] The deliberations of the Badinter Arbitration Commission were politically influenced and, in turn, had considerable political effects.[109] It seems that the arbitrators based their opinions on common sense, while taking strongly into consideration the EC's policy aims in the Yugoslav

---

104 Arbitration Commission, Interlocutory Decision, 32 *ILM* (1992) at p. 1520, point 2: '[...] the intention was to create a body capable of resolving, on the basis of law, the differences which were to be submitted to it by the parties, which precisely constitutes the definition of arbitration [...].' It continued inn para. 9, stating that 'the Commission can give a judgment only in law, in the absence of any express authorization to the contrary by the parties, it being specified that in this case it is called upon to express opinions on the legal rules applying.'

105 See Craven, loc. cit. n. 98, at pp. 337-349, who refers, *inter alia*, to the International Law Commission's 1958 Model Rules on Arbitral Procedure, GA Official Records, 13th Session, Suppl. No. 9, UN Doc. A/3859, at 5-8.

106 However, the SFRY and all the republics implicitly accepted the existence and competences of the Arbitration Commission by participating in the EC Conference on Yugoslavia and, for the first opinions, in the arbitral procedure.

107 See Pellet, loc. cit. n. 100, at p. 335.

108 See Ragazzi, loc. cit. n. 100, at p. 1490.

109 For example, in Opinion No. 8, the Arbitration Commission quotes the statement of the Council of 27 June 1992 to prove that the SFRY had ceased to exist. Subsequently, in the EPC Joint Statement of 20 July 1992, the EC expressly refers to the Arbitration Commission's conclusions concerning the succession of Yugoslavia.

crisis and in Europe.[110] But even if the Badinter Arbitration Commission cannot be seen as an independent judicial body *stricto sensu*, it was certainly independent of the disputing parties. Also, it attempted to conduct its activities in a broadly judicial manner and it sought to found its opinions on general international law. As such, its opinions may be treated as non-binding but authoritative statements of the relevant law.[111]

2.6.2 *Arbitral opinions*

The Badinter Arbitration Commission issued a total of fifteen opinions, dealing with a range of issues of international law including questions of statehood, recognition, self-determination and succession. From November 1991 until July 1992, the Commission issued ten opinions, one interlocutory decision and one comment concerning Croatia's constitutional law on minorities.[112] There are two groups of opinions in this first batch. One set of opinions was given at the initiative of Lord Carrington, the chairman of the Conference on Yugoslavia, and includes Opinions Nos. 1 (actual status of the SFRY), 2 (status of the Serbian people in Croatia and Bosnia-Herzegovina), 3 (boundaries), 8 (dissolution of Yugoslavia), 9 (state succession) and 10 (has the SFRY been transformed into the FRY, a state comprising two constituent republics, Serbia and Montenegro?). The questions underlying Opinions Nos. 2 and 3 were first raised by the Republic of Serbia but were redrafted by the chairman. The second group of opinions (Nos. 4 to 7), in which the Arbitration Commission considered the question of recognition of four Yugoslav republics (Slovenia, Croatia, Bosnia-Herzegovina and Macedonia), was delivered in accordance with a mandate given by the EC Council of Ministers on 16 December 1991 in its 'Declaration on the "Guidelines on the Recognition of New States in Eastern Europe and in the Soviet Union"' and its 'Declaration on Yugoslavia'.[113] Following this first batch of opinions, the co-chairmen of the steering committee of the ICFY submitted a further six questions to the Arbitration Commission on 20 April 1993, concerning succession of state property, archives and debts. These issues were addressed in Opinions 11-15.[114] It is beyond the scope of this study to address all issues raised in all arbitral opinions. For that reason, a brief presentation will be given below of the contents of

---

110 See Lopandić, loc. cit. n. 26, at p. 331.

111 See Craven, loc. cit. n. 98, at p. 334.

112 All texts are published in 31 *ILM* (1992) p. 1494 et seq. One of the most striking points of the arbitral opinions, apart from the speed at which they were delivered, is their extreme brevity. Both legally and politically complex and difficult questions were dealt with in two to three pages on average, almost without discussion of the contradictory arguments and without motivation or explanation of the reasoning of the Arbitration Commission.

113 *Bull. EC* 12-1991, points 1.4.5 and 1.4.6; and 31 *ILM* (1992) at p. 1486.

114 32 *ILM* (1993) at p. 1586 et seq.

the first ten opinions, after which a number of legal and political issues will be selected for discussion.[115]

- Opinion No. 1 (29 November 1991): The question was whether the ongoing process in Yugoslavia was a secession of some republics from the federation or the dissolution of the SFRY. The opinion was that the SFRY was 'in the process of dissolution'.[116]
- Opinion No. 2 (11 January 1992): The question was whether the Serbian population in Croatia and Bosnia-Herzegovina, as one of the constituent peoples, had the right to self-determination. The answer was that, because 'the right of self-determination must not involve changes to existing frontiers', the Serbian population in Bosnia-Herzegovina and Croatia was entitled to the protection given to minorities ('as opposed to 'peoples') under international law.
- Opinion No. 3 (11 January 1992): The question was whether the internal boundaries between the Yugoslav republics could be considered as frontiers under international law. The answer was that 'the former boundaries become frontiers protected by international law'.
- Opinion No. 4 (11 January 1992): The opinion was that Bosnia-Herzegovina was not yet entitled to recognition because 'the will of the peoples of Bosnia-Herzegovina' was not fully established. It was proposed to organise a referendum.
- Opinion No. 5 (11 January 1992): The opinion was that Croatia did not fully comply with the provisions concerning the special status for minorities in chapter II, section 2(c) of Lord Carrington's draft Convention (autonomy in respect of local government, local law enforcement and the judiciary, educational systems and other specific matters)[117] but that it otherwise met 'the necessary conditions for its recognition'.
- Opinion No. 6 (11 January 1992): The opinion was that Macedonia satisfied the test for recognition.
- Opinion No. 7 (11 January 1992): The opinion was that Slovenia satisfied the test for recognition.
- Opinion No. 8 (4 July 1992): The question was whether the dissolution of the SFRY was complete. The answer was affirmative.

---

115 For further details and discussion on the background, composition, (revised and clarified) rules of procedure and the opinions of the 'reconstituted' 1993 Arbitration Commission, see 32 *ILM* (1993) at p. 1572 et seq.; Terrett, op. cit. n. 93, at pp. 199-253; and Craven, loc. cit. n. 98, at pp. 396-409.

116 This opinion was given *after* the Community and its Member States had decided to adopt sanctions, precisely because Yugoslavia was dissolving. See *supra* section 2.2.1.

117 See *infra* section 2.6.4.

- Opinion No. 9 (4 July 1992): The question was how to settle the problems of succession of the SFRY. The answer was that the successor states must negotiate equitable solutions, based on the principles of the 1978 Vienna Convention on Succession of States in Respect of Treaties.
- Opinion No. 10 (4 July 1992): The question was whether the Federal Republic of Yugoslavia (the federation of Serbia and Montenegro, including Kosovo) was a new state eligible for recognition in accordance with the 'Guidelines' adopted by the EC. The answer was positive.

2.6.3 *The question of self-determination*

One of the most important contributions of the Badinter Arbitration Commission's practice in connection with the dissolution of Yugoslavia was the primacy given to the right of self-determination over the other principles of integrity of the state, non-intervention in internal matters and inviolability of borders.[118] In 1990, Hurst Hannum wrote that

> [p]erhaps no contemporary norm of international law has been so vigorously promoted or widely accepted as the right of all peoples to self-determination. Yet the meaning and content of that right remain as vague and imprecise as when they were enunciated by President Woodrow Wilson and others at Versailles.[119]

Precisely because self-determination is 'one of those unexceptionable goals that can be neither defined nor opposed',[120] I will make use of a working definition so as not to unnecessarily complicate the nature of this study. Generally speaking, the right to self-determination is the right of all peoples of existing states to freely determine their political and legal status (external self-determination) and to choose for themselves a form of democratic government and pursue their economic, social and cultural development (internal self-determination).[121]

Self-determination is enshrined as a principle in Article 1 of the UN Charter and as right of all peoples in Article 1 of the 1966 UN Conventions on Human Rights as well as in a number of other international documents.[122] Today, it is

---

[118] See Terrett, op. cit. n. 93, at pp. 254-308.

[119] H. Hannum, *Autonomy, Sovereignty, and Self-Determination: The Accommodation of Conflicting Rights* (Philadelphia, University of Pennsylvania Press 1990) at p. 27.

[120] M. Halperin, D. Scheffer and P. Small, *Self-Determination in the New World Order* (Washington D.C., Carnegie Endowment for International Peace 1992) at p. xi.

[121] This begs the question what is meant by the term 'peoples'. It is generally accepted that this entails all persons living in a given state that comprise a distinctive grouping on the basis of race, ethnicity, religion, etc. For detailed legal analyses, see the literature referred to *infra* n. 123.

[122] E.g., Final Act of the Helsinki Conference, Part III, Principle 8; and Art. 20 of the 1981 African Charter of Human and Peoples' Rights.

generally accepted that self-determination is not merely a political principle but a legally enforceable collective human right of a peremptory nature.[123] However, before the collapse of the Berlin Wall, the right of self-determination was generally applied only to the situations of colonised and dependent peoples overseas (from Europe, i.e., in Africa and Asia). The question as to whether it could be applied in a post-colonial context and within an existing state was more controversial at the beginning of the nineties than it is now. In its first statement mentioning self-determination in the Yugoslav context, the Community did not solve the dilemma and just quoted parts of the Paris Charter: 'the right of peoples to self-determination in conformity with the Charter of the UN and with the relevant norms of international law, including those relating to the territorial integrity of states.'[124] It was not until a few months later, in their 'Guidelines on the Recognition of New States', that the EC Member States adopted a more clear-cut attitude and declared: 'The Community and its Member States confirm their attachment to the principles of the Helsinki Final Act and the Charter of Paris, in particular the principle of self-determination.'[125] With that document, and the 'Declaration on Yugoslavia',[126] they declared their readiness to recognise different Yugoslav republics on the basis of unilateral declarations of independence and without consideration of the fact that there no agreement had been reached within the Yugoslav federation or between the republics themselves.[127]

Interestingly, several provisions of the 1974 Constitution of Yugoslavia expressly proclaimed that Yugoslavia was based upon and actually constituted an incarnation of the principle of self-determination of peoples, nations and nationalities and also pursued self-determination as an objective of foreign policy.[128] But

---

123 See, e.g., C. Tomuschat, ed., *Modern Law of Self-Determination* (Dordrecht, Martinus Nijhoff Publishers 1993); A. Cassese, *Self-Determination of Peoples – A Legal Appraisal* (Cambridge, Cambridge University Press 1995); and D. Raič, *Statehood and the Law of Self-Determination* (The Hague, Kluwer Law International 2002).

124 EPC Joint Statement of 5 July 1991, *Bull. EC* 7/8-1991, point 1.4.3.

125 *Bull. EC* 12-1991, point 1.4.5.

126 *Bull. EC* 12-1991, point 1.4.6.

127 For the reaction from the side of the remaining federal bodies, see 32 *Yugoslav Survey* (1991) at p. 4. The Federal Assembly, composed only of Serbian, Montenegrin and some Bosnian and Macedonian representatives, adopted a declaration on 21 December 1991 which stated: 'Unilateral acts of recognition of individual Yugoslav Republics, by individual states or groups of states would be incompatible with the principles and provisions of the Charter of the United Nations, the Declaration on Principles of International Law Concerning Friendly Relations and Cooperation among States, and the Declaration on the Inadmissibility of Intervention and Interference in the Internal Affairs of States, as well as with those of the CSCE. Consequently, such acts would be a gross violation of the sovereignty and territorial integrity of the SFRY and of the principle of inviolability of its frontiers.'

128 The 1974 Constitution is reprinted in S. Trifunovska, ed., *Yugoslavia Through Documents: From its Creation to its Dissolution* (Dordrecht, Martinus Nijhoff Publishers 1994) at pp. 125-134. See, e.g., the Preamble ('Introductory Part – Basic Principles'), Principles I, III and VII, as well as Arts. 1, 2, 244-249. The 1974 Constitution was amended in 1988 but no right of self-determination was provided for.

the Constitution did not make specific provision for the right of one of the six constituent republics to secede. On the contrary, Article 5(4) stipulated that '[t]he frontiers of the [SFRY] may not be altered without the consent of all Republics and Autonomous Provinces.' The achievement of independence by Slovenia, Croatia, Bosnia-Herzegovina and Macedonia could therefore be seen as a revolutionary process that had taken place beyond the control of the existing body of laws.[129]

The Badinter Arbitration Commission tackled some general legal problems in its first three opinions. In doing so, the Commission did not directly consider the applicability of the principle of self-determination in relation to the acts of independence of the various republics, but it did stress the importance of the 'rights of peoples and minorities' and even defined the norms that provided for these as part of *jus cogens*.[130] In the following four opinions, the Commission made pronouncements on the requests for recognition made by four of the six republics. In all four opinions, the Commission ascertained, in particular, whether referenda on independence had been held in each republic and whether each republic had committed itself to respecting the rights of individuals, groups and minorities. Strikingly, whereas in the cases of Croatia, Macedonia and Slovenia it was found that these requirements had been satisfied, in the case of Bosnia-Herzegovina it was emphasised that no referendum had been held involving the *whole* population[131] and therefore that not all criteria for statehood had been fulfilled. The Commission went on to say that this appraisal could be modified if 'safeguards' were established by Bosnia-Herzegovina, 'if necessary by way of a referendum in which all citizens of the Republic were to participate, under international supervision.'[132]

There is little doubt that Opinion No. 1 and the legal reasoning in the other opinions of the Badinter Arbitration Commission, together with the practice of the EC Council, have legally recognised the right of secession of federal units,

---

[129] However, the Yugoslav breakaway republics deemed it fit to hold referenda before declaring their independence. Slovenia: on 23 December 1990, 94.5 per cent voted in favour of independence; Croatia: on 19 May 1991, 93.2 per cent voted in favour of independence; Macedonia: on 8 September 1991, 95 per cent voted in favour of independence. On 11 April 1991, the presidents of the six republics reached agreement to hold a referendum in each of the republics except for Slovenia (thus including Bosnia-Herzegovina) on the future of the country. However, the referendum proposals ran into problems towards the end of April as divisions occurred on the scheduling of the vote.

[130] See Opinion No. 1.

[131] Instead, a plebiscite had been held on 10 November 1991 by the 'Serbian people of Bosnia-Herzegovina,' which had opted for a 'common Yugoslav state'.

[132] From 29 February to 1 March 1992, a Bosnian referendum was held. The turnout was 63 per cent. The overwhelming majority of Bosnian Serbs, accounting for 31 per cent of the population, boycotted the vote. Of those voting, 99.4 per cent opted for independence. Subsequently, on 6 April 1992, the EC and the twelve Member States granted their recognition, followed the next day by the United States and Croatia. Bosnia-Herzegovina was admitted to the United Nations on 22 May 1992.

albeit under the basic condition that a referendum is held in which *all* the citizens of a republic are to participate. The Badinter Arbitration Commission thus elevated the referendum, the 'internal' dimension of self-determination, to the status of a basic requirement to legitimate unilateral secession. Hence, the Yugoslav crisis reveals that, as a consequence of the dissolution of a state, peoples are not legally precluded from exercising a qualified right to unilateral secession, even outside the colonial context.[133]

The Badinter Arbitration Commission (as well as the EC and its Member States, for that matter) stopped short of granting all peoples a right to secession, regardless of the circumstances. It seems to have made a distinction between two types of situations. On the one hand, the right to external self-determination was granted to peoples inhabiting regional units, the territorial limits of which had previously been defined by an autonomous government and administration *and* which were direct constituent parts of the federation (i.e., 'republics'). Contrary to what was laid down in the 1974 Constitution of the SFRY, the Serbian 'autonomous provinces' of Kosovo and Vojvodina, which were represented at the federal level but which belonged to the Republic of Serbia, were not granted the same right to external self-determination. On the other hand, a special status was granted to persons belonging to groupings (i) that were minorities within republics (e.g., Serbs in Croatia); (ii) that belonged to a majority living in another republic of the SFRY or another state altogether (e.g., Albanians of Kosovo); and (iii) whose territorial limits were not predefined (e.g., Serbs or Croats in Bosnia-Herzegovina). Such minorities were offered legal protection under Article 27 of the 1966 UN Convention on Civil and Political Rights.[134] In the Yugoslav case, it therefore seems that the Badinter Arbitration Commission, the EC and its Member States linked the granting of the right to external self-determination to territorial units dubbed 'republics' and not directly to the peoples inhabiting them.[135] This is especially clear from Opinions Nos. 2 and 4 concerning the question of the Serbian 'population' in Bosnia-Herzegovina and the recognition of Bosnia-Herzegovina, respectively. In Opinion No. 2, Serbs in Bosnia-Herzegovina were declared to be a minority, entitled to minority and human rights recognised in international law but not to the right of secession.[136] In Opinion No.

133 See Weller, loc. cit. n. 70, at p. 606; J. Crawford, 'State Practice and International Law in Relation to Secession', 69 *BYIL* (1999) pp. 85-117; and Raič, op. cit. n. 123, at pp. 308-397, in particular at pp. 342-366 and 386-394.

134 For a critical note in this respect, see Craven, loc. cit. n. 98, at pp. 390-391.

135 Contrary to what is laid down in the 1974 Constitution of the SFRY, which speaks in its preamble and Article 1 of the right to self-determination and secession of the Yugoslav peoples, not of the administrative units.

136 The Arbitration Commission, while discussing their rights, did not take into consideration the internal and constitutional aspects of the position of the national communities in Bosnia-Herzegovina and Croatia. Opinion No. 2 was issued several months before Bosnia-Herzegovina was recognised,

4, as discussed above, the 'citizens' of Bosnia-Herzegovina, without distinction, were recognised as having a unilateral right of self-determination by means of referendum.[137]

The underlying idea for the Community's stance towards the implementation of the right to self-determination was, of course, to pose certain limits on the disintegration of states in order to safeguard, as far as possible, the principle of inviolability of borders and, thus, to be able to counter claims from existing states to agree to a real territorial autonomy of their minorities abroad.[138] However, it is dubious whether the level of protection of national minorities would have been better if there was a parallel tendency to offer less protection to the stability of the existing republics.[139]

2.6.4 *The question of recognition*

As has been highlighted already, another question considered during the first episode of the Yugoslav crises concerned the conditions of recognition of the former federal units which had declared independence. Contrary to the case of the former Soviet Union, there was no internal agreement on the independence of the federal units of the SFRY, and the question of recognition was dealt with in parallel with the armed conflict.[140] In its 'Guidelines on the Recognition of New States',[141] the EC warned that it would not recognise entities that were the result of aggression, which seemed applicable only to newly emerging entities (i.e.,

---

but the entire opinion was based on principles of international law only. For the Serbian position on the question of self-determination, see the position of the Presidency of the SFRY, published in 43 *Review of International Affairs* (1992) pp. 21-23.

[137] There was no 'majority' nation/people in Bosnia-Herzegovina. Consequently, 'self-determination' was not based on the right of a 'people' but of all 'citizens'.

[138] See C. Warbrick, 'Recognition of States (Current Developments)', 41 *ICLQ* (1992) at p. 480: 'The idea of self-determination looks to be an inherently destabilizing notion.'

[139] A good example is the situation in Croatia. The self-determination granted to the Croat people greatly contributed to the disappearance of the SFRY. On the other hand, the Serb community in Croatia was deprived the status of 'equal' and 'constitutive' people of Croatia, granted by the 1974 Constitution of the SFRY. Serbs were promised a 'special status', but Croatia was recognised in spite of the fact that it did not fulfil its obligations concerning this status. Moreover, it is difficult to see how the creation of small 'nation states' in the Balkans, replacing the SFRY, would in any way improve the position of minorities *within* each of those states. As for the protection given by international law, Pellet states: 'A vrai dire, "les droits reconnus aux minorités par les conventions internationales en vigueur" se limitent à peu de choses.' Pellet, loc. cit. n. 100, at p. 339.

[140] On the recognition of states, see, e.g., R. Bieber, 'European Community Recognition of Eastern European States: A New Perspective for International Law?', 86 *Proceedings of the ASIL* (1992) p. 374 et seq.; R. Rich, 'Recognition of States: The Collapse of Yugoslavia and the Soviet Union', 4 *EJIL* (1993) pp. 36-65; C. Warbrick, 'Recognition of States: Part 2', 42 *ICLQ* (1993) pp. 433-442; Weller, loc. cit. n. 70; and P. Hilpold, 'Die Anerkennung der Neustaaten auf dem Balkan', 31 *Archiv des Völkerrechts* (1993) pp. 387-408.

[141] *Bull. EC* 12-1991, point 1.4.5.

after 16 December 1991), but not to the former federal units engaged in the struggle.

The 'Guidelines' prescribed that only states that fulfilled 'the normal standards of international practice' (i.e., statehood)[142] and 'the political realities'[143] would be entitled to recognition, if they had:

(i) 'constituted themselves on a democratic basis' (i.e., if they had organised referenda on independence);
(ii) accepted the appropriate international obligations (e.g., the UN Charter, the Helsinki Final Act and the Charter of Paris); and
(iii) 'committed themselves in good faith to a peaceful process and to negotiations'.

Furthermore, the EC enumerated all the conditions for the recognition of the countries of Central and Eastern Europe, including respect for the rule of law, democracy, human and minority rights, respect for borders and a commitment to disarmament and to peaceful dispute settlement by way of arbitration. In addition, the Yugoslav republics were to accept the 'draft Convention' under consideration by the Conference on Yugoslavia, and especially the provisions of chapter II on human rights and the rights of national and ethnic groups.[144] It is interesting to note that the principal issues of discussion in the Badinter Arbitration Commission concerned not so much the legal conditions of recognition, but the political requirements, such as the principle of effective control, a classic criterion for recognition of states but absent from the 'Guidelines on the Recognition of New States' and the 'Declaration on Yugoslavia.'[145]

Although the EC and its Member States reiterated, in various ways, their reliance on traditional international legal criteria for recognition, their policy of non-recognition of various states was far from being a consistent application of legal criteria.[146] Thus, Slovenia, which had fulfilled all traditional criteria since July 1991 (Opinion No. 7), remained unrecognised by the EC until mid-January 1992.

---

142 Art. 1 of the 1933 Montevideo Convention on Rights and Duties of States, 165 *LNTS* 19 (1933): 'The state as a person of international law should possess the following qualifications: (a) a permanent population; (b) a defined territory; (c) government; and (d) capacity to enter into relations with other states.' On the concepts of and (traditional and additional) criteria for statehood, see, extensively, Raič, op. cit. n. 123, at pp. 19-168.

143 Rich, loc. cit. n. 140, at p. 43, observes that this rider is a stark reminder of Lauterpacht's comment that recognition of states is a matter of policy, but that it has rarely been expressed in such a direct way. See H. Lauterpacht, *Recognition in International Law* (Cambridge, Cambridge University Press 1947) at p. 1.

144 EPC 'Declaration on Yugoslavia', *Bull. EC* 12-1991, point 1.4.6.

145 See Warbrick, loc. cit. n. 138, at p. 482.

146 It is important to note that the Badinter Arbitration Commission itself was accurate and consistent in its Opinions Nos. 4-8.

Macedonia, which also fulfilled all criteria, at least since the end of 1991 (Opinion No. 6), remained unrecognised for a much longer period due to a dispute over its name.[147] Serbia and Montenegro, as republics with equal standing in law, constituted a new state (the FRY) and were recognised as such by the Badinter Arbitration Commission in Opinion No. 8, a decision which was not heeded with serious action by the EC and its Member States. On the other hand, Croatia was recognised even though it had not fully implemented the provisions concerning the 'special status' for the Serb minority (Opinion No. 5), a fact which remained without consequences for months.[148] Bosnia-Herzegovina, which was unable to fulfil the criterion of effective control, was recognised in April 1992 after it had organised a referendum, as it had been urged to do by the Badinter Arbitration Commission in its Opinion No. 4.[149]

It is clear that the legal conditions incorporated in the 'Guidelines on the Recognition of New States' and the 'Declaration on Yugoslavia', as imposed on the breakaway states of the former Yugoslavia by the Badinter Arbitration Commission in its opinions, were manipulated by the EC Member States to influence and direct the behaviour of the recipients.[150] EC recognition of the ex-Yugoslav

[147] This problem was eventually spelled out in an EPC Statement of 2 May 1992, *Bull. EC* 5-1992, in which the EC Member States referred to the former Yugoslav republic of Macedonia and said that they were 'willing to recognise that state as a sovereign and independent state within its existing borders and under a name that can be accepted by all parties concerned.' At the European Council summit in Lisbon on 26-27 June 1992, the EC even went a step further when it once again declared its willingness to recognise that republic 'under a name which does not include the term Macedonia.' See *Bull. EC* 6-1992, point I-1. The latter condition was unacceptable to Macedonia. See M. Craven, 'What's in a Name? The Former Yugoslav Republic of Macedonia and Issues of Statehood', 16 *Australian YIL* (1995) pp. 199-239.

[148] See the Badinter Arbitration Commission's comments on Croatia's constitutional law of 4 December 1991, as amended on 8 May 1992, 31 *ILM* (1992) at p. 1505.

[149] D. Türk, 'Recognition of States: A Comment', 4 *EJIL* (1993) pp. 66-71 at p. 69 argues that 'it would be wrong to conclude that recognition and admission of Bosnia-Herzegovina to the UN was necessarily a political mistake. The recognition of Bosnia-Herzegovina was not only fair and just, but also – paradoxically, in accordance with state practice. In the case of Bosnia-Herzegovina it should have been clear that the emerging state would need more than formal recognition, admission to the UN and establishment of diplomatic relations. The Conference on Yugoslavia could have been – but was not – used for the purpose of creating appropriate guarantees for the independence of Bosnia-Herzegovina. This omission was probably due to (i) divergent opinions among the major powers regarding the approach to the Yugoslav crisis in general, and (ii) the lack of readiness to act by force, if necessary, to protect the independence of Bosnia-Herzegovina and thus to give credibility to the international support for Bosnia's independence.'

[150] See J. Charpentier, 'Les declarations des Douze sur la reconnaissance des nouveaux Etats', 96 *RGDIP* (1992) p. I-343 et seq. at p. I-353. It could also be argued that the two declarations made the process of recognition more difficult because they purport to retain the 'normal standards of international practice' while adding a series of new requirements. Rich is of the opinion that, in fact, 'the new requirements have tended to supplant the previous practice [on the recognition of states,] which was largely based on meeting the traditional criteria for statehood.' In his view, these two documents have significantly transformed recognition law. See Rich, loc. cit. n. 140, at pp. 42-43. For a recent analysis of the strategic logic of conditional recognition by the EC in the case at hand,

republics was an entirely optional and discretionary political act. The recognition of states at a stage where they had not really consolidated their authority over the claimed territory would have constituted an illegal intervention under the traditional standards of international law. Nevertheless, the EC Member States recognised Bosnia-Herzegovina and Croatia, thus transforming 'early recognition' into a regulatory mechanism in order to secure the precedence of the right of self-determination over the competing claim for sovereignty still raised by the so-called 'federal' authorities.[151] Admittedly, there are good reasons for using recognition in such a way. A community of Western European states which has lifted self-determination to the heights of being one of the fundamental principles of international law – a norm of *jus cogens* – should not look aside when a ruthless regime tries to smother justified claims of self-determination in a bloodbath.[152] Doing so would mean that the international community degrades its fundamental norms to pure rhetoric.

2.6.5 *The question of frontiers*

A state can be recognised without its frontiers being fully defined.[153] The question of recognition is therefore not directly linked to border disputes. This was acknowledged by the EC in its EPC Joint Statement of 31 December 1991:

> Recognition shall not be taken to imply acceptance by the European Community and its Member States of the position of any of the republics concerning the territory which is the subject of a dispute between two or more republics.[154]

---

see R. Caplan, *Europe and the Recognition of New States in Yugoslavia* (Cambridge, Cambridge University Press 2005) at pp. 49-72.

151 See S. Oeter, 'Selbstbestimmungsrecht im Wandel: Überlegungen zur Debatte um Selbstbestimmung, Sezessionsrecht und 'vorzeitige' Anerkennung', 52 *ZaöRV* (1992) pp. 741-780.

152 In fact, even heavier duties rest upon the shoulders of the international community of states to make sure that human rights and fundamental freedoms – of a *jus cogens* nature – are not grossly and persistently violated. On the (conditional) duty to intervene (if need be militarily) in a state's internal affairs on humanitarian grounds, see, e.g., M. Sornarajah, 'Internal Colonialism and Humanitarian Intervention', 11 *Georgia Journal of International and Comparative Law* (1981) p. 75 et seq.; H.G. Schermers, 'The Obligation to Intervene in the Domestic Affairs of States', in A. Delissen and G. Tanja, eds., *Humanitarian Law of Armed Conflict – Challenges Ahead. Essays in Honour of Frits Kalshoven* (Dordrecht, Martinus Nijhoff Publishers 1991) pp. 583-593; V.P. Nanda, 'Tragedies in Northern Iraq, Liberia, Yugoslavia, and Haiti – Revisiting the Validity of Humanitarian Intervention under International Law – Part I', 20 *Denver Journal of International Law and Policy* (1992) pp. 305-334; A. Cassese, 'Ex Iniuria Ius Oritur: Are We Moving towards International Legitimation of Forcible Humanitarian Countermeasures in the World Community?', 10 *EJIL* (1999) pp. 23-30; S. Blockmans, Moving into UNchartered Waters: An Emerging Right of Unilateral Humanitarian Intervention', 12 *LJIL* (1999) pp. 759-786.

153 Cf., Albania (1912) and Israel (1948).

154 *Bull. EC* 12-1991, point 1.4.13.

The argument that self-determination must not involve changes to existing frontiers at the time of independence can easily be accepted as regards established international borders.[155] The real question was whether the formerly internal boundaries that demarcated the various republics within the SFRY for administrative purposes, especially between Serbia, Croatia and Bosnia-Herzegovina, could be regarded as international borders. This was vehemently opposed by Serbia and the remaining federal representatives (from Serbia, Montenegro, Bosnia-Herzegovina and Macedonia), which linked the issue to the question of self-determination of 'constituent nations' in each of the republics (e.g., the Serbs in Bosnia-Herzegovina). The Federal Presidency stated that the republican borders were drawn up by the Communist regime in 1945, without democratic or public procedure and without consideration of ethnic, economic, political or other principles.[156] It argued that these borders should consequently be regarded as mere administrative demarcations. According to the Federal Presidency, prior to the recognition of separate republics, 'borders between the new states would have to be drawn with due respect for the relevant international legal norms.'[157] The position of the other Yugoslav republics was that the internal administrative borders should automatically become international frontiers.

In its Opinion No. 3 of 11 January 1992, the Badinter Arbitration Commission took the view that

> [e]xcept where otherwise agreed, the former boundaries become frontiers protected by international law. This conclusion follows from the principle of respect for territorial status quo and, in particular, from the principle of *uti possidetis*, which is today recognized as a general principle.

As explained by the ICJ in the *Burkina Faso and Mali Frontier Dispute* case, *uti possidetis juris* 'is a general principle, which is logically connected with the phenomenon of the obtaining of independence, wherever it occurs. Its obvious purpose is to prevent the independence and stability of new states being endangered by fratricidal struggles.'[158] The Commission's decision to generally apply the principle of *uti possidetis juris* outside the context of decolonisation – which was new for Europe[159] – is explained by Marc Weller as the enlargement of the

155 See, e.g., 'Declaration on the granting of independence to colonial countries and peoples', UNGA resolution 1514 (1960); and 'Declaration on Principles of International Law Concerning Friendly Relations and Co-operation Among States in Accordance with the Charter of the United Nations', UNGA resolution 2625 (1970).

156 See 43 *Review of International Affairs* (1992) at p. 23.

157 Ibid.

158 *ICJ Reports* 1986, at 554.

159 For an overview of the subtle changes in the evolution of the principle of *uti possidetis*, see J. Klabbers and R. Lefeber, 'Africa: Lost between Self-Determination and Uti Possidetis', in C. Brölmann, R. Lefeber and M. Zieck, eds., *Peoples and Minorities in International Law* (Dordrecht, Martinus Nijhoff Publishers 1993) pp. 37-42; and Raič, op. cit. n. 123, at pp. 293-305.

protection of international law to the 'nascent states' on the territory of the former Yugoslavia.[160] As a question of policy, there is a strong case for arguing an expansive view of the principle's field of application. The application of *uti possidetis* in the Yugoslav case was preferable, in the short term at least, to the delimitation of boundaries on the basis of unstable and shifting forces of nationalist sentiment or on the basis of a strict application of the principle of effective control. The escalation of violence, provoked essentially by territorial disputes, prompted the EC Member States to take a more defined view and urge Belgrade to commit itself to the 'respect for the integrity of all borders of all republics.'[161] Nevertheless, one may question whether this is a legal technique that will provide a permanent and pacific settlement of the underlying territorial disputes. If *uti possidetis* is to apply to all cases of 'independence', there is nothing to preclude its further application within each of the republics even after their statehood has been established.

Ultimately, two different processes are at work here. Firstly, the identification of presumptive units of statehood, whether it be in virtue of the principle of effective control or self-determination. And secondly, the determination of boundaries within which those entities are to be confined. In its original guise, the principle of *uti possidetis* only serves to address the second question and does not provide a coherent basis for establishing the statehood of the emerging entities. The manner in which the Badinter Arbitration Commission addressed the issue, however, was to use *uti possidetis* as a tool for establishing the presumptive statehood of the entities to emerge from the dismemberment of the SFRY and to deny the autonomous provinces of Kosovo and Vojvodina, as well as the self-proclaimed Serbian republics in Krajina and Bosnia-Herzegovina, the benefit of that presumption. If the Arbitration Commission's first opinions are taken together as a coherent whole – which is not unreasonable given the fact that the first three were handed down on the same day – one is left with the view that, owing to a collapse in central government, the SFRY fell into a process of dismemberment in which, through application of the principle of *uti possidetis*, the succeeding entities were presumptively deemed to be the six republics. This being the case, it is clear that the principle of self-determination had little overall influence on territorial settlement. It is also apparent that the principle of effective control played only a subordinate role – it being suggested that in virtue of the internationalisation of their borders, each of the constituent republics of the former SFRY enjoyed *prima facie* statehood, irrespective of the effectiveness of their government. The principle of *uti possidetis* was employed *a priori* to protect the integrity of the constitutionally-defined territorial units which were then, and

---

160 See Weller, loc. cit. n. 70, at p. 589.

161 EPC Joint Statement of 5 May 1992, *Bull. EC* 5-1992, point 1.3.4.

only then, able or entitled to exercise some form of external self-determination, whether that be full independence or integration into a confederation of states. In other words, a principle of boundary delimitation was used as the primary determining tool not only for the shape of the new territorial entities but also for their international personality as states.

2.6.6 *The question of succession*

Another object of disagreement between the six republics was whether, legally speaking, some of them seceded from the SFRY or whether the federation simply dissolved and disappeared. Of course, the differences had more important political – rather than legal – implications for the republics.

The Vienna Conventions on Succession of States in Respect of Treaties (1978)[162] and Succession in Respect of State Property, Archives and Debts (1983)[163] lay down, in a similar fashion, the rules of succession in the cases of dismemberment and secession. Perhaps the most important difference between the two scenarios concerns the membership of a state in international organisations, which is automatic in the case of the continuity of the state. In the Declaration on the Promulgation of the Constitution of the FRY of 27 April 1992, the parliament of the new federation stated that:

> The Federal Republic of Yugoslavia, continuing the state, international legal and political personality of the SFRY, shall strictly abide by all the commitments that the SFRY assumed internationally in the past.[164]

The Badinter Arbitration Commission declared on 4 July 1992 that 'the process of dissolution of the SFRY is now complete and that the SFRY no longer exists.'[165] It also ruled that 'the FRY (Serbia and Montenegro) is a new state which cannot be considered the sole successor of the SFRY.'[166] The consequences of the foregoing were that the FRY should not automatically succeed to the SFRY's seats in international organisations or its property abroad. The property had to be divided equitably between the SFRY's various successor states by agreement or arbitration.[167] Unsurprisingly, the EC Council of Ministers adopted the same position: '[i]t is for Serbia and Montenegro to decide whether they wish to form a

---

162 Reprinted in 72 *AJIL* (1978) p. 971.

163 22 *ILM* (1983) p. 306.

164 Cited in Lopandić, loc. cit. n. 26, at p. 345.

165 See Opinion No. 8.

166 See Opinion No. 10.

167 The UN Security Council dealt with the question in a more definitive way in its resolution 777 of 19 September 1992. This resolution, and UNGA resolution 47/1 of the same date, settled the continuity issue by specifically denying the FRY's claims.

new federation. But this new federation cannot be accepted as the sole successor to the former Socialist Federal Republic of Yugoslavia.'[168]

For reasons already mentioned, these decisions made political sense. But, from a legal point of view, this attitude is questionable, as neither the Badinter Commission nor the EC and its Member States took into account that there was no formal interruption in the functioning of the Yugoslav federal organs and that Serbia and Montenegro did not declare their independence from the SFRY, as the other republics did. In addition, the FRY had the advantage of possession. The SFRY's foreign service had been progressively stripped from its non-Serbian or non-Montenegrin representatives, and the personnel in the Yugoslav missions abroad were consequently by and large loyal to Belgrade. It is also interesting to point out the different approaches of the EC to the question of state succession in the cases of the USSR and Yugoslavia.[169] In the first case, Russia was accepted as continuing the international position and obligations of the former Soviet Union, including its status in the United Nations. For political reasons, however, the FRY was denied the right to continue the status of the former SFRY without a renewed application to the United Nations.[170]

2.6.7 *General legal observations*

On the basis of the foregoing, some observations can be made concerning the 'European' application of international law in the first phase of the Yugoslav crisis. Firstly, the opinions of the Badinter Arbitration Commission represent a unique and important examination of a whole range of legal issues relating to statehood, recognition, self-determination, territorial integrity and succession in relation to the break-up of a single state. Secondly, it has become clear that the

---

168 EPC Joint Statement of 20 July 1992, *Bull. EC* 7/8-1992, point 1.5.5.

169 See M. Bohte and C. Schmidt, 'Sur quelques questions de succession posées par la dissolution de l'URSS et celle de la Yougoslavie', 96 *RGDIP* (1992) p. II-811 et seq.; R. Mullerson, 'The Continuity and Succession of States by Reference to the Former USSR and Yugoslavia', 42 *ICLQ* (1993) pp. 473-493; O. Schachter, et al., 'Symposium: State Succession in the Former Soviet Union and in Eastern Europe', 33 *Virginia JIL* (1993) pp. 253-350. On succession of states, see generally M. Shaw, 'State Succession Revisited', 5 *Finnish YIL* (1994) pp. 34-98; M. Craven, 'The Genocide Case, the Law of Treaties and State Succession', 68 *BYIL* (1998) pp. 127-163; M. Mrak, *Succession of States* (The Hague, Martinus Nijhoff Publishers 1999); and J. Klabbers, M. Koskenniemi, O. Ribbelink and A. Zimmermann, eds., *State Practice Regarding State Succession and Issues of Recognition: The Pilot Project of the Council of Europe* (The Hague, Kluwer Law International 1999).

170 The official attitude towards the FRY is contested as contrary to UN practice in Y. Blum, 'UN Membership of the "New" Yugoslavia: Continuity or Break?', 86 *AJIL* (1992) pp. 830-833. See also M. Scharf, 'Musical Chairs: The Dissolution of States and Membership in the United Nations', 28 *Cornell ILJ* (1995) pp. 29-69; and K. Bühler, *State Succession and Membership in International Organizations: Legal Theories versus Political Pragmatism* (The Hague, Kluwer Law International 2001) at pp. 180-272.

use of international legal norms was extremely politically oriented. International law was an instrument which directly and immediately had to serve the political objectives of the EC and its Member States. Only the rules which matched these objectives were applied. Thirdly, international law was used in order to regulate a conflict which was – at the outset – an internal one. Fourthly, some principles, such as respect for human and minority rights and the almost absolute prohibition on the use of force, were a priority for the EC and its Member States in dealing with the Yugoslav crises, while the principle of the integrity of states and the stability of social and political orders seemed less important. The process of dismemberment did not identify *per se* the presumptive units for future statehood. The Badinter Arbitration Commission established that this was to be determined not by resort to the principle of self-determination, nor by a strict application of the principle of effective control of government over the claimed territory, but rather in virtue of the principle of *uti possidetis*: independent territorial units that exist within the borders of a former administrative unit have to establish their statehood as against the presumptive effectiveness of the unit as a whole. Finally, the right to self-determination was closely linked to respect for human rights, while at the same time it could provide grounds for the secession of federal units of the former Yugoslavia if some basic political conditions were met (i.e., the holding of a referendum representing the whole population). In the latter situation, the SFRY was not allowed to use force against democratic secessionist movements. In sum, a principle of boundary delimitation was used as the primary determining tool for the international personality of new territorial entities as states.

2.7 Impact of EC intervention

Despite all the efforts during one year of sanctions policies, troika mediation, the deployment of the EC Monitoring Mission, the organisation of the Conference on Yugoslavia and the work of the Badinter Arbitration Commission, the EC did not succeed in preventing the further escalation of the Yugoslav crisis. In August 1992, when a new and bigger peace conference (ICFY) was organised in London, now under the auspices of the United Nations, the problems created by the destruction of Yugoslavia and the war in Bosnia-Herzegovina looked much more difficult and complicated to resolve than a year before. Whatever the reasons for this, suffice it to say that the European Community was not prepared for such a difficult and complex conflict: it did not possess the appropriate instruments to influence developments on the ground and lacked the military muscle to back up its diplomatic efforts if need be. Its classic foreign policy instrument, the EPC, was crippled by the differing positions of the Member States and by the slow and consensual nature of its decision making. The *Alleingang* of Germany, which did not wait until the end of the arbitration process to recognise Slovenia and Croatia (23 December 1991), blew the EC's cover. And while the Badinter Arbitration

Commission on 11 January 1992 recommended that only Slovenia and Macedonia be granted recognition, the EC and its Member States chose to ignore its opinions.[171] Slovenia *and* Croatia were recognised (15 January 1992), while Macedonia was not, as its recognition was vetoed by Greece, which objected to the name of the country on the grounds that it implied territorial ambition towards Greece's own northern province of the same name.

Thus, the EC's first confident experiment in common foreign policy making ended in shambles, the Community's own carefully formulated legal and diplomatic mechanisms shot down by old-fashioned political expediency. It was a major blow to the principles of foreign policy, exactly at the time of signature of the Maastricht Treaty.[172] With hindsight, one can state that perhaps the most important elements in the Community's policy towards the Yugoslav crisis were the adoption of the 'Guidelines on the Recognition of New States', the opinions rendered by the Badinter Arbitration Commission and the subsequent premature recognition of Croatia. While the political fall-out of the EC Council's decisions destroyed the chances for a comprehensive solution (as well as its own role in that process)[173] and precipitated the catastrophe in Bosnia-Herzegovina,[174] the European Community did make serious attempts to limit the consequences of the violent dissolution of Yugoslavia and cajole the most bloodthirsty of warring parties into accepting a peaceful resolution of the conflict. The EC certainly showed imagination by creating specific instruments to reach a peaceful settlement: a peace conference, arbitration and monitoring. In the development of these initiatives, the EC remained consistent in advocating peaceful means for solving the conflict. It condemned and tried to limit and dissuade the use of force, and

---

171 See Türk, loc. cit. n. 149, at p. 70: 'In short, the opinions of the Arbitration Commission of the Conference on Yugoslavia were legally consistent and correct, notwithstanding their inconsistent implementation and the silence of the Commission with regard to some questions which were of obvious relevance. The latter shortcoming was caused by political barriers and was not consequent from a decision of the Arbitration Commission itself.'

172 Ironically, some claim that the Yugoslav case was 'sacrificed' by the United Kingdom and France in order to satisfy the German desire to recognise Croatia and thus to achieve a balance in the negotiations in the pre-Maastricht IGC. See Caplan, op. cit. n. 150, at p. 48.

173 Recognition hardened Slovenia's and Croatia's demands but further alienated Serbia and, as such, brought an effective end to the EC-sponsored peace talks in the framework of the Conference on Yugoslavia. In Lord Carrington's words: '[Recognition] torpedo[ed] the conference,' cited in Caplan, op. cit. n. 150, at p. 96.

174 See D. Owen, *Balkan Odyssey* (New York, Harcourt Brace & Co. 1995) at p. 46: '[L]ike pouring petrol on a smouldering fire.' Richard Caplan has criticised the general reading that recognition, more than any other single factor, has aggravated and extended the war in Yugoslavia. He has convincingly argued that 'in at least one critical respect the debate over recognition is misconceived: for the real relevance of recognition lies with the opportunities for more effective international action that it created. It was the failure to seize these opportunities, rather than the strategic effects of recognition, that better explains the tragic events that ensued.' Caplan, op. cit. n. 150, at pp. 97-98.

repeated without fail the importance of respect for human and minorities rights, democracy and the need for a negotiated compromise.

3. SURFING THE WAVES OF INTERNATIONAL MEDIATION (1992-1998)

3.1 Political objectives

As of 11 January 1992, the EC/EU gave way to the efforts of others to stop the escalation of war and violence in ex-Yugoslavia. The United Nations, and later the Contact Group and NATO, built on the record and experience of European mediation. All financial sanctions, visa and travel bans adopted by the EC/EU during this period were basically an implementation of the restrictive measures adopted by the UN Security Council against the Federal Republic of Yugoslavia. All restrictions aimed at calling a halt to the breaches of international peace and security in the region and the unacceptable loss of human life and material damage. The measures adopted to this end were also geared at dissuading the FRY from further violating the integrity and security of Bosnia-Herzegovina and at inducing the federation of Serbia and Montenegro to cooperate in the restoration of dialogue with the other parties to the conflict. For reasons explained above, the discussion here will only focus on unilaterally adopted sanctions by the European Union.[175] During the period under review, only one autonomous sanction decision was adopted by the European Union. It has been mostly overlooked in the literature and is therefore worth pointing out.

At the end of 1995, a controversial peace agreement reached after heavy American arm-twisting on the Patterson-Wright air force base in Dayton (Ohio) ended the war in Bosnia-Herzegovina and therefore also the need for international sanctions.[176] One commentator has argued that, while all restrictions on economic and financial relations with the Federal Republic of Yugoslavia were terminated by the European Union on 18 December 1996 following the adoption of UN Security Council resolution 1074 (1996),[177] a whole 'outer wall of EU sanctions'

---

175 See *supra* nn. 5-7 and accompanying main text.

176 The present structure of the Republic of Bosnia-Herzegovina was established under the General Framework Agreement for Peace, initialled at Dayton on 21 November 1995 and signed at the Royaumont Palace in Paris on 14 December 1995, 35 *ILM* (1996) p. 75 et seq. For a brilliant account of the negotiations leading up to Dayton, see R. Holbrooke, *To End a War* (New York, Random House 1998). For an analysis of the problems concerning the implementation of the peace agreements, see S. Bose, *Bosnia after Dayton – Nationalist Partition and International Intervention* (London, Hurst & Company 2002).

177 Common Position 96/708/CFSP of 9 December 1996 defined by the Council on the basis of Article J.2 of the Treaty on European Union concerning the termination of restrictions on economic

remained in place: a set of political conditions for the normalisation of relations between the FRY and the European Union, ranging from respect for the Dayton Agreement and cooperation with the ICTY, via the introduction of democratic reforms and respect for human and minority rights, especially in Kosovo, to good neighbourly relations with the other countries of the former Yugoslavia and membership of the Council of Europe and the World Trade Organisation.[178] Whereas the European Union certainly gave the impression of paternalism by relying on a rigorous form of conditionality to normalise relations with the FRY, these conditions cannot be qualified as punitive measures but should be seen as elements of enforcement of the (then newly adopted) Regional Approach, an European Union strategy of engagement that accompanied the multilateral Royaumont Process for Stability and Good Neighbourliness in South-Eastern Europe.[179]

3.2 Arms embargo

While the UN arms embargo on the states of the former Yugoslavia was lifted in accordance with Security Council resolution 1021 of 22 November 1995, the European Union continued its own arms embargo of 5 July 1991 to ensure the safety of the international troops and civilian personnel stationed in Bosnia-Herzegovina and Croatia during the implementation of the Dayton Agreement.[180] The EU Council decided, firstly, that during the period of the deployment of IFOR and UNTAES, as well as other operations including the IPTF, the EU arms embargo on arms, munitions and military equipment[181] would be maintained

---

and financial relations with the Federal Republic of Yugoslavia (Serbia and Montenegro), the United Nations Protected Areas in the Republic of Croatia and those areas of the Republic of Bosnia and Herzegovina under the control of the Bosnian Serb forces, *OJ* 1996 L 328/3; and Council Regulation (EC) No. 2382/96 of 9 December 1996 repealing Regulations (EEC) No. 990/93 and (EC) No. 2471/94 and concerning the termination of restrictions on economic and financial relations with the Federal Republic of Yugoslavia (Serbia and Montenegro), the United Nations Protected Areas in the Republic of Croatia and those areas of the Republic of Bosnia and Herzegovina under the control of Bosnian Serb forces, *OJ* 1996 L 328/1.

178 See B. Alendar, 'Conditions for the Normalization of Relations between FR Yugoslavia and the European Union – The Outer Wall of Sanctions of the European Union', 49 *Review of International Affairs* (1998) at p. 7.

179 Council Conclusions of 29 April 1997 on the principle of conditionality governing the development of the EU's relations with certain countries of South East Europe, in *Bull. EU* 4-1997, point 2.2.1. Conditionality, i.e., making cooperation and assistance dependent on progress by a 'partner' – was indeed a strong feature in the EU-FRY relationship. See chapter 5.

180 Council Common Position 96/184/CFSP of 26 February 1996 defined by the Council on the basis of Article J.2 of the Treaty on European Union concerning arms exports to the former Yugoslavia, *OJ* 1996 L 58/1.

181 As listed in the Member States' embargo list of 5 July 1991. See *supra* section 2.2.1.

towards Bosnia-Herzegovina, Croatia and the Federal Republic of Yugoslavia.[182] Transfers of equipment needed for demining activities were not covered by the embargo. Secondly, subject to UN Security Council resolution 1021 (1995), export licence applications to Slovenia and Macedonia would be considered on a case-by-case basis.[183] This provision was adopted on the understanding that the Member States would show restraint in their arms export policy towards Slovenia and Macedonia, based on the common criteria for arms exports contained in the conclusions of the Luxembourg European Council of 28-29 June 1991 and the Lisbon European Council of 26-27 June 1992.[184] They would also take into account the objectives of the European Union's policy in the region, 'fundamentally aimed at pacification and stabilisation in the area, including the need for arms control and reduction to the lowest level and confidence-building measures.' On the understanding that the Member States would rigorously apply the EU Code of Conduct on arms exports adopted on 8 June 1998,[185] the EU arms embargo was lifted first for Slovenia (1998),[186] then Croatia (2000)[187] and the FRY (2001),[188] so as to take account of the improved circumstances in these countries. The embargo remained in place against Bosnia-Herzegovina until it was finally repealed on 23 January 2006, to take account of the overall progress made by the country, most crucially the fact that Bosnia-Herzegovina had adopted (and started implementing) EU-proof legislation on exports, imports and the transit of arms.[189]

3.3 Effectiveness of EU sanctions

As is amply demonstrated in the scholarly literature, proving the effectiveness of sanctions in changing the behaviour of their addressees is fraught with difficulties of measurement.[190] Drawing reliable conclusions on the effectiveness of the EU

---

[182] Art. 2(i) of Common Position 96/184/CFSP.

[183] Art. 2(ii) of Common Position 96/184/CFSP.

[184] See *Bull. EC* 6-1991, point I-1; and *Bull. EC* 6-1992, point I-1.

[185] Council Doc. No. 8675/2/98 REV 2, Brussels, 5 June 1998, available at: <http://www.consilium.europa.eu/uedocs/cmsUpload/08675r2en8.pdf>.

[186] Council Decision 98/498/CFSP of 10 August 1998 amending Common Position 96/184/CFSP defined by the Council on the basis of Article J.2 of the Treaty on European Union concerning arms exports to the former Yugoslavia, *OJ* 1998 L 225/1.

[187] Council Common Position 2000/722/CFSP of 20 November 2000 amending Common Position 96/184/CFSP concerning arms exports to the former Yugoslavia, *OJ* 2000 L 292/1.

[188] Council Common Position 2001/719/CFSP of 8 October 2001 amending Common Position 96/184/CFSP concerning arms exports to the former Yugoslavia and Common Position 98/240/CFSP on restrictive measures against the Federal Republic of Yugoslavia, *OJ* 2001 L 268/49.

[189] Council Common Position 2006/29/CFSP of 23 January 2006 repealing Common Position 96/184/CFSP concerning arms exports to the former Yugoslavia, *OJ* 2006 L 19/34.

[190] See, e.g., J. Devin and J. Dashti-Gibson, 'Sanctions in the Former Yugoslavia: Convoluted Goals and Complicated Consequences', in T. Weiss, et al., eds., *Political Gain and Civilian Pain:*

arms embargo in the period from 22 November 1995 (the suspension of UN sanctions) to 28 February 1998 (adoption of new EU sanctions against the FRY) is hampered by insufficient data. Nonetheless, the following general remarks can be made. While the EU arms embargo and the prohibition on the supply of equipment for internal repression and terrorism was targeted against Bosnia-Herzegovina, Croatia and the FRY, EU sanctions were not applied against neighbouring Slovenia (which saw 'only' ten days of armed conflict) and Macedonia (which had been completely spared warfare). While Member States were expected to exercise restraint in their deliveries of weapons to Slovenia and Macedonia, the effectiveness of this clause was undermined by poor monitoring and enforcement. As a result of the sheer volume of weapons sloshing around the region, the enormous profit potential in moving arms from where they were in surplus to where they were in demand and poor sanction monitoring, weapons still flowed through the porous new borders and found their way to those still wanting to settle old scores and those in need of defending themselves against waves of ethnic violence.[191] As such, the EU arms embargo did not prevent the eruption of armed violence in Kosovo (1998) and in Macedonia (2001).

4. EU SANCTIONS AGAINST THE FRY OVER THE WAR IN KOSOVO (1998-2001)

4.1 **Political objectives**

In the third episode of the wars in the former Yugoslavia (from 28 February 1998 to 5 November 2001), the European Union took a range of new restrictive measures against the Federal Republic of Yugoslavia because of its role in Kosovo.[192] EU actions were not based on resolutions of the UN Security Council,

---

Humanitarian Impacts of Economic Sanctions (Lanham, Rowman & Littlefield Publishers Inc. 1997) at pp. 149-187; R. Pape, 'Why Economic Sanctions Do Not Work', 22 *International Security* (1997) pp. 90-136; K. Elliot, 'The Sanctions Glass: Half Full or Completely Empty?', 23 *International Security* (1998) pp. 50-65; D. Baldwin, 'The Sanctions Debate and the Logic of Choice', 24 *International Security* (1999) pp. 80-107. For an analysis of the effectiveness of UN sanctions against Yugoslavia (1991-1995), see the Report of the Copenhagen Round Table on UN Sanctions in the Case of the Former Yugoslavia, annexed to the letter dated 24 September 1996 from the Chairman of the UNSC Committee established pursuant to resolution 724 (1991) concerning Yugoslavia addressed to the President of the Security Council, UN Doc. S/1996/776. For an analysis of the political effectiveness of EC/EU sanctions against the SFRY and the FRY, see De Wilde d'Estmael, op. cit. n. 2, at pp. 281-305.

[191] See M. Kaldor, V. Bojičić and I. Vejvoda, 'Reconstruction in the Balkans: A Challenge for Europe?', 2 *EFA Rev.* (1997) pp. 329-350 at pp. 330 and 333.

[192] Fighting began on 28 February 1998 between the Kosovo Liberation Army and a Serbian police patrol in Likosane. The last EU sanctions against the FRY for its role in the Kosovo crisis were suspended on 5 November 2001. For a political narrative of the fight for Kosovo, see T. Judah, *Kosovo – War and Revenge*, 2nd edn. (New Haven, Yale University Press 2002).

but instead formed a source of inspiration for restrictive measures adopted by the United Nations. The EU sanctions during this period were generally more comprehensive than the sanctions which the UN Security Council required its Member States to implement.

The inspiration for most of the European Union's sanctions came from the Contact Group on Yugoslavia, which consisted of the United States, France, the United Kingdom, Germany, Italy and Russia.[193] The problem which the EU members of the Contact Group faced was that they could not implement most of the sanctions themselves. They had to act through the European Union and therefore needed to obtain the agreement of the other Member States. That agreement was in most cases reached by keeping the wording of the common positions vague and/or ambiguous, leaving it to the European Commission to find a more precise interpretation that would form the basis for the directly applicable EC legislation.[194]

Over time, the objectives of the EU sanctions gradually shifted. Initially, the goal was ending the use of force against and the continued oppression of the Albanian population in Kosovo. Later the goal was to convince the FRY regime to negotiate a political solution in Kosovo. Finally, the goal became bringing about regime change in Belgrade to enable such a political solution and to create lasting stability in the whole Balkan region. The European Union justified the increasing severity of its sanctions by pointing to the FRY regime's continued violation of international humanitarian law and fundamental human rights.

In the spring of 1999, the policy of using sanctions to coerce the FRY regime into compliance with the demands of the Contact Group was replaced by a policy of using military force. In a declaration on Kosovo on 15 June 1998, the Cardiff European Council ordered the regime of President Milošević to comply with a set of conditions to normalise the situation. Unless the regime responded without delay,

> [...] a much stronger response, of a qualitatively different order, will be required from the international community to deal with the increased threat to regional peace and security. The European Council welcomed the acceleration of work in international security organisations on a full range of options, including those which may require an authorisation by the UN Security Council under chapter VII of the UN Charter.[195]

---

193 See chapter 2.

194 See A. de Vries, 'European Union Sanctions Against the Federal Republic of Yugoslavia from 1998 to 2000: A Special Exercise in Targeting', in D. Cortright and G. Lopez, eds., *Smart Sanctions – Targeting Economic Statecraft* (Lanham, Rowman & Littlefield Publishers Inc. 2002) pp. 87-108 at pp. 90-91.

195 *Bull. EU* 6-1998, point I-35.

The failure of the Rambouillet negotiations at the end of 1998 and the serious deterioration of the situation in Kosovo in early 1999 led to the announced stronger response (i.e., the NATO intervention occurring between March and June 1999), which was conducted without the authorisation of the UN Security Council.[196]

As a means of supporting the military intervention, existing sanctions were strengthened and an oil embargo was imposed. Financial sanctions were reinforced and investments were banned, but these measures took effect only in June 1999, just after the government of the FRY had agreed to withdraw its army from Kosovo and NATO military air raids had been suspended. The aims of the sanctions were redirected towards reaching lasting regional stability in the Balkans, as indicated in Common Position 1999/318/CFSP of 10 May 1999.[197] Following the September and December 2000 electoral victories of the democratic opposition in the FRY and the end of President Milošević's rule, most of the sanctions were lifted.[198] As noted before, the arms embargo and the ban on the sale and supply of equipment which might be used for internal repression or terrorism remained in place until 8 October 2001, when they were lifted in order to give effect to UN Security Council resolution 1367 (2001).[199] The financial sanctions against the late Milošević, those persons associated with him and ICTY indictees remain in place until today.[200]

The EU sanctions imposed against the FRY can be divided into the following broad categories: an arms embargo, including a prohibition on equipment for internal repression and terrorism; travel restrictions, including a visa and a flight ban; an oil embargo; and financial sanctions, including a ban on new investment. The terms 'targeted' or 'smart' sanctions are often used for such restrictive measures. In principle, 'targeted sanctions' are restrictive measures that are designed and implemented in such a way as to affect only those (groups of) persons that are held responsible for breaches of or threats to international peace and security.[201] However, arms embargoes may withhold arms from both armed

---

196 See chapter 2.

197 Common Position 1999/318/CFSP of 10 May 1999 adopted by the Council on the basis of Article 15 of the Treaty on European Union concerning additional restrictive measures against the Federal Republic of Yugoslavia, *OJ* 1999 L 123/1.

198 See, e.g., Council Regulation (EC) No. 2156/2001 of 5 November 2001 repealing Regulation (EC) No. 926/98 concerning the reduction of certain economic relations with the Federal Republic of Yugoslavia, *OJ* 2001 L 289/5. Other measures are included in the sections below.

199 Council Common Position 2001/719/CFSP of 8 October 2001 amending Common Position 96/184/CFSP concerning arms exports to the former Yugoslavia and Common Position 98/240/CFSP on restrictive measures against the Federal Republic of Yugoslavia, *OJ* 2001 L 268/49.

200 Commission Regulation (EC) No. 68/2006 of 16 January 2006 amending Council Regulation (EC) No. 2488/2000 maintaining a freeze of funds in relation to Mr Milosevic and those persons associated with him, *OJ* 2006 L 11/11. Despite his death, the assets of Milošević remain frozen.

201 Based on the definition used in the so-called Interlaken Process, the first comprehensive attempt to examine the feasibility of targeted financial sanctions, initiated by the Swiss government

rebel groups and legitimate governments, flight bans may hit innocent travellers more heavily than members of the targeted regime and financial sanctions can also have strong effects on general commerce by denying the possibility of payment. It may thus be useful to add to the definition that targeted sanctions are intended not to hurt innocent parties or cause 'collateral' damage, or at least to minimise such effects, because they are concentrated on those (groups of) persons that are held accountable for the violation of international law.

4.2 Arms embargo

At the beginning of 1998, in view of the Kosovo crisis, the UN Security Council imposed a new arms embargo against the FRY.[202] The arms embargo targeted the FRY regime as well as the Kosovar organisations that used arms to promote their causes (notably the Kosovar Liberation Army). Since the EU arms embargo of 5 July 1991 had been extended in 1996 and had remained in place until then,[203] the European Union could suffice on 19 March 1998 by confirming the existing arms embargo and imposing an extra prohibition on the export to the FRY of equipment that could be used for internal repression and terrorism.[204] Here again, parties on both sides of the conflict were targeted. After long discussions, the Council of Ministers agreed on a list of prohibited equipment used for internal repression and terrorism.[205] The list did not contain dual-use goods, but Member States were subject to the European Community's regime and procedures on the exports of dual-use goods in their exports to the FRY.[206]

On 10 September 2001, The UN Security Council adopted resolution 1367, thereby terminating the prohibition to sell or supply arms to the FRY. The European Union considered that its arms embargo and ban on the supply of equipment that might be used for internal repression or for terrorism had thereby

---

in 1998. See *A Manual for Design and Implementation of Targeted Financial Sanctions – Contributions from the Interlaken Process* (2001), available at: <http://www.watsoninstitute.org>.

202 S/RES/1160 (1998) of 31 March 1998.

203 Common Position 1996/184/CFSP of 26 February 1996 defined by the Council on the basis of Article J.2 of the Treaty on European Union concerning arms exports to the former Yugoslavia, *OJ* 1996 L 58/1.

204 Common Position 98/240/CFSP of 19 March 1998 defined by the Council on the basis of Article J.2 of the Treaty on European Union on restrictive measures against the Federal Republic of Yugoslavia, *OJ* 1998 L 95/1.

205 Council Regulation (EC) No. 926/98 of 27 April 1998 concerning the reduction of certain economic relations with the Federal Republic of Yugoslavia, *OJ* 1998 L 130/1.

206 Council Regulation (EC) No. 3381/94 of 19 December 1994 setting up a Community regime for the control of exports of dual-use goods, *OJ* 1994 L 367/1 (as amended); and Council Decision 94/942/CFSP of 19 December 1994 on the joint action adopted by the Council on the basis of Article J.3 of the Treaty on European Union concerning the control of exports of dual-use goods, *OJ* 1994 L 367/8 (as amended).

also become redundant. Both sets of sanctions were lifted on 6 November 2001, it being understood that, with respect to arms exports to the FRY, the Member States would strictly apply the EU Code of Conduct for Arms Exports adopted on 8 June 1998.[207]

4.3 Visa restrictions

The package of restrictive actions adopted by the European Union on 19 March 1998 included a visa ban with respect to persons who had been identified as having clear security responsibilities as well as other senior FRY and Serbian representatives responsible for repressive action in Kosovo.[208] A list of ten persons, on which President Milošević himself did not appear, was published initially. It was announced that other senior FRY and Serbian representatives would be added to the visa ban list in the case of a failure by the authorities to respond to the demands of the international community. A second list of nineteen persons was established in December 1998.[209] This list contained the names of persons deemed to have played a major role in diminishing and curtailing the role of the independent media, thereby violating recognised international norms and showing a further lack of respect for democratic principles. Again, President Milošević was not listed. It was only in May 1999, when all hope of Milošević agreeing to a negotiated resolution of the conflict was abandoned, that the president himself was subjected to the visa ban, together with his family, all ministers and senior officials of the FRY and Serbian governments and persons close to the regime whose activities supported the president.[210] This latter category included a number of military leaders, as well as directors and other chief executives of companies and organisations. After January 2000, members of the police and security forces and of the judiciary were also

---

[207] Art. 2 of Common Position 98/240/CFSP was repealed by Council Common Position 2001/719/CFSP of 8 October 2001 amending Common Position 96/184/CFSP concerning arms exports to the former Yugoslavia and Common Position 98/240/CFSP on restrictive measures against the Federal Republic of Yugoslavia, *OJ* 2001 L 268/49. See also Council Regulation (EC) No. 2156/2001 of 5 November 2001 repealing Regulation (EC) No. 926/98 concerning the reduction of certain economic relations with the Federal Republic of Yugoslavia, *OJ* 2001 L 289/5.

[208] Common Position 98/240/CFSP of 19 March 1998 defined by the Council on the basis of Article J.2 of the Treaty on European Union on restrictive measures against the Federal Republic of Yugoslavia, *OJ* 1998 L 95/1.

[209] Common Position 1998/725/CFSP of 14 December 1998 defined by the Council on the basis of Article J.2 of the Treaty on European Union on restrictive measures to be taken against persons in the Federal Republic of Yugoslavia acting against the independent media, *OJ* 1998 L 345/1.

[210] Common Position 1999/318/CFSP of 10 May 1999 adopted by the Council on the basis of Article 15 of the Treaty on European Union concerning additional restrictive measures against the Federal Republic of Yugoslavia, *OJ* 1999 L 123/1; and Council Decision 1999/319/CFSP of 10 May 1999 implementing Common Position 1999/318/CFSP concerning additional restrictive measures against the Federal Republic of Yugoslavia, *OJ* 1999 L 123/3.

added to the list. Between May 1999 and August 2000, the list grew from about 280 to almost 800 names.[211]

The selection of persons to be included on the list was mostly based on reports from the ICTY and the diplomatic representatives of the Member States and the European Commission in Belgrade. In January 2000, Common Position 2000/56/CFSP was adopted, identifying the categories of persons against whom visa restrictions would be imposed:

- persons indicted for crimes as defined in Articles 1 to 5 of the [ICTY] statute;
- the following persons: President Milošević, his family and all Ministers and senior officials of the Federal and Serbian Governments;
- persons whose activities support President Milošević politically and/or financially (including publishers, editors-in-chief and SPS party members);
- leaders of the military and police forces and those responsible for intelligence or security services;
- persons involved in repression activities.[212]

These categories were rather broad, and a considerable degree of discretionary power and political compromise was necessary to keep the list restricted to those who really mattered. In the same common position, the Council also indicated that persons to whom the criteria were no longer applicable would be deleted from the list.[213]

---

[211] See Council Decisions 1999/424/CFSP of 28 June 1999, *OJ* 1999 L 163/86; 1999/612/CFSP of 13 September 1999, *OJ* 1999 L 242/32; 2000/177/CFSP of 28 February 2000, *OJ* 2000 L 56/2; 2000/348/CFSP of 22 May 2000, *OJ* 2000 L 122/7; 2000/370/CFSP of 5 June 2000, *OJ* 2003 L 134/1; and 2000/495 of 3 August 2000, *OJ* 2000 L 200/1.

[212] Art. 1(2) of Council Common Position 2000/56/CFSP of 24 January 2000 amending and supplementing Common Position 1999/318/CFSP concerning additional restrictive measures against the Federal Republic of Yugoslavia (FRY), *OJ* 2000 L 21/4.

[213] Art. 1(3) of Council Common Position 2000/56/CFSP. Art. 1(7) of the Common Position also stated that '[i]n exceptional cases, exemptions may be made if this would further vital Union objectives and be conducive to political settlement [...].' Still, the burden of proof of mistakes was left with the person listed and there was no recourse to judicial authorities within the European Union. On the (lack of) judicial protection within the legal order of the European Union against targeted sanctions, see S. Blockmans, 'De EU toont haar melktanden. Het instellen en implementeren van gerichte sancties ter handhaving of herstel van de internationale vrede en veiligheid', in T.M.C. Asser Instituut, *'Veiligheid' en het recht van de Europese Unie* (The Hague, T.M.C. Asser Press 2002) pp. 85-96 at pp. 91-96. For a contextual discussion on the recent judgments of the CFI, in Joined Cases T-306/01 *Ahmed Ali Yusuf and Al Barakaat International Foundation* v. *Council and Commission* [2005] *ECR* II-3533 and T-315/01 *Yassin Abdullah Kadi* v. *Council and Commission* [2005] *ECR* II-3649, in which the CFI noted the lack of judicial protection of persons placed on sanctions lists, see R. Wessel, 'The Invasion by International Organizations. De toenemende samenhang tussen de mondiale, Europese en nationale rechtsorde', Inaugural Lecture, University of Twente, 2006, and the literature referred to *supra* n. 6.

Following the democratic elections that removed Milošević from the presidency, the visa ban was confined to Milošević and the natural persons associated with him.[214] While the black list was considerably reduced, it still contained a substantial number of persons identified for non-admission to the European Union.[215] After the free and fair legislative elections in Serbia in December 2000, the Council further confined the visa restrictions to Milošević, his family and persons indicted by the ICTY (just thirteen persons in all).[216]

4.4 Flight ban

Following the deterioration of the situation in Kosovo, the European Union complemented the sanctions it had adopted in the course of 1998 with Regulation (EC) No. 1901/98 of 7 September 1998, which imposed a flight ban against the FRY.[217] While the Council had already decided in June 1998 to ban all flights by Yugoslav carriers between the Federal Republic of Yugoslavia and the European Union,[218] the delay in rendering the decision effective was caused by the fact that the flight ban could form a violation of bilateral air services agreements that several Member States had concluded with the FRY.[219] Greece and the United Kingdom initially agreed that the flight ban could only take effect after the end of the mandatory notification period for terminating their agreements (six and twelve months respectively). In September, the United Kingdom rallied to the position of the other thirteen Member States and the Commission that the flight ban did not necessitate a termination of the bilateral air services agreement but was justified as a countermeasure against the breaches by the FRY of its *erga*

---

214 Council Common Position 2000/696/CFSP of 10 November 2000 on the maintenance of specific restrictive measures directed against Mr Milosevic and persons associated with him, *OJ* 2000 L 287/1.

215 Council Decision 2000/697/CFSP of 10 November 2000 implementing Common Position 2000/696/CFSP concerning the maintenance of specific restrictive measures against Mr Milosevic and persons associated with him, *OJ* 2000 L 287/2. Some 330 persons remained listed.

216 Council Common Position 2001/155/CFSP of 26 February 2001 amending Common Position 2000/696/CFSP on the maintenance of specific restrictive measures directed against Mr Milosevic and persons associated with him and repealing Common Position 98/725/CFSP, *OJ* 2001 L 57/3. See also the following sections.

217 Council Regulation (EC) No. 1901/98 of 7 September 1998 concerning a ban on flights of Yugoslav carriers between the Federal Republic of Yugoslavia and the European Community, *OJ* 1998 L 248/1. See generally, S. Karaggianis, 'Sanctions internationales et droit communautaire. A propos du règlement 1901/98 sur l'interdiction de vol des transporteurs yougoslaves', 35 *RTDE* (1999) p. 363; D. Wibaux, 'A propos de quelques questions juridiques posées par l'interdiction des vols des compagnies yougoslaves', 44 *AFDI* (1998) p. 262.

218 Common Position 98/426/CFSP of 29 June 1998 defined by the Council on the basis of Article J.2 of the Treaty on European Union concerning a ban on flights by Yugoslav carriers between the Federal Republic of Yugoslavia and the European Community, *OJ* 1998 L 190/3.

219 See De Vries, loc. cit. n. 194, at p. 107, n. 14.

omnes obligations.[220] In an implicit preambular reference to the violation of such higher norms, the Council stated:

> Whereas the Government of the FRY has not stopped the use of indiscriminate violence and brutal repression against its own citizens, which constitute serious violations of human rights and international humanitarian law, and has not taken effective steps to find a political solution to the issue of Kosovo through a process of peaceful dialogue with the Kosovar Albanian community in order to maintain the regional peace and security[.][221]

The flight ban did not apply to EU carriers or to those of third countries.[222] In the same regulation, a symbolic but nevertheless important exemption was made for charter series flights between Leipzig and Tivat by Montenegro Airlines. In January 1999, the scope of this exemption was broadened to cover all individual or charter series flights by Montenegro Airlines between Montenegro and the European Union, on the condition that the Montenegrin government provided conclusive evidence to the Commission that neither the Serbian nor the FRY authorities would benefit, directly or indirectly, from the revenues resulting from the flights authorised.[223] Primarily aimed at JAT (*Jugoslovensko Aviontransport*), a state-owned company and the Yugoslav national flag carrier, the flight ban was a targeted measure intended to deprive the FRY regime of revenues from air traffic services.[224] The European Union clearly broke new ground in adopting this flight ban (i) as a countermeasure by relying on (ii) the violation of *erga omnes* obligations by the FRY.[225]

---

220 *Barcelona Traction, Power & Light Co.* case, *ICJ Reports* 1970, para. 33. Certain fundamental human rights and rules of humanitarian law (*jus cogens*) should be protected at all times and impose obligations *erga omnes*; i.e., they give rise to a claim for their execution that accrues to any other member of the international community. Examples are the prohibition of genocide, torture, slavery and racial discrimination. See P. Weil, 'Towards Relative Normativity in International Law?', 77 *AJIL* (1983) pp. 413-442.

221 Preamble to Council Regulation (EC) No. 1901/98.

222 Another exemption related to emergency landings on the territory of the Community and ensuing take-offs. See Art. 3 of Council Regulation (EC) No. 1901/98.

223 Council Regulation (EC) No. 214/99 of 25 January 1999 amending Regulation (EC) No. 1901/98 concerning a ban on flights of Yugoslav carriers between the Federal Republic of Yugoslavia and the European Community, *OJ* 1999 L 23/6.

224 Art. 1 of Council Regulation (EC) No. 1901/98. However, JAT was allowed to make flights over the European Union. Not allowing these overflights, it was feared, would lead the FRY to deny EU carriers the rights to fly over the FRY, which would impose significant costs on these EU carriers.

225 The measure has not been challenged before the CFI and/or ECJ, either by way of direct action against the institutions or via a preliminary ruling from a national court. The ban was challenged in the Belgian courts, however, where JAT requested provisional measures. The Cour d'Appel de Bruxelles rejected the request on several grounds. In considering the legality of Regulation (EC) No. 1901/98 itself, it was considered to fulfil the following conditions: 'ces mesures

The flight ban was extended to cover all flights between the European Union and the FRY when the NATO intervention began in 1999.[226] An exemption was made for strictly humanitarian flights.[227] In the autumn of 1999, the Council decided to expand the existing exemptions for flights to and from the Republic of Montenegro and the Province of Kosovo as well as for Montenegro Airlines.[228] These two exemptions to the flight ban were clearly intended to support the opposition of the Montenegrin government to the FRY regime in Belgrade.

A six-month suspension of the flight ban was decided in March 2000 and was later extended for another six months in August 2000.[229] This suspension was officially presented as a concession to the Yugoslav opposition, which claimed that the flight ban was hitting innocent Yugoslavs harder than members of the regime.[230] It was assumed that the visa ban would be sufficient to prevent the FRY's ruling elites from using air traffic services. The flight ban was completely lifted in the first half of October 2000.[231]

---

répondent à une violation antérieure du droit international; cette violation autorise les contre-mesures; ces contre-mesures ne sont pas d'une illicitée absolue; elles sont proportionnées à la violation initiale du droit international; leur mise en oeuvre est précédée d'une sommation adressée à l'État responsable de mettre fin à la violation initiale du droit international.' Cour d'Appel de Bruxelles (9ème Chambre), Case 1998/KR/528 (*Jugoslovensko Aerotransport* v. *l'État Belge*), *J.T.* (1999), 693. See generally, P. Palchetti, 'Reactions by the European Union to Breaches of Erga Omnes Obligations', in E. Cannizzaro, ed., *The European Union as an Actor in International Relations* (The Hague, Kluwer Law International 2002) pp. 219-230.

226 Common Position 1999/318/CFSP; and Council Regulation (EC) No. 1064/1999 of 21 May 1999 imposing a ban on flights between the European Community and the Federal Republic of Yugoslavia, and repealing Regulation (EC) No. 1901/98, *OJ* 1999 L 129/27.

227 Art. 3(2) and (3) of Council Regulation (EC) No. 1064/1999. See *infra* n. 235 for the consultation procedure on the basis of which the Commission could monitor, on a case-by-case basis, the authorisations of flights by the Member States.

228 Art. 2 of Council Common Position 1999/604/CFSP of 3 September 1999 amending Common Position 1999/273/CFSP concerning a ban on the supply and sale of petroleum and petroleum products to the Federal Republic of Yugoslavia (FRY), and Common Position 1999/318/CFSP concerning additional restrictive measures against the Federal Republic of Yugoslavia, *OJ* 1999 L 236/1; and Council Regulation (EC) No. 2151/1999 imposing a ban on flights between the territories of the Community and the Federal Republic of Yugoslavia other than the Republic of Montenegro or the Province of Kosovo, and repealing Council Regulation (EC) No. 1064/1999, *OJ* 1999 L 264/3.

229 Common Position 2000/176/CFSP of 28 February 2000, *OJ* 2000 L 56/1; and Council Regulation (EC) No. 607/2000 of 20 March 2000, *OJ* 2000 L 73/4; Common Position 2000/454/CFSP of 20 July 2000, *OJ* 2000 L 183/1; and Council Regulation (EC) No. 1746/2000 of 3 August 2000, *OJ* 2000 L 200/24.

230 This does not exclude the fact that strong lobbying from the European business community, notably the EC air carriers, also helped to convince the Council to suspend this type of sanction.

231 Council Common Position 2000/599/CFSP of 9 October 2000 on support to a democratic FRY and the immediate lifting of certain restrictive measures, *OJ* 2000 L 255/1; and Council Regulation (EC) No. 2227/2000 of 9 October 2000 repealing Regulation (EC) No. 2151/1999 imposing a ban on flights between the territories of the Community and the Federal Republic of Yugoslavia other than the Republic of Montenegro or the Province of Kosovo, *OJ* 2000 L 255/2.

4.5 Oil embargo

At the end of April 1999, when NATO was already engaged in air strikes in Kosovo, the EU Council decided to impose an oil embargo on the whole of the FRY in order to deprive its army of essential supplies of petroleum and petroleum products.[232] The EU oil embargo against the FRY initially also covered the Republic of Montenegro (with its oil import facilities in the ports of Bar and the Bay of Kotor) and Kosovo. For the selection of products to be embargoed, the Commission proposed to copy the list of petroleum and petroleum products that was established for the implementation of the UN Security Council oil embargoes imposed on Angola and Sierra Leone. This was done to avoid protracted technical debates in the Council. The proposal was adopted without discussion.[233]

Exemptions from the oil embargo were approved for sales, supplies or exports for verified and strictly humanitarian purposes, in particular for the needs of internally displaced persons and returnees.[234] With a view to avoiding different interpretations by the Member States of the term 'strictly humanitarian', a specific consultation system was set up.[235] Another exception concerned sales, supplies, and exports to diplomatic and consular missions of the Member States and the international military peacekeeping presence within the FRY.[236] This was necessary to allow the aircraft involved in the NATO air strikes to 'import' fuel into the FRY. An initiative from some Member States to allow NATO naval forces to check and search ships in the international waters of the Adriatic Sea failed to obtain the necessary support.[237]

---

232 Common Position 1999/273 of 23 April 1999 defined by the Council on the basis of Article J.2 of the Treaty on European Union concerning a ban on the supply and sale of petroleum and petroleum products to the Federal Republic of Yugoslavia (FRY), *OJ* 1999 L 108/1; and Council Regulation (EC) No. 900/1999 of 29 April 1999 prohibiting the sale and supply of petroleum and certain petroleum products to the Federal Republic of Yugoslavia (FRY), *OJ* 1999 L 114/7.

233 See De Vries, loc. cit. n. 194, at p. 95.

234 Art. 2(1)b of Council Regulation (EC) No. 900/1999.

235 Commission Regulation (EC) No. 1084/1999 of 26 May 1999 establishing the list of competent authorities referred to in Article 2 of Council Regulation (EC) No. 900/1999 prohibiting the sale and supply of petroleum and petroleum products to the Federal Republic of Yugoslavia, *OJ* 1999 L 131/29, as amended by Commission Regulation (EC) No. 1971/1999 of 15 September 1999, *OJ* 1999 L 244/40. Before any Member State could authorise the sale, supply or export of petroleum or petroleum products to the FRY, it had to notify its intention to do so to the other Member States and the Commission. If the Commission or any other Member State questioned the strictly humanitarian character of the intended sale, supply or export, it needed to notify the other Member States and the Commission within one working day of its objection to the authorisation. In such a case, the Commission would convene a meeting with all Member States to discuss the character of the transaction. Only after such a meeting took place could the Member State that intended to grant an export authorisation do so, on the condition that, if it did, it had to report to the Commission and the other Member States why it still considered the transaction to be serving strictly humanitarian purposes.

236 Art. 2(1)a of Council Regulation (EC) No. 900/1999.

237 See De Vries, loc. cit. n. 194, at p. 95.

The oil embargo was continued after the end of the military intervention. In September 1999, a common position was adopted calling for exceptions for the Republic of Montenegro and the Province of Kosovo.[238] The Council regulation to this effect entered into force in October 1999.[239] The delay of the partial lifting of the embargo was needed for the Commission to create a system whereby the exceptions would not create loopholes through which petroleum and petroleum products could slip into the rest of the FRY.[240] The Commission cooperated with the competent authorities of the Republic of Montenegro to establish a control mechanism that would guarantee the effectiveness of the EU oil embargo. A similar agreement could not be reached with the UN administration in Kosovo because its mandate did not authorise cooperation with third parties on an oil embargo against the FRY.[241] As a result, petroleum exports from the European Union to Kosovo could only take place if the competent authorities within the European Union obtained conclusive evidence that the products sold, supplied or exported stayed within that province. Under the circumstances, such evidence was difficult to obtain. The oil embargo was partially suspended in March 2000 and then lifted in October 2000, following the electoral victory of the democratic opposition in the FRY and the end of President Milošević's rule.[242]

4.6 Financial sanctions

The first financial sanctions imposed against the FRY were included in the package adopted on 19 March 1998 and concerned a moratorium on government-financed export credit support for trade and investment, including government

238 Council Common Position 1999/604/CFSP of 3 September 1999 amending Common Position 1999/273/CFSP concerning a ban on the supply and sale of petroleum and petroleum products to the Federal Republic of Yugoslavia (FRY), and Common Position 1999/318/CFSP concerning additional restrictive measures against the Federal Republic of Yugoslavia, *OJ* 1999 L 236/1.

239 Council Regulation (EC) No. 2111/1999 of 4 October 1999 prohibiting the sale and supply of petroleum and certain petroleum products to certain parts of the Federal Republic of Yugoslavia (FRY) and repealing Regulation (EC) No. 900/1999, *OJ* 1999 L 258/12.

240 See De Vries, loc. cit. n. 194, at p. 95.

241 Ibid.

242 Council Regulation (EC) No. 607/2000 of 20 March 2000 suspending, for a limited period, Regulation (EC) No. 2151/1999 imposing a ban on flights between the territories of the Community and the Federal Republic of Yugoslavia other than the Republic of Montenegro or the Province of Kosovo and amending Regulations (EC) No. 1294/1999 and (EC) No. 2111/1999 as regards payments and supplies in relation to flights during the period of suspension, *OJ* 2000 L 73/4; followed by Council Common Position 2000/599/CFSP of 9 October 2000 on support to a democratic FRY and the immediate lifting of certain restrictive measures, *OJ* 2000 L 255/1; and Council Regulation (EC) No. 2228/2000 of 9 October 2000 repealing Regulation (EC) No. 2111/1999 prohibiting the sale and supply of petroleum and certain petroleum products to certain parts of the Federal Republic of Yugoslavia (FRY), *OJ* 2000 L 255/3.

financing for privatisations, in Serbia.[243] The prohibition of financing for privatisation was intended to deny financial benefits to the FRY/Serbian governments as owners of the companies to be privatised. But of course the general denial of trade or investment support hurt all companies in Serbia. The Republic of Montenegro was exempted from this measure. These sanctions were lifted in November 2000.[244]

In June 1998, the Council ordered by Regulation (EC) No. 1295/98 that all funds held outside the territory of the FRY and belonging to the government of the FRY and/or the government of the Republic of Serbia were to be frozen or denied.[245] Financial institutions in the European Union were prohibited from making funds available, directly or indirectly, to or for the benefit of those governments. The funds to be frozen or denied were defined in Article 1 of the regulation as 'funds of any kind, including interest, dividends or other value accruing to or from any such funds.' When it was realised that this approach did not cause real financial problems for the FRY/Serbian regime, the Council in June 1999 decided to strengthen the financial sanctions by extending the range of targets and the scope of funds to be frozen. According to Council Regulation (EC) No. 1294/1999, the targets of financial sanctions included not only the government of the FRY and the Republic of Serbia, but all

> [...] agencies, bodies or organs, companies, undertakings, institutions and entities owned or controlled by that Government, including all financial institutions and State-owned and socially-owned entities organized in the Federal Republic of Yugoslavia as of 26 April 1999, any successors to such entities, and their respective subsidiaries and branches, wherever located, and any persons acting or purporting to act for or on behalf of any of the foregoing.[246]

At the same time, the scope of the assets to be frozen and prohibited was expanded to include:

---

243 Art. 3 of Common Position 98/240/CFSP of 19 March 1998 defined by the Council on the basis of Article J.2 of the Treaty on European Union on restrictive measures against the Federal Republic of Yugoslavia, *OJ* 1998 L 95/1; and Art. 2 of Council Regulation (EC) No. 926/98 of 27 April 1998 concerning the reduction of certain economic relations with the Federal Republic of Yugoslavia, *OJ* 1998 L 130/1.

244 Common Position 2000/599/CFSP of 9 October 2000 on support to a democratic FRY and the immediate lifting of certain restrictive measures, *OJ* 2000 L 255/1; and Council Regulation (EC) No. 2488/2000 of 10 November 2000 maintaining a freeze of funds in relation to Mr Milosevic and those persons associated with him and repealing Regulations (EC) Nos. 1294/1999 and 607/2000 and Article 2 of Regulation (EC) No. 926/98, *OJ* 2000 L 287/19.

245 Council Regulation (EC) No. 1295/98 of 22 June 1998 concerning the freezing of funds held abroad by the Governments of the Federal Republic of Yugoslavia and the Republic of Serbia, *OJ* 1998 L 178/33.

246 Art. 1(2) of Council Regulation (EC) No. 1294/1999 of 15 June 1999 concerning a freeze of funds and a ban on investment in relation to the Federal Republic of Yugoslavia (FRY) and repealing Regulations (EC) No. 1295/98 and (EC) No. 1607/98, *OJ* 1999 L 153/63.

> [...] financial assets and economic benefits of any kind, including, but not necessarily limited to, cash, cheques, claims on money, drafts, money orders and other payment instruments; deposits with financial institutions or other entities, balances on accounts, debts and debt obligations; publicly and privately traded securities and debt instruments, including stocks and shares, certificates representing securities, bonds, notes, warrants, debentures, derivatives contracts; interest, dividends or other income or value accruing from or generated by assets; credit, right of set-off, guarantees, performance bonds or other financial commitments; letters of credit, bills of lading, bills of sale; documents evidencing an interest in funds or financial resources, and any other instrument of export-financing.[247]

The government of Montenegro and all its agencies, bodies and organs at any level, as well as the UN administration in Kosovo, were excluded from these sanctions.

It was the Council's intention to safeguard the Yugoslav private sector from the financial sanctions insofar as persons in that sector did not act on behalf of or for the benefit of the FRY or Serbian governments.[248] To highlight this aspect of the sanctions regime, the Commission proposed to attach a so-called 'white list' to the regulation that would contain the names and other relevant data of companies that would not be subjected to the sanctions. Initially, the Council did not adopt this proposal, no doubt for fear that publicising the identity of such companies would make them targets for ownership or control by the FRY or Serbian governments.[249] But not providing such a list meant that only the most conspicuously targeted companies in the FRY were subject to the freeze of funds. This situation prevailed until April 2000, when the Council finally adopted the necessary amendments in Regulation (EC) No. 723/2000 in order to better target the freeze of funds and enhance the effectiveness of the existing financial sanctions.[250] This was done, *inter alia*, by closing loopholes and improving enforcement. In this regulation, the Council established a 'white list' of companies in Serbia (minus the Province of Kosovo and the Republic of Montenegro) that were deemed not to be owned or controlled by the FRY/Serbian governments, directly or indirectly. To qualify for this white list, companies in the FRY had to submit evidence to that effect. If a company in Serbia was not listed, it was

247 Ibid., Art. 1(3).

248 See De Vries, loc. cit. n. 194, at p. 97.

249 Ibid.

250 Council Regulation (EC) No. 723/2000 of 6 April 2000 amending Regulation (EC) No. 1294/1999 concerning a freeze of funds and a ban on investment in relation to the Federal Republic of Yugoslavia (FRY), *OJ* 2000 L 86/1. Because most Member States were not able to execute the screening of FRY companies within the foreseen deadline, the most relevant articles dealing with the increased targeting of the FRY/Serbian regime entered into force only on 1 July 2000 by way of Council Regulation (EC) No. 1059/2000 of 18 May 2000 amending Regulation (EC) No. 723/2000 amending Regulation (EC) No. 1294/1999 concerning a freeze of funds and a ban on investment in relation to the Federal Republic of Yugoslavia (FRY), *OJ* 2000 L 119/1.

deemed to fall within the scope of one or more of the four so-called 'black lists' which were also included in Regulation (EC) No. 723/2000 to target the freeze of funds of companies, undertakings, institutions or entities which were owned or controlled by the FRY/Serbian governments.[251] By reversing the burden of proof, it was expected that better targeting would be possible.[252] Regulation (EC) No. 723/2000, in Article 1(6), sub 2, stipulated that a company, undertaking, institution or entity in Serbia would be presumed to be 'white' if it fulfilled any of the following criteria:

- [being] able to withhold from the Government of the FRY and the Government of the Republic of Serbia, its revenues obtained from transactions with natural or legal persons within the Community;
- [being] engaged in transactions with natural or legal persons within the Community not exceeding, on a monthly basis, a value of EUR 100,000; [or]
- [not being active in] the following sectors: banking and financial services, energy and fuel supply, production of or trade in military or police equipment, transport, petrochemicals, iron and steel.

A first – and as it turned out last – list of about 190 'white' companies was published on 1 July 2000.[253] As noted before, the financial sanctions against companies were already lifted in November 2000, as a consequence of the democratically held presidential elections of 24 September 2000.[254]

The strengthened financial sanctions of June 1999 also applied to individuals. Annex 1 to Regulation (EC) No. 1294/1999 contained a list of names of individuals to whom the assets freeze would be applied. This list was identical to the list drawn up for the visa ban. It was regularly updated in conformity with the updates of the visa ban list, although the criteria for being listed were oriented to involvement in economic and financial activities rather than police, security, military or judicial activities. The assets freeze against individuals was the only financial sanction that was not lifted in November 2000, although the list of persons to which it applied was significantly reduced, mostly by deleting a large

---

[251] For the text of the white and black lists, see Art. 1(3) of Council Regulation (EC) No. 723/2000.

[252] This reversal of the burden of proof did not apply to the Republic of Montenegro and the Province of Kosovo. Indeed, in those two areas the sanctions were alleviated to the extent that only companies deemed to be owned or controlled by the FRY/Serbian governments were put on a black list. If not on the black list, any company in the Republic of Montenegro or the Province of Kosovo would be considered to be 'white'.

[253] Commission Regulation (EC) No. 1440/2000 of 30 June 2000 amending Annex VI to Council Regulation (EC) No. 1294/1999 concerning a freeze of funds and a ban on investment in relation to the Federal Republic of Yugoslavia (FRY), *OJ* 2000 L 161/68.

[254] Common Position 2000/599/CFSP and Council Regulation (EC) No. 2488/2000.

number of military officials.[255] In June 2001, the Commission further reduced the number of persons listed in Annex I to bring it in line with the list that was used to deny Milošević, his family and persons indicted by the ICTY admission to the EU Member States.[256]

4.7 Investment bans

In July 1998, Council Regulation (EC) No. 1607/98 imposed a general ban on new investments in the Republic of Serbia.[257] However, the prohibition concerned only the transfer of funds or other financial assets to Serbia 'insofar as such funds or other financial assets are transferred for the purposes of establishing a lasting economic link with the Republic of Serbia, including the acquisition of real estate there.' An exemption was made for the transfer of funds used solely for projects in support of democratisation, humanitarian and educational activities and independent media. A year later, the investment ban was strengthened in Regulation (EC) No. 1294/1999 by prohibiting any participation in or ownership or control of any real estate, company, undertaking, institution or entity located, registered or incorporated within the Republic of Serbia or, wherever else located, registered or incorporated, owned or controlled by the government of the FRY or the government of the Republic of Serbia.[258] The ban concerned not only state-

[255] Common Position 2000/696/CFSP of 10 November 2000 on the maintenance of specific restrictive measures directed against Mr Milosevic and persons associated with him, *OJ* 2000 L 287/1; and Council Regulation (EC) No. 2488/2000 of 10 November 2000 maintaining a freeze of funds in relation to Mr Milosevic and those persons associated with him and repealing Regulations (EC) Nos. 1294/1999 and 607/2000 and Article 2 of Regulation (EC) No. 926/98, *OJ* 2000 L 287/19. Annex I still listed thirty-seven persons against whom a freeze of funds was maintained: Slobodan Milošević, five of his family members and thirty-one members of the FRY government.

[256] Commission Regulation (EC) No. 1205/2001 of 19 June 2001 amending, for the first time, Council Regulation (EC) No. 2488/2000 maintaining a freeze of funds in relation to Mr Milosevic and those persons associated with him, *OJ* 2001 L 163/14. In January 2006, the regulation was amended, albeit just to take account of the changed addresses of some EU financial institutions. Commission Regulation (EC) No. 68/2006 of 16 January 2006 amending Council Regulation (EC) No. 2488/2000 maintaining a freeze of funds in relation to Mr Milosevic and those persons associated with him, *OJ* 2006 L 11/11. So far, no amendment has been adopted to take account of the death of Milošević on 11 March 2006. Thus, the former president's assets remain frozen.

[257] Council Regulation (EC) No. 1607/98 of 24 July 1998 concerning the prohibition of new investment in the Republic of Serbia, *OJ* 1998 L 209/16. The regulation was based on Common Position 98/374/CFSP of 8 June 1998 defined by the Council on the basis of Article J.2 of the Treaty on European Union concerning the prohibition of new investment in Serbia, *OJ* 1998 L 165/1. Earlier, Common Position 98/240/CFSP and Council Regulation (EC) No. 926/98 had already prohibited (a) 'the provision and/or use of government and/or other official financial support, insurance and/or guarantees in respect of new export credit for trade with or investment in the Republic of Serbia [...]; (b) the provision or use of government and/or other official financing for privatizations in the Republic of Serbia [...].'

[258] Art. 4(1).

owned or state-controlled companies but also private companies in Serbia. Investments in the Republic of Montenegro were exempted, although this exemption only applied to companies that were not owned or controlled by the FRY or Serbian governments. In principle, the investment ban covered the Province of Kosovo, but investments in that province could be authorised to avoid serious damage to an EU company or industry or to the interests of the Community itself.[259] The investment ban was lifted in November 2000.[260]

4.8 Effectiveness of EU sanctions

Assessing the effectiveness of specific types of targeted sanctions is extremely difficult, especially when they are applied in combination with one another *and* in combination with UN sanctions, like during the Kosovo crisis. Nevertheless, a few observations can be made on the impact of each of the above-mentioned specific measures adopted by the European Union.[261]

A basic requirement for judging the effectiveness of smart sanctions is whether such measures deny targets the fulfilment of what they may consider an important or essential need. Evidence to that effect in the case of the visa ban is not available. Also unknown is the extent to which the targeted individuals were able to use false passports. While this ban may have annoyed those listed, it did not necessarily make them change their behaviour. The same can be said of the arms embargo, which targeted the armies of the FRY and the KLA. As the embargo was poorly enforced, it did not prevent the warring parties from obtaining what they needed. The oil embargo was intended to deprive the army of the FRY of the means to prolong its repressive activities in Kosovo. Thanks to the cooperation of the FRY's neighbouring states, the embargo was effectively implemented during NATO's intervention and may have assisted in prompting Belgrade's decision to withdraw from Kosovo. After NATO's intervention, however, the embargo crumbled and may have even had the opposite effect, as the regime profited from smuggling. But, again, concrete evidence is lacking. It is also difficult to judge the effectiveness of the flight ban. Of course, the clear visibility of the measure made it difficult to ignore. The resistance of the FRY against the ban could be interpreted as proof that this sanction was a real hit.[262] On the other hand, the countermeasures and threats made by the FRY could also be seen as a sign of confidence that the measure was not sustainable or at least could become very costly to the European Union itself.

---

259 Art. 8.

260 By Common Position 2000/599/CFSP and Council Regulation (EC) No. 2488/2000.

261 See De Vries, loc. cit. n. 194, at p. 87.

262 Serbian authorities imposed a $30 per passenger tax against EU carriers applying the ban. When most of the carriers refused to pay the tax, because payment would have been a violation of the EU financial sanctions, they were threatened with non-approval of their seasonal flights.

On the other hand, the investment ban may have had a major impact on the FRY regime. The biggest and most powerful companies in Serbia were owned or controlled by the FRY/Serbian governments. The investment ban deprived those companies of access to new capital, debt relief, capital goods and patents. As a result, those companies could not transfer funds to the FRY or Serbian governments. The investment ban thus hit the regime more than the private sector.

The freezing of funds may have been the most effective in pressurising the regime in Belgrade to comply with international law, although, here again, one should guard against strong conclusions. The initial financial sanctions, precisely because they were too narrowly targeted, may not have deprived the regime of access to hard foreign currency. Even the strengthening of the freezing of funds in June 1999 had little effect. The freezing of assets of designated individuals did not result in the seizure of a significant amount of funds with regard to companies. Most EU Member States continued to permit payments into accounts of Yugoslav banks and companies. The competent authorities of the Member States did not devote sufficient resources to determining which companies were to be sanctioned. Unless there was strong evidence to the contrary, most FRY companies received the benefit of the doubt. The provision of significant loans to companies in the FRY seems not to have taken place, but this may have been due not only to the freezing of funds but also to the poor state of the Yugoslav economy, which provided sufficient grounds for a reluctance to provide loans. The introduction of the reversal of the burden of proof in July 2000 stopped almost all payments to the FRY. But because of the very limited number of 'white' companies, many non-targeted companies were hit by the sanctions. Moreover, those companies that were listed as white companies were hit by retaliatory measures by the FRY regime. This factor and the almost indiscriminate nature of the financial sanctions may have contributed significantly to the massive opposition to the regime as expressed by the electoral outcome of 23 September 2000 and the protests during the following weeks. Thus, by becoming less targeted, the financial sanctions may have had their biggest effect on regime change in Belgrade.

Partly as a consequence of their relative success, a number of the European Union's smart sanctions were maintained and reinforced after the Kosovo conflict had ended. In this regard, their aim was not so much to dissuade parties from escalating the conflict but to target (individuals who aided or abetted) persons who were suspected to have committed crimes against humanity not only during the war in Kosovo but also during the wars in Bosnia and Croatia.[263]

---

263 See Council Common Position 2003/280/CFSP of 16 April 2003 in support of the effective implementation of the mandate of the ICTY, *OJ* 2003 L 101/22, renewed for another twelve months by Council Common Position 2007/150/CFSP of 5 March 2007 renewing measures in support of the

5. EU SANCTIONS AGAINST EXTREMISTS IN FYROM

In the context of the Macedonian crisis of 2001,[264] the Council adopted a common position to impose a visa ban on Albanian extremists who endangered peace and stability in Macedonia and thereby blocked international efforts to settle their dispute with the government in a peaceful manner.[265] However, the decisions needed to implement the visa ban were never taken, as a peace deal that ended the crisis was already reached three weeks later. Despite an overall improvement of the situation during the two-and-a-half years after the signing of the Ohrid Framework Agreement, certain individuals continued to promote or take part in violent activities challenging the agreement's basic principles of stability, territorial integrity and the unitary and multi-ethnic character of Macedonia. These actions undermined the concrete implementation of the Ohrid Agreement. In 2004, targeted measures in the form of restrictions on the admission on the territory of the Member States were adopted against twelve such individuals, some of whom resided outside Macedonia.[266] In 2005, the application of these restrictive measures was extended for a year and nine persons were added to the list of extremists.[267] Following the second review of Common Position 2004/133/CFSP, the Council in 2006 and 2007 extended the admission ban for another year and

---

effective implementation of the mandate of the International Criminal Tribunal for the former Yugoslavia (ICTY), *OJ* 2007 L 66/21. In parallel, Council Common Position 2004/694/CFSP of 11 October 2004 on further measures in support of the effective implementation of the mandate of the International Criminal Tribunal for the former Yugoslavia (ICTY), *OJ* 2004 L 315/52, and Council Regulation 1763/2004 of 11 October 2004 imposing certain restrictive measures in support of effective implementation of the mandate of the International Criminal Tribunal for the former Yugoslavia (ICTY), *OJ* 2004 L 315/14, were adopted, by which efforts were stepped up to close the net around Karadžić, Mladić, Gotovina and other persons publicly indicted by the ICTY for war crimes and who were not in the custody of the Tribunal. Most recently amended by Commission Regulation (EC) No. 1053/2006 of 11 July 2006 amending, for the 10th time, Council Regulation (EC) No. 1763/2004 imposing certain restrictive measures in support of effective implementation of the mandate of the International Criminal Tribunal for the former Yugoslavia (ICTY), *OJ* 2006 L 189/5.

264 See chapter 4, section 3.1.2.

265 Council Common Position 2001/542/CFSP of 16 July 2001 concerning a visa ban against extremists in FYROM, *OJ* 2001 L 194/55.

266 Council Common Position 2004/133/CFSP of 10 February 2004 on restrictive measures against extremists in the Former Yugoslav Republic of Macedonia (FYROM) and repealing Common Position 2001/542/CFSP, *OJ* 2004 L 39/19.

267 Council Common Position 2005/80/CFSP of 31 January 2005 extending and amending Common Position 2004/133/CFSP on restrictive measures against extremists in the Former Yugoslav Republic of Macedonia (FYROM), *OJ* 2005 L 29/45. Apart from the EEA countries, Bulgaria and Romania, as acceding countries, and Turkey and Croatia, as candidate countries, declared that they shared the objectives of the Council's Common Position and stated that they would ensure that their national policies would conform to this decision. See Declaration by the Presidency, Doc. 6243/1/05 REV 1 (Presse 29) P 11/05, 10 February 2005.

reviewed the list of targeted persons.[268] Like in previous sanctions policies, the restrictive measures come with a procedure for exemptions that can be granted by Member States in cases where travel is justified on the grounds of urgent humanitarian need or for the purpose of attending intergovernmental meetings (including those promoted by the European Union) where a political dialogue is conducted that directly promotes democracy, human rights and the rule of law in Macedonia.[269]

6. CONCLUDING REMARKS

As well as political and diplomatic questions, the crises in the former Yugoslavia raised a number of (European and international) legal issues to which the EC/EU had to provide an answer. At the beginning, the basic problem was how to treat a conflict that was at the same time inter-republican and inter-ethnic. Internal conflict and civil war were intermixed with international legal issues and increasing foreign involvement. The tendency was to 'simplify' the conflict by transforming it from the internal, federal, constitutional issues of a state called Yugoslavia to an international problem of relations between former Yugoslav republics. One of the first steps in that direction was the suspension of the EEC-SFRY Cooperation Agreement. The issue arose whether this action was legal under the rules of international law. Another step was the transformation of internal, inter-republican relations into international relations by way of recognition of the right to self-determination for individual federal units, that is to say, the Yugoslav republics. Incidentally, the internal borders between these federal units were recognised as international. At the same time, the EC had to deal with the political and legal questions revolving around the continuity and succession of the former Yugoslavia. The aim of the first part of this chapter was to investigate whether the EC was simply applying the classic rules of international law or whether we have witnessed the emergence of some new rules adopted to satisfy the new European realities. The answer to this question tends to include both of the elements just raised.

---

268 Council Common Position 2006/50/CFSP of 30 January 2006 extending and amending Common Position 2004/133/CFSP on restrictive measures against extremists in the Former Yugoslav Republic of Macedonia (FYROM), *OJ* 2006 L 26/24; and Council Common Position 2007/86/CFSP of 7 February 2007 extending and amending Common Position 2004/133/CFSP on restrictive measures against extremists in the former Yugoslav Republic of Macedonia, *OJ* 2007 L 35/32.

269 See Art. 3(2) of Council Common Position 2004/133/CFSP: 'A Member State wishing to grant exemptions [...] shall notify the Council in writing. The exemption will be deemed to be granted unless one or more of the Council Members raises an objection in writing within 48 hours of receiving notification of the proposed exemption. In the event that one or more of the Council Members raises an objection, the Council, acting by a qualified majority, may decide to authorise the proposed exemption.'

From 1991 until the end of the war in Bosnia (i.e., phases one and two of the Yugoslav wars), the EC/EU, much like other international actors, was preoccupied with attempts to contain and ultimately end the violent conflicts in the former SFRY. Despite a number of mostly reactive and punitive initiatives against the SFRY, and later the FRY, no coherent EC/EU sanctions policy existed in its own name. In fact, most of the sanctions imposed by the EC/EU on these targets were derivatives from obligations that originated at the level of the United Nations and were terminated once the Security Council decided to that effect. The only exceptions thereto, and thus the only examples of autonomous EU action during this period, were the precursors to the multilateral sanctions in 1991 (the arms embargo of July and the unilateral withdrawal of trade preferences in November) and the continuation of the arms embargo after the United Nations lifted its embargo on the states of the former Yugoslavia in 1995.

The third episode of the wars waged on the territory of the former SFRY shows a distinctively more ambitious development of the European Union's own sanctions policy. When studying the EU sanctions against the FRY as a reaction to the war in Kosovo, one notices a development from a very narrow targeting of the FRY and Serb governments in the first half of 1998 to a broader range of measures extending the impact to a larger group of persons and entities, becoming almost non-targeted in the cases of the oil embargo and the flight ban in mid-1999. After that, the sanctions were once again narrowed down to the Milošević regime, diminishing the impact on non-targeted sectors of the population, although in the summer of 2000 the financial sanctions severely impacted on many non-targeted companies and entities. After the elections of 24 September 2000, most of the sanctions were lifted, although a limited visa ban and assets freeze affecting approximately 600 individuals remained in place as of January 2001. The need for unanimity to adopt common positions that had allowed the more reluctant Member States to limit the scope and severity of the initial sanctions in 1998 gave the Member States that favoured stronger sanctions the leverage in 2000 to trade off the suspension of the flight ban and mitigation of the oil embargo against a strengthening of the financial sanctions.[270] Of course, such divergences in opinion within the Council put the Commission in a difficult spot with respect to the design and execution of sanctions. This lack of conviction and the resulting inaction in the implementation of sanctions may have allowed the FRY regime to ignore the sanctions.

At a time when the European Union is actively seeking to increase its capacity to master international conflicts on its own or to be an equal partner with other countries, notably the United States, concrete steps should be taken to ensure that military and non-military means and procedures can be deployed rapidly and

270 See De Vries, loc. cit. n. 194, at p. 87.

effectively to manage crises and prevent conflicts. One would expect that the sanctions described in this chapter, as non-military coercive instruments, would have a place in the arsenal of the European Union. But they apparently do not sit well with most Member States. A discussion on the role of sanctions as instruments of the Common Foreign and Security Policy has not even started yet. If that remains the case, the probability is that any new sanctions adopted by the European Union will display the same characteristics as the sanctions against the FRY.

CHAPTER 4

THE WESTERN BALKANS AS A TESTING GROUND FOR A COMMON FOREIGN AND SECURITY POLICY*

1. THE GRADUAL DEVELOPMENT OF THE CFSP/ESDP

History has shown that rogue leaders with bad intentions only understand the language of diplomacy backed by force.[1] Since the entry into force of the Treaty of Maastricht, the Member States of the European Union have actively used the diplomatic structures with which they endowed 'their' Common Foreign and Security Policy (CFSP). At first, this manifested itself primarily in reaching political agreement internally to adopt economic and other sanctions against (leaders of) third states.[2] But since the entry into force of the Treaty of Amsterdam, Javier Solana, Secretary-General/High Representative for the CFSP (SG/HR), supported by his staff at the Council, has made the most of the cautious wording of his tasks in Article 26 TEU. In the Western Balkans, the European Union, by way of its SG/HR, was instrumental in brokering a peace deal between the government and the Albanian separatists in Macedonia (2001) and in hammering out the Belgrade Agreement (2002) to prevent the Federal Republic of Yugoslavia from falling apart and having a knock-on effect on the precarious balance reached in Kosovo. The question remains, however, whether such diplomatic constructs can sustain the disintegrative forces at work in the Western Balkans. For long it has been clear that the European Union is in need of other, more persuasive instruments to force parties (that are intent on) fighting each other in an armed conflict not to commit heinous crimes such as ethnic cleansing and religious persecution and to settle their differences in a peaceful manner.

The need to move beyond the paper security structures that were introduced in the Treaty on European Union during the 1991 IGC quickly became apparent with the violent disintegration of Yugoslavia at the end of that year and the war in Bosnia-Herzegovina (BiH) (1992-1995). In the absence of its own security and defence capabilities, the European Union could avail itself of the Western European Union (WEU) to elaborate and implement decisions and actions of the

---

* An earlier version of this chapter was published as 'Role and Impact of the EU's Common Foreign and Security Policy towards the Western Balkans (2001-2006)', in 2 *Croatian Yearbook of European Law and Policy* (2006) pp. 209-264.

1 See R. Holbrooke, *To End a War* (New York, Random House 1998) at p. 146.

2 See chapter 3.

Council that had 'defence' implications.[3] The word 'defence' was to be interpreted in a broad sense, since it explicitly did not include the common defence of the territory of the European Union. The term referred to military cooperation in 'out-of-area' actions. Reviewing the significant changes that had taken place in the security situation in Europe after the outbreak of the Yugoslav crisis, the WEU Council of Ministers, at its meeting in Petersberg (near Bonn) on 19 June 1992, redefined its operational role so as to include the deployment of military units of WEU Member States for 'humanitarian and rescue tasks, peacekeeping tasks and tasks of combat forces in crisis management, including peacemaking' to implement conflict prevention or crisis management measures adopted within the framework of the OSCE or the United Nations.[4] While military units of the ten WEU Member States (all EU Member States) conducted operations in the Adriatic[5] and on the Danube,[6] they did not do so in support of the European

---

[3] Article J.4(2) TEU. See also the document on the 'Relations between the Union and the WEU', adopted by the Council of the European Union on 26 October 1993 and accepted by the WEU Council of Ministers on 22 November 1993, published in *Bull. EU* 10-1993 and as Document 1412 of the Assembly of the WEU, 8 April 1994. For more details on the legal relationship between the two international organisations, see R. Wessel, 'The EU as a Black Widow: Devouring the WEU to Give Birth to a European Security and Defence Policy', in V. Kronenberger, ed., *The European Union and the International Legal Order: Discord or Harmony?* (The Hague, T.M.C. Asser Press 2001) pp. 405-434.

[4] The WEU Declaration of 19 June 1992 is reproduced in C. Hill and K. Smith, *European Foreign Policy: Key Documents* (London, Routledge 2000) pp. 205-211. On the question whether the WEU, in extending its original collective defence task to completely new functions, was acting *ultra vires*, see R. Wessel, 'The Legality of the New Functions of the Western European Union: The Attribution of Powers Reconsidered on the Occasion of the 50th Anniversary of the Brussels Treaty', in A. Deighton and E. Remacle, eds., *The Western European Union, 1948-1998: From the Brussels Treaty to the Treaty of Amsterdam*, published as 1-2 *Studia Diplomatica* (1998) pp. 15-28.

[5] See: <http://www.weu.int>. In July 1992, the WEU Ministerial Council decided that WEU naval forces would participate in monitoring the UN embargo against the former Yugoslavia in the Adriatic. NATO was also conducting its own operation at the time. On 8 June 1993, the WEU and NATO Councils met to approve a combined concept for a joint operation in support of UNSC resolution 820 (1993). The agreement established a unified command for Operation *Sharp Guard*, which began on 15 June 1993. In the course of that operation, the WEU deployed four ships and some six maritime patrol and early warning aircraft. Almost 6,000 ships were inspected at sea, and more than 1,400 were diverted and inspected in port. Six ships were caught while attempting to break the embargo.

[6] Ibid. Following an extraordinary meeting of the WEU Council of Ministers in Luxembourg on 5 April 1993, it was agreed that WEU Member States would provide assistance to Bulgaria, Hungary and Romania in their efforts to enforce the UN sanctions on the Danube. In June 1993, the three riparian states accepted this offer and agreed with the WEU on the setting-up of a police and customs operation. Some 250 WEU personnel were involved when the operation was at its height. Equipped with eight patrol boats and forty-eight vehicles, WEU personnel carried out 6,748 inspection and monitoring operations resulting in the discovery of 422 infringements. This operation was a practical example of concrete cooperation with the Associate Partners, within the WEU, and of OSCE-WEU coordination, through the WEU Presidency delegation to the OSCE Sanctions Coordination Committee in Vienna. Following the Dayton Peace Agreement and the termination of the UN arms embargo, the Adriatic and Danube operations were wound up.

Union. The only official request from the Union during the first half of the 1990s to make use of WEU capabilities in the Western Balkans was related to support for the EU administration of the Bosnian town of Mostar (1994).[7] Unfortunately, this operation was generally perceived as a failure, especially by the parties to the conflict.[8] With the crises in Albania (1997) and Kosovo (1999), the European Union was further embarrassed at how little it could contribute to the prevention and/or 'management' of conflicts on its doorstep. Reliance upon US diplomacy and NATO's military strength condemned the Union to paying the bills for reconstruction while not moving the emphasis to conflict prevention and crisis management.

Frustration at such inadequacies and calls for change by others, notably the United States, led France and the United Kingdom, the EU Member States that pack the most military punch, to prod their colleagues at the Helsinki European Council in December 1999 into carrying forward work on the development of the Union's own military (and non-military) crisis management capability, with the objective of a strengthened and credible European policy on security and defence.[9] At its meeting in Helsinki, the European Council underlined its determination to develop an autonomous capacity to take decisions and, where NATO as a whole was not engaged, to launch and conduct EU-led military operations in response to international crises.[10] To this end, the European Council agreed that:

> by the year 2003, cooperating together voluntarily, [Member States] will be able to deploy rapidly and then sustain forces capable of the full range of Petersberg tasks as set out in the Amsterdam Treaty, including the most demanding, in operations up to corps level (up to 15 brigades or 50,000-60,000 persons). These forces should be militarily self-sustaining with the necessary command, control and intelligence capabilities, logistics, other combat support services and additionally, as appropriate, air and naval elements. Member States should be able to deploy in full at this level within 60 days, and within this to provide smaller rapid response

---

7 Three later requests by the European Union for WEU support pursuant to Article J.4(2) TEU concerned: the clearance of landmines in Croatia, general security surveillance of the Kosovo region and the provision of advice and training to instructors of the Albanian police. See *infra* section 2.2.

8 See *infra* section 2.1.

9 As a result of a meeting between French President Jacques Chirac and British Prime Minister Tony Blair at Saint-Malo, a joint Franco-British declaration on European defence was issued on 4 December 1998, stating that '[t]he Union must have the capacity for autonomous action, backed up by credible military forces, the means to decide to use them and a readiness to do so, in order to respond to international crises.' The joint declaration is reproduced in Hill and Smith, op. cit. n. 4, pp. 243-244.

10 The WEU Council facilitated this ambition of the European Union by deciding 'to prepare the WEU legacy and the inclusion of those functions of the WEU, which will be deemed necessary by the EU to fulfil its new responsibilities in the area of crisis-management tasks.' See WEU Ministerial Council, Luxembourg Declaration, 23 November 1999, para. 4.

> elements available and deployable at very high readiness. They must be able to sustain such a deployment for at least one year. This will require an additional pool of deployable units (and supporting elements) at lower readiness to provide replacements for the initial forces.[11]

This so-called 'common European headline goal' represented a political commitment by the Member States to develop a Rapid Reaction Force (RRF) and to progressively improve the Union's military capabilities for crisis management operations. In subsequent steps, the European Council agreed to the institution of new political and military bodies, structures and procedures to be established within the Council to ensure political guidance and strategic direction;[12] the principles for consultation and cooperation with non-European allies and NATO in crisis management;[13] measures to enhance the Union's civilian capabilities in the area of crisis management;[14] the European Security Strategy (ESS), the Union's first comprehensive approach to security issues;[15] measures to enhance

---

11 *Bull. EU* 12-1999, Annexes to the Presidency Conclusions, Annex 1 to Annex IV.

12 Following up on an agreement reached by the defence ministers of the European Union at their informal meeting at Sintra on 28 February 2000, the interim structures that prepared the ground for the Political and Security Committee, the EU Military Committee and the EU Military Staff started their activities in Brussels on 1 March 2000. See *Bull. EU* 3-2000, point I-20. In December 2000, the Council decided to make the interim committees permanent in the year 2001. See *Bull. EU* 12-2000, point I.6. The process to enhance European capabilities has recently been given a fresh impetus with the creation of the European Defence Agency. See Council Joint Action 2004/551/CFSP of 12 July 2004 on the establishment of the European Defence Agency, *OJ* 2004 L 245/17. See A. Ambos, 'The Institutionalisation of CFSP and ESDP', in D. Mahncke, A. Ambos and C. Reynolds, eds., *European Foreign Policy: From Rhetoric to Reality?* (Brussels, Peter Lang 2004) pp. 165-192.

13 On the so-called 'Berlin Plus' arrangements of 16 December 2002, which allow the European Union to draw on some of NATO's military assets in its own peacekeeping operations, see *infra* section 4.2.1.

14 The June 2000 Feira European Council decided to set up a European Security and Intelligence Force (ESIF) which is eventually meant to consist of 5,000 well-armed police officers, of whom 1,000 are to be deployable within thirty days, able to carry out preventive as well as repressive actions in support of global peacekeeping missions. See *Bull. EU* 6-2000, point I.8.11. See further Council Decision 2000/354/CFSP of 22 May 2000 setting up a Committee for civilian aspects of crisis management, *OJ* 2000 L 127/1; and Council Conclusions of 12 December 2005, Press Release No. 14960/05 (Presse 317) on the Civilian Headline Goal 2008. See A. Nowak, ed., *Civilian Crisis Management: the EU Way* (Paris, EUISS 2006).

15 *Bull. EU* 12-2003, point I.32.83. The ESS, on page 8, includes the following reference to the Western Balkans when listing strategic objectives for the Union: 'Our task is to promote a ring of well-governed countries to the East of the European Union and on the borders of the Mediterranean with whom we can enjoy close and cooperative relations. The importance of this is best illustrated in the Balkans. Through our concerted efforts with the US, Russia, NATO and other international partners, the stability of the region is no longer threatened by the outbreak of major conflict. The credibility of our foreign policy depends on the consolidation of our achievements there. The European perspective offers both a strategic objective and an incentive for reform.' On the ESS, see, *inter alia*, R. Kissack, 'The European Security Strategy: A First Appraisal' 2 *CFSP Forum* (2004) pp. 19-20; S. Duke, 'The European Security Strategy in a Comparative Framework: Does it Make for

EU military capabilities (the new Headline Goal 2010); and a timetable for carrying forward work on all these issues.[16]

Thus, in a very short timeframe, the European Union disentangled itself from the WEU[17] and developed what was needed to create an ability of its own to undertake the full range of Petersberg tasks.[18] These developments found their way into the Treaty of Nice of December 2000.[19] The European Security and Defence Policy (ESDP) was – somewhat prematurely – declared operational at the European Council of Laeken on 14 and 15 December 2001.[20] The most striking manifestation – and *raison d'être* – of this policy is the Union's capacity to back its diplomatic efforts by action on the ground, namely its crisis management operations. Since 2001, the European Union has affirmed its operational capability through the launching of sixteen ESDP operations, five of which – nearly one third of all EU operations – took or are still taking place in the Western Balkans: the EU Police Mission (since 2003) and EUFOR Althea (since 2004) in Bosnia-Herzegovina and Concordia (2003), Proxima (2003-2005) and

---

Secure Alliances in a Better World?', 9 *EFA Rev.* (2004) pp. 459-481; A. Toje, 'The 2003 European Union Security Strategy: A Critical Appraisal', 10 *EFA Rev.* (2005) pp. 117-134; A. Bailes, *The European Security Strategy. An Evolutionary History* (Stockholm, SIPRI 2005); and S. Biscop, *The European Security Strategy – A Global Agenda for Positive Power* (Aldershot, Ashgate 2005).

16 For an overview of the Union's efforts to build an ESDP, see, e.g., S. Blockmans, 'A New Crisis Manager at the Horizon – The Case of the European Union', 13 *LJIL* (2000) pp. 255-263; S. Duke, *The EU and Crisis Management: Development and Prospects* (Maastricht, EIPA 2001); A. Deighton, 'The European Security and Defence Policy', 40 *Journal of Common Market Studies* (2002) pp. 719-741; H. Neuhold and E. Sucharipa, eds., *The CFSP/ESDP After Enlargement: A Bigger EU = A Stronger EU?* (Vienna School of International Studies, Favorita Papers 2003); N. Gnesotto, ed., *EU Security and Defence Policy: The First Five Years (1999-2004)* (Paris, EUISS 2004); S. Biscop, 'Able and Willing? Assessing the EU's Capacity for Military Action', 9 *EFA Rev.* (2004) pp. 509-527; and S. Biscop, ed., *E Pluribus Unum? Military Integration in the European Union* (Brussels, Academia Press 2005).

17 In the Marseille Declaration of 13 November 2000, the WEU Council decided on the transfer of some WEU institutions (the Satellite Centre and the EUISS) and suspended the routine consultation mechanisms between the WEU and the European Union and between the WEU and NATO. The European Union agreed to take over the WEU institutions as well as the WEU activities that were still running (MAPE; the Demining Assistance Mission to the Republic of Croatia was continued under the responsibility of Sweden until 9 May 2001, when its mandate expired). The WEU thus returned to the organisation that was originally set up to deal with collective defence matters in 1948, namely, the Brussels Treaty Organisation. See Wessel, loc. cit. n. 3.

18 The content of which had already been codified to a great extent in Art. 17(2) TEU by the Treaty of Amsterdam.

19 In Art. 17 TEU, as amended, all references to the WEU were deleted. See R. Wessel, 'The State of Affairs in European Security and Defence Policy: The Breakthrough in the Treaty of Nice', 8 *Journal of Conflict & Security Law* (2003) pp. 265-288.

20 *Bull. EU* 12-2001, points I.5.6 and I.28. The Thessaloniki European Council of 19 and 20 June 2003 admitted recognised shortfalls in the European Union's operational capability across the full range of Petersberg tasks, but considered that they could be alleviated by the further development of the Union's military capabilities. See *Bull. EU* 6-2003, point I.23.56.

EUPAT (2005-2006) in Macedonia.[21] At the time of writing, the European Union is preparing for its biggest civilian ESDP operation in Kosovo.[22]

This chapter explores a variety of legal and political aspects of the European Union's actions in the Western Balkans that helped shape the CFSP during the early stages of its development. One ESDP operation *avant la lettre* is discussed: the civilian administration of the town of Mostar (1994-1996) (section 2).[23] After that, attention is paid to the European Union's diplomatic efforts to prevent or suppress violent conflicts in Macedonia, between Serbia and Montenegro and in Kosovo (section 3). Subsequently, the role and impact of the five ESDP operations that have been launched in the Western Balkans since 2001 are examined (section 4). Answers are provided to the question whether these operations have been or are being conducted *selon la lettre*. Conclusions will be drawn in section 5. This chapter is not concerned with the institutional changes of the Union's CFSP and ESDP as a result of the conflicts in the Western Balkans.[24]

2. ESDP OPERATIONS *AVANT LA LETTRE*

2.1 EU Administration of Mostar[25]

The geography, history, and population of Mostar are special. Mostar embraces both banks of the Neretva river. The proximity of mountains makes the left river bank steep, while the right bank is flatter and extended. Mostar was named either after the bridge keepers (*mostari*) or after the two towers from where they worked (*mostare*). Right in the centre of Herzegovina, the town of Mostar has long been the seat of both a *mufti*, an Orthodox episcopacy and – since the middle of the last century – a Catholic bishop. Until the annexation of Bosnia-Herzegovina to the Austro-Hungarian monarchy in 1878, Mostar had been under Ottoman rule. During the two World Wars, Mostar was heavily damaged. In 1991, the historical capital of Herzegovina was one of the most culturally cosmopolitan and nationally diverse towns in Yugoslavia. Of the 76,000 inhabitants, 34 per cent were

---

21 For a list of ESDP operations, see: <http://ue.eu.int/cms3_fo/showPage.asp?id=268&lang=EN&mode=g>.

22 See *infra* section 3.3.4.

23 For the EUMM – the other CFSP/ESDP mission *avant la lettre* – see chapter 3, section 2.4.

24 See, *inter alia*, S. Duke, 'From Amsterdam to Kosovo: Lessons for the Future of CFSP', 2 *Eipascope* (1999) pp. 2-15; C. Piana, 'The EU's Decision-Making Process in the Common Foreign and Security Policy: The Case of the Former Yugoslav Republic of Macedonia', 7 *EFA Rev.* (2002) pp. 209-226; and P. Latawski and M. Smith, *The Kosovo Crisis and the Evolution of Post-Cold War European Security* (Manchester, Manchester University Press 2003) in particular pp. 120-142.

25 The facts about Mostar are largely drawn from H. Boškailo-Šikalo, *Mostar* (Mostar, Microbook Publishing 2004).

Muslim, 29 per cent Croat and 19 per cent Serb, while as many as 18 per cent were self-declared 'Yugoslavs'. In 1992, Mostar again came under attack. As a result of the conflict in the former Yugoslavia, the eastern part of Mostar became Muslim-controlled while Bosnian-Croat forces controlled the western parts of town. The overwhelming majority of the town's Serb population fled or was expelled. On 9 November 1993, soldiers of the Croatian army destroyed the Old Bridge (1566) over the Neretva. Broadcasts of the demolition went all over the world and shocked the international community into action. As a result, the ongoing peace negotiations between the Bosnian Muslims and Croats gained more momentum.

Because the fate of Mostar was one of the key points of contention between Croats and Muslims during the peace negotiations that led to the Washington Agreement of March 1994, which established the Federation of Bosnia-Herzegovina (FBiH),[26] the reintegration of the town was viewed by the international community as a key indicator of the viability of that precarious federation. Mostar was therefore subject to a special degree of international attention.[27] Between July 1994 and January 1997, the town was placed under a special supervisory regime: the European Union Administration of Mostar (EUAM).[28] The aim was to overcome Mostar's ethnic division through a process of reconstruction, a feat that was to provide a much-needed model of cooperation for the rest of the FBiH. The European Commission effectively ran the civilian administration in Mostar from 23 July 1994 to 22 July 1996 in what must be regarded as the first civilian crisis management operation of the European Union.[29] Hans Koschnick, former mayor of Bremen, took up the post as 'EU Administrator' of the divided town.[30] At the request the Council of the European Union, the WEU

26 The text is available at: <http://www.usip.org/library/pa/bosnia/washagree_03011994.html> (last visited 19 March 2006).

27 Mostar's status was determined in the Agreement Implementing the Federation of Bosnia-Herzegovina, para. 1 *juncto* Annex on Mostar, 10 November 1995, 35 *ILM* (1996) pp. 170-183.

28 The EUAM was established by Council Decision 94/308/CFSP of 16 May 1994 adapting and extending the application of Decision 93/603/CFSP concerning the joint action decided on by the Council on the basis of Article J.3 of the Treaty on European Union on support for the convoying of humanitarian aid in Bosnia and Herzegovina, *OJ* 1994 L 134/1; and Council Decision 94/790/CFSP of 12 December 1994 concerning the joint action, adopted by the Council on the basis of Article J.3 of the Treaty on European Union, on continued support for European Union administration of the town of Mostar, *OJ* 1994 L 326/2. The Memorandum of Understanding approved by the Council at its meeting on 13 and 14 June 1994 and signed in Geneva on 5 July 1994 set out the conditions of application of Council Decision 94/790/CFSP. See *Bull. EU* 7/8-1994. The constituent instruments of the EUAM were repeatedly extended and eventually terminated on 22 July 1996; see *infra* n. 35.

29 See, A. Nowak, *L'Union en action: la mission de police en Bosnie* (Paris, ISS 2003); P. Jakobsen, 'The Emerging EU Civilian Crisis Management Capacity – A "Real Added Value" for the UN?', Background paper for the Copenhagen Seminar on Civilian Crisis Management arranged by the Royal Danish Ministry of Foreign Affairs, 8-9 June 2004.

30 The Council formally appointed Koschnick during its meeting on 18 April 1994. See *Bull. EU* 4-1994. A controversy over the size of a neutral 'central zone' in the decimated town-centre (strongly resisted by the Croats) led to the resignation of Koschnick in March 1996. See S. Bose, 'Mostar:

contributed a police contingent to the EUAM.[31] The aim of the WEU Police Force was to monitor the demilitarisation of Mostar with UNPROFOR, to restore and maintain public order with local police forces and to establish and train a unified police force in Mostar (UPFM) capable of carrying on after the final departure of the EUAM and the WEU Police Force.[32]

In the two years of its administration of Mostar, the European Union spent a total of ECU 144 million 'winterising' damaged residences and rebuilding damaged schools, medical facilities, courthouses, government offices, hotels, a theatre and railway and bus stations.[33] With this money, the Union also funded the reconstruction of Mostar's infrastructure, rebuilding water and electricity lines, repairing streets and restoring bridge connections over the Neretva river.[34] Most of this work was concentrated in East Mostar, which was far more damaged in the war than West Mostar. The European Union hoped that equalising conditions in the town's two halves would foster reconciliation. However, its success in reconstructing Mostar's ruined buildings and infrastructure took place against the background of its inability to reconstruct Mostar's ruined political, social and cultural institutions.[35]

In line with Article 4 (1) of the MoU signed at Geneva on 5 July 1994, the EUAM's mandate ended on 22 July 1996. In order to ensure the gradual transfer of the responsibilities exercised by the EUAM to the newly elected unified local administration and consequently ensure the objective of phasing out the EUAM, the European Union appointed Sir Martin Garrod as its Special Envoy in Mostar.[36] It was his task to ensure the rapid integration of Mostar into the overall

International Intervention in a Divided Bosnian Town, 1994-2001', in P. Siani-Davies, ed., *International Intervention in the Balkans since 1995* (London, Routledge 2003) pp. 68-87 at pp. 74 and 85. The Council of Ministers on 25 March endorsed the appointment of Spain's Ricardo Perez Casado to replace Koschnick. See *Bull. EU* 3-1996, point 1.4.55.

31 See: <http://www.weu.int>. The request of the Council was not presented in an official decision. The cooperation was not based on Art. J.4(2) TEU since no defence issues were involved. See J.-F. Paganon, 'Western European Union's Pivotal Position Between the Atlantic Alliance and the European Union', in A. Deighton, ed., *Western European Union 1954-1997: Defence, Security, Integration* (Oxford, European Independent Research Unit 1997) pp. 93-102 at p. 97.

32 The WEU's mandate in reproduced in Special Report No. 2/96 concerning the accounts of the Administrator and the European Union Administration, Mostar (EUAM) accompanied by the replies of the Commission and the Administrator of Mostar, *OJ* 1996 C 287/1, Annex 1, sub c. In May 1995, the Permanent Council of the WEU accepted the offer of contributions to the police force from Austria, Finland and Sweden, which enabled it to reach its maximum strength of 181 personnel during the summer of that year. Ibid., paras. 15 and 51.

33 Ibid., paras. 31-39.

34 Ibid., paras. 13-30.

35 See F. Pagani, 'L'administration de Mostar par l'Union européenne', 42 *AFDI* (1996); and S. Bose, 'Mostar: International Intervention in a Divided Bosnian Town, 1994-2001', in Siani-Davies, op. cit. n. 30, pp. 68-87.

36 See Joint Action 96/442/CFSP of 15 July 1996 adopted by the Council on the basis of Article J.3 of the Treaty on European Union, on the nomination of a Special Envoy of the European Union in

structures for the implementation of the Dayton Peace Agreement for Bosnia-Herzegovina.[37] The WEU police contingent continued to assist him until he transferred his public order executive powers to the local authorities on 15 October 1996. The EUAM was replaced by the Office of the High Representative (OHR) for Bosnia-Herzegovina, headed by Carl Bildt.

The EU Administration of Mostar was the first major CFSP joint action of the European Union. By way of the EUAM and the Office of the Special Envoy in Mostar, the Union demonstrated its commitment to peace, reconciliation and stability in Bosnia-Herzegovina in a very concrete way. The EUAM was undertaken in the extremely difficult circumstances of the conflict in Bosnia-Herzegovina. The objectives that were set for the mission were extremely ambitious, and the EUAM did not itself control the key elements that influenced whether or not the objectives could be achieved.[38] Progress on the primary objective of the EUAM – ensuring the establishment of a basis for a functioning unified local administration in the town with a joint police force – was extremely slow, due to the unwillingness of the local parties to work together. In the end, the elected authorities assumed the main responsibility for the management of the town's affairs, albeit under the auspices of the OHR. However, considerable progress was achieved in the areas of rehabilitation, reconstruction and redevelopment. Until the late summer of 1995, while the town was still subject to sporadic shelling, the only significant rehabilitation effort in the east was that undertaken by the EUAM. However, many problems persisted in Mostar after the European Union handed over its administrative authority, including continuing expulsions, harassment, intimidation and the influence of organised crime. Some local parties continued to obstruct political progress.[39] Hence, in terms of taking away the root causes of conflict in Mostar, the Union was not very successful.[40] Then again, a major reconstruction and reconciliation effort was needed throughout the whole of Bosnia-Herzegovina – a task that was not assigned to the European Union.

---

the city of Mostar, *OJ* 1996 L 185/1; Joint Action 96/476/CFSP adopted by the Council on 26 July 1996 on interim arrangements concerning the phasing out of the European Union Administration of Mostar, *OJ* 1996 L 195/1; Council Decision 96/508/CFSP of 9 August 1996 setting the date on which Joint Action 96/442/CFSP adopted by the Council on 15 July 1996 shall take effect, *OJ* 1996 L 212/1; and Council Decision 96/744/CFSP of 20 December 1996 on the phasing out of European Union operations in Mostar, *OJ* 1996 L 340/1.

37 On the UN-supervised International Police Task Force (responsible for police monitoring, training and restructuring), the OSCE (responsible for framing electoral rules and conducting elections), NATO's Stabilisation Force (guarantor of overall security) and the Office of the High Representative, see chapter 2.

38 See J. Monar, 'Mostar: Three Lessons for the European Union', 2 *EFA Rev.* (1997) pp. 1-5.

39 *Bull. EU* 12-1996, point I.37, Declaration of the European Council on former Yugoslavia.

40 For (very) critical assessments of the European Union's performance in Mostar, see, e.g., S. Orucević, 'Mostar: Europe's Failure', 15 *Bosnia Report* (1996); and S. Markotich, 'Pursuing Balkan Peace', 30 *OMRI Special Report* (1996).

2.2 EU interventions by way of the WEU

During the second half of the 1990s, the European Union requested WEU support pursuant to Article J.4(2) TEU on three occasions: for the provision of advice to and training of instructors of the Albanian police, for general security surveillance in the Kosovo region and for the clearance of landmines in Croatia.

2.2.1 *Multinational Advisory Police Element to Albania*

Although the crisis which erupted at the beginning of 1997 in Albania in the wake of the collapse of the 'pyramid' speculation systems would have lent itself *par excellence* for the launch of a so-called 'Petersberg mission' of the European Union, the principal responsibility for managing the chaos and violence in Albania was left to a military operation launched by a 'coalition of the willing' under Italian leadership in the context of the OSCE (*Operazione Alba*).[41] In May 1997, the WEU Council decided to send a Multinational Advisory Police Element to Albania (MAPE) as part of the efforts undertaken in that country by the OSCE.[42] A key part of MAPE's work was to provide advice to the Ministry of Public Order on restructuring the Albanian police. A new State Police Law was drawn up with MAPE's support and contained the foundations for building a democratic police to internationally accepted standards. In addition, approximately 3,000 police officers were trained in the Tirana Training Centre (Police Academy), in a second training centre in Durres and through field training programmes.[43]

On 2 February 1999, the WEU Council approved plans for an enhanced MAPE mission with a mandate until April 2000.[44] This mission was conducted by WEU at the request of the European Union on the basis of Article J.4(2) TEU, among other things enabling a major part of the costs to be met from the EU budget.[45] MAPE enhanced its geographical coverage and increased its operational mobility. The mission expanded its training and advice to selected ministries,

---

41 See, e.g., G. Kostakos and D. Bourantonis, 'Innovations in Peace-keeping: The Case of Albania', 29 *Security Dialogue* (1998) pp. 49-58; and E. Foster, 'Ad hoc in Albania: Did Europe Fail? A Rejoinder', 29 *Security Dialogue* (1998) pp. 213-219.

42 See chapter 2, section 8.7.

43 For background information on MAPE, see: <http://www.weu.int>.

44 Ibid.

45 See Council Decision 98/547/CFSP of 22 September 1998, adopted on the basis of Article J.4(2) of the Treaty on European Union, on the study of the feasibility of international police operations to assist the Albanian authorities, *OJ* 1998 L 263/1; Council Joint Action 1999/189/CFSP concerning a contribution by the European Union to the re-establishment of a viable police force in Albania, *OJ* 1999 L 63/1; and Council Decision 1999/320/CFSP concerning an EU contribution to the collection and destruction of weapons in Albania, *OJ* 1999 L 123/12.

directorates and 'low risk' police districts down to the operational unit level. MAPE consisted of 143 personnel by mid-1999. The WEU's mission played an important role during the Kosovo refugee crisis from April 1999 by supporting the Albanian police in their responsibilities for receiving, registering, supervising and escorting refugees. The MAPE mission terminated on 31 May 2001.[46]

2.2.2 *General security surveillance mission in Kosovo*

In November 1998, the WEU Satellite Centre embarked on a mission of general security surveillance in the Kosovo region. The aim of the mission was (i) to gather information for the European Union as well as the NATO and OSCE missions in Kosovo on the state of implementation of the agreements signed in Belgrade between the Federal Republic of Yugoslavia and the OSCE on 16 October 1998 and between the FRY and NATO on 15 October 1998; (ii) to provide full support for the OSCE and its Kosovo Verification Mission; and (iii) to provide support to the European Union's readiness to contribute to the assistance to refugees and displaced persons.[47] Again, this mission was launched at the request of the European Union pursuant to Article J.4(2) TEU. The mission was conducted in close coordination with the WEU Military Staff, which provided additional information for each of the Satellite Centre reports transmitted to the European Union, NATO and the OSCE. In view of the changed situation in Kosovo, with KFOR troops and other representatives of the international community on the ground, the Satellite Centre from July 1999 concentrated its work on the finalisation of a geographic information system (GIS) on Kosovo. The GIS was a digital map of the entire Kosovo region with visualisation and analysis tools and could be used to assist in several aspects of reconstruction work (including demining) in Kosovo.[48]

2.2.3 *WEU Demining Assistance Mission in Croatia*

On 9 November 1998, the Council of the European Union adopted two decisions with the aim of launching a mission to supervise and train mine clearance specialists in Croatia. In Council Decision 98/627/CFSP, an amount of up to ECU 435,000 (charged to the EC budget) was reserved to cover the operational

---

46 Council Joint Action 2000/798/CFSP supplementing Joint Action 1999/189/CFSP concerning a contribution by the European Union to the re-establishment of a viable police force in Albania, *OJ* 2000 L 324/1, which was not prolonged after it ceased to apply on 31 May 2001.

47 Council Decision 98/646/EC of 13 November 1998, adopted on the basis of Article J.4(2) of the Treaty on European Union, on the monitoring of the situation in Kosovo, *OJ* 1998 L 308/1. For the background to the NATO and OSCE operations in Kosovo, see chapter 2, sections 7.3 and 8.4.

48 See: <http://www.weu.int>.

expenditure to which the implementation of the decision would give rise.[49] In Council Decision 98/628/CFSP, the European Union requested the WEU to implement the demining assistance mission.[50] Unlike the former, the latter decision was based on Article J.4(2) TEU because the action would require staff having military expertise. The institutions of the WEU had already given their agreement to the practical arrangements set out in the annex to Decision 98/628/CFSP.[51] Within the framework of the WEU Demining Assistance Mission in Croatia, which began operations on 10 May 1999, the WEU provided advice, technical expertise and training support to the Croatian Mine Action Centre in the areas of programme management, planning, project development and geographic information.[52] Sweden acted as lead nation for this mission. The mission terminated on 30 November 2001.[53]

2.3 Evaluation

In the 1990s, the European Union's CFSP towards the Western Balkans was largely of a declaratory nature.[54] This is logical if one considers the lack of operational capabilities and hardware at the European Union's disposal. In the military field, the Union was obliged to outsource 'its' actions in the Western Balkans. Only in those relatively minor areas of post-conflict rehabilitation left by the international protagonists (the United States and NATO) could the Union make use of WEU capabilities in support of its actions. As such, the WEU conducted operations in Albania, Kosovo and Croatia, while the European Union paid the bills. The Union's civilian administration of Mostar was the only operation over which the Union itself kept control; the only ESDP operation *avant la lettre*. While it was supported by a WEU police contingent, the European Union's Administrator pulled the levers. Unfortunately for the Union, the EUAM

---

49 Council Decision 98/627/CFSP of 9 November 1998 adopted on the basis of Article J.3 TEU concerning a specific action of the Union in the field of assistance for mine clearance, *OJ* 1998 L 300/1. See also Council Decision 2000/231/CFSP of 20 March 2000 supplementing Decision 98/627/CFSP concerning a specific action of the Union in the field of assistance for mine clearance, *OJ* 2000 L 73/2.

50 Council Decision 98/628/CFSP adopted on the basis of Article J.4(2) TEU on the implementation of a Council Decision concerning a specific action of the Union in the field of assistance for mine clearance, *OJ* 1998 L 300/2.

51 Ibid., preamble.

52 See: <http://www.weu.int>.

53 The budget for the mission was prolonged for the second and last time – until 30 November 2001 – by Council Decision 2001/328/CFSP of 24 April 2001 supplementing Decision 98/627/CFSP concerning a specific action of the European Union in the field of assistance for mine clearance, *OJ* 2001 L 116/1.

54 The Member States, by way of the Presidency or through the Council, adopted a huge number of declarations, statements and common positions concerning the situation in ex-Yugoslavia.

was generally perceived as a failure, especially by the parties to the conflict. With the crisis in Kosovo (1999), the European Union was further embarrassed at how little it could contribute to conflict prevention and crisis management in its own 'backyard.' Kosovo made it clear to the Union that, if it ever wanted to play a more important role on the international scene, it had to put its M&M (men and money) where its mouth was. At the turn of the millennium, the Member States carried 'their' CFSP agenda forward to narrow what has been famously called the 'capabilities-expectations' gap.[55] The crises in Macedonia (2001) and the Federal Republic of Yugoslavia (2001-2002) proved more fertile ground for the development of a more comprehensive CFSP.

3. DIPLOMATIC ENDEAVOURS

3.1 *Coupe macédoine*[56]

3.1.1 *Protecting minority rights*[57]

In 2001, a conflict erupted between Albanian and Slavic Macedonians that brought the country to the brink of an outright civil war. Macedonia had never really succeeded in integrating its Albanian citizens. The Albanian Macedonians boycotted the 1991 referendum on independence from the SFRY and the attendant census because the Macedonian Constitution did not recognise them as a constituent nation of Macedonia.[58] In January 1992, they held a plebiscite of their own in which they opted for autonomy. They publicly and recurrently rejected the results of the 1994 internationally monitored census (according to which Albanians made up 23 per cent of the population, amended by a later census to 26 per cent). Many Albanians in Western Macedonia felt closer to their kith and kin in

[55] See C. Hill, 'The Capability-Expectations Gap, or Conceptualizing Europe's International Role', 31 *Journal of Common Market Studies* (1993) pp. 305-328; and C. Hill, 'Closing the Capabilities-Expectations Gap?', in J. Peterson and H. Sjursen, eds., *A Common Foreign Policy for Europe: Competing Visions of the CFSP* (London, Routledge 1998) pp. 18-38. See *supra* section 1.

[56] A dessert consisting of a mixture of fresh fruit. For analyses on the history of Macedonia since the break-up of Yugoslavia, see J. Pettifer, ed., *The New Macedonian Question* (Basingstoke, Palgrave 2001).

[57] The facts described in this paragraph are primarily based on the Balkan Crisis Reports of the London-based Institute for War & Peace Reporting, available at: <http://www.iwpr.net>.

[58] The Constitution of Macedonia was altered in 1989 from '[Macedonia is] the state of the Macedonian people and the Albanian and the Turkish minorities' to read '[Macedonia is] the national state of the Macedonian nation'. The Albanians demanded to be explicitly mentioned in the Constitution as a 'constituent nation'. In the 1946 and 1974 Constitutions of the former Yugoslavia, constituent nations had the right to secede. It is therefore no wonder the Macedonians rejected this formulation.

Kosovo than to the Macedonian state. Albanians occasionally accused the Slavic Macedonians of discrimination in the labour market, in secondary and higher education, in expenditure on infrastructure (many Albanian villages still lack proper roads and are not connected to the national water and electricity grids) and in public administration. Albanians claimed that police brutality, discriminatory legislation and the exclusive use of the Macedonian language violated their human and civil rights. Gradually, they lost faith in the Slavic Macedonians' will to accommodate their demands, however legitimate. To this the Macedonians would retort that Albanians made up a hefty chunk of the informal economy, thus distorting official unemployment figures; that Albanians in Western Macedonia largely did not pay taxes; that their under-representation in state administration was due to the lack of properly qualified and educated people; and that infrastructure all over the country was decrepit. Macedonians intermittently accused the Albanians of illegal construction, purchases of real estate at inflated prices, mass immigration from Kosovo, repopulation of Macedonian villages abandoned by their inhabitants, ethnic cleansing of urban neighbourhoods by intimidation, nationalist indoctrination under the guise of religious instruction, pressuring other Muslims to declare themselves as Albanians and irredentism.[59]

On top of these simmering tensions, during much of the 1990s, there was the growing problem of Albanian refugees from Kosovo in Macedonia following Milošević's crackdown on Albanians in Kosovo and NATO's air campaign of March-June 1999.[60] Repeatedly, the Macedonian government warned the international community that it could not allow more refugees on its soil, both for economic reasons and for fear of disrupting the fragile ethnic fabric of the country. In addition, there was a lot of evidence of massive arms smuggling activity in the northern regions of Macedonia bordering Kosovo and southern Serbia. Reports showed that Albanians in the Macedonian border villages were preparing themselves for an armed uprising.[61] Finally, the international community failed to establish a link between the crisis of the Preševo Valley in June 1999 and a possible crisis in Macedonia.[62] The attention of the European Union,

---

[59] See the December 2001 Progress Report of the Rome-based 'Ethnobarometer' network, published online as K. Balalovska, A. Silj and M. Zucconi, *Minority Politics in Southeast Europe: Crisis in Macedonia* (2002), available at: <http://www.ethnobarometer.org>.

[60] Some 400,000 Kosovar refugees flooded into Macedonia (equal to 20 per cent of the population).

[61] See: <http://www.macedonia.org/crisis/timeline.html>.

[62] The crisis surfaced after the end of the war in Kosovo, when Serbian military and police forces were withdrawn from Kosovo and deployed in the Preševo Valley and when the pressure of the Serbian administration on the Albanian families there increased, forcing them to leave a number of villages. From June 1999 onwards, thousands of Albanians fled, mostly to Kosovo and Macedonia. See B. Huszka, 'The Presevo Valley of Southern Serbia alongside Kosovo: The Case for Decentralisation and Minority Protection', *CEPS Policy Brief*, No. 120, January 2007.

indeed of the international community as a whole, was focused on Kosovo and Serbia, whereas Macedonia was regarded as a relatively stable country in the Western Balkans. While it is true that the European Commission, in the months preceding the crisis, was engaged in Macedonia with different projects, these actions did not prevent inter-ethnic tensions from reaching fever pitch during the presidential elections of 17 November 1999, when the late President Boris Trajkovski's win was attributed by the opposition to mass electoral fraud among Albanian voters.[63] Over the next year, Macedonia continued to run on a dangerously high voltage. In that year, the National Liberation Army (NLA) (the Macedonian version of the Kosovar Liberation Army) emerged, claiming equal rights for ethnic Albanians by force. There was sporadic ethnically motivated violence in the form of terrorist bomb attacks.

At the beginning of 2001, the Macedonian pressure cooker exploded. On 25 January, Albanian guerrillas claimed responsibility for a rocket attack on a police station which left one officer dead and wounded another three. On 11 February, the first sod was turned and construction of the disputed SEE University at Tetovo began.[64] On 19 February, ethnic Albanian insurgents wearing the insignia of the NLA clashed with a military patrol in Macedonia. Due to the increasing violence, Macedonia put its troops on alert along the border with Kosovo to prevent ethnic Albanian fighters from infiltrating. Amid growing evidence that Albanian separatist guerrillas were using the Ground Safety Zone (GSZ) around Kosovo to stage incursions into both southern Serbia and Macedonia, NATO agreed to start dismantling the buffer zone (Operation *Eagle*).[65] At the fourth

63 In the eyes of some, the European Union was even seen as siding with the Albanians by providing support to strengthen their administrative and judicial capacities and by contributing financial means to set up the South East European University in Tetovo, the first official university institute in Macedonia (partly) committed to the Albanian culture, language and population. See: <http://www.seeu.edu.mk/english/general/history.asp>.

64 Construction was completed within less than six months. This is even more remarkable when one considers that the Tetovo region witnessed some of the heaviest inter-ethnic skirmishes between March and August of 2001. The academic year started in October 2001.

65 At the end of NATO's air campaign against Serbia, the UN Security Council adopted resolution 1244 (1999), which enabled NATO to deploy KFOR troops in Kosovo. Simultaneously, KFOR's First Commander, Sir Michael Jackson, and the Yugoslav military authorities agreed, *inter alia*, to the withdrawal of the Yugoslav army and police from Kosovo and the creation of a demilitarised, five-kilometre wide *Ground Safety Zone* in western Montenegro and southern Serbia along the border of Kosovo. See P. Janković and S. Gligorijević, 'Burying the Hatchet', *NATO Review* (Summer 2004). Part of the GSZ, around the village of Tanuševci, in the corner where the borders of Kosovo, Southern Serbia and Macedonia meet, had become a sort of no-man's land after the withdrawal of UNPREDEP. The NLA had prospered there thanks to different kinds of trafficking and other illegal activities. The pending ratification by the Macedonian parliament of a Yugoslav-Macedonian border agreement, which had been negotiated without the participation of the Albanians, was another reason for the NLA to launch an armed uprising. See R. Detrez, *Macedonië: land in de wachtkamer* (Antwerp, Houtekiet 2002) at p. 223.

Summit of the Heads of State and Government of the South-East Europe Cooperation Process (SEECP), which – ironically – was held under Macedonian chairmanship in Skopje on 22 February 2001, all delegates (including Javier Solana and Chris Patten, then Commissioner for External Relations) distanced themselves from the ethnic Albanian armed extremism and reiterated their strong attachment to the principle of inviolability of borders, including the territorial integrity of Macedonia.[66] The EU Presidency delivered tough warnings to Albanian leaders and called on all involved 'to isolate the extremists'.[67] NATO Secretary General George Robertson called the rebels 'a bunch of murderous thugs whose objective is to destroy a democratic Macedonia and who are using civilians as human shields' in a cynical bid to provoke 'another Balkan bloodbath'.[68] Strengthened by the international disapproval of the NLA's actions, the Macedonian army called for a general mobilisation on 5 March and launched an offensive against the NLA's stronghold in Tanuševci. While the Macedonian army seized control of the village and its surroundings, it was not able to prevent the violence from spreading.[69]

The crowning achievement of the Albanians was their success in internationalising the conflict. In this, they were aided by a panic-stricken Macedonian establishment. When the leaders of the NLA, at the end of March, emphasised that their sole goal for action constituted the protection of those rights for which they had been fighting by peaceful means for the past ten years, and not the ambition to create a 'Greater Albania', they must have convinced the 'wise men of the West' – Javier Solana, Lord Robertson, and US Secretary of State Colin Powell – to put pressure on the Macedonian government to start negotiations with the NLA to solve the conflict.[70]

---

66 See: <http://www.seecp.gov.mk>. The SEECP represents a comprehensive framework for regional cooperation aimed at close cooperation with other international organisations and regional initiatives. Of particular importance are the United Nations, the European Union, the OSCE, NATO, the Council of Europe, the Black Sea Initiative, SECI, the CEI and the BSEC. See also chapter 5, section 3.3.2.

67 *Bull. EU* 1/2-2001, point 1.6.41. 'The European Union urges all parties to respect the border demarcation agreement between the FRY and the Former Yugoslav Republic of Macedonia signed in Skopje on 23 February, and reiterates its strong attachment to the principle of inviolability of borders, including the territorial integrity of the Former Yugoslav Republic of Macedonia. A peaceful and stable Former Yugoslav Republic of Macedonia – within internationally recognised borders – is an important condition for furthering the integration of the Former Yugoslav Republic of Macedonia within the European Union, soon through the signing of the Stabilisation and Association Agreement.'

68 As reported in 'Macedonia "on brink of abyss"', *BBC News*, 7 March 2001.

69 The conflict spread out and in the ensuing months ethnic Albanian militants successfully 'liberated' other villages in Northern Macedonia, including Aračivono in June, from where they threatened to launch mortar attacks on the outskirts of Skopje and on the international airport.

70 See Detrez, op. cit. n. 65, at pp. 230-231; and *The Position of the EU and NATO on the Current Situation in the Republic of Macedonia*, available at: <http://www.macedonia.org/crisis/story3.html>.

3.1.2 *A partnership of 'honest' brokers?*

At the beginning of April 2001, a number of EU representatives visited Skopje to prepare for the signing of the Stabilisation and Association Agreement (SAA) with Macedonia on 9 April in Luxembourg.[71] The SAA would establish legal obligations for Macedonia to approximate its legislation to the *acquis communautaire* and to cooperate with the other countries of the Western Balkans. It involved the perspective of the establishment of a free trade area between the European Community and the country, provisions on cooperation in a wide range of fields, including justice and home affairs, and the provision of financial assistance to help Macedonia achieve the objectives of the agreement. Macedonia was the first and at the same time the least prepared country that was offered such an agreement. It was meant to repair the shattered confidence of Macedonia in the European Union and to make the government more amenable to Western diplomatic initiatives. Javier Solana, who had been 'invited' by the European Council at its Stockholm summit of 23 and 24 March 'to follow the situation in the region, to stay in close touch with the leaders and in consultation with the Commission and to make recommendations to the Council',[72] used the prospect of the pending signature and ratification of the SAA as a strong lever to persuade the Macedonian government to engage in negotiations to reform the Constitution and establish equal rights for both communities.[73] The Albanians found comfort in this approach because they expected that Macedonia would never accede to the European Union if the Albanian question was not resolved according to 'European standards'. When the Macedonian government realised that negotiations on a political agreement with the Albanian militants had become unavoidable, it decided to build a government of national unity by expanding the existing government with moderate Albanian politicians. In this way, the coalition would share the responsibility for the amendments to the Constitution and other laws with the two biggest ethnic Albanian parties, and it would be able to find the necessary two-thirds majority needed to push the reforms through parliament.

While the fighting on the ground and the talks on forming a grand coalition dragged on, Western diplomats tried to hammer out a politically acceptable implementation plan for the future accord. At the end of June, Robert Badinter,[74] US Special Envoy James Pardew and François Léotard, the freshly appointed EU

---

[71] Negotiations were closed on 24 November 2000 and the SAA was initialled on the same date, during the Zagreb Summit. See COM(2001) 90 final, Brussels, 19 February 2001. See also chapter 5, section 3.

[72] See *Bull. EU* 3-2001, point I.36.66.

[73] In line with the European Parliament's resolution of 5 April 2001. See *Bull. EU* 4-2001, point 1.6.1.

[74] See chapter 3.

Special Representative in Macedonia,[75] were sent to Skopje to mediate in the negotiations on a ceasefire and a political agreement between the parties to the conflict.[76] The ceasefire agreement of 5 July was breached by Albanian extremists. This caused the negotiations to stall. As a reaction, the European Union adopted punitive sanctions against the ethnic extremists.[77] On 25 July, NATO's Special Envoy Peter Feith secured a limited ceasefire agreement in and around Tetovo. The following day, Solana and Robertson, accompanied by the Chairman-in-Office of the OSCE, Mircea Geoana, travelled to Skopje to blow new life into the negotiations.[78] On 28 July, the negotiators decided to move the talks to Villa Biljana, on the idyllic shores of Lake Ohrid. Despite some heavy fighting in the first two weeks of August, a political deal was struck at Ohrid on 8 August.

It can be said that the new institutional framework for the CFSP and the ESDP allowed EU action in Macedonia to produce a more positive outcome than in previous Balkan crises. Nonetheless, in terms of conflict prevention *stricto sensu*, the Union failed to identify, let alone address, some of the early signs that pointed to the possibility that a crisis might emerge in FYROM, long before it actually did in January 2001.[79] The Albanian armed insurgency amounted to low intensity warfare but nevertheless created a humanitarian catastrophe when one considers the numbers of ethnic Albanian refugees that fled into Kosovo (approximately 65,000) and internally displaced persons in Macedonia (approximately 35,000).[80] To a large extent, the Union's success in preventing a further escalation of violence into full-blown civil war and suppressing the conflict is due to its 'preventive' diplomacy and the leading role played by Javier Solana. The SG/HR travelled to Skopje on countless occasions, sometimes accompanied by Chris Patten. Supported on the ground by François Léotard, the European Union's resident envoy, and José Pinto Teixeira, Head of the Commission Delegation, the SG/HR put considerable pressure on both the Macedonian and the Albanian side to engage in dialogue.[81] The looming signature of the SAA between the European Union and FYROM was certainly the strongest incentive at Solana's disposal to

---

75 Council Joint Action 2001/492/CFSP, *OJ* 2001 L 180/1.

76 In the meantime, an agreement on a broad coalition government had been struck. See *Bull. EU* 5-2001, point 1.6.12.

77 Council Common Position 2001/542/CFSP concerning a visa ban against extremists in the Former Yugoslav Republic of Macedonia, *OJ* 2001 L 194.

78 See Presidency statement on behalf of the European Union on the situation in the Former Yugoslav Republic of Macedonia of 26 July 2001, in *Bull. EU* 7/8-2001, point 1.6.10.

79 See, e.g., S. Clément, *Conflict Prevention in the Balkans: Case Studies of Kosovo and the FYR of Macedonia* (Paris, ISS 1997) at pp. 13-16 and 24-27. Clément draws the same conclusion about the limited preventive measures adopted by the international community, 'in particular the European Union', in the case of Kosovo, at pp. 21-23. See also S. Clément, 'Former Yugoslav Macedonia, the Regional Setting and European Security: Towards Balkan Stability?', in J. Pettifer, ed., *The New Macedonian Question* (Basingstoke, Palgrave 2001) pp. 285-302.

80 UNHCR estimates reported in 261 *IWPR Balkan Crisis Report* (2001).

81 See N. Whyte, N. Arbatova and D. Allin, 'The Macedonian Crisis and Balkan Security', *ESF Working Papers* (2001).

force the two parties in the conflict to arrive at an agreement by political means. To this end, the Commission's brand new Rapid Reaction Mechanism (RRM) was also utilised.[82]

But the Union could not have managed to broker the peace deal at Ohrid without the support of NATO and, to a lesser extent, the United States and the OSCE. NATO's involvement was evident if one considers that KFOR's supply routes and logistical bases were in Macedonia. From a more geopolitical perspective, NATO's southern flank – comprising the ever-adversarial Turkey and Greece – could be destabilised by an inter-religious conflict in the Balkans. Add to this the destabilising and radicalising impact upon the delicate fabric of Kosovo of the throngs of ethnic Albanian refugees from Macedonia and Lord Robertson's active engagement becomes more understandable, as does his relentless pressure on local politicians to deliver a peace agreement.

3.1.3 *Ohrid Framework Agreement (2001)*

The Ohrid Framework Agreement was signed at a ceremony at the residence of President Trajkovski in Skopje on 13 August 2001.[83] With their presence, Solana, Robertson, Geoana, Pardew and Léotard emphasised the importance that the international community attached to the agreement. The text of the Ohrid Framework Agreement contained a series of commitments, in the form of basic principles and legislative modifications, which the parliament had to apply through constitutional amendments and implementing laws. Among the basic principles, the parties to the agreement rejected the use of violence in pursuit of political aims, recognised Macedonia's sovereignty, its territorial integrity and the multi-ethnic character of its society, and underlined the development of local self-government to encourage the participation of citizens in democratic life and promote respect for the identity of communities. The parties agreed to a complete cessation of hostilities, after which the ethnic Albanian armed groups would be completely disarmed and disbanded with the assistance of NATO. The rest of the

---

[82] Council Regulation (EC) No. 381/2001 creating a rapid-reaction mechanism, *OJ* 2001 L 57/5. The RRM allows the Commission to dispatch Community funds rapidly in case of an emergency. It can be used both to conduct once-off actions arising out of a crisis situation and to 'kick-start' projects or programmes which will require longer-term follow-up through other assistance instruments. The RRM funds measures aimed at restoring the conditions of stability under which the main Community cooperation programmes can achieve their objectives. These can include measures to restore the rule of law, promote democracy and human rights, peacebuilding and mediation initiatives, the demobilisation and reintegration of combatants, the reconstruction of infrastructure and the strategic planning of the economic, administrative and social rebuilding of countries affected by crisis. The funds available through the RRM were €20 million for 2001 and €25 million for 2002. The RRM was first used in March 2001 to pay for the reconstruction of houses destroyed or damaged by the fighting in the areas of Tetovo and Skopska Crna Gora.

[83] The agreement is available at: <http://faq.macedonia.org/politics/framework_agreement.pdf>.

agreement was devoted to the more concrete revision of legislation on, *inter alia*, local self-government,[84] the revision of municipal boundaries one year after a new census (to be held by the end of 2001) and employment in public administration.[85]

Special parliamentary procedures were agreed to for the amendment of the Constitution and the Law on Local Self-Government: a qualified majority of two-thirds of votes, 'within which there must be a majority of the votes of representatives claiming to belong to the communities not in the majority in the population of Macedonia.'[86] The same clause applied to the majority of votes required for the revision of laws affecting culture, the use of language, education, personal documentation and the use of symbols, as well as laws on local finances, local elections, the city of Skopje and boundaries of municipalities.

With respect to primary and secondary education, instruction would be provided in the students' native languages. State funding would be provided for university level education in languages spoken by at least 20 per cent of the population of Macedonia. It was agreed that Macedonian would be the official language of the country. Any other language spoken by at least 20 per cent of the population was also recognised as an official language and could be used for communication with central government and with and/or within decentralised authorities. In criminal and civil judicial proceedings at any level, an accused person or any other party was said to have the right to translation at state expense of all proceedings as well as documents. Local authorities were given the right to place emblems marking the identity of the majority community in the municipality on the front of local public buildings, next to the emblem of the 'Republic of Macedonia'.

The Constitutional amendments attached to the Ohrid Framework Agreement in Annex A had to be presented to parliament immediately. The parties committed themselves to take all measures to assure the adoption of these amendments within forty-five days of the signature of the agreement. The legislative modifications identified in Annex B were expected to be adopted in accordance with the timetables specified therein. Finally, the parties invited the international community to convene an international donor conference to address, in particular, macro-financial assistance and the financing of the measures to be undertaken for the purpose of implementing the Framework Agreement.

---

[84] To reinforce the powers of elected local officials and to expand their competences in the areas of public services, urban and rural planning, environmental protection, local economic development, culture, local finances, education, social welfare and health care.

[85] To assure the equitable representation of communities in all central and local public bodies, especially the police services, and at all levels of employment within such bodies, while respecting the rules concerning competence and integrity that govern public administration.

[86] Ohrid Framework Agreement, section 5.1.

Annex C to the Framework Agreement contained a number of issues that concerned the international community. The parties 'invited' the international community to facilitate, monitor and assist in the implementation of the provisions of the agreement and its annexes, and 'requested' such efforts to be coordinated by the European Union in cooperation with the newly established Stabilisation and Association Council (SAC).[87] The Council of Europe and the European Commission were asked to supervise the conduction of a census. The OSCE and other international organisations were invited to send observers to the parliamentary elections of 2002. Furthermore, the parties pledged to work to ensure the return of refugees and internally displaced persons to their homes within the shortest possible timeframe and invited the UNHCR, in particular, to assist in these efforts. The parties invited the European Union, the OSCE and the United States to support and assist with the implementation of the commitment to ensure that by 2004 the police services would generally reflect the composition and distribution of the population of Macedonia, in particular through the screening and selection of candidates and their training. In addition, the European Union, the OSCE and the United States were invited to deploy international monitors and police advisors in sensitive areas as soon as possible. Finally, the parties invited the international community to assist in the training of lawyers, judges and prosecutors from members of communities not in the majority in Macedonia, in order to increase their representation in the judicial system.

A major flaw in the Framework Agreement came in the form of the special governmental privileges (in respect of education and the use of languages). As noted, they were only granted to minorities making up 'at least 20 percent of the population'.[88] Ironically, the preamble of the agreement asserted that it 'will promote the peaceful and harmonious development of civil society while respecting the ethnic identity and the interests of all Macedonian citizens.' With thousands of Macedonian citizens of various ethnic backgrounds making up less than 20 per cent of the population,[89] the Ohrid Framework Agreement unequivocally discriminated against these citizens.[90]

---

87 On the SAC, see chapter 5, section 3.

88 Ohrid Framework Agreement, section 6.

89 Macedonian 64.2 per cent, Albanian 25.2 per cent, Turkish 3.9 per cent, Roma 2.7 per cent, Serb 1.8 per cent, Other 2.2 per cent (2002 census). See CIA World Factbook, available at: <http://www.cia.gov/cia/publications/factbook/geos/mk.html>.

90 See S. Gligorov and M. Koloski, 'Decentralization, or Euro-Discrimination?', 4 November 2004, available at: <http://www.maknews.com/html/articles/koloski/koloski8.html> (last visited 19 March 2006): 'Public pressure against fulfilment of the Framework Agreement surfaced in the form of large public protests against race-based decentralisation. The Constitutional requirement for Referendum put democratic power back in the hands of the people when over 150,000 signed a petition against the Framework.'

3.1.4 *Sustainability of the diplomatic efforts*

While the Ohrid Framework Agreement has been criticised as a continuation of 'the infamous tradition of compacts imposed by a war-weary West on helpless and hapless small nations' and was doomed to fail,[91] it did, in the medium term,[92] bring an end to several months of violence between ethnic Albanian groups and the state security forces. In the second half of 2001, NATO collected 4,000 pieces of weapons from the NLA (Operation *Essential Harvest*).[93]

The Ohrid Framework Agreement provided for a decentralised system of governance, an equitable representation for ethnic Albanians in the Macedonian state structures and the recognition of the Albanian language and culture. It is true, however, that additional 'carrots and sticks' were necessary to persuade the former rivals to adhere to their commitments. In October 2001, for example, the Commission adopted a decision to finance a Confidence Building Programme for Macedonia, including the use of funds of the RRM. This package, worth €10.3 million, was inextricably linked to the full ratification of all the amendments to the Macedonian Constitution (16 November 2001), as well as the new Law on Local Self-Government (24 January 2002).[94] Withholding financial incentives by postponing the donor conference to which the international community had been 'invited' proved another useful tool to clear hurdles in the implementation process of the Framework Agreement. At that conference, which was held in Brussels on 12 March 2002, the international community pledged €307 million to reform in Macedonia – €50 million more than the country had asked for.[95] Finally, the threat by the European Union to revise the one-year-old SAA was another (doubtful) method used by the Union to cajole the Macedonian parliament into adopting the necessary laws on the use of languages in April 2002.[96]

After a series of constitutional amendments and changes to more than seventy laws, the adoption of the law on use of flags of the communities on 15 July 2005 meant that Macedonia completed the legislative agenda set out in the Ohrid

---

[91] See S. Vaknin, 'Macedonia's Framework Agreement', 20 August 2005, available at: <http://www.globalpolitician.com/articleshow.asp?ID=1106&cid=3&sid=10> (last visited 19 March 2006).

[92] In the months following the signing of the Ohrid Framework Agreement, ethnic Albanian gangs continued with isolated armed provocations and terrorist attacks, such as placing bombs in residential areas and intimidating Slavic Macedonians by destroying their homes and preventing their safe return.

[93] See chapter 2, section 7.2.

[94] European Commission Conflict Prevention and Crisis Management Unit, Rapid Reaction Mechanism End of Programme Report Former Yugoslav Republic of Macedonia, November 2003, available at: <http://europa.eu.int/comm/external_relations/cpcm/rrm/fyrom.pdf>.

[95] Ibid.

[96] See Detrez, op. cit. n. 65, at p. 257.

Framework Agreement.[97] Despite the criticism on the Ohrid Framework Agreement, its implementation has spurred a process of rapid stabilisation and normalisation of the situation in Macedonia.[98] The country is now definitely in much better shape than in 2001. Instead of facing a destructive conflict, it is currently engaged in a constructive effort to gain membership of the European Union. It is to be hoped that the basis for this rapid transformation process – the principles of multi-ethnicity, sovereignty and territorial integrity of Macedonia as laid down in the Framework Agreement – will stand the test of time.

3.2 The death of the third 'Yugoslavia'[99]

3.2.1 *The need to restructure relations between Serbia and Montenegro*

The relations between Belgrade and Podgorica had been deadlocked ever since Milo Djukanović and his Democratic Party of Socialists (DPS) beat Milošević's confederates in Montenegro on a pro-independence ticket in the 1997 presidential and 1998 parliamentary elections.[100] Djukanović's victory revealed the fundamental flaw of the Federal Republic of Yugoslavia (FRY), the two-state federation created in April 1992 from the remainder of Tito's Socialist Federal Republic of

97 See SG/HR's statement to mark the occasion, *Javier Solana, EU High Representative for the CFSP, welcomes the completion of the legislative agenda of the Ohrid Framework Agreement*, S259/05, 15 July 2005: 'While the completion of the legislative agenda of the Framework Agreement marks the end of an important process, it does not mean that the Ohrid agenda is fulfilled. Mission accomplished can only be declared when rules are respected, realities on ground have changed, and long-term reforms such as decentralisation and equitable representation have been fully carried out. Further clarification might be needed in the area of use of languages. Tackling these challenges will form part the future European reform agenda.'

98 From the side of the Council, this process was overseen by a series of EU Special Representatives. By means of Council Joint Action 2001/760/CFSP of 29 October 2001, *OJ* 2001 L 287, Alain Le Roy was appointed as the EUSR in Macedonia to replace François Léotard. One year later, Le Roy was replaced by Alexis Brouhns; see Council Joint Action 2002/832/CFSP of 21 October 2002, *OJ* 2002 L 258/12. Brouhns' mandate was prolonged and widened by Council Joint Action 2002/963/CFSP of 10 December 2002, *OJ* 2002 L 334/7 and Council Joint Action 2003/870/CFSP of 8 December 2003, *OJ* 2003 L 326/39, *inter alia*, to draw clearer lines of command and to give guidance to the first ESDP missions in the country (see *infra* section 4.2). Brouhns was replaced by Michael Sahlin; see Council Joint Action 2004/565/CFSP of 26 July 2004, *OJ* 2004 L 251/18. He was replaced by Erwan Fouéré by means of Council Joint Action 2005/724/CFSP of 17 October 2005, *OJ* 2005 L 272/26. His mandate was amended and extended until 29 February 2008 by Council Joint Action 2006/123/CFSP of 20 February 2006, *OJ* 2006 L 49/20 and Council Joint Action 2007/109/CFSP of 15 February 2007, *OJ* 2007 L 46/68.

99 The facts described in this paragraph are based primarily on the Balkan Crisis Reports of the London-based Institute for War & Peace Reporting, available at: <http://www.iwpr.net>.

100 See F. Bieber, 'Montenegrin Politics Since the Disintegration of Yugoslavia', in F. Bieber, ed., *Montenegro in Transition: Problems of Identity and Statehood* (Baden-Baden, Nomos 2003) pp. 11-42.

Yugoslavia: the equality of the two unequal partners in the federation.[101] Between the inauguration of Djukanović as president of Montenegro in January 1998 and the fall of Milošević two and a half years later, tensions between Serbia and Montenegro steadily increased. In the light of the escalating conflict in Kosovo and the participation of the Serbian Radical Party in the Serbian government in early 1998, the Serbian authorities adopted an increasingly belligerent tone, using the considerable army presence in Montenegro to put pressure on the republican authorities.[102] Simultaneously, the Djukanović government adopted an increasingly independence-minded policy, leading eventually to an outright call for Montenegro's secession from Serbia.[103] Montenegro effectively ended most economic ties with Serbia, *inter alia*, by adopting the German mark in November 1999 as a parallel currency and, as of November 2000, as an exclusive one (before switching to the euro in early 2002).[104] In response, Serbia established checkpoints at the border between the two republics and started collecting customs duties, thus in fact confirming Montenegro's independence in all but name. The FRY had become a dead letter.

The deadlock in relations between Belgrade and Podgorica became an acute political dilemma after Milošević was removed from the presidential *peluche* in the wake of the epochal elections in October 2000. In the course of just a few months, all major players managed to manoeuvre themselves into an untenable position. Djukanović, expecting Milošević to win, had boycotted the federal elections. As a consequence, his natural allies, the reform-oriented and pro-Western Democratic Opposition of Serbia (DOS), took over power in Serbia but had to make a coalition at the federal level with the reactionary Montenegrin opposition. The reform drive and international credibility of the political programme of the late Zoran Djindjić, the new prime minister of Serbia, fell prey to the stand-off over competences between federation and republic. The newly

---

[101] Serbia is sixteen times bigger than Montenegro in terms of population and six times in terms of landmass. See CIA World Fact Book, available at: <http://www.cia.gov/cia/publications/factbook/geos/yi.html>. In 2006, the population of Serbia and Montenegro stood at roughly 10.5 million with approximately 8 million living in Serbia, 1.9 million in Kosovo and 600,000 in Montenegro. The total landmass of Serbia and Montenegro is 102,350 sq km: Serbia accounts for 77,535 sq km, Kosovo for 10,877 sq km and Montenegro for 13,938 sq km.

[102] See E. Schmitt, 'Crisis in the Balkans: The Military; NATO Commander Says Milošević is Moving Forces into Pro-Western Montenegrin Republic', *New York Times*, 2 July 1999; and 'Armed Yugoslav Troops Take over Montenegro's Main Airport', *New York Times*, 9 December 1999.

[103] See S. Erlanger, 'Montenegrins See Split with Serbia', *New York Times*, 18 October 1999.

[104] The dispute over Montenegro's status has been considerably informed by economic considerations. See B. Huszka, 'The Dispute over Montenegrin Independence', in Bieber, op. cit. n. 100, at pp. 43-62. The successful introduction of the euro is by no means an indication of economic strength or aptitude: Podgorica is not bound by any criteria of economic convergence. The currency is more convenient for legal and not-so-legal international dealings than for an ailing local economy. See ICG, 'Montenegro's Independence Drive', *Europe Report*, No. 169, 7 December 2005.

installed president, Vojislav Koštunica, saw his lead in popularity diminish in comparison with Djindjić and other younger reformers, a development partly due to the powerlessness of his position. The nationalist opposition of former Milošević parties witnessed the once proud Yugoslavia become defunct, with a quasi-independent state in Montenegro and a quasi-protectorate in Kosovo. In Podgorica, his narrow victory on 22 April 2001 in the parliamentary elections and the rising popularity of the Socialist People's Party of Montenegro (SNP) in the polls determined Djukanović's reluctance to implement his promise for a referendum on independence.[105] Thus, after the euphoria at the end of 2000 of finally having democratic negotiating partners and two constructive and apparently compatible platforms,[106] the actual talks between Belgrade and Podgorica soon stalled in a 'consent not to consent'. As all players came to realise that they had manoeuvred themselves into a 'lose-lose' situation, the perspective of closer relations with the European Union provided economic incentives as well as a welcome excuse to accept mediation of the Union's High Representative for the CFSP.

3.2.2 *The EU as an honest broker?*

From December 2001 onwards, when Javier Solana took on the 'mission impossible' to find the middle ground between Belgrade and Podgorica and prevent a spring referendum on the independence of Montenegro, criticism grew louder and louder. No doubt, Solana's role went far beyond merely offering 'good offices'.[107] As participants to the negotiations have indicated, Solana often dangled the carrot of opening negotiations on a prospective Stabilisation and Association Agreement

---

105 See M. Tadić, 'Montenegrin Independence on Hold', 240 *IWPR Balkan Crisis Report* (2001).

106 The Montenegrin negotiation position was put to paper by Djukanović on 29 December 2000. The joint reply by Federal President Koštunica and Serbian Prime Minister Djindjić was presented on 10 January 2001. The full text of both positions is reproduced in *CEPS Europa South-East Monitor*, Issue 19, January 2001. Typically, whereas the Djukanović platform dwells on the injustices of past Montenegro-Serbia relations and Montenegro's 'inalienable right to self-determination', the preamble of the response by Koštunica and Djindjić highlights the merits of federal arrangements, historic and cultural ties as well as joint economic interests.

107 In its original meaning, good offices are aimed only at the initiation or resumption of negotiations, with no active participation of the third party. In a mediatory process, on the other hand, the third party tries to bring the conflicting parties to an agreement for peaceful settlement by actively participating in the process of negotiations. In practice, however, the borderline between the two methods is often blurred. The Hague Convention for the Pacific Settlement of International Disputes (1907) set up the same rules for offering and handling good offices and mediation (Arts. 2-8). The text of the Convention reproduced on the website of the Permanent Court of Arbitration, available at: <http://www.pca-cpa.org/ENGLISH/BD/1907.htm>, is a translation of the French text adopted at the 1907 Peace Conference. Nowadays, the term 'good offices' is generally accepted to mean the supply of mediation services by persons of high moral standing and acknowledged impartiality to find an amicable settlement of a dispute between states.

between the FRY and the European Union, with its immediate economic advantages and its alluring promise of future EU membership.[108] But the SG/HR was also reported to have threatened Montenegro with cutting off at least half of EU financial aid if Podgorica pursued its plans to stage a referendum on independence.[109] On 14 February 2002, the Brussels-based Centre for European Policy Studies (CEPS) and International Crisis Group (ICG) published an open letter to the SG/HR concerning Montenegro.[110] One part of the think tanks' critique concerned Solana's methods of applying extreme pressure to just one side in order to 'bulldozer' Podgorica towards the European Union's preferred solution. In their view, the Union used its hegemony as a regional economic power to force a state union on 'unwilling partners'.[111] The other half of the critique concerned the dictated outcome of the negotiations: 'a democratic Montenegro in a democratic (FR)Yugoslavia.'[112] This solution was considered 'economically and politically unwise'.[113] Solana's attempts to keep Serbia and Montenegro together were more often than not understood as blunt efforts to preserve the status quo, with some minor, cosmetic modifications. Consequently, the European Union would end up polarising the parties and supporting the line of the reactionary SNP nationalists in Montenegro and the parties of the former Milošević coalition in Serbia.

Once both Koštunica and Djindjić had expressed their willingness to consider a new form of federation with Montenegro (albeit not at all costs), Solana indeed ended up siding with the reactionary forces at the federal level and in Montenegro, cajoling the pro-independence parties into making major concessions to their programme.[114] Publicly, the European Union failed to distance its stabilisation objective from the die-hard conservatism of the local pro-Yugoslav forces. Nevertheless, the final agreement, which constituted a compromise between the two original position papers, ultimately favoured the reformers rather than the reactionaries. The 'creation' of the new state union of 'Serbia and Montenegro' and a temporary freezing of the status issue allowed pro-Western politicians in both republics to pursue their reform agendas with more zeal.

---

[108] See G. Barrett, 'EU and Serbia and Montenegro', in D. Lopandić and V. Bajić, eds., *Serbia and Montenegro on the Road to the European Union – Two Years Later* (Belgrade, European Movement in Serbia 2003) pp. 37-45.

[109] See M. Tadić, 'Montenegro: Djukanović Cornered over Independence', 319 *IWPR Balkan Crisis Report* (2002); and M. Wisse Smit, 'Comment: Squabbling Yugoslav Republics Set for Divorce', 322 *IWPR Balkan Crisis Report* (2002).

[110] The open letter is reproduced in *CEPS Europa South-East Monitor*, Issue 31, January/February 2002.

[111] Ibid.

[112] See Council Conclusions throughout 2001, published in *Bull. EU* 2001.

[113] *CEPS Europa South-East Monitor*, Issue 31, January/February 2002.

[114] See Wisse Smit, loc. cit. n. 109.

3.2.3 *Belgrade Agreement (2002)*

A document called 'Proceeding Points for the Restructuring of Relations Between Serbia and Montenegro' – commonly known as the Belgrade Agreement, after the place were it was signed on 14 March 2002 – was the outcome of the trilateral negotiations between the governments of Serbia, Montenegro and the Federal Republic Yugoslavia, with the SG/HR as mediator and 'witness' to the agreement.[115] In the most principal set of issues, international status and representation, the Belgrade Agreement contains only one short reference to 'elements of Serbian and Montenegrin statehood, stemming from the present-day factual situation and the historic rights of the two member states.' The agreement largely follows the Serb position with a veto on unilateral secession. Montenegro was not granted its desired international legal personality, but in return Serbia (and the European Union) accepted the option of a referendum on independence three years after the adoption of the Constitutional Charter which was to implement the agreement. To protect Montenegro's interests from being swamped by Serb domination of the joint institutions and international representative positions, specific safeguards were built in for proportional representation by rotation.

As far as the more tangible issues of the relations between the federation and the composite republics and the division of competences are concerned, the Belgrade Agreement is largely uninformative. The range of joint competences and ministries – defence, foreign affairs, internal and international economic relations as well as human and minority rights (including cooperation with the ICTY) – copied the Montenegrin proposal, with the exception of the common market and the convertible currency (euro). As the composite republics were allowed to keep their separate economies, currencies and customs services, the actual competences of the federation in internal and international economic relations were not clearly formulated. In the sphere of defence, conscripts would not be forced to serve outside their own republic against their will. There would be only one federal army – a lesson from Bosnia.

In terms of state institutions and decision making, the Belgrade Agreement followed the more pragmatic Serbian approach based on operability rather than a strict interpretation of equality. The impracticable system of having two republican ministers of defence and two republican ministers of foreign affairs taking

---

115 The 'Proceeding Points for the Restructuring of Relations between Serbia and Montenegro' have been reproduced in *CEPS Europa South-East Monitor*, Issue 31, January/February 2002. For further analyses and commentaries, see, e.g., N. Bentzen, *Fata Solana. Die Staatsunion Serbien-Montenegro – eine Spiegelung zwischen 'Balkan' und EU?* (Vienna University, Interdisziplinäre Balkanstudien – IDM 2004), available at: <http://homepage.univie.ac.at/Vedran.Dzihic/balkan_bentzen.pdf>; and W. van Meurs, 'The Belgrade Agreement: Robust Mediation Between Serbia and Montenegro', in Bieber, op. cit. n. 100, pp. 63-79.

turns in the respective nominal positions at the federal level was replaced with an 'exchange of roles' by these two federal ministers and their respective deputies from the other republic. In line with the limited competences of the federal government, the Belgrade Agreement did not foresee a prime minister. The supervision of the ministerial council would be in the hands of the president. The unicameral parliament elected by all citizens of the federation pointed in the same direction, ignoring demands for a parallel system of republican parity next to individual democratic rights.

In short, apart from the clear decision to rename the FRY, most of the contentious issues had been left open, awaiting a constructive negotiation process to fill in the gaps. Thus, the Belgrade Agreement was essentially a declaration of intent rather than a constitutional blueprint. The modalities for the achievement of the goals set out in the agreement were to be elaborated in parallel with the Constitutional Charter. The substantiation of the agreement by a mixed commission from the two republican parliaments and the federal parliament proved no easy task.[116] The commission presented a Constitutional Charter in June 2002. Thereafter, newly elected republican parliaments and eventually a federal parliament elected by the entire constituency of 'Serbia and Montenegro' passed democratic judgement on the new federation. The Constitutional Charter was adopted and proclaimed on 4 February 2003 by the parliament of Serbia and Montenegro.[117]

3.2.4 *Sustainability of the European Union's diplomatic efforts?*

The Belgrade Agreement left a number of questions unanswered. An obvious question concerned the state's ambiguous character between a federation and a confederation. Effectively, 'Serbia and Montenegro' was a continuation of the 1992 Federal Republic of Yugoslavia.[118] At the same time, however, the fact that the Constitutional Charter had to be passed by the parliaments of the composite republics after elections indicated an institutional break with the past. Many in Serbia, nostalgic for the days of Tito, regretted the loss of the name 'Yugoslavia' and the ideal of a multi-ethnic state it once implied. To others in the region, 'Yugoslavia' stood only for Serb ethno-nationalism and ethnic cleansing. After the extradition of Milošević, dropping the name 'Yugoslavia' was a second reassuring symbol, a farewell to the era of ethnic conflict and human tragedy. Of

---

[116] For an elaboration on the open questions, hidden caveats and difficult negotiation process, see Van Meurs, loc. cit. n. 115, pp. 73-78; and G. Noutcheva, 'Negotiating a Viable State Union of Serbia and Montenegro', *CEPS Commentary* (2002).

[117] See Official Gazette of Serbia and Montenegro No. 1 of 4 February 2003, available at: <http://www.osce.org/documents/fry/2003/02/133_en.pdf>. For the European Union's reaction, see Council Conclusions of 24 February 2003, Press Release No. 6604/03 (Presse 52).

[118] Recognised by not only by the European Union but also the United Nations. Serbia and Montenegro took the seat of the FRY in the General Assembly.

course, the argument that Yugoslavia in its three forms – the Kingdom of Serbs, Croats and Slovenes (1918-1945), the Socialist Federal Republic of Yugoslavia (1945-1992) and the Federal Republic of Yugoslavia (1992-2002) – was an historic error or that the FRY was an anti-European and anti-democratic state reintroduced the ideal of nation-states through the backdoor.

Another deficit of the Belgrade Agreement concerned the economic integration of the two composite republics: each member of the state union retained its own economic, financial and customs systems, and Montenegro retained the euro. Both the EU mediators and the negotiating parties clearly gave priority to easing tensions over the status question, hoping that new economic momentum spurred by the Stabilisation and Association Process (SAP) would make up for the evident disadvantages of economic separation.[119]

The principal issue was the impact of the Belgrade Agreement on stability in the region. One of the reasons why the European Union had strongly objected to the idea of Montenegrin independence ever since Djukanović took office, although the Badinter Commission had confirmed Montenegro's right to self-determination,[120] was concern that allowing a referendum on independence would create further tensions within a very divided society.[121] The chief reason, however, was the Union's worry for a precedent followed by yet another round of state fragmentation in a region traditionally suffering from too many state- and nation-building projects. The European Union was afraid that unravelling the Yugoslav federation would open the way to independence for unstable Kosovo and potentially even for the Republika Srpska. Kosovo's unresolved status was the main obstacle to Montenegro's independence, although political leaders in Podgorica and Priština never tired of denying any such nexus.[122]

What the Belgrade Agreement achieved was gaining time rather than playing for time. It erased the illusion of a viable FRY and stabilised relations between the two republics. The agreement, given hands and feet by the Constitutional Charter of Serbia and Montenegro, prescribed a three-year cooling-off period before any of the composite republics could hold a referendum on independence.[123] Even if the new state union were only a transitional solution, it ended the

---

119 See D. Reljić, 'Serbien und Montenegro einigen sich über zukünftige staatliche Gemeinschaft', *SWP-Brennpunkte* (2002). On the SAP, see chapter 5.

120 See chapter 3.

121 The high cost of integrating an independent Montenegro into the European Union has been mentioned as another reason for the Union's opposition. See Wisse Smit, loc. cit. n. 109.

122 Recent history has shown that Kosovar politicians have indeed not abandoned their aspirations for independence, no matter what kind of constitutional acrobatics the Montenegrins perform.

123 Incidentally, it gave the pro-independence movement in Montenegro ample time to prepare for a referendum.

constitutional confusion and political deadlock, without impeding the progress of either towards European integration.[124] Most importantly, it gave the international community time to find a way to tackle the final status question for Kosovo. The price that the European Union was willing to pay for that was the acceptance of secession by Montenegro, counter to international rules on the inviolability of borders, as long as the vote would be 'legitimate', that is to say, that there would be a 50 per cent threshold for participation and a 55 per cent threshold for the approval of any result.[125]

In the end, the Belgrade Agreement was a mere stopgap before a narrow majority of the Montenegrin voters (55.5 per cent) chose independence in a nationwide referendum held on 21 May 2006.[126] In a special session on 3 June, the parliament in Podgorica passed a declaration on the independence of the Republic of Montenegro. On 5 June, the parliament in Belgrade declared the Republic of Serbia the legal successor to the state union and gave all state institutions forty-five days to complete the separation. On 12 June, the Council of the European Union recognised that the parliamentary acts were taken in conformity with the arrangements and procedures foreseen in the Belgrade Agreement as well as Article 60 of the Constitutional Charter. International recognition of the two new states followed soon afterwards.

Fifteen years since the break-up of Yugoslavia, Montenegro is both lucky and unfortunate. It is lucky because it has achieved independence while avoiding war. It has not seen inter-ethnic relations poisoned by ethno-nationalist mobilisation as elsewhere in the former Yugoslavia.[127] It is unfortunate because its economic and social situation leaves it in a precarious position. Despite a series of political, administrative and economic reforms, Montenegro is still among the world's

---

[124] In the period from the signing of the Belgrade Agreement until the adoption of the so-called 'twin-track approach' in November 2004, the effectiveness of the Union's approach towards Serbia and Montenegro did, however, suffer from incoherence and inconsistencies between the demands of the SG/HR and the Council, on the one hand, and of the European Commission, on the other. See N. Tocci, 'EU Intervention in Ethno-Political Conflicts: The Cases of Cyprus and Serbia-Montenegro', 9 *EFA Rev.* (2004) pp. 551-573; and R. Keane, 'The Case of the Solana Process in Serbia and Montenegro: Coherence in EU Foreign Policy', 11 *International Peacekeeping* (2004) pp. 1-17. More positively, see J. Batt, 'The EU's "Soft Power" at Work in the Balkans', *EUISS Newsletter*, July 2006. See also chapter 5, section 3.2.4.

[125] See Council Conclusions of 27 February 2006, Press Release No. 6344/06 (Presse 46).

[126] The referendum was deemed to have been conducted in line with OSCE and Council of Europe commitments and other international standards for democratic electoral processes. See, *inter alia*, Declaration by the Presidency on behalf of the European Union regarding the referendum in Montenegro, Press Release P 73/06, Doc. 9730/06 (Presse 152), Brussels, 23 May 2006. See also ICG, 'Montenegro's Referendum', 42 *Europe Briefings* (2006); and J. Batt, 'Montenegro and Serbia After the Referendum', *EUISS Analysis*, May 2006.

[127] See F. Bieber, 'Preface', in Bieber, op. cit. n. 100, at pp. 7-9.

largest recipients in terms of international assistance per capita.[128] It will take years before Montenegro will be in the position to join the European Union.[129]

3.3 The European Union in Kosovo

3.3.1 *Embedded in an international reconstruction effort*

The violence in Kosovo that lead to the NATO campaign against the Federal Republic of Yugoslavia triggered important qualitative changes in the European Union's policy towards South-Eastern Europe as a whole. If the United States and NATO had done the dirty work of defeating Milošević militarily, the European Union offered what the rest of the international community expected it to do: generating economic growth and political stability in the region.[130] By initiating the Stability Pact for South-Eastern Europe, the European Union resurrected the idea of the 'hour of Europe'.[131] Adopted on 10 June 1999, the day that NATO's air campaign against Serbia came to an end, the Stability Pact's founding documents solemnly declared that '[t]he EU will draw the region closer to the perspective of full integration of these countries [in South-Eastern Europe] into its structures.'[132] However, it was rather unclear how the Stability Pact squared with accession to the European Union. It remained, by and large, a regional post-conflict reconstruction strategy funded by the international financial institutions, the Union and its Member States.[133] In terms of its approach, the Stability Pact

128 See ICG, 'Montenegro's Independence Drive', *Europe Report*, No. 169, 7 December 2005: 'Accusations of simulated reforms to please Western donors seem plausible. A significant part of economic activity – an estimated 40 to 60 per cent – is related to black market, mainly car rackets and cigarettes smuggling. The involvement of political parties and state administration is a foregone conclusion. The state needs foreign aid for social peace in a poverty-ridden country of rising unemployment, frequent electric power cuts and high inflation. Its economic openness (3 per cent tariff average) may be an asset, but tourism certainly is not its main industry at the moment.'

129 See J. Batt, 'Making a Success of Montenegrin Independence – Lessons from Slovakia', *DANAS*, Weekend Supplement, 25-26 June 2006; and K. Evenson, 'Becoming Democratic: Now for the Real Work', *Transitions Online*, 13 July 2006.

130 See Agreement on the principles (peace plan) to move towards a resolution of the Kosovo crisis presented to the leadership of the Federal Republic of Yugoslavia by the President of Finland, Martti Ahtisaari, representing the European Union, and Viktor Chernomyrdin, Special Representative of the President of the Russian Federation, UN Doc. S/1999/649, 3 June 1999. See also chapter 2, section 7.3.2.

131 See chapter 1; declaration of Jacques Poos, Luxembourg's Foreign Minister, to the international press, 29 June 1991.

132 For the final text of the Stability Pact of 10 June 1999, see: <http://www.stabilitypact.org>. The quote is to be found on p. 20 of the text. For more on the Stability Pact, see chapter 5, section 2.2.

133 See, e.g., D. Bechev, 'Between Enlargement and CFSP: the EU and the Western Balkans', paper presented at the LSE European Foreign Policy Conference, 2-3 June 2004; and D. Vignes, 'The Stability Pact for South Eastern Europe', in C. Tomuschat, ed., *Kosovo and the International Community: A Legal Assessment* (The Hague, Kluwer Law International 2002) pp. 317-325.

was not an accession platform. Although initiated by the German Presidency of the European Union and sanctioned by the European Council at its Cologne summit,[134] it was placed under the umbrella of the OSCE. The Union was just one, albeit the most important, stakeholder amongst many. In fact, the Stability Pact exemplified a trend for the European Union in Kosovo: in July 1999, the Council of Ministers fulfilled the UN Secretary-General's wish to entrust to the Union the task of managing the economy pillar within the United Nations' administration in Kosovo,[135] thus sharing responsibility for the reconstruction of Kosovo with a vast range of international actors.

On the same day as the Stability Pact was launched, the UN Security Council passed resolution 1244 (1999), authorising the United Nations Mission in Kosovo (UNMIK) to begin a process of building peace, democracy, stability and self-government, designed to determine Kosovo's future status.[136] By deciding that a political solution to the Kosovo crisis would have to take account of the Rambouillet Accords[137] and be based on the general principles developed by the G-8,[138] as further elaborated in the principles and other required elements in Annex 2 to the resolution, the Security Council endorsed what later became known as the so-called 'standards before status' policy. In essence, Kosovo was expected to make progress on the eight standards to be achieved by the Provisional Institutions of Self-Government (PISG) before its final status could be addressed. Those standards concerned: functioning democratic institutions, the rule of law, freedom of movement, returns and reintegration, the economy, property rights, dialogue with Belgrade and the professional training of the Kosovo Protection Corps, the successor organisation to the Kosovo Liberation Army.[139] The implementation of the 'standards before status' policy was the core political project of UNMIK and was given fresh momentum by the adoption of the Kosovo Standards Implementation Plan of 31 March 2004.[140]

---

134 *Bull. EU* 6-1999, point I.26.71.

135 Council Joint Action 1999/522/CFSP of 29 July 1999 concerning the installation of the structures of the UNMIK, *OJ* 1999 L 201/1.

136 See chapter 2, section 6.7.

137 Rambouillet Accords: Interim Agreement for Peace and Self-Government in Kosovo, UN Doc. S/1999/648, 7 June 1999. The Accords were concluded under the auspices of the members of the Contact Group and the European Union. See also chapter 2, section 6.7.

138 See Statement by the Chairman on the conclusion of the meeting of the G-8 foreign ministers held at the Petersberg Centre on 6 May 1999, reproduced in Annex 1 to UNSC resolution 1244 (1999).

139 The 'Standards for Kosovo' were agreed between the PISG and UNMIK and subsequently launched by the Special Representative of the Secretary-General (SRSG) Harry Holkeri and Kosovo's Prime Minister Bajram Rexhepi on 10 December 2003. See Press Release UNMIK/PR/1078 of that date. The 'Standards' were endorsed by the Security Council on 12 December 2003. See Presidential Statement S/PRST/2003/26.

140 See further chapter 2, section 6.7.

In the first-ever operation of its kind, the United Nations brought together four so-called 'pillars' under overall UNMIK leadership:[141] police and justice (Pillar I) and civil administration (Pillar II) under the direct responsibility of the United Nations,[142] democratisation and institution building (Pillar III) under the responsibility of the OSCE and economic reconstruction, recovery and development (Pillar IV) under the responsibility of the European Union.[143] Since 1999, the work of the European Union in Pillar IV has been geared towards modernising the economic framework of Kosovo, with a view to developing the structures and instruments that form the basis of a competitive, efficient market economy.[144] That is not to say that 'Europe's' influence is only felt within the framework of Pillar IV. The EU Member States' presence also extends to the other three pillars, for example through their participation in the work that KFOR and the OSCE carry out for UNMIK.[145] In fact, since the end of the crisis, the European Union and its Member States have devoted the lion's share of their resources – military, financial and human – to repairing the damage of war and decades of underinvestment and neglect, increasing the capacity of local administration and fostering reforms. Since 1999, the European Community has devoted over €1.6 billion to

---

141 UNMIK is currently headed by the SRSG Joachim Rücker (Germany).

142 Pillar II has since been integrated into the Office of the SRSG.

143 Pillar IV is headed by Acting Deputy SRSG Paul Acda since March 2006. Council Joint Action 1999/522/CFSP was extended by Council Joint Action 1999/864/CFSP of 21 December 1999, *OJ* 1999 L 328/67 and Council Joint Action 2000/175/CFSP of 28 February 2000, *OJ* 2000 L 55/78; Council Regulation (EC) No. 1080/2000 of 22 May 2000 on support for the United Nations Interim Mission in Kosovo (UNMIK) and the Office of the High Representative in Bosnia and Herzegovina (OHR), *OJ* 2000 L 122/27; Council Regulation (EC) No. 2098/2003 of 27 November 2003 amending Regulation (EC) No. 1080/2000 on support for the United Nations Interim Mission in Kosovo (UNMIK) and the Office of the High Representative in Bosnia and Herzegovina (OHR), *OJ* 2003 L 316/1.

144 Included among the achievements attributed by the European Union to its work in Pillar IV are the creation of a modern market economy through the introduction of commercial and economic legislation conforming to European standards; the launch of the privatisation process stimulating economic development and investment; the successful switch to the euro as the single currency; the creation of a working banking system with nine commercial banks including over 240 branches; the initiation of free trade agreements and the integration of Kosovo into various regional and European economic structures; the transformation of the customs service into a modern organisation collecting over 70 per cent of the Kosovo Consolidated Budget funds; the introduction of various measures to counter economic crime and corruption; and the stabilisation of Kosovo's fragile power situation. See: <http://www.euinkosovo.org/uk/about/about_pillar.php>. See also Commission Staff Working Document, Kosovo (under UNSCR 1244) 2006 Progress Report, COM (2006) 649 final, Brussels, 8 November 2006. For a more critical evaluation of UNMIK's activities and achievements, with a special focus on the European Union in Pillar IV, see D. Papadimitriou, P. Petrov and L. Greiçevci, 'To Build a State: Europeanization, EU Actorness and State-Building in Kosovo', 12 *EFA Rev.* (2007) pp. 219-238 at pp. 229-231 and 233-237.

145 For an overview of the experiences in EU-UN cooperation in Kosovo so far, see M. Karnitschnig, 'The UN and the EU in Kosovo – The Challenges of Joint Nation-Building', in J. Wouters, F. Hoffmeister and T. Ruys, eds., *The United Nations and the European Union: An Ever Stronger Partnership* (The Hague, T.M.C. Asser Press 2006) pp. 323-351.

Kosovo, money which has been channelled via ECHO (which was phased out of the province in 2003 as the humanitarian crisis was over),[146] the European Agency for Reconstruction (managing the bulk of CARDS funds),[147] the operating costs of Pillar IV[148] and the Kosovo Consolidated Budget via the decision of DG ECFIN (the European Commission's Directorate General for Economic and Financial Affairs) on exceptional financial assistance.[149]

Despite the attention and resources devoted to Kosovo by the international community, and the European Union in particular, economic performance remained in shambles and unemployment remained very high. UN Security Council resolution 1244 (1999) effectively kept the Provisional Institutions for Self-Government weak. At the same, the powerful private actors, oligarchs and criminal syndicates generated by the wars of the 1990s largely escaped scrutiny and remained influential. Cumulatively, this caused the 'standards before status' policy to run out of steam. This was also due to the slowness of the Albanian leadership in Kosovo in implementing reforms to meet the UN-set standards because of its insistence on a 'status before standards' policy.[150] Gradually, the international community became convinced that the open-ended mandate of UN Security Council resolution 1244 (1999) had outlived its purpose and that a political process had to be initiated in order to reach a settlement on Kosovo's final status if the province was to move forward.[151]

3.3.2 *Final status talks*

On 10 November 2005, the UN Security Council endorsed the Secretary-General's intention to appoint Martti Ahtisaari, former president of Finland, as his Special Envoy to lead the political process, and established the following guiding principles for the process, as agreed to by the Contact Group:

> 1. The settlement of the Kosovo issue should be fully compatible with international standards of human rights, democracy and international law and contribute to regional security.

---

146 See the thematic booklet published by the European Commission, *ECHO in the Balkans – 12 Years of Humanitarian Action 1991-2003* (Brussels, ECHO 2003).

147 See chapter 5, section 3.4.

148 Unlike the first three pillars of UNMIK, the operational expenditure of Pillar IV is almost fully financed out of the European Commission's budget. See Council Regulation (EC) No. 2098/2003 of 27 November 2003 amending Regulation (EC) No. 1080/2000 on support for UNMIK and OHR, *OJ* 2003 L 316/1.

149 Data available on the EU Pillar's website, at: <http://www.euinkosovo.org/uk/about/about_pillar.php>.

150 See also chapter 2, section 6.7.

151 See B. Knoll, 'From Benchmarking to Final status? Kosovo and the Problem of an International Administration's Open-ended Mandate', 16 *EJIL* (2005) pp. 637-660.

2. The settlement of Kosovo's Status should conform with democratic values and European standards and contribute to realizing the European perspective of Kosovo, in particular, Kosovo's progress in the stabilization and association process, as well as the integration of the entire region in Euro-Atlantic institutions.
3. The settlement should ensure multi-ethnicity that is sustainable in Kosovo. It should provide effective constitutional guarantees and appropriate mechanisms to ensure the implementation of human rights for all citizens in Kosovo and of the rights of members of all Kosovo communities, including the right of refugees and displaced persons to return to their homes in safety.
4. The settlement should provide mechanisms to ensure the participation of all Kosovo communities in government, both on the central and on the local level. Effective structures of local self-government established through the decentralization process should facilitate the coexistence of different communities and ensure equitable and improved access to public services.
5. The settlement of Kosovo's status should include specific safeguards for the protection of the cultural and religious heritage in Kosovo. This should include provisions specifying the status of the Serbian Orthodox Church's institutions and sites and other patrimony in Kosovo.
6. The settlement of Kosovo's status should strengthen regional security and stability. Thus, it will ensure that Kosovo does not return to the pre-March 1999 situation. Any solution that is unilateral or results from the use of force would be unacceptable. There will be no changes in the current territory of Kosovo, i.e., no partition of Kosovo and no union of Kosovo with any country or part of any country. The territorial integrity and internal stability of regional neighbours will be fully respected.
7. The Status settlement will ensure Kosovo's security. It will also ensure that Kosovo does not pose a military or security threat to its neighbours. Specific provisions on security arrangements will be included.
8. The settlement of Kosovo's status should promote effective mechanisms to strengthen Kosovo's ability to enforce the rule of law, to fight organized crime and terrorism and safeguard the multi-ethnic character of the police and the judiciary.
9. The settlement should ensure that Kosovo can develop in a sustainable way both economically and politically and that it can cooperate effectively with international organizations and international financial institutions.
10. For some time Kosovo will continue to need an international civilian and military presence to exercise appropriate supervision of compliance of the provisions of the Status settlement, to ensure security and, in particular, protection for minorities as well as to monitor and support the authorities in the continued implementation of standards.[152]

It is within these parameters – no partition of Kosovo, no union with a neighbouring state and no return to pre-1999 conditions – that the UN Special Envoy had to find a compromise agreement between Priština and Belgrade.[153] Ahtisaari started

152 See UN Doc. S/2005/709.

153 On 7 November 2005, the Council of the European Union endorsed the appointment of Stefan Lehne as EU representative to support the UN Status Envoy in the implementation of his mandate. See Council Conclusions of 7 November 2005, Press Release No. 13622/05 (Presse 274).

the final status talks on 21 November 2005 with a fact-finding mission to both capitals. What he found were two irreconcilable positions. The approximately 1.5 million ethnic Albanians in Kosovo envisaged only one outcome: an independent Kosovo. Bajram Kosumi, then prime minister, was reported as having said: 'A small country like Kosovo would feel insecure if it didn't have a UN seat.'[154] For Belgrade, however, independence was anathema. Kosovo is considered to be the 'cradle of Serbia', a sacrosanct place in Serbian history with a collection of churches, monasteries and other sites used for religious purposes to prove it. The Serbs, who entered the final status negotiations with the puzzling slogan 'more than autonomy, less than independence', were ready to concede *de facto* self-government as long as they retained sovereignty *de jure*.[155] With the no-compromise Radical Party riding high in the polls, Prime Minister Vojislav Koštunica[156] had little negotiating space. An independent Kosovo was – and still is – a taboo subject. It remains historic Serb territory which no politician can give away. Boris Tadić, the president of Serbia and Montenegro, was reported as having said: 'For Serbia it's unacceptable to see Kosovo with a seat in the UN.'[157] The 'secession' of Montenegro in June 2006 complicated the Kosovo question. While Serbs believe that they did not lose Montenegro in the sense that they face 'losing' Kosovo to the ethnic Albanians, the break-away republic of Montenegro scarred the Serbian soul and reduced the room for compromise even more.

In this context, it is interesting to note that the question what consequences the dissolution of the 'third Yugoslavia' would have for the guarantee of its 'sovereignty and territorial integrity' in Security Council resolution 1244 (1999) has been raised, all the more so because this resolution referred to Kosovo as part of the FRY, not of Serbia. The Belgrade Agreement of 2002 included an explicit precaution for a possible disintegration after three years: 'If Montenegro withdraws from the state union, international documents related to the FRY, the UN Security Council resolution 1244 in particular, shall relate to and fully apply on Serbia as its successor.'[158] Thus, this weaving fault in resolution 1244 was

---

[154] See S. Wagstyl, 'Why Kosovo might hold the key to the Balkans' future', *Financial Times*, 19 February 2006.

[155] Under his formula, Kosovo would largely manage its own affairs – have its own executive, legislative and judicial authorities – but remain nominally part of Serbia and forgo diplomatic representation abroad – a single minister of foreign affairs, a single minister of defence and a single seat at the United Nations. The 100,000 Kosovo Serbs would have to benefit from a high level of minority rights protection.

[156] See *supra* section 3.2.1. Koštunica became prime minister in the spring of 2004.

[157] See S. Wagstyl, 'Why Kosovo might hold the key to the Balkans' future', *Financial Times*, 19 February 2006.

[158] Proceeding Points for a Restructuring of Relations between Serbia and Montenegro, reproduced in *CEPS Europa South-East Monitor*, Issue 31, January/February 2002.

repaired.[159] The suggestion that this provision violated the resolution and reintroduced Serb sovereignty over Kosovo seems far-fetched. Resolution 1244 (1999) could not deny Kosovo being a province of the Serbian republic under the Yugoslav Constitution, and Serbia could theoretically have upheld the defunct 'shell' of the FRY even after Montenegro's secession if only because of Kosovo.

At the outset of the final status process, the Contact Group avoided taking sides, but it was clear that the United States and the United Kingdom were increasingly leaning towards independence for Kosovo.[160] France and other EU Member States were more cautious, concerned that early discussion of independence could take the pressure off Priština to negotiate and risk a Serb walk-out of the negotiations.[161] The Contact Group agreed that minority rights had to be guaranteed, peacekeeping troops had to stay and an international civilian mission – probably run by the European Union – had to be put in place.[162] Russia and China, which had previously worried that an independent Kosovo would set a precedent for their claimed territories of Chechnya, Tibet and Taiwan, were reported as having told the US Secretary of State Condoleezza Rice that they would not block the independence of Kosovo, because they considered the situation of Kosovo 'unique'.[163] But Russia has since swung back to its earlier position and is prepared to vote against a proposed UN Security Council resolution granting independence to Kosovo.[164]

Instead of tackling the status question head-on, Ahtisaari initially opted for a bottom-up approach. On 20-21 February 2006, the first round of direct negotiations between Serbs and Kosovar Albanians took place in Vienna. Middle-ranking officials met under the auspices of Deputy UN Special Envoy Albert

---

159 Strictly speaking, only the unlikely case of Serbia's secession would unhinge resolution 1244.

160 See 'Kosovo's future', *SEEUROPE.NET*, 15 February 2006.

161 Ibid.

162 See *infra* section 3.3.4.

163 See G. Dinmore and D. Dombey, 'Russia and China "pledge not to block new Kosovo"', *Financial Times*, 14 March 2006. On the qualification of Kosovo's 'uniqueness', one should observe that Kosovo is, of course, unique. But so is any other territory seeking independence or autonomy. Bosnia was and is fundamentally different from Croatia and both are entirely different from East Timor. Even the secessionist regions on the fringes of the former Soviet Union that receive support from Moscow – Abkhazia, Nagorno-Karabach, South Ossetia and Transnistria – are different to each other. However, Kosovo is in all likelihood becoming independent, not because of its uniqueness *per se*, but because that uniqueness is of such a nature that it leaves independence as just about the only conceivable solution. In other words, Kosovo is becoming independent because NATO stopped Serbia from terrorising it and expelled it from the province and because no one outside Serbia can argue with a straight face that letting Serbia back in any shape or form would be conducive to peace. But this does not mean that other regions will not be able to convincingly cite Kosovo's independence as a precedent for their own secessionist cause. To argue that an independent Kosovo will not represent such a precedent is simply an insult to common sense.

164 See J. Headley, 'Kosovo: Déjá vu for Russia', *Transitions Online*, 28 May 2007.

Rohan (Austria) to discuss rival schemes for the devolution of powers from Kosovo's central authorities to the municipalities. Effective provisions for the decentralisation of government will be crucial to the status settlement, as decentralisation can ensure that minority communities such as the Kosovo Serbs remain a vital part of Kosovo's future. Decentralisation should also give impetus to the return of displaced persons who should be able to choose where they live in Kosovo. Although no agreement was reached on the issue, the negotiations were generally perceived to be largely constructive. After meeting government representatives in Belgrade, Ahtisaari announced that he would dispatch technical teams to Belgrade and Priština to pave the way for continuing negotiations on practical questions. On 17 March, talks resumed in Vienna. Prime Minister Bajram Kosumi, who stepped down over accusations of ineffectiveness by members of his coalition, was replaced by former KLA commander Agim Çeku, against whom Serbia had issued an arrest warrant. Despite protests from Belgrade, the European Union supported the replacement.[165] The show had to go on. In their second round, the talks focused on cultural and religious heritage, minority rights and the economy, local financing, cooperation and relations between municipalities. Although the sides were again unable to reach agreement, participants described the talks as constructive and scheduled the next round.

After seven unsuccessful rounds of technical negotiations, the final status talks convened in Vienna at the highest political level under the chairmanship of Martti Ahtisaari. But that meeting only served as a confirmation of the entrenched positions: the Serb 'everything but independence' versus the Kosovo Albanian 'nothing but independence'. While negotiations at the technical level continued in the second half of 2006, they were effectively dead. In October, Ahtisaari started openly doubting that a negotiated settlement for Kosovo would be possible, as the two parties remained diametrically opposed on the final status issue.[166]

While the final status process was expected to last for several months, the Contact Group, together with the EU High Representative, the EU Presidency, the European Commissioner for Enlargement, NATO's Secretary-General, the UN Special Status Envoy and the SRSG, had expressed the belief that all possible efforts should be made to achieve a negotiated settlement before the end of 2006.[167] But this deadline was pushed back after a narrow majority of the Serbian electorate (51.6 per cent) in the 28-29 October referendum approved Serbia's new Constitution, which claims sovereignty over the province of Kosovo, and general

---

[165] See Statement S074/06, 'Javier Solana, High Representative for the CFSP, welcomes confirmation of new Kosovo government', 10 March 2006.

[166] As reported in M. Abramovitz and J. Lyon, 'Another Balkan High Noon', *The Guardian*, 24 October 2006.

[167] Kosovo Contact Group Statement, London, 31 January 2006, available at: <http://ue.eu.int/ueDocs/cms_Data/docs/pressdata/EN/declarations/88236.pdf>.

elections were called for.[168] After consulting with the Contact Group, UN Special Envoy Ahtisaari decided to delay the presentation of his 'recommendations' on the future of Kosovo in order to avoid inflaming tension ahead of Serbia's elections on 21 January 2007.[169] Further delay was deemed risky, as it would be taken by Belgrade not as a cue to cooperate with an orderly process but as a further opportunity to wreck it.[170] Further delay would also severely test Kosovo Albanian cohesion. The longer the Kosovo Albanians were forced to wait, the greater the chance that they would discredit themselves with unilateral independence moves or riots. That would have virtually finished prospects for retaining the Serb minority in a multi-ethnic Kosovo.[171] Instead of finally closing the question of Western Balkan borders with an orderly settlement for Kosovo, a new chapter of destabilisation would be opened.

3.3.3 *Proposed outcome*

On 2 February 2007, UN Special Envoy Martti Ahtisaari presented his 'Comprehensive Proposal for the Kosovo Status Settlement' to Serbian President Boris Tadić[172] and to Prime Minister Agim Çeku.[173] Rejected in Belgrade and welcomed in Priština, Ahtisaari's draft sets out the basis for a viable, stable and sustainable Kosovo. While the Comprehensive Proposal offers independence to Kosovo in all but name (symbols, security forces, representation in international organisations, etc.),[174] Ahtisaari's plan is first and foremost a document designed to make Kosovo a multi-ethnic society. This means that the non-Albanian communities (Serb, Roma, Ashkali, Gorani, Egyptian, Turk and Bosniak) that make up 10 per cent of the population have been granted substantial powers in all government institutions and in all sectors.[175] A high degree of autonomy for the Serb community,

168 See ICG, 'Serbia's New Constitution: Democracy Going Backwards', 44 *Europe Briefing* (2006), and T. Judah, 'Making Moves', *World Today*, December 2006, pp. 17-18.

169 In fact, it was feared that an early recognition of Kosovo's independence might bring the ultranationalist Radical Party to power in Serbia. See further T. Judah, 'Finding the right balance for Kosovo', *European Voice*, 26 October-1 November 2006, at p. 17.

170 See ICG, 'Kosovo Status: Delay is Risky', 177 *Europe Reports* (2006).

171 See ICG, 'Kosovo's Status: Difficult Months Ahead', 45 *Europe Briefing* (2006).

172 Caretaker Prime Minister Koštunica said that he could not receive Ahtisaari because no government had yet been formed after the elections of 21 January.

173 A few days earlier, Ahtisaari had informed the Contact Group of his plan. The version of the Comprehensive Proposal of 2 February was only briefly available at: <http://www.unosek.org>, the website of the UN Office of the Special Envoy for Kosovo. A slightly amended version of the proposal was included in the addendum to the Letter dated 26 March 2007 from the Secretary-General addressed to the President of the Security Council, UN Doc. S/2007/168/Add.1.

174 See Art. 1 of the Comprehensive Proposal.

175 See especially the provisions of Annex I (Constitutional Provisions), Annex II (The Rights of Communities and Their Members), Annex III (Decentralisation), Annex IV (Justice System) and Annex V (Religious and Cultural Heritage) to the Comprehensive Proposal.

including in areas such as healthcare, education and cultural and religious sites, is a *conditio sine qua non* for a sustainable solution. The proposed decentralisation of Kosovo could enable Serb-majority municipalities to develop links with each other and – crucially – with the municipal authorities across the border in Serbia.[176] In a limited and transparent manner, the Serbian government could be allowed to provide economic assistance to these municipalities.[177]

In essence, Ahtisaari designed an asymmetric state with supervised independence. A future International Civilian Mission (ICM) should monitor the implementation of the status settlement, as well as – implicitly – compliance with European standards under the SAP,[178] and intervene when the implementation is at risk. As such, the proposed ICM, which should be headed by the 'double-hatted' International Civilian Representative (ICR)/EU Special Representative, is a leaner and 'Europeanised' version of the Office of the High Representative in Bosnia-Herzegovina, with no less intrusive powers than the OHR,[179] working in cooperation with an International Military Presence (IMP) to ensure the security of Kosovo (provided for by NATO's KFOR)[180] and a civilian ESDP Mission (focused on the rule of law)[181] in support of local authorities. The ICM would be led by the European Union,[182] but non-EU Member States such as Russia and the United States could also be given a role.

---

176 See Annex III (Decentralisation) to the Comprehensive Proposal. Particular attention should be paid to Article 13, proposing the official 'division' of Mitrovica into two municipalities, governed by a Joint Board (composed on the principle of parity and headed by an international representative selected by the International Civilian Representative) to carry out functional cooperation in the areas of their own competences as agreed to by the municipalities.

177 Ibid., Arts. 10-11.

178 On the SAP, see chapter 5, section 2.3.

179 See Art. 2 of Annex IX to the Comprehensive Proposal, which prescribes that the ICR shall be the 'final authority in Kosovo regarding interpretation of the civilian aspects of this Settlement', who ensures its effective implementation 'through the execution of specific tasks accorded' to him. To that end, the ICR can 'take corrective measures to remedy, as necessary, *any* actions taken by the Kosovo authorities that [he] deems to be a breach of this Settlement, or seriously undermine the rule of law, or to be otherwise inconsistent with the terms or the spirit of this Settlement; such corrective measures may include, but are not limited to, annulment of laws or decisions adopted by the Kosovo authorities' [emphasis added]. 'In cases of serious or repeated failures to comply with the letter or spirit of this Settlement, and/or in instances of serious obstruction in the work of the ICR and/or ESDP Mission, the ICR shall have the authority to sanction or remove from office any public official or take other measures, as necessary, to ensure full respect for this Settlement and its implementation.' Also, the ICR is proposed to have the power to directly appoint persons to a number of posts and ensure that cases of war crimes, terrorism, organised crime, corruption, inter-ethnic and other serious crimes are properly investigated, prosecuted and adjudicated and that decisions in such cases are properly enforced. Compare with the overview given of OHR's tasks, functions and powers in chapter 2, section 6.4.

180 See Art. 13 and Annex XI to the Comprehensive Proposal.

181 See Art. 12 and Annex X to the Comprehensive Proposal.

182 See in this respect the preparatory actions of the European Union foreseen in Council Joint Action 2006/623/CFSP of 15 September 2006 on the establishment of a EU-team to contribute to the

After almost eight years in limbo, there is now a roadmap that leads Kosovo directly to statehood. Of course, the Comprehensive Proposal is not Ahtisaari's magic wand that will instantly make things right in the province and in the region.[183] In fact, deadly violence erupted almost instantly in Kosovo and in Belgrade thousands took to the streets.[184] Two weeks of intensive consultations between Belgrade and Priština at the end of February ended without success. Following a final meeting between the two parties in Vienna on 9 and 10 March 2007, Ahtisaari declared that the year-long process of negotiations had been exhausted, leaving no common ground between Belgrade and Priština. On 26 March, the UN Secretary-General shifted the talks to the Security Council. Tough work lies ahead to rally all the members of the UN Security Council behind the plan. The stakes are high. If the Security Council does not get Kosovo right, then chaos will likely ensue and probably violence too. Kosovo's Albanian-dominated parliament will no doubt declare independence and some countries, led probably by the United States and the United Kingdom, will recognise the new state. In this situation, the Serbian-dominated north of the province will, in effect, secede and Serbs living in enclaves in the centre of the province will probably flee or be 'ethnically cleansed'. Kosovo would become perpetually prone to unrest or stay frozen in a decades-long stalemate like Cyprus. Unless there is a new Security Council resolution on the future of Kosovo, then EU Member States will probably not endorse an ESDP mission. Faced with this prospect, it is hardly surprising that EU diplomats insist that there can be no alternative to the Comprehensive Proposal by Ahtisaari.

Equally important – and despite the fact that Kosovo is unusual because of NATO's military intervention in 1999 – the international community's handling of Kosovo will be read around the globe as having broader meaning for what it says about minority rights, self-determination and the way to deal with breakaway territories (territorial integrity and sovereignty of states).[185] Kosovo's future independence is seemingly evident. But does this decision not retroactively justify the use of force and military actions to change borders and status? And what

preparations on the establishment of a possible international civilian mission in Kosovo, including a European Union Special Representative component (ICM/EUSR Preparation Team), *OJ* 2006 L 253/29. The mandate of the EU team was extended until 31 July 2007 by Council Joint Action 2007/203/CFSP of 27 March 2007, *OJ* 2007 L 90/94. At the same time, the financial reference amount of €869,000 was increased by €807,000 to cover expenditure from 15 September 2006 to 31 July 2006.

183 See A. Beatty, 'Rumbles over Kosovo', *European Voice*, 8-14 February 2007, at p. 13.

184 See F. Terdevci, 'Kosovo's status: ready to blow', *Transitions Online*, 20 February 2007.

185 See M. Goodwin, 'From Province to Protectorate to State? Speculation on the Impact of Kosovo's Genesis upon the Doctrines of International Law', 8 *German Law Journal* (2007) pp. 1-20; and S. Cvijić, 'Self-determination as a Challenge to the Legitimacy of Humanitarian Intervention: The Case of Kosovo', 8 *German Law Journal* (2007) pp. 57-79.

message does this decision send to the Republika Srpska or the Albanian community in Macedonia, or even the Hungarian minority in Vojvodina? Whatever the way out, there seems to be no easy and elegant exit from the 'Kosovo trap'.[186]

3.3.4 *Future EU intervention in Kosovo*

At first sight, the European Union's role in Kosovo since 1999 has been limited. 'Embedded' in the international reconstruction effort, the Union acted under the responsibility of the United Nations. Yet, Europe's impact on the ground has been tangible, as the European Union and its Member States devoted the lion's share of their resources – military, financial and human – to repairing the damage of war and of decades of underinvestment and neglect, to increasing the capacity of local administration and fostering reforms. Unfortunately, paying the bills has not translated itself into greater visibility for the Union. But, this is about to change. The appointment by the UN Security Council of Martti Ahtisaari represented one of the first occasions since Lord Owen's rocky involvement in the early phases of the Bosnian war that a European has been given such pre-eminence in Balkan diplomacy.[187] One of the lessons learned from Bosnia-Herzegovina is that, unless the chief negotiator has real powers, many in the Balkans will assume that this person is simply answering to his US deputy or more powerful handlers in the White House.[188] With a European future for Kosovo, it was only logical that Europe should not only wield real power in the final status negotiations but also in the implementation process. And thus, a bigger role for the European Union in Kosovo looms on the horizon. If and when a settlement on the final status of Kosovo, with internationally recognised borders, is handed down, UNMIK will have to oversee the transfer of authority from Kosovo's PISG to institutions established under the settlement during a final transitional stage of 120 days.[189] The UN Security Council already made it clear in the guiding principles that it adopted for the final status process that, for some time, 'Kosovo [would] continue to need an international civilian and military presence to exercise appropriate supervision of compliance of the provisions of the Status settlement, to ensure security and, in particular, protection for minorities as well as to monitor and support the authorities in the continued implementation of standards.'[190] In

---

[186] See I. Berend, 'Editorial: The Kosovo Trap', 14 *European Review* (2006) pp. 413-414.

[187] As noted before, the European Union fully participates in the status negotiations through its representative Stefan Lehne. However, his influence has been held back by the difficulties of EU Member States in forming a common stance on (conditional) independence for Kosovo (United Kingdom v. France).

[188] See J. Norris, 'Kosovo: Get It Right, Now', *Le Monde Diplomatique*, 12 October 2005.

[189] See Art. 14 (Transitional arrangements and final provisions) of the Comprehensive Proposal.

[190] See UN Doc. S/2005/709, 10 November 2005.

October 2005, the SGSR initiated consultations with a view to preparing a technical assessment of the need for possible future international involvement in Kosovo, without prejudice to the outcome of the future status process.[191] This ongoing assessment is conducted by UNMIK, together with the European Union, the OSCE and NATO, as well as with the UN funds and agencies and the bilateral donors present in Kosovo. It focuses on four main areas: the rule of law; good governance; democratisation, human rights and minority issues; and economic and fiscal issues.

It is believed that, for some time to come, NATO will continue to perform the hardcore security tasks and that the European Union will restrict its future role in Kosovo to civilian crisis management. In December 2005, the European Union's General Affairs and External Relations Council discussed a joint report by the SG/HR and the European Commissioner for Enlargement on the Union's future role in and contribution to Kosovo.[192] The report suggested that the Union should take over responsibility for policing Kosovo from UNMIK and train judges, prosecutors and prison staff to guarantee the rule of law. The report also called for increased aid to Kosovo and talked of a tangible European prospect, whatever the outcome of the status talks. The Council asked the SG/HR and the Commission 'to continue examination of these issues in coordination with other international actors, particularly in the areas of police and the rule of law (including contingency planning for a possible ESDP mission), economic development and fostering Kosovo's European perspective, and to keep the relevant Council bodies actively engaged in order to ensure continuing timely preparation of an EU role in Kosovo.'[193] To this end, a Council/Commission joint mission was dispatched to Kosovo in February 2006, and a joint action was adopted by the Council on 10 April 2006 to send an EU Planning Team (EUPT Kosovo) to the province, charged with designing an EU role in the fields of justice, police and rule of law issues as well as the smooth takeover of such selected tasks from UNMIK.[194] At the end of 2006, the mandate of EUPT Kosovo was widened to include planning and taking action in relation to selected UNMIK tasks *and* 'a possible EU crisis

191 Report of the Secretary-General on the United Nations Interim Administration Mission in Kosovo, UN Doc. S/2006/45, 25 January 2006, para. 14.

192 See Council Conclusions of 12 December 2005, Press Release No. 14961/05 (Presse 318).

193 Ibid.

194 Council Joint Action 2006/304/CFSP of 10 April 2006 on the establishment of an EU Planning Team (EUPT Kosovo) regarding a possible EU crisis management operation in the field of rule of law and possible other areas in Kosovo, *OJ* 2006 L 112/19. See also Olli Rehn, 'The Western Balkans', speech to the AFET Committee of the European Parliament, Brussels, 23 February 2006, SPEECH/06/125. The SG/HR and the EU Commissioner for Enlargement again reported, in their third joint report to the Council in July 2006. See Press Release No. S200/06, 'The Future EU Role and Contribution in Kosovo', 12 July 2006.

management operation in the field of the rule of law and other areas that might be identified by the Council in the context of the future status process.'[195]

At the time of writing, the political leaders of the Member States are not expected to assemble enough courage to let 'their' European Union enter the high-risk territory of Kosovo by taking over the military operation from KFOR (assuming that the government of Kosovo would actually prefer EU involvement over that of the United States within NATO). It seems that the Union is still doubtful about its own military capabilities. This is a pity, as most of the approximately 16,000 KFOR troops are European anyway.[196] Already in February 2006, US Secretary of Defence Donald Rumsfeld indicated that he hoped that US troop levels – currently standing at 1,700 – could be further reduced.[197] A reorganisation of the European Union's military involvement in Bosnia-Herzegovina[198] and invoking the necessary 'Berlin Plus' arrangements would enable the European Union to seize an historic opportunity and finally face up to the task of securing crisis situations on the continent without having to rely on US military might.

A final point concerns representation. In the event that the European Union indeed launches a civilian ESDP mission in Kosovo, it will have to work side-by-side with NATO, UN agencies and the international financial institutions. It would benefit the international community's goals and actions if it were to speak with a single voice. The double-hatted ICR/EUSR proposed by the Ahtisaari plan draws on the lessons learned from the OHR in Bosnia-Herzegovina, UNMIK in Kosovo and other international and ESDP civilian missions elsewhere and should therefore be welcomed.[199]

---

195 Art. 1(1) and (2) of Council Joint Action 2006/918/CFSP of 11 December 2006 amending and extending Joint Action 2006/304/CFSP on the establishment of an EU Planning Team (EUPT Kosovo) regarding a possible EU crisis management operation in the field of rule of law and possible other areas in Kosovo, *OJ* 2006 L 349/57. The EUPT Kosovo was extended until 1 September 2007 in principle, this date being subject to ongoing work in the United Nations and up for evaluation on 15 July 2007. See Council Joint Action 2007/334/CFSP of 14 May 2007, *OJ* 2007 L 125/29. The fourth joint report by the SG/HR and the EU Commissioner for Enlargement was sent to the Council on 29 March 2007. See Press Release No. S113/07 of that date.

196 Levels of the thirty-seven troop-contributing nations are available on KFOR's website, at: <http://www.nato.int/kfor>. See also the monthly reports to the United Nations on the operations of KFOR, e.g., UN Doc. S/2006/167, 15 March 2006, covering the period from 1 November to 31 December 2005.

197 See D. Sevastopulo and D. Dombey, 'Rumsfeld wants to cut US presence in Kosovo', *Financial Times*, 3 February 2006.

198 As suggested by Günter Platter, the Austrian Minister of Defence, at the informal meeting of EU Defence Ministers on 6-7 March 2006 in Innsbruck. Platter was reported as having said that EUFOR Althea could be reduced by 700 troops in the second half of 2006 and to 2,500 in the longer term. See 'EU-vredesmacht Bosnië verkleinen', *NRC Handelsblad*, 7 March 2006. On EUFOR Althea, see *infra* section 4.1.2.

199 See M. Karnitschnig, 'The UN and the EU in Kosovo – The Challenges of Joint Nation-Building', in J. Wouters, F. Hoffmeister and T. Ruys, eds., *The United Nations and the European Union: An Ever Stronger Partnership* (The Hague, T.M.C. Asser Press 2006) pp. 323-351. For an alternative view, see G. Niessen and J. te Velde, 'In Kosovo is geen plaats voor het Bosnisch model', 60 *Internationale Spectator* (2006) pp. 148-150.

4. ESDP OPERATIONS *SELON LA LETTRE*?

4.1 Bosnia-Herzegovina

4.1.1 *EU Police Mission to Bosnia-Herzegovina*

On 1 January 2003, the European Union launched its first-ever civilian crisis management operation within the framework of the ESDP: the European Union Police Mission (EUPM) in Bosnia-Herzegovina.[200] The Union thereby provided a follow-on mission to the United Nations International Police Task Force (IPTF). The aim of the EUPM, the mandate of which was adjusted and extended for another two years, is to consolidate the achievements of the IPTF and the international community's work to establish sustainable policing arrangements under Bosnian ownership in accordance with best European and international standards.[201] This overall goal is to be achieved in particular through monitoring, mentoring and inspecting the Bosnian police at the appropriate level, as well as through training and technical support.[202] Understandably, the EUPM does not have a mandate to enact legislation or to enforce the law in Bosnia-Herzegovina. To possess either would be to undermine the principle of an independent, non-politicised police service that the international community is seeking to instil more than ten years after the war ended.

At the time of writing, a total of thirty-four countries (the twenty-seven EU Member States and seven third countries) are contributing to a force of 207 police officers and support staff.[203] In accordance with Article 25 TEU, the Political and Security Committee (PSC, most commonly referred to by its French acronym

---

200 As explained in section 3, the European Union had already conducted civilian crisis management missions in cooperation with both the WEU and the United Nations. The EUPM was the first operation for which the European Union alone assumed leadership and responsibility. After having been invited thereto in the statement by the President of the Security Council of 12 December 2002 (UN Doc. S/PRST/2002/33), the European Union does, however, report to the Security Council on the activities of the EUPM. For the most recent report, covering the period from 1 January to 31 December 2005, see UN Doc. S/2006/125, 23 February 2006.

201 See Council Joint Action 2002/210/CFSP of 11 March 2002 on the European Union Police Mission, *OJ* 2002 L 70/1, which applied until 31 December 2005; and Council Joint Action 2005/824/CFSP of 24 November 2005 on the European Union Police Mission (EUPM) in Bosnia and Herzegovina (BiH), *OJ* 2005 L 307/55, applicable from 1 January 2006 to 31 December 2007.

202 Ibid. The total cost of the EUPM amounted to €38 million in 2003. See Council Decision 2002/968/CFSP of 10 December 2002 concerning the implementation of Joint Action 2002/210/CFSP on the European Union Police Mission, *OJ* 2002 L 335/1. Member States funded €18 million through staff secondment. The remaining €20 million in operational costs was financed through the Community budget. The latter figure dropped to €17.5 million per year in 2004 and 2005.

203 Canada, Iceland, Norway, Russia, Switzerland, Turkey and Ukraine have contributed police officers to the EUPM. The European Union has based itself on Art. 24 TEU to conclude agreements with these states on their (forces') participation in the EUPM. For updates on contribution levels, see: <http://www.eupm.org>.

COPS) is tasked with exercising political control and strategic direction over the mission. The Head of Mission/Police Commissioner is in operational control of the mission, reporting to the SG/HR through the EU Special Representative in Bosnia.[204] In order to support the domestic police forces in their work, the EUPM initially co-located over 400 of its officers with BiH officers at medium and senior level in all the police forces of Bosnia-Herzegovina, that is to say, in the police forces of the two entities that make up Bosnia-Herzegovina, the Muslim-Croat Federation of Bosnia-Herzegovina (FBiH) and the Republika Srpska (RS), and the police force of the independently administered Brčko District.[205] It is the officers' joint task to implement the EUPM's seven core programmes in crime policing, criminal justice, internal affairs, police administration and public order.[206] Each programme is implemented through a number of concrete projects, such as the Major and Organised Crime project and the Fight and Intervention against Human Trafficking project. In the field of internal affairs, one of the EUPM's main tasks is to encourage the domestic authorities to deal with cases of non-compliance such as obstruction of the EUPM, failure to adhere to the terms of the Dayton Agreement or failure to uphold democratic policing principles.

---

204 Sven Christian Frederiksen was appointed Head of Mission by Council Decision 2002/212/CFSP of 11 March 2002 concerning the appointment of the Head of Mission/Police Commissioner of the European Union Police Mission (EUPM), *OJ* 2002 L 70/8. Bartholomew Kevin Carty was appointed as his successor by Council Decision 2004/188/CFSP of 23 February 2004, *OJ* 2004 L 58/27. His mandate was extended until 31 December 2005 by Council Decision 2005/81/CFSP of 31 January 2005, *OJ* 2005 L 29/48. Carty was replaced by Vincenzo Coppola by PSC Decision EUPM/1/2005 (2005/922/CFSP) of 25 November 2005, *OJ* 2005 L 335/58. On 1 February 2006, Christian Schwarz-Schilling (Germany) succeeded Paddy Ashdown (United Kingdom) as High Representative and EUSR in Bosnia-Herzegovina. See Council Joint Action 2006/49/CFSP of 30 January 2006 appointing the European Union Special Representative in Bosnia and Herzegovina, *OJ* 2006 L 26/21. His mandate was amended and extended until 30 June 2007 by Council Joint Action 2007/87/CFSP of 7 February 2007 amending and extending the mandate of the European Union Special Representative in Bosnia and Herzegovina, *OJ* 2007 L 35/35. Lord Ashdown was appointed EUSR to Bosnia-Herzegovina by Council Joint Action of 11 March 2002 on the appointment of the EU Special Representative in Bosnia and Herzegovina, *OJ* 2002 L 70/7. This 'double-hatting' greatly facilitated the coordination of the rule of law reform programmes between the United Nations and the European Union.

205 The present structure of the State of Bosnia and Herzegovina was established under the General Framework Agreement for Peace, initialled in Dayton on 21 November 1995 and signed in Paris on 14 December 1995, 35 *ILM* (1996) at p. 75.

206 On the activities of the EUPM in Bosnia-Herzegovina, see the Agreement of 4 October 2002 between the EU and Bosnia-Herzegovina, annexed to Council Decision 2002/845/CFSP of 30 September 2002 concerning the conclusion of the Agreement between the European Union and Bosnia and Herzegovina (BiH) on the activities of the European Union Police Mission (EUPM) in BiH, *OJ* 2002 L 293/1. In coordination with the HR/EUSR, international organisations in Bosnia-Herzegovina, as well as senior BiH police authorities, the EUPM's first Head of Mission, Police Commissioner Frederiksen, set two priorities for the mission, namely combating organised crime and guaranteeing the safe return of refugees and internally displaced persons, particularly those returning to an area where the ethnic group to which they belong is in the minority. The EUPM's priorities developed over the course of the mission.

Only if the local authorities are seen to be failing in their duty to properly apply the disciplinary procedures will the matter be taken up by the EUPM. In the last instance, the EUPM Commissioner can recommend the removal of non-compliant officers to the HR/EUSR.[207] Any officer so removed would be barred from any future service in the police.[208]

It is difficult to objectively assess how successful the EUPM has been in the performance of its tasks since its inception. It is very much a question of whether one sees the bottle as half-full or half-empty. In the wake of the tenth anniversary of Dayton, travelling outside the remarkably safe and pleasant environment of Sarajevo, one gets a sense that Bosnia is settling into a sort of normality. People expelled during the war are returning. The cost of life is relatively cheap. But while an end to war has brought a peace dividend, elections and freedom of expression, it has also brought organised crime and hard drugs. On the basis of official press releases in the first year of operations, it seems that the EUPM was 'learning by doing'.[209] It increased border security after the assassination of Serbian Prime Minister Djindjić, it raided night clubs after reports of human trafficking and it increased surveillance after indications of smuggling activity via the beaches at Neum (the twelve-kilometre strip between Dubrovnik and Split that provides Bosnia-Herzegovina with access to the Adriatic). Eight months down the road, the EUPM acknowledged that the time had come to move beyond responding to violent incidents after they have occurred and formulate a security doctrine that would enable it to prevent the eruption of renewed violence. A stable and secure environment in Bosnia, underpinned by a military presence, was – and still is – an essential element for the success of the EUPM. At the outset, the European Union was dependent on the military presence of NATO/SFOR to secure this environment, making close consultation between the EUPM on the one hand, and the other international actors, in particular SFOR, on the other, imperative for establishing the rule of law in Bosnia-Herzegovina.[210] Procedures were simplified when, on 2 December 2004, the Union launched EUFOR Althea as a follow-on for SFOR.[211] But this move did not translate itself into a qualitative or quantitative improvement of the EUPM's record. While the EUPM was

207 Para. 6 of the Annex to Council Joint Action 2002/210/CFSP.

208 See C. Mace, 'European Union Security and Defence Policy Comes of Age in the Balkans', *EPC Working Papers* (2003), available at: <http://www.TheEPC.be>.

209 See also A. Nowak, *L'Union en action: la mission de police en Bosnie* (Paris, ISS 2003).

210 To this end, Council Joint Action 2003/188/CFSP of 17 March 2003 amending Joint Action 2002/210/CFSP on the European Union Police Mission, *OJ* 2003 L 73/9 was adopted to amend the original mandate of the EUPM to give the SG/HR the authorisation to release classified information and documents up to the level 'CONFIDENTIEL UE' to NATO/SFOR, the host state and the third parties associated with the EU Joint Action, and up to the level 'RESTREINT UE' to the Office of the High Representative, the United Nations and the OSCE.

211 See *infra* section 4.1.2.

supposed to turn local police into more efficient crime fighters, the International Crisis Group found that statistics collected by the entity police forces indicated that crime had in fact risen significantly since the EUPM's mandate began.[212] The most visible failure, however, was the inability of the EUPM to conclude an agreement between the various local parties on police reform.[213]

Substantive police reform was long overdue in Bosnia-Herzegovina. During the 1992-1995 war, the police were a key instrument of ethnic cleansing – particularly in the Republika Srpska and the Croatian areas of the FBiH.[214] The war left Bosnia with three police forces: Bosniak, Croat and Serb, each with its own jurisdictions. The first two merged fairly swiftly, at least nominally, but police throughout the whole country remained highly politicised, carrying out the orders of policymakers to obstruct the implementation of the Dayton Peace Agreement, in particular regarding refugee return, and were heavily involved in organised crime. The force in the Republika Srpska was filled with war criminals and actively supported persons indicted by the ICTY.[215] While the EUPM was empowered to request the HR/EUSR to remove obstructionist police officers, this proved such a cumbersome and protracted process that the EUPM has never exercised the power.[216] For a long time, police reform (of the structure of the police forces, their financing and their relationship to the courts) remained hopelessly blocked due to obstruction from the Serbian side. The leading party in the Republika Srpska – the Serbian Democratic Party (SDS) – openly blocked all reform efforts and received active encouragement from the Serbian government in Belgrade, the Serbian Orthodox Church and Serbia's security structures, which wished to annex the Republika Srpska in the context of a Kosovo final status

---

212 See ICG, 'Bosnia's Stalled Police Reform: No Progress, No EU', *Europe Report*, 6 September 2005. John Erik Jensen, Chief of Quality Control of the EUPM, was reported as having said that crime had risen approximately 40 per cent since the EUPM began, but that the statistics used by local police agencies were extremely unreliable.

213 The EUPM can claim formation of the State Investigation and Protection Agency, a state-level police agency, as a success, though one that must be shared with the OHR. The Council was proud to devote attention to this fact by publishing a positive press report on the issue in the first issue of its ESDP Newsletter in December 2005. See 'Wächter im Splitterstaat', *Süddeutsche Zeitung*, 20 October 2005. For a more critical view, see M. Merlingen and R. Ostrauskaite, 'ESDP Police Missions: Meaning, Context and Operational Challenges', 10 *EFA Rev.* (2005) pp. 215-235; and, more elaborately, M. Merlingen and R. Ostrauskaite, *European Union Peacebuilding and Policing: Governance and the European Security and Defence Policy* (London, Routledge 2006).

214 See L. Silber and A. Little, *The Death of Yugoslavia*, rev. edn. (London, Penguin Books 1996).

215 Although the Srebrenica Report of the Republika Srpska's government listed hundreds of individuals who took part in that massacre as still being active duty officers, the EUPM did not remove them or otherwise follow up. See ICG, 'Bosnia's Stalled Police Reform: No Progress, No EU', *Europe Report*, 6 September 2005. See, more generally, S. Bose, *Bosnia After Dayton: Nationalist Partition and International Intervention* (London, Hurst & Company 2002).

216 See ICG, loc. cit. n. 215.

settlement.[217] The OHR, the EUPM and other international agencies in Bosnia-Herzegovina proved incapable of convincing the Serbs to cooperate. A narrow interpretation of the EUPM's rather weak mandate – to 'monitor, mentor and inspect' – did not help to break to deadlock. It was not until heavy political pressure was applied on both Banja Luka and Belgrade, *inter alia*, by making police reform a necessary precondition for Bosnia-Herzegovina to open SAA negotiations with the European Union,[218] that the Bosnian Serb parliament on 6 October 2005 backed down from blocking a key police law.[219]

Keen to score an early success for its nascent European Security and Defence Policy, the European Union underestimated both the size and the complexity of the task in Bosnia-Herzegovina. The EUPM took over poorly prepared and lacking in inspiration and expertise on how to devise a hard-hitting and non-negotiable strategy for 'Europeanising' the police in Bosnia-Herzegovina. At the end of 2005, the Council reassessed the disappointing performance of the EUPM and used the expiration of its mandate on 31 December 2005 to replace it with an institution charged, until 31 December 2007, with supervising the implementation of the fight against organised crime and the agreed police reforms.[220] It seems unlikely that, with this marginal widening of the EUPM's mandate, a robust police mission has been created that will remove recalcitrant police officials and earn respect in – as well as outside – Bosnia-Herzegovina.[221]

4.1.2 *EUFOR Althea*

At the Copenhagen European Council in December 2002, the European Union stated its willingness to follow on from a strong NATO-led military operation in Bosnia-Herzegovina by mid-2004.[222] This ambition was restated by President Chirac and Prime Minister Blair at the Franco-British summit in Le Touquet in February 2003. SFOR, which operated under a robust chapter VII mandate,[223] was set up in Bosnia in December 1996, following the Dayton Agreement that ended

---

217 Ibid.

218 See chapter 5, section 3.2.3.

219 See M. Beunderman, 'Bosnia set to follow Croats and Serbs on EU track', *EUObserver.com*, 6 October 2005. But problems with the implementation of the agreement have since remained, blocking the conclusion of the SAA. See, e.g., D. Raduski, 'Written Interview of Javier Solana', *Nezavisne Novine*, 5 December 2006.

220 Art. 2 of Council Joint Action 2005/824/CFSP of 24 November 2005 on the European Union Police Mission (EUPM) in Bosnia and Herzegovina (BiH), *OJ* 2005 L 307/55; and Council Decision 2006/865/CFSP of 28 November 2006 implementing Joint Action 2005/824/CFSP on the European Union Police Mission (EUPM) in Bosnia and Herzegovina (BiH), *OJ* 2006 L 335/46.

221 See S. Penksa, 'Policing Bosnia and Herzegovina 2003-2005: Issues of Mandates and Management in ESDP Missions', *CEPS Working Document*, No. 255, December 2006.

222 *Bull. EU* 12-2002, point I.9.29.

223 S/RES/1088 (1996).

the civil war in the republic. It had a mandate to provide security and stability as well as to capture alleged war criminals and transfer them to the International Criminal Tribunal for the former Yugoslavia (ICTY) in The Hague. In June 2004, SFOR consisted of some 7,000 troops (reduced from 40,000 at the start, 33,000 in 1999 and 16,000 in 2002 as part of a restructuring exercise), with European states contributing the majority of the force.[224] Yet, leading an operation of this size would certainly represent a major task for the European Union. The United States had initially given a cautious welcome to the Union's proposal, emphasising the need for a successful initial military operation in Macedonia before any takeover from SFOR could be considered. At the beginning of June 2003, however, the United States put the brakes on the European Union's plans to take over the large NATO-led mission, citing security reasons, the complexity of the mission, and continuing problems with the transfer of war criminals to the ICTY.[225] High-level EU diplomats were not easily persuaded that, by postponing the European Union's takeover of NATO's mission, the United States was in fact doing the Union a favour and not attempting to thwart its efforts at giving the ESDP real visibility, which the Union's third military operation certainly would provide.[226]

Discontent over the spat between the United States and a divided Europe over the war in Iraq certainly fuelled the Union's eagerness to prove its military capabilities by taking over some of the tasks performed by NATO and the United Nations, especially in the nearby Western Balkans. Yet, as most of the region increasingly shed its dependency on large international military forces (some 7,000 NATO-led troops in Bosnia, up to 20,000 in Kosovo and a few hundred in Macedonia) and slowly moved towards the stage of state- and institution-building, the need for professionally trained police forces capable of providing security was growing. It was acknowledged that military missions could neither be open-ended nor carried out separately from building civilian structures. As such, the existing military mission in Bosnia-Herzegovina had to be part of a comprehensive approach in the country and, in particular, geared towards providing the necessary security regime to allow for the deployment of civilian missions aimed at integrating police forces, improving training and overhauling

224 Data available on SFOR's website, at: <http://www.nato.int/sfor>.

225 See: <http://www.europeanvoice.com/current/article.asp?id=18147>; and J. Dempsey, in N. Gnesotto, *EU Security and Defence Policy: The First Five Years (1999-2004)* (Paris, EUISS 2004) at p. 199.

226 See J. Dempsey, 'A Case of Overloaded Agendas', *Financial Times*, 3 June 2003, in which the author points to the overloaded agenda from which the European Union was suffering at the time: it was, *inter alia*, going through the most ambitious enlargement process in the history of European integration; it was involved in one of its most intense treaty amendment debates; it was working on its own 'security doctrine'; and it was already carrying out two military operations: 'Concordia' in Macedonia and 'Artemis' in Bunia (DRC).

the judiciary and penal systems.[227] In a decision hailed by the UN Security Council and Member States of both organisations, NATO announced at its 28-29 June 2004 summit in Istanbul that SFOR would be replaced by an EU-led peacekeeping force by the end of 2004.[228] The motives, however, had less to do with the real security situation in Bosnia-Herzegovina than with the European Union's eagerness to bolster its credibility as a security actor and the desire of the United States to declare at least one of its long-term military deployments successfully over.

On the surface, EUFOR merely had to pick up where the NATO peacekeepers had left off: patrolling the country, carrying out weapons collections and providing reassurance to local people. But the mission also faced two key challenges. The first was to deal with the issue of war criminals. While NATO managed to arrest twenty-eight people indicted by the ICTY, it singularly failed to arrest the two people at the top of the most wanted list: the former Bosnian Serb leaders Radovan Karadžić and Ratko Mladić. Although NATO maintained a residual military presence comprising a small 200-strong headquarters in Sarajevo (NHQSa) to advise the government of Bosnia-Herzegovina on defence reform, counter-terrorism *and* the capture of suspected war criminals, the spotlight shifted to EUFOR: could it do better in catching the big fish? Secondly, EUFOR would have to prove that it really could carry out a serious peacekeeping mission with thousands of troops on the ground. The question was whether the internal structures within the European Union would allow for such a mission. If so, then EUFOR could boost the Union's self-confidence in the field of the EDSP and lead to the launching of similar missions in other trouble spots.

Authorised by UN Security Council resolution 1575 (2004) for an initial planned period of twelve months,[229] EUFOR Althea embarked on a mission to provide deterrence[230] and continued compliance with the Dayton Agreement and

---

227 The European Council summit of 17-18 June 2004 adopted such a comprehensive policy towards Bosnia-Herzegovina. See *Bull. EU* 6-2004, point I.12.51.

228 See Istanbul Summit Communiqué issued by the Heads of State and Government participating in the meeting of the North Atlantic Council, NATO Press Release (2004) 096, 28 June 2004; Summary of remarks by Javier Solana, EU High Representative for the CFSP, at the Istanbul NATO summit Istanbul, 28 June 2004, S0179/04; and UNSC resolution 1551 (2004), adopted on 9 July 2004.

229 S/RES/1575 (2004), adopted on 22 November 2004. In para. 13, the Security Council expressed its intention to consider the terms of further authorisation as necessary in the light of developments in the implementation of the Dayton Peace Agreement and the situation in Bosnia-Herzegovina. In para. 18, the Security Council requested the Member States acting through or in cooperation with the European Union (and NATO) to report to it on the activities of EUFOR (and NHQSa) at least at three-monthly intervals.

230 That is to say, EUFOR would guarantee the peace by deterring anyone who might try to upset it.

to contribute to a safe and secure environment in Bosnia-Herzegovina.[231] The handover ceremony from NATO to EU peacekeepers took place at Camp Butmir, NATO's main base near Sarajevo, on 2 December 2004.[232] With the adoption of resolution 1575 (2004) under chapter VII of the UN Charter, the Security Council authorised the Member States acting through EUFOR to take 'all necessary measures' to effect the implementation of and to ensure compliance with Annexes 1-A and 2 of the Dayton Peace Agreement, and stressed that the parties to those agreements would continue to be subject to such enforcement action by EUFOR (and NHQSa) as might be necessary to ensure the protection and the defence of EUFOR (and the NATO presence). The resolution thus allowed for the use of force as applied by EUFOR troops in the gun battle that ensued after they stormed a house in Bosnia to apprehend Bosnian Serb war crimes suspect Dragomir Abazović.[233]

In terms of operation and command, the PSC, under the responsibility of the Council, is tasked with exercising political control and strategic direction over the military operation. The Council authorised the PSC to take the relevant decisions in accordance with Article 25 TEU.[234] This authorisation included the power to take further decisions on the appointment of the EU Operation Commander and/or the EU Force Commander and to amend the planning documents, including the operation plan, the chain of command and the rules of engagement. The powers of decision with respect to the objectives and termination of EUFOR, however, remained vested in the Council, assisted by the SG/HR.

As part of the 1999 'Berlin Plus' arrangements, EUFOR is drawing on NATO assets and capabilities for Althea.[235] The EU Operation Headquarters (EU OHQ) at Supreme Headquarters Allied Powers Europe (SHAPE) in Mons (Belgium) oversees EUFOR Althea. The EU OHQ draws on EU and NATO staff. The EU

---

231 Council Decision 2004/803/CFSP of 25 November 2004 on the launching of the European Union military operation in Bosnia and Herzegovina, *OJ* 2004 L 353/21, adopted on the basis of Art. 17 TEU, provided the legal basis for the launching of EUFOR Althea. Art. 3 states that, '[w]ithout prejudice to Article 17 of Joint Action 2004/570/CFSP, this Decision shall remain in force until the Council decides to end the EU military operation in Bosnia and Herzegovina.' For EUFOR Althea's mission statement, see Art. 1 of Council Joint Action 2004/570/CFSP of 12 July 2004 on the European Union military operation in Bosnia and Herzegovina, *OJ* 2004 L 252/10.

232 See Javier Solana, European Union High Representative for the Common Foreign and Security Policy, 'Launch of the EU "ALTHEA" operation in Bosnia and Herzegovina', Sarajevo, 2 December 2004, S0337/04: 'Today the EU assumes a new responsibility and commitment: here with the same spirit of generosity and efficiency as its predecessor from NATO. EUFOR will mesh with the EU's substantial engagement in so many areas: a formidable economic commitment, a Police mission deployed, a solid political relationship. All this is part of the journey to the only possible direction: the EU institutions.'

233 See T. Küchler, 'EU troops kill wife of Bosnian war crimes suspect', *EUObserver.com*, 6 January 2006.

234 Art. 6(1) of Council Joint Action 2004/570/CFSP.

235 Art. 1(3) of Council Joint Action 2004/570/CFSP.

Command Element at NATO's Joint Forces Command in Naples (Italy) and the EUFOR HQ at Camp Butmir in Sarajevo have control of the operation, reporting to EU OHQ. On 24 July 2004, Admiral Rainer Feist (Germany), NATO's Deputy Supreme Allied Commander for Europe (D-SACEUR), was appointed EU Operation Commander,[236] but he was succeeded (in both posts) by General John Reith (United Kingdom) before he could even start working for EUFOR.[237] The EU Military Committee (EUMC) monitors the proper execution of the EU military operation conducted under the responsibility of the EU Operation Commander.[238] Major General David Leakey (United Kingdom) was appointed as first EU Force Commander.[239] On 5 December 2005, he was replaced by Major General Gian Marco Chiarini (Italy),[240] who in turn was replaced by Rear Admiral Hans-Jochen Witthauer (Germany).[241] The EU Force Commander maintains contact with the local authorities, in close coordination with the HR/EUSR, on issues relevant to his mission.[242] Without prejudice to the chain of command, the EU Commanders coordinate closely with the HR/EUSR with a view to ensuring consistency of the EU military operation with the broader context of the international community's activities in Bosnia-Herzegovina.[243] At the end of 2006, a total of thirty-four countries (twenty-four EU Member States and ten third countries) were contributing to a force of about 7,000 troops that operated under the renewed UN chapter VII mandate of Security Council resolution 1722 (2006).[244] In line with the revised operational plan agreed to by the PSC and

236 Art. 2 of Council Joint Action 2004/570/CFSP.

237 PSC Decision BiH/2/2004 of 24 September 2004 on the appointment of an EU Operation Commander for the European Union military operation in Bosnia and Herzegovina (2004/733/CFSP), *OJ* 2004 L 324/22.

238 Art. 8(1) of Council Joint Action 2004/570/CFSP.

239 Art. 4 of Council Joint Action 2004/570/CFSP.

240 PSC Decision BiH/6/2005 of 14 June 2005 on the appointment of an EU Force Commander for the European Union Military Operation in Bosnia and Herzegovina (2005/483/CFSP), *OJ* 2005 L 173/14.

241 PSC Decision BiH/9/2006 of 27 June 2006 on the appointment of an EU Force Commander for the European Union Military Operation in Bosnia and Herzegovina (2006/497/CFSP), *OJ* 2006 L 196/25.

242 Art. 9 of Council Joint Action 2004/570/CFSP.

243 Art. 10 of Council Joint Action 2004/570/CFSP.

244 Facts and figures are drawn from <http://www.euforbih.org>. See PSC Decision BiH/5/2004 of 3 November 2004 amending Decision BiH/1/2004 on the acceptance of third States' contributions to the European Union military operation in Bosnia and Herzegovina and Decision BiH/3/2004 on the setting-up of the Committee of Contributors for the European Union military operation in Bosnia and Herzegovina (2004/822/CFSP), *OJ* 2004 L 357/39. Albania, Argentina, Canada, Chile, Macedonia, Morocco, New Zealand, Norway, Switzerland and Turkey have contributed troops. The European Union has based itself on Art. 24 TEU to conclude agreements on the participation of some of these third states' forces in EUFOR. See, e.g., Council Decision 2006/477/CFSP of 30 June 2006 concerning the conclusion of the Agreement between the European Union and the former Yugoslav Republic of Macedonia on the participation of the former Yugoslav Republic of Macedonia in the

endorsed by the Council on 5 March 2007,[245] EUFOR was downsized to 2,500 troops contributed by Hungary, Poland, Spain and Turkey (backed up by 'over-the-horizon' reserve forces in case of crisis). In accordance with Article 28(3) TEU, the operational expenditure for EUFOR Althea is paid through contributions by Member States to a financial mechanism (ATHENA) based on GDP.[246]

It is now more than two years since EUFOR took over from SFOR in Bosnia-Herzegovina. The transition from SFOR to EUFOR was seamless and did not result in a security gap. Thanks to its operational set-up and the symbiotic relationship with NATO and the rest of the 'EU family' in Bosnia-Herzegovina, EUFOR has managed to establish its credibility and robustness from the outset.[247] A good start was crucial for the consolidation of the European Union's ESDP, as EUFOR Althea is its most ambitious and significant operation within that framework. With approximately 7,000 personnel, EUFOR Althea is not only the largest EU military mission to date,[248] but is also still part of a comprehensive endeavour to give Bosnia-Herzegovina the perspective of EU membership.[249] The immediate goal of Operation Althea was to contribute to maintaining a secure environment for the implementation of the Dayton Agreement. In this respect, EUFOR Althea has proved to be a success. As part of its operations, EUFOR has conducted searches of companies suspected of pursuing activities in contravention of the Dayton Agreement, and it has conducted operations to disrupt illegal

---

European Union military crisis management operation in Bosnia and Herzegovina (Operation ALTHEA), *OJ* 2006 L 188/10. Denmark, Cyprus and Malta have not contributed troops. In conformity with Article 6 of the Protocol on the position of Denmark annexed to the Treaty of Amsterdam, *OJ* 1997 C 340/101, Denmark does not participate in the elaboration and implementation of decisions and actions of the European Union that have defence implications. Therefore, Denmark does not participate in the implementation of Joint Action 2004/570/CFSP, nor in the financing of the operation. Under the 'Berlin Plus' arrangements, Cyprus and Malta are excluded from taking part in EU military operations using NATO assets and capabilities. See *infra* section 4.2.1. The neutral EU countries of Finland, Sweden and Ireland have contributed troops to EUFOR Althea. Major troop contributions came from Germany (1,014), Italy (955), the United Kingdom (706) and France (402).

245 See Council, 'Operation ALTHEA in Bosnia and Herzegovina: EU confirms decision on transition', Press Release No. 6896/07 (Presse 43), 28 February 2007; and Council Conclusions of 5 March 2007, Press Release No. 6756/07 (Presse 39).

246 Art. 12 of Council Joint Action 2004/570/CFSP. On ATHENA, see Council Decision 2004/197/CFSP of 23 February 2004 establishing a mechanism to administer the financing of the common costs of European Union operations having military or defence implications, *OJ* 2004 L 63/68; and Council Decision 2007/91/CFSP of 12 February 2007 amending Decision 2004/197/CFSP, *OJ* 2007 L 41/11.

247 See a happy J. Solana, 'Foreword', EUFOR FORUM, 2 December 2005.

248 The two military operations that the European Union carried out prior to launching EUFOR Althea, 'Concordia' (FYROM) and 'Artemis' (DRC). 'Concordia' consisted of 400 troops.

249 See Remarks of Javier Solana, EU High Representative for the CFSP, at the EUFOR Change of Command Ceremony, Sarajevo, 6 December 2005, S402/05: 'This comprehensive approach is what modern crisis management is all about.'

activities by those involved in organised crime. EUFOR has also supported demining operations and regularly carries out weapons collection activities across the country. Cooperating closely with the EUPM, EUFOR puts pressure on criminal networks.[250] By doing so, it has also helped to disrupt support to ICTY indictees.[251] In short, EUFOR's activities have helped to create the conditions under which Bosnia-Herzegovina was able to make progress in several important respects.[252] For example, in September 2005, the Republika Srpska and the FBiH agreed on a long-debated military reform; a number of weeks later they agreed on the issue of police reform. This progress has been rewarded with the opening of negotiations on a Stabilisation and Association Agreement with the European Union.[253]

As noted when discussing the role of the EUPM, however, much progress is still to be made. Ongoing disagreement about police reform now forms the obstacle to concluding the SAA negotiation process. However stable Bosnia-Herzegovina is, the potential for instability still exists: the country is awash with weapons; the three constituent peoples do not all share a common vision for the future, and this is evident in daily politics, which is driven by nationalistic agendas; and progress towards self-sustainability is significantly hindered by widespread organised crime and corruption, which are deeply intermingled with public life. The reform agenda, including the defence and police reforms, still needs to be implemented. In 2006, a new multi-ethnic professional army under a central general staff and one defence ministry at federal level was created. The new army has replaced the military structures of the BiH entities. As the reform of the BiH armed forces and the build up of the BiH security sector continues, EUFOR (in cooperation with the NHQSa) will have to stand ready to hand over more and more of its responsibilities to Bosnia-Herzegovina. Cooperation with the ICTY must continue and be enhanced. In this respect, EUFOR Althea risks receiving the same criticism that NATO has had to endure: Karadžić and Mladić

250 Asked what had been the main shortcomings of EUFOR in its first year of operations, Major General Leakey, Commander of the force, mentioned that in supporting the fight against organised crime, EUFOR very much had to learn by doing: 'This new task has been demanding for everyone, from the soldiers on the ground to myself. Nevertheless, all EUFOR personnel have performed extremely well in this regard.' Leakey also admitted that in running a multinational headquarters as efficiently as possible, one needs to overcome practical challenges such as language, different cultures and modus operandi. 'But I believe that EUFOR has, again, risen to the challenge successfully.' See 'Interview with Major General David Leakey, Commander of the stabilisation force (EUFOR)', in 1 *ESDP Newsletter* (2005) at p. 23.

251 Information available on EUFOR's website, at: <http://www.euforbih.org>. See also N. Hawton, 'Forces target Karadzic "network"', *BBC News*, 15 March 2006.

252 For the European Union's own account of the achievements of EUFOR, see the Factsheet, ATH/08 (update 8) attached to the Council's Press Release No. 6896/07 (Presse 43), 28 February 2007.

253 See chapter 5, section 3.2.3.

are still at large. Determining that the situation in the region continues to constitute a threat to international peace and security, the UN Security Council was therefore right in extending EUFOR's robust chapter VII mandate until November 2007.[254]

4.2 **Macedonia**

4.2.1 *Operation Concordia*

As part of its larger commitment to Macedonia,[255] the European Union deployed its inaugural military operation to contribute further to a stable and secure environment in the country. On 31 March 2003, it launched Operation Concordia to ensure the follow-up of NATO's Operation *Allied Harmony*.[256] The European Union had already hoped to take over from NATO in Macedonia when the mandate of the Alliance's Operation *Amber Fox* came to an end in December 2002.[257] However, the EU-led operation could not go ahead until an agreement was reached with Turkey, within NATO, on EU access to NATO assets and capabilities (the so-called 'Berlin Plus' arrangements). The negotiations between the European Union and Turkey were deadlocked for months, until a breakthrough finally came on 12 December 2002, when the European Council of Copenhagen agreed that the 'Berlin Plus' arrangements and the implementation thereof would 'only apply to those EU Member States which are also either NATO members or parties to NATO's "Partnership for Peace", and which have consequently concluded bilateral security agreements with NATO'.[258] This formulation, which effectively excludes Cyprus (and Malta) from taking part in EU military operations using NATO assets, was sufficient to overcome Turkish objections and secure access to NATO assets.[259] At the same summit, the European Council

---

[254] S/RES/1639 (2005) and S/RES/1722 (2006), both of 21 November.

[255] See *supra* section 3.1 and chapter 5.

[256] See Council Decision 2003/202/CFSP of 18 March 2003 relating to the launch of the EU military operation in the Former Yugoslav Republic of Macedonia, *OJ* 2003 76/43. On NATO's role in Macedonia, see chapter 2, section 7.2.

[257] See *Bull. EU* 6-2002, point I.7.14.

[258] *Bull. EU* 12-2002, points I.9.27 and I.17.

[259] The finalisation of the 'Berlin Plus' arrangements was concluded with the signing of a Security of Information Agreement between the European Union and NATO on 14 March 2003. See Council Decision 2003/211/CFSP of 24 February 2003 concerning the conclusion of the Agreement between the European Union and the North Atlantic Treaty Organisation on the Security of Information, *OJ* 2003 L 80/35. The agreement itself is not publicly accessible. For background and analysis, see M. Reichard, 'Some Legal Issues Concerning the EU-NATO Berlin Plus Agreement', 73 *Nordic JIL* (2004) pp. 37-67. After a more thorough examination of the characteristics of 'Berlin Plus', the same author comes to the conclusion that the document underpinning the arrangements does not meet 'enough' requirements to qualify as an international treaty under the 1969 Vienna Convention on the Law of Treaties and the 1986 Vienna Convention on the Law of Treaties between

confirmed the Union's readiness to take over the military operation in Macedonia as soon as possible, in consultation with NATO.[260] The European Council invited the relevant EU bodies to finalise work on the overall approach to the operation, including the development of military options and relevant plans. The Union's wish eventually became reality at the end of March 2003. A total of twenty-seven countries (thirteen EU Member States[261] and fourteen non-EU countries[262]) contributed to a force of 350 soldiers plus fifty support staff.[263]

It is worth pointing out that the Irish government decided that it was unable to contribute personnel to Concordia due to the lack of *explicit* UN Security Council authorisation for the operation.[264] Indeed, without referring to its legal basis in the UN Charter or determining the situation in Macedonia a threat to international peace and security, Security Council resolution 1371 (2001), the single non-EU basis for the adoption of Joint Action 2003/92/CFSP on the establishment of Concordia,[265] called for the full implementation of resolution 1345 (2001) and further simply *welcomed* international efforts, including those of the OSCE, the European Union and NATO, in cooperation with the Macedonian government, and other states, 'to prevent the escalation of ethnic tensions in the area and to facilitate the full implementation of the Framework Agreement, thus contributing

---

States and International Organisations. See M. Reichard, *The EU-NATO Relationship: A Legal and Political Perspective* (Aldershot, Ashgate 2006) at pp. 288-300, in particular at p. 300: 'The strongest evidence supporting such a conclusion are the title as 'Declaration', lack of specific treaty-making capacity of the EU, and its half-secret nature, hinting at NATO's lack of consent to be bound.' It is Reichard's view, however, that 'Berlin Plus' is a non-binding agreement that can, on the basis of the application of regional customary law and the principle of estoppel, create the possibility of redress for the aggrieved party. Ibid., at pp. 301-310.

260 *Bull. EU 12-2002*, point I.9.28.

261 Denmark, for reasons already mentioned (see *supra* n. 244), did not participate in the elaboration, implementation and financing of Council Joint Action 2003/92/CFSP of 27 January on the European Union military operation in the Former Yugoslav Republic of Macedonia, *OJ* 2003 L 34/26. In accordance with Art. 28(3) TEU, the operational expenditure arising from the Joint Action having military implications were charged to the Member States according to a formula based on GDP. Such costs totalled €6.2 million. The remaining costs were funded by participating states on a 'costs lie where they fall' basis.

262 Bulgaria, Canada, Czech Republic, Estonia, Hungary, Iceland, Latvia, Lithuania, Norway, Poland, Romania, Slovakia, Slovenia and Turkey.

263 The status of the EU-led forces in FYROM was the subject of an agreement between the European Union and the government of the Macedonia, concluded on the basis of Article 24 TEU. See Council Decision 2003/222/CFSP of 21 March 2003 concerning the conclusion of the Agreement between the European Union and the Former Yugoslav Republic of Macedonia on the status of the European Union-led Forces (EUF) in the Former Yugoslav Republic of Macedonia, *OJ* 2003 L 82/45, to which the so-called SOFA is annexed.

264 Nevertheless, Ireland did contribute to the mission's joint costs and played a full role in the Committee of Contributors. See PSC Decision FYROM/1/2003 of 18 February 2003 on the setting-up of the Committee of Contributors for the European Union Military Operation in the Former Yugoslav Republic of Macedonia, *OJ* 2003 L 62/1.

265 Council Joint Action 2003/92/CFSP, preamble, recital 4.

to peace and stability in the region.'[266] Resolution 1345 (2001) did little more than call on states and appropriate international organisations to consider how they could best give practical help to efforts in the region to strengthen democratic, multi-ethnic societies and assist in the return of displaced persons (para. 11).[267] The legal basis for the adoption of this resolution was also elusive, but like resolution 1371 (2001) it recalled resolution 1244 (1999) on Kosovo, which had determined that the situation 'in the region' constituted a threat to international peace and security and gave NATO a chapter VII mandate to deploy KFOR troops. While Ireland was probably right in insisting that resolution 1244 (1999), adopted in the wake of NATO's armed intervention in Kosovo, could not serve as an appropriate legal basis for the deployment of an EU peacekeeping mission in neighbouring Macedonia in 2003, it could hardly use this argument to not contribute troops to Operation Concordia. After all, the European Union (supposedly) acted on the explicit request of the Macedonian government, not the other way around.[268]

As said at the beginning, the aim of Operation Concordia was to contribute further to a stable and secure environment to allow the Macedonian government to implement the 2001 Ohrid Framework Agreement in order to arrive at a situation where an international security presence was no longer needed. The command and control arrangements for Operation Concordia were drawn up in accordance with the 'Berlin Plus' arrangements so as to create an EU chain of command that recognised the need for coordination with NATO.[269] Admiral Rainer Feist, Deputy Supreme Allied Commander for Europe (D-SACEUR),[270] was appointed as the first EU Operation Commander.[271] The Council appointed

---

266 S/RES/1371 (2001) of 26 September 2001.

267 S/RES/1345 (2001) of 21 March 2001. The resolution also called on all states in the region to respect each other's territorial integrity and to cooperate on measures that foster stability and promote regional political and economic cooperation in accordance with the UN Charter, the basic principles of the OSCE and the Stability Pact for South Eastern Europe (para. 12).

268 President Trajkovski is supposed to have sent a formal invitation letter to the SG/HR on 17 January 2003. See Council Joint Action 2003/92/CFSP, preamble, recital 5. But proof of the existence of this letter could not be found. On 13 March 2003, the SG/HR allegedly received a further letter from President Trajkovski, inviting the European Union to launch an operation in Macedonia. See Council Decision 2003/202/CFSP, preamble, recital 1. Proof of the existence of this letter could also not be found.

269 Arts. 1-5, 7, 8, 10, and 11 of Council Joint Action 2003/92/CFSP. It serves little purpose to repeat the arrangements here. They have been described in detail when discussing EUFOR Althea, *supra* section 4.1.2. It should be emphasised, however, that the command and control arrangements for Althea were copied from those for Operation Concordia. See also C. Mace, 'European Union Security and Defence Policy Comes of Age in the Balkans', *EPC Working Papers* (2003), available at: <http://www.TheEPC.be>.

270 See *supra* section 4.1.2.

271 Art. 2 of Council Joint Action 2003/92/CFSP.

Brigadier-General Pierre Maral (France) as EU Force Commander.[272] One of his tasks was to maintain contact with local authorities on issues relevant to his mission. Javier Solana and Alexis Brouhns (the EUSR in Macedonia at the time),[273] each within his own mandate, acted as primary points of contact with the Macedonian authorities for matters relating to the implementation of Joint Action 2003/92/CFSP.[274]

In terms of crisis management, the European Union has fared well in the case of Macedonia. Building on the success of three NATO operations in the country (*Essential Harvest*, *Amber Fox* and *Allied Harmony*), Operation Concordia provided continuity by carrying out classic peacekeeping tasks such as patrolling Macedonia's crisis areas, mostly near the Kosovo border.[275] While it is true that, overall, the situation in Macedonia was relatively straightforward when compared to other Balkan conflicts, the security situation in the country nevertheless remained precarious. Incidents that took place at the beginning of 2003 and that apparently were the work of ethnic Albanian extremists unhappy with the Ohrid Framework Agreement had served as a reminder of the potential for a resurgence of ethnic violence Macedonia.[276] Although Concordia was a relatively small force, its deployment was an important first test for both the European Union's military crisis management capabilities and the 'Berlin Plus' arrangements. The Union was successful on both counts. Concordia's deployment heralded a period of normalisation and stabilisation. Initially expected to last for a period of six months,[277] the Council on 29 July 2003 agreed to extend Operation Concordia for one additional period until 15 December 2003, in line with the request made to the European Union by the president of Macedonia.[278] This shows the level of confidence that the Macedonian government had in the European Union as a

---

272 See Council Press Release No. 6158/03 (Presse 38), 7 February 2003. Maral was replaced by Major General Luís Nelson Ferreira dos Santos (Portugal) as of 1 October 2003. On that date, Concordia took over from France the responsibilities at the force's headquarters level. See Art. 2 of Council Decision 2003/563/CFSP of 29 July 2003 on the extension of the European Union military operation in the Former Yugoslav Republic of Macedonia, *OJ* 2003 L 190/20.

273 See *supra* n. 98.

274 Art. 6 of Council Joint Action 2003/92/CFSP.

275 For an overview of Concordia's activities, see Concordia's website: <http://www.delmkd.cec.eu.int/en/Concordia/main.htm>.

276 See, e.g., T. Stojcevski, 'Abductions rattle Macedonians', 395 *IWPR Balkan Crisis Report* (2003); T. Stojcevski, 'Lions menace ends', 401 *IWPR Balkan Crisis Report* (2003); T. Stojcevski, 'Militants threaten with renewed conflict', 403 *IWPR Balkan Crisis Report* (2003); and T. Stojcevski, ''Extremists' target Macedonians' homes', 410 *IWPR Balkan Crisis Report* (2003).

277 Art. 3 of Council Decision 2003/202/CFSP.

278 Council Decision 2003/563/CFSP of 29 July 2003 on the extension of the European Union military operation in the Former Yugoslav Republic of Macedonia, *OJ* 2003 L 190/20 refers to Trajkovski's letter of 4 July 2003, addressed to the SG/HR, in which the president invited the European Union to extend Operation Concordia until 15 December 2003 with the existing mandate and legal framework.

crisis manager. Or perhaps it was the SG/HR who bought extra preparation time by convincing Trajkovski to wait until the end of the year before the Union's first-ever military mission would be transformed into a police mission.[279]

4.2.2 *EUPOL Proxima*

On 15 December 2003, a ceremony and a military parade in Skopje marked the official end of Operation Concordia. Immediately afterwards, the opening ceremony of the EU Police Mission in Macedonia (EUPOL Promixa) took place at the mission's new headquarters. Javier Solana spoke on both occasions.[280] In both speeches, the SG/HR stressed the continued engagement of the European Union in Macedonia, a country which had moved from a situation where the main threat to stability was no longer armed conflict but criminality. Hence the need to shift the emphasis in the Union's support actions from the military to the police.

At the invitation of Prime Minister Branko Crvenkovski,[281] the European Union assumed responsibility for its second-ever police mission in the framework of the ESDP – its fourth ESDP mission of 2003. Proxima was launched for an initial period of twelve months.[282] A planning team had been preparing its operations since 1 October 2003.[283] As part of the SAP aimed at strengthening the rule of law in the region, Proxima aimed to support Macedonian efforts in moving closer towards the European Union.[284] In particular, Proxima's aim was to consolidate public confidence in policing by monitoring, mentoring and advising the local police and thus help fight organised crime more effectively. Proxima would achieve this goal by means of a comprehensive reform of the Ministry of the Interior, including the creation of a border police force and the development of an efficient and professional police service living up to European standards of policing, as required within the implementation of the Ohrid Framework Agreement.[285] To this end, thirty-five states (the fifteen EU Member States, the ten acceding countries, the three candidate countries and seven third states[286]) contributed to a 200- strong police mission that was placed under the day-to-day

---

279 Already ten weeks after the European Union launched Operation Concordia, President Trajkovski suggested that the force be transformed into one that advises on border controls and the police. See E. Jansson, 'Macedonia Seeks Greater Role for Balkans', *Financial Times*, 9 June 2003.

280 Javier Solana, EU High Representative for CFSP, attends ceremonies for termination of Operation Concordia and launch of Mission Proxima, Skopje, S0256/03, 15 December 2003.

281 Letter dated 16 September 2003.

282 Council Joint Action 2003/681/CFSP of 29 September 2003 on the European Union Police Mission in the Former Yugoslav Republic of Macedonia (FYROM), *OJ* 2003 L 249/66.

283 The planning team was foreseen by Arts. 1 and 2 of Council Joint Action 2003/681/CFSP.

284 See chapter 5.

285 Art. 3 of Council Joint Action 2003/681/CFSP.

286 Canada, Iceland, Norway, Russia, Switzerland, Ukraine and the United States.

supervision of Head of Mission/Police Commissioner Bart D'Hooge, who had also acted as the Police Head of Mission/Head of the Planning Team.[287] He was obliged to report to the SG/HR through the EUSR.[288] Like with other ESDP operations, the PSC provided political control and strategic direction. Uniformed police personnel were seconded by the Member States.[289] Officers were co-located at appropriate levels in Skopje, Tetovo, Kumanovo, Gostivar and Ohrid.[290]

EUPOL Proxima was extended by one year in response to a request of the Macedonian Prime Minister Hari Kosotov on 1 October 2004.[291] Brigadier General Jürgen Scholz was appointed as D'Hooge's replacement.[292] Under the political guidance of the EUSR in Skopje, Ambassador Michael Sahlin, and in partnership with the local authorities, Proxima police experts continued to monitor, mentor and advise the country's police, focusing on middle and senior management. It also assisted further in the creation of a border police force. During its second year of activities, EUPOL Proxima focused on urgent operational needs within three programmes: Public Peace and Order, Organised Crime and Border Police. As a consequence, the mission expanded its geographical coverage to a country-wide deployment, while maintaining a higher presence in the former crisis area.

---

287 Council Decision 2003/682/CFSP of 29 September 2003 concerning the appointment of the Head of Mission/Police Commissioner of the European Union Police Mission (EUPOL) in the Former Yugoslav Republic of Macedonia, *OJ* 2003 L 249/70. In accordance with Art. 13 of Council Joint Action 2003/681/CFSP, the Council adopted – by written procedure and on the basis of Art. 24 TEU – a decision concerning the conclusion of the Agreement between the European Union and the Former Yugoslav Republic of Macedonia on the status and activities of the European Union Police Mission in the Former Yugoslav Republic of Macedonia (EUPOL Proxima), *OJ* 2004 L 16/66. The agreement included, where appropriate, the privileges, immunities and further guarantees necessary for the completion and smooth functioning of the police mission. The Head of Mission had to sign a contract with the Commission. See Art. 5(2) of Council Joint Action 2003/681/CFSP.

288 The SG/HR gave guidance to the Head of Mission/Police Commissioner through the EUSR. Art. 7 of Council Joint Action 2003/681/CFSP.

289 Each Member State had to bear the costs related to the police officers seconded by it, including salaries, medical coverage, allowances other than per diems and travel expenses to and from Macedonia. See Art. 6(2) of Council Joint Action 2003/681/CFSP. All police officers remained under full command of the appropriate national authority. National authorities transferred operational control to the Head of Mission (Art. 5(3)).

290 For an overview of the operational challenges faced by Proxima, see M. Merlingen and R. Ostrauskaite, 'ESDP Police Missions: Meaning, Context and Operational Challenges', 10 *EFA Rev.* (2005) pp. 213-235.

291 Council Joint Action 2004/789/CFSP of 22 November 2004 on the extension of the European Union Police Mission in the Former Yugoslav Republic of Macedonia (EUPOL PROXIMA), *OJ* 2004 L 348/40.

292 PSC Decision PROXIMA/2/2004 of 30 November 2004 concerning the appointment of the Head of Mission of the EU Police Mission in the former Yugoslav Republic of Macedonia, EUPOL Proxima (2004/846/EC), *OJ* 2004 L 367/29.

The European Union's second ESDP police mission was successfully terminated on 9 December 2005.[293] The closing of EUPOL Proxima preceded the decision of the European Council summit of 15-16 December 2005 to award candidate country status to Macedonia as a reward for the 'significant progress' it had made in the previous years towards meeting the political criteria for EU membership.[294] Thus, the European Union's relationship with Macedonia moved from post-conflict stabilisation to pre-accession integration.

4.2.3 *EUPAT*

The end of EUPOL Proxima did not signify the end of EU support to police reform in Macedonia. With the establishment of the EU Police Advisory Team (EUPAT), the European Union continued its efforts in supporting local authorities.[295] EUPAT was launched on 15 December 2005 for a single period of six months.[296]

The main objective of EUPAT was to help the Macedonian government modernise police structures, a priority reform area for further progress towards the European Union.[297] The team consisted of thirty experts seconded from EU Member States.[298] They acted under the day-to-day leadership of Brigadier General Scholz, whose stay in Macedonia was thereby prolonged.[299] Scholz, in turn, acted under the guidance of EUSR Erwan Fouéré and in partnership with the Macedonian authorities.[300] Very much like the staff of its predecessor, EUPOL

---

293 Statement by Javier Solana, EU High Representative for CFSP, on the occasion of the ceremony marking the end of the EU Police Mission in the former Yugoslav Republic of Macedonia, Skopje, S406/05, 9 December 2005.

294 *Bull. EU* 12-2005, points I.12.23 and 24.

295 During consultations with the European Union, the Macedonian government had indicated that it would welcome, under certain conditions, a police mission to bridge the gap between the end of EUPOL Proxima and a planned project funded by CARDS aimed at providing technical assistance in the field of police reform.

296 Council Joint Action 2005/826/CFSP of 24 November 2005 on the establishment of an EU Police Advisory Team (EUPAT) in the Former Yugoslav Republic of Macedonia (fYROM), *OJ* 2005 L 307/61.

297 Art. 1(2) of Council Joint Action 2005/826/CFSP.

298 Art. 5(4) of Council Joint Action 2005/826/CFSP. The staff comprised both EU police officers and civilian experts (including law enforcement monitors), assisted by twenty national staff. The headquarters for the head of EUPAT and his staff were in Skopje, while EUPAT mobile units were co-located in Skopje, Tetovo, Ohrid, Bitola and Stip, thereby covering all police regions. The necessary arrangements were made regarding the extension of the agreement between the European Union and Macedonia on the status and activities of EUPOL Proxima to EUPAT.

299 PSC Decision EUPAT/1/2005 of 7 December 2005 concerning the appointment of the Head of the EU Police Advisory Team Mission in the former Yugoslav Republic of Macedonia (fYROM), EUPAT, *OJ* 2005 L 346/46.

300 Fouéré was the Head of the Commission's Delegation in Skopje. Under the terms of Council Joint Action 2005/724/CFSP of 17 October 2005, *OJ* 2005 L 272/26, Fouéré's mandate as EUSR expired on 28 February 2006. It was extended and amended by Joint Action 2006/123/CFSP of 20 February 2006, *OJ* 2006 L 49/20.

Proxima, EUPAT experts monitored and advised the Macedonian police (primarily the middle and senior management levels) in fields spanning border management, public order and the fight against corruption and organised crime. EUPAT put emphasis on the implementation of police reforms, cooperation between the police and the judiciary, professional standardisation and internal control.[301] The European Union set aside €1.5 million for this mission in Macedonia.[302]

When EUPAT's mandate ended on 14 June 2006, it handed over to a European Commission funded CARDS project that would continue to provide police advisors at central and local level.[303] This evolution shows how far Macedonia has come in just five years. It also illustrates the European Union's ability to adapt its different tools to specific situations with specific needs. The Union thus began by taking over a military operation from NATO, continued with an ESDP police mission and followed up with EUPAT and the European Commission projects.

5. CONCLUDING REMARKS

The European Union has come a long way in the Western Balkans in just a few years. During the 1990s, while it stood by and watched the Balkans burn, it was the United States, in the framework of NATO, that had to put the fire out. In the aftermath of the Kosovo crisis, the Union finally found its voice to say no to violent conflict in the heart of Europe. In Macedonia, it for the first time acted quickly and in a unified way to head off the plunge into inter-ethnic warfare. Thanks to the heavy involvement of SG/HR Javier Solana, and with the support of NATO and the OSCE, the European Union brokered the Ohrid Framework Agreement (2001), which defined the road to a new inter-ethnic arrangement in Macedonia. The creation of the state union of Serbia and Montenegro marked a second important feat for the Union and its High Representative for the CFSP. This temporary arrangement helped the region to 'cool off', while it bought the international community time to find ways to face the next challenges, most notably that of Kosovo's final status, the determination of which is the key to creating sustainable peace and stability in the Western Balkans.

The European sword is being forged in the Western Balkans, in order to back up words with force if need be. The European Union has taken its first steps in the field of the ESDP with the launch of its first-ever police and military missions. Macedonia and Bosnia-Herzegovina have served as good testing grounds for

301 Art. 2 of Council Joint Action 2005/826/CFSP.
302 Art. 8 of Council Joint Action 2005/826/CFSP.
303 On CARDS, see chapter 5, section 3.4.

making forthcoming ESDP missions a success. Lessons learned from these operations should be taken to heart when the Union embarks on its biggest civilian mission in the high-risk territory of Kosovo.

In this context, it is clear that the European Union cannot afford to fall prey to the consequences of a half-hearted policy or another 'Balkan fatigue'. The Western Balkans may offer the Union's one and only chance of developing credible and lasting foreign policy, security and defence arrangements. The Western Balkans will require continued attention and support from the European Union if the region is to become stable and secure. The need for further investment in peacebuilding in the Western Balkans is clear. Complicated issues need to be tackled urgently if the Union is to get a return on its investment in the region. In order to succeed, the short-term intervention actions must be underpinned by reinforced policies to address the root causes of radical discontent. Organised crime and widespread corruption need to be eradicated quickly and the sustainable return of internally displaced persons is vital for ethnic reconciliation. During the last seven years, the European Union's SAP has made a critical contribution to progress achieved throughout the region in promoting peace and stability. The European Union's evolving relationship with the Western Balkans centres around the application of the conditionality principle. This will be the topic of the next chapter.

CHAPTER 5

THE EUROPEAN UNION'S APPLICATION OF THE CONDITIONALITY PRINCIPLE TO THE WESTERN BALKANS*

1. INTRODUCTION

As noted in the previous chapter, the recent establishment of a real and credible Common Foreign and Security Policy towards the Western Balkans and the launching of the first-ever EU military and police missions in the framework of the European Security and Defence Policy are helpful in restoring order in the region. Maintaining the 'negative peace' (absence of armed hostilities) is a necessary condition for establishing and maintaining a 'positive peace' (social justice and equality) within and among the countries of the Western Balkans. However, it does not single-handedly deal with the underlying causes and conditions of the symptoms of violent conflicts in the region. The determinants of security stabilisation in the Western Balkans are not just political and military. A comprehensive approach towards reconstruction and reconciliation is key to the efforts geared at stabilising the region. This implies the establishment of autonomous communities and the creation of new or reformed administrative, legislative and judicial structures that guarantee the rule of law instead of the 'law of the ruler'. Moreover, the establishment of effective democratic structures has to go hand in hand with macroeconomic stabilisation and liberalisation.[1] Finally, a good approach will adapt to local and regional differences. This is the consequence of the disintegration and fragmentation of the former Yugoslavia. Hence, what is needed is a flexible, multi-layered approach that recognises these specificities and provides a form of assistance that is designed to encourage political, economic and social integration in the Western Balkans and in Europe; a process that would render states and borders relatively unimportant. Only such a comprehensive strategy for lasting peace can create an opposite logic to that of war.

To fill the relative 'Hobbesian void' in south-eastern Europe with conflict controlling and resolving mechanisms, and to create a belt of security, stability and prosperity stretching from Slovenia in the north-west to Greece in the south-east,

---

* This chapter is a revised and extended version of my contribution 'Western Balkans', in S. Blockmans and A. Łazowski, eds., *The European Union and Its Neighbours: A Legal Appraisal of the EU's Policies of Stabilisation, Partnership and Integration* (The Hague, T.M.C. Asser Press 2006) pp. 315-355.

[1] See M. Kaldor, V. Bojičić and I. Vejvoda, 'Reconstruction in the Balkans: A Challenge for Europe?', 2 *EFA Rev.* (1997) pp. 329-350 at pp. 344-346.

the European Union has, for some years now, engaged in longer-term conflict prevention, for which it is far better equipped. It has committed itself to a stabilisation process that capitalises on the Union's greatest asset, namely, the promise of association and future membership.

The adoption by the General Affairs Council of a Regional Approach towards the Western Balkans on 29 April 1997 represented the European Union's first step towards the formulation of its own strategy designed to favour a progressive process of stabilisation and association of the countries in the region.[2] Over the years, this strategy has been defined, refined and redefined. Central to the European Union's relations with the Western Balkans is the application of the conditionality principle. While the conditionality principle, in one way or another, has always been part of EC/EU policies towards third countries, the Union's strategies towards the Western Balkans have played a significant role in the development of this concept. Building on earlier legal and political studies on the evolving nature of EU conditionality,[3] this chapter examines the integration of the principle into the main EU policy instruments targeting the Western Balkans. The Regional Approach, the Stability Pact for South-Eastern Europe and the Stabilisation and Association Process will therefore be analysed (section 2). Particular attention is devoted to the Stabilisation and Association Agreements, the most prestigious legal instruments aimed at defining the relationship between the European Union and each of the states of the Western Balkans (section 3). This chapter also explores whether the European Partnerships introduce new elements of conditionality and whether they can bolster the European Union's Stabilisation and Association Process to integrate the Western Balkan countries into the European Union (section 4). The specific nature of the (potential) membership

[2] Council conclusions on the principle of conditionality governing the development of the EU's relations with certain countries of South East Europe, *Bull. EU* 4-1997, point 2.2.1.

[3] See, e.g., O. Stokke, 'Aid and Political Conditionality: Core Issues and State of the Art', in O. Stokke, ed., *Aid and Political Conditionality* (London, Frank Cass 1995) pp. 1-87; K. Smith, 'The Use of Political Conditionality in the EU's Relations with Third Countries: How Effective?', 3 *EFA Rev.* (1998) pp. 253-274; E. Lannon, K. Inglis and T. Haenebalcke, 'The Many Faces of EU Conditionality in Pan-Euro-Mediterranean Relations', in M. Maresceau and E. Lannon, eds., *The EU's Enlargement and Mediterranean Strategies – A Comparative Analysis* (London, Palgrave 2001) pp. 97-138; F. Hoffmeister, 'Changing Requirements for Membership', in A. Ott and K. Inglis, eds., *Handbook on European Enlargement – A Commentary on the Enlargement Process* (The Hague, T.M.C. Asser Press 2002) pp. 90-102; K. Smith, 'The Evolution and Application of EU Membership Conditionality', in M. Cremona, ed., *The Enlargement of the European Union* (Oxford, Oxford University Press 2003) pp. 105-139; C. Hillion, 'The Copenhagen Criteria and their Progeny', in C. Hillion, ed., *EU Enlargement: A Legal Approach* (Oxford, Hart Publishing 2004) pp. 1-22; M. Cremona, 'EU Enlargement: Solidarity and Conditionality', 30 *EL Rev.* (2005) pp. 3-22; and K. Inglis, 'EU Enlargement: Membership Conditions Applied to Future and Potential Member States', in Blockmans and Łazowski, eds., *The European Union and Its Neighbours: A Legal Appraisal of the EU's Policies of Stabilisation, Partnership and Integration* (The Hague, T.M.C. Asser Press 2006) pp. 61-92.

perspective of the Western Balkans (section 5) will be analysed in the light of the Union's current constitutional impasse (section 6). In this respect, it is argued that the commitment to enlarge the European Union with Croatia, which is likely to be the first entrant for which no institutional arrangements have been made, offers a good opportunity to find practical solutions to reconcile the 'deepening' and 'widening' agendas of the Union. As such, the chapter touches upon the level of commitment of both the European Union and the Western Balkans and recommends the use of positive conditionality in the form of medium and long-term benefits attached to the fulfilment of the different criteria (sections 7-9). Conclusions will be drawn at the end of the chapter (section 10).

2. MAIN POLICY INSTRUMENTS

2.1 Regional approach

At the end of 1995, the Dayton Agreement ended the war in Bosnia-Herzegovina. At first, as a consequence of the its subsidiary role in the US-led efforts to end the Bosnian war and bring 'positive peace' to the region, the European Union's objectives were embedded in the international community's initiative to adopt a comprehensive and encompassing approach to deal with the plethora of issues in south-eastern Europe. At the Royaumont Summit of 13 December 1995, which brought together the Ministers of Foreign Affairs of the EU Member States, representatives of four ex-Yugoslav republics (Bosnia-Herzegovina, Croatia, the FRY and FYROM), representatives of neighbouring countries in the region, delegations from the United States and Russia as well as representatives from NATO, the OSCE and the Council of Europe to formalise the Dayton Agreement, the international community unveiled the 'Process for Stability and Good Neighbourliness in South-Eastern Europe'.[4] The so-called 'Royaumont Process' was geared towards supporting the implementation of the Dayton Agreement and to encourage democratisation through regional projects in fields such as human rights, culture and civil society.[5]

As a complement to the Royaumont Process, the European Union launched its own 'Regional Approach', designed for those countries which at the time did not qualify for the conclusion of Europe Agreements.[6] As the Council had already

4 See Council Conclusions and Declaration on former Yugoslavia, *Bull. EU* 1/2-1996, point 1.4.108.

5 See H.-G. Ehrhart, 'Prevention and Regional Security: The Royaumont Process and the Stabilisation of South-Eastern Europe', 4 *OSCE Yearbook* (1998) pp. 327-346.

6 See Council Conclusions and Declaration on former Yugoslavia, *Bull. EU* 1/2-1996, point 1.4.108.

signed Europe Agreements with Romania and Bulgaria,[7] and as a Europe Agreement with Slovenia was being negotiated,[8] Albania remained the only country outside the borders of the former Yugoslavia that could be integrated into the Regional Approach. Within the framework of the Regional Approach, the European Union offered financial assistance and unilateral trade preferences, subject to the Western Balkan countries' commitment to restore economic cooperation with each other. Since none of the countries involved had any significant contractual relations with the European Union, with the exception of Albania, which had concluded a Trade, Commercial and Economic Agreement with the EC,[9] it was hoped that the prospect of a comprehensive cooperation agreement, enabling them to gain improved access to the internal market for a large number of their products, would serve as an incentive for economic reforms and the development of good neighbourly relations.[10]

Apart from strong commitments to regional cooperation and the free market ideal, political conditionality was also at the heart of the Union's Regional Approach. The Council made it clear that any consideration of establishing contractual relations would 'depend on the willingness of the countries concerned to work towards consolidating peace and to respect human rights, the rights of minorities and democratic principles.'[11] In addition, the Union's offers were coupled to a clear expectation that all republics that had emerged from the violent implosion of the Socialist Federal Republic of Yugoslavia would fully comply with their commitments under the Dayton Agreement, in particular those regarding the return of internally displaced persons and refugees to their place of origin and cooperation with the ICTY. The Council warned that, in the case of non-compliance by any of the parties, it would consider taking 'specific measures' in response.[12]

---

[7] The EAs with Romania and Bulgaria were signed on 8 March 1993 and published in *OJ* 1994 L 357/2 and *OJ* 1994 L 358/3, respectively.

[8] Negotiations on the Europe Agreement with Slovenia started in March 1995. The Agreement was signed on 10 June 1996 and entered into force in January 1997. For the text of the EA, see *OJ* 1996 L 51/3.

[9] *OJ* 1992 L 343/1. The agreement is still in force, but Articles 3 to 14 have been suspended by the Interim Agreement on trade and trade-related matters between the European Community, of the one part, and the Republic of Albania, of the other part, *OJ* 2006 L 239/2, which entered into force on 1 December 2006; see Council Information, *OJ* 2006 L 318/26. The 1992 Trade, Commercial and Economic Agreement will be fully replaced once the SAA Albania enters into force. See *infra* section 3.2.2.

[10] See F.-L. Altmann, 'Die Balkanpolitik der EU – Regionalansatz und Prinzip der Konditionalität', 47 *Südosteuropa* (1998) pp. 503-515 at p. 504; and O. Kovać, 'Regional Approach of the European Union to Cooperation among Countries of the Former Yugoslavia', 47 *Review of International Affairs* (1996) pp. 1-5.

[11] *Bull. EU* 1/2-1996, point 1.4.108.

[12] Ibid. See also European Commission, Common Principles for Future Contractual Relations with Certain Countries in South-Eastern Europe, COM (1996) 476 final, Brussels, 2 October 1996.

The new strategy was soon put into legal practice. On 25 July 1996, the Council adopted Regulation (EC) No. 1628/96 relating to aid for Bosnia-Herzegovina, Croatia, Macedonia and the FRY (the so-called 'OBNOVA' Regulation), which in Article 2 explicitly identified respect for democratic principles, the rule of law and human rights and fundamental freedoms as 'essential elements' for the application of the entire programme.[13] The OBNOVA conditionality clause went one step further than comparable human rights and democracy clauses in earlier trade, cooperation and association agreements concluded by the Community with third states,[14] by stating that the 'specific conditions' defined by the Council for the former Yugoslav republics were also to be regarded as essential elements of the regulation and, hence, their fulfilment a precondition for the granting of Community aid. The specific conditions mentioned in the regulation referred to the Council Conclusions of 26 February 1996 and the simultaneously adopted Declaration on former Yugoslavia.[15]

However, the criteria listed in these documents were formulated in broad terms and thus fairly fuzzy. This problem was addressed by the Council on 29 April 1997, with the adoption of specific guidelines in the form of 'Conclusions on the principle of conditionality governing the development of the European Union's relations with certain countries of south-east Europe'.[16] These guidelines, for the first time, distinguished conditions which applied to all countries of the region from conditions which applied to individual countries only. The guidelines also established a graduated approach, within which trade preferences, financial assistance and the establishment of contractual relations were subject to different degrees of conditionality. This was meant to solve a principal dilemma of the European Union's Western Balkans policy, manifested in the its desire to differentiate more effectively between the countries concerned in terms of their political and economic development, while at the same time continuing to apply a coherent strategy towards the region as a whole. Hence, while the Council reaffirmed that all offers continued to be available to all countries of the region and that the Union's strategy was meant as an incentive, not an obstacle, to the countries to meet the relevant criteria, the refined approach towards conditionality

---

13 *OJ* 1996 L 204/1. 'Obnova' means 'reconstruction' in the language formerly known as Serbo-Croat. The regulation was repealed in December 2000 and replaced by a new funding instrument, the so-called CARDS Regulation. See *infra* section 3.4.

14 See, generally, M. Cremona, 'Human Rights and Democracy Clauses in the EC's Trade Agreements', in N. Emiliou and D. O'Keeffe, eds., *The European Union and World Trade Law: After the GATT Uruguay Round* (London, Wiley 1996) pp. 62-77; F. Hoffmeister, *Menschenrechts- und Demokratieklauseln in den vertraglichen Außenbeziehungen der Europäischen Gemeinschaft* (Berlin, Springer 1998) pp. 117-175; E. Riedel and M. Will, 'Human Rights Clauses in External Agreements of the European Communities', in P. Alston, ed., *The European Union and Human Rights* (Oxford, Oxford University Press 1999) pp. 723-754; and M. Bulterman, *Human Rights in the Treaty Relations of the European Community* (Antwerp, Intersentia 2001).

15 *Bull. EU* 1/2-1996, point 1.4.108.

16 *Bull. EU* 4-1997, point 2.2.1.

followed the basic principle that the closer a country wanted to move towards the European Union, the more conditions it had to fulfil. The Guidelines of 29 April 1997 clearly reflected a combination of both positive and negative conditionality. Progressive compliance with the conditions established by the Council was rewarded with intensified bilateral cooperation, including the establishment of contractual relations. However, in the case of serious and repeated non-compliance with the conditions underpinning the respective levels of cooperation, trade preferences could be withdrawn, Community assistance frozen and, where applicable, an agreement suspended.[17]

Thus, the contours of a distinctive model of EU conditionality towards the Western Balkans became visible. EU conditionality with regard to the Western Balkans was based on the 1993 Copenhagen criteria, the defining components of the Union's relations with the Central and Eastern European countries (CEECs),[18] but extra conditions were added in the April 1997 guidelines to reflect the special need to stabilise the region.[19] This led to an exceptionally broad range of political and economic conditions used by the Council:

- Democratic principles: representative government and accountable executive; government and public authorities to act in a manner consistent with the constitution and the law; separation of powers (government, administration, judiciary); free and fair elections at reasonable intervals by secret ballot.
- Human rights, rule of law: freedom of expression, including independent media; right of assembly and demonstration; right of association; right to privacy, family, home and correspondence; right to property; effective means of redress against administrative decisions; access to courts and right to fair trial; equality before the law and equal protection by the law; freedom from inhuman or degrading treatment and arbitrary arrest.
- Respect for and protection of minorities: right to establish and maintain their own educational, cultural and religious institutions, organisations or associations; adequate opportunities for minorities to use their own language before courts and public authorities; adequate protection of refugees and displaced persons returning to areas where they represent an ethnic minority.
- Market economy reform: macroeconomic institutions and policies necessary to ensure a stable economic environment; comprehensive liberalisation of prices, trade and current payments; setting-up of a transparent and stable legal and regulatory framework; demonopolisation and privatisation of state-owned or socially-owned enterprises; establishment of a competitive and prudently managed banking sector.[20]

---

17 For a detailed account of these measures and their legal bases, see C. Pippan, 'The Rocky Road to Europe: The EU's Stabilisation and Association Process for the Western Balkans and the Principle of Conditionality', 9 *EFA Rev.* (2004) pp. 219-245 at pp. 229-238.

18 *Bull. EU* 6-1993, point 13. See Hillion, loc. cit. n. 3.

19 *Bull. EU* 4-1997, point 2.2.1, sections on 'PHARE' and 'Contractual Relations'.

20 Ibid., Annex I.

With this demonstrative list of standards, the European Union has helped to clarify the normative content of the conditionality principle that it applies towards the Western Balkans.

The European Union's Regional Approach represented an ambitious attempt to deal with the Western Balkans on a regional basis, recognising that all political issues and conflicts in the region were interconnected components of a larger whole: to deal effectively with any one issue or conflict means that, ultimately, the others have to be dealt with as well, if not simultaneously then certainly in sequence. Although the aim of the Regional Approach was never to put the Yugoslav jigsaw puzzle back together, betting on the results of such an approach for the Western Balkans was extremely risky at the time of its adoption. For no sooner had each breakaway republic become independent – in essence given *itself* a new identity – than it needed to integrate again on a regional basis and eventually become a member of a new entity. While the European Union's efforts looked good on paper, in reality regional cooperation and bilateral relations barely progressed in the post-1997 period, and negative conditionality prevailed in the form of limited contractual relations and exclusions from association agreements. In the period from 28 February 1998 to 5 November 2001, the European Union even adopted a whole new range of sanctions against the FRY, because of its role in Kosovo.[21]

2.2 Stability Pact for South-Eastern Europe

The Kosovo crisis of 1999 revealed the shortcomings of the Royaumont Process in addressing the complex and volatile situation in the Western Balkans and triggered a response by the international community. On 17 May 1999, amid ongoing NATO air strikes against Serbia, the EU Ministers for Foreign Affairs, following an initiative by the German Presidency, launched the Stability Pact for South-Eastern Europe to replace the previous reactive crisis intervention policy in south-eastern Europe with a comprehensive, long-term conflict prevention strategy.[22]

Although initiated by the European Union within its Common Foreign and Security Policy, the Stability Pact is not an EU instrument. The Pact was endorsed at an international meeting held on the fringes of the European Council summit in Cologne on 10 June 1999 – the day that NATO's seventy-eight-day bombing

---

21 See chapter 3, section 4.

22 Common Position 1999/345/CFSP of 17 May 1999 adopted by the Council on the basis of Article 15 of the Treaty on European Union, concerning a Stability Pact for South-Eastern Europe, *OJ* 1999 L 133/1. For background and analysis, see D. Phinnemore and P. Siani-Davies, 'Beyond Intervention? The Balkans, the Stability Pact and the European Union', in P. Siani-Davies, ed., *International Intervention in the Balkans Since 1995* (London, Routledge 2003) pp. 172-193.

campaign against the FRY ended – and its further development and implementation was vested in the OSCE.[23] The Stability Pact is a political declaration of commitment and a framework agreement on cooperation to develop an international strategy for stability and growth in a region wider than the Western Balkans.[24] The Stability Pact has not, from a legal and institutional perspective, emerged as a new international organisation. It does not have any independent financial resources or implementing structures. Organisationally, the Stability Pact relies on the Special Coordinator, appointed by the European Union in consultation with the OSCE, and his Brussels-based team of approximately thirty members.[25] The Special Coordinator's most important task is to bring the participants' political strategies in line with one another, to coordinate existing and new initiatives in the region and, thereby, to help avoid unnecessary duplication of work.[26] To these ends, the Special Coordinator chairs the Regional Table, the most important political forum of the Stability Pact. The Regional Table is responsible for the coordination of the activities of the more than forty participating and facilitating states, international organisations and regional initiatives, which contribute in varying degrees to the so-called Working Tables on (1) Democratisation and Human Rights; (2) Economic Reconstruction, Cooperation and Development; and (3) Security Issues. In short, the Stability Pact serves as an international platform for cooperation and is geared towards supporting the implementation of the Dayton Agreement, facilitating political stability and economic prosperity and improving the coordination between and, as a result of

---

23 See also *Bull. EU* 6-1999, point I.26.71. For the final text of the Stability Pact of 10 June 1999, see the Stability Pact's website at: <http://www.stabilitypact.org>. See also chapter 2, section 8 and chapter 4, section 3.3.1.

24 The partners to the Stability Pact include, *inter alia*, Albania, Bosnia-Herzegovina, Croatia, Macedonia, Moldova, Montenegro and Serbia; the EU Member States; the European Commission; Canada, Japan, Norway, Russia, Switzerland, Turkey and the United States; the United Nations, the OSCE, the Council of Europe, the UNHCR, NATO, the OECD, the World Bank, the IMF, the EBRD, the EIB, the Council of Europe Development Bank; the Black Sea Economic Cooperation, the Central European Initiative, the Southeast European Cooperative Initiative and the South-East Europe Cooperation Process.

25 The first incumbent of this post was Bodo Hombach. The post is currently held by Erhard Busek, who was appointed in December 2001. His mandate was renewed until 31 December 2007 by Council Decision 2006/921/EC of 11 December 2005 on the appointment of the Special Coordinator of the Stability Pact for South-Eastern Europe, *OJ* 2006 L 351/19. Interestingly, the Council Decision refers to the whole EC Treaty, instead of a particular provision thereof, as its legal basis for adoption.

26 Likewise, the Pact does not implement the projects that were placed under its auspices during the first regional funding conference of March 2000 but is an instrument for coordinating and facilitating the implementation of the projects of all its partners.

this, the efficiency of all actors in the region.[27] As such, it resembles the model of the late Conference on Security and Cooperation in Europe (CSCE).[28]

What marked a fundamental shift in the European Union's own strategy towards the Western Balkans was the Council's self-declared willingness to draw the countries of the region closer to the perspective of full integration into EU structures, through a new kind of contractual relationship, 'with a *perspective* of EU membership on the basis of the Treaty of Amsterdam once the Copenhagen criteria have been met.'[29] This explicit *offer* of future EU membership for the countries of the Western Balkans was firmly endorsed by the European Council at its summit in Santa Maria da Feira on 19-20 June 2000.[30] It seems that, against the backdrop of yet another violent crisis in the Western Balkans, the political leaders of the European Union reached the conclusion that a policy aimed at economic reconstruction, political reform and regional cooperation was, as such, not enough to bring lasting peace and stability to the region. The additional prospect of full EU membership was needed to trigger the reforms necessary to achieve 'positive peace'.[31] Hence, the Union brought its policy for the Western Balkans in line with the logic behind its decision to fully open its doors to the CEECs in the early 1990s.

It has been argued that, in respect of the South Eastern European countries' *rapprochement* to the European Union, 'the Council's unilateral "Common Position" on the Union's launching of the Pact was, at the time of its adoption,

27 See H.-J. Axt, 'Der Stabilitätspakt für Südosteuropa: Politischer Aktionismus oder langfristig tragfähiges Konzept?', 48 *Südosteuropa* (1999) pp. 401-416; R. Biermann, 'The Stability Pact for South-Eastern Europe: Potential, Problems and Perspectives', C56 *ZEI Discussion Papers* (1999) at pp. 15-19; T. Buchsbaum, 'The OSCE and the Stability Pact for South-Eastern Europe', 11 *Helsinki Monitor* (2000) pp. 62-79; L. Friis and A. Murphy, '"Turbo-charged negotiations": The EU and the Stability Pact for South-Eastern Europe', 7 *Journal of European Public Policy* (2000) pp. 767-786; M. Cremona, 'Creating the New Europe: the Stability Pact for South-Eastern Europe in the Context of EU-SEE Relations', in A. Dashwood and A. Ward, eds., *The Cambridge Yearbook of European Legal Studies – Volume 2, 1999* (Oxford, Hart Publishing 2000) pp. 463-506; D. Papadimitriou, 'The EU's Strategy in the Post-Communist Balkans', 3 *Journal of Southeast European and Black Sea Studies* (2001) pp. 69-94; F. Cameron and A. Kintis, 'Southeastern Europe and the European Union', 2 *Journal of Southeast European and Black Sea Studies* (2001) pp. 94-112; P. Jureković, ed., *The Stability Pact for South East Europe – Dawn of an Era of Regional Co-operation* (Vienna, National Defence Academy 2002); D. Vignes, 'The Stability Pact for South-Eastern Europe', in C. Tomuschat, ed., *Kosovo and the International Community: A Legal Assessment* (The Hague, Kluwer Law International 2002) pp. 317-325; and U. Dusjin, 'The Stability Pact for South-Eastern Europe: An Avenue to EU Membership', 53 *Zbornik PFZ* (2003) pp. 629-652.

28 See Phinnemore and Siani-Davies, loc. cit. n. 22, at p. 176.

29 Common Position 1999/345/CFSP, preamble, recital 7 [emphasis added].

30 *Bull. EU* 6-2000, point I.49.67.

31 See T. King, 'The European Community and Human Rights in Eastern Europe', 23 *LIEI* (1996) pp. 93-125 at p. 123; and P. Pantev, 'Security Risks and Instabilities in Southeastern Europe', in W. van Meurs, ed., *Beyond EU Enlargement, Volume 2: The Agenda of Stabilisation for Southeastern Europe* (Gütersloh, Bertelsmann Foundation Publishers 2001) pp. 118-138.

probably of more importance than the Pact itself.'[32] Indeed, back in 1999, the Stability Pact was rather pompously presented as a sort of contemporary Eldorado: a pledge on behalf of the international community to pour billions into the Balkans.[33] But with the creation of expectations that, in view of the available resources,[34] it cannot hope to meet, the Stability Pact remains 'one of the most enigmatic political inventions' for south-eastern Europe of the last century.[35] Strategically, the Stability Pact is an EU project, closely intertwined with the perspective of EU candidacy. But the European Union is only one out of many implementing partners, and the recipient countries' participation in the Stability Pact does not lead to EU membership.[36] Moreover, the Pact has been largely outdone by strategies developed in parallel, most importantly by its leading partner, the European Union.[37] After all, since the declaration of the European Council at Santa Maria da Feira, the accession of Albania, Bosnia-Herzegovina, Croatia, Macedonia, Serbia (including Kosovo under the terms of UN Security Council resolution 1244) and Montenegro to the European Union is no longer a matter of *if* but of *when* and *how*. As to the *how*, it is reassuring to note that, by referring in Common Position 1999/345/CFSP to both Article 49 TEU and the Copenhagen criteria, the Council has emphasised that the political and economic criteria formulated by the European Council in June 1993 for the enlargement of the Union remain fully valid. In the light of the European Union's decision at

[32] See, *inter alia*, Pippan, loc. cit. n. 17, at p. 227.

[33] Former US President Bill Clinton has likened the aid needed for the Balkans to America's Marshall Plan. See 'New "Marshall Plan" for the Balkans', *USA Today*, 25 July 1999.

[34] The Stability Pact secured funding for projects worth €5.4 billion at two donors' conferences. In March 2000, €2.4 billion was raised in Brussels to fund 244 projects in the so-called 'Quick Start Package'. At a second regional conference in October 2001 (Bucharest), an additional €3 billion was committed, mainly for infrastructure (€2.4 billion) and refugee issues (€0.5 billion). According to the Pact's mandate, these funds are used to support projects of two, three or more countries, thereby engaging the governments in a process of regional cooperation. As these sums are limited in their ability to address the huge reconstruction efforts needed in south-eastern Europe, this money is spent in 'strategic projects' with a view to mobilising vital private investment and facilitating reforms. All projects in the Stability Pact framework are administered through implementing partners, such as the international financial institutions. More data is available on the Stability Pact's website at: <http://www.stabilitypact.org>.

[35] See W. van Meurs, 'The Stability Pact Beyond EU Enlargement', in D. Lopandić, ed., *Regional Cooperation in South Eastern Europe – Conference Proceedings* (Belgrade, European Movement in Serbia 2002) pp. 39-45. For an exploratory assessment of the effectiveness of the Stability Pact to serve as a conflict prevention regime, see D. Sandole, 'The Balkans Stability Pact as a Regional Conflict Management and Prevention "Space": An Evaluation', in P. Jureković, ed., *The Stability Pact for South East Europe – Dawn of an Era of Regional Co-operation* (Vienna, National Defence Academy 2002) pp. 20-36.

[36] In this respect, one can understand the admission of Moldova as a recipient country under the Stability Pact in 2001. The former Soviet republic lacked – as it still does – the perspective of EU accession given to the countries of the Western Balkans. See A. Skvortova, 'Moldova', in Blockmans and Łazowski, op. cit. n. 3, pp. 549-574.

[37] On the Pact's future, see chapter 6, section 2.1.1.3.

Santa Maria da Feira, it is evident that the perspective of integration of the countries of the Western Balkans into the structures of the European Union requires a long-term commitment on both sides. The Union, for its part, responded to this challenge by transforming its Regional Approach into a more sophisticated policy framework: the Stabilisation and Association Process.

2.3 Stabilisation and Association Process

Initiated by the Commission in 1999,[38] the Stabilisation and Association Process (SAP) specifically aims to assist each of the countries of the Western Balkans in meeting the relevant EU criteria and being *ultimately* accepted as official candidates for membership. The one incentive that the SAP shrank from providing, however, was an explicit *promise* of EU membership. At the 2000 Santa Maria da Feira Council, the European Union stated that the SAP countries were 'potential candidates', which undisputedly represented a promotion compared with the Regional Approach but not a breakthrough that went all the way.[39]

The SAP was built on the Union's Regional Approach and consists of modified and new offers to the states of the Western Balkans, including enhanced trade liberalisation, improved financial and economic assistance, a regular political dialogue, cooperation in justice and home affairs and, in particular, a new, tailor-made category of contractual relations: Stabilisation and Association Agreements (SAAs). The instruments covered by the SAP are open to all countries of the region on equal terms. Their actual availability, however, continues to depend on each country's compliance with the general and country-specific conditions set out by the European Union. Hence, conditionality remains the glue of the Stabilisation and Association Process. Although anchored in a common set of political and economic conditions, the approach of the SAP is flexible enough to allow each country to move ahead at its own pace. An annual review mechanism assesses each country's performance in meeting the conditions. The recommendations contained in the Commission's 'progress' reports and the Council's annual assessment are intended to help the SAP countries focus their attention for the year ahead on specific priority areas. Thus, the emphasis of the SAP is placed on *differentiation* according to the specific needs and situations of each country, as well as on improvements in the relations within the entire region.

The 24 November 2000 Zagreb Summit of Heads of State and Government of the EU Member States and the SAP countries set the seal on the SAP by gaining

---

38 See COM (1999) 235 final, Brussels, 26 May 1999.

39 *Bull. EU* 6-2000, point I.49.67. For a critical view on this promise of a perspective of membership, see O. Anastasakis and D. Bechev, *EU Conditionality in South East Europe: Bringing Commitment to the Process* (Oxford, SEESP 2003). On the use of the concept of 'potential' candidate countries, see *infra* section 5.

the region's agreement to the applicable set of objectives and conditions.[40] At the 21 June 2003 EU-Western Balkans Summit in Thessaloniki, it was acknowledged that the SAP would remain the framework for the European course of the Western Balkan countries, 'all the way to their future accession'.[41] Crucially, it was agreed that the SAP (and the prospects it offers) would serve as the anchor for reform in the Western Balkans, in the same way that the accession process has done in Central and Eastern Europe. To this end, the SAP needed to be strengthened and enriched with elements from the enlargement process so that it would be better equipped to meet the new challenges, as the countries move from stabilisation and reconstruction to sustainable development, association and integration into European structures. In light of the latter, the European Council endorsed the Thessaloniki Agenda for the Western Balkans: Moving Towards European Integration.[42] The Thessaloniki Agenda served both to confirm the conditionality developed under the SAP and to list the domains in which progress was to be made:

> [...] the EU will continue to work closely with the Western Balkan countries to further consolidate peace and to promote stability, democracy, the rule of law, and respect for human and minority rights. Inviolability of international borders, peaceful resolution of conflicts and regional co-operation are principles of the highest importance. Terrorism, violence and extremism, be it ethnically, politically or criminally motivated, should be unequivocally condemned.
>
> The EU reiterates its support for the full implementation of Resolution 1244 of the UN Security Council on Kosovo and of the 'standards before status' policy. On this basis, the people of a multiethnic and a democratic Kosovo will have their place in Europe. The Dayton/Paris agreements and subsequent Peace Implementation Council decisions, and the Ohrid and Belgrade agreements, are key elements of EU policy. Full compliance by all countries and parties concerned is essential.
>
> Recalling that all Western Balkan countries are parties to the International Criminal Court, the EU urges them to support, fully and in deed, its work and the integrity of its statute, in line with the relevant EU decisions.
>
> The EU urges all concerned countries and parties to co-operate fully with the International Criminal Tribunal for the former Yugoslavia. Recalling that respect for international law is an essential element of the SAP, the EU reiterates that full co-operation with ICTY, in particular with regard to the transfer to The Hague of all indictees and full access to documents and witnesses, is vital for further movement towards the EU.[43]

---

[40] *Bull. EU* 11-2000, point I.6.57.

[41] For the full text of the declaration of the EU-Western Balkans Summit at Thessaloniki, see *Bull. EU* 6-2003, point 1.6.70.

[42] For the text of the Thessaloniki Agenda, see Annex A to Council Conclusions of 16 June 2003, Press Release No. 10369/03 (Presse 166).

[43] Ibid., para. 1.

As such, the European Union and the Western Balkans agreed on an 'agenda' for the pre-accession process of the countries of the region, very much like Agenda 2000 set the tune for the countries that joined the European Union in its fifth wave of enlargement. In addition, the Thessaloniki Agenda was meant to further strengthen and enhance the political visibility of the SAP, *inter alia*, by launching the high-level multilateral EU-Western Balkans Forum and 'European Partnerships' (reminiscent of the Accession Partnerships for the CEECs) as well as by promoting the decisions for enhanced cooperation in the areas of political dialogue and the Common Foreign and Security Policy, parliamentary cooperation, support for institution-building, the opening of Community programmes and regional economic development. Each of these elements will be elaborated upon below.

3. STABILISATION AND ASSOCIATION AGREEMENTS

3.1 **Legal basis**

Article 310 TEC, on the basis of which the European Economic Area was established and the Europe Agreements (EAs) with the CEECs were concluded, provides the legal basis for the SAAs that the European Union is offering to countries in the Western Balkans.[44] Content-wise, the SAAs are also based on the existing EAs, even if they include new elements respecting the specific situation of the Western Balkan countries.[45] This was to be expected given the short period of time that the Commission had to develop the SAAs. In crisis situations – in the context of the Western Balkans even in a literal sense – the European Union traditionally acts conservatively and instinctively falls back on an existing policy approach (so-called 'path dependency behaviour').[46] Nevertheless, the Commission was keen to differentiate between this 'new type of contract' and the EAs.[47] The Commission argued that the conclusion of SAAs would provide an appropriate alternative to the EAs, which are regarded as leading to EU membership, and the Partnership and Cooperation Agreements (PCAs), which have been concluded with almost all the successor states to the Soviet Union and have far less ambitious

44 See D. Phinnemore, *Association: Stepping-Stone or Alternative to EU Membership?* (Sheffield, Sheffield Academic Press 1999).

45 Analysis of the two existing SAAs shows considerable similarities with the earlier EAs. See D. Phinnemore, 'Stabilisation and Association Agreements: Europe Agreements for the Western Balkans?', 8 *EFA Rev.* (2003) pp. 77-103 at pp. 79-81.

46 See J. Peterson, 'The European Union as a Global Actor', in J. Peterson and H. Sjursen, *A Common Foreign Policy for Europe?* (London, Routledge 1998) pp. 3-17.

47 See COM (1999) 235 final, Brussels, 26 May 1999.

goals.[48] As David Phinnemore explains, the reasons were essentially twofold. Firstly, the challenges in the Western Balkans went beyond those concerning economic and political transition that had been posed by the CEECs over the last decade. Therefore, a new type of relationship responding to the particular needs of the Western Balkans was deemed necessary. Secondly, by the spring of 1999, the European Union was making headway towards realising its most ambitious enlargement to date. The prospect of up to twelve new entrants over the next few years was unprecedented. Added to this was the question of admitting Turkey into the accession process. Faced with such an overwhelming enlargement agenda, there was little enthusiasm for widening it further by offering EAs to the countries of the Western Balkans, thereby raising expectations of pre-accession aid and encouraging membership applications. Mindful of this and anxious about causing concern among the candidate countries about their position in the enlargement process, the European Union had to avoid any formulation that might raise objections and potentially undermine reform efforts in those countries. This was recognised in the title of the SAAs: their purpose was not just association but first and foremost, in the short term at least, stabilisation.

3.2 Procedure

In the procedure for the conclusion of an SAA, the application of conditionality has to be seen as a graduated process, with the start of SAA negotiations requiring a lower level of compliance than the conclusion of the agreements. Before negotiations on the conclusion of an SAA can start, a certain level of progress must be made. The Commission observes and evaluates the situation in the country, in particular the fulfilment of the relevant conditions set out in the Council's Guidelines of 29 April 1997, such as the presence of functioning democratic structures, respect for human rights, fundamental freedoms and the rule of law, as well as cooperation with neighbouring countries. In doing so, the Commission is guided by reports of other international organisations, committees or institutions that are active in the region, such as NATO, the OSCE and the Council of Europe. The results are published in annual country reports, in which the Commission reviews the compliance of each of the countries concerned with

---

[48] On the EAs, see, *inter alia*, M. Maresceau, ed., *Enlarging the European Union: Relations Between the EU and Central and Eastern Europe* (London, Longman 1997); and A. Mayhew, *Recreating Europe: The European Union's Policy towards Central and Eastern Europe* (Cambridge, Cambridge University Press 1998). On the PCAs, see C. Hillion, *The Evolving System of European Union External Relations as Evidenced in the EU Partnerships with Russia and Ukraine* (Leiden, Ph.D thesis 2005).

the European Union's political and economic criteria.[49] Once the Commission judges that a country has made sufficient progress in its domestic reform process, it starts, with the approval of the Council, to carry out a study on the feasibility of opening negotiations for an SAA. Following the completion of this so-called 'feasibility study' and a positive assessment by the Council that a Western Balkan country has indeed made sufficient progress in meeting the SAP conditions and that it has the capacity to negotiate and implement the far-reaching political and economic obligations under an SAA, the Commission submits a formal proposal on the negotiating directives for the SAA concerned. If adopted by the Council, the negotiations are conducted by the Commission in consultation with a special committee created by the Council for that purpose. SAAs, like EAs, are mixed agreements. Hence, in order to enter into force, they require the approval of the Council (by way of a Council decision),[50] the assent of the European Parliament (Articles 300(3) and 310 TEC) as well as ratification by all EU Member States and the non-Member State concerned. In anticipation of the full ratification of an SAA, the trade provisions may enter into force via interim agreements. Political dialogue can already be established as well.

3.2.1 *Macedonia and Croatia*

At the time of writing, only the SAAs with Macedonia (signed on 9 April 2001)[51] and Croatia (signed on 29 October 2001)[52] have entered into force. Ratification in both Macedonia and Croatia followed shortly after the agreements were signed (on 12 April 2001 and 5 December 2001 respectively). The European Parliament was also quick to give its assent to the agreements (on 3 May 2001 and 12 December 2001 respectively). In anticipation of the full ratification of both SAAs, the trade

---

49 The individual country reports are annexed to the Commission's annual reviews of the SAP. For the European Commission's three SAP reports, see COM (2002) 163 final, Brussels, 4 April 2002; COM (2003) 139 final, Brussels, 26 March 2003; and COM (2004) 202 final, Brussels, 30 March 2004. In a speech to the EU-Western Balkan Forum on his first day in office as Commissioner for Enlargement, Olli Rehn announced that the Commission's Annual Report on the SAP would be moved to the autumn to make it coincide with the Regular Reports on the candidate countries. See SPEECH/04/487, Brussels, 22 November 2004. Indeed, the Commission's 2005 Enlargement Strategy Paper combines general reports on the progress made by Turkey and the Western Balkans. See COM (2005) 561 final, Brussels, 9 November 2005. This facilitates a more consistent and systematic approach to assessing and advising both candidate and 'potential' candidate countries on their track towards EU integration.

50 Since the transfer of responsibility for relations with the Western Balkans from the Directorate General for External Relations to the Directorate General for Enlargement in November 2004, SAAs are signed by a ministerial representative of the country holding the Presidency of the Council, the EU Commissioner for Enlargement and a ministerial representative of the Western Balkan country concerned.

51 See COM (2001) 90 final, Brussels, 19 February 2001.

52 See COM (2001) 371 final, Brussels, 9 July 2001.

provisions already entered into force via interim agreements.[53] After ratification by the then still fifteen Member States of the European Union, the SAA FYROM entered into force on 1 April 2004.[54] While a majority of the Member States also ratified the SAA Croatia within the usual time frames, the Netherlands, the United Kingdom and Italy for a long time withheld (notification of) ratification of the agreement because of their negative perception of Croatia's willingness to cooperate with the ICTY.[55] Like mixed agreements, SAAs are open to national interpretation, but this raises the question whether individual Member States should maintain the power to impose political conditionality on SAA candidates unilaterally and at such a late stage. Such action undermines the authority of the Commission to evaluate the fulfilment of the key conditions for association and blocks the Union's efforts to build a common policy to engage associates. In the second half of 2004, when it became clear that cooperation with the ICTY would become a strict condition for Croatia to open accession negotiations with the

---

53 Interim Agreement on trade and trade-related matters between the European Community, of the one part, and the former Yugoslav Republic of Macedonia, of the other part, *OJ* 2001 L 124/2; and Interim Agreement on trade and trade-related matters between the European Community, of the one part, and the Republic of Croatia, of the other part, *OJ* 2001 L 330/3. The Interim Agreements entered into force on 1 June 2001 and 1 March 2002, respectively. On the Interim Agreement with Albania, see *supra* n. 9 and *infra* section 3.2.2.

54 Stabilisation and Association Agreement between the European Communities and their Member States, of the one part, and the former Yugoslav Republic of Macedonia, of the other part, *OJ* 2004 L 84/13. The SAA FYROM replaced the Cooperation Agreement between the European Community and the former Yugoslav Republic of Macedonia, *OJ* 1997 L 348/2, which had been in force since 1 January 1998. On 21 February 2005, the Council and the Commission adopted Decision 2005/192/EC, *OJ* 2005 L 63/21, on the conclusion of the Protocol to the SAA FYROM to take account of the accession to the European Union of the ten new Member States. For the text of the Protocol, see *OJ* 2004 L 388/3. With the entry into force of an SAA, a new set of joint bodies is established at ministerial level (Stabilisation and Association Council), at senior official level (Stabilisation and Association Committee) and at technical level (subcommittees). Following the entry into force of the SAA FYROM, the first meeting of the Stabilisation and Association Committee took place on 3 June 2004 in Skopje. The committee is meant to ensure the continuity of the association relationship between Macedonia and the European Union and the proper functioning of the SAA. It decided to set up seven subcommittees (on trade, industry, customs and taxation; agriculture and fisheries; internal market and competition; economic and financial issues; justice and home affairs; human resources, research, technological development and social policy; and transport, environment, energy and regional development) covering all areas of cooperation under the SAA.

55 See S. Rodin, 'Croatia', in Blockmans and Łazowski, op. cit. n. 3, pp. 357-389. These countries referred to Croatia's apparent inability to arrest indicted General Ante Gotovina and hand him over to the ICTY in The Hague. Gotovina, the UN tribunal's third most wanted fugitive, disappeared the day before the ICTY made his indictment public, in July 2001, and was finally arrested on 7 December 2005 in a hotel in the resort of Playa de las Americas in Tenerife and subsequently transferred to The Hague. He is indicted for ordering the killing of more than 100 ethnic Serbs and expelling 150,000 more during and after Zagreb's final offensive in August 1995 to recapture Croatian lands seized by Serb forces (Operation Storm). The pressure on Croatia to find and arrest Gotovina has provoked negative feelings towards the European Union, as many Croatians perceive him as a war hero rather than a war criminal.

European Union,[56] the obstructive trio dropped its opposition towards ratification of the SAA. Thanks to this, an Enlargement Protocol to the SAA Croatia could also be negotiated in order to take account of the accession of ten new Member States to the European Union on 1 May 2004. On 21 December 2004, the Protocol was signed.[57] Via the Enlargement Protocol, the new Member States became party to the SAA.[58] The SAA Croatia entered into force on 1 February 2005.[59]

3.2.2 *Albania*

On the basis of a positive evaluation of the political stability and progress on reforms, the Commission opened negotiations on an SAA with Albania on 31 January 2003, but talks soon stalled. This was largely due to the Commission's firm opinion that Albania was not demonstrating a great determination to fight organised crime, all types of 'trafficking', money laundering and corruption.[60] The 3 July 2005 general elections were widely seen as an important test of the country's democratic credentials and a condition for reviving the SAA talks. The Commission, in its Progress Report of 9 November 2005, paved the way for the conclusion of SAA negotiations.[61] By considering that the political situation in the country had improved, it seems that the Commission gave precedence to political expediency over concerns about the killing of three in electoral violence, the OSCE's statement that the election complied only partially with democratic norms and a political comeback that was unprecedented even in the revolving-doors world of Balkan politics. Sali Berisha – a former president (and personal physician to Albania's late Stalinist leader Enver Hoxha) who was forced out of office in 1997 when fraudulent pyramid savings schemes sparked civil unrest –

---

56 See *infra* section 5 and chapter 6, section 4.2.2.

57 Council and Commission Decision 2005/205/EC of 21 February 2005, *OJ* 2005 L 68/30.

58 Protocol to the Stabilisation and Association Agreement between the European Communities and their Member States, of the one part, and the Republic of Croatia, of the other part, to take account of the accession of the Czech Republic, the Republic of Estonia, the Republic of Cyprus, the Republic of Hungary, the Republic of Latvia, the Republic of Lithuania, the Republic of Malta, the Republic of Poland, the Republic of Slovenia and the Slovak Republic to the European Union, *OJ* 2005 L 26/222.

59 Stabilisation and Association Agreement between the European Communities and their Member States, of the one part, and the Republic of Croatia, of the other part, *OJ* 2005 L 26/3.

60 See the Commission's Third Annual SAP Report, COM (2004) 202 final, Brussels, 30 March 2004. See also M. Bogdani and J. Loughlin, *Albania and the European Union: The Tumultuous Journey Towards Integration and Accession* (London, I.B. Tauris 2007). More generally, see C. de Waal, *Albania Today: A Portrait of Post-Communist Turbulence* (London, I.B. Tauris 2005).

61 See COM (2005) 561, Brussels, 9 November 2005, SEC (2005) 1421. In a similar vein, see Council Decision 2005/809/EC of 7 November 2005 concerning the conclusion of the Agreement between the European Community and the Republic of Albania on the readmission of persons residing without authorization, *OJ* 2005 L 304/14.

and his newly installed Democratic Party government must have somehow convinced the Commission of the sincerity of their pledge to step up reforms and fight organised crime and corruption, as well as solving property issues and improving the work of the customs administration. European Commission President Barroso himself announced the conclusion of the SAA negotiations on 18 February 2006.[62] The SAA Albania was signed on 12 June 2006.[63] Pending the full ratification of the SAA, the trade and trade-related provisions of the agreement entered into force on 1 December 2006 after full ratification of the Interim Agreement.[64] Pursuant to Article 56 of the Interim Agreement, Articles 3-14 of the 1992 Trade, Commercial and Economic Cooperation Agreement were suspended. The Trade, Commercial and Economic Agreement will be fully replaced once the SAA Albania enters into force.

3.2.3 *Bosnia-Herzegovina*

The substantial completion of the so-called 'Road Map' for Bosnia-Herzegovina and the establishment of the first elected government for a four-year term were rewarded by the Commission with the launching of a feasibility study in June 2003.[65] The study was adopted on 18 November 2003.[66] Nevertheless, in its Third Annual Report on the SAP, the Commission identified sixteen new priorities on which it demanded further political and economic reform and progress in 2004 to make the country a self-sustaining state based on the rule of law before negotiations on the SAA would be considered.[67] In particular, cooperation with the ICTY

---

[62] José Manuel Barroso, 'Building for the future: Making a success of the Stabilization and Association Agreement', Parliament of Albania, Tirana, 18 February 2006, SPEECH/06/103.

[63] See COM (2006) 138 final, Brussels, 21 March 2006.

[64] Interim Agreement on trade and trade-related matters between the European Community, of the one part, and the Republic of Albania, of the other part, *OJ* 2006 L 239/2. On the entry into force of the Interim Agreement, see Council Information, *OJ* 2006 L 318/26. In addition, see Council Regulation (EC) No. 1616/2006 of 23 October 2006 on certain procedures for applying the Stabilisation and Association Agreement between the European Communities and their Member States, of the one part, and the Republic of Albania, of the other part, and for applying the Interim Agreement between the European Community and the Republic of Albania, *OJ* 2006 L 300/1; and Council Decision 2007/239/EC of 5 March 2007 on a Community Position concerning Decision 1/2007 of the Joint Committee referred to in the Interim Agreement on trade and trade-related mattes between the European Community, of the one part, and the Republic of Albania, of the other part, adopting its Rules of Procedure including the Terms of Reference and Structure of the EC-Albania Working Parties, *OJ* 2007 L 104/32. The undated Decision 1/2007 of the Joint Committee is attached to Council Decision 2007/239/EC.

[65] The Road Map was presented by the Commission in March 2000 and set out eighteen essential steps to be undertaken by Bosnia-Herzegovina before the European Union would consider any further advance of the country within the SAP. The Road Map is available at: <http://www.esiweb.org/bridges/bosnia/EURoadMap.pdf>.

[66] COM (2003) 692 final, Brussels, 18 November 2003.

[67] COM (2004) 202 final, Brussels, 30 March 2004.

was declared less than satisfactory. In the Federation of Bosnia-Herzegovina, serious inadequacies were noted on the part of the Bosnian Croats. The Republika Srpska was dismissed for its failure to locate or arrest even a single indicted fugitive. After a wave of extraditions of both Bosnian Serb and Muslim indictees to the ICTY in the first three months of 2005, the European Commissioner for Enlargement announced that Bosnia-Herzegovina could start negotiations on an SAA by the end of 2005, on the condition that cooperation with the ICTY would continue and would lead to 'full cooperation'.[68] Despite the fact that the two most wanted Bosnian Serb indictees, Radovan Karadžić and Ratko Mladić, were still at large – reportedly thanks to well-organised systems of support[69] – the Commission on 21 October 2005 nonetheless recommended the opening of negotiations on an SAA with Bosnia-Herzegovina and presented draft negotiating directives for adoption by the Council.[70] The move was widely seen as a reward for the difficult agreements reached between the Federation and the Republika Srpska on military and police reforms.[71] SAA negotiations were officially opened on 25 November 2005, in the same week that the world celebrated the tenth anniversary of the Dayton Agreement. It took Bosnia-Herzegovina one year to negotiate the terms of an SAA with the European Union. But due to the ongoing problems concerning the implementation of the agreement to reform the police, the restructuring of the public broadcasting sector and the establishment of a single economic space, the European Commission decided to postpone the formal final round of the SAA talks until all these criteria have been met.[72]

3.2.4 *Serbia* and *Montenegro*

Internal disputes surrounding the endorsement of the Internal Market and Trade Action Plan by the State Assembly of Serbia and Montenegro led the Commission

68 See E. Vucheva, 'Bosnia and Herzegovina a step further on the EU path', *EUObserver.com*, 21 March 2005.

69 The former was thought to be changing his hiding places across the borders of Serbia, Montenegro and Republika Srpska, while the latter was thought to be in hiding in Serbia. Interestingly, the outspoken Minister of Foreign Affairs of Serbia and Montenegro, Vuk Drasković, has claimed on several occasions that Mladić was hiding with the help of Serbian security forces. See, e.g., E. Jansson, 'Serbian authorities "know where Mladić is hiding"', *Financial Times*, 5 April 2005; and 'Serbia Min: Mladic Sheltered By Milosevic Allies – Report', *Dow Jones Newswires*, 1 March 2006.

70 Communication from the Commission to the Council on the progress achieved by Bosnia and Herzegovina in implementing the priorities identified in the Feasibility Study on the preparedness of Bosnia and Herzegovina to negotiate a Stabilisation and Association Agreement with the European Union (COM (2003) 692 final), COM (2005) 529 final, Brussels, 21 October 2005.

71 See M. Beunderman, 'Bosnia set to follow Croats and Serbs on EU track', *EUObserver.com*, 6 October 2005. See also chapter 4, section 4.1.1.

72 See 'Rehn welcomes the finalisation of technical talks for a SAA with Bosnia and Herzegovina and encourages further reform', *European Newsletter*, 15 December 2006.

to stall the feasibility study on an SAA with the state union. It took a full endorsement of the European Union's so-called 'twin-track' approach by the political leaders of both Serbia and Montenegro to relaunch the feasibility study in October 2004. The twin-track approach to SAA negotiations meant that the European Union dealt with the two republics on policies that they conducted separately, notably trade, economic and sectoral policies, while it continued to work with the state union where it was the competent authority, for example in the field of international political obligations and human rights, including cooperation with the ICTY.

As far as the latter is concerned, the state union was under enormous pressure from the European Union's SG/HR and the Commission to extradite alleged war criminals in order to finalise the feasibility report on 12 April 2005. As a result, the authorities made serious headway in their cooperation with the ICTY by 'arresting' half a dozen suspects that were believed to be hiding in Serbia in the first three months of 2005.[73] This change of attitude in Belgrade was rewarded by the Commission with the adoption of the feasibility report on 12 April 2005.[74] On 3 October 2005, the General Affairs Council gave the Commission a mandate to conduct negotiations on an SAA with Serbia and Montenegro.[75] The opening of negotiations by European Commissioner Olli Rehn in Belgrade on 10 October 2005 marked the fifth anniversary of the democratic uprising that removed Slobodan Milošević from the presidential *peluche*. On this occasion, Rehn warned that the conclusion of SAA negotiations would only be possible if Karadžić and Mladić were handed over to The Hague tribunal in the meantime.[76] However, after the ICTY's Chief Prosecutor told the BBC in February 2006 that General Mladić was within 'immediate reach' of the Belgrade authorities, a statement that provoked a flurry of media reports which first claimed and later denied that Mladić had been captured, the European Union hardened its tone.[77]

---

[73] The media have reported the adoption of legislation in Serbia in 2004 to provide pensions to its indicted war criminals. The law would give indictees a full salary, plus unspecified 'compensation' for family and legal expenses. Allegedly, Serbian General Vujadin Popović received a bonus of $1 million when he turned himself in on 14 April 2005. Popović was the commander of the Drina Corps in Bosnia, which conducted some of the worst ethnic-cleansing campaigns in the region. See R. Nordland, 'Pensions for War Criminals', *Newsweek*, 25 July 2005. Mladić was thought to be negotiating a similar package with the Serbian authorities.

[74] See Press Release IP/05/421, Brussels, 12 April 2005.

[75] On 12 July 2005, the Commission had submitted to the Council a mandate for negotiations with Serbia and Montenegro on an SAA. See Press Release IP/05/915, Brussels, 12 July 2005. On the adoption of the mandate, see Council Conclusions of 3 October 2005, Press Release No. 12515/1/05 REV 1 (Presse 242).

[76] European Commission, 'Serbia and Montenegro Open Association Talks with EU', in *Enlargement Newsletter*, 28 October 2005.

[77] See L. Kubosova, 'Reports on Mladic capture spark confusion', *EUObserver.com*, 22 February 2006.

Although not laid down black on white in the Council Conclusions of 27 February 2006, the Union was reported as having given Serbia and Montenegro a one-month deadline to send Mladić to The Hague or face disruption of the SAA talks.[78] While Belgrade came under increased pressure from the ICTY and the European Union to capture Mladić in the wake of the death of Slobodan Milošević on 11 March 2006, the controversies over the circumstances of the death and the burial of the former president complicated the authorities' efforts to transfer the war-time general to The Hague.[79] Implicitly, this was recognised by the ICTY's Chief Prosecutor, when she reported positively in Brussels on Serbia and Montenegro's cooperation with the Tribunal. Accordingly, the European Union opened the political round of SAA talks with Serbia and Montenegro on 5 April 2006, while at the same time keeping up the pressure by extending Belgrade's deadline by one month.[80] As Belgrade was also unable to meet the new deadline, the Council supported the Commission's decision to call off the SAA negotiating round scheduled for 11 May, in line with its conclusions of 3 October 2005 and 27 February 2006.[81]

In a parallel development, the European Union had declared that it was ready to accept any outcome of the referendum on independence that Montenegro had scheduled for 21 May 2006 – be it independence or federation with Serbia – as long as the vote would be 'legitimate', that is to say, that there would be a 50 per cent threshold for participation and a 55 per cent threshold for approval of the result.[82] On 21 May, 55.5 per cent of the majority of Montenegrin voters opted for independence in a nationwide referendum that was considered to be free and fair. In a special session on 3 June, the parliament in Podgorica passed a declaration on the independence of the Republic of Montenegro. On 5 June, the parliament in Belgrade declared the Republic of Serbia the legal successor to the state union and gave all state institutions forty-five days to complete the separation. On 12

[78] See E. Krasniqi, 'EU ministers back Balkans war crimes ultimatum', *EUObserver.com*, 27 February 2006; and Council Conclusions of 27 February 2006, Press Release No. 6344/06 (Presse 46): 'The Council noted with concern recent comments by ICTY Chief Prosecutor Carla del Ponte about Serbia and Montenegro's unsatisfactory cooperation with ICTY. The Council strongly supported the recent messages delivered by the Commission in Belgrade and Sarajevo that full cooperation with the ICTY must be achieved to ensure that the SAA negotiations are not disrupted. Recalling its conclusions of 3 October 2005 and of 30 January 2006, the Council urged both Serbia and Montenegro and Bosnia and Herzegovina to take decisive action to ensure that all remaining fugitive indictees, notably Radovan Karadzic and Ratko Mladic, are finally brought to justice without delay. The Council asked the Presidency and the Commission to remain in close contact with the Chief Prosecutor and to continue to keep the Council fully informed.'

[79] See S. Wagstyl, D. Dombey and N. Macdonald, 'Death increases pressure for capture of other war suspects', *Financial Times*, 13 March 2006.

[80] See O. Lungescu, 'EU pleased with Serbia "progress"', *BBC News*, 31 March 2006.

[81] See Council Conclusions of 15 May 2006, Press Release No. 9001/06 (Presse 126).

[82] See Council Conclusions of 27 February 2006, Press Release No. 6344/06 (Presse 46).

June, the Council of the European Union recognised that the parliamentary acts were taken in conformity with the arrangements and the procedures foreseen in the Belgrade Agreement and Article 60 of the Constitutional Charter, and decided to develop bilateral relations with the new sovereign and independent Republic of Montenegro.[83] The pro-independence vote in Montenegro required the European Union to completely disentangle the SAA talks with the two republics. In practice, this proved not to be a problem, as the 'twin-track' approach had become a standard working method for the Commission. The Commission submitted for adoption by the Council new draft negotiating directives for Montenegro and, as the successor state of the state union, amended negotiating directives for Serbia.[84] On 17 July, the General Affairs Council hinted that it would approve the Commission's recommendation to continue separate SAA negotiations with Montenegro and with Serbia.[85] On 24 July, the Justice and Home Affairs Council adopted the decisions authorising the Commission to negotiate an SAA with Montenegro.[86] At the same time, the Council amended the negotiating directives for the SAA with Serbia. The decisions have no implications for the Commission's decision on 3 May 2006 to freeze the SAA negotiations as long as Serbia's obligations to cooperate fully with the ICTY are not fulfilled. However, the adoption of this amendment will enable the Commission to resume the negotiations as soon as the obligations are fulfilled. To this end, Serbia presented the European Union with a new action plan in July 2006, including ways and means to arrest and extradite Ratko Mladić. But reactions were divided afterwards as to whether the European Union might endorse the SAA with Serbia if the action plan was fully implemented. Some EU Member States, like the Netherlands, demanded the actual arrest of the top fugitive.[87]

As two independent countries, Serbia and Montenegro are now in different positions in terms of establishing closer links with the European Union: not only

---

83 See Council Conclusions of 12 June 2006, Press Release No. 9947/06 (Presse 162). See also chapter 4, section 3.2.4.

84 See Commission Press Release IP/06/941 of 6 July 2006.

85 See Council Conclusions of 17 July 2006, Press Release No. 11575/06 (Presse 219): 'The Council took note of the fact that all EU Member States have recognized the Republic of Montenegro as a sovereign and independent state. In line with the Stabilisation and Association Process and the Thessaloniki Agenda, the Council decided to extend bilateral political dialogue at ministerial level to Montenegro. A joint declaration will be prepared to that end. The Council also agreed to invite Montenegro to align itself with EU demarches, declarations and common positions on CFSP issues.'

86 See Council Conclusions of 12 June 2006, Press Release No. 11556/06 (Presse 216). On 15 September 2006, the European Union and Montenegro agreed to establish a regular political dialogue to accompany and consolidate their *rapprochement*. See Joint Declaration on political dialogue between the European Union and Montenegro, *OJ* 2006 C 242/6. SAA negotiations with Montenegro were (re)opened on 26 September 2006.

87 See E. Krasniqi, 'EU states divided on Serbia strategy', *EUObserver.com*, 18 July 2006. For a critique on this particular point, see chapter 6, section 4.2.

in terms of cooperation with the ICTY but also because the republics have quite different economies. While the Serbian economy is based on production, industry and agriculture and its internal market needs some protection, Montenegro's economy is quite open and based mainly on services. Logically speaking, Montenegro should therefore be in a better position than Serbia to make swift progress on closer relations with the European Union.[88]

3.2.5 *Kosovo*

The European perspective of the Western Balkans, as stated in the Zagreb Declaration of November 2000, is also open to Kosovo.[89] However, pending a final settlement on its legal status,[90] UN-administered Kosovo (as defined by UN Security Council resolution 1244 (1999)) was not able to participate as a full member in the SAP. To ensure that UNMIK and the PISG would follow EU-compatible practices in the political, economic and sectoral reform process, UNMIK and the European Commission agreed that an instrument was needed to monitor and drive the process. It was deemed profitable for Kosovo to follow the methodology and substance of the SAP and thus avoid isolation from the path of EU-compatible transition and development of the rest of the region.[91] To that end, on 6 November 2002, the Commission commenced the so-called 'Stabilisation and Association Process Tracking Mechanism' (STM).[92] The STM is a joint technical working group of the European Commission, UNMIK and Kosovo's PISG that is intended to help the authorities in Kosovo prepare for reinforced policy-making relations within the framework of the Union's Stabilisation and Association Process.[93] It tracks the progress made in the implementation of the European Partnership[94] and provides policy advice on building EU-compatible institutional, legislative, economic and social frameworks. As such, Kosovo benefits from all the elements of the SAP, with the notable exception of the

88 For a note of caution, see chapter 4, section 3.2.4.

89 *Bull. EU* 11-2000, point I.6.57. On 20 April 2005, the European Commission adopted a Communication entitled 'A European Future for Kosovo,' which reinforces the Commission's commitment to Kosovo. See COM (2005) 156 final, Brussels, 20 April 2005.

90 On the final status talks, see chapter 4, sections 3.3.2-3.3.4.

91 The European Union was also eager to apply the same standards to the whole region. See chapter 2, section 6.7.

92 EU Ministers endorsed the launch of technical talks at the Thessaloniki Summit on 21 June 2003, *Bull. EU* 6-2003, point 1.6.70.

93 In fact, STM meetings are the main channel for dialogue between the Commission and Kosovo. To date, eight STM meetings have taken place. The sixth STM meeting, which was held on 16 February 2005 in Priština, was the first meeting with the newly elected government.

94 The STM and the Annual Progress Report are the main instruments of the European Commission for monitoring Kosovo's progress in the SAP. On the European Partnership, see *infra* section 4.

possibility of contractual relations with the European Union. However, depending on the outcome of status process, Kosovo may in due course engage in contractual relations with the Union as appropriate.

At the time of writing, the European Union's main focus is on improving capacity-building through regular cooperation and joint initiatives with a number of line ministries, particularly the Ministry of Finance and Economy and the Ministry of Trade and Industry.[95] Together with these ministries, the EU Pillar in UNMIK has led free trade negotiations and facilitated Kosovo's involvement in a number of regional and wider European initiatives, such as the Energy Community Treaty, the South East European Transport Observatory, the European Common Aviation Area and the European Charter for Small Enterprises.[96]

3.3 General principles

3.3.1 *Essential elements*

The SAAs that have already entered into force set out various principles to which the parties are committed.[97] The preamble and Article 1(2) of both agreements describe the objectives of the new associations: the establishment of an appropriate framework for political dialogue between the associate and the European Union, the approximation of the associate's legislation to that of the European Union, the development of a climate conducive to increased trade and investment, the transition of the associate's economy into a market economy, EC support for reform and regional cooperation in all fields covered by the SAA. To these ends, both SAAs confirm in almost identical provisions that the conclusion and implementation of the agreements come within the framework of the Council Conclusions of 29 April 1997 and that they are based on individual merits of the respective SAP partner (Art. 3). The conditionality clause used in Article 2 of the SAAs includes such 'essential elements' as the

---

[95] For factual details, see D. Papadimitriou, P. Petrov and L. Greiçevci, 'To Build a State: Europeanization, EU Actorness and State-Building in Kosovo', 12 *EFA Rev.* (2007) pp. 219-238.

[96] See Council Decision No. 2006/56/EC of 30 January 2006 on the principles, priorities and conditions contained in the European Partnership with Serbia and Montenegro including Kosovo as defined by the United Nations Security Council Resolution 1244 of 10 June 1999 and repealing Decision 2004/520/EC, *OJ* 2006 L 35/32.

[97] The same goes for the SAA with Albania, which will remain outside the scope of these sections because it has not yet entered into force. For an analysis of the SAAs with Macedonia and Croatia, see J. Marko and J. Wilhelm, 'Stabilisation and Association Agreements', in Ott and Inglis, op. cit. n. 3, pp. 165-174; and Phinnemore, loc. cit. n. 45, at pp. 79-81. It should be noted that the analysis of Marko and Wilhelm was conducted prior to the publication of the SAAs in the *Official Journal* of the European Union.

> [r]espect for the democratic principles and human rights as proclaimed in the Universal Declaration of Human Rights and as defined in the Helsinki Final Act and the Charter of Paris for a New Europe, respect for international law principles and the rule of law as well as the principles of market economy as reflected in the Document of the CSCE Bonn Conference on Economic Cooperation [...].

Unlike the EAs, 'respect for international law principles and the rule of law' is also mentioned among the general principles of the SAAs. In the case of Croatia, a commitment to the right of return for all refugees and compliance with the 1995 Dayton and Erdut Agreements is also reaffirmed (preamble).

By classifying the criteria mentioned in Article 2 as 'essential elements' of the contractual relationship, both SAAs borrow the language of the 1969 Vienna Convention on the Law of Treaties. Article 60(3) VCLT allows for the unilateral suspension or termination of international agreements by one of the parties in cases of 'material breach' of a treaty, caused, for instance, by '(b) the violation of a provision *essential* to the accomplishment of the object or purpose of the treaty'.[98] In line with the EC's international treaty practice, the essential elements clause of Article 2 is complemented by a standard non-compliance clause. This so-called 'Bulgarian clause' enables either party to take 'appropriate measures', that is to say, measures taken in accordance with international law (e.g., principle of proportionality, etc.) if it considers that the other party has failed to fulfil an obligation under the SAA.[99] The party considering such measures must, 'except in cases of special urgency, first supply the Stabilisation and Association Council (SAC) with all relevant information required for a thorough examination of the situation with a view to find a solution acceptable to both parties.' A joint declaration annexed to the Final Act of each SAA clarifies that the notion 'cases of special urgency' should be interpreted to mean 'cases of material breach of the Agreement by one of the two Parties'. A material breach of the SAA is considered to consist of 'repudiation of the Agreement not sanctioned by the general rules of international law [and] violation of the essential elements of the Agreement as set out in Article 2.' As a result, any infringement of democratic principles, human rights and fundamental freedoms, international law principles (e.g., full and unequivocal cooperation with the ICTY), the rule of law and principles of market economy constitutes, at least in principle, a case of special urgency, entitling the sanctioning party to take appropriate measures, without the need for prior consultations in the SAC. It would seem that the immediate

98 Emphasis added.

99 See Art. 118(2) SAA FYROM and Art. 120(2) SAA Croatia. If a party takes a measure in a case of special urgency pursuant to these articles, the other party may avail itself of a dispute settlement procedure. For an explanation on the emergence and importance of the 'Bulgarian clause', see Bulterman, op. cit. n. 14, at pp. 204-205.

adoption of such measures, without a prior attempt to find an adequate solution in the SAC, is reserved for gross, widespread and persistent violations of one or more of the requirements enshrined in the essential elements clause.

Christian Pippan has rightly argued that, with their references to the rights and freedoms contained in the 1948 Universal Declaration of Human Rights (UDHR), the 1975 Helsinki Final Act and the 1990 Charter of Paris for a New Europe, as well as the political and economic principles enshrined in the Document of the CSCE Bonn Conference on Economic Cooperation, the essential elements clauses in the SAAs with Macedonia and Croatia set out a considerably high standard. From the time of the entry into force of the SAAs, the parties to these bilateral relationships are contractually bound, for example, to undertake 'to build, consolidate and strengthen democracy as the only system of government.'[100] This requires, *inter alia*, a representative and pluralistic government, which is 'based on the will of the people, expressed regularly through free and fair elections', and which ensures 'accountability to the electorate' as well as 'justice administered impartially'.[101] Under the SAAs, the creation of – or the return to – a non-democratic form of government by one of the treaty partners is therefore illegal.[102] This is not only an important regional contribution to a general trend in contemporary international law that increasingly outlaws military or one-party civil regimes and endorses pluralistic, democratic governance as the only legitimate expression of the peoples' right to (internal) self-determination. It is also a remarkable normative advancement given the fact that the UDHR, as well as the Helsinki Final Act and the Charter of Paris are, as such, legally non-binding instruments.[103]

3.3.2 *Regional cooperation*

Whereas regional cooperation was encouraged among the countries that signed EAs with the European Union, it was never made a distinct feature of their associations. In the case of the SAAs, regional cooperation is viewed as key to the

---

[100] Charter of Paris for a New Europe, section on Human Rights, Democracy and the Rule of Law, para. 1, 21 *ILM* (1982) at 58.

[101] Ibid., paras. 3 and 4.

[102] As SAAs are mixed agreements, this conclusion is also applicable to the EU Member States. For thoughts on what would happen when democracy derails in one of the Member States, see my articles 'Oostenrijk in quarantaine – de voorwaarden voor het beëindigen van het lidmaatschap van een internationale organisatie' [Austria in quarantine – conditions for terminating membership of an international organisation], 9 *Ars Aequi* (2000) pp. 629-637; and 'Van Wenen naar Nice: nieuwe voorwaarden voor het instellen van sancties door de EU tegen een lidstaat die de grondrechten schendt' [From Vienna to Nice: New conditions for imposing EU sanctions against a Member State that violates fundamental rights], 5 *Ars Aequi* (2001) pp. 331-338.

[103] See Pippan, loc. cit. n. 17, at pp. 237-238.

stabilisation of the Western Balkans and has been made an explicit condition before the countries of the region can join the European Union (Art. 3). However difficult it is to enforce this additional conditionality, the importance attached to it has been underlined by the Commission, which noted in its first annual report on the SAP: '[i]ntegration with the EU is only possible if future members can demonstrate that they are willing and able to interact with their neighbours as EU Member States do.'[104] In Article 4, SAA signatories commit themselves to 'continue and foster cooperation and good neighbourly relations with the other countries of the region.' The SAAs explicitly refer to such relations covering the movement of persons, goods, capital and services, as well as the development of projects of common interest. In the SAA Croatia, specific examples are given: 'refugee return and combating organised crime, corruption, money laundering, illegal migration and trafficking'. To achieve regional cooperation on these issues, the SAA countries are expected to conclude conventions between each other. SAA signatories are also obliged to engage in regional cooperation with the other countries covered by the SAP (Art. 13). The political dialogue, held within a multilateral framework (Arts. 7 and 8), is also meant to contribute to the development of regional cooperation and good neighbourly relations. In fact, these provisions codify a proliferation process that was already underway in south-eastern Europe. Apart from a matrix of bilateral free trade agreements,[105] a whole range of regional initiatives for political dialogue has been developed. Notable examples are the Central European Initiative (CEI), the Black Sea Economic Cooperation (BSEC), the Central European Free Trade Agreement (CEFTA),[106] the South East Europe Cooperation Process (SEECP), the Southeast European Cooperation Initiative (SECI) and the Adriatic-Ionian Initiative (AII).[107] The biggest achievement of these initiatives is without doubt the sustainable political dialogue between the countries involved in these frameworks. But with partly overlapping memberships and agendas indicating lack of complementarities, competitiveness is growing among them. Many regional initiatives have been criticised because of the modesty of their objectives and the limited concrete results they have yielded.[108] Moreover, most of them are only addressing the

---

104 See COM (2002) 163 final, Brussels, 4 April 2002, at p. 11.

105 A matrix of the free trade agreements in south-eastern Europe is available at: <http://en.wikipedia.org/wiki/Stability_Pact_for_South_Eastern_Europe#FTA_Progress>. See also European Commission, 'Trade in South Eastern Europe', MEMO/06/155, Brussels, 5 April 2006.

106 See chapter 6, section 2.1.1.3.

107 For an overview and analysis of these and other initiatives, see D. Lopandić, *Regional Initiatives in South Eastern Europe* (Belgrade, European Movement in Serbia 2001). See also E. Busek, ed., *10 Years Southeast European Cooperative Initiative: From Dayton to Brussels* (Vienna, Springer 2006).

108 See O. Anastasakis and V. Bojičić-Dželilović, *Balkan Regional Cooperation and European Integration* (London, Hellinic Observatory LSE 2002); and A. Petričušić, 'Regional Cooperation in the Western Balkans – A Key to Integration into the European Union', 1 *Croatian Yearbook of European Law and Policy* (2005) pp. 213-233.

immediate post-conflict situation, and all but the SEECP have been created as a consequence of external incentives by resuscitating and broadening existing initiatives. It seems that, in the search for the most appropriate regional initiative, valuable resources are being wasted.[109]

3.3.3 *Approximation of legislation*

The approximation of the associate's legislation to that of the European Union is another important aspect of the SAAs as far as the perspective of future integration is concerned. The existing SAAs define the rules of the internal market as *priorities* for legislative approximation by Macedonia and Croatia.[110] The focus on internal market law bears a risk of an unbalanced situation in the approximation process, leaving behind other essential areas such as social or environmental policy. Yet, it is a critical component within the SAA, essentially extending to the Western Balkans the European Union's own philosophy that the adoption of the hard core of economic standards based on a free market economy is a route to national as well as regional peace, stability and growth and that such integration serves the mutual interests of all countries concerned.

The SAA Croatia declares that this legislative approximation process will be fully implemented within six years of the entry into force of the agreement (Arts. 5 and 69), that is to say, before 1 February 2011. In the case of Macedonia, the approximation will take place in a timeframe of ten years divided into two successive stages (Arts. 5 and 68). In the first phase of the implementation of the SAA FYROM (until 9 April 2009), the approximation will cover fundamental elements of the internal market *acquis* and other trade-related areas. This includes competition law, intellectual property law, standards and certification law, public procurement law and data protection law. During the second phase (until 9 April 2014), the remaining elements of the *acquis* will be covered. The reasoning behind the shorter timeframe and the absence of stages in the SAA Croatia reflect the belief among the Member States of the European Union that Croatia is in a better position, both economically and politically, to meet its obligations under the SAA. Full implementation of the SAAs will help the countries of the Western Balkans in their preparations for EU membership. They are assisted in this task by the Commission with technical advice and financial assistance.

---

[109] See J. Minić, 'Summary and Recommendations of the Conference', in Lopandić, op. cit. n. 35, at pp. 9-17. For suggestions for restructuring regional cooperation, see chapter 6, section 2.1.1.3.

[110] This is clearly an advance compared to the one-size-fits-all approach prescribed in the EAs. See A. Łazowski, 'Approximation of Laws', in Ott and Inglis, op. cit. n. 3, at pp. 631-639.

3.4 Financial and technical assistance

As an overarching, multi-country strategy, the SAP commits the European Union to providing not only political but also financial and technical support to the six countries of the Western Balkans. From 2000 to 2006, the CARDS (Community Assistance for Reconstruction, Development and Stabilisation) programme was the Community's main funding instrument dedicated to the region of the Western Balkans and supported the actions undertaken within the SAP and under the SAAs.[111] It replaced the OBNOVA[112] and PHARE[113] programmes and established a single legal framework for EU assistance to the countries of the region.[114] In addition, a special European Agency for Reconstruction (EAR) was entrusted with the local administration of EC assistance to Kosovo, Macedonia, Serbia and Montenegro.[115]

---

111 Council Regulation (EC) No. 2666/2000 of 5 December 2000 on assistance for Albania, Bosnia and Herzegovina, Croatia, the Federal Republic of Yugoslavia and the Former Yugoslav Republic of Macedonia, repealing Regulation (EC) No. 1628/96 and amending Regulations (EEC) No. 3906/89 and (EEC) No. 1360/90 and Decisions 97/256/EC and 1999/311/EC, *OJ* 2000 L 306/1 (as amended). In addition, funding was provided through other budget lines as well.

112 Council Regulation (EC) No. 1628/96 of 25 July 1996 relating to aid for Bosnia and Herzegovina, Croatia, the Federal Republic of Yugoslavia and the former Yugoslav Republic of Macedonia, *OJ* 1996 L 204/1. See *supra* section 2.1.

113 The PHARE programme was one of the pre-accession instruments financed by the European Union to assist the applicant countries from Central and Eastern Europe in their preparations to join the Union. PHARE was created in 1989 to assist Poland and Hungary in their *rapprochement* to the Community. See Council Regulation (EC) No. 3906/89 of 18 December 1989 on economic aid to the Republic of Hungary and the Polish People's Republic, *OJ* 1989 L 375/11. In 1990, the PHARE programme was enlarged with, *inter alia*, Yugoslavia. See Council Regulation (EEC) 2690/90 of 17 September 1990, *OJ* 1990 L 257/1. This decision reflected the upbeat attitude of the EC towards increased cooperation, potentially even association, with the SFRY. See M. Maresceau, 'Zuidoost-Europa en de Europese Unie', in R. Detrez, ed., *Ontmoeting met de Balkan* (Brussels, KVAB 2005) pp. 9-43 at pp. 11-14. Until 2000, Albania, Bosnia-Herzegovina, Croatia and Macedonia were also recipients of PHARE assistance. See, respectively, Council Regulation (EEC) No. 3800/91 of 23 December 1991 amending Regulation (EEC) No. 3906/89 in order to extend economic aid to include other countries in central and eastern Europe, *OJ* 1991 L 357/10; Council Regulation (EC) No. 753/96 of 22 April 1996 amending Regulation (EEC) No. 3906/89 with a view to extending economic aid to Bosnia and Herzegovina, *OJ* 1996 L 103/5; Council Regulation (EC) No. 1366/95 of 12 June 1995 amending Regulation (EEC) No. 3906/89 in order to extend economic aid to Croatia, *OJ* 1995 L 133/1; and Council Regulation (EC) No. 463/96 of 11 March 1996 amending Regulation (EEC) No. 3906/89 with a view to extending economic assistance to the Former Yugoslav Republic of Macedonia, *OJ* 1996 L 65/3.

114 For a breakdown of the grand total of €5.55 billion in Community support to the SAP region during the 1991-2000 period, see Annex 4 to European Commission, CARDS Assistance Programme to the Western Balkans: Regional Strategy Paper 2002-2006, Brussels, 22 October 2001, available at: <http://europa.eu.int/comm/enlargement/cards/publications_en.htm>.

115 Council Regulation (EC) No. 2667/2000 of 5 December 2000 on the European Agency for Reconstruction, *OJ* 2000 L 306/7. The EAR has its headquarters in Thessaloniki and runs operational centres in Belgrade, Priština, Podgorica and Skopje. It is accountable both to the Council and the European Parliament and overseen by a governing board composed of the Commission and representatives from EU Member States. The EAR is due to close down by the end of 2008. More information is available on the EAR's website at: <http://www.ear.eu.int/agency/agency.htm>.

Under the unified procedures of CARDS, which became fully operational in 2002, the Commission drew up multi-annual country strategies as well as a regional strategy in collaboration with the Western Balkan countries, EU Member States, other donors and, insofar as possible, representatives of civil society. These strategy papers formed the basis for annual programmes for each of the countries concerned.[116] Under the CARDS programme, a budget of €4.65 billion was agreed for the 2000-2006 period.[117] However, Table 1 below shows that the eventual amount of CARDS funding during this period was closer to €5.13 billion (or even €5.385 billion when including funding to Croatia during its first pre-accession period). To achieve its objective of facilitating the SAP, CARDS assistance financed investment, institution-building and other programmes in four major areas: (i) reconstruction, democratic stabilisation, reconciliation and the return of refugees; (ii) institutional and legislative development, including approximation of domestic legislation with EU norms to underpin democracy and the rule of law, human rights, civil society and the media, as well as the operation of a free market economy; (iii) sustainable economic and social development, including structural reform; and (iv) the promotion of closer relations and regional cooperation between SAP countries and between the SAP countries, the EU Member States, the acceding countries (Bulgaria and Romania) and candidate country Turkey.[118]

In one regional strategy paper and a series of country strategy papers, the European Union set out its priorities for the implementation of the SAP and the legally binding bilateral agreements between the Union and each associate. The Commission has identified the strategy papers as key tools for integrating conflict prevention in the programming of its development cooperation.[119] As such, they

---

[116] The 2002-2006 Strategy Papers and the most recent Annual Programmes can be retrieved from: <http://europa.eu.int/comm/enlargement/cards/publications_en.htm>.

[117] Annex B to the first annual review of the SAP, COM (2002) 163 final, Brussels, 4 April 2002, at p. 23.

[118] In 2005-2006, CARDS financial assistance covered both the 'potential' candidate countries (Albania, Bosnia-Herzegovina, Serbia *and* Montenegro (including Kosovo under UN administration)) and the candidate countries of the Western Balkans (Croatia and Macedonia). The latter remain part of the SAP and continue to be eligible for regional funding. Upon receiving candidate status (see *infra* section 5), Croatia was included as a beneficiary of PHARE, ISPA, and SAPARD by way of Council Regulation (EC) No. 2257/2004 amending Regulations (EEC) No. 3906/89, (EC) No. 1267/1999, (EC) No. 1268/1999 and (EC) No. 2666/2000, to take account of Croatia's candidate status, *OJ* 2004 L 389/1. See also the Framework Agreement between the European Community and the Republic of Croatia on the general principles for the participation of the Republic of Croatia in Community programmes, *OJ* 2005 L 192/16; and Commission Decision 2006/658/EC of 29 September 2006 conferring management of aid on implementing agencies for pre-accession measures in agriculture and rural development in Croatia in the pre-accession period, *OJ* 2006 L 271/83. At the time of writing, similar decisions concerning Macedonia, which received candidate country status in December 2005 (see *infra* section 5), had not been taken.

[119] COM (1999) 235 final, Brussels, 26 May 1999.

complement the political dialogue backed up by the annual reviews of the SAP. When drafting the political analysis section of the strategy papers, risk factors are systematically checked. For that purpose, the Commission is using the indicators developed for the so-called 'checklist for root causes of conflict'.[120] This checklist looks at issues such as the balance of political and economic power, the control of the security forces, the ethnic composition of the government of ethnically divided countries, the human rights situation, the level of organised crime, the potential degradation of environmental resources, the level of corruption and so forth. On the basis of this conflict analysis, attention is then drawn to activities focused on conflict prevention that should be targeted by external aid.

The CARDS Assistance Programme to the Western Balkans: Regional Strategy Paper 2002-2006 was adopted by the Commission on 22 October 2001 and provided a strategic framework for programming the regional envelope of the CARDS programme during the 2002-2006 period.[121] Some 10 per cent of the available CARDS budget was to be directed towards raising the levels of regional cooperation between the countries of the Western Balkans. The Regional Strategy Paper earmarked funds for support in four priority areas: (i) integrated border management to help tackle cross-border crime, to facilitate trade across borders and to stabilise the border regions themselves; (ii) institutional capacity-building to help raise awareness of EU policy and laws that the region should increasingly be moving towards; (iii) democratic stabilisation to help cement advances in democracy and boost the involvement of civil society in the region's development; and (iv) integration of the region's transport, energy and environmental infrastructure into the wider European networks. These areas were selected because of their contribution to regional cooperation or because the support could be best delivered at the regional level. The so-called 'multi-annual indicative programme' attached to the Regional Strategy Paper provided strategic guidance for implementing the CARDS regional assistance. The CARDS regional financial allocation for 2005-2006 amounted to €85 million.[122]

The country strategy papers were adopted to provide the strategic framework in which EC assistance would be provided to each country during the 2000-2006 period. Each country strategy paper set out cooperation objectives, policy response and priority fields of cooperation based on a thorough assessment of the

---

120 Available at: <http://europa.eu.int/comm/external_relations/cpcm/cp/list.htm>. For background and analysis, see J. Niño-Pérez, 'Conflict Indicators Developed by the Commission: The Check-list for Root Causes of Conflict/Early Warning Indicators', in V. Kronenberger and J. Wouters, eds., *The European Union and Conflict Prevention: Policy and Legal Aspects* (The Hague, T.M.C. Asser Press 2004) pp. 3-19.

121 See *supra* n. 114.

122 Priority areas for regional CARDS assistance in 2005-2006 were institution-building (€16-18 million), justice and home affairs (€5-6 million), cross-border cooperation (€33-39 million), private sector development (€2.5-3.5 million) and infrastructure development (€21-26 million).

partner country's policy agenda and political and socio-economic situation. The multi-annual indicative programme attached to the each country strategy paper set out the EU response in more detail, highlighting programme objectives, expected results and conditionality in the priority fields of cooperation. Malfunctioning governance, combined with organised crime, corruption and smuggling, constituted the most serious obstacle to a rapid improvement of the situation in most of the Western Balkan countries.[123] In this context, and taking into account the objectives of the SAP, it is worth noting that the EU response under the CARDS programme to the partner countries focused on the sustainable return of refugees and displaced persons, the full integration of ethnic minorities into society, democratic stabilisation, administrative capacity-building, an effective and accountable legal system, economic and social development, the environment and natural resources, and justice and home affairs.[124]

The main beneficiaries of CARDS assistance were the central governmental institutions, but regional and local bodies, social partners, cooperatives, associations and NGOs were also eligible to apply.[125] In the past, the latter has proven to be of particular importance, as this creates the possibility of a direct, 'decentralised' form of cooperation that can be maintained even if the state's central government falls short of complying with the conditions set out by the European Union for official Community assistance.[126]

Political conditionality was explicitly included in Article 5 of Council Regulation (EC) No. 2666/2000 on CARDS:

> 1. Respect for the principles of democracy and the rule of law and for human and minority rights and fundamental freedoms is an essential element for the application of this Regulation and a precondition for Community assistance. If these principles are not respected, the Council, acting by qualified majority on a proposal from the Commission, may take the appropriate measures.
> 2. Community assistance shall also be subject to the conditions defined by the Council in its Conclusions of 29 April 1997, in particular as regards the recipients' undertaking to carry out democratic, economic and institutional reforms.

---

123 Bosnia-Herzegovina faced even greater challenges over the medium term, notably strengthening the state and reinforcing the administration. The country strategy papers for Serbia and Montenegro and Macedonia set out an approach that was designed to require the least modification possible, whatever the outcome of the final status talks on Kosovo.

124 For 'facts and figures' on assistance to each of the Western Balkan countries, see the Regional Strategy Paper 2002-2006, the country strategy papers, the multi-annual indicative programmes and a sample of case studies from the hundreds of ongoing projects in all sectors, regions and countries, all available at: <http://www.europa.eu.int/comm/external_relations>. See also the joint initiative of the European Commission and the World Bank in economic reconstruction and development in south-eastern Europe, available at: <http://www.seerecon.org>.

125 Art. 1(2) of Council Regulation (EC) No. 2666/2000.

126 See Pippan, loc. cit. n. 17, at p. 233.

Table 1: CARDS programme allocation for 2000-2006 (€ millions)

	2000	2001	2002	2003	2004	2005	2006	TOTAL
Albania	33.4	37.5	44.9	46.5	63.5	44.2	45.5	**315.5**
Bosnia and Herzegovina	90.3	105.2	71.9	63.0	72.0	49.4	51.0	**502.8**
Croatia (transfer to pre-accession from 2005)	16.8	60.0	59.0	62.0	81.0	-	-	**278.8**
The former Yugoslav Republic of Macedonia	13.0	56.2	41.5	43.5	59.0	45.0	40.0	**298.2**
Serbia and Montenegro[a]	650.5	385.5	351.6	324.3	307.9	282.5	257.5	**2,559.8**
Interim Civilian Administrations	10.0	24.5	33.0	32.0	35.0	36.0	35.0	**205.5**
Regional	20.2	20.0	43.5	31.5	23.0	47.9	43.5	**229.6**
Other[b]	141.5	118.0	11.0	17.0	22.5	19.7	16.1	**345.8**
Macro-Financial Assistance (grants)[c]	70.0	120.0	100.0	15.0	16.0	33.0	50.0	**404.0**
TOTAL	**1,045.7**	**926.9**	**756.4**	**634.8**	**679.9**	**557.7**	**538.6**	**5,130.2**
Croatia, pre-accession 2005-2006						105	140	**245**
TOTAL including Croatia, 2005-2006						**662.7**	**678.6**	**5,385**

Notes:

1. Figures include assistance from PHARE and OBNOVA where relevant in 2000 and from CARDS in 2001 and onwards.
2. 2005 budget implementation: reuse of recoveries from 2004-2005, i.e., above budget allocation 2005: €6 million for the former Yugoslav Republic of Macedonia, €7.5 million for regional programme.

a. Includes the Republic of Serbia, the Republic of Montenegro, and the Province of Kosovo, which is currently under UN administration. Amounts for Serbia in 2002-2003 include assistance from Regional Programme for Integrated Border Management destined for the whole of FRY/Serbia and Montenegro. In 2004, €8 million for that purpose is shown under the regional programme.

b. Until 2001 (inclusive): humanitarian aid, specific measures, rapid intervention operations, EIDHR and CFSP. From 2001 (inclusive): administrative costs and the Western Balkans' contribution to the European Training Foundation.

c. For 2000-2002: disbursements and not commitments.

Source: <http://europa.eu.int/comm/enlargement/financial_assistance.htm> (31 December 2006)

This provision represented one of the most comprehensive conditionality clauses ever embodied in a Community legal instrument regulating external assistance.[127] Apart from giving expression, in its first paragraph, to the importance of the 'political' part of the 1993 Copenhagen criteria as a precondition for Community assistance, it also explicitly incorporated the entire range of political and economic conditions entailed in the April 1997 Council Conclusions on conditionality as additional conditions for EU financial support to the countries of the Western Balkans. Moreover, the CARDS Regulation did not only rely on punitive measures in order to promote the exceptionally broad range of political and economic standards applied by the European Union towards the countries concerned. It also provided for the application of positive measures, namely, the financing of projects and programmes aimed at supporting 'the creation of an institutional and legislative framework to underpin democracy, the rule of law and human and minority rights, reconciliation and the consolidation of civil society'.[128]

In an attempt to harmonise (insofar as possible) the pre-accession financial instruments – PHARE, ISPA, SAPARD, the Turkish pre-accession instrument and CARDS – the Council has recently adopted a regulation creating a single Instrument for Pre-Accession Assistance (IPA) for the period covered by the financial perspective for 2007-2013.[129] This new funding mechanism for the Western Balkans (and Turkey) will be discussed in chapter 6 of this book.

3.5 Trade preferences

In addition to the significant amounts of aid that the countries of the Western Balkans receive from the European Union, all states benefit from generous trade preferences. In March 2000, the Lisbon European Council decided that future association agreements with the Western Balkans had to be preceded by a regime

---

127 Ibid., at p. 232.

128 Art. 2(2)(b) of Council Regulation (EC) No. 2666/2000. Between 1998 and 2002, EC assistance devoted to the field of 'democratic stabilisation' (including aid to refugees) represented 20 per cent of the total assistance allocated to the Western Balkans. See COM (2003) 139 final, Brussels, 26 March 2003, at 23.

129 See Council Regulation (EC) No. 1085/2006 of 17 July 2006 establishing an Instrument for Pre-Accession Assistance (IPA), *OJ* 2006 L 210/82. IPA is part of a wider reorganisation of the European Union's financial framework for relations with third states, which includes a new European Neighbourhood and Partnership Instrument (ENPI), a new development cooperation instrument, the Instrument for Stability and a financing instrument for the promotion of democracy and human rights. The IPA Regulation provides a total envelope of €11.5 billion over the next seven years for the countries with candidate status (currently Croatia, Macedonia and Turkey) and potential candidate status (Albania, Bosnia-Herzegovina, Montenegro and Serbia (including Kosovo)). As a result, all Western Balkan countries will receive less than before. This point is made more poignantly in chapter 6, section 2.1.1.2.

of asymmetrical trade liberalisation.[130] The decision to improve access for exporters from the Western Balkans to the single market creates a win-win situation, as it meets a paramount interest of the countries of the region (the European Union is by far their most important trading partner) and involves as good as no economic risks but plenty of benefits for the European Union.[131] As part of the SAP, the Council of Ministers implemented the decision taken by the European Council at Lisbon by adopting Council Regulation (EC) No. 2007/2000, which provided for duty and quota free access to the EU market for nearly all industrial products and most agricultural products from the Western Balkan countries.[132] Preferential quotas were retained, however, for baby-beef, fisheries and wine products.[133] While Council Regulation (EC) No. 2007/2000 was initially limited to Albania, Bosnia-Herzegovina, Croatia and certain 'territories' linked to the SAP (Kosovo and Montenegro),[134] its application was soon extended to Macedonia and, after the political uproar that led to the fall of the Milošević regime, to the whole territory of Serbia and Montenegro.[135] Council Regulation (EC) No. 2563/2000 improved the existing autonomous trade preferences and

---

130 *Bull. EU* 3-2000, point I.21.47.

131 The general level of imports from the Western Balkan countries is less than 1 per cent of all Community imports, whereas 70 per cent of all Croatian exports, for example, currently go to the European market. This means that the EU market can profit from an increased product diversification without having to fear that it will be swamped by products from the Western Balkans. Moreover, the market of the Western Balkans offers a huge potential for European exporters. See European Commission, Trade in South Eastern Europe, MEMO/06/155, 5 April 2006, and the portal of the WIIW Balkan Observatory for more statistics and research in relation to economic developments in south-eastern Europe, at: <http://www.wiiw.ac.at/balkan>.

132 Council Regulation (EC) No. 2007/2000 of 18 September 2000 introducing exceptional trade measures for countries and territories participating in or linked to the European Union's Stabilisation and Association process, amending Regulation (EC) No. 2820/98, and repealing Regulations (EC) No. 1763/1999 and (EC) No. 6/2000, *OJ* 2000 L 240/1, as amended by Council Regulation (EC) No 530/2007 of 8 May 2007, *OJ* 2007 L 125/1 to take account of the new contractual regime with Albania. The period of validity of Regulation (EC) No. 2007/2000 was prolonged until 31 December 2010 by Council Regulation (EC) No. 1946/2005 of 14 November 2005, *OJ* 2005 L 312/1.

133 See, e.g., Commission Regulation (EC) No. 2008/2006 of 22 December 2006 laying down detailed rules for the application in 2006 of the tariff quotas for baby beef products originating in Croatia, Bosnia and Herzegovina, the former Yugoslav Republic of Macedonia and Serbia and Montenegro, *OJ* 2006 L 379/105; and Commission Regulation (EC) No. 2088/2004 of 7 December 2004 amending Regulation (EC) No. 2497/2001 and Commission Regulation (EC) No. 2597/2001 as regards tariff quotas for certain fish and fishery products originating in Croatia and for certain wines originating in Croatia, the former Yugoslav Republic of Macedonia and Slovenia, *OJ* 2004 L 361/3.

134 In the case of Kosovo and Montenegro, limited trade preferences were granted for certain products that were not produced in other parts of the FRY, which remained excluded from EC trade preferences until November 2000.

135 Council Regulation (EC) No. 2563/2000 of 20 November 2000 amending Regulation (EC) No. 2007/2000 by extending to the Former Yugoslav Republic of Macedonia and the Federal Republic of Yugoslavia the exceptional trade measures for countries and territories participating in or linked to the European Union's stabilisation and association process and amending Regulation (EC) No. 2820/98, *OJ* 2000 L 295/1. Council Regulation (EC) No. 2007/2000 was also amended by Council Regulation (EC) No. 1946/2005 to take account of the fact that the Republic of Montenegro, the Republic of Serbia and Kosovo each constitute separate customs territories.

provided for an autonomous trade liberalisation of 95 per cent for all of the Western Balkan countries' exports to the European Union, meaning that imports of such products into the Union were to be admitted without quantitative restrictions or measures having equivalent effect. These arrangements were even more generous than those enjoyed by the ten new Member States before they joined the Union.[136] The Enlargement Protocols to the SAAs with Macedonia and Croatia did not change this, as they simply adapted the trade provisions of the SAAs to increase the volume of tariff quotas in order to take into account traditional trade between Macedonia and Croatia, on the one hand, and the ten new Member States, on the other. The quotas for fisheries and wine products from Macedonia and Croatia have thus been increased, thereby providing new export opportunities for these SAA countries.

The preamble to Council Regulation (EC) No. 2007/2000 on exceptional trade preferences refers to the political conditions enshrined in the Council Conclusions of 29 April 1997. The granting of autonomous trade preferences is linked to respect for fundamental principles of democracy and human rights, but political conditionality is not repeated in the operative part of the regulation. Article 2 links the granting of improved autonomous trade preferences in favour of countries participating in the SAP to their readiness to engage in effective economic reforms and regional cooperation, in particular through the establishment of free trade areas in line with Article XXIV of the 1994 GATT and other relevant WTO provisions. In addition, the entitlement to benefit from autonomous trade preferences is conditional on the beneficiaries' involvement in effective administrative cooperation with the Community in order to prevent any risk of fraud. According to the same Article 2, the Council may, in the event of non-compliance by one of the beneficiary countries, take 'appropriate measures' – thus including the suspension or withdrawal of exceptional trade preferences – by a qualified majority vote, on the basis of a Commission proposal. From a legal standpoint, exceptional trade preferences, which by definition go beyond the Community's general obligations stemming from its WTO membership, do not reflect a legally binding commitment on the part of the EC *vis-à-vis* beneficiary countries, provided that such preferences are not governed by bilateral agreements.[137] Therefore, any subsequent decision to suspend or withdraw these preferences in a specific situation remains at the discretion of the competent EU institutions. As indicated in the preamble to Council Regulation (EC) No. 2007/2000, such a decision will be based on all requirements set out by the

136 For a comparison, see P. Koutrakos, 'Free Movement of Goods under the Europe Agreements', in Ott and Inglis, op. cit. n. 3, pp. 369-390 at pp. 375-381.

137 See B. Brandtner and A. Rosas, 'Trade Preferences and Human Rights', in Alston, op. cit. n. 14, pp. 699-722 at p. 706.

Council in respect of the granting of autonomous trade preferences in its 29 April 1997 Conclusions, including respect for the fundamental principles of democracy and human rights. Hence, political conditionality is introduced via the back door.[138]

4. EUROPEAN PARTNERSHIPS: CONDITIONS AND CONSEQUENCES

At the Thessaloniki Summit in June 2003, it was determined that the SAP should be bolstered by new methods based on the experience of previous enlargements of the European Union. The chief of these is the introduction of the so-called 'European Partnerships'.[139] On 30 March 2004, the Council of Ministers approved the first-ever European Partnerships with Bosnia-Herzegovina, Macedonia, Albania and Serbia and Montenegro (including Kosovo as defined by UN Security Council resolution 1244 of 10 June 1999).[140] The first European Partnership with Croatia was published at the same time as the Commission's positive *avis* on Croatia's application for membership.[141] Due to the unsettled status of Kosovo, the Commission had proposed a separate list of priorities and recommendations, based on the 'Standards for Kosovo'.[142] Thus, the European Partnership with Serbia and Montenegro strengthened the existing 'standards before status' policy of the international community, even though this policy had long been declared dead in the region. At the same time, however, by treating Kosovo's priorities separately, the European Partnership gave tacit support for a decentralisation process, something Serbia vehemently opposed.[143] In the wake of the proclamation of independence by Montenegro on 3 June 2006, it was appropriate to

---

138 See Pippan, loc. cit. n. 17, at p. 231.

139 See *Bull. EU* 6-2003, point 1.6.70.

140 Council Decisions 2004/515/EC, 2004/518/EC, 2004/519/EC and 2004/520/EC, *OJ* 2004 L 221/10, L 222/20, L 223/20 and L 227/21, respectively. These acts were repealed and replaced by Council Decisions 2006/55/EC, 2006/57/EC, 2006/54/EC and 2006/56/EC, *OJ* 2006 L 35/19, 57, 1 and 32, respectively.

141 See Council Decision 2004/648/EC on the principles, priorities and conditions contained in the European Partnership with Croatia, *OJ* 2004 L 297/19, repealed and replaced by Council Decision 2006/145 on the principles, priorities and conditions contained in the *accession* partnership with Croatia, *OJ* 2006 L 55/30 [emphasis added] so as to reflect the new status of Croatia as a candidate for EU accession.

142 See chapter 4, section 3.3.1.

143 This situation was not remedied in the latest European Partnership with Serbia and Montenegro, including Kosovo, even though it was already clear at the moment of its adoption that final status talks would commence. This shows the EU Member States' firm belief that, by gradually merging the Standards for Kosovo into the European Partnership, the European Commission was creating a framework for credibly monitoring and accompanying Kosovo's development towards a stable and multi-ethnic society in the European mainstream.

establish a new European Partnership with Montenegro on the basis of the parts relating to it in the European Partnership with Serbia and Montenegro, updated in view of the 2006 progress report and supplemented with priorities addressing the challenges faced by the newly independent state. The first European Partnership with Montenegro was adopted on 22 January 2007.[144]

Modelled on the Accession Partnerships developed to prepare past aspirants for EU membership, the European Partnerships were heralded as a milestone in the relations between the European Union and the Western Balkan countries, but the difference in the qualifying adjective suggests otherwise: this time around, the emphasis is on 'partnership' rather than 'accession'. This impression is reinforced when one considers that, while the partnerships for the Western Balkan countries were first announced as 'European Integration Partnerships' in the Commission's proposal from 2003,[145] they were tellingly re-dubbed as 'European Partnerships' in Council Regulation (EC) No. 533/2004 of 22 March 2004, the basic legal act by which they are established.[146]

The first Accession Partnerships were endorsed by the European Council of Luxembourg in December 1997 as a key element for strengthening the pre-accession strategy for the candidate countries at the time. They set out the priorities for each country as they were preparing themselves to become members of the European Union. The first accession strategies were decided in March 1998 for the ten CEECs, in 2000 for Cyprus and Malta and in 2003 for Turkey. They highlighted the main instruments and financial resources available, which had to be maximised to target the objectives effectively. Each candidate country was supposed to establish a 'National Programme for the Adoption of the Acquis' (NPAA), setting out in detail the way in which the priorities would be realised. The Commission assessed each country's progress annually in its regular reports.[147]

---

144 Council Decision 2007/49/EC of 22 January 2007 on the principles, priorities and conditions contained in the European Partnership with Montenegro, *OJ* 2007 L 20/16. The adoption of a new constitution, the completion of the establishment of the legal and institutional set-up required for an independent country, including the signature and ratification of the international instruments to which the state union of Serbia and Montenegro had adhered, and the continuation of efforts to implement the reform of the public administration and the judiciary were mentioned as short-term key priorities.

145 European Commission, The Western Balkans and European Integration, COM (2003) 285 final, Brussels, 21 May 2003.

146 Council Regulation (EC) No. 533/2004 of 22 March 2004 on the establishment of the European Partnerships in the framework of the stabilisation and association process, *OJ* 2004 L 86/1. The Council rephrased the policy instrument as early as 16 June 2003. See Thessaloniki Agenda, in Annex A to Council Conclusions of 16 June 2003, Press Release No. 10369/03 (Presse 166).

147 See K. Inglis, 'The Europe Agreements Compared in the Light of Their Pre-accession Reorientation', 37 *CML Rev.* (2000) pp. 1173-1210 at p. 1184; K. Inglis, 'The Pre-Accession Strategy and the Accession Partnerships', in Ott and Inglis, op. cit. n. 3, pp. 103-111; and M. Maresceau, 'Pre-accession', in Cremona, op. cit. n. 3, pp. 9-42 at pp. 30-32.

While the European Partnerships are very similar to the Accession Partnerships, their legal basis is nevertheless different. Council Regulation (EC) No. 533/2004[148] is based on Article 181a(2) TEC rather than Article 308 TEC (ex Art. 235 TEC), which was the legal basis for Regulation (EC) No. 622/98 on the establishment of Accession Partnerships.[149] Since the entry into force of the Treaty of Nice, Article 181a(2) provides a specific legal basis for the adoption of European Partnerships, because it is the only provision that is capable of referring both to association agreements and agreements still 'to be concluded with the states which are candidates for accession to the Union'. As such, Article 181a(2) could appropriately serve as a legal basis for the adoption of European Partnerships with SAP countries that have either already signed an SAA (Macedonia and Croatia) or will do so in the future (Albania, Bosnia-Herzegovina, Montenegro and Serbia). But this conclusion hinges on the assumption that the interpretation of 'candidates' in Article 181a(2) equals 'potential candidates'. Unfortunately for the SAP countries, this liberal interpretation does not constitute a Freudian slip on the part of the EU institutions in the sense that, with the adoption of Council Regulation (EC) No. 533/2004, all Western Balkan states have indirectly been promoted to the level of candidate states. European Partnerships do not endow their addressees with candidate country status and cannot be thought of as pre-accession instruments in the same way as the Accession Partnerships, because they are used to programme the work of a range of states even *prior to* the existence of contractual relations with the European Union. The Accession Partnerships, on the other hand, were proposed to candidate countries that were recognised as such and already signatories to a Europe Agreement.[150]

On paper, the European Partnerships and the Accession Partnerships seem to offer the same framework, the same organisation and the same means of assessment. They are both structurally divided into short and medium-term priorities. Based on the Commission's annual SAP reports, the European Partnerships are tailored to each Western Balkan country's specific needs, setting out priorities for the short term (one to two years) and the medium term (three to four years). The Partnerships are intended to help governments concentrate reform efforts and available resources where they are most needed. The competent authorities are expected to respond with a detailed plan for the implementation of their state's European Partnership priorities, setting out the concrete measures to be taken, a

148 As amended by Council Regulation (EC) No. 269/2006 of 14 February 2006 on the establishment of the European Partnerships in the framework of the stabilisation and association process, *OJ* 2006 L 47/7, to take account of the establishment of an Accession Partnership for Croatia.

149 Council Regulation (EC) No. 622/98 of 16 March 1998 on assistance to the applicant States in the framework of the pre-accession strategy, and in particular on the establishment of Accession Partnerships, *OJ* 1998 L 85/1.

150 In a similar vein, see Inglis, loc. cit. n. 3.

timetable and demonstrating what human and financial resources will be devoted to the tasks involved – basically a sort of NPAA. The priorities identified in the European Partnerships will also influence the allocation of the financial assistance from the European Union. Thus, clearly, European Partnerships cannot be regarded as agreements. They are EU policy tools to encourage reforms and serve as checklists against which to measure progress. Furthermore, they provide guidance for Community and Member State financial assistance. They reflect the particular stages of development of each country and, to that end, all contain a conditionality clause: according to common recital 5 of the preamble to the European Partnerships, non-compliance with the 1993 Copenhagen political criteria and a lack of progress in meeting the specific priorities of the European Partnerships themselves could lead the Council to unilaterally suspend Community assistance under the SAP.[151] Community assistance is also subject to the conditions defined by the Council in its Conclusions of 29 April 1997 and 21-22 June 1999, in particular as regards the recipients' undertaking to carry out democratic, economic and institutional reforms.

In short, the added value of the European Partnerships lies primarily in the fact that their adoption represents a new step towards further integration with the European Union, as the SAP is increasingly being modelled on the pre-accession process of the CEECs. These policy instruments finally provide each of the countries with a timetable and a road map towards EU membership. The partnerships are necessary to measure progress and build motivation to persist with the painful reforms that are necessary to attract private domestic and foreign direct investment, help stimulate economic growth and overcome high unemployment. The timeframe for their implementation will of course depend on the pace of political and economic reform in each country.

5. FROM 'POTENTIAL' TO FULL MEMBERSHIP PERSPECTIVE

5.1 The meaning of 'potential' candidate country status

In contrast to the preambular reference to accession in the Europe Agreements, the preambles of the SAAs recall not simply the European Union's readiness to integrate Macedonia and Croatia 'to the fullest possible extent [...] into the political and economic mainstream of Europe' but also the status of the two associates as 'potential' candidates for EU membership. The membership perspective is set out in the final recital of the preamble to the two existing SAAs:

---

[151] The conditionality clause invokes Article 5 of the CARDS Regulation.

> [The contracting parties recall] the European Union's readiness to integrate to the fullest possible extent the [associate] into the political and economic mainstream of Europe and its status as a potential candidate for EU membership on the basis of the Treaty on European Union and fulfilment of the criteria defined by the European Council in June 1993, subject to successful implementation of this Agreement, notably regarding regional cooperation.

From the wording of the recital, as well as its *travaux préparatoires*, it becomes clear that, for reasons already explained, the inclusion of the membership perspective came against a background of reticence towards any firm commitment to admit the SAP countries into the European Union at a future date.[152] This is apparent in the Commission's May 1999 Communication on the SAP, which made no explicit mention of the word 'membership' at all, but instead referred to the SAAs as 'draw[ing] the region closer to the perspective of full integration into EU structures.'[153] One month later, the Cologne European Council agreed to a similar wording but acknowledged that this would be done 'with a prospect of EU membership on the basis of the Treaty of Amsterdam and fulfilment of the criteria defined at the Copenhagen European Council in June 1993.'[154] In the course of drawing up the SAAs, the European Union watered down the strength of the commitment.[155] The current wording of the recital follows declarations that were made at the June 2000 European Council in Santa Maria da Feira and at the Zagreb Summit of November 2000, to the effect that the Western Balkan countries are 'potential candidates' for EU membership.[156] Although this notion has no official definition and does not confer on the holder a legally enforceable right to membership, politically speaking, the term 'potential candidate' recognises the Union's willingness to see membership ambitions of the status holder realised in the future. In the words of Friis and Murphy:

> This promise, however vague and conditional, cannot be withdrawn [...]. [I]t will force the Union to increase its level of engagement with the region and to advance the on-going enlargement process [...]. [The] genie is now out of the bottle.[157]

---

152 See *supra* section 2.1. See also R. Biermann, 'Die Europäische Perspektive für den westlichen Balkan', 51 *Osteuropa* (2001) pp. 922-937 at pp. 926-927.

153 COM (1999) 235 final, Brussels, 26 May 1999, at 4.

154 *Bull. EU* 6-1999, point I.26.72.

155 See Biermann, loc. cit. n. 27, at pp. 15-19.

156 *Bull. EU* 6-2000, point I.49.67; and *Bull. EU* 11-2000, point I.6.57.

157 L. Friis and A. Murphy, 'Enlargement of the European Union: Impacts on the EU, the Candidates and the "Next Neighbours"', 14 *ECSA Rev.* (2001). Looked at from the perspective of Ukraine, for example, 'potential candidate' status is a rather significant commitment and one that was not, after all, offered to the CEECs.

However half-hearted the Member States' commitment to enlarging 'their' Union with the countries of south-eastern Europe may at first have seemed, the repeated confirmation of it[158] has provided the 'able and willing' governments of the Western Balkan states with a justification for difficult political and economic reforms and a means to rally support for tough decisions at home.[159] Croatia's bid for membership on 20 February 2003,[160] Macedonia's application for accession on 22 March 2004,[161] the eagerness of political leaders to guide Bosnia-Herzegovina into the European Union[162] and the successful efforts of Podgorica on a peaceful withdrawal from the state union of Serbia and Montenegro to speed up the process of European integration[163] all attest to the fact that the only worthwhile 'carrot' the European Union can offer the Western Balkan countries in exchange for concerted efforts to create lasting peace and stability in the region is the prospect of full membership.[164] The Union should therefore grant candidate country status to Albania, Bosnia-Herzegovina, Montenegro and Serbia (and – if independent – Kosovo) if and when these potential candidate countries formally apply for membership and meet all the relevant conditions (ex Art. 49 TEU).[165]

5.2 Revised procedure for accession negotiations

5.2.1 *Transitional v. permanent arrangements*

The European Council, at its 16-17 December 2004 summit in Brussels, agreed on a revised framework for every future round of accession negotiations, to be created 'according to own merits and specific situations and characteristics of

---

158 Most vocally at Zagreb in 2000 and Thessaloniki in 2003, *Bull. EU* 11-2000, point I.6.57 and *Bull. EU* 6-2003, point I.17, respectively.

159 Others have criticised the European Union's unwillingness to make a full commitment to integrate the countries concerned and have pointed out that an integration strategy that revolves around the promise of the perspective of membership does not necessarily trigger the reforms most needed in instable societies. See, e.g., Anastasakis and Bechev, op. cit. n. 39; and D. Triantaphyllou, 'The Balkans between Stabilisation and Integration', in J. Blatt, et al., 'Partners and Neighbours: A CFSP for a Wider Europe', 64 *Chaillot Papers* (2003) pp. 60-76.

160 See Doc. 6991/03 ELARG 19 COWEB 28.

161 See Council Conclusions of 17 May 2004, Press Release No. 9210/04 (Presse 149).

162 For a country whose governance is supervised by the international community and where the EU will maintain a military force (EUFOR Althea) and a police mission (EUPM) for some time to come, even 2014 seems an optimistic target date.

163 See chapter 4, section 3.2.4.

164 Increasingly louder calls from Western European political leaders for the European Union to grant so-called 'privileged partnerships' instead of full membership to countries like Turkey and Ukraine have recently been extended to include the Western Balkans. On these related developments, see *infra* section 6.4.

165 For an elaboration on this point, see chapter 6, section 2.1.1.1.

each candidate state.'[166] It adopted this new approach to soothe worries in some Member States over its decision to open accession talks with Turkey (most vocally France, Cyprus and Austria)[167] and, to a lesser extent, with Croatia (the Netherlands, the United Kingdom and Italy).[168] The European Council stressed, for instance, that long transition periods, derogations and specific arrangements could in the future be imposed in areas such as freedom of movement of persons, structural policies or agriculture.[169] The proliferation of different sorts of transitional arrangements in previous accession treaties[170] and the safeguard clauses included in the Accession Treaty with Bulgaria and Romania are indicative in this respect.[171] With respect to the latter, the proper use of a membership postponement clause, that is to say, in the absence of a promised date of entry (which is the new norm), an economic safeguard clause and internal market and JHA safeguard clauses are temporary measures that could act as a powerful lever for reform. More problematic is the fact that the European Council even went so far as to suggest that permanent safeguard clauses, defined as 'clauses which are permanently available as a basis for safeguard measures', could be imposed.[172] Although the introduction of permanent safeguard clauses seems reasonable from the political point of view of some Member States, it is highly questionable as a permanent solution for a 'constitutional' legal order like that of the European Union, for it would violate one of the most fundamental legal principles upon which it is built: the prohibition of discrimination on the ground of nationality.[173]

---

166 See *Bull. EU* 12-2004, point I.8.23.

167 For background and analysis, see E. Lenski, 'Turkey (including Northern Cyprus)', in Blockmans and Łazowski, op. cit. n. 3, pp. 283-313.

168 See *infra* section 5.3.

169 And all matters relating to freedom of movement of persons will allow 'a maximum role of [those] individual Member States' that are afraid that their labour market will be flooded by Turkish workers. The European Council emphasised that transitional arrangements or safeguards should be reviewed regarding their impact on competition or the functioning of the internal market.

170 See, e.g., K. Inglis, 'The Union's Fifth Accession Treaty: New Means to Make Enlargement Possible', 41 *CML Rev.* (2004) pp. 937-973; and K. Inglis, 'The Accession Treaty and Its Transitional Arrangements: A Twilight Zone for the New Members of the Union', in Hillion, op. cit. n. 3, pp. 77-109.

171 See A. Łazowski, 'And Then They Were Twenty-Seven... A Legal Appraisal of the Sixth Accession Treaty', 44 *CML Rev.* (2007) pp. 401-430 at pp. 410-419.

172 See *Bull. EU* 12-2004, point I.8.23.

173 See U. Becker, 'EU-Enlargements and Limits to Amendments of the EC Treaty', 15 *Jean Monnet Working Paper* (2001), available at: <http://www.jeanmonnetprogram.org>; A. Bodnar, 'Transitional Periods for Employment – "Second Class" EU Citizenship?', in O. Zetterquist, ed., *Law and Modernity* (Kraków, Polpress 2004) pp. 121-138; C. Hillion, 'The European Union is dead. Long live the European Union...', 29 *EL Rev.* (2004) pp. 583-612 at p. 593; and C. Hillion, 'You Cannot Have Your Cake and Eat It! The Limits to Member States' Discretion in EU Enlargement Negotiations', Inaugural lecture, Leiden University, 21 March 2006. For a more optimistic view, see D. Thym, *Ungleichzeitigkeit im Europäischen Verfassungsrecht* (Baden-Baden, Nomos 2002) at p. 341.

5.2.2 *Benchmarking*

Like in previous pre-accession rounds, all Member States will take part in chapter-by-chapter negotiations with each candidate. However, there will be more chapters to be negotiated by present and future candidate countries. Instead of the thirty-one chapters that Bulgaria and Romania had to negotiate, Croatia and Turkey are looking at thirty-five chapters. This is the result of both a technical rearrangement – certain chapters were considered too big and were chopped up and smaller ones were merged[174] – and the introduction of a new package on judiciary and human rights. The latter reflects a normative advancement in comparison with previous rounds of accession negotiations, as the political Copenhagen criteria on respect for democracy, human rights and the rule of law have now been incorporated into a so-called '*acquis* chapter'.[175] From now on, candidate countries will have to show that they have the administrative capacity to effectively apply and implement the *acquis* on democracy, the rule of law, human rights and – crucially when dealing with Western Balkan countries – minority rights.

Another novelty in the revised procedure agreed to by the December 2004 European Council concerns the right of the Council, acting by unanimity on a proposal by the Commission, to lay down benchmarks for the provisional closure and, where appropriate, (re)opening of each chapter. Depending on the chapter concerned, these benchmarks will refer to legislative alignment and a satisfactory track record of implementation of the *acquis* as well as obligations deriving from contractual relations with the European Union. Thus, after agreement has been reached between the Union and the candidate country on an individual chapter of the negotiations, and once the set benchmarks have been met, the respective chapter is considered *temporarily* closed. The formal decision is made by the Intergovernmental Conference at ministerial level. If, before the Accession Treaty has been concluded, new *acquis* falling within the scope of a specific chapter is developed or if the candidate country does not meet the set benchmarks or obligations assumed under the chapter concerned, negotiations on that chapter can be reopened. The revised procedure thus provides for an extra 'stick behind the door' to make sure that candidate countries deliver on each of the chapters,

---

174 For example, the chapter on free movement of persons was divided into a chapter on free movement of workers and one dealing with the right of establishment and the free movement of services; the chapter on agriculture was separated into a chapter on agriculture and rural development and one on food safety, veterinary and phytosanitary policy. On the other hand, the chapters on industrial policy and small and medium-sized enterprises were merged into one chapter on enterprise and industrial policy.

175 For a critical legal appraisal of the European Union's application of pre-accession conditionality in the fields of democracy and the rule of law in the run-up to the two previous rounds of enlargements, see D. Kochenov, *The Failure of Conditionality* (Groningen, Ph.D thesis 2007).

something about which the Commission had become distrustful since the fifth round of enlargement negotiations. In fact, the December 2004 European Council stated that the new frameworks for negotiations would be established by the Council on a proposal by the Commission, 'taking account of the experience of the fifth enlargement process and of the evolving *acquis*'. Under the terms of the frameworks, 'the shared objective of the negotiations is accession', but 'the outcome cannot be guaranteed beforehand.'

In one way, the European Council merely stated the obvious, namely that accession negotiations have – and have always had – an open-ended character, but the political signal towards new candidate countries cannot be underestimated. They have to comply with the conditions and stick to the rules or see their pre-accession path (partially) blocked by the European Union. In cases where a candidate seriously and persistently breaches the principles of liberty, democracy, respect for human rights, fundamental freedoms and the rule of law, negotiations can be suspended altogether. In such cases, the Commission will, on its own initiative or at the request of one third of the Member States, recommend the suspension of negotiations and propose conditions for their eventual resumption. On receiving such a recommendation, the Council will decide by qualified majority, after having heard the candidate state, whether to suspend the negotiations and what the conditions for their resumption should be. The procedure further prescribes that Member States will act in the IGC in accordance with the Council decision, without prejudice to the general requirement for unanimity in the IGC, and that the European Parliament will be informed. However, if a candidate is not in a position to assume in full all the obligations of membership – diplomatic language for a failure in negotiating accession – the European Union will nevertheless ensure 'that the candidate state concerned is fully anchored in the European structures through the strongest possible bond'. Supposedly, the one-time candidate would then fall back to its status as an associate.[176]

5.3 **Croatia**

On 17-18 June 2004, the European Council finally crossed the Rubicon when it decided to follow up on the Commission's positive *avis* on Croatia's application for membership and grant candidate status to the country, thereby opening it up to increased financial and technical assistance.[177] At its Brussels summit in December 2004, the European Council requested the Council of Ministers to agree on a negotiating framework with a view to opening accession negotiations with

---

176 See S. Blockmans and A. Łazowski, 'Conclusions: Squaring the Circle of Friends', in Blockmans and Łazowski, op. cit. n. 3, pp. 613-639.

177 For the *avis*, see COM (2004) 257 final, Brussels, 20 April 2004; for the decision by the European Council, see *Bull. EU* 6-2004, point I.7.31. See further *supra* n. 118.

Croatia on 17 March 2005, thereby rewarding Croatia's ongoing preparations for membership with a firm date for starting accession talks.[178] The opportunity, however, was subject to an equally firm condition: full and unequivocal cooperation with the ICTY. Croatia was given exactly three months to 'smoke Ante Gotovina out of his hole' and hand him over to the ICTY in The Hague.[179] Despite strong eleventh-hour lobbying by Croatia to prevent the consequences of its failure to arrest and extradite Gotovina, 'the absence of a common agreement' among the twenty-five EU Member States on the issue of full cooperation with the ICTY led the Council to take the unprecedented decision to postpone the start of membership talks.[180] The Council was careful, however, to underline that accession negotiations with Croatia could open as soon as there was proof that Croatia was fully cooperating with the Tribunal. To prove its point, but without offering an early resolution of the standoff, the Council adopted the negotiating mandate for the Commission[181] and created a special task force to monitor Zagreb's cooperation with the ICTY.[182] Just hours ahead of the crucial 'enlargement' meeting of the Council of Ministers on 3 October 2005 in Luxembourg, the task force gave its positive opinion after it was informed by the Chief Prosecutor of the ICTY that, despite the fact that Gotovina remained at large, Croatia was 'cooperating fully' with the Tribunal.[183] Noting the clear commitment by the

---

[178] See *Bull. EU* 12-2004, point I.6.16. For a description and analysis of the road travelled by Croatia to get to that point, and a little further, see D. Jović, 'Croatia and the European Union: A Long Delayed Journey', 8 *Journal of Southern Europe and the Balkans* (2006) pp. 85-103.

[179] See *supra* n. 55.

[180] Council Conclusions of 16 March 2005, Press Release No. 6969/05 (Presse 44); reproduced in *Bull. EU* 3-2005, point 1.5.1.

[181] Ibid.

[182] See L. Kubosova, 'EU to send monitoring team to Croatia', *EUObserver.com*, 23 March 2005. Chaired by the Minister of Foreign Affairs of Luxembourg, the task force brought together representatives of the Commission, the SG/HR and the next two EU Presidencies (the United Kingdom and Austria). These two countries held diametrically opposed views during the Council debate of 16 March 2005. The United Kingdom was against the opening of negotiations because it was convinced that Croatia was not fully cooperating with the ICTY. Austria, on the other hand, wanted to open membership talks with Croatia on 17 March 2005, because such a decision would enhance Austria's economic and political position in the region.

[183] Carla del Ponte was heavily criticised by her own staff for the sudden U-turn in the approach taken towards Croatia. She was reported as having said at a press conference in Luxembourg, that '[f]or a few weeks now, Croatia has been cooperating fully with us and is doing everything it can to locate and arrest Ante Gotovina.' This statement stood in sharp contrast to what the Chief Prosecutor said after a one-and-a-half-hour meeting with Prime Minister Ivo Sanader and President Stipe Mesić in Zagreb on 30 September 2005: 'You cannot imagine how disappointed I am. [The] prime minister has promised me full cooperation but we still have the same problem. Gotovina is still at large.' It is thought that del Ponte succumbed to heavy political pressure. The Chief Prosecutor herself denied such allegations. See 'Carla del Ponte bescheinigt Zagreb überraschend "uneingeschränkte Zusammenarbeit" bei der Kriegsverbrecher-Suche', *Süddeutsche Zeitung*, 4 October 2005. Whatever the case may be, del Ponte's announcement on 3 October greatly facilitated agreement by Austria – a strong ally of Croatia – on the opening of accession talks with Turkey, which Vienna had blocked until the last minute. Incidentally or otherwise, Gotovina was arrested on 7 December 2005. See *supra* n. 55.

Croatian Prime Minister that full cooperation would be maintained until the last remaining indictee was in The Hague and as long as required by the ICTY, the Council of Ministers concluded that Croatia had fulfilled the outstanding condition for the start of accession negotiations.[184] The accession negotiations were officially launched immediately after the Council meeting, that is to say, in the early hours of 4 October 2005.[185]

The formal start of the accession negotiations was followed by the opening of the so-called 'screening process' by the Commission on 20 October 2005. In the course of this process, the degree of harmonisation of national legislation with the *acquis* is subjected to an analytical examination. This examination is conducted individually for each chapter. Following the screening process in respect of Croatia, which was completed on 23 October 2006, the decision on opening the negotiations on individual chapters, depending on the evaluated readiness of Croatia, is made by the Member States within the Council.[186] During this phase, the subject of the negotiations is the conditions under which Croatia will have to adopt and implement the *acquis* in the respective chapter, including the transitional periods that Croatia may have requested during the screening phase. Chapters that might raise difficulties in Croatia's accession negotiations include: 'free movement of capital' (in view of the currently very tolerant Croatian laws that allow EU citizens to purchase real estate), 'competition policy' (in view of the fact that Croatia spends a greater percentage of its national wealth on state aid to companies than any EU Member State) and 'judiciary and human rights' (rights of minorities, refugee return, impartial prosecution of war crimes trials, judicial and public administration reform and fighting corruption).[187] It was in a

---

[184] See Council Conclusions of 3 October 2005, Press Release No. 12514/1/05 REV 1 (Presse 241). The Council confirmed that sustaining full cooperation with the ICTY would remain a requirement for progress throughout the accession process. It invited the Commission to continue to monitor this closely, on the basis of regular reports from the ICTY, and report back to the Council if full cooperation was not maintained. The Council noted that an assessment of cooperation with the ICTY would form part of the Commission's reports to the Council on Croatia's fulfilment of the political criteria. The Council agreed that less than full cooperation with the ICTY at any stage would affect the overall progress of the negotiations and could be grounds for triggering the mechanism in para. 12 of the negotiating framework.

[185] The UK Presidency insisted that negotiations had been opened on 3 October 2005, that is to say, before 24:00 hrs GMT.

[186] According to the European Council, the difficult policy dossiers, such as those on administrative and judicial reforms and the fight against corruption, will be opened early. See European Council Conclusions of 14-15 December 2006, Press Release No. 16879/06 CONCL 3, Brussels, 15 December 2006, para. 7. In this way, the European Union avoids giving the impression that the negotiations will be easy.

[187] These items were highlighted by the President of the Commission in his speech to the Croatian *Sabor*. See J. Barroso, 'Leading by example: Croatia's road to EU membership', Zagreb, 16 February 2006, SPEECH/06/96. More generally, see T. Ćapeta, D. Mihelin and S. Rodin, 'Croatia', in A.E. Kellermann, J. Czuczai, S. Blockmans, A. Albi and W.Th. Douma, *The Impact of EU Accession on the Legal Orders of New EU Member States and (Pre-)Candidate Countries* (The Hague, T.M.C. Asser Press 2006) pp. 69-112; and S. Rodin and I. Goldner, 'National Report for Croatia', presented at FIDE 2006 (<http://www.fide2006.org>).

different dossier, however, that Croatia has the dubious honour of being the first candidate country ever to experience the discomfort of the revised accession negotiation procedure.[188] In an unprecedented move, Slovenia briefly blocked the opening of EU-Croatia negotiations on the next chapter of EU legislation by not giving its approval to a European Commission screening report on the extent to which Croatia's fisheries legislation conformed to the *acquis*. Slovenia argued that Croatia had failed to implement a bilateral border agreement on the basis of which Slovenian fishermen (operating from the Bay of Piran, Slovenia's sole outlet to sea and the object of a dispute between the two countries since their secession from the SFRY in 1991) should be able to enjoy a right of passage through Croatian waters.[189] The blockage by Slovenia served as a brief beating of the drums to raise awareness among EU members of the country's outstanding land and sea border disputes with Croatia and to warn the latter to solve the matter or risk a real interruption of the accession negotiations process.[190]

From here onwards, until the conclusion of the Accession Treaty, the revised procedure as described above will be applied.[191] Croatia is hoping to conclude its EU membership talks by 2008, so that it can take part in the European Parliament elections of 2009.[192]

---

188 In a much more widely publicised incident, Turkey was the first candidate country to see the opening of eight of its accession negotiation chapters suspended by the European Union until it opens its air and seaports to planes and ships from EU Member State Cyprus. See European Council Conclusions of 14-15 December 2006, Press Release No. 16879/06 CONCL 3, Brussels, 15 December 2006, para. 10, with reference to the conclusions of the Council of Ministers (GAERC), Press Release No. 16289/06 (Presse 352), 11 December 2006, at 8-9. See S. Blockmans, 'Reconciling "Widening" and "Deepening" of the European Union: Consolidating the Enlargement Agenda for South Eastern Europe', in S. Blockmans, S. Prechal and W.Th. Douma, eds., *Reconciling 'Deepening' and 'Widening' of the European Union* (The Hague, T.M.C. Asser Press 2007), forthcoming.

189 See H. Mahony, 'Slovenia blocks EU-Croatia talks over fishing dispute', *EUObserver.com*, 19 October 2006; and N. MacDonald, 'Rocky Road from Independence to EU Accession', *Financial Times*, 30 October 2006. See also the warning in the conclusions of the Council of Ministers (GAERC), Press Release No. 16289/06 (Presse 352), 11 December 2006, at 10.

190 A call from MEPs on Croatia and Slovenia to resolve this issue in arbitration if negotiations would be unsuccessful was kept out of the European Parliament's report on Croatia's progress towards accession in 2006. See EP Committee on Foreign Affairs, Report on Croatia's 2006 progress report (2006/2288 (INI)), No. A6-0092/2007 final, 29 March 2007, prepared by rapporteur Hannes Swoboda; and 'EP President urges Croatia, Slovenia to resolve border dispute without international arbitration', *Southeast European Times*, 15 March 2007.

191 For more details on the negotiations on the accession of Croatia to the European Union, see the website specifically designed by the Ministry of Foreign Affairs and European Integration for the Negotiating Team for the Accession of the Republic of Croatia to the European Union, at: <http://www.eu-pregovori.hr/default.asp?ru=447&sid=&akcija=&jezik=2>.

192 See K. Grabar-Kitarović, 'Guest Editorial. The Stabilization and Association Process: The EU's Soft Power at Its Best', 12 *EFA Rev.* (2007) pp. 121-125. In a speech for the French Parliament on 6 June 2006, Olli Rehn had shut the European Union's doors until 2010, or at least until new rules on the internal functioning of the Union had entered into force. See O. Rehn, 'Elaborer un nouveau consensus sur l'élargissement', Paris, 6 June 2006, SPEECH/06/345.

5.4 Macedonia

When the Council requested the Commission to give its opinion on Macedonia's application for accession on 1 October 2004, the Commission submitted to the Macedonian authorities a questionnaire with over 2,500 questions on the political, economic and administrative situation in the country. The answers, which were transferred to the Commission on 14 February 2005, formed the basis for the *avis* on the start of accession negotiations. In the preparation of its opinion, the Commission also used feedback from its delegation in Skopje and from the international organisations active in the country, as well as statistical and economic information from sources such as the OECD and the IMF. On 9 November 2005, the Commission published its *avis*.[193] Despite the Commission's positive stance towards the opening of accession negotiations with Macedonia, the granting of candidate country status was thrown into doubt when France threatened the other Member States that they would have to put all enlargement issues aside if the Council could not agree on its financial perspective for 2007-2013, the first budget to include the ten new Member States.[194] After two days of nervous negotiations, the European Council of December 2005 reached an agreement on the financial perspective,[195] thereby averting the threat of deep political rifts within the Union as well as delays over further enlargement. Macedonia was granted EU candidate country status in the early morning hours of 17 December 2005.[196] The European Council spoke highly of Macedonia's 'significant progress' in implementing the Ohrid Framework Agreement, securing minority rights, implementing the SAA and fulfilling the political criteria for EU membership, but made it clear that Skopje's new status did *not* automatically mean the opening of accession negotiations. For that, Macedonia would first have to show 'further significant progress' in each of the above-mentioned domains.[197] Crucially, the European Council also referred to the debate on the 2005 Enlargement Strategy Paper,[198] as first provided for by the Council on 12 December 2005,[199] and the Union's own 'absorption capacity' as two of the 'specific

---

193 COM (2005) 562, Brussels, 9 November 2005.

194 See A. Rettman, 'Macedonia should not be held hostage, Denmark says', *EUObserver.com*, 15 December 2005.

195 *Bull. EU* 12-2005, point I.4.6.

196 *Bull. EU* 12-2005, point I.12.24.

197 *Bull. EU* 12-2005, point I.12.25.

198 COM (2005) 561 final, SEC (2005) 1421-1424, 1426, 1428 and 1433, Brussels, 9 November 2005.

199 *Bull. EU* 12-2005, point 1.5.4. The Council concluded that the 2005 Enlargement Strategy Paper prepared by the Commission was a good basis for discussion on enlargement in 2006, but it also noted that 'care should be taken to anchor and develop support for the enlargement process across the EU, to ensure effective conditionality at all stages of the process in a fair and rigorous way, and to reiterate encouragement to reform and stability to all candidate countries, particularly the western Balkans.'

benchmarks' for taking 'further steps'.[200] Thus, the start of Macedonia's entry talks has been tied to the much broader debate among the EU Member States on the Union's future and its ability to absorb more newcomers. Bilateral issues may also feature. The Greek government, for example, has announced that it will veto Macedonia's accession to the European Union if the country seeks to accede as 'Macedonia', as opposed to its internationally recognised name, currently the Former Yugoslav Republic of Macedonia.[201] Accordingly, it may take months, possibly years, before Skopje actually opens membership talks. This casts a gloomy spell over the rest of the region's membership prospects.

6. INTEGRATION CAPACITY OF THE EUROPEAN UNION

6.1 Shortcomings of the Treaty of Nice

EU enlargement conditionality does not only include conditions, incentives and disincentives that apply to candidate countries but also focuses on the European Union. The Copenhagen European Council of June 1993 made the Union responsible for ensuring its own 'capacity to absorb new members, while maintaining the momentum of European integration'.[202] Institutional reform has been a constant in the EC/EU's history and each enlargement since 1973 has emphasised the dilemma of the strain that 'widening' puts on the 'deepening' of the European integration process. However, the need to reform the institutional architecture of the Union to keep the motor of the integration process running became increasingly pressing with the prospect of the accession of ten new Member States in 2004. Although the pre-Nice IGC did not effectively deal with the so-called 'Amsterdam left-overs' (e.g., the size of the Commission, voting weights in the Council and further moves towards qualified majority voting),[203] enlargement went ahead as scheduled. It has stretched the operational capacity of the EU institutions to the maximum. Further enlargements will accentuate – almost certainly aggravate – the problems facing the Union in terms of its decision-making capacity and the continued evolution, implementation and enforcement of the *acquis*. Moreover, the current legal framework, as provided for by the Treaty of Nice, does not cater for the integration of any other states than those with

---

200 *Bull. EU* 12-2005, point I.12.25.

201 See 'Greece to say "No" to FYROM', *Euractiv.com*, 2 September 2005. On the name issue, see chapter 1, section 5.1 and chapter 3, section 2.6.4.

202 *Bull. EU* 6-1993, point 13. See, e.g., Olli Rehn, 'The European Community and the Challenge of a Wider Europe', *Sussex Working Papers in Contemporary European Studies*, No. 6, July 1994.

203 See G. Edwards, 'Reforming the Union's Institutional Framework: A New EU Obligation?', in Hillion, op. cit. n. 3, pp. 23-43.

which accession negotiations had already started prior to the Nice summit (Bulgaria and Romania).[204] Therefore, the institutional arrangements for taking in today's candidate countries – Croatia, Macedonia and Turkey – are still to be made.

6.2 Constitutional impasse

The Treaty establishing a Constitution for Europe (TCE), which was signed on 29 October 2004 in Rome by the Heads of State and Heads of Government of the twenty-five Member States and Bulgaria, Romania and Turkey in their capacity as candidate countries and observers to the IGC, was intended to improve the democracy, transparency and efficiency of the European Union's decision-making processes in light of, *inter alia*, the ongoing enlargement process.[205] After its signing, the Constitutional Treaty was ratified by more than half of the Member States, representing more than half of the Union's population.[206] According to Article IV-447 TCE, the Constitutional Treaty could only enter into force when ratified by each of the high contracting parties in accordance with their own constitutional procedures and the ratification was officially notified by all the signatory states (excluding Turkey). The entry into force of the Constitutional Treaty was thrown into doubt after voters in France and the Netherlands rejected the text of the Treaty in referenda held on 29 May 2005 and 1 June 2005, respectively.[207] In the light of these results and facing a clear risk of a similar outcome in referenda that had been scheduled in Denmark and Ireland, as well as the decision of the British government to suspend the parliamentary ratification process, the European Council, meeting on 16 and 17 June 2005, considered that the date initially planned for a report on ratification of the Treaty (1 November 2006 according to Art. IV-447 TCE), was no longer tenable, since those countries which had not yet ratified the Treaty would be unable to furnish a clear reply before mid-2007.[208] A period of reflection, explanation and discussion was announced by the Commission for all countries, whether or not they had ratified

---

[204] *OJ* 2001 C 80/1, Declaration No. 20 on the enlargement of the European Union.

[205] *OJ* 2004 C 310/1. For background and analysis on the Constitutional Treaty, see, *inter alia*, D. Curtin, A.E. Kellermann and S. Blockmans, eds., *The EU Constitution: The Best Way Forward?* (The Hague, T.M.C. Asser Press 2005).

[206] An up-to-date overview is presented at: <http://europa.eu.int/constitution/index_en.htm>.

[207] By 54.68 per cent and 61.6 per cent of the voters, respectively (turnout was 69.3 per cent and 62.8 per cent). For background and analysis, see J. Ziller, 'France: Revision of the Constitution and Popular Rejection', in A. Albi and J. Ziller, eds., *The European Constitution and National Constitutions: Ratification and Beyond* (The Hague, Kluwer Law International 2007) pp. 103-112; and L. Besselink, 'The Netherlands: Ratification Referendum and Impact on the Constitution', ibid., pp. 113-123.

[208] *Bull. EU* 6-2005, point I-30.

the EU Constitution.[209] The state of discussions on the ratification of the Constitutional Treaty and the future of the Union was again examined by the European Council at its summit of December 2006,[210] on the basis of the Commission's communication on the enlargement strategy and – in Annex I thereof – its special report on the European Union's capacity to integrate new members.[211] The European Council agreed with the Commission that after the completion of the sixth wave of enlargement, with the accession of Bulgaria and Romania, an institutional settlement should precede any further enlargement of the Union. This way, the efficient and harmonious functioning of the Union would be ensured. To this end, the European Council set a timetable for continuing the institutional reform, starting with a political declaration adopted in Berlin on 25 March 2007, the day that the Member States celebrated the fiftieth anniversary of the Treaties of Rome.[212] The necessary steps to achieve a new institutional settlement (i.e., a new IGC and ratification of a reform treaty) should have been taken by mid-2009, so that the newly-appointed Commission and newly-elected European Parliament can start working under the new rules. Therefore, the Constitutional Treaty as we know it in the form of the document published in the *Official Journal* in October 2004 is dead.[213]

6.3 Enlargement as a casualty?

The resounding 'No' votes in France and the Netherlands have been said to reflect a variety of factors. The French 'No' is widely thought to have been due to the voters' stubborn dislike of being ordered around by their own politicians and

---

209 EC Press Release IP/05/995, 'Listen, Communicate, Go Local – New Commission approach to dialogue and communication with European citizens', Brussels, 20 June 2005.

210 More or less in line with Declaration No. 30 on the ratification of the Treaty establishing a Constitution for Europe, annexed to the Final Act of the IGC: 'The Conference notes that if, two years after the signature of the Treaty establishing a Constitution for Europe, four fifths of the Member States have ratified it and one or more Member States have encountered difficulties in proceeding with ratification, the matter will be referred to the European Council.'

211 See European Council Conclusions of 14-15 December 2006, Press Release No. 16879/06 CONCL 3, Brussels, 15 December 2006; and Communication from the Commission to the European Parliament and the Council, Enlargement Strategy and Main Challenges 2006-2007 Including annexed special report on the EU's capacity to integrate new members, COM (2006) 649 final, Brussels, 8 November 2006. For a critical analysis of the concept of integration capacity, see M. Emerson, et al., *Just what is this 'Absorption Capacity' of the European Union* (Brussels, CEPS 2006); and F. Amtenbrink, 'On the European Union's Institutional Capacity to Cope with Further Enlargement', in S. Blockmans, S. Prechal and W.Th. Douma, eds., *Reconciling 'Deepening' and 'Widening' of the European Union* (The Hague, T.M.C. Asser Press, 2007), forthcoming.

212 The Berlin Declaration is available on the website of the German EU Presidency, at: <http://www.eu2007.de>.

213 In this respect, see already Paul Magnette at the symposium on the future of the constitutional process of the European Union, organised by the Constitutional Affairs' Committee of the European Parliament, Brussels, 13-14 October 2005, as reported in *NRC Handelsblad*, 14 October 2005, but not in the European Parliament's press release on the event, Ref. No. 20051010IPR01195, 'EU Constitution: seeking a way forward'.

bureaucrats; worries that the Constitutional Treaty would move the European Union in an 'Anglo-Saxon' direction economically; general concerns about the development of the Union, especially a perceived reduction of France's influence in the enlarged Union, combined with a perceived threat posed by the proverbial Polish plumber to the French labour force; and last, but certainly not least, opposition to the possible future EU membership of Turkey.[214] The referendum in the Netherlands embraced all the insecurities that have led to the disenchantment of voters: from unemployment and strained welfare systems, to immigration and cultural cohesion.[215]

It is striking to note that the negative outcome of both referenda was to a considerable extent due to hostility to enlargement. One year after the 'big bang' enlargement of the European Union, French and Dutch voters seemed to suffer from both 'enlargement blues' (the impact of the 2004 enlargement) and 'enlargement fears' (the prospect of further expansion of the Union). As far as the latter is concerned, France's CSA polling institute found in an exit-poll on the day of the referendum that, for 79 per cent of all French 'No' voters, Turkey's possible entry into the European Union was a reason for their opposition.[216] In its exit poll on the day of the referendum, the renowned Maurice de Hond institute in the Netherlands found that 41 per cent of the Dutch 'No' voters were motivated by opposition to enlargement.[217] The same proportion of Dutch opponents to the Constitutional Treaty saw the prospect of Turkey's entry into the European Union as a threat to cherished liberal and secular values.[218]

Whereas early indicators pointed out that enlargement was one of the main, if not the most important reason for the astounding 'No' votes in France and the Netherlands, this reading of the outcome of the referenda was heavily played down in the following weeks, especially by the European Commission. In-depth voter analyses conducted by the Commission's Directorate General for Press and Communication showed that further enlargement of the European Union featured very far down on the list of reasons why the French and the Dutch voted against the EU Constitution. Eurobarometer studies on the referenda in France and the Netherlands had 3 per cent of French and 8 per cent of the Dutch 'No' voters saying that enlargement was the reason for their negative vote.[219] And only 6 per

214 See Ziller, loc. cit. n. 207.

215 See Besselink, loc. cit. n. 207.

216 See CSA, *Le vote au référendum sur le traité constitutionnel: explication du vote et perspectives politiques*, sondage sortie des urnes réalisé le 29 mai 2004, available at: <http://www.csa-tmo.fr/dataset/data2005/opi20050529d.pdf>.

217 Data available at: <http://www.peil.nl>.

218 Figures reproduced in W. Horsley, 'EU's 'enlargement blues'', *BBC News*, 3 June 2005.

219 European Commission, Flash EB 171, 'La Constitution européenne: sondage post-référendum en France', June 2005, available at: <http://europa.eu.int/comm/public_opinion/flash/fl171_fr.pdf>; and Flash EB 172, 'The European Constitution: post-referendum survey in the Netherlands', June 2005, available at: <http://europa.eu.int/comm/public_opinion/flash/fl172_en.pdf>.

cent and 3 per cent of them, respectively, allegedly said specifically that further expansion to include Turkey was the reason.[220] European Commissioner for Enlargement Olli Rehn added to the spinning of the referenda results by saying that 'it would be a misinterpretation to highlight [the] issue [of enlargement] as the decisive cause of the No vote, when the sense of insecurity and social discontent stemming from high unemployment played a much bigger role.'[221] While the latter may be true, it does seem slightly odd that no explanations were giving for the Commission's dramatically different insights into the motives of French and Dutch voters to reject the Constitutional Treaty. But the rationale behind the Commission's totally different take on the disastrous referenda is obvious. It feared that the Union's enlargement plans could get snarled up in a much bigger argument between rival groups of Member States that disagree about the long-term objectives of the Union, its shape and final borders and that this could lead certain Member States suffering from enlargement *fatigue* to retreat from the Union's commitments under the consolidated enlargement agenda towards south-eastern Europe.[222]

6.4 **'Privileged partnerships'**

On several occasions since the 'big bang' enlargement, half a score of primarily French and German political leaders have insisted that the European Union should pause for breath, consolidate and grant a 'privileged partnership' instead of full EU membership to big neighbouring countries such as Turkey and Ukraine.[223] From those statements, it is not clear what exactly is to be understood by the concept of 'privileged partnership', other than the creation of 'arrangements that would bring maximum benefits to all sides without endangering the EU itself.'[224] While one's first thoughts immediately go in the direction of the

---

[220] Ibid.

[221] See O. Rehn, 'Europe at a Crossroads: Enlargement, Constitution and the Future of the EU', Brussels, 20 June 2005, SPEECH/05/363.

[222] See D. Phinnemore, 'Beyond 25 – The Changing Face of EU Enlargement: Commitment, Conditionality and the Constitutional Treaty', 8 *Journal of Southern Europe and the Balkans* (2006) pp. 7-26.

[223] See, e.g., L. Harding and N. Watt, 'Turkey's EU dream dealt double blow as Chirac and Merkel raise doubts', *The Guardian*, 27 August 2005; L. Kubosova, 'Sarkozy calls for definition of "borders of Europe"', *EUObserver.com*, 31 March 2006; V. Giscard d'Estaing, 'A better European bridge to Turkey', *Financial Times*, 25 November 2004; and A. Leparmentier, 'UE: les turcosceptiques durcissent leurs positions', *Le Monde*, 16 November 2004. Austrian Chancellor Wolfgang Schüssel used the argument as *ultimum remedium* to block a unanimous decision on the opening of accession talks with Turkey until the other Member States agreed to do the same for Croatia. See A. Browne, 'Turkey left out in cold as Austria digs in heels over EU entry talks', *The Times*, 3 October 2005.

[224] A poor definition offered by Wolfgang Schäuble (then deputy head of Germany's CDU/CSU group which brought Angela Merkel to power after winning the parliamentary elections in 2005) in a response to an article by David Phillips in Foreign Affairs. See W. Schäuble, 'A Still-European Union', 83 *Foreign Affairs* (2004) at p. 134.

partnership and 'privileges' offered by the European Union in the framework of the European Neighbourhood Policy (ENP),[225] this is apparently not what the likes of Germany's Chancellor Angela Merkel and France's President Nicolas Sarkozy have in mind. Turkey and Ukraine are too big and strategically important for the Union, in (geo)political as well as economic terms, to be put in the same category with countries like Azerbaijan and Lebanon. The Union cannot suffice by granting these countries enhanced trade relations and increased financial and technical assistance. Some sort of 'third way' is implied, whereby Turkey and Ukraine would be granted a special status in relation to the Union that would go beyond a customs union but would not envisage any Turkish or Ukrainian participation in the Union's common policies (e.g., structural funds and agriculture), except – for obvious reasons – in the fields of security and defence. The free movement of goods, services and even capital would be guaranteed, but the Union's labour market would remain closed.[226] This situation could be created either by granting *full* membership to the countries in question, albeit with the permanent safeguard clauses proposed under the revised procedure for accession negotiations,[227] or by concluding an international agreement between the European Union and the countries concerned that is based on a customs union and otherwise comes as close to the *acquis* as politically acceptable. Setting aside the legal obstacles, both options represent a position that, politically speaking, is unwise to adopt when one is concerned with the positioning of the European Union on the international scene. By abandoning the commitments made towards Turkey, the Union would create an image of itself as an unreliable negotiating partner and potentially destabilise domestic politics in Turkey, with all imaginable consequences.

More troubling, especially in the context studied here, is the fact that German Chancellor Angela Merkel was the first Head of Government to publicly suggest a loose partnership option for the Western Balkans.[228] Merkel's statement came just days after EU Ministers of Foreign Affairs struggled to find common wording for their aims towards the region after their (ultimately not so) informal

225 See Communication from the Commission, European Neighbourhood Policy Strategy Paper, COM (2004) 373 final, Brussels, 12 May 2004. Related strategy papers, action plans, progress reports and other relevant documents are available on the Commission's ENP website, at: <http://europa.eu.int/comm/world/enp/index_en.htm>. From the growing body of literature on the ENP, see, e.g., M. Cremona, 'The European Neighbourhood Policy: Legal and Institutional Issues', *CDDRL Working Papers* No. 25, 2 November 2004; M. Emerson, *European Neighbourhood Policy: Strategy or Placebo?* (Brussels, CEPS 2004); R. Dannreuther, ed., *European Union Foreign and Security Policy: Towards a Neighbourhood Strategy* (London, Routledge 2004); and Blockmans and Łazowski, loc. cit. n. 176.

226 See J. Horstmann, 'Türkei: Ungeliebtner Partner', *cafebabel.com*, 27 February 2004.

227 For a legal critique, see *supra* section 5.2.1.

228 See E. Krasniqi and M. Beunderman, 'Merkel moots "privileged partnership" for Balkans', *EUObserver.com*, 17 March 2006.

meeting with leaders from the Western Balkans in Salzburg on 10-11 March 2006. A draft statement had avoided the term 'membership' while confirming the EU accession goal in more general terms. After strong overnight pressure from the Balkan states, the final statement read:

> [T]he EU confirms that the future of the Western Balkans lies in the European Union. […] All [Western Balkans states] have in the last year made significant steps along their road towards the EU, with EU membership as ultimate goal in conformity with the Thessaloniki Declaration.[229]

But diplomats from the Western Balkans lost the battle to remove the notion 'absorption capacity' from the final text. 'The EU also notes that its absorption capacity has to be taken into account,' the statement reads.[230] France and the Netherlands strongly insisted on keeping the absorption capacity paragraph, as they saw perceptions of uncontrolled enlargement as a key reason why their citizens voted down the Constitutional Treaty in the national referenda. The French Minister of Foreign Affairs Philippe Douste-Blazy was reported as having said: 'We cannot act as if the people do not exist. […]. We must not rush headlong into enlargement.'[231] His Dutch counterpart Bernard Bot indicated: 'We should not go too fast, we should pay attention to our public opinion,' adding that a 'very long process' lies ahead.[232]

In spite of the more or less clear message on the future membership of Turkey sent by the French and Dutch voters, it would be unwise, dangerous even, to renege on the commitments made *vis-à-vis* the countries of the Western Balkans, as this could disrupt a valuable process that is helping to build stable states in the region. In the words of Olli Rehn in a speech before the European Parliament: 'If [the European Union] were to go wobbly about the Western Balkans' European perspective, [its] beneficial influence would be seriously eroded, just when the region enters a difficult period of talks on Kosovo's status.'[233] The debate on how to increase the absorption capacity of the European Union or the final borders of Europe should not be used to question the existing commitments under the consolidated enlargement agenda for the Western Balkans. Seen in this light, the

---

229 Salzburg EU/Western Balkans Joint Press Statement of 11 March 2006, Press Release No. 7283/06 (Presse 77).

230 Ibid. In a similar vein, see EP Committee on Foreign Affairs, Report on the Commission's 2005 Enlargement Strategy Paper (2005/2206(INI)), No. A6-0025/2006 final, 3 February 2006, prepared by rapporteur Elmar Brok, and adopted by the European Parliament on 16 March 2006, P6_TA-PROV(2006)0096.

231 See M. Beunderman, 'EU membership goal clarified under Balkan pressure', *EUObserver.com*, 11 March 2006.

232 Ibid.

233 See O. Rehn, 'Commission's Enlargement Strategy', Strasbourg, 15 March 2006, SPEECH/06/171.

opposition to the EU Constitution, as expressed in the disruptive referenda in France and the Netherlands, has to give way to the responsibilities of the European Union in ensuring security and stability on the continent by continuing the process of enlargement. After all, the perspective of full membership is the most powerful incentive that the European Union can offer to the (potential) candidate countries in return for reform. Of course, further enlargements cannot be self-defeating, in the sense that they would weaken the fabric of the Union to such an extent that they would threaten the very aims of peace, prosperity, stability and security on the European continent that they seek to achieve.[234] The best way forward for the European Union is to reconcile its 'deepening' and 'widening' agendas without creating second-class members.

6.5 Reconciling 'deepening' and 'widening': can 'widening' save 'deepening'?

While the membership provisions of the Nice Treaty, as applied through the Copenhagen conditionality, are still perfectly suitable for the purposes of future EU enlargements, the institutional architecture is not. If the potential for institutional reform, *inter alia*, through the adoption of secondary legislation has been exhausted and the political stalemate over the current constitutional impasse lingers on beyond the Union's self-imposed new 'deadline' of mid-2009,[235] 'deepening' of the Union might in fact be saved by 'widening'. Theoretically, the conclusion of the seventh accession treaty could serve as a vehicle to introduce institutional reform via the backdoor. After all, accession treaties, acts of accession and the annexes thereto constitute primary law, as they are intended to amend provisions of the constituent treaties of the European Union.[236] However, the argument hinges on a liberal interpretation of Article 49(2) TEU:

> The conditions of admission and the adjustments to the Treaties on which the Union is founded which such admission entails shall be the subject of an agreement between the Member States and the applicant State. This agreement shall be submitted for ratification by all contracting States in accordance with their respective constitutional requirements.

The words 'adjustments to the Treaties on which the Union is founded', a phrase which so far has only been used for the introduction of the acceding country's

---

234 A response to Inglis, loc. cit. n. 3.

235 For an exploration of the legal scenarios for moving the integration process forward in case of an ongoing constitutional crisis, see B. de Witte, 'The Process of Ratification and the Crisis Options: A Legal Perspective', in Curtin, Kellermann and Blockmans, op. cit. n. 205, pp. 21-38.

236 See ECJ, Joined Cases 194/85 and 241/85 *Commission* v. *Greece* [1988] *ECR* 1037; and Joined Cases 31/86 and 35/86 *LAISA et al.* v. *Council* [1988] *ECR* 2285.

number of weighted votes in the Council, seats in the European Parliament and so forth could be interpreted so as to apply to the reform of the entire institutional apparatus of the Union, from the composition of the Commission and decision-making procedures in the Council to revisiting the distribution of powers. This functional interpretation of Article 49(2) TEU could be regarded as supporting the achievement of one of the goals for which the Union was set up, namely ensuring the effectiveness of the mechanisms and the institutions (Art. 2 TEU). However, as noted earlier, there are obvious limits to the introduction of institutional reforms through accession treaties: they may not have the intent or effect of undermining the foundations of the European integration process. For example, they may not violate the principle of non-discrimination on the ground of nationality.[237]

The argument is also based on the assumption that the ratification process of the accession treaty with Croatia will proceed unhindered.[238] This is not a foregone conclusion when one considers the lukewarm response that the Accession Treaty with Bulgaria and Romania received in the national parliaments of some enlargement-wary Member States.[239] But Croatia seems to hold a better hand. If it jumps through all the hoops that the Commission is holding out for it, which it seems able and willing to do, then it is difficult to see for what reasons a majority of voters in Ireland or the national parliaments of the other twenty-six Member States could oppose the entry of a small and increasingly prosperous country that currently holds the No. 1 position of European holiday destinations.

7. THE MULTI-DIMENSIONAL NATURE OF EU CONDITIONALITY AS APPLIED IN THE CASE OF THE WESTERN BALKANS: SYNOPSIS

EU membership conditionality is primarily defined by the requirements of Articles 49 and 6(1) TEU. According to Article 49 TEU, 'any European state'

---

[237] See *infra* section 5.2. On the advantages, previous examples and legal limits to the introduction of institutional reform of the founding treaties in accession treaties, see S. Blockmans, 'Reconciling Widening and Deepening: Enlargement as a Vehicle to Break the Union's Constitutional Deadlock', in Albi and Ziller, op. cit. n. 207, pp. 249-259; and C. Hillion, 'Can "Widening" Serve as a Vehicle for "Deepening"? Potential and Limits of the Use of Accession Treaties to Achieve Institutional Reforms', in Blockmans, Prechal and Douma, op. cit. n. 211.

[238] Art. 49(2) TEU, second sentence. Whereas Ireland holds an obligatory referendum, most Member States confine themselves to a parliamentary majority, sometimes requiring a special quorum. In France, the Constitution was amended to include a provision that prescribes the organisation of enlargement referenda after Bulgaria, Romania and Croatia have joined.

[239] See, e.g., the negative stance adopted by the CDA, the main coalition party in the Dutch cabinet, on the accession of the countries in 2007, in 'Kamer wil toetreding Roemenië en Bulgarije', *Elsevier*, 2 February 2006. See also M. Buenderman, 'Romania disappointed by French delay on accession ratification', *EUObserver.com*, 21 March 2006.

that respects the principles set out in Article 6(1) TEU (liberty, democracy, respect for human rights and fundamental freedoms, and the rule of law) may apply to become a member of the Union. The application of these articles (in their previous forms and numbers: Art. 237 EEC, Art. 98 ECSC, Art. 205 EAEC and Art. O TEU) proved sufficient to allow the EC/EU to expand to fifteen members without undermining its functioning.[240] But the prospect of the 'reunification of Europe' after the fall of the Iron Curtain and the entry of twelve or more mostly poor post-Communist members triggered the June 1993 European Council Summit in Copenhagen to develop more stringent criteria to measure the level of preparedness of both the candidates and the European Union itself. Since 1993, EU membership requires:

(a) that the candidate country has achieved stability of institutions guaranteeing democracy, the rule of law, human rights and respect for and protection of minorities;
(b) the existence of a functioning market economy, as well as the capacity to cope with competitive pressures and market forces within the Union;
(c) the ability to take on the obligations of membership, including adhering to the aims of political, economic and monetary union;
(d) the Union's capacity to absorb new members, while maintaining the momentum of European integration, is also an important consideration in the general interest of both the Union and the candidate countries.

To reflect the special need to stabilise the region, EU conditionality towards south-eastern Europe was defined by the interpretation given to the Copenhagen criteria in the specific guidelines adopted by the Council on 29 April 1997.[241] Multi-dimensional in nature, the instrument was subsequently geared towards reform and integration of the countries of the region into the structures of the Union. Economic, political, social and security-related, the nature of EU conditionality towards south-eastern Europe is positive as well as negative and develops in parallel with the European Union's *acquis*. Special requirements reflect the distinct historical trajectory and peculiar problems of the Western Balkans. In addition to the membership conditions of Articles 49 and 6(1) TEU and the 1993 Copenhagen criteria, pre-accession conditionality for the Western Balkans is established by:

---

240 See F. Hoffmeister, 'Changing Requirements for Membership', in Ott and Inglis, op. cit. n. 3, at pp. 90-102; and K. Smith, 'The Evolution and Application of EU Membership Conditionality', in Cremona, op. cit. n. 3, at pp. 105-139.

241 *Bull. EU* 4-1997, point 2.2.1, reproduced in section 2.1 of this chapter.

(a) the conditions flowing from the 1999 Stability Pact for South-Eastern Europe and the Stabilisation and Association Process, which reiterate the Copenhagen criteria and add the condition of regional cooperation through political dialogue and the conclusion of (free trade) agreements with countries in South Eastern Europe; and
(b) the country-specific conditions for the opening and conclusion of SAA talks, that is to say, the conditions that arise out of the peace agreements and political deals (e.g., the Dayton and Ohrid Agreements, UN Security Council resolution 1244 and future arrangements).

In its annual reports, the European Commission closely monitors progress in fulfilling the seemingly ever-increasing body of membership conditions. Through the screening process and the accession negotiations, the Commission identifies the main weaknesses and technical adaptations needed by the (potential) candidate countries and accordingly sets out priorities and benchmarks and directs EU funds towards relevant projects. Similarly, the SAP is monitored and reviewed annually in order to highlight the key priorities and channel funds to the Western Balkans. On top of all this, the Union is, for the first time in its history, applying the fourth Copenhagen criterion, namely, the Union's capacity to absorb new members while maintaining the momentum of European integration.

8. DIFFICULTIES IN APPLYING EU CONDITIONALITY IN THE WESTERN BALKANS

8.1 Flawed assumptions?

While the European Union has established one single framework to govern relations with all SAP countries, it is developing bilateral ties at different speeds. This reflects the pace at which reforms are being introduced by the governments concerned. As such, frontrunners are distinguished from laggards. As Othon Anastasakis and Dimitar Benchev have explained, the European Union, in applying conditionality, relies upon three implicit assumptions:

(1) that differentiation among the countries generates a positive climate of competition on the way towards accession;
(2) that the reform process enjoys consensus and support from the local elites and populations; and
(3) that the guidelines and templates developed by the European Union are equally beneficial for all of the countries.[242]

---

242 See Anastasakis and Bechev, op. cit. n. 39, at p. 9.

While the application of the conditionality principle has worked well in the CEECs, its ability to generate EU-proof reform in the Western Balkans has been less conclusive, especially in Albania and the international protectorates of Bosnia-Herzegovina and Kosovo.[243] This may reflect flaws in the implicit assumptions underpinning the application of EU conditionality in the Western Balkans as well as its effectiveness. Each of the three above-mentioned points will briefly be touched upon below.

8.2 Regional approach

As noted before, differences are huge in the Western Balkans. This fragmentation is a consequence of centuries of recompositioning in the region. This *a priori* differentiation is at the root of the varying progress in bilateral relations with the European Union, which in turn exacerbates local disparities. Croatia is undoubtedly the frontrunner in light of its economic performance and the pace of its administrative reforms. Although Croatia's progress has long been inhibited by political problems such as an aversion to cooperating with the ICTY and to Serb refugee return, technically it has been moving closer to EU standards. Full cooperation with the ICTY was rewarded by the European Union with the opening of accession negotiations. Macedonia is keen to follow the Croatian example, but its ability to meet conditions is clearly more limited. Its spectacular progress in barely five years time has earned it EU candidate country status, but further progress, such as the cultivation of a democratic decision-making process based on the principle of political compromise, is needed before it will be able to open membership talks. A weak state and a gangster economy make Albania, the third SAA signatory, one of the laggards in the process. Serbia possesses the know-how and capacity to meet the conditions set by the European Union, but its cooperation with the ICTY will have to be improved before further progress can be made. After its withdrawal from the state union with Serbia, Montenegro will have to focus on constitutional and judicial reform and administrative capacity-building before real steps towards the European Union can be made. Bosnia-Herzegovina and Kosovo have the longest way to go, as both are still under international administration. A sustainable solution for the latter's status will also have to be found.

This heterogeneity contradicts those elements of Stability Pact and SAP conditionality that promote a greater degree of regional cooperation. In fact, the contribution of the Stability Pact to the process of European integration is often contested, for it creates unnecessary coordination problems and sometimes hinders

---

243 See International Commission on the Balkans, *The Balkans in Europe's Future* (Sofia, Centre for Liberal Strategies 2005) at p. 14.

a more effective application of the conditionality principle by the European Union.[244] For their part, most Western Balkan states tend to regard regional schemes with suspicion, sceptical of the benefits they can generate or concerned that they might impede closer bilateral relations with the Union.[245] In such a context, it is difficult to see how the differentiating effect of conditionality can generate healthy competition among Western Balkan states when the stronger feel that they are delayed by the weaker and the weaker do not benefit from the progress of the stronger.[246]

8.3 Local support

EU conditionality can have an important catalytic role in prompting reforms. For instance, good progress reports tend to raise (foreign) investors' confidence, which is essential for growth and further reforms. However, a sustainable reform process also requires certain domestic conditions, such as the presence of reformist parties that alternate in power and a broad societal consensus as to the necessity of EU-guided reforms. The experience of a number of Western Balkan countries suggests that EU conditionality does not generate popular consensus, even if it is understood to be necessary in principle.[247] Thus, the European Union does not help political parties to win elections.[248]

One must take into account that many people in the Western Balkans still perceive the European Union in a rather ambivalent way. Although, overall, the polls show a considerable rate of approval for the Union,[249] this seems to be offset by a lack of confidence in what it actually does or has done in the region. In a way, there are two clashing conceptions of the Union cohabiting in local perceptions. One is related to the image of 'EUtopia', representing prosperity, democratic values and peace. The other raises the not-so-distant memories of EU

---

244 See Van Meurs, loc. cit. n. 35.

245 See Anastasakis and Bojičić-Dželilović, op. cit. n. 108; and D. Bechev, 'Carrots, Sticks and Norms: The EU and Regional Cooperation in Southeast Europe', 8 *Journal of Southern Europe and the Balkans* (2006) pp. 27-43.

246 For recommended reinforcements in this field, see chapter 6, section 2.1.1.3.

247 In Croatia, for instance, general support for EU membership fell dramatically in the year ahead of the European Union's decision to open accession negotiations. According to a poll by the Puls agency, conducted in September 2004, just 49 per cent of those questioned backed accession, while 41 per cent of the respondents were opposed to joining the Union. This represented a massive drop in support for EU membership since January 2004, when more than 70 per cent of voters supported joining the Union. The drop in public support for accession was largely due to the European Union's pressure to transfer Ante Gotovina to The Hague. See L. Kirk, 'EU entry talks with Croatia could start in April', *EUObserver.com*, 14 December 2004. See also Jović, loc. cit., n. 178.

248 This conclusion is supported by the results of the survey conducted by the International Commission on the Balkans, op. cit. n. 243, at p. 40, fig. 2.

249 Ibid., at p. 49, fig. 16, and at p. 52, fig. 19.

blunders in dealing with the Yugoslav wars. This feeling is strongest in Kosovo, where a widespread perception exists that European powers did not do enough to protect the Albanian population in Kosovo against Serb aggression, and in Serbia, where memories of EU Member States' fighter jets participating in the air campaign waged by NATO in 1999 over the crisis in Kosovo are still fresh. Such contradictory attitudes erode the efficiency and legitimacy of EU conditionality, especially when the European Union is perceived to lack a real commitment towards the Western Balkans. Opening accession negotiations with Croatia has given the Union a boost in popular perception in the region, but this advantage risks being lost if Macedonia is kept in limbo.

In essence, EU conditionality is considered as a necessary but also unwelcome imposition from outside. These perceptions are of immense political importance because they reinvigorate the image of the European Union as a necessary evil, a picture that is further boosted by its one-way approach to priorities-setting.

8.4 One-way approach

EU conditionality has hitherto been a one-way process: conditions are defined exclusively by the European Union and its Member States and must be accepted unconditionally by the (potential) candidates.[250] This unequal relationship has been aimed at the transposition of policy templates that reflect EU preferences and past practices.[251] The templates used for the post-Communist CEECs, which followed the 'classic' transition path, are not the most conducive to effecting EU-proof change in all corners of a war-torn region, especially in those corners where a state-building process is still underway. The European Union seems to assume that its prescriptions have universal applicability and should therefore be adopted and implemented irrespective of the particularities of countries or regions. As Laza Kekić has pointed out, there are some indicative areas in which harmonisation with the EU's *acquis* and policies can be detrimental to the hoped-for economic growth in the Western Balkans, for example capital account liberalisation and competition policies.[252] This paradox reflects the shortcomings of the one-way approach in setting policy targets. Moreover, local priorities often prove to be out of sync with those of the European Union. Especially in the international protectorates, to people who see their country dominated, for better or worse, by

---

250 See M. Cremona, 'Flexible Models: External Policy and the European Economic Constitution', in G. de Búrca and J. Scott, eds., *Constitutional Change in the EU: From Uniformity to Flexibility?* (Oxford, Hart Publishing 2000) pp. 59-94 at pp. 64-65.

251 See D. Chandler, 'The European Union and Governance in the Western Balkans: An Unequal Partnership', 1/2 *European Balkan Observer* (2003) pp. 5-9.

252 See L. Kekić, 'The EU and the Balkans – To Harmonise or Not to Harmonise', *Economist Intelligence Unit* (Viewshire, 2002).

foreign masters, the European Union's demands ring hollow. An extreme example is provided by the reactions in the region to the Union's support for the United Nations' 'standards before status' policy for Kosovo.

There is little point in the European Union constantly blowing against the wind, especially when that wind is coming from the Western Balkans. By doing so in the past couple of years, the international community, including the European Union, has bred an unsustainable status quo that might drive parts of the region towards a new period of highly dangerous instability.[253] Regional input in the Union's policies towards the Western Balkans is a *conditio sine qua non* for effectively stabilising the region. There is one big problem, however. Regional input not only requires a perceptive and understanding donor that can demonstrate vision and flexibility but also presupposes sovereign governments that are capable of articulating their needs and demands. The reality is that sovereignty is still a scarce resource in some parts of the Western Balkans. When one considers the extensive powers of the High Representative/European Union Special Representative in Bosnia-Herzegovina and the Special Representative of the Secretary-General in Kosovo, one may question the domestic ability to address needs and priorities. The result is the definition of a form of EU conditionality that does not involve regional input, does not necessarily generate broad domestic consensus for reform and poisons relations between the populations and the political elites and, by extension, between the countries concerned and international actors.[254]

9. IMPROVING EU CONDITIONALITY FOR THE WESTERN BALKANS

While conditionality is inherently asymmetric and the European Union must not step down from its role of as a promoter of reform, there is much to be done in terms of establishing a viable partnership with the Western Balkans. Beyond any doubt, EU conditionality has to be based on a process of 'adaptive learning' by paying closer attention to the signals coming from the region.[255] There is general agreement across the region, verified by opinion polls, that social and economic

---

[253] This observation is supported by the results of the survey conducted by the ICB, op. cit. n. 243, at p. 10.

[254] See I. Krastev, 'The Balkans: Democracy without Choices', 13 *Journal of Democracy* (2002). One move in the right direction has so far been the greater consideration of the recipients' interests in the timing, for example, of the approximation of legislation. See the rationale behind the shorter timeframe and the absence of stages for the approximation of legislation in the SAA Croatia as compared to the SAA FYROM, as discussed *supra* section 3.3.3.

[255] See Chandler, loc. cit. n. 251.

matters – as opposed to the old ethno-political repertoire – are the real concern.[256] High unemployment, poverty and corruption typically score high on the list of problems that preoccupy people in the Balkans. It is only when its commitment is better linked to addressing those issues that matter to citizens that the European Union will be able to sell its conditionality approach.[257]

Although EU membership conditionality leads, by definition, to bilateralism and competition, the Western Balkans also require a region-wide strategy. While packaging the countries into a single region is not viable, the institutionalisation of the dialogue between Brussels and the Western Balkans has been a step in the right direction. It is imperative that the countries in the region are involved in setting the regional cooperation agenda. The European Union should also take a clear stand on the Stability Pact. As far as the Western Balkans are concerned, the Pact has been overtaken by the more preferred and comprehensive Stabilisation and Association Process. Moreover, after the accession of Bulgaria and Romania to the Union, the Pact's 'theatre' is almost limited to the Western Balkans. There is little point in maintaining the 'working tables' as a forum for relations with Turkey and Moldova. Turkey has a customs union with the European Union and is covered by the pre-accession process, while Moldova is covered by the ENP. At long last, the European Union has accepted that it must let go of the Stability Pact and prioritise relations with the Western Balkans through a reorganised SAP. For those countries, regionalism would thus be more closely linked to the EU integration project than it is at present. In view of the need for the countries of the region to take ownership of the regional cooperation process, the plan to transform the Stability Pact into a Regional Cooperation Council, with a Secretariat and a Secretary General, should be welcomed.[258] This Regional Cooperation Council would not be a substitute for EU membership but only a way to speed up integration with the European Union.

10. CONCLUDING REMARKS

In the aftermath of the Kosovo crisis of 1999, the Stability Pact for South-Eastern Europe and the Stabilisation and Association Process replaced and updated the European Union's Regional Approach. While the Stability Pact focuses on regional cooperation in the fields of politics, economics and security, the SAP is intended to act primarily as a mechanism for upgrading bilateral relations

256 Based on an extensive survey of public attitudes conducted by the International Institute for Democracy and Electoral Assistance during January and February 2002, available at: <http://www.idea.int>.

257 See Anastasakis and Bechev, op. cit. n. 39.

258 See more elaborately in chapter 6, section 2.1.1.3.

between the European Union and the individual countries. The two elements are interrelated in that the conditionality instituted by the SAP urges the Western Balkan states to engage in regional cooperation activities, partly in the framework of the Stability Pact. It places a particular emphasis on projects like the establishment of free trade in south-eastern Europe. The SAP countries are also required to demonstrate commitment to democratic and market reforms and respect for human rights, to work for the return of refugees, to cooperate with the ICTY and to build up their capacity in the domain of justice and home affairs. Rightly, it has been noted that the structural tension between a regional approach and bilateral conditionality may endanger the coherence of international action towards a region still known to many as a powder keg. This is because the best pupils of the class will 'leave' the region by acquiring a different contractual status in their relations with the Union, thereby increasing rather than reducing the disparities within the region.[259] While official EU documents have always shunned a prioritisation between the Stability Pact and the SAP, it is clear that, in practice, the Stabilisation and Association Agreements (as part of the SAP) are seen, both by the countries in the region and the European Union, as the most important instruments to achieve lasting peace and stability in the Western Balkans, because they offer the prospect of EU membership. For these countries, there is no need to pursue the Stability Pact.

With the principle of conditionality firmly and explicitly built into all phases of the SAP, the countries of the Western Balkans have a clearly marked path and timetable to follow and are aware of the consequences of not abiding by the conditions imposed upon them by the European Union: postponement or cancellation of political negotiations and/or suspension or termination of contractual relations. At the same time, the European Union has recently confirmed the tangible prospect of EU membership, the most powerful instrument for transformation of the Western Balkans, as the SAP's *finalité*. This gives the governments that were still in doubt as to whether or not to take the Union's 'perspective of membership' offer seriously a strong incentive and clear message to convince their electorates of the advantages of ethnic reconciliation and the tightening of belts to reform their countries' administrative, legislative and economic structures.

In many ways, Croatia stands out as a model for the rest of the region.[260] For the Croatian case to serve as a positive example, the rest of the SAP countries should be persuaded that the European Union is serious about settling the legacy of the Yugoslav wars of the 1990s and does not apply a double standard. Consistency is

---

259 Van Meurs, loc. cit. n. 35, at p. 41.

260 Of course, so does Slovenia. But for reasons explained in chapter 1, section 5.1, comparisons with Slovenia are harder to make.

crucial. Seen in this light, the Union was right to play hard-ball with Croatia and enforce its conditionality principle by not opening accession talks when Croatia failed to show full cooperation with the ICTY before 17 March 2005. An equally strong signal was certainly received in Belgrade over its failure to transfer Ratko Mladić to the ICTY. Now that membership negotiations have opened with Croatia, the European Union will have to continue to apply pressure to make sure that Croatia holds up its end of the deal. As noted, the revised framework for accession negotiations offers new possibilities in this respect.

The decision to open accession negotiations with Croatia, the granting of candidate country status to Macedonia and the progress made on the SAAs with the other countries of the Western Balkans do not allow for the conclusion that any of these countries is likely to join the European Union as a full member any time soon. But these developments do provide the European Union's overall approach towards the Western Balkans with a radically new strategic objective: the further expansion of the European Union south-eastwards. This strategic reorientation should prompt the Union to vigorously reinforce a guiding principle that has characterised its relations with third countries in general: the principle of conditionality. But it is important that the Union does not give the impression that membership is too distant, as this might lead to rapid domestic deterioration. A balanced application of the conditionality principle is central to closer relations between the European Union and the Western Balkans.

CHAPTER 6

RECOMMENDATIONS FOR REINFORCING THE EUROPEAN UNION'S ROLE IN THE WESTERN BALKANS

1. IN SEARCH OF SUSTAINABLE SOLUTIONS

Over the past two decades, most parts of the Western Balkans have been touched by forms of autocratic governance, armed conflict, ethnic cleansing and secession. Ever since the fighting ended, it has been recognised that systemic political, economic and social reforms are needed to build legitimacy, transparency and the rule of law. Set in motion by the international community, this transition process is far from over. The problem is that, until recently, the Western Balkans were regarded primarily as a post-war region. This approach has led to a raft of provisional solutions to constitutional problems and policies based on what might be termed 'constructive ambiguity', which have been imposed on their recipients and embodied in documents like the Dayton Agreement (1995), UN Security Council resolution 1244 (1999), the Ohrid Framework Agreement (2001) and the Belgrade Agreement (2002). At the same time, the international community has been working on the assumption that economic development would reduce the pressing need to solve the remaining status issues. Unfortunately, this assumption has turned out to be false. Economic stagnation has generated massive unemployment. On top of that, thousands of refugees and displaced persons still await return or resettlement; prominent accused war criminals remain at large; key institutions have resisted reform; and political and legal reforms are impeded by corruption and by entrenched obstructionist forces that advance narrow, personal or ethnically driven interests. In those circumstances, unresolved status issues are potentially a very harmful source of instability. Neglecting these challenges by pursuing policies that either maintain the status quo or amount to international dicta that find very little support on the ground could have severe and destabilising consequences for parts of the Western Balkans, including a greater likelihood of political extremism, armed conflict and further human displacement. A renewal of armed conflict, however limited, would be devastating for the region and beyond, especially for the European Union and its Member States. It would amount to a policy failure with damaging implications for the European security architecture. In short, it is high time for the international community to change its current approach to problem-solving in the Western Balkans, reverse the vicious circles and turn them into virtuous ones. Failure to do so could result in a costlier and more dangerous intervention down the line and act as an unnecessary irritant in international relations.

While a continued international presence in some parts of the Western Balkans is imperative, the current structure of the international involvement in the region is poorly organised, sometimes even counterproductive. Throughout the Western Balkans, *ad hoc* structures (e.g., the OHR, UNMIK and Stability Pact), regional missions (e.g., of the OSCE, the Council of Europe and NATO) and the European Union work independently, with coordination that ranges from close to non-existent. Although this jungle of largely uncoordinated agencies was perhaps inevitable – given that the international presence in each country was created at different times, by different actors and under different circumstances – it has prevented the international community from mounting a concerted campaign against the core elements that inhibit progress. It is increasingly obvious that the *ad hoc* nature of the international presence is an impediment to effective action on the most pressing issues. The makeshift structure puts an extra layer between the states of the Western Balkans and the Euro-Atlantic institutions to which they aspire. This arrangement inhibits the effectiveness of the international agencies on the ground, confuses local actors when the signals coming from the various international institutions are competing or unclear and may become a source of resentment for governments anxious to demonstrate to their citizens that, after several years of hard choices, they are full partners in the main pillars of the European security architecture. If this confusion and resentment continue to grow, the international presence will become less effective over time, just when the states of the region will have to tackle some of the most difficult issues, impeding their integration with the rest of Europe. Thus, it is time to reduce the number of international officials and organisations that are able to set priorities and make decisions.

In the previous chapters, this study has identified both the measures taken by the key international stakeholders in stabilising the Western Balkans and – along those lines – the progress made by the different parts of the region in getting back on track. It now turns towards crafting general recommendations targeted at those international organisations that make up the European security architecture. In doing so, it takes a 'tough love' approach to long-term peacebuilding, paying particular attention to measures to strengthen those who promote moderation and growth while weakening those who oppose progress. Accordingly, this chapter tries to devise a realistic agenda for general actions that make wiser use of the remaining resources in support of regional and Euro-Atlantic interests: achieving a sustainable ('positive') peace by preventing the region from becoming a vacuum in which organised crime and corruption predominate and poverty and insecurity fuel migration to the European Union and beyond.

The overall vision for the countries of the Western Balkans centres on their full integration into the European Union and NATO – both in terms of shared structures and institutions and in terms of shared norms and ideals. A coordinated international effort with these objectives and clear lines of responsibility can, in cooperation with reform-oriented local leaders, put all Western Balkan states on the path to full integration with the European Union and NATO. Such an effort will encourage and assist a wide-ranging transformation of the political, economic, legal and administrative systems in the region that will make it possible, over the next years, for the European security architecture to reduce its presence in an orderly fashion and transfer full sovereignty and responsibilities to capable domestic actors and institutions. Achieving the goal of putting the Western Balkans on the path of integration with the European Union and NATO will therefore require sustained assistance, organised around three guiding principles:

(i) the rationalisation of the international presence in the Western Balkans, led by the European Union and supported by NATO (section 2);
(ii) the adoption of policies that seek to resolve the remaining constitutional and status questions and focus on political, social, economic and legal reform (section 3); and
(iii) the assumption by the citizens of the Western Balkan countries and their political leaders of responsibility for their own future (section 4).[1]

2. RESTRUCTURING THE INTERNATIONAL PRESENCE

2.1 More European Union and NATO

The vision formulated above for the Western Balkans requires a continued, albeit reconfigured and rebalanced engagement by the international community. In any rational reconfiguration of the international presence in the Western Balkans, the European Union and NATO will take the lead. The aim of the countries in the region is to establish closer ties with the main pillars of the European security architecture, because these provide the best rationale, leverage and political cover for promoting tough political, economic and social changes. For reasons already mentioned, it is in the interest of these international organisations, the European Union in particular, to provide the 'carrots and sticks' that will keep the states of the Western Balkans on the path of progress and reform. Therefore, the international presence can be reorganised most effectively around the Union's Stabilisation and Association Process and NATO's Membership Action Plan and Partnership for Peace programme. However, the SAP and the MAP/PfP will require streamlining and systematising to meet today's challenges in the region.

---

[1] The same could be said of EU citizens and their political leaders. See chapter 5, section 6.

2.1.1 *Strengthening the Stabilisation and Association Process*

The current Stabilisation and Association Process is not strong enough a framework to build Member States out of the weak states and international protectorates of the Western Balkans. More and better quality technical and financial assistance is needed before the laggards in the process – Bosnia-Herzegovina and Kosovo – will be able to close the gap with the frontrunner – Croatia – and face up to the challenges posed by EU membership. In this context, it has been rightly suggested that, in their drive towards EU accession, the Western Balkans are in need of a 'Member State-building' strategy.[2] It is argued here that the implementation of this new strategy should be facilitated by three important improvements to the SAP: (i) overcoming the 'potential' candidate country status; (ii) mitigating the effects of a tough love approach towards granting financial and technical assistance; and (iii) enhancing cooperation in the region.

2.1.1.1 Choosing a 'Helsinki moment'

Firstly, a so-called 'Helsinki moment' should be created for the Western Balkans. This is a reference to the historic decision of the European Council gathered at Helsinki in December 1999 to grant candidate country status to Turkey.[3] In a similar historic spirit, the European Council should use one of its forthcoming summits to review the achievements of the Western Balkans in satisfying the pre-accession criteria and grant candidate country status to Albania, Bosnia-Herzegovina, Montenegro, Serbia and Kosovo (if independent). These countries (including Macedonia in case accession negotiations have still not been opened) should then be presented with their accession road maps. The experience of the CEECs illustrates best how the institutionalisation of the EU integration perspective is the most efficient way to foster and accelerate the overall political, economic, administrative and legal reforms in aspirant countries. This does not mean that all Western Balkan countries should join the European Union at the same time. On the contrary, each country should only join when all conditions have been fulfilled. But giving the 'potential' candidate countries a real membership perspective would mean an end to the growing fears in some of these countries that they might be left out of the accession process altogether. The enlargement summit should be held soon after the last SAA has entered into force

---

[2] See International Commission on the Balkans, *The Balkans in Europe's Future* (Sofia, Centre for Liberal Strategies 2005) at p. 14.

[3] *Bull. EU* 12-1999, point I.3.2. The phrase was first coined by the European Stability Initiative, *The Helsinki Moment – European Member State Building in the Balkans* (Berlin, ESI 2005).

and all applications for EU membership have been received (pursuant to Art. 49 TEU). Working on the assumption that the European Commission will meet its ambition to conclude the remaining SAAs in 2007, a new 'Helsinki moment' could come as early as the second half of 2008.[4] To that end, popular anxiety over any further EU enlargements, now very apparent in the internal politics of some Member States,[5] should be countered, as the European Union definitely 'cannot take a sabbatical' from enlargement while it sorts out its internal rules.[6] Convincing the Union's enlargement-wary citizens will not be an easy task, but it is necessary if the Union wants to keep a firm grip on its most effective tool for stabilising the troubled region of the Western Balkans.

2.1.1.2 Embedding financial and technical assistance

The second improvement of the SAP should concern the flanking policies of the financial and technical assistance given to the candidate – and especially the potential candidate – countries of the Western Balkans. Over the years, the European Union has developed a system of different aid programmes addressed, *inter alia*, to the candidate countries of Central and Eastern Europe (PHARE, SAPARD and ISPA and the Turkish pre-accession instrument), the (potential) candidate countries of the Western Balkans (CARDS), the neighbouring countries on the Mediterranean Sea (MEDA) and those built on the ashes of the Soviet Union (TACIS). In September 2004, the European Commission presented plans to harmonise (insofar as possible) the existing aid programmes for the period covered by the financial perspective for 2007-2013.[7] With regard to the candidate and potential candidate countries, the Council adopted Regulation (EC) No. 1085/2006 of 17 July 2006 establishing an Instrument for Pre-Accession Assistance (IPA), thereby replacing the five existing instruments by a single one.[8]

---

4 At the beginning of 2005, the ICB suggested to first organise a 'Helsinki'-type summit in the second half of 2006 and then to conclude Europe Agreements with those countries that would not start accession negotiations directly. In view of the aim to conclude all the SAAs in 2007, there seems little point to negotiate and conclude a type of agreement that is so similar to the SAAs. See chapter 5, section 3. The third pointer in the ICB's strategy was to start accession negotiations around 2009/2010.This would make accession of all Western Balkan countries possible on or before 28 June 2014. ICB, op. cit. n. 2, at pp. 6 and 14.

5 See chapter 5, section 6.

6 Dixit Olli Rehn, quoted in G. Parker and C. Condon, 'Some Balkan states may find EU's door closed', *Financial Times*, 7 April 2006. Of course, it would be best if institutional reform were to precede the next wave of enlargement.

7 See, *inter alia*, European Commission, Proposal for a Council Regulation establishing an Instrument for Pre-Accession Assistance (IPA), COM (2004) 627 final, Brussels, 29 September 2004.

8 *OJ* 2006 L 210/82. IPA is part of a wider reorganisation of the European Union's financial framework for relations with third states, which includes a new European Neighbourhood and Partnership Instrument (ENPI), a new development cooperation instrument, the Instrument for Stability and a financing instrument for the promotion of democracy and human rights worldwide.

The IPA Regulation is problematic on two levels. Firstly, following its adoption, there are no more ways of mobilising additional EU pre-accession funds within the new budget cycle. The envelope that the Regulation foresees for the pre-accession process will force the European Union to reduce its assistance to the Western Balkans in the coming years. As can be seen from Table 1 below, the region is due to receive around €2.7 billion over the next four years.

Table 1: IPA funds allocation for 2007-2010 (in € millions)

Country	2007	2008	2009	2010	2007-2010
Croatia	141.2	146.0	151.2	154.2	592.6
Former Yugoslav Republic of Macedonia	58.5	70.2	81.8	92.3	302.8
Serbia	186.7	190.9	194.8	198.7	771.1
Kosovo*	68.4	64.7	66.1	67.3	266.5
Montenegro	31.4	32.6	33.3	34.0	131.3
Bosnia-Herzegovina	62.1	74.8	89.1	106.0	332.0
Albania	61.0	70.7	81.2	93.2	306.1
Total Western Balkans	**609.3**	**649.9**	**697.5**	**745.7**	**2702.4**

* under UN Security Council resolution 1244 (1999)
Source: European Commission[9]

The IPA Regulation provides a total envelope of €11.5 billion over the next seven years for the countries with candidate status (currently Croatia, Macedonia and Turkey) and potential candidate status (Albania, Bosnia-Herzegovina, Montenegro and Serbia (including Kosovo)). This amount is less than the €14.65 billion proposed by the Commission in its heavily criticised proposal of 2004.[10] As a

---

9 European Commission, MEMO/07/169, 8 May 2007. In addition, the Western Balkans will benefit, together with Turkey, through horizontal and regional programmes, from almost €560 million in additional funding over the same period.

10 Section 2.1 of Annex 2 to the Draft Regulation of 2004 set out the total envelope of funds available for assistance to both candidate and potential candidate countries, but not the allocation for each country. However, section 5.1.1 of the Explanatory Memorandum to the Draft Regulation stated the principles according to which funds would be allocated to the official candidates: Croatia, Turkey and, in due course, Macedonia. The Draft Regulation stated: 'The intention is that future candidate countries should be treated broadly the same as past candidate countries. As the countries of the Western Balkans become candidate countries it is proposed that they will receive per capita per year about the level of assistance established in the financial perspective 2000-2006 [...] for the 10 candidate countries in central and eastern Europe.' The European Stability Initiative, a non-profit research and policy institute with bases in Berlin, Brussels and Istanbul calculated that, according to this formula, each of the candidates would receive around €27 per capita per year. For Croatia, this would boil down to €120 million per year and for Macedonia around €54 million per year. See ESI, *Breaking Out of the Balkan Ghetto: Why IPA Should Be Changed* (Berlin, ESI 2005).

result, most Western Balkan countries (with the exception of Croatia and FYROM, which have received candidate country status) will receive virtually the same funding as they receive now, but it should be noted that CARDS funding has already fallen to a lower level since 2000.[11] In Kosovo, the decline in EU assistance will be particularly steep, even in view of the exceptional Community financial assistance given in 2007 under the previous budget cycle.[12] Consequently, signing an SAA will not be 'rewarded' with the increase in EU financial assistance that the potential candidates hope for. At a time when some of the most delicate steps in the region are expected to be taken, namely the implementation of the decisions concerning Kosovo's final status and ending the international governance of Bosnia-Herzegovina, the European Union's financial engagement in the region will be almost at its lowest level since the war over Kosovo. Following the difficult compromise on the financial perspective for 2007-2013 reached at the European Council of 17 December 2005,[13] hope should only be vested in the willingness of individual Member States that are genuinely committed to the eventual integration of the Western Balkans into the European Union to provide extra funds on a bilateral basis.

The second reason why the IPA Regulation is problematic is that the negative consequences of the instrument's 'tough love' approach are currently insufficiently mitigated. Under the rules of the IPA Regulation, pre-accession assistance will not be made automatically and fully available to the potential candidate countries.[14] Official candidates *will* and potential candidate countries *may* receive support under three headings: regional development, rural development and human resources development. Likewise, the regional development component, the human resources development component and the rural development components will only be accessible to candidate countries accredited to manage funds in a decentralised manner. This qualitative differentiation between the two categories of countries is significant and will exacerbate the differences in the Western

11 See Table 1 in chapter 5, section 3.4.

12 See Council Decision of 30 November 2006 providing exceptional Community financial assistance to Kosovo, *OJ* 2006 L 339/36.

13 *Bull. EU* 12-2005, points I.1 and I.4.6.

14 Section 1 of the Explanatory Memorandum to the Draft Regulation already described that the potential candidates were to be offered a continuation of the same kinds of assistance provided in recent years under the CARDS programme: 'Potential Candidate Countries will continue to receive assistance along the lines currently laid down in the CARDS Regulation: Institution Building and Democratisation, Economic and Social Development, Regional and Cross-Border Co-operation and some alignment with the *acquis communautaire*, in particular where this is in the mutual interest of the EU and the beneficiary country.' The official candidates, however, were to receive the full package of pre-accession assistance, in order to prepare them more intensively for EU membership: 'Candidate Countries will receive the same kind of assistance [as the potential candidates], and will additionally receive assistance in the preparation for the implementation of Structural and Rural Development Funds after Accession, as well as concerning the full implementation of the *acquis communautaire*.'

Balkans if it is not compensated for in other domains. Its implementation will mean that all those living in rural areas and declining industrial towns in Albania, Bosnia-Herzegovina, Montenegro, Serbia and Kosovo, who are already suffering from inadequate education systems and a seriously deficient infrastructure, will see the development gap separating them from the rest of Europe – and from their immediate neighbours in candidate countries – grow wider. To prevent the emergence of a new 'Balkan ghetto'[15] – comprising most of the region's difficult to reconcile Albanians and Serbs, brought together behind a wall of trade and visa restrictions – in the heart of an integrating subcontinent, IPA needs to be supported by attractive flanking policies. In this respect, visa facilitation will be an important improvement for ordinary citizens in the region, enabling them to travel to, study in and make business cheaper with the European Union. Easier access to visas will make the European perspective more concrete to all citizens of the region, in particular those from the potential candidate countries.[16] The conclusion of negotiations between the EC and the countries of the region on agreements to facilitate procedures for issuing short-stay visas and on the readmission of people who are residing in the Union illegally represents a step in the right direction.[17] Such new agreements will promote people-to-people contacts between the European Union and the Western Balkan countries and will increase the opportunities for travel, especially for the younger generation. The inclusion of the potential candidate countries in the *Tempus* and *Erasmus Mundus* programmes is another symbolic example of an IPA flanking policy, but it is obvious that more scholarships should be made available for this to have a real impact.[18]

2.1.1.3 Enhancing regional cooperation

For the European Union, the third policy challenge in the improvement of the Stabilisation and Association Process emerges as a conundrum: how to effectively reconcile the regional approach that is essential for the stabilisation of the

---

[15] The term is from ESI, op. cit. n. 10.

[16] See A. Pulaj, 'Visa or no visa? That's still the question in the Balkans', *Southeast European Times*, 26 February 2007.

[17] The draft agreements with Albania, Bosnia-Herzegovina, Macedonia and Montenegro were initialled on 12 April 2007; the one with Serbia on 16 May 2007. Albania only negotiated a visa facilitation agreement as a readmission agreement had been in force since 1 May 2006. See Agreement between the European Community and the Republic of Albania on the readmission of persons residing without authorisation, *OJ* 2005 L 124/22. In this context, see F. Trauner, 'EU Justice and Home Affairs Strategy in the Western Balkans', *CEPS Working Document* No. 259, February 2007.

[18] See 'The European Commission launches new scholarship scheme outside the EU', Press Release IP/06/1721, Brussels, 11 December 2006. The plan allows for up to 100 (in the future 500) students from the region to undertake postgraduate studies in EU master's courses. In the 2006-2007 academic year, only four students from Albania, one from Bosnia-Herzegovina, four from Macedonia, three from Serbia and Montenegro and three from Kosovo participated in the programme.

Western Balkans with the requirement of evaluating countries on the basis of their individual performances, a concept that lies at the heart of the EU accession process? The SAP tried to answer this question by emphasising the central need for regional cooperation as part of the SAAs. The past five years, however, have demonstrated that this works only to a limited extent. The laggards in the pre-accession process – Bosnia-Herzegovina and Serbia (including Kosovo) – no longer perceive the SAP as a fast integration track. The lesson from this is that only real incentives can bring real reforms.

The creation of a free trade area in south-eastern Europe would provide the missing incentive for regional cooperation. After all, the economic interdependence of the countries of the Western Balkans is vital for the future of the region.[19] The economic sustainability of their small and unattractive markets depends on the creation of a common economic area that will attract foreign direct investment. Thus, in an economic sense, a regional approach is a necessary precondition for development. In this respect, the Energy Community Treaty, which creates an Energy Community between the European Community, on the one hand, and Albania, Bulgaria, Bosnia-Herzegovina, Croatia, Macedonia, Montenegro, Romania, Serbia and the United Nations Mission in Kosovo (pursuant to UN Security Council resolution 1244 (1999) on behalf of the entity), on the other, is a development that should be welcomed.[20] The Treaty entered into force on 1 July 2006 for a period of ten years. The Energy Community Treaty is not a mixed agreement, as the scope of the treaty is fully covered by Community competence (Arts. 43(2), 55, 83, 89, 95, 133 and 175 TEC). However, the (geographically most concerned) EU Member States may become participants without voting rights in the institutions of the Energy Community pursuant to Article 95 of the Treaty. While this form of 'enhanced multilateralism'[21] is limited

19 On the high levels of intra-regional trade, see European Commission, 'Trade in South Eastern Europe', MEMO/06/155, Brussels, 5 April 2006. For up to date data, see the portal of the WIIW Balkan Observatory, at: <http://www.wiiw.ac.at/balkan>. For an overview of recent macroeconomic and structural developments in the countries of the Western Balkans, as well as contributions on various topics that represent a common challenge for all the economies in the region, see European Commission (DG ECFIN), 'Western Balkans in Transition', 30 *Enlargement Papers* (2006).

20 See Council Decision of 29 May 2006 on the conclusion by the European Community of the Energy Community Treaty, *OJ* 2006 L 198/16. The text of the Treaty itself follows on page 18. For an analysis of these and other peculiarities of the Energy Community Treaty, see F. Hoffmeister, 'Die Beziehungen der Europäischen Union zu den Staaten des Westbalkans', in S. Kadelbach, ed., *Die Außenbeziehungen der Europäischen Union* (Baden-Baden, Nomos 2006) pp. 125-150 at pp. 132-138.

21 See S. Blockmans and A. Łazowski, 'Conclusions: Squaring the Ring of Friends', in S. Blockmans and A. Łazowski, eds., *The European Union and its Neighbours: A Legal Appraisal of the EU's Policies of Stabilisation, Partnership and Integration* (The Hague, T.M.C. Asser Press 2006) pp. 613-639; and A. Łazowski, 'Box of Chocolates Integration: The European Economic Area and Swiss Model Revisited', in S. Blockmans, S. Prechal and W. Douma, eds., *Reconciling 'Deepening' and 'Widening' of the European Union* (The Hague, T.M.C. Asser Press 2007, forthcoming).

to the creation of an integrated market in natural gas and electricity,[22] the Energy Community Treaty does provide a legal framework (i.e., a new international organisation equipped with autonomous decision-making powers and legal instruments) for exporting and extending the EC's *acquis* on energy, the environment, competition and renewables to the Western Balkans.[23] As such, the Treaty aims to create a stable regulatory and market framework capable of attracting investment so that all parties have access to the continuous supply of gas and electricity that is essential for economic development and social stability. The Energy Community Treaty provides a model for the integration of the relatively small markets of south-eastern Europe in other segments of the European Union's single market. An example of the latter is the creation of a European Common Aviation Area (ECAA) by 2010.[24] Just like the integration efforts of the six founding states of the ECSC in the field of coal and steel were a precursor to the decision to expand their cooperation to other domains of their economies with the creation of the EEC, the Energy Community Treaty heralds the resuscitation of a much broader platform for realising their economic ambitions, namely the Central European Free Trade Agreement (CEFTA).

CEFTA will provide the countries of the Western Balkans with a broader platform to realise their economic ambitions and meet two important requirements of EU pre-accession conditionality: regional cooperation and readiness for the competitive impact of participating in the Union's single market. Since its enactment in 1992, the agreement's aim has been to ensure the free commercial

---

22 At a later stage, the integrated market may involve other energy products and carriers, such as liquefied natural gas, petrol, hydrogen or other essential network infrastructures.

23 See Title II of the Treaty. Article 94 of the Treaty provides that the institutions of the Energy Community shall interpret any term or concept used in the Treaty that is derived from EC law in conformity with the case law of the ECJ or the CFI. Where no interpretation from those courts is available, the Ministerial Council of the Energy Community will give guidance in interpreting the Treaty, not prejudging any interpretation of the *acquis* by the ECJ or the CFI at a later stage.

24 See, e.g., European Commission, Proposal for a Council Decision on the conclusion of the Multilateral Agreement between the Republic of Albania, Bosnia and Herzegovina, the Republic of Bulgaria, the Republic of Croatia, the European Community, the Republic of Iceland, the former Yugoslav Republic of Macedonia, the Kingdom of Norway, Serbia and Montenegro, Romania and the United Nations Interim Administration Mission in Kosovo on the Establishment of a European Common Aviation Area (ECAA), COM (2006) 113 final, Brussels, 14 March 2006. See also the study prepared by the European Commission – World Bank Office for South East Europe, *The European Common Aviation Area and the Western Balkans: Domestic Reforms and Regional Integration in Air Transport*, February 2007. The EC and the countries of the region have already concluded bilateral agreements in this field. See, e.g., Agreement between the European Community and Serbia and Montenegro on certain aspects of air services, *OJ* 2006 L 169/37; Agreement between the European Community and Bosnia and Herzegovina on certain aspects of air services, *OJ* 2006 L 169/48; Agreement between the European Community and the former Yugoslav Republic of Macedonia on certain aspects of air services, *OJ* 2006 L 217/17; and Agreement between the Council of Ministers of the Republic of Albania and the European Community on certain aspects of air services, *OJ* 2006 L 294/52.

flow of products and services between countries sharing a common EU perspective and political stability in Central and Eastern Europe.[25] As such, CEFTA has made a valuable contribution in preparing the CEECs for the competitive forces within the single market and – ultimately – accession to the European Union. The founding members of CEFTA (the Czech Republic, Hungary, Poland and Slovakia) left CEFTA when they acceded to the European Union in 2004. So did Slovenia. In view of the departure of Bulgaria (party since 1998) and Romania (party since 1997) following their accession to the Union on 1 January 2007, CEFTA was preserved by extending its membership to cover the Western Balkan states, thereby replacing the 'spaghetti bowl' of bilateral free trade agreements between them.[26] On 6 April 2006, nine Heads of Government and one Minister of Foreign Affairs from the Balkans, and the Special Representative of UNMIK on behalf of Kosovo, adopted a joint declaration underpinning their political commitment to start negotiations on the enlargement and amendment of CEFTA in May.[27] Eight months later, on 19 December 2006, the political leaders of the countries and territories involved signed a new Central European Free Trade Agreement.[28] Included in the enlarged CEFTA are Albania, Bosnia-Herzegovina, Croatia (since 2002), Macedonia (since 2006), Moldova, Montenegro, Serbia and the United Nations Interim Administration Mission in Kosovo. The agreement focuses on the promotion of simpler and less bureaucratic procedures and the introduction of modern trade provisions in areas such as harmonisation, competition, state aid, services and the protection of intellectual property rights. As such, the agreement assists Montenegro and Serbia (including Kosovo) in their preparation for WTO membership, because the two processes are rooted in the same goals and rules of progressive trade liberalisation. The European Union, which is not a party to the agreement, had strongly supported an agreement on the enlargement of CEFTA because of the complementary nature of the regional cooperation stemming from CEFTA's principles within the EU integration process.[29]

---

25 The original 1992 Agreement is reproduced entirely in 34 *ILM* (1995) pp. 8-42, with an accompanying note from P. Kornfeld, 'CEFTA', 34 *ILM* (1995) pp. 3-7. See also D. Lopandić, *Regional Initiatives in South Eastern Europe* (Belgrade, European Movement in Serbia 2001) at pp. 93-102.

26 A matrix of the free trade agreements in the region is available at: <http://en.wikipedia.org/wiki/Stability_Pact_for_South_Eastern_Europe#FTA_Progress>. The quote is from European Trade Commissioner Peter Mandelson's 'Remarks at the launch of CEFTA expansion negotiations', SPEECH/06/228, Bucharest on 6 April 2006.

27 Joint Declaration by Prime Ministers, South Eastern Europe Summit, Bucharest, 6 April 2006, available at: <http://www.stabilitypact.org/trade/documents/tradeFINAL-joint%20declaration.pdf>.

28 See 'A New Regional Agreement to Develop Trade in South Eastern Europe', MEMO/06/502, Brussels, 19 December 2006.

29 See Council Conclusions of 20 March 2006, in Press Release No. 7035/06 (Presse 69). Others have made the argument that extending the matrix of bilateral trade agreements into a pan-regional

Based on the foregoing, we should witness substantial progress in regional economic cooperation in the coming years. As a result of the greater ownership of the countries of the Western Balkans in these forms of regional cooperation, a review of the *ad hoc* structures and methods of regional cooperation has become necessary. It has been acknowledged by at least one of those structures, the Stability Pact, that the time has come to pass the buck to the countries of the region. In May 2006, the Regional Table of the Stability Pact adopted a roadmap for a regionally-owned cooperation framework in south-eastern Europe.[30] The roadmap foresees in the creation of a Regional Cooperation Council (RCC) to take over the responsibilities of the Stability Pact in early 2008. A Secretariat will be established in Sarajevo and a Secretary General has recently been elected.[31] The RCC and its Secretariat will provide the SEECP, for a long time the only regionally-owned initiative,[32] with operational capabilities as well as a framework for the continued involvement of the international donor community in the region. Priority areas for cooperation in the framework of the RCC are economic and social development, infrastructure, justice and home affairs, security cooperation, building human capital and parliamentary cooperation. Social cohesion and gender mainstreaming will also be given due attention. As such, these activities will complement and build on achievements within CEFTA, the ECAA and the Energy Community and should be welcomed.

2.1.2 *Focus on the Membership Action Plan and the Partnership for Peace*

Until it develops a forceful military arm of its own, NATO remains a crucial partner for the European Union in the Western Balkans, and its continued engagement is imperative. The Western Balkans is the region where the 'Berlin Plus' arrangements have finally paid off. EUFOR Althea in Bosnia-Herzegovina is a case in point.[33] In the short to medium term, NATO's support for the EU-led security forces is crucial. The formulation by NATO of a long-term strategy for the Western Balkans, beyond the situation-specific deployments in Bosnia-Herzegovina and Kosovo, will enhance the security context in the entire region.

---

trade association is likely to be inadequate. See D. Kernohan, 'Reverse Balkanisation? Trade Integration in South-East Europe', *CEPS Working Document* No. 249, August 2006. Kernohan argues that it would be better to extend the present customs union with Turkey to include trade with the entire south-east European zone of countries linked to the European Union.

30 See Chairman's Conclusions, Regional Table of the Stability Pact, 30 May 2006, Belgrade; available at: <http:// www.stabilitypact.org>.

31 The Croatian deputy Foreign Minister Hido Biscević was elected during a SEECP meeting in Zagreb on 10-11 May 2007. See N. Radić, 'Croatian diplomat to lead new Regional Co-operation Council', *Southeast European Times*, 25 May 2007.

32 See chapter 5, section 3.3.2.

33 See chapter 4, section 4.1.2.

The underlying goal for this strategy is the development in each Western Balkan state of a security capacity under civilian democratic control, as well as the eventual transition of the role played by NATO units from security forces to security *development* forces. To put it in the words of the International Commission on the Balkans: '[p]aradoxically, membership in NATO is the only effective instrument for demilitarising this most militarised part of Europe.'[34]

The Membership Action Plan, the Partnership for Peace programme and joint military exercises are the basis for this strategy. NATO played the role of a fast integration track for the CEECs, and it should do the same for the Western Balkans. On the basis of the progress achieved on their Membership Action Plans, Albania, Croatia and Macedonia should receive invitations to join NATO at the Alliance's summit in the spring of 2008. And in order for NATO enlargement to fulfil its regional role, the Alliance should offer membership in the Membership Action Plan to PfP programme partners Bosnia-Herzegovina, Montenegro and Serbia as soon as possible. In this way, ever closer and deeper relations with the Alliance would be forged with a view to all Western Balkan states becoming full members. In the process, the countries of the region would have to undergo comprehensive and demanding reforms covering a wide variety of areas, extending well beyond defence and security issues and military structures. In this respect, NATO enlargement can be a complementary tool to the European Union's efforts to take away some of the root causes of conflicts in south-eastern Europe and contribute to the extension of the zone of lasting peace and stability in Europe.

2.2 Fewer *ad hoc* arrangements

2.2.1 *The role of the United Nations*

The establishment of an enhanced Stabilisation and Association Process and the orientation on NATO's Membership Action Plan and Partnership for Peace programme as the basic road maps for the region's evolution and the subsequent transfer of responsibilities to EU officials, or preferably capable local leaders, implies that *ad hoc* arrangements such as the Office of the High Representative in Bosnia-Herzegovina and the UN Mission in Kosovo can be phased out. The international community seems set to restructure its presence in Bosnia-Herzegovina in 2008.[35] The United Nations has started its 'wind-down' operation and a change of guard with the European Union is being prepared pending consideration of status issues in Kosovo.[36]

---

[34] ICB, op. cit. n. 2, at p. 15.
[35] See, more extensively, *infra* section 3.3.2.
[36] See, more extensively, *infra* section 3.3.1.

As has been indicated by a dozen or more NGO's and think tanks active in the region, the international organisations and operations ought to prepare and publicise their transition plans to ease the process. These plans must identify the local government offices or ministries that will assume responsibility for specific issues and tasks, detail how the transition will occur and within what timeframe and identify a follow-up plan, specifying which offices or agencies within EU and NATO structures will retain responsibility for coordination with local actors on the major tasks required by the SAP and the MAP/PfP after the transition period is completed.

2.2.2 *The role of the OSCE and the Council of Europe*

The involvement of the Organisation for Security and Cooperation in Europe and the Council of Europe should be limited to those fields of action in which the European Union can benefit from their specialised expertise. For the OSCE this means election monitoring through ODIHR and conflict prevention through the High Commissioner on National Minorities. The Council of Europe could continue to assist its members (and the European Union) with human rights monitoring and advice on constitutional issues (Venice Commission).[37]

2.2.3 *The role of the United States and Russia*

Experience over the last seventeen years has shown that the military presence of the United States is still indispensable to ensure security and maintain stability in the Western Balkans and that EU efforts are most effective when closely coordinated with and supported by the United States, whether exercised unilaterally or through NATO. Notwithstanding the leading role of the European Union in shaping the future of the Western Balkans and the diversion of US attention from the region after the terrorist attacks against the United States on 11 September 2001, there is a strong case for continued engagement by the United States.[38] It is based partly on the US interest in the ongoing project of building a free and undivided Europe and partly on the need for the hard political and military power of the United States to confront security threats posed by a vacuum of authority in the Western Balkans. The main question for the United States is whether, in view of its difficulties in reconciling its 'deepening' and 'widening' agendas, the European Union has the staying power and political will to see its stabilisation strategy for the Western Balkans through. It is strongly in the interests of the United States to help the Union stay the course and ensure that it remains politically accountable for its end of the deal. The exact nature of US involvement will

[37] See, more extensively, chapter 2, sections 8 and 9.
[38] This is acknowledged by the ICB, op. cit. n. 2, at p. 38.

change with the situation, but an active presence in the region will remain necessary, as the United States possesses a unique combination of authority and capabilities that are still needed in parts of the Western Balkans. The European Union's nascent efforts to build up a rapid reaction force may help in limited circumstances, but for the foreseeable future this will not replace the capacity of NATO (as a *longa manus* of the United States) to assure basic security in the most fragile parts of the region.

Any discussion of the international community's role in the Western Balkans would be incomplete without considering the interests of Russia, which for centuries has seen itself as an important player in the region, a defender of the region's Orthodox populations. But Russia's influence in the region has waned after most of the Western Balkan countries started looking westward towards a European future. So far, Russia has acquiesced in NATO's expansion plans in the region and has even played a constructive role by participating in NATO-led missions. As such, the region has become a laboratory for cooperation between Russia and the Euro-Atlantic partners. But a reassertion of Russia's role on the international political scene, through energy politics and other questionable means, could again cause problems for the Euro-Atlantic players, especially over the final status of Kosovo.[39]

3. FACING CONSTITUTIONAL AND STATUS ISSUES

3.1 The current constitutional environment

Between 1994 and 2002, international negotiators and local parties designed (i) several constitutional frameworks for the Federation of Bosnia-Herzegovina (1994), which was to become one of the entities within the Republic of Bosnia-Herzegovina; (ii) a Constitution for that Republic, as part of the Dayton Accord (1995); (iii) changes to the Constitution of the Republika Srpska (1996); (iv) a constitutional framework for Kosovo as requested by the Special Representative of the UN Secretary-General (2001); (v) Macedonia's new constitutional framework, known as the Ohrid Agreement (2001); and (vi) the Constitutional Charter for the state union of Serbia and Montenegro, underpinned by the Belgrade Agreement (2002). These constitutional frameworks have several features in common. First, they were shaped by elites associated with armed conflicts. The processes that led to the Constitutions were not informed by popular mandates but by cold-blooded trade-offs to stop the fighting or avoid other destabilising acts. A second similarity is that each of the constitutional frameworks allocated power on

---

39 See *infra* section 3.3.1.

the basis of ethnicity. For example, in the Constitution of the Republic of Bosnia-Herzegovina, the Ohrid Agreement and the constitutional framework for Kosovo, members of various ethnic groups were assured specified quotas in the central institutions. While it is probably true that without these allocations of jobs and decision-making powers the peace agreements would have failed, the question is how long these undemocratic provisions should be tolerated. Third, the constitutional frameworks created weak states. Each state must compete with strongly decentralised powers, especially in the case of Bosnia-Herzegovina and (previously) in Serbia and Montenegro. State weakness is perpetuated in those states where there are influential international actors on the scene. The posts of the High Representative in Bosnia-Herzegovina and the Special Representative of the UN Secretary-General in Kosovo were established during crises. Years later, both continue to exercise extraordinary powers, including the authority to override local decisions. Neither the reach of these powers nor the occasions for their use are clearly defined or well understood. In both Bosnia-Herzegovina and Kosovo there has been an irresistible temptation for both international representatives and local governments to shift political accountability onto one another. Citizens are left guessing who is responsible for what.

A consequence of the patchwork regulatory environment is that state actors have become cumulatively weaker while powerful private actors, oligarchs and criminal syndicates generated by the wars of the 1990s have remained influential and have largely escaped scrutiny. This means that, in some areas, non-state institutions provide basic public services that traditionally fall under the responsibility of the state. It also means that some individuals receive pensions, health care and education from neighbouring states. The best example is provided by the Serbs of Mitrovica (Northern Kosovo), who are subsidised by Belgrade. The emphasis on decentralisation in Kosovo may accelerate the trend.[40]

3.2 The perceptions map: ICB survey

International stakeholders have frequently argued that postponing the resolution of key status issues is the lesser of two evils. While they concede that the status quo is not ideal, they maintain that it is nonetheless essential to maintain regional peace and stability. The results of the survey conducted by the International Commission on the Balkans (ICB) in 2005 show a more complex reality.[41] The key findings demonstrate that Bosnia-Herzegovina is no longer a highly contested state. Most Serbs in Serbia and almost half of the Serbs in Bosnia-Herzegovina view the separation of the Republika Srpska from Bosnia-Herzegovina as both undesirable

---

40 See ICG, 'Bridging Kosovo's Mitrovica Divide', *Europe Report* No. 165, 13 September 2005.

41 See ICB, op. cit. n. 2, Annex.

and unlikely.[42] It is important to note that the ICB's survey indicates that there is no ethnic group intent on threatening the existence of the state of Bosnia-Herzegovina and that the international community's nightmare that Kosovo's independence would automatically provoke the disintegration of Bosnia-Herzegovina has no foundation in reality. Still, it would be premature to conclude from this that nation-building among Serb communities across the region has been settled. Such a conclusion hinges on the implementation of the results of the final status talks for Kosovo. An indication of what can be expected was given when, in the wake of the pro-independence referendum results in Montenegro of 21 May 2006, even the Prime Minister of the Serb community in Bosnia-Herzegovina renewed calls for the independence of the Republika Srpska.[43]

As noted before, determining Kosovo's status is a contested process which, if mismanaged, could have a ruinous effect on the settlement of Serb-Albanian interests.[44] According to the survey conducted by the ICB, the establishment of a 'Greater Albania' is a development that could destabilise the region. The results of the survey show a relatively high acceptance of the idea of a Greater Albania among the Albanian populations of both Kosovo and Albania.[45] As a whole, they differ from other groups in the region in their view that a future unification of Kosovo and Albania is both desirable and possible.[46] This suggests that the process of nation-building among Albanian communities in the Western Balkans is still in progress. If the European Union fails to offer a convincing membership perspective to Albania and – if independent – Kosovo, it might bolster support for a Greater Albania among Albanians. This would almost certainly provoke a Serb reaction.

In contrast, when it comes to the territorial integrity of Macedonia, the survey shows that a great majority of Albanians in Macedonia reject the idea of dividing the country: 77.5 per cent of ethnic Albanians (and 85 per cent of ethnic Macedonians) support the territorial integrity of the Macedonian state.[47]

3.3 Balkan endgame[48]

Unresolved status issues and provisional constitutional frameworks are major obstacles for the process of European integration of parts of the Western Balkans.

---

42 Ibid., figure 5.

43 See T. Loza, 'Balkan Eye: Watch Out, Milorad', *Transitions Online*, 8 January 2007, referring to Milorad Dodik.

44 See chapter 4, section 3.3.

45 Even if this has been rejected by Albanian Prime Minister Sali Berisha on numerous occasions.

46 See ICB, op. cit. n. 2, Annex, figure 6.

47 Ibid., figure 7.

48 The term is taken from, *inter alia*, R. Bassett, 'Balkan Endgame?', *JDW* (1999); S. Biserko, 'Comment: Balkan Endgame', 23 *IWPR Balkan Crisis Report* (1999); and E. Pond, *Endgame in the Balkans: Regime Change, European Style* (Washington, Brookings Institution Press 2006).

While all states aspire to EU membership it is unclear how many will actually emerge from the current constitutional chaos. The integration of Bosnia-Herzegovina and Serbia (including Kosovo) into the European Union is unimaginable in the current circumstances of constitutional uncertainty.

3.3.1 *Kosovo's final status*

Time is running out in Kosovo. The international community has clearly failed in its attempts to stabilise and develop the province. The social and economic situation in the protectorate is depressing. Power cuts are regular. The province never boasted a self-sustaining economy, and chances are small that it will develop one now. In 2006, the official unemployment rate was more than 40 per cent.[49] A multi-ethnic Kosovo does not exist. The events of March 2004, July 2005 and February 2007 amount to the strongest signals yet that the situation could explode. UNMIK has demonstrated neither the capacity nor the courage to reverse this trend.[50] Serbs in Kosovo are living imprisoned in their enclaves with no freedom of movement, no jobs and with neither hope nor opportunity of meaningful integration into Kosovo's society.[51] The position of the Serbian minority in Kosovo is the greatest challenge to the European Union's willingness and ability to defend and export its proclaimed values.[52]

By endorsing final status talks, the UN Security Council on 24 October 2005 implicitly accepted that the 'standards before status' approach needed to be replaced by a 'status and standards' strategy. While the result of the negotiations will not solve all the territory's problems, postponement of the final status talks would no doubt have led to a further deterioration in the situation in the province. It is argued here that the European Union should play a much more prominent role in guiding this process.[53] The rationale behind this is simple. The determination of the final status of Kosovo should concentrate on offering real incentives to Belgrade, Priština and Tirana, so that all may find the prospect of an independent

---

[49] See European Commission (DG ECFIN), 'Western Balkans in Transition', 30 *Enlargement Papers* (2006) at p. 86.

[50] Indirectly, this has been acknowledged by the United Nations' outgoing Special Representative for Kosovo, Søren Jessen-Petersen. See 'UN mission head says Kosovo status-quo unsustainable', *DTT-NET.COM*, 26 August 2005.

[51] See ICG, loc. cit. n. 40.

[52] In the judgement of the UN Secretary-General's Special Envoy Kai Aide, the protectorate has made insufficient progress towards meeting internationally agreed standards with regard to human rights, respect for minorities and law and order. See UN Doc. S/PRST/2005/51.

[53] Compare with the current situation, as described in chapter 4, section 3.3.1. See further, ICG, 'Kosovo: Challenge of Transition', *Europe Report* No. 170, 17 February 2006. On the limits of the European Union's role as a state-builder in Kosovo, see D. Papadimitriou, P. Petrov and L. Greiçevci, 'To Build a State: Europeanization, EU Actorness and State-Building in Kosovo', 12 *EFA Rev.* (2007) pp. 219-238.

Kosovo as a future member of the European Union acceptable. The enhanced EU pre-accession process can provide such incentives. Thus, the implementation of the decision on the final status of Kosovo should be an integral part of the overall process of European integration of the Western Balkans. Of course, the European Union should be backed up by its international partners. The active engagement of the United States is of particular importance for a successful outcome of the negotiating process, as Kosovo Albanians still view the United States as the best guarantor of their independence.[54]

In this context, the ICB has recommended a helpful and realistic agenda for achieving Kosovo's independence and EU accession in four stages.[55] The first stage would see the de facto separation of Kosovo from Serbia. This stage is implicit in UN Security Council resolution 1244 (1999), which transformed Kosovo into a UN protectorate, even if the 'weaving fault' has been repaired and the text of the resolution now fully applies to Serbia.[56] The second stage (independence without full sovereignty) would see Kosovo as an independent entity but one where the international community reserves its powers in the fields of human rights and the protection of minorities – the areas that are essential for meeting the Copenhagen 'Plus' criteria. Legally, Kosovo would remain a protectorate, but the United Nations' authority, as defined by chapter VII of the UN Charter, would be transferred from UNMIK to the European Union. NATO's KFOR would preserve both its mandate and its size. Kosovo would be treated as an independent state but not as a sovereign one at this stage, allowing it to further develop a capacity for self-government. It would be assisted in this task by an EU administration for Kosovo and a civilian ESDP mission. The provisions in the final status agreement on the decentralisation of power (guaranteeing, *inter alia*, self-government and development for the Kosovo Serbs), the return of refugees and the clarification of property rights would be the key provisions to be implemented at this stage. The special arrangements for the areas around Mitrovica and the Serbian monasteries would have to be enforced by the transitional EU administration for Kosovo, backed up by KFOR. The third stage (guided sovereignty) would coincide with Kosovo's recognition as a candidate for EU membership. As the European Union cannot open accession negotiations with itself, that is to say, with a protectorate it controls, it would at this stage hand over its powers to the government of Kosovo. The Union would further exercise influence through the negotiation process alone. The fourth stage (sovereignty) would mark the accession of Kosovo to the European Union and its adoption of the shared sovereignty to which all EU Member States are subject. Martti

---

54 See ICB, op. cit. n. 2, Annex, figure 20.

55 Ibid., at pp. 18-23.

56 Chapter 4, section 3.3.3.

Ahtisaari's blueprint for the status settlement is a good and crucial first step in this process and should therefore be supported.[57]

3.3.2 *Bosnia-Herzegovina: from Bonn to Brussels*

Since the world celebrated the tenth anniversary of the Dayton Agreement, attention is increasingly being focused on how Bosnia-Herzegovina can move from the tutelage of the international community to a full-fledged, decentralised, modern, sovereign, democratic state. The need for constitutional change is high on the political agenda in Bosnia-Herzegovina. For Bosnians who have grown accustomed to the awkward political system established under the Dayton Agreement of 1995, this is revolutionary. There are few greater frustrations in Bosnia-Herzegovina than the country's multi-tiered political system with its rotating leadership positions shared by members of the three main ethnic groups, its many levels of administration and overlapping jurisdictions – all set up under Dayton and overseen by the international community's High Representative. While all involved agree that the present constitutional architecture is dysfunctional, deeper agreement about what Bosnia-Herzegovina's new Constitution should look like has long eluded the parties to the process. On 18 March 2006, the leaders of the main political parties reached a deal on constitutional changes.[58] They agreed to increase the number of ministries in central government and change the powers of the current three-member presidency into a single rotating one with two vice-presidents, each of them representing one of the country's main ethnic groups. The last stumbling block concerned the election of the members of the presidency and was only cleared after the Venice Commission of the Council of Europe gave its opinion on the issue.[59] Bosnian Muslims, Serbs and Croats finally agreed that the members of the presidency would be elected by the national Parliament (in accordance with the wishes of the Bosnian Croats, who represent the smallest ethnic community) and not by direct vote. Like Dayton, this agreement on a new Constitution was the fruit of painful compromise. It was hailed by the Council of the European Union as representing a significant step towards strengthening Bosnia-Herzegovina's state institutions and boosting the country's ability to meet European standards.[60]

Along with the need for constitutional change, the main problem that Bosnia-Herzegovina faces today is the transition from its current status as a protectorate that is defined by the Bonn powers to a sustainable self-governed state guided by

---

[57] See chapter 4, section 3.3.4.

[58] As reported in 'BiH parties agree to constitutional reforms', *Southeast European Times*, 19 March 2006.

[59] See Opinion No. 374/2006, CDL-AD(2006)004, Strasbourg, 20 March 2006.

[60] Council Conclusions of 20 March, in Press Release No. 7035/06 (Presse 69).

the process of EU accession. The coercive authority of the High Representative was originally developed for an unstable environment in the wake of armed conflict. When its intrusive powers to intervene in and overrule domestic institutions were developed in mid-1997, these were intended to head off threats to public order and attempts by the former warring parties to challenge the integrity of the state. However, as the agenda of politics in Bosnia-Herzegovina has shifted to very different issues like democratic consolidation and development, the powers and activities of the High Representative continue to dominate Bosnian politics. This has blocked the development of self-government, which is a precondition to becoming an EU candidate state.[61] After the success of the first elections to be run and managed entirely by domestic institutions rather than the international community, the challenge for the next political leaders of Bosnia-Herzegovina will be to complete the stalled police and constitutional reforms. With their joint report on the European Union's future presence in Bosnia-Herzegovina, the SG/HR and the European Commissioner for Enlargement expressed their conviction that these reforms could be implemented before 30 June 2007, the date on which the Office of the High Representative was provisionally scheduled for closure and the Bonn powers of the High Representative could be transferred back to the domestic authorities.[62] The report noted that progress in Bosnia-Herzegovina justified the transfer of full responsibility to its elected leaders by end-June 2007 and stated that 'only threats to the country's peace and stability ought to change that timeline.'[63]

Unfortunately, these plans were pushed back by one year when the Steering Board of the Peace Implementation Council, which reviews the stabilisation of the country, decided on 27 February 2007 to extend the mandate of the OHR by one year (until 30 June 2008) due to the still volatile situation in Bosnia-Herzegovina.[64] With a continued visible military and police presence on the ground, the plan is now that a reinforced office for the EU Special Representative should guarantee the smooth transition from the international community's caretaker role to the European Union's role as a strong supporter for further reforms under domestic governance.[65] The EUSR for Bosnia-Herzegovina would

61 In a similar vein, see S. Recchia, 'Beyond International Trusteeship: EU Peacebuilding in Bosnia and Herzegovina', Occasional Paper No. 66, February 2007, EUISS, Paris.

62 See joint report by the EU SG/HR and the EU Commissioner for Enlargement on a reinforced EU presence in Bosnia and Herzegovina in the context of the envisaged closure of the Office of the High Representative, 17 October 2006.

63 Ibid.

64 See Council Conclusions of 5 March 2007, in Press Release No. 6756/07 (Presse 39) at 10. The PIC Steering Board will again review the situation in Bosnia-Herzegovina in October 2007 and February 2008.

65 See also the recommendations by the ICG, 'Ensuring Bosnia's Future: A New International Engagement Strategy', *Europe Report* No. 180, 15 February 2007. It should be noted that the joint report by the EU SG/HR and the EU Commissioner for Enlargement also recommended maintaining the coalition of the international community as an important coordination forum.

remain as the overall coordinator of the activities of the EU family in the country (EUFOR Althea, EUPM and others) and would work alongside the European Commission's delegation in Sarajevo.[66] The office of the EUSR would concentrate on political and security-related issues, offer political advice, facilitate political and legal processes, especially in relation to further constitutional reform, and promote the rule of law. It could also offer advice on rationalising structures. As noted before, the enhanced Stabilisation and Association Process could provide the framework that provides the requisite incentives for strengthening the state's federal structures and developing policy-making capacity.

4. BUILDING MEMBER STATES IN THE WESTERN BALKANS

The success of EU enlargement is one of the few unambiguously positive achievements of the post-Cold War world, nothing short of a revolution, as European Enlargement Commissioner Olli Rehn is fond of saying. In little over a decade, the prospect of EU membership succeeded in consolidating democratic and market reforms and transforming societies throughout Central and Eastern Europe. The European Union likes to repeat that it can do the same for the Western Balkans. There are, however, three critical differences compared to previous pre-accession rounds: the problem of weak states; the Union's lack of experience in integrating them; and the presence of other – powerful – international actors on the ground. Enlargement of the Union with most of the countries of the Western Balkans is therefore not a matter of business as usual. Functioning state administrations have to be developed – in one case even in the absence of a state (Kosovo) – the quality of political representation has to be improved and the economy has to be reformed. This section will only focus on institution-building and constituency-building. For suggestions on how to realise economic revitalisation and 'Europeanisation', suffice it to refer to what has already been said about the creation of a regional markets and their integration into the European Union's single market.[67]

4.1 Institution-building

The Member-State-building strategy that is advocated by the International Commission on the Balkans and think tanks like the European Stability Initiative and the International Crisis Group holds the middle ground between the 'authoritarian' model of international tutelage, as applied in Bosnia-Herzegovina and

---

66 Over time, a similar construction as in Macedonia could perhaps be opted for by combining the posts of head of the delegation of the Commission and the EUSR. This double-hatting could increase the coherence and consistency of the European Union's role in the country.

67 See *supra* section 2.1.1.3.

Kosovo, and the EU accession process as typified by the enlargements of 2004 and 2007. The objective is not 'simply' to build stable, legitimate states whose own citizens will seek to strengthen and not destroy them. Rather, it is the establishment of states that the European Union can accept as full members. The trouble is that there is not a single model EU Member State. In the absence thereof, and in view of the wide variety of Member States' practices and constitutional arrangements in fields such as justice or tax administration, the European Commission is wary to recommend specific institutional solutions to candidate countries. The International Commission on the Balkans has regarded this as a 'serious obstacle' and has called upon the European Commission to 'assume the responsibility for some of the institutional choices that the applicants are forced to make'.[68] Disregarding the fact that, in this respect, the European Commission could only make recommendations to and execute such responsibility for the Council, imposing institutional choices on Kosovo would in the long run be counter-productive. For Member-State-building to be truly effective over time, homebred choices would have to be carried by democratic majorities. The extent to which the European Union can win local hearts and minds by mobilising the carrot of Kosovo's future entry to the club remains a key challenge, particularly in a context where the pro-Europeanism of local elites cannot be taken for granted.[69] In this respect, the instrument of benchmarking in the SAP should be cautiously applied when facing the most challenging reform issues: administrative capacity-building and reform of the judiciary. These issues, which in previous accession rounds were tackled last, should be included as the principal objectives of the future negotiating frameworks for Macedonia and the other countries of the Western Balkans.[70] The progress of the candidates in the field of institutional capacity-building could then be monitored by measuring the level of implementation of the *acquis* – not just its adoption – in the light of annual progress reports and accession partnerships.[71]

---

68 ICB, op. cit. n. 2, at p. 30.

69 Much of the scepticism towards 'Europe' has its roots in the European Union's early debacles over the handling of the disintegration of the SFRY and, more importantly, a widespread perception that European powers did not do enough to protect the Albanian population in Kosovo against Serb aggression.

70 The ICB has rightly suggested that instead of starting with the White Book on the Single Market, the countries of the Western Balkans would be much better served by a White Book on Freedom, Security and Justice. In practical terms, this would mean that assisting the countries from the region in the field of justice and home affairs would be the overriding priority for the accession process and that the state of the rule of law would be the major criterion in evaluating the progress of Western Balkan countries on their journey to the European Union. See ICB, op. cit. n. 2, at p. 30.

71 See S. Blockmans, 'Impact of EU Accession on the Role of (Potential) Candidate Countries' Executives', in A. Kellermann, J. Czuczai, S. Blockmans, A. Albi and W. Douma, eds., *Impact of EU Accession on the Legal Orders of New Member States and (Pre-)Candidate Countries: Hopes and Fears* (The Hague, T.M.C. Asser Press 2006) pp. 291-300.

4.2 Constituency-building

A state is not only a legal and administrative entity, it is also a social phenomenon. The growing gap between a state's public administration and its citizens is a critical risk to the success of the European Union's transformative policies.[72] Political mobilisation and participation is essential. In the Western Balkans, the modernisation of the political culture and discourse is also necessary. The emphasis should be on the future, while progress is made by dealing with the past. Three challenges stick out: (i) assuring minority rights protection in decentralised systems of governance; (ii) achieving justice and reconciliation on war crimes; and (iii) the fight against organised crime. These will be discussed in turn.

4.2.1 *Assuring minority rights protection*

As observed at the outset of this study, war and ethnic cleansing on the territory of the former Yugoslavia have resulted in significant demographic shifts. While all countries of the Western Balkans still contain multi-ethnic areas, most countries are now nation-states with majorities amounting to 80 per cent or more of the population. Albania, Croatia, Serbia (excluding Kosovo) and Kosovo (as a separate entity) have strong majorities, and most minorities live in a relatively compact part of the country and account for 10 to 20 per cent of the population. Only Bosnia-Herzegovina, Macedonia and Montenegro are multi-ethnic, with little or no dominance by one community.[73] Decentralisation policies aggravate the ethnic separation in certain parts of the Western Balkans. Albanian areas around Tetovo in Northern Macedonia and the predominantly Serb area around Mitrovica in Northern Kosovo are cases in point. While the argument for decentralisation (with more competences exercised at local level minorities are able to govern themselves to a larger degree, which in turn should increase their loyalty to the state) is perfectly acceptable, its reality in the Western Balkans is not. Human rights violations by regional authorities against minority elements (e.g., Roma and residents or returnees of a different ethnicity) largely escape international monitoring.[74] Hence, what is needed is the recognition of minorities at municipal level and the international monitoring of their fundamental rights.[75]

---

72 Again, the same might be said of the transformation process of the European Union itself.

73 See F. Bieber, 'Minority Rights in Practice in South Eastern Europe', Discussion Paper, King Baudouin Foundation, 30 September 2004.

74 Ibid.

75 See ICB, op. cit. n. 2, at pp. 32-33.

4.2.2 *Reinterpreting ICTY conditionality*

The second challenge to constituency-building in the Western Balkan societies concerns justice and reconciliation on war crimes. Since 1993, the ICTY has played a decisive role in bringing war criminals to justice. However, it has failed to take away the distrust of local people regarding its mission to achieve justice and reconciliation in the Western Balkans.[76] The European Union has defined full cooperation with the ICTY as a threshold conditionality when it comes to the process of integration.[77] The challenge facing the Union at present is how to translate the post-war conditionality of the ICTY, which is charged with examining concrete crimes in the cases of Gotovina, Mladić and Karadžić, into one that looks towards the future and concentrates on the strengthening of European values across the region. While the unprecedented decision by the Council to postpone the start of membership talks with Croatia was – incidentally or not – followed by the arrest of General Gotovina and his transfer to The Hague, a similar decision to suspend negotiations on an SAA with Serbia failed to cajole Belgrade into compliance with ICTY conditionality. Of course, full cooperation with the ICTY should remain mandatory for the opening of accession negotiations with the European Union. However, failure to transfer a single high-profile fugitive to the Tribunal should not hold back the development of entire countries when it comes to negotiating and signing SAAs. In partial recognition of this, and despite the opposition of the United Kingdom and the Netherlands, the strict requirement of handing over Mladić to the ICTY seems to have been dropped by the Council in an attempt to lessen the blow of an internationally imposed decision to let Kosovo secede from Serbia.[78] As was to be expected, the European Union won the scorn of Carla del Ponte, the ICTY's Chief Prosecutor.[79] But what should be learned from these experiences is that ICTY conditionality, at least in the phase of negotiating and signing SAAs, should be understood more broadly than just the need to transfer one or two suspected war criminals to The Hague.[80] Instead, it should concentrate on the willingness of Western Balkan societies as a

---

76 See, P. Hazan, *Justice in a Time of War: The True Story Behind the International Criminal Tribunal for the Former Yugoslavia* (Texas, A&M University Press 2004).

77 In addition, the European Union regards the success of the ICTY as critical in its struggle to confer legitimacy on the International Criminal Court.

78 In February 2007, the Council confirmed the European Union's readiness to resume SAA negotiations with a new government in Belgrade 'provided it shows clear commitment and takes concrete and effective action *for* full co-operation with the ICTY.' See Council Conclusions of 12 February 2007, in Press Release No. 6037/07 (Presse 18) at 13 [emphasis added].

79 See 'Del Ponte again urges EU not to resume SAA talks with Serbia', *Southeast European Times*, 16 February 2007.

80 For the counterarguments, see G. Evans and J. Lyons, 'No Mladic, no talks', *International Herald Tribune*, 21 March 2007; and S. Freizer and A. Stroehlein, 'The EU's inexcusable pardon for Serbia', *European Voice*, 29 March 2007.

whole to examine the causes and consequences of their troubled past. Hence, the European Union should attach more importance than it does now to the readiness and ability of the domestic judicial, religious and educational authorities to deal with the war-related crimes of the past and to promote tolerance and reconciliation. In this respect, recent judgments by Bosnian, Croatian and Serbian courts convicting war criminals to long prison sentences should be taken as a positive sign.[81] The European Union was therefore right to look at the broader picture and no longer outsource the decision-making on compliance with ICTY conditionality to the single-minded Chief Prosecutor of the Tribunal.

4.2.3 *Fighting organised crime*

A third challenge in the movement towards moderation and modernisation in the Western Balkans is posed by so-called 'politico-criminal syndicates'. In every country of the region, there are people in high places with the motivation and resources to undermine local reformers' efforts to modernise and clean up their governments and economies.[82] Strengthened by the profits from pirate privatisation and bolstered by cross-border illegal connections, the revenue and survival of these syndicates depend on their ability to suppress efforts to introduce transparency and accountability into the political and economic systems of the states in which they operate. Their combination of influence, access, resources and superficially appealing ideology makes it difficult for new and weak governments to mount sustained campaigns against them. Until the Western Balkan governments have the capacity and will to fight these politico-criminal groups, the Office of the High Commissioner, the European Union and UNMIK have launched such campaigns in Bosnia-Herzegovina, Macedonia and Kosovo, that is to say, where the extent and authority of these international institutions are greatest. Arrests of ethnic extremists, seizure of weapons, control of border crossings, the enforcement of travel and financial restrictions on key leaders and improved law enforcement and intelligence cooperation have played important roles in reducing ethnic violence in these parts of the Western Balkans.[83] While

---

[81] See, e.g., 'Croatian Court Charges Glavas, Six Others with 1991 Crimes Against Ethnic Serbs', *Southeast European Times*, 11 April 2007; N. Wood, 'Serbian court convicts 4 in Srebrenica murders', *International Herald Tribune*, 10 April 2007; and N. Wood, 'Serbia praised over trials of alleged war criminals', *International Herald Tribune*, 3 January 2006.

[82] In the Western Balkans, a prime example concerns the assassination in March 2003 of the pro-reform Prime Minister of Serbia Zoran Djindjić by Milorad Ulemek, former member of the secret police and condemned, together with his superiors, to a forty-year jail term for the kidnapping and murder of Serbia's former President Ivan Stambolić. See 'Serb president's killers jailed', *Financial Times*, 18 July 2005.

[83] In Bosnia-Herzegovina, in particular, progress in moving the country toward European standards of governance was only made when the OHR confronted the syndicates' power over industry,

these efforts have been limited, the underlying lesson is clear: decisive actions aimed at the levers of power controlled by the politico-criminal groupings produce results and help reformers' efforts to modernise the state. The international community should therefore continue the seizing of criminal institutions and the pursuit, prosecution and removal from office of individuals associated with illegal intersections of government and financial power until local institutions acquire the ability and the will to take it upon themselves.

5. CONCLUDING REMARKS

The European Union has come a long way in the Western Balkans in just a few years. During the 1990s, while it stood by and watched the Balkans burn, it was the United States, in the framework of NATO, that acted decisively to stop the war in Bosnia-Herzegovina and the crisis in Kosovo. In the aftermath of the Kosovo crisis, the European Union finally found its voice to say no to new armed conflict in the heart of Europe. It adopted sanctions, brokered political agreements, launched its first-ever police and military missions and directed economic, legal and administrative reforms. Yet, despite the comprehensive nature of the Union's actions, its strategy towards the Western Balkans has been marked by confusion. While the European Union actively courted the countries of the region to form a closer relationship, it scaled down the level of financial support to tackle complicated issues that form the root causes of radical discontent and instability. Thus, the Union's Stabilisation and Association Process has made a critical contribution to progress achieved throughout the region, but the returns on its investment are dwindling. In contrast to the CEECs, the Western Balkans still contain the possibility of a genuine security threat. Therefore, there is currently a real imperative to move the region as a whole from the stage of international protectorates and weak states to the stage of accession to the European Union and NATO. This scenario not only presupposes a reinvigorated drive for reform by the countries concerned but also presumes a continued, albeit reconfigured engagement by the Euro-Atlantic security organisations under the leadership of the European Union. Such a strategy would be significant not just practically but

---

government finances, borders and the media. Examples include the 1997 removal of media from nationalist control in the Republika Srpska; the seizure in 2001 of a bank controlled by hard-line Croats who had stolen from their own people; the March 2002 decision by the OHR to remove constitutional provisions that helped nationalist parties retain control of public institutions and resources; and the December 2004 sackings of senior Bosnian Serb security officials accused of harbouring war crimes suspects, including Ratko Mladić. See the six-monthly reports of the High Representative for implementation of the Dayton Peace Agreement to the UN Secretary-General, available on the OHR's website at: <http://www.ohr.int>.

symbolically as well: if the Western Balkans were to be successfully integrated into the European Union, it would finally banish the possibility of a revival of the type of armed conflict that so plagued the continent's nineteenths and twentieth century history. Incidentally, defusing the 'powder keg' would also be a landmark achievement for the European Union in its quest for a more prominent role internationally.

By opening accession negotiations with Croatia and granting candidate country status to Macedonia, the European Union has finally shown its commitment to the countries of this troubled region. One can only hope that, despite the constitutional impasse and the enlargement *fatigue* from which it is currently suffering, the Union will not shy away from offering a real membership perspective to the other Western Balkan countries as well. By transcending the 'potential members' mindset and showing its commitment to Albania, Bosnia-Herzegovina, Montenegro, Serbia and Kosovo, the Union will render the Stabilisation and Association Process a much more credible framework. But it will have to do more than that to prevent these least stable parts of the Western Balkans from turning into a new ghetto. The Union will have to address the remaining constitutional and status issues and put its money where its mouth is. While nation-building in the Western Balkans has entered its final stages with the functional separation of Serbia and Montenegro, the search for the end of international governance in Bosnia-Herzegovina and a final status for Kosovo, the EU Member States seem unwilling to release the necessary funds to see these defining processes through. Only a bigger effort based on a fair but firm application of the conditionality principle will lead to the integration of the Western Balkans into the European mainstream. This means that countries should gain substantial rewards if they meet tough political, economic and legal conditions and that rewards will be denied or withdrawn if they lapse back into bad habits. Today, probably more than ever, tough love is required.

A CHRONOLOGY OF KEY EVENTS IN THE HISTORY OF THE WESTERN BALKANS

1389 – On 28 June, a coalition of Serbs, Hungarians, Bosnians, Bulgarians and Albanians under the leadership of the Serbian Prince Lazar meets the Ottoman army for a battle on the Field of Blackbirds (*Kosovo Polje*, in Serbian). The coalition suffers a crushing defeat. Much of the region falls under the influence of the Ottoman Empire.

1878 – In the wake of the Russo-Turkish War of 1877-1878, Europe's Great Powers and the Ottoman Empire decide on the reorganisation of the Balkans at the Congress of Berlin. Ceding to Russian pressure, Serbia and Montenegro are declared independent principalities. Bosnia and Herzegovina are placed under the administration of Austria-Hungary. The establishment of a border between Greece and Turkey is not accomplished. The Congress sows the seeds of further conflicts, including two Balkan Wars and World War I.

1908 – Austria-Hungary annexes Bosnia and Herzegovina.

1912 – First Balkan War. The Balkan League (Bulgaria, Greece, Montenegro and Serbia) conquer Ottoman-held Macedonia and northern Greece and subsequently fall out over the division of the spoils.

1913 – Second Balkan War (Serbia, Greece and Romania v. Bulgaria over Macedonia). Serbia wrests control of Kosovo from Albania.

1914 – On 28 June, Serbian nationalist Gavrilo Princip assassinates Archduke Franz Josef, the heir to the Austrian Empire, in Sarajevo. One month after the assassination, Austria-Hungary declares war on Serbia. Serbia's ally Russia declares war on Austria-Hungary. Austria-Hungary's ally Germany declares war on Russia and World War I begins.

1918 – Following the end of World War I, the Treaty of Versailles establishes the principle of self-determination and the League of Nations. In the resulting break-ups of the Austro-Hungarian and Ottoman Empires, the Kingdom of the Serbs, Croats and Slovenes is created. Serbia dominates the kingdom.

1919 – The Communist Party is founded in the Kingdom of Serbs, Croats and Slovenes.

1920 – The Kingdom of Serbs, Croats and Slovenes joins the so-called 'Little Entente' (with France, Czechoslovakia and Romania) against what remains of the Austria-Hungary.

1929 – The Kingdom of the Serbs, Croats and Slovenes is renamed Yugoslavia. The parliamentary system is abolished in favour of a royal dictatorship. Macedonians are forbidden from having political parties and from speaking Macedonian in public.

1939 – Croatia earns a certain degree of autonomy within Yugoslavia with the creation of the *Banovina* (Duchy) of Croatia.

1940 – Nazi Germany occupies Denmark, Norway, Belgium and the Netherlands. It establishes the puppet Vichy government in much of France. Italy invades Greece.

1941 – Nazi Germany invades Yugoslavia from Hungary, Bulgaria and Romania. Germany and Italy divide Slovenia. Italy also takes parts of Dalmatia and Montenegro, as well as Kosovo and Western Macedonia on behalf of Albania. Bulgaria gets the rest of Macedonia. Hungary gets part of Vojvodina. Bosnia is officially 'independent'. Serbia comes under German military occupation. Croatia becomes a fascist puppet regime of the Nazis under the *Ustaše*. Ethnic cleansing of Serbs begins. Serbs respond with Chetnik guerrilla forces of their own. Josip Broz (Tito) leads the Communist partisan movement (primarily Serbs) against the *Ustaše* and the Nazis, as well as the Chetniks.

1943 – The Western alliance discontinues aiding the Chetniks under Draz Mihajlović and starts aiding Tito's partisans. Proclamation of Communist Yugoslavia.

1944 – Tito's partisans, aided by the Soviets and the British, push the Nazis out of Yugoslavia. The pre-war borders between Bulgaria, Greece and Yugoslavia are restored.

1945 – World War II ends. Tito comes to power. The Communists abolish the monarchy and establish the Federal People's Republic of Yugoslavia.

1946 – A new constitution is adopted, whereby six constituent republics (Bosnia-Herzegovina, Croatia, Macedonia, Montenegro, Serbia and Slovenia) are established.

1948 – Tito breaks with Stalin.

1950s – Yugoslavia is at the forefront of the international non-aligned movement.

1963 – The new constitution proclaims Yugoslavia to be a socialist republic (Socialist Republic of Yugoslavia, SFRY) and Tito is named president-for-life.

1967 – The national movement in Croatia enjoys a resurgence as Croatian intellectuals protest against the suppression of the Croatian language in Yugoslavia.

1968 – Kosovo becomes an autonomous province of the SFRY. Hungarian is recognised as an official language in Vojvodina.

1971 – Officials in Zagreb circulate proposals for Croatia to secede from Yugoslavia. Tito responds by suppressing organisations and sending several officials to jail (including future Croatian President Franjo Tudjman).

1973 – The European Economic Community (EEC) concludes a trade agreement with the SFRY.

1974 – The new constitution of the SFRY strengthens the powers of the autonomous provinces of Kosovo and Vojvodina within the Serbian republic.

1980 – The EEC signs a cooperation agreement with the SFRY. Tito dies. A collective presidency rules until 1991.

1984 – On 8 February, the XIVth Winter Olympic Games open in Sarajevo, introducing the world to a city of cosmopolitan flair in the heart of the Balkans.

1985 – The Serbian Academy of Sciences condemns Tito for leaving Serbia poorer than Croatia and Slovenia and proposes an independent Serbian state.

1986 – Slobodan Milošević becomes head of the Serbian Communist Party.

1988 – Ethnic Albanians protest against Serb domination in Kosovo.

1989 – On 28 June, one million Serbs gather at the site of the Battle of Kosovo to commemorate its 600th anniversary. Milošević, newly elected president of Serbia, uses the occasion to promote Serbian nationalism and strip Kosovo of all autonomy.

1990

January – The Yugoslav Communist Party splits along ethnic lines. Deadly riots in Kosovo result in an intervention by the Yugoslav Army (JNA).

February – A multi-party system is adopted in Bosnia-Herzegovina.

April – A pro-independence coalition wins in Slovenia.

May – HDZ (Croatian Democratic Union Party) wins the parliamentary elections in Croatia. HDZ's leader Franjo Tudjman advocates a Yugoslav confederation of sovereign states.

June – In Serbia, a referendum is organised in opposition to ethnic autonomy for Kosovo and Vojvodina and in favour of retaining a one-party state. In Croatia, HDZ proposes that the constitution be amended to allow for a confederated system of sovereign states.

July – The League of Communists of Serbia and the Socialist Alliance of the Working People of Serbia merge to become the Socialist Party of Serbia. Slobodan Milošević is elected president by the delegates. Albanian delegates of the Parliament of Kosovo declare independence from Yugoslavia. Belgrade responds by banning the Kosovo shadow government led by Ibrahim Rugova and shutting down or taking over the local media. The Slovenian legislature declares Slovenia a sovereign state. Croatia adopts the proposed amendments to the constitution which replace the flag and declares that it is no longer a socialist republic. The Bosnian legislature adopts constitutional amendments declaring that Bosnia-Herzegovina is a democratic state with equality for all its ethnic groups.

August – As Croatia's move towards independence seems likely, ethnic Serbs in Krajina argue for greater autonomy by way of their newly established Serbian National Council (i.e., the Parliament of the Knin-based Serbian Autonomous *Oblast* (SAO) Krajina).

November – A Macedonian party advocating a confederation of sovereign states comes to power in the republic's first multi-party elections. Bosnia-Herzegovina also holds its first multi-party elections. Nationalistic parties win.

December – Milošević wins the presidency of Yugoslavia. Ethnic Albanians boycott the elections. The new Croatian constitution recognises ethnic Serbs as a minority but does not grant rights to minority groups. In a plebiscite in Slovenia, nearly 90 per cent of voters favour sovereignty.

1991

January – Macedonia elects a new president and adopts pro-sovereignty legislation. Slovenia announces it will start legislative procedures towards independence.

February – Tensions mount in the Croatian but largely Serbian-populated regions of Slavonia and Baranja.

March – Milošević orders a crackdown on opposition protests in Serbia. The Serbian National Council, with Milošević's approval, declares Krajina's independence from Croatia. Violence between ethnic Croats and ethnic Serbs in Croatia intensifies. Serbia assumes authority over the dissolved Kosovo legislature. In response to the increased tensions in Yugoslavia, the European Communities declare their support for diplomacy and political dialogue over force and promote unity and democracy in Yugoslavia.

April – At a meeting of the six presidents of the Yugoslav republics, it is agreed that each republic should hold a referendum on a future confederation or federation.

May – Serbs resist the election of Stipe Mesić to the rotating presidency of the SFRY. In a referendum in Croatia, over 90 per cent votes for sovereignty and independence. The Krajina Serbs boycott the referendum.

June – Macedonia and Bosnia-Herzegovina unsuccessfully propose a Yugoslav commonwealth of sovereign republics. On 25 June, Croatia and Slovenia proclaim their independence from Yugoslavia. JNA army tanks and helicopters attack Slovenia. After the Slovenian militia captures 2,000 JNA soldiers, it trades their release for the right to control its own borders. The war in Slovenia lasts for a total of ten days. Fighting between Serbian and Croatian militias, which starts on 27 June, is more severe, especially in regions of Krajina, Baranja and Slavonia. The United States states its support for the unity and democracy of Yugoslavia and for sovereignty determined through mutual agreement rather than unilateral secession. The EC sends a troika to Belgrade and Zagreb to leverage a ceasefire accord by threatening to block trade and withdraw economic aid. Jacques Poos, Luxembourg's prime minister, declares that 'the hour of Europe has dawned'.

July – The Zagreb ceasefire accord brokered by the EC is broken. On 5 July, the Council of Ministers decides to impose an arms embargo on all Yugoslav republics and suspends some aid and trade concessions. Under the political sponsorship of the EC, the Brioni ceasefire agreement of 7 July is signed and hailed as a triumph of European diplomacy. In accordance with this document, the SFRY stops all hostilities on Slovenian territory, thus ending the Slovenian war, while Slovenia and Croatia freeze independence activities for a period of three months.

August – JNA tanks and aircraft drive refugees from Vukovar and Dubrovnik. The fighting escalates. The EC threatens to impose economic sanctions on Serbia and recognise the other republics seeking independence.

September – In a referendum in Kosovo, ethnic Albanians vote for independence. The UN Security Council enacts an arms embargo against all former Yugoslav republics and an economic embargo against Serbia and Montenegro. Resolution 713 states that a continuation of the situation in Yugoslavia would constitute 'a threat to international peace and security'. The EC hosts a Peace Conference on Yugoslavia in The Hague. A ceasefire is signed between Serbia and Croatia. An EC Monitoring Mission is deployed to supervise the ceasefire. In spite of this, fighting continues. ECMM is maintained until it is restructured and renamed in 2000.

October – Croat and Muslim parties in Bosnia-Herzegovina unite against Bosnian Serbs and plan for a referendum on the future of Bosnia-Herzegovina. President Tudjman of Croatia and President Milošević of Serbia agree to a ceasefire. But the JNA remains in Croatia. With the navy, it starts its siege of the UNESCO-protected town of Dubrovnik. The EC's Peace Conference on Yugoslavia reconvenes in The Hague. Co-chairman Lord Carrington submits a proposal that supports independence and recognition of former Yugoslav republics and protection of the rights of ethnic minorities. Serbia refuses to agree to the proposal even after changes are made, on the grounds that it does not support the unity of Yugoslavia. Albania's Parliament recognises Kosovo as an independent republic. The Bosnian Muslim government declares itself a sovereign state.

November – The Council of Ministers decides to unilaterally suspend all coordinated assistance to Yugoslavia. For the first time in the history of the European Communities, a cooperation agreement with a third country is denounced. 90 per cent of Bosnian Serbs vote to remain within Yugoslavia. The Macedonian legislature proposes a new constitution declaring Macedonia sovereign and independent.

December – The EEC restores trade links, the Generalised System of Preferences and economic and financial aid terms with all Yugoslav republics, except Serbia and Montenegro. Under German pressure, the European Communities invite republics seeking diplomatic recognition to submit applications by 24 December. To this end, special 'Guidelines on the Recognition of New States in Eastern Europe and the Soviet Union' are adopted. Bosnia-Herzegovina, Croatia, Macedonia and Slovenia rise to the occasion. Germany does not wait for the end of the 'arbitration' process and recognises Croatia and Slovenia. UN Special Envoy Vance's peace plan provides UN peacekeepers to Eastern Slavonia, Western

Slavonia and Krajina, following a ceasefire, the withdrawal of troops and the disbanding of irregulars, but offers no specific solutions to the ethnic conflict. The Bosnian Serbs adopt a resolution to form the Serbian Republic of Bosnia-Herzegovina (Republika Srpska). Leaders of the SAO Krajina, the SAO Eastern Slavonia, Baranja and Western Srem announce that the areas are being joined to form a single Serbian 'state' in Croatia: the Republic of Serbian Krajina (Republika Srpska Krajina). Dubrovnik sustains its worst shelling on 6 December.

1992

January – On 3 January, the fourteenth cease-fire takes effect. The UN Security Council sends monitors. On 11 January, the Badinter Arbitration Commission opines that only Macedonia and Slovenia meet all the criteria to be recognised as new states. Nevertheless, the EEC and its Member States on 15 January choose to recognise Croatia and Slovenia. Macedonia is not, as its recognition is vetoed by Greece on account of the republic's name.

February – On 7 February, the Treaty of Maastricht is signed. On 21 February, the Security Council establishes the UN Protection Force (UNPROFOR). On 29 February, Bosnia-Herzegovina declares its independence and the Bosnian Serbs declare their own separate state.

March – The fighting in Croatia spreads to Bosnia.

April – The United States recognises Croatia and Bosnia-Herzegovina as independent sovereign states. Bosnian Serb forces start to drive Muslims out of small villages; many of these refugees flee to the larger Bosnian cities of Žepa, Srebrenica, Tuzla and Sarajevo. Bosnian Serbs, holding the high ground on the perimeter of the city, begin their siege of Sarajevo. On 28 April, Serbia and Montenegro, the two remaining republics of the SFRY, establish the Federal Republic of Yugoslavia (FRY).

May – The Croatian army liberates Dubrovnik and its surroundings from the suffocating Serbo-Montenegrin grip. Croatia is accepted as a full member in the United Nations. International sanctions are adopted against the FRY, the two remaining republics of the SFRY. Ethnic Albanian writer Ibrahim Rugova is elected president of Kosovo in an election unsanctioned by the 'Yugoslav' government.

June – Croatia joins the war in Bosnia on the side of the Muslims.

August – UNPROFOR is authorised to use force to deliver humanitarian supplies to Bosnia-Herzegovina, two-thirds of which is now under Serbian domination.

First international media reports of 'ethnic cleansing', rapes, Bosnian Serb concentration camps, and mass executions in Bosnia. The United Nations convenes an International Conference on Yugoslavia in London.

September – The FRY is expelled from the United Nations.

October – Serb and ethnic Albanian leaders in Kosovo hold peace talks. The United Nations imposes a no-fly zone over Bosnia-Herzegovina.

November – The EEC concludes a Trade, Commercial and Economic Cooperation Agreement with Albania.

1993

January – Croatia launches an offensive in Krajina. The Geneva peace talks get underway. Under discussion is the Vance-Owen Plan, which would partition Bosnia-Herzegovina and provide for a rotating presidency but require no Serb troop withdrawals.

March – Bosnian Croats and Muslims begin fighting over the 30 per cent of Bosnia not yet seized by the Bosnian Serbs.

April - May – In resolutions 819 and 824, the Security Council declares six 'safe areas' for Bosnian Muslims: Sarajevo, Tuzla, Bihać, Srebrenica, Žepa and Goražde. The International Criminal Tribunal for the former Yugoslavia (ICTY) is established by UN Security Council resolution 827. Bosnian Serb leaders reject the Vance-Owen Plan.

June – Bosnian Serb President Radovan Karadžić proposes several partition deals that would leave Serbs about half of Bosnia. The Bosnian Muslim government rejects this plan. The Copenhagen criteria, the defining component of the EC's relations with the countries of Central and Eastern Europe, are adopted. They are named after the European Council summit meeting in the Danish capital on 21 and 22 June. WEU naval forces start participating in operations in the Adriatic and on the Danube to monitor the implementation of UN sanctions imposed on the former Yugoslavia.

July – Krajina Serbs vote to join the Bosnian Serbs in 'Greater Serbia'.

September – Bosnian Muslims reject the Owen-Stoltenberg Peace Plan to separate Bosnia into Muslim, Croat and Serb sections.

November – On 1 November, the Treaty of Maastricht enters into force, thereby creating the European Union. On 9 November, Bosnian Croatian artillery units destroy the Stari Most (Old Bridge) in the Bosnian town of Mostar.

1994

January – Yasushi Akashi is appointed as the UN Secretary-General's Special Representative. NATO offers all states participating in the North Atlantic Cooperation Council (including Albania) the opportunity to join the Partnership for Peace programme.

February – A Bosnian Serb mortar shell kills sixty-eight people in Sarajevo's central Markale market. The attack increases international attention for Bosnia and western nations threaten air strikes if the Bosnian Serbs do not stop shelling Sarajevo and withdraw their heavy weapons outside a perimeter established by NATO. On 28 February, NATO jets shoot down four Serb aircraft over central Bosnia. This is the Alliance's first use of force since it was founded in 1949.

March – A US-brokered peace accord on the constitution of the Federation of Bosnia-Herzegovina is signed in Washington by Bosnian Muslims and Croats. The Krajina Serbs sign a ceasefire and agree to zones of separation between Serbs and Croats. At the end of the month, Bosnian Serb forces launch a big offensive against the safe area of Goražde.

April – After UN military observers in Goražde are endangered by Serb shelling, UNPROFOR's command requests NATO to use its air support for the defence of UN personnel. On 10 and 11 April, aircraft belonging to NATO states bomb Bosnian Serb positions. NATO threatens more air strikes if the Bosnian Serbs do not pull back from Goražde, Tuzla, Žepa, Bihać and Srebrenica.

May – NATO starts air strikes against Bosnian Serb positions but halts them as UN peacekeepers are taken hostage by the Bosnian Serb army and used as 'human shields'.

July – The European Union takes over the civilian administration in Mostar.

August - September – Twice more, UNPROFOR calls in NATO warplanes to hit Serbian heavy weapons violating the exclusion zone around Sarajevo.

October - December – The war in Bosnia-Herzegovina continues unabated.

1995

January – On New Year's Day, former US President Jimmy Carter brokers a truce between Bosnian Serbs and Muslims. It holds reasonably well for four months.

March – Negotiations on a Europe Agreement with Slovenia start.

May – When Serbs ignore a UN order to remove heavy weapons from the Sarajevo area, NATO aircraft attack a Serb ammunition depot. In retaliation, Serbs begin shelling UN-protected 'safe areas'. Krajina Serbs shell Zagreb. Croatia seizes Western Slavonia.

July – Bosnian Serb forces enter the 'safe areas' of Srebrenica (11 July) and Žepa (25 July) in Eastern Bosnia. In what is considered the first genocide in Europe since World War II, as many as 8,000 Bosnian Muslims are killed by Bosnian Serb forces under the command of General Ratko Mladić. Croatia expels ethnic Serbs from the Krajina region. Nearly seventy ethnic Albanians in Kosovo are sentenced to jail for setting up a parallel police force. Radovan Karadžić and Ratko Mladić are indicted for war crimes by the ICTY.

August – On 4 August, General Ante Gotovina launches Croatia's *Operation Storm*, an offensive against Serb-held territory in Eastern Croatia, killing hundreds and sending 150,000 Serb citizens fleeing. On 19 August, three diplomats from US Envoy Richard Holbrooke's peace mission are killed when their armoured personnel carrier plunges off a road on Mount Igman, near Sarajevo. On 30 August, NATO warplanes begin a fierce air campaign against Serb positions around Sarajevo.

September – The Serbs around Sarajevo hold their ground until 20 September. The foreign ministers of Bosnia-Herzegovina, Croatia and the FRY agree to the division of Bosnia-Herzegovina into Serb and Muslim-Croat entities.

October – A ceasefire is declared in Bosnia.

November – On 1 November, peace talks between Bosnia-Herzegovina, Croatia and the FRY begin at the Wright-Patterson Air Force Base in Dayton, Ohio. On 21 November, the leaders of the three countries agree to a settlement. Despite UN Security Council resolution 1021 on the lifting of the arms embargo against the states of the former Yugoslavia, the European Union continues its own embargo of 5 July 1991 against Bosnia-Herzegovina, Croatia and the FRY (until long after the start of the Kosovo crisis in 1998).

December – The Dayton Peace Agreement is signed in Paris on 14 December and puts an end to a war that engulfed the Balkans for nearly four years, claimed more than 200,000 lives and displaced six million people. The accord gives 51 per cent of Bosnian territory to the Muslim-Croat Federation and 49 per cent to the Bosnian Serbs. It also authorises a right for refugees to return to their pre-war homes and a NATO-led international force (IFOR) to implement the peace plan. With regard to Croatia, the Dayton Agreement recognises the country's pre-war borders (including Eastern Slavonia). On 20 December, NATO launches its largest military mission to date: *Operation Joint Endeavour*.

1996

February – In its Conclusions and Declaration on former Yugoslavia, the Council of the European Union calls for a broad regional approach and the negotiation and conclusion of association agreements, taking account of each country's individual situation.

March – The United Nations ends its embargo on small arms for the region.

April – Bosnian Muslim and Croat officials sign a federation accord to jointly collect customs duties and have a common flag. The FRY and Macedonia establish diplomatic relations. The international community pledges to raise $1.2 billion for the reconstruction of Bosnia-Herzegovina.

May – The ICTY opens in The Hague. This is the first war crimes tribunal since the Nuremberg Trials after World War II. Radovan Karadžić is succeeded by Biljana Plavsić as leader of the Bosnian Serbs.

June – The Europe Agreement with Slovenia is signed on 10 June.

July – Leaders of Serbia, Croatia and Bosnia-Herzegovina sign an agreement to reduce their arsenals of heavy weapons. The Bosnian Federation approves the merger of the Muslim and Croat armies. Mass graves are discovered at Srebrenica. The EU Administration in Mostar is replaced by the Office of the High Representative of the international community in Bosnia-Herzegovina, headed by Carl Bildt. The Council of the European Union adopts Regulation (EC) No. 1628/96 on reconstruction in Bosnia-Herzegovina, Croatia, Macedonia and the FRY (the so-called 'OBNOVA' Regulation).

August – Serbia and Croatia agree to establish diplomatic relations.

September – Bosnia-Herzegovina holds the first national ('entity') elections since the end of the war. Bosnian Muslim Alija Izetbegović becomes the first chairman of the new, rotating presidency to be shared with Serbian Momcilo Krajisnik and Croat Kresimir Zubak.

December – Following UN Security Council resolution 1074, the European Union terminates all restrictions on economic and financial relations with the FRY. After Milošević annuls local election results, Serbs take to the streets in protests.

1997

January – In Albania, the first of a series of pyramid savings schemes collapses, triggering riots. IFOR is renamed Stabilisation Force (SFOR). The Kosovo Liberation Army (KLA), a banned ethnic Albanian militia group, is suspected of having had a hand in the car bomb targeting the Serb rector of Priština University. A KLA leader is killed by the police.

March – Albania is in chaos. The government loses control over the south of the country. Many in the army and police force defect and a million weapons are looted from depots. Evacuation of foreign nationals and mass emigration of Albanians begins. The government is forced to resign. The country descends into anarchy and a near civil war in which some 2,000 people are killed. President Berisha is deposed. Four people are injured when a bomb explodes in the centre of Priština, Kosovo.

April – Authorised by UN Security Council resolution 1101, an Italian-led coalition of willing states under the flag of the OSCE deploys a military and humanitarian mission (*Operazione Alba*). Adoption by the Council of the European Union of its 'Conclusions on the principle of conditionality governing the development of the European Union's relations with certain countries of South-East Europe', combining the Union's regional and bilateral approach towards the countries of the Western Balkans.

May – The WEU Council decides to send a Multinational Advisory Police Element to Albania (MAPE), as part of the efforts undertaken by the OSCE.

July – The ICTY convicts Serbian police officer Dusan Tadić to twenty years in prison for war crimes and crimes against humanity. He is the first person to be found guilty by the Tribunal after a full trial. He appeals against the conviction.

August - December – *Operazione Alba* draws to a close on 12 August. The first municipal elections since the end of the war take place in Bosnia-Herzegovina on 13 and 14 September. The Treaty of Amsterdam is signed on 2 October. The pro-Western Milo Djukanović wins the November presidential elections in Montenegro. The December European Council of Luxembourg decides to convene bilateral IGCs in the spring of 1998 to begin accession negotiations with Slovenia and five other candidate countries.

1998

January – Milo Djukanović is inaugurated as president of Montenegro.

February – Fighting erupts between the KLA and a Serbian police patrol in Likosane.

March – Between twenty and fifty ethnic Albanians are killed during battles in the Kosovar village of Prekaz. Ethnic Albanians vote in presidential and parliamentary elections, but the elections are declared illegal by Belgrade. The European Union publishes its first sanctions list to impose travelling restrictions on senior FRY and Serbian representatives deemed to be responsible for repressive action in Kosovo.

April – A Serbian referendum opposes Western intervention in Kosovo. The United States sets new sanctions against Serbia, including the freezing of its leaders' assets abroad.

May – Peace talks between ethnic Albanians and Serbs are conducted as fighting continues.

June – The Council of the European Union decides that all funds held outside the territory of the FRY and belonging to the governments of the FRY and/or Serbia are to be frozen. The Council also adopts the EU Code of Conduct on arms exports.

July – Kosovo Albanians inaugurate their outlawed Parliament. Serbian police order legislators to disperse.

August – Serbian forces capture the KLA stronghold of Junik. The United Nations calls for a ceasefire in Kosovo.

September – NATO issues an ultimatum to Serbia to stop violence in Kosovo or face air strikes. The European Union imposes a flight ban against the FRY.

October – The United Nations condemns massacres of Kosovo Albanians by Serbian troops. NATO threatens air strikes in spite of Russian protests. Holbrooke and Milošević engage in talks. Serbian forces appear to pull back, and the negotiations lead to the Kosovo Verification Agreement of 12 October: OSCE monitors will check whether violence has ended.

December – The peace negotiations on Kosovo fail in Rambouillet, near Paris.

1999

January – Violence escalates in Kosovo. OSCE monitors discover the bodies of at least forty-five ethnic Albanians in Racak in southern Kosovo. ICTY's Chief Prosecutor Louise Arbour is refused entry to Kosovo to probe the killings. NATO once again threatens air strikes.

February – Peace talks between Serbs and Albanians are again held in Rambouillet. Kosovo Albanians conditionally accept a ceasefire and a draft accord in exchange for broad autonomy for Kosovo. The Serbs accept conditional autonomy. Serb forces expand in Kosovo.

March – Peace talks resume in Paris. The Kosovo Albanians sign the accord, but Serbia rejects international peacekeepers on its territory and boycotts the event. OSCE monitors withdraw from Kosovo. In spite of last-minute diplomatic efforts to seek a peaceful solution, Serbia continues to reject any talk of NATO peacekeepers in Kosovo. NATO launches air strikes against military targets of the FRY. Russia suspends cooperation with NATO. The FRY breaks off diplomatic relations with the United States, France, Germany and Britain. Hundreds of thousands of ethnic Albanian refugees flee to Albania, Macedonia and Montenegro.

April – The refugee crisis in Albania and Macedonia continues with the influx of as many as 20,000 people per day. The FRY closes refugee exit points. Macedonia refuses to let NATO and the United Nations set up more camps. NATO bombs hit a passenger train south of Belgrade and a convoy of ethnic Albanian refugees. The FRY rules out a foreign military force in Kosovo but says it is willing to discuss a civilian presence. The FRY breaks off diplomatic relations with Albania. Yugoslav and Kosovo Albanian troops exchange fire at the border. NATO missiles hit the headquarters of Milošević's Serbian Socialist Party, his private residence, Serbian State Television and the Defence Ministry in Belgrade. The European Union imposes an oil embargo on the FRY.

May – On 1 May, the Treaty of Amsterdam enters into force. President Milošević is listed by the European Union under the visa ban adopted in March 1998. NATO missiles mistakenly hit a civilian bus north of Priština, the Chinese Embassy in Belgrade and a crowded bridge in central Serbia. NATO begins intensive bombing of the FRY's electricity and water grids, disrupting supplies. The ICTY indicts President Milošević for crimes against humanity. On 17 May, EU Ministers of Foreign Affairs launch the Stability Pact for South Eastern Europe, stating their willingness to draw the countries of the region closer to the perspective of full integration into EU structures through a new kind of contractual relationship, 'with a perspective of EU membership on the basis of the Treaty of Amsterdam once the Copenhagen criteria have been met'. To this end, the European Commission initiates the European Union's Stabilisation and Association Process (SAP) on 26 May.

June – The FRY seemingly accepts a peace plan from the European Union and Russia but refuses to agree to NATO's terms. NATO's bombing campaign intensifies. Serb forces start their withdrawal from Kosovo. Redeployments in the

Preševo Valley cause thousands of ethnic Albanians to flee to Macedonia. On 10 June, Serbian forces withdraw from Kosovo and NATO halts its seventy-eight-day bombing campaign against the FRY. Russian peacekeepers from Bosnia enter Kosovo and take control of Priština airport. Ethnic Albanian refugees start to return home. The KLA promises to disarm. The Stability Pact for South Eastern Europe is endorsed at an international meeting held on the fringes of the European Council summit in Cologne, also on 10 June 1999. The Pact's further development and implementation is vested in the OSCE.

November – Boris Trajkovski's win in the presidential elections is attributed by the opposition to mass electoral fraud among Albanian voters. The Montenegrin government introduces the German Mark as a parallel currency.

December – Croatian President Tudjman dies of cancer.

2000

January – Serbian business man, paramilitary leader and indicted war criminal Arkan is assassinated in a Belgrade hotel. The Milošević government denies involvement, although rumours spread that Arkan was ready to provide evidence at the ICTY against Milošević. The first case tried in the ICTY ends. Following the appeals procedure, Bosnian Serb Dusan Tadić is sentenced to twenty years for crimes against humanity.

February – Ethnic Albanians in Kosovo spar with UN troops over their protection of Kosovo Serbs. The new Croatian government promises to support internal democratic reforms and the independence of Bosnia rather than stimulate a separatist movement among the Bosnian Croats. The Serbian Minister of Defence is assassinated.

March – Serbia's independent media are shut down by the government, and Serbia seals its border with Montenegro. Several Bosnian Serbs are arrested by NATO troops and charged with committing war crimes between 1992 and 1994 in Bosnia. Meanwhile, the new Croatian government hands over to the ICTY a Bosnian Croat who had commanded irregular forces against Bosnian Muslims from 1993 to 1994. Street battles in Mitrovica in northern Kosovo result in the deaths of civilians and French peacekeepers.

April – In the Federation of Bosnia-Herzegovina, the Social Democrats win the elections. The Serbian Democratic Party narrowly wins in the Republika Srpska. An ally of Milošević, the head of the Yugoslav airline company JAT, is shot death in Serbia.

May – The head of the Vojvodina regional government is shot dead. President Milošević blames the political opposition for the murder. The opposition holds rallies in favour of free elections. Milošević continues his crackdown on the independent media. Albania, Bulgaria, Macedonia and Slovenia are among nine countries petitioning for NATO membership by 2002. A Serbian court convicts nearly 150 ethnic Albanians on terrorism charges stemming from the 1999 NATO bombings. President Milošević closes universities early. The security advisor to the Montenegrin president is shot dead.

June – Elections in Montenegro are split. Although the pro-Western government of Milo Djukanović wins, pro-Milošević representatives win in predominantly Serbian areas. The Serb opposition figure Vuk Drasković survives an assassination attempt in Montenegro. Montenegro informs the United Nations that it does not wish to be represented by the FRY. The European Council at its summit in Santa Maria da Feira endorses its offer of future EU membership for the five countries of the Western Balkans by dubbing them 'potential' candidate countries.

July – President Milošević adjusts the constitution of the FRY to reduce Montenegro's power in the legislature and allow himself to run for re-election.

September – Elections take place in the FRY. In spite of widespread fraud and the refusal by most Montenegrins and Kosovo Albanians to participate, opposition leader Vojislav Koštunica is elected. The Milošević government insists that the opposition's 'victory' represents less than 50 per cent of the votes and declares that a second round of voting will take place in October. The opposition refuses to accept a second round and leads nationwide protests and strikes.

October – Serb protesters storm the parliament building and official state media outlets in Belgrade. Milošević concedes power to Koštunica, who is sworn in as the new president. Alija Izetbegović, citing poor health, steps down from the Bosnian joint presidency. As the last of the wartime leaders, his decision marks a new era in Balkan leadership. The European Union lifts its flight ban and oil embargo completely.

November – On 21 November 2000, the Zagreb Summit of Heads of State and Government of EU Member States and Western Balkan countries set the seal on the Stabilisation and Association Process by gaining the region's agreement on the applicable set of objectives and conditions. The European Union lifts its financial sanctions against companies in the FRY. The assets freeze against listed individuals is continued. Montenegro adopts the German Mark as its exclusive currency.

December – The Montenegrin negotiation position on the future of the FRY is presented by Prime Minister Djukanović. The Community Assistance for Reconstruction, Development and Stabilisation (CARDS) programme replaces OBNOVA as the Community's funding instrument to support actions undertaken within the SAP and under the future Stabilisation and Association Agreements (SAAs).

2001

January – Federal President Koštunica and Serbian Prime Minister Djindjić present a reply to the Montenegrin position on the future of the FRY. Albanian guerrillas claim responsibility for a deadly rocket attack on a Macedonian police station.

February – In Macedonia, construction begins of the disputed SEE University in Tetovo. A border demarcation agreement between the FRY and Macedonia is signed in Skopje. The Macedonian National Liberation Army (NLA) clashes with a military patrol. Both the European Union and NATO issue sharp warnings to Albanian leaders and call on all involved to isolate the extremists. The Parliament of the FRY passes an amnesty law for 650 ethnic Albanians held in jails since the 1999 Kosovo war. On 21 February, the Treaty of Nice is signed.

March – The Macedonian army calls for a general mobilisation and launches an offensive against the NLA's stronghold of Tanuševci, near the border with Kosovo. The conflict spreads.

April – On 9 April, the EC and their Member States sign the first SAA with Macedonia. The European Union uses the SAA to leverage the Macedonian authorities into negotiations with the NLA to solve the conflict by peaceful means. The European Union also concludes agreements with Macedonia and the FRY on the activities of the European Union Monitoring Mission (EUMM) in these countries. Slobodan Milošević is arrested in Belgrade. The Serbian government vows to try him at home rather than send him to The Hague. Survivors of Srebrenica storm UN headquarters in Sarajevo following reports that a Bosnian Muslim commander who defended the town would be charged with war crimes against Bosnian Serbs.

June – At the end of June, Robert Badinter, François Léotard – the freshly appointed EU Special Representative in Macedonia – and US Special Envoy James Pardew are sent to Skopje to mediate in the negotiations on a ceasefire and a political agreement between the parties to the conflict. On the anniversary of his 'Field of Blackbirds' speech in Kosovo, Slobodan Milošević is extradited to The Hague. Milošević refuses to cooperate and the ICTY issues a not guilty plea on his behalf.

July – A ceasefire agreement is breached by Albanian extremists. This causes the peace talks on Macedonia to stall. The European Union adopts punitive sanctions against the ethnic extremists. Fighting continues as government forces battle with Albanian rebels in the northern town of Tetovo. On 25 July, NATO secures a limited ceasefire agreement in and around Tetovo. The following day, the EU High Representative for the Common Foreign and Security Policy, Javier Solana, and NATO Secretary General Lord Robertson, accompanied by the Chairman-in-Office of the OSCE, Mircea Geoana, travel to Skopje to blow new life into the negotiations.

August – On 13 August, the Macedonian government signs the Ohrid Framework Agreement with the Albanian rebels. A British-led NATO force enters the country to disarm the guerrillas (Operation *Essential Harvest*). Bosnian Serb General Radislav Krstić is found guilty of genocide for his role in the July 1995 Srebrenica execution of 7,000 Muslim men and boys.

October – On 29 October, the EC and its Member States sign a second SAA, now with Croatia.

November – The last EU sanctions against the FRY for its role in the Kosovo crisis are suspended, pursuant to UN Security Council resolution 1367.

December – Slobodan Milošević is charged with genocide by the ICTY.

2002

February – The trial of Slobodan Milošević opens, with the defendant representing himself.

March – After more than one year of difficult trilateral negotiations among the governments of Montenegro, Serbia and the Federation, with Javier Solana as mediator, the 'Proceeding Points for the Restructuring of Relations between Serbia and Montenegro' are agreed to and signed in Belgrade on 14 March.

April – The Dutch Government resigns amidst a scandal over Dutch UN troops not preventing the 1995 Srebrenica massacre.

May – Paddy Ashdown succeeds Wolfgang Petritsch as High Representative of the international community in Bosnia-Herzegovina.

July – The presidents of Bosnia-Herzegovina, Croatia and the FRY meet for the first time since the war. The countries pledge to cooperate on the repatriation of refugees and the fight against organised crime and assist each other in economic development. The United States extends its peacekeeping mission in Bosnia-Herzegovina amidst negotiations over Americans being granted immunity from prosecution by the International Criminal Court.

October – Former Bosnian-Serb President Biljana Plavsić confesses to committing crimes against humanity during the 1992-1995 Bosnian war against Croats and Muslims.

November – NATO invites Slovenia to join the alliance, along with other Central and Eastern European countries.

December – NATO's mandate for Operation *Amber Fox* comes to an end. Operation *Allied Harmony* secures the follow-up.

2003

January – As a follow-on mission to the United Nations' International Police Task Force, the European Union launches its first-ever civilian ESDP operation, the EU Police Mission (EUPM) in Bosnia-Herzegovina. Negotiations on an SAA with Albania are opened by the Commission.

February – On 4 February, the Parliament of the Federal Republic of Yugoslavia votes to rename the country Serbia and Montenegro and thereby adopts the new Constitutional Charter. The new federation includes a joint administration of defence and foreign affairs. The Constitutional Charter prescribes a three-year time period before any of the composite republics can hold a referendum on independence. Croatia applies for EU membership on 20 February. Plavsić is sentenced to eleven years in jail by the ICTY.

March – The Treaty of Nice enters into force on 1 March. Serbian Prime Minister Zoran Djindjić is assassinated in Belgrade on 12 March. Likely suspects are organised criminals with ties to Milošević. On 31 March, the European Union launches its inaugural military Operation *Concordia* in Macedonia as a follow-on to NATO's Operation *Allied Harmony*.

April – Slovenia and nine other countries meet in Athens to sign the fifth EU Accession Treaty. Mirko Sarović, the Bosnian Serb member of the tripartite presidency, is forced to resign following a scandal over military exports to Iraq.

June – The EU-Western Balkans Summit in Thessaloniki on 21 June acknowledges that the SAP will remain the framework for the European course of the Western Balkan countries, 'all the way to their future accession'. 'The Thessaloniki Agenda for the Western Balkans: Moving Towards European Integration' is adopted to further strengthen and enhance the political visibility of the SAP.

July – After twenty months of work, the president of the Convention on the Future of Europe, Valéry Giscard d'Estaing, presents the draft text of the EU Constitution to the EU Presidency.

November - December – Political parties associated with nationalism in the 1990s gain power in Croatia and Serbia and Montenegro. HDZ, the party of the late Franjo Tudjman, wins more than 40 per cent of the seats in parliamentary elections in Croatia. In Serbia and Montenegro, the Serbian Radical Party of Vojislav Seselj walks away with the most votes. Seselj and Milošević both win seats in spite of being held by the ICTY on war crimes charges. Bosnian Serb commanders are convicted of war crimes for their part in commanding the siege of Sarajevo (1992-1994) and the 1995 massacre in Srebrenica. The European Union's military Operation *Concordia* is replaced by the EUPOL Proxima police mission, in line with the objectives of the Ohrid Framework Agreement.

2004

March – Macedonia applies for EU membership on 22 March. In Kosovo, NATO is unable to prevent the eruption of riots between ethnic Albanians and Serbs, which last for four days and leave nineteen dead and at least ten Orthodox churches and 100 Serbian homes destroyed. The Council of the European Union adopts the first-ever European Partnerships with each of the Western Balkan states to guide them in their reform efforts towards accession.

April – The SAA with Macedonia enters into force on 1 April.

May – On 1 May, the European Union expands with ten new Member States, including Slovenia.

June – The European Council grants candidate country status to Croatia. At its summit in Istanbul, NATO announces that SFOR will be replaced by an EU-led peacekeeping force by the end of 2004.

October – Political leaders of both Serbia and Montenegro endorse the so-called 'twin-track' approach whereby the European Union will deal with the two republics on policies that they conduct separately, while it will continue to work with the state union where the latter is the competent authority. The Commission relaunches the feasibility study on an SAA. After an IGC of more than a year, the Treaty establishing a Constitution for Europe is signed in Rome on 29 October.

December – As a follow-on from NATO's SFOR, the European Union launches its second-ever military operation – EUFOR Althea – in Bosnia-Herzegovina. Paddy Ashdown sacks senior Bosnian Serb security officials accused of harbouring war crimes suspects, including Ratko Mladić. The European Council agrees on a revised framework for every future round of accession negotiations. It requests the Council of Ministers to agree on a negotiating framework with a view to opening accession negotiations with Croatia on 17 March 2005, provided the country fully cooperates with the ICTY.

2005

January – In a wave of extraditions, half a dozen Bosnian Serb and Serb indictees are transferred to the ICTY.

February – The SAA with Croatia enters into force on 1 February.

March – In an unprecedented move, the Council of the European Union decides on 16 March to postpone the granting of EU candidate country status to Croatia until the country fully cooperates with the ICTY. After having been indicted, Kosovo's Prime Minister Ramush Haradinaj resigns and surrenders to the ICTY.

May - June – The Treaty establishing a Constitution for Europe is rejected in French and Dutch referenda. The negative outcome plunges the European Union into a political crisis. During their summit on 16-17 June, political leaders steer clear of discussing further enlargement of the European Union.

July – Sali Berisha returns to power as Prime Minister of Albania after winning the 3 July general elections. Despite the OSCE's statement that the elections complied 'only partially' with democratic norms, the Commission is in favour of reviving the stalled SAA talks. Macedonia completes the legislative agenda set out in the 2001 Ohrid Framework Agreement.

August – Car bombs explode and two Serbs are killed in Priština, ahead of UN Special Envoy Kai Eide's visit to Kosovo to evaluate the province's progress in the last year and the chances of success of possible final status talks.

October – On 3 October, the Council of the European Union decides to open accession negotiations with Croatia after being informed by the Chief Prosecutor of the ICTY that Croatia is cooperating fully with the Tribunal. The accession negotiations are officially launched in the early hours of 4 October. Four months into its 'constitutional crisis', the European Union reasserts its commitment to the Western Balkans. The opening of SAA negotiations with Serbia and Montenegro on 10 October marks the fifth anniversary of the democratic uprising that ousted Slobodan Milošević from the presidential seat. On 25 October, the Energy Community Treaty, the first-ever multilateral treaty in south-eastern Europe, is signed between the European Union and Croatia, Bosnia-Herzegovina, Serbia,

Montenegro, Macedonia, Albania, Romania, Bulgaria and UNMIK on behalf of Kosovo. The UN Security Council endorses final status talks for Kosovo.

November – On 10 November, the UN Security Council endorses the Secretary-General's intention to appoint Martti Ahtisaari as his Special Envoy to lead the negotiations on the final status for Kosovo and establishes the guiding principles for the process as agreed to by the Contact Group. The Council of the European Union endorses the appointment of Stefan Lehne as EU Representative to support the UN Status Envoy in the implementation of his mandate. Ahtisaari kicks off the final status process with a fact-finding mission to Priština on 21 November. SAA negotiations with Bosnia-Herzegovina are officially opened on 25 November, in the same week that the world celebrates the tenth anniversary of the Dayton/ aris Peace Accords.

December – Following the compromise reached on the financial perspective for 2007-2013, the European Council grants candidate country status to Macedonia, but no date is set for the opening of accession negotiations. A decision on the country's entry is linked to a future debate among the EU-25 on the Union's future and its ability to absorb more newcomers. The European Union launches an EU Police Advisory Team in Macedonia after the termination of the mandate of EUPOL Proxima. Former Croatian General Ante Gotovina is arrested in Tenerife and transferred to the ICTY.

2006

January – In the gun battle that ensues after the storming of a house in Bosnia, EUFOR troops apprehend Bosnian Serb war crimes suspect Dragomir Abazović but kill his wife. On 21 January, Kosovo's President Ibrahim Rugova dies.

February – Christian Schwarz-Schilling succeeds Paddy Ashdown as High Representative in Bosnia-Herzegovina. On 4 February, the three-year period mentioned in the Constitutional Charter of Serbia and Montenegro as barring the composite republics from holding a referendum on independence lapses. The Montenegrin Parliament schedules a referendum for 21 May. On 10 February Fatmir Sejdiu is elected as the new president of Kosovo. On 20-21 February, the first round of direct negotiations between Serbs and Kosovo Albanians on the final status of Kosovo takes place in Vienna under the auspices of UN Special Envoy Ahtisaari. The talks focus on decentralisation and are perceived to be largely constructive. After the ICTY's Chief Prosecutor tells the BBC that Mladić is within 'immediate reach' of the Belgrade authorities, the Council of the European Union gives Serbia and Montenegro a one-month deadline to send the war crimes suspect to the ICTY or else face 'disruption' of SAA negotiations.

March – On 11 March, Slobodan Milošević dies in his prison cell in The Hague, where he was on trial before the ICTY on sixty-six charges of crimes against humanity (including two counts of genocide). His death and burial spark controversy in Serbia. EU Ministers of Foreign Affairs, assembled in Salzburg at a Gymnich meeting with political leaders from the Western Balkans, greet Milošević's death by reaffirming their support for the Thessaloniki Agenda and the SAP, thereby renewing their promise that the countries of the region will join the European Union. In Kosovo, Prime Minister Bajram Kosumi steps down over accusations by members of his coalition of being ineffective. He is replaced by former KLA commander Agim Çeku, against whom Serbia has issued an arrest warrant. Solana rebuffs Serbian opposition to the move and welcomes the replacement. On 17 March, technical talks on the future status of Kosovo resume in Vienna. They focus on cultural and religious heritage, minority rights and the economy, local financing and relations between municipalities. Although no agreement is reached, all participants describe the talks as constructive. On 18 March, the main political parties in Bosnia-Herzegovina reach agreement on constitutional reform for the country.

April – The European Union recognises that controversies over the death and burial of Milošević have complicated Belgrade's efforts to transfer Mladić to The Hague and gives Belgrade one extra month to transfer the war-time general. Thus, the political round of SAA negotiations with Serbia and Montenegro goes ahead as planned on 5 April. On 26 April, Bosnia-Herzegovina's Parliament fails to adopt the proposed constitutional amendments. Swan song for Serbia and Montenegro as the country withdraws from the Eurovision song contest after a row over its competition to find a song for this year's event.

May – As Belgrade is unable to meet the deadline over the transfer of Mladić, the European Union cancels the political round of SAA talks with Serbia and Montenegro. The US suspends $7 million in assistance to Serbia over Mladić. On 21 May, 55.5 per cent of the Montenegrin voters choose for independence in a nation-wide referendum that is considered to be free and fair. Elements in the Serb community in Bosnia-Herzegovina renew calls for the independence of the Republika Srpska.

June – In a special session on 3 June, the Parliament of Montenegro passes a declaration on the independence of the Republic of Montenegro. On 5 June, the Parliament in Belgrade declares the Republic of Serbia the legal successor to the state union and gives all state institutions forty-five days to complete the separation. On 12 June, the Council of the European Union recognises that the parliamentary acts were taken in conformity with the arrangements and the procedures foreseen in the Belgrade Agreement and with Article 60 of the

Constitutional Charter. The SAA Albania is signed in the margins of the Council meeting. An interim agreement is also signed, allowing for the trade part of the SAA to take effect immediately. On 15 June, Serbia recognises Montenegro as an independent state. On 21 June, Montenegro joins the OSCE.

July – The Energy Community Treaty enters into force on 1 July. Despite violent incidents within the Albanian community during the election campaign, the OSCE considers the general elections in Macedonia to have been conducted in a generally peaceful and orderly manner. Serbia presents the European Union with a new action plan for achieving full cooperation with the ICTY, including ways and means to arrest and extradite Mladić. European Commission President José Manuel Barroso states that the European Union might endorse the SAA with Serbia by the end of 2006 if the action plan is fully implemented. Taking note of the fact that all Member States have recognised the Republic of Montenegro as a sovereign and independent state, the Council of the European Union decides to extend bilateral political dialogue under the SAP at ministerial level. On 24 July, the Justice and Home Affairs Council authorises the Commission to negotiate an SAA with Montenegro. At the same time, the Council amends the negotiating directives for the SAA with Serbia, in order to take account of Montenegro's independence. After seven unsuccessful rounds of technical negotiations, the final status talks in Vienna convene at the highest political level under the chairmanship of Martti Ahtisaari. The positions of the Serbs (everything but independence) and the Kosovo Albanians (nothing but independence) remain far apart.

August – Serbia's Prime Minister Koštunica insists that Kosovo will remain part of Serbia, even if that means delaying EU membership. On 7 August, talks on the future of Kosovo resume at a technical level, with the Kosovo Serb delegation boycotting the negotiations. Following comments by Martti Ahtisaari that, with regard to Kosovo, Serbs as a nation would have to pay the price for their past and the policies of ex-President Milošević, Koštunica declares that his government will start a diplomatic campaign against the serious preconceptions of the UN envoy. At the ICTY in The Hague, one of the biggest joint trials tackling the 1995 Srebrenica massacre kicks off.

September – The European Union expresses concern over looming instability in Macedonia amid strong dissatisfaction on the part of ethnic Albanians, whose preferred party has been excluded from the new government. General elections in Montenegro are largely conducted in line with international standards. During a week of heightened tensions in Kosovo, Contact Group ministers meeting in New York reaffirm their commitment that all possible efforts will be made to achieve a negotiated settlement in the course of 2006 and make it clear that they would permit neither Belgrade nor Priština to 'unilaterally' block negotiations to decide the disputed territory's future status. But attempts to reach a negotiated solution in Vienna remain deadlocked. On 26 September, Bulgaria and Romania receive the go-ahead from the European Commission to enter the European Union as planned on 1 January 2007. Commission President Barroso tells the European Parliament an institutional settlement for the European Union should precede any further enlargement. European Commissioner for Enlargement Olli Rehn adds that it should be possible to reach such an institutional settlement in 2008, that is to say, before the next likely enlargement of the European Union with candidate country Croatia. Also on 26 September, SAA negotiations with Montenegro are resumed. The talks continue from the point at which they were interrupted by the European Union in May under the twin-track approach for the state union of Serbia and Montenegro. During a special session, Serbia's Parliament unanimously approves a new constitution that claims sovereignty over the UN administered province of Kosovo.

October – For the first time since 1995, Bosnia-Herzegovina holds general elections on 1 October that are managed entirely by its own institutions. The elections are largely in accordance with international standards. In Montenegro, outgoing Prime Minister Djukanović, whose coalition won the September elections, retires from government. In an unprecedented move, Slovenia blocks the opening of EU-Croatia negotiations on the next chapter of EU legislation by not giving its approval to a European Commission screening report on the extent to which Croatia's fisheries legislation conforms to the *acquis*. Slovenia argues that Croatia has failed to implement a bilateral border agreement on the basis of which Slovenian fishermen should be able to enjoy a right of passage through Croatian waters. Meanwhile, Ahtisaari says he doubts a negotiated settlement for Kosovo is possible as the two parties remain diametrically opposed on the final status issue. At its 16-17 October meeting, the Council of the European Union again chides Serbia for not doing enough to transfer Mladić to the ICTY. Solana and Rehn present a joint report on a reinforced EU presence in Bosnia-Herzegovina after the envisaged closure of the Office of the High Representative on 30 June 2007. In the weekend of 28-29 October, voters in Serbia and Kosovo are asked whether or not they support the adoption of a new constitution which states, *inter alia*, that Kosovo is a 'constituent' part of Serbia. Other innovations include the abolition of the death penalty, a ban on human cloning and the safeguard of minority rights. The one million ethnic Kosovo Albanians boycott the referendum. Despite international warnings not to prejudge status talks and amid allegations of electoral fraud, Prime Minister Koštunica declares that 51.6 per cent of the total population has voted in favour of the new constitution. Solana congratulates Serbia for the orderly conduct of the referendum, but recalls that Kosovo's status will be determined by the ongoing status process.

November – Political leaders in Serbia issue calls for UN Special Envoy Martti Ahtisaari to step down, accusing him of writing biased proposals on the future status of Kosovo. EU Ministers of Foreign Affairs welcome Ahtisaari's decision, after consulting with the Contact Group, to delay the presentation of his recommendations on the future of Kosovo in order to avoid inflaming tension ahead of Serbia's elections on 21 January 2007. Kosovo's Prime Minister Agim Çeku warns that if the United Nations does not proclaim independence soon, then local institutions will do it themselves. In turn, Bosnian Serb officials warn that a unilateral proclamation of Kosovo's independence by the ethnic-Albanian leadership could provoke a similar move in the Republika Srpska. Representatives of several international organisations caution political leaders in the region against unilateral moves. On 8 November, in its annual enlargement package, the European Commission recommends holding off on EU enlargement with the Western Balkans until the 'medium to long term', urging all six states in the region to do more on political and economic reform before the accession process can move forward. On 28 November, UNMIK police and local security forces use teargas to disperse thousands of ethnic Albanian protesters in Priština. At its Riga summit on 29 November, NATO Heads of State and Government declare that the Alliance intends to extend further invitations to Albania, Croatia and Macedonia to join NATO at the next summit (in the spring of 2008) if these countries meet NATO standards. Bosnia-Herzegovina, Montenegro and Serbia are invited to join the Partnership for Peace programme. On 30 November, the Commission launches negotiations on readmission and relaxing the visa regime for the citizens of Bosnia-Herzegovina, Serbia, Montenegro and Macedonia and relaxing the visa regime for the citizens of Albania.

December – The SAA Interim Agreement between the EC and Albania enters into force on 1 December. Montenegro wraps up technical negotiations on its SAA with the European Union. The fifth and final round of technical talks on an SAA between Bosnia-Herzegovina and the EC are held in Sarajevo. EU Commissioner Olli Rehn says that Bosnia-Herzegovina must implement key reforms (especially restructuring of the police sector) before SAA negotiations can be formally concluded. Russia hints at its intention to use its veto power in the UN Security Council to block a plan for the future status of Kosovo if it does not satisfy both the ethnic Albanian majority and Serbia. The Joint Committee of SFRY Successor States convenes in Zagreb to divide assets of sixty-seven diplomatic and consular offices. Survivors and relatives of the victims of the 1995 Srebrenica massacre criticise the Dutch government for giving medals to UN peacekeepers who served in the city. Most of the 300 Dutch military staff of EUFOR will leave Bosnia-Herzegovina in April 2007. On 14 December, Bosnia-Herzegovina, Montenegro and Serbia join NATO's Partnership for Peace programme. After seven months of intense negotiations, the prime ministers of south-eastern European countries and territories sign a new Central European Free Trade Agreement on 19 December. At its 'enlargement' summit, the European Council agrees that the Commission's 'enlargement strategy based on consolidation, conditionality and communication, combined with the European Union's capacity to integrate new members, forms the basis for a renewed consensus on enlargement'. While deciding to delay the opening of eight of the thirty-five chapters in the accession negotiations with Turkey, due to the country's continued failure to open up its ports and airports to ships and planes from Cyprus, the European Union 'keeps its commitments towards the countries that are in the enlargement process', according to the summit conclusions. The European Council confirms that the future of the Western Balkans lies in the European Union.

2007

January – On 1 January, Bulgaria and Romania accede to the European Union. Thirteen 'old' Member States and one of the ten that joined in 2004 invoke their right to impose transitional arrangements in the field of the free movement of workers. After a stalemate of more than a year, the twelve political parties that make up the governing coalition in Albania reach a deal on electoral reforms, clearing the way for local elections in February. On 21 January, Serbia holds general elections that are declared to have been conducted in a free and fair manner. With 28.5 per cent of the vote, the ultranationalist Radical Party emerges as the biggest party, but pro-EU parties gather enough votes to establish a coalition government. On 28 January, a bomb explodes in the Kosovar town of Gnjilane, damaging a building but causing no injuries. On 29 January, Christian Schwarz-Schilling announces that he will step down as High Representative for Bosnia-Herzegovina when his mandate expires on 30 June. On 31 January, the Constitutional Court of Bosnia-Herzegovina strips the Republika Srpska and the Federation of Bosnia-Herzegovina of their symbols (flag, anthem and coat of arms) because the entities failed to harmonise them with the constitution.

February – On 2 February, UN Special Envoy Martti Ahtisaari presents his proposals on a settlement for Kosovo's final status. During a press conference, he states that his draft proposal is a reflection of the fifteen rounds of direct negotiations and twenty-six missions to Belgrade and Priština over the previous year. NATO, the European Union and the United States welcome Ahtisaari's plan and firmly support the his intension of holding intensive talks with and between the two sides on the basis of the proposals. Serbian Prime Minister Kostunica rejects the plan. The government of Kosovo supports it. Russian Minister of Defence Ivanov warns that Russia might veto a Security Council resolution granting independence to Kosovo. Two persons die and seventy are injured when UNMIK police officers use excessive force in their efforts to disperse a violent demonstration on 10

February. On 12 February, the Council of the European Union voices strong support for Ahtisaari's plan and welcomes the Commission's readiness to resume SAA negotiations with a new Serbian government, provided it shows a clear commitment to and takes concrete and effective action for full cooperation with the ICTY. On 16 February, Serbia's new Parliament rejects the Ahtisaari plan. In a series of bomb explosions, a blast in Priština on 20 February damages three UNMIK vehicles. A group calling itself the Kosovo Liberation Army claims responsibility for the attack. On 21 February, Ahtisaari starts a two-week consultative process with delegations from Belgrade and Priština on all aspects of his draft comprehensive proposal for the Kosovo status settlement. On 26 February, a new blast damages seven vehicles of the OSCE in Peja. On 27 February, 20,000 people gather in front of the US embassy in Belgrade to protest against Ahtisaari's settlement proposal for Kosovo. On the same day, the International Court of Justice clears Serbia of direct responsibility for the 1995 'genocide' in Srebrenica but rules that it breached international law by failing to stop the killings and punish those responsible. The ICJ criticises Serbia for failing to cooperate fully with the ICTY and hand over war crimes fugitives, including Ratko Mladić. Also on 27 February, the Council of the European Union decides on a transition plan for the Union's EUFOR Althea military operation in Bosnia-Herzegovina. EUFOR will scale down its troops to 2,500. Tensions during the local elections in Albania on 18 February prompt a response from the European Union, with both Olli Rehn and Javier Solana saying that the shortcomings in the preparation and conduct of the elections reflect the need for improved cross-party cooperation to fulfil Albania's international commitments.

March – On 1 March, the Steering Board of the Peace Implementation Council, which reviews Bosnia-Herzegovina's stabilisation, extends the mandate of the Office of the High Representative until the end of June 2008, due to the still potentially volatile situation in the country. Stating that the ICJ's ruling demonstrated that blame lies with individuals who must be brought to justice, Serbian President Tadić calls on all war crimes fugitives to surrender to the ICTY. The government of the Republika Srpska officially expresses its deep regret for the crimes committed against non-Serbs during the 1992-1995 war in Bosnia-Herzegovina and condemns all persons who took part in these crimes. Former Kosovo Prime Minister Haradinaj returns to The Hague to stand trial before the ICTY. On 2 March, talks between Belgrade and Priština in Vienna end without success. About 4,000 activists of the Self-Determination Movement march past UNMIK's headquarters in a peaceful demonstration on 5 March. Following a final meeting between the two parties in Vienna on 9 and 10 March, Ahtisaari says that the one-year long negotiations have been exhausted, leaving no 'common ground' between Belgrade and Priština. The talks shift to the UN Security Council. On his tour through the Western Balkans in mid-March, Olli Rehn issues an usually stark warning to Macedonia, criticising all political parties for 'obstruction [of] and lack of faith' in the democratic decision-making process. In Tirana, the Enlargement Commissioner calls upon political parties to develop a democratic culture of compromise. In Sarajevo he issues a tough warning to political leaders to push forward with the required (police) reforms or see the SAA with Bosnia-Herzegovina put on ice. On 16 March, Rehn and the Montenegrin Prime Minister Sturanović initial the SAA between the European Union and Montenegro. Ahead of his visit to Podgorica, Rehn says that the Union expects Montenegro to draft a constitution in line with European standards and strengthen its institutions and judicial and administrative capacities. After two months of bickering over who will fill the post of prime minister, negotiations on a coalition start in Serbia. On 25 March, the European Union celebrates the fiftieth anniversary of the Treaties of Rome. On 26 March, the High Representative in Bosnia-Herzegovina annuls Parliament's approval of the new government of the Federation of Bosnia-Herzegovina. On 30 March, the ICTY transfers its first war crimes case to Serbia. In a five-day span, three bomb attacks against Serb-owned houses take place in Mitrovica. An informal meeting of EU Ministers of Foreign Affairs in Bremen sees Slovakia, Romania and Greece raise serious objections to the European Union's endorsement of Ahtisaari's proposals for supervised independence for Kosovo, with Spain, Italy and Cyprus also voicing reservations on the blueprint.

April – On 3 April, the UN Security Council holds its first meeting on the status plan for Kosovo. It later decides to send a fact-finding mission to the region. On 10 April, the Serbian war crimes court sentences four Serb paramilitaries filmed killing Bosnian Muslims during the 1995 Srebrenica massacre. Six months of negotiations are concluded with the initialling of agreements between the EC and Albania, Bosnia-Herzegovina, Macedonia and Montenegro on visa facilitation and the readmission of persons. On 17 April, the former Minister of the Interior of Macedonia goes on trial before the ICTY. The Osjiek County Court indicts Croatian MP Glavas and six others for war crimes committed against Serb civilians in 1991. Ongoing EU disunity over Kosovo's future knocks the topic off the agenda of the General Affairs Council on 23 April. Russia threatens to use its veto on an EU and US-backed draft UN resolution to give independence to Kosovo, denting hopes that it might abstain from the vote. Deputy Prime Minister Titov explicitly states that a decision based on Ahtisaari's draft proposals will 'not get through' the Security Council without the support of both Belgrade and Priština. A delegation of the Security Council completes a five-day fact-finding mission to Brussels, Vienna, Belgrade and Kosovo on 28 April saying that the Security Council will need more time to make a decision on the province's future.

May – Hard-line nationalists pledge allegiance to a new paramilitary force (the Guard of Tzar Lazar) willing to fight and die to save Kosovo as part of Serbia. Twenty-seven volunteers are arrested by the Serbian police. The international community expresses concern about the election of the leader of the Serbian Radical Party, Tomislav Nikolić, as speaker of the Serbian Parliament. Nikolić calls on Russia to devise a way to unite countries that are against US hegemony and the European Union, saying that Serbia should not become a member of the European Union. On 11 May, the United States and the European Union circulate a draft resolution endorsing independence for Kosovo under international supervision. Russia circulates elements for a rival resolution calling for additional talks between Belgrade and Priština and increased efforts to meet the UN-endorsed 'Standards for Kosovo'. Montenegro joins the Council of Europe as its forty-seventh member. Serbia takes over the two-month chairmanship of the Committee of Ministers of the Council of Europe. Decisions on transforming the Stability Pact for South-Eastern Europe into a regionally-owned Regional Cooperation Council are taken at the meeting of the Pact's Regional Table and the SEECP in Zagreb. The Belgrade regional court finds twelve men guilty of the 2003 assassination of Zoran Djindjić. Agreements on visa facilitation and readmission between the EC and Serbia are initialled. After one week in the post, Nikolić resigns as speaker of the Parliament in a deal between opposition parties to form Serbia's next government. Twenty-eight minutes before the expiration of the deadline, the Serbian Parliament approves a new government led by Vojislav Kostunica. Olli Rehn confirms that the European Union is ready to resume SAA talks with Serbia as soon as the new government's programme on cooperation with the ICTY is 'rigorously being implemented'. On 31 May, General Zradvko Tolimir, a close aid to Ratko Mladić accused of helping to plan and carry out the Srebrenica massacre, is arrested in Bosnia, apparently after close cooperation between Serbian and Bosnian Serb authorities. With his arrest, only five of the 161 people indicted by the ICTY remain at large. Russia dismisses the slight changes in a new draft UN resolution tabled by the United Kingdom, saying it wants more negotiations to see if the ethnic Albanians and Serbs in Kosovo can reach an agreement.

The question of Kosovo's future status, relations with Serbia and Bosnia-Herzegovina's assumption of greater ownership of its governance will continue to top EU priorities for the Western Balkans in 2007.

BIBLIOGRAPHY

1. BOOKS

A

A. Albi, *EU Enlargement and the Constitutions of Central and Eastern Europe* (Cambridge, Cambridge University Press 2005).
P. Alston, ed., *The EU and Human Rights* (Oxford, Oxford University Press 1999).
C. Amerasinghe, *Principles of Institutional Law of International Organizations* (Cambridge, Cambridge University Press 1996).
O. Anastasakis and V. Bojičić-Dželilović, *Balkan Regional Cooperation and European Integration* (London, Hellenic Observatory LSE 2002).
A. Aust, *Modern Treaty Law and Practice* (Cambridge, Cambridge University Press 2003).
G. Aybet, *A European Security Architecture After the Cold War: Questions of Legitimacy* (New York, St. Martin's Press 2000).

B

A. Bailes, *The European Security Strategy. An Evolutionary History* (Stockholm, SIPRI 2005).
E. Bakker and B. Bomert, *The OSCE and the Netherlands as Chairman-in-Office* (The Hague, Netherlands Helsinki Committee 2003).
T. Barkhuysen, M. Kuijer and R.A. Lawson, eds., *55 jaar EVRM* (Leiden, NJCM 2006).
D. Bethlehem and M. Weller, eds., *The 'Yugoslav' Crisis in International Law: General Issues (Part I)* (Cambridge, Cambridge University Press 1997).
R. Bideleux and I. Jeffries, *The Balkans: A Post-Communist History* (London, Routledge 2007).
F. Bieber, ed., *Montenegro in Transition: Problems of Identity and Statehood* (Baden-Baden, Nomos 2003).
S. Biscop, *The European Security Strategy – A Global Agenda for Positive Power* (Aldershot, Ashgate 2005).
S. Biscop, ed., *E Pluribus Unum? Military Integration in the European Union* (Brussels, Academia Press 2005).
S. Blockmans and A. Łazowski, eds., *The European Union and Its Neighbours: A Legal Appraisal of the EU's Policies of Stabilisation, Partnership and Integration* (The Hague, T.M.C. Asser Press 2006).
S. Blockmans, S. Prechal and W.Th. Douma, eds., *Reconciling 'Deepening' and 'Widening' of the European Union* (The Hague, T.M.C. Asser Press 2007).

W. Blockmans, *A History of Power in Europe* (Antwerp, Mercatorfonds 1997).

A. Bloed, L. Leicht, M. Nowak and A. Rosas, eds., *Monitoring Human Rights in Europe: Comparing International Procedures and Mechanisms* (Dordrecht, Martinus Nijhoff Publishers 1993).

A. Bloed and R.A. Wessel, *The Changing Functions of the Western European Union (WEU): Introduction and Basic Documents* (Dordrecht, Martinus Nijhoff 1994).

N.M. Blokker and H.G. Schermers, eds., *Proliferation of International Organizations: Legal Issues* (The Hague, Kluwer Law International 2001).

N.M. Blokker and N.J. Schrijver, eds., *The Security Council and the Use of Force: Theory and Reality – A Need for Change?* (Leiden, Koninklijke Brill NV 2005).

M. Bogdani and J. Loughlin, *Albania and the European Union: The Tumultuous Journey Towards Integration and Accession* (London, I.B. Tauris 2007).

S. Bose, *Bosnia after Dayton – Nationalist Partition and International Intervention* (London, Hurst & Company 2002).

H. Boškailo-Šikalo, *Mostar* (Mostar, Microbook Publishing 2004).

M. Bothe, N. Ronzitti and A. Rosas, eds., *The OSCE in the Maintenance of Peace and Security: Conflict Prevention, Crisis Management, and Peaceful Settlement of Disputes* (The Hague, Kluwer Law International 1998).

C. Brölmann, R. Lefeber and M. Zieck, eds., *Peoples and Minorities in International Law* (Dordrecht, Martinus Nijhoff Publishers 1993).

K. Bühler, *State Succession and Membership in International Organizations: Legal Theories versus Political Pragmatism* (The Hague, Kluwer Law International 2001).

M. Bulterman, *Human Rights in the Treaty Relations of the European Community – Real Virtues or Virtual Reality?* (Antwerp, Intersentia 2001).

G. de Búrca and J. Scott, eds., *Constitutional Change in the EU: From Uniformity to Flexibility* (Oxford, Hart Publishing 2000).

E. Busek, ed., *10 Years Southeast European Cooperative Initiative: From Dayton to Brussels* (Vienna, Springer Verlag 2006).

C

E. Cannizaro, ed., *The European Union as an Actor in International Relations* (The Hague, Kluwer Law International 2002).

R. Caplan, *Europe and the Recognition of New States in Yugoslavia* (Cambridge, Cambridge University Press 2005).

A. Cassese, *Self-Determination of Peoples – A Legal Appraisal* (Cambridge, Cambridge University Press 1995).

A. Cassese, *International Law* (Oxford, Oxford University Press 2001).

D. Chandler, *Bosnia: Faking Democracy after Dayton*, 2nd edn. (London, Pluto Press 2000).

A. Chayes and A. Chayes, *The New Sovereignty. Compliance with International Regulatory Agreements* (Cambridge (Mass.), Harvard University Press 1995).

S. Chesterman, *Just War or Just Peace? Humanitarian Intervention and International Law* (Oxford, Oxford University Press 2001).

N. Chomsky, *The New Military Humanism: Lessons from Kosovo* (Monroe, Courage 1999).

J. Cohen, *Conflict Prevention in the OSCE: An Assessment of Capacities* (The Hague, Netherlands Institute of International Relations 'Clingendael' 1999).

A. Conze, *Die völkerrechtliche Haftung der Europäische Gemeinschaft* (Baden-Baden, Nomos 1987).

P. Craig and G. de Búrca, *The Evolution of EU Law* (Oxford, Oxford University Press 1999).

M. Cremona, ed., *The Enlargement of the European Union* (Oxford, Oxford University Press 2003).

D. Curtin, A.E. Kellermann and S. Blockmans, eds., *The EU Constitution: The Best Way Forward?* (The Hague, T.M.C. Asser Press 2005).

D

I. Daalder and M. O'Hanlon, *Winning Ugly: NATO's War to Save Kosovo* (Washington, Brookings Institution 2000).

R. Dannreuther, ed., *European Union Foreign and Security Policy: Towards a Neighbourhood Strategy* (London, Routledge 2004).

A. Dashwood and C. Hillion, eds., *The General Law of the EC External Relations* (London, Sweet & Maxwell 2000).

E. Decaux and L.-A. Sicilianos, eds., *La CSCE: Dimension humaine et règlement des différends* (Paris, Montchrestien 1993).

R. Detrez, *De Balkan: van burenruzie tot burgeroorlog*, 4th edn. (Antwerp, Hadewijch 1993).

R. Detrez, *Macedonië: land in de wachtkamer* (Antwerp, Houtekiet 2002).

R. Detrez, ed., *Ontmoeting met de Balkan* (Brussels, KVAB 2005).

P. Duignan, *NATO: Its Past, Present, and Future* (Stanford, Hoover Press 2000).

S. Duke, *The Elusive Quest for European Security: From EDC to CFSP* (London, MacMillan/St Antony's 2000).

S. Duke, *The EU and Crisis Management: Development and Prospects* (Maastricht, EIPA 2001).

E

P. Eeckhout, *The External Relations of the European Union: Legal and Constitutional Foundations* (Oxford, Oxford University Press 2004).

M. Emerson, *European Neighbourhood Policy: Strategy or Placebo?* (Brussels, CEPS 2004).

M. Emerson, et al., *Just what is this 'Absorption Capacity' of the European Union* (Brussels, CEPS 2006).

EUISS, *EU Security and Defence: Core Documents 2004*, Vol. V (Paris, ISS 2005).

F

E. Fierro, *The EU's Approach to Human Rights Conditionality in Practice* (The Hague, Martinus Nijhoff 2003).

R. Frid, *The Relations between the EC and International Organizations: Legal Theory and Practice* (The Hague, Kluwer Law International 1995).

G

H.-D. Genscher, *Erinnerungen* (Berlin, Siedler Verlag 1995).

A. Gerolymatos, *The Balkan Wars: Conquest, Revolution, and Retribution from the Ottoman Era to the Twentieth Century and Beyond* (New York, Basic Books 2002).

V.-Y. Ghébali and D. Warner, eds., *The Operational Role of the OSCE in South-Eastern Europe: Contributing to Regional Stability in the Balkans* (Aldershot, Ashgate 2001).

C. Giersch, *Konfliktregulierung in Jugoslawien 1991-1995: Die Rolle von OSZE, EU, UNO und NATO* (Baden-Baden, Nomos 1998).

R. Ginsberg, *The European Union in International Politics – Baptism by Fire* (Lanham, Rowman & Littlefield Publishers 2001).

M. Glenny, *The Fall of Yugoslavia*, 3rd edn. (London, Penguin Books 1996).

M. Glenny, *The Balkans: Nationalism, War, and the Great Powers, 1804-1999* (London, Penguin Books 2001).

N. Gnesotto, ed., *EU Security and Defence Policy: The First Five Years (1999-2004)* (Paris, ISS 2004).

V. Gowlland-Debbas, ed., *United Nations Sanctions and International Law* (The Hague, Kluwer Law International 2001).

H

M. Halperin, D. Scheffer and P. Small, *Self-Determination in the New World Order* (Washington D.C., Carnegie Endowment for International Peace 1992).

H. Hannum, *Autonomy, Sovereignty, and Self-Determination: The Accommodation of Conflicting Rights* (Philadelphia, University of Pennsylvania Press 1990).

R. Hayden, *Blueprints for a House Divided: The Constitutional Logic of the Yugoslav Conflicts* (Ann Arbor, The University of Michigan Press 2000).

P. Hazan, *Justice in a Time of War: The True Story Behind the International Criminal Tribunal for the Former Yugoslavia* (Texas, A&M University Press 2004).

R. Higgins, *Problems and Process: International Law and How We Use It* (Oxford, Clarendon Press 1994).

C. Hill, ed., *The Actors in Europe's Foreign Policy* (London, Routledge 1996).

C. Hill and K. Smith, eds., *European Foreign Policy: Key Documents* (London, Routledge 2000).

C. Hillion, ed., *EU Enlargement: A Legal Approach* (Oxford, Hart Publishing 2004).

F. Hoffmeister, *Menschenrechts- und Demokratieklauseln in den vertraglichen Außenbeziehungen der Europäischen Gemeinschaft* (Berlin, Springer 1998).

R. Holbrooke, *To End a War* (New York, Random House 1998).

N. Horbach, R. Lefeber and O. Ribbelink, eds., *Handboek Internationaal Recht* (The Hague, T.M.C. Asser Press 2007).

I

K. Inglis and A. Ott, eds., *The Constitution for Europe and an Enlarging European Union: Unity in Diversity?* (Groningen, Europa Law Publishing 2005).

International Commission on the Balkans, *The Balkans in Europe's Future* (Sofia, Centre for Liberal Strategies 2005).

J

O. Jacot-Guillarmod, *Droit communautaire et droit international public* (Geneva, Libraire de l'université 1979).

C. Jameson and J. Charlton, *The Rocky Road to the EU: Who Wins the Rally?* (Brussels/Leiden, Vlaams-Nederlandse Denktank voor de Westerse Balkan 2005).

T. Judah, *Kosovo: War and Revenge*, 2nd edn. (New Haven, Yale University Press 2002).

P. Jureković, ed., *The Stability Pact for South East Europe – Dawn of an Era of Regional Co-operation* (Vienna, National Defence Academy 2002).

P. Jureković, ed., *Building Stability in Weak States: The Western Balkans* (Vienna, National Defence Academy 2002).

T. Jürgens, *Die gemeinsame Europäische Aussen- und Sicherheitspolitik* (Cologne, Carl Heymanns Verlag 1994).

K

E. Kalpyris, R. Vork and A. Napolitano, *Les sanctions des Nations Unies dans le conflit de l'ex-Yougoslavie* (Brussels, Bruylant 1995).

R. Kaplan, *Balkan Ghosts: A Journey Through History* (New York, Vintage Books 1994).

A.E. Kellermann, ed., *De Europese Politieke Samenwerking* (The Hague, T.M.C. Asser Instituut 1979).

A.E. Kellermann, ed., *Externe Bevoegdheden van de Europese Unie* (The Hague, T.M.C. Asser Instituut 1994).

A.E. Kellermann, J.W. de Zwaan and J. Czuczai, eds., *EU Enlargement: The Constitutional Impact at EU and National Level* (The Hague, T.M.C. Asser Press 2001).

A.E. Kellermann, J. Czuczai, S. Blockmans, A. Albi and W.Th. Douma, eds., *Impact of EU Accession on the Legal Orders of New Member States and (Pre-) Candidate Countries – Hopes and Fears* (The Hague, T.M.C. Asser Press 2006).

I. Kempe and W. van Meurs, eds., *Beyond EU Enlargement, Volume 2: The Agenda of Stabilisation for Southeastern Europe* (Gütersloh, Bertelsmann Foundation Publishers 2001).

S. Keukeleire, *Het buitenlands beleid van de Europese Unie* (Deventer, Kluwer 1998).

I. King and W. Mason, *Peace at Any Price: How the World Failed Kosovo* (Ithaca, Cornell University Press 2006).

F. Kirgis, *International Organisations in Their Legal Setting*, 2nd edn. (St. Paul, West 1993).

J. Klabbers, *An Introduction to International Institutional Law* (Cambridge, Cambridge University Press 2002).

J. Klabbers, M. Koskenniemi, O. Ribbelink and A. Zimmermann, eds., *State Practice Regarding State Succession and Issues of Recognition: The Pilot Project of the Council of Europe* (The Hague, Kluwer Law International 1999).

T. Knudsen and C. Laustsen, *Kosovo Between War and Peace: Nationalism, Peacebuilding and International Trusteeship* (London, Routledge 2006).

D. Kochenov, *The Failure of Conditionality: Pre-Accession Conditionality. Pre-accession Conditionality in the Fields of Democracy and the Rule of Law: A Legal Appraisal of EU Enlargement* (Groningen, Ph.D thesis 2007).

C. Koenig and M. Pechstein, *Die Europäische Union*, 3rd edn. (Tübingen, J.C.B. Mohr 2000).

M. Koskenniemi, ed., *International Law Aspects of the European Union* (The Hague, Kluwer Law International 1998).

P. Koutrakos, *Trade, Foreign Policy & Defence in EU Constitutional Law* (Oxford, Hart Publishing 2001).

P. Koutrakos, *EU International Relations Law* (Oxford, Hart Publishing 2006).

H. Krieger, ed., *The Kosovo Conflict and International Law: An Analytical Documentation 1974-1999* (Cambridge, Cambridge University Press 2001).

V. Kronenberger, ed., *The European Union and the International Legal Order: Discord or Harmony?* (The Hague, T.M.C. Asser Press 2001).

V. Kronenberger and J. Wouters, eds., *The European Union and Conflict Prevention: Policy and Legal Aspects* (The Hague, T.M.C. Asser Press 2004).

M. Kuijer, *The Blindfold of Lady Justice: Judicial Independence and Impartiality in Light of the Requirements of Article 6 ECHR* (Nijmegen, Wolf Legal Productions 2004.

L

F. Larrabee, ed., *The Volatile Powder Keg: Balkan Security After the Cold War* (Washington D.C., American University Press 1994).

S. Larrabee, *NATO Enlargement: Prague and Beyond* (Brussels, CEPS 2001).

P. Latawski and M. Smith, *The Kosovo Crisis and the Evolution of post-Cold War European Security* (Manchester, Manchester University Press 2003).

H. Lauterpacht, *Recognition in International Law* (Cambridge, Cambridge University Press 1947).

R.A. Lawson and H.G. Schermers, *Leading Cases of the European Court of Human Rights*, 2nd edn. (Nijmegen, Ars Aequi Libri 1999).

A. Leenen, *Gemeenschapsrecht en volkenrecht* (Deventer, Kluwer 1984).

D. Lopandić, *Regional Initiatives in South Eastern Europe* (Belgrade, European Movement in Serbia 2001).

D. Lopandić, ed., *Regional Cooperation in South Eastern Europe – Conference Proceedings* (Belgrade, European Movement in Serbia 2002).

D. Lopandić and V. Bajić, eds., *Serbia and Montenegro on the Road to the European Union – Two Years Later* (Belgrade, European Movement in Serbia 2003).

S. Lucarelli, *Europe and the Breakup of Yugoslavia. A Political Failure in Search of a Scholarly Explanation* (The Hague, Kluwer Law International 2000).

M

I. MacLeod, I. Hendry and S. Hyatt, *External Relations of the European Communities* (Oxford, Clarendon Press 1996).

M. MacMillan, *Peacemakers – The Paris Conference of 1919 and Its Attempt to End War* (London, John Murray 2003).

M. Maresceau, ed., *Enlarging the European Union: Relations Between the EU and Central and Eastern Europe* (London, Longman 1997).

M. Maresceau and E. Lannon, eds., *The EU's Enlargement and Mediterranean Strategies – A Comparative Analysis* (London, Palgrave 2001).

B. Marković, *Yugoslav Crisis and the World: Chronology of Events January 1990 – December 1995* (Belgrade, Institute of International Politics and Economics 1995).

A. Mayhew, *Recreating Europe: The European Union's Policy towards Central and Eastern Europe* (Cambridge, Cambridge University Press 1998).
M. Mazower, *The Balkans: From the End of Byzantium to the Present Day*, 4th edn. (London, Phoenix 2003).
D. McGoldrick, *International Relations Law of the European Union* (London, Longman 1997).
M. Merlingen and R. Ostrauskaite, *European Union Peacebuilding and Policing: Governance and the European Security and Defence Policy* (London, Routledge 2006).
M. Mrak, *Succession of States* (The Hague, Martinus Nijhoff Publishers 1999).
T. Musgrave, *Self-Determination and National Minorities* (Oxford, Oxford University Press 2000).

N

NATO, *NATO Handbook* (Brussels, NATO Office of Information and Press 2001).
H. Neuhold and E. Sucharipa, eds., *The CFSP/ESDP After enlargement: A Bigger EU = A Stronger EU?* (Vienna School of International Studies, Favorita Papers 2003).
H.-H. Nöll, *Die Völkerrechtssubjectivität der Europäische Gemeinschaften und deren Bindung an das Allgemeine Völkerrecht* (Baden-Baden, Nomos 1986).
J. Nolan, ed., *Global Engagement: Cooperation and Security in the 21st Century* (Washington D.C., Brookings Institution 1994).
A. Nowak, ed., *Civilian Crisis Management: The EU Way* (Paris, EUISS 2006).
S. Nutall, *European Political Cooperation* (Oxford, Clarendon Press 1992).
L. Nyholm, ed., *OSCE – A Need for Co-operation* (Copenhagen, The Danish United Nations Association 1998).

O

A. Orford, *Reading Humanitarian Intervention: Human Rights and the Use of Force in International Law* (Cambridge, Cambridge University Press 2003).
OSCE, *OSCE Handbook*, 3rd edn. (Vienna, OSCE Secretariat 2000).
A. Ott and K. Inglis, eds., *Handbook on European Enlargement – A Commentary on the Enlargement Process* (The Hague, T.M.C. Asser Press 2002).
D. Owen, *Balkan Odyssey* (New York, Harcourt, Brace & Co. 1995).

P

J. Peterson and H. Sjursen, eds., *A Common Foreign Policy for Europe? Competing Visions of the CFSP* (London, Routledge 1998).
J. Pettifer, ed., *The New Macedonian Question* (Basingstoke, Palgrave 2001).

D. Phinnemore, *Association: Stepping-Stone or Alternative to EU Membership?* (Sheffield, Sheffield Academic Press 1999).

A. Pijpers, E. Regelsberger and W. Wessels, eds., *European Political Cooperation in the 1980s – A Common Foreign Policy for Western Europe?* (Dordrecht, Martinus Nijhoff Publishers 1988).

E. Pond, *Endgame in the Balkans: Regime Change, European Style* (Washington, Brookings Institution Press 2006).

R

D. Raič, *Statehood and the Law of Self-Determination* (The Hague, Kluwer Law International 2002).

E. Regelsberger, P. de Schoutheete de Tervarent and W. Wessels, eds., *Foreign Policy of the European Union: From EPC to CFSP and Beyond* (Boulder, Lynne Rienner Publishers 1997).

M. Reichard, *The EU-NATO Relationship: A Legal and Political Perspective* (Aldershot, Ashgate 2006).

S

H.G. Schermers and N.M. Blokker, *International Institutional Law – Unity within Diversity*, 4th edn. (Boston, Martinus Nijhoff Publishers 2003).

A. Schmid, *Thesaurus and Glossary of Early Warning and Conflict Prevention Terms* (Rotterdam, Erasmus University 1998).

I. Seidl-Hohenveldern and G. Loibl, *Das Recht der Internationale Organisationen einschließlich der Supranationalen Gemeinschaften*, 5th edn. (Cologne, Carl Heymanns Verlag 1992).

P. Siani-Davies, ed., *International Intervention in the Balkans Since 1995* (London, Routledge 2003).

R. Siekmann, *National Contingents in United Nations Peace-keeping Forces* (Dordrecht, Martinus Nijhoff 1991).

L. Silber and A. Little, *The Death of Yugoslavia*, Rev. edn. (London, Penguin Books 1996).

B. Simma, ed., *The Charter of the United Nations: A Commentary*, 2nd edn. (Oxford, Oxford University Press 2002).

H. Sokalski, *An Ounce of Prevention: Macedonia and the UN Experience in Preventive Diplomacy* (Washington D.C., Endowment of the US Institute of Peace 2003).

T

S. Terrett, *The Dissolution of Yugoslavia and the Badinter Arbitration Commission: A Contextual study of Peace-making Efforts in the Post-Cold War World* (Aldershot, Ashgate 2000).

M. Todorova, *Imagining the Balkans* (Oxford, Oxford University Press 1997).

C. Tomuschat, ed., *Modern Law of Self-Determination* (Dordrecht, Martinus Nijhoff Publishers 1993).

C. Tomuschat, ed., *Kosovo and the International Community: A Legal Assessment* (The Hague, Kluwer Law International 2002).

P. van Tongeren, H. van de Veen and J. Verhoeven, *Searching for Peace in Europe and Eurasia: An Overview of Conflict Prevention and Peace-building Activities* (Boulder, Lynne Rienner 2002).

D. Triantaphyllou, ed., *What Status for Kosovo?* (Paris, ISS 2001).

S. Trifunovska, ed., *Yugoslavia Through Documents: From Its Creation to Its Dissolution* (Dordrecht, Martinus Nijhoff Publishers 1994).

M. Trybus and N.D. White, eds., *European Security Law* (Oxford, Oxford University Press 2007).

U

UN Department of Public Information, *The Blue Helmets: A Review of United Nations Peace-keeping*, 3rd edn. (New York, UNDPI 1996).

V

J. Vanhamme, *Volkenrechtelijke beginselen in het Europees recht* (Groningen, Europa Law Publishing 2001).

W

C. de Waal, *Albania Today: A Portrait of Post-Communist Turbulence* (London, I.B. Tauris 2005).

C. Walter, *Vereinte Nationen und Regionalorganisationen. Eine Untersuchung zu Kapitel VIII der Satzung der Vereinten Nationen* (Heidelberg, Springer 1996).

J.H.H. Weiler, ed., *The Constitution of Europe – 'Do the New Clothes have an Emperor?' and Other Essays on European Integration* (Cambridge, Cambridge University Press 1999).

T. Weiss, et al., eds., *Political Gain and Civilian Pain: Humanitarian Impacts of Economic Sanctions* (Lanham, Rowman & Littlefield Publishers Inc. 1997).

M. Weller, *The 'Yugoslav' Crisis in International Law: General Issues (Part I)* (Cambridge, Cambridge University Press 1997).

R.A. Wessel, *The European Union's Foreign and Security Policy – A Legal Institutional Perspective* (The Hague, Kluwer Law International 1999).

R. West, *Black Lamb and Grey Falcon: A Journey through Yugoslavia*, 4th edn. (Edinburgh, Canongate Books 2001).

E. de Wet, *The Chapter VII Powers of the United Nations Security Council* (Oxford, Hart Publishing 2004).

T. de Wilde d'Estmael, *La dimension politique des relations économiques extérieures de la Communauté européenne: sanctions et incitants économiques comme moyens de politique étrangère* (Brussels, Émile Bruylant 1998).

A. Williams, *Reorganizing Eastern Europe: European Institutions and the Refashioning of Europe's Security Architecture* (Aldershot, Dartmouth Publishing Group 1994).

S. Woodward, *Balkan Tragedy: Chaos and Dissolution After the Cold War* (Washington D.C., Brookings Institution 1995).

J. Wouters, F. Hoffmeister and T. Ruys, eds., *The United Nations and the European Union: An Ever Stronger Partnership* (The Hague, T.M.C. Asser Press 2006).

Z

J. Zielonka, ed., *Paradoxes of European Foreign Policy* (The Hague, Kluwer Law International 1998).

J. Zielonka, ed., *Europe Unbound: Enlarging and Reshaping the Boundaries of the European Union* (London, Routledge 2002).

J.W. de Zwaan, J. Jans, F. Nelissen and S. Blockmans, eds., *The European Union: An Ongoing Process of Integration – Liber Amicorum Alfred E. Kellermann* (The Hague, T.M.C. Asser Press 2004).

M. Zwanenburg, *Accountability of Peace Support Operations* (Leiden, Martinus Nijhoff 2005).

2. ARTICLES, BOOK CONTRIBUTIONS AND REPORTS

A

A. Ackerman, 'International Intervention in Macedonia: From Preventive Engagement to Peace Implementation', in P. Siani-Davies, ed., *International Intervention in the Balkans Since 1995* (London, Routledge 2003) pp. 105-119.

F. Alabrune, 'La pratique des comités des sanctions du Conseil de sécurité depuis 1990', 45 *AFDI* (1999) pp. 226-279.

B. Alendar, 'Conditions for the Normalization of Relations between FR Yugoslavia and the European Union – The Outer Wall of Sanctions of the European Union', XLIX *Review of International Affairs* (1998) pp. 7-12.

P. Alston and J.H.H. Weiler, 'An "Ever Closer Union" in Need of a Human Rights Policy: The European Union and Human Rights', in P. Alston, ed., *The EU and Human Rights* (Oxford, Oxford University Press 1999) pp. 3-66.

F.-L. Altmann, 'Die Balkanpolitik der EU – Regionalansatz und Prinzip der Konditionalität', 47 *Südosteuropa* (1998) pp. 503-515.

A. Ambos, 'The Institutionalisation of CFSP and ESDP', in D. Mahncke, A. Ambos and C. Reynolds, eds., *European Foreign Policy: From Rhetoric to Reality?* (Brussels, Peter Lang 2004) pp. 165-192.

M. Amor and M. Estebanez, 'The High Commissioner on National Minorities: Development of the Mandate', in M. Bothe, N. Ronzitti and A. Rosas, eds., *The OSCE in the Maintenance of Peace and Security: Conflict Prevention, Crisis Management, and Peaceful Settlement of Disputes* (The Hague, Kluwer Law International 1998) pp. 123-165.

F. Amtenbrink, 'On the European Union's Institutional Capacity to Cope with Further Enlargement', in S. Blockmans, S. Prechal and W.Th. Douma, eds., *Reconciling 'Deepening' and 'Widening' of the European Union* (The Hague, T.M.C. Asser Press, 2007).

O. Anastasakis and D. Bechev, 'EU Conditionality in South East Europe: Bringing Commitment to the Process', *SEESP Papers* (2003).

H.-J. Axt, 'Der Stabilitätspakt für Südosteuropa: Politischer Aktionismus oder langfristig tragfähiges Konzept?', 48 *Südosteuropa* (1999) pp. 401-416.

B

R. Badinter, 'L'Europe du droit', 4 *EJIL* (1993) pp. 15-23.

E. Bakker, 'A Culture of Conflict Prevention: OSCE Experience and Cooperation with the EU', in V. Kronenberger and J. Wouters, eds., *The European Union and Conflict Prevention: Policy and Legal Aspects* (The Hague, T.M.C. Asser Press 2004) pp. 393-413.

D. Baldwin, 'The Sanctions Debate and the Logic of Choice', 24 *International Security* (1999) pp. 80-107.

G. Barrett, 'EU and Serbia and Montenegro', in D. Lopandić and V. Bajić, eds., *Serbia and Montenegro on the Road to the European Union – Two Years Later* (Belgrade, European Movement in Serbia 2003) pp. 37-45.

R. Barry, 'After the Bombing – the OSCE in the Aftermath of the Kosovo Crisis', 5 Institute for Peace Research and Security Policy at the University of Hamburg, ed., *OSCE Yearbook 1999* (Baden-Baden, Nomos 2000) pp. 49-57.

R. Bassett, 'Balkan Endgame?', 31 *JDW* (1999) pp. 22-25.

D. Bechev, 'Carrots, Sticks and Norms: The EU and Regional Cooperation in Southeast Europe', 8 *Journal of Southern Europe and the Balkans* (2006) pp. 27-43.

U. Becker, 'EU-Enlargements and Limits to Amendments of the EC Treaty', 15 *Jean Monnet Working Paper* (2001).

I. Berend, 'Editorial: The Kosovo Trap', 14 *European Review* (2006) pp. 413-414.

L. Besselink, 'The Netherlands: Ratification Referendum and Impact on the Constitution', in A. Albi and J. Ziller, eds., *The European Constitution and National Constitutions: Ratification and Beyond* (The Hague, Kluwer Law International 2007) pp. 113-123.

D. Bethlehem, 'Regional Interface between Security Council Decisions and Member States Implementation: The Example of the European Union', in V. Gowlland-Debbas, ed., *United Nations Sanctions and International Law* (The Hague, Kluwer Law International 2001) pp. 291-305.

F. Bieber, 'Preface', in F. Bieber, ed., *Montenegro in Transition: Problems of Identity and Statehood* (Baden-Baden, Nomos 2003) pp. 7-9.

F. Bieber, 'Montenegrin Politics Since the Disintegration of Yugoslavia', in F. Bieber, ed., *Montenegro in Transition: Problems of Identity and Statehood* (Baden-Baden, Nomos 2003) pp. 11-42.

F. Bieber, 'Minority Rights in Practice in South Eastern Europe', Discussion Paper, King Baudouin Foundation, 30 September 2004.

R. Bieber, 'European Community Recognition of Eastern European States: A New Perspective for International Law?', 86 *Proceedings of the ASIL* (1992) p. 374 et seq.

R. Biermann, 'The Stability Pact for South Eastern Europe: Potential, Problems and Perspectives', C56 *ZEI Discussion Papers* (1999) at pp. 15-19.

R. Biermann, 'Die Europäische Perspektive für den westlichen Balkan', 51 *Osteuropa* (2001) pp. 922-937.

S. Biscop, 'Able and Willing? Assessing the EU's Capacity for Military Action', 9 *EFA Rev.* (2004) pp. 509-527.

J. Blatt, et al., 'Partners and Neighbours: A CFSP for a Wider Europe', 64 *Chaillot Papers* (2003).

A. Bleckmann, 'Die Position des Völkerrechts im inneren Rechtsraum der Europäischen Gemeinschaften. Monismus oder Dualismus der Rechtsordnungen?', 18 *JIR* (1975) pp. 300-319.

S. Blockmans, 'Moving into UNchartered Waters: An Emerging Right of Unilateral Humanitarian Intervention', 12 *LJIL* (1999) pp. 759-786.

S. Blockmans, 'A New Crisis Manager at the Horizon – The Case of the European Union', 13 *LJIL* (2000) pp. 255-263.

S. Blockmans, 'Oostenrijk in quarantaine – De voorwaarden voor het beëindigen van het lidmaatschap van een internationale organisatie', 49 *Ars Aequi* (2000) pp. 629-637.

S. Blockmans, 'Van Wenen naar Nice: Nieuwe voorwaarden voor het instellen van sancties door de EU tegen een lidstaat die de grondrechten schendt', 50 *Ars Aequi* (2001) pp. 331-338.

S. Blockmans, 'De EU toont haar melktanden. Het instellen en implementeren van gerichte sancties ter handhaving of herstel van de internationale vrede en veiligheid', in T.M.C. Asser Instituut, *Veiligheid en het recht van de Europese Unie* (The Hague, T.M.C. Asser Press 2002) pp. 85-96.

S. Blockmans, 'EU Conflict Prevention in the Western Balkans', in V. Kronenberger and J. Wouters, eds., *The European Union and Conflict-prevention – Policy and Legal Aspects* (The Hague, T.M.C. Asser Press 2004) pp. 293-321.

S. Blockmans, 'The European Union's Troubled Relations with the Federal Republic of Yugoslavia (1991-2001)', in J.W. de Zwaan, J. Jans, F. Nelissen and S. Blockmans, eds., *The European Union: An Ongoing Process of Integration – Liber Amicorum Alfred E. Kellermann* (The Hague, T.M.C. Asser Press 2004) pp. 337-356.

S. Blockmans, 'Impact of EU Accession on the Role of (Potential) Candidate Countries' Executives', in A.E. Kellermann, J. Czuczai, S. Blockmans, A. Albi and W.Th. Douma, eds., *Impact of EU Accession on the Legal Orders of New Member States and (Pre-)Candidate Countries – Hopes and Fears* (The Hague, T.M.C. Asser Press 2006) pp. 291-300.

S. Blockmans, 'The European Union and Its Neighbours: Questioning Identity and Relationships', in S. Blockmans and A. Łazowski, eds., *The European Union and Its Neighbours: A Legal Appraisal of the EU's Policies of Stabilisation, Partnership and Integration* (The Hague, T.M.C. Asser Press 2006) pp. 3-18.

S. Blockmans, 'Western Balkans', in S. Blockmans and A. Łazowski, eds., *The European Union and Its Neighbours: A Legal Appraisal of the EU's Policies of Stabilisation, Partnership and Integration* (The Hague, T.M.C. Asser Press 2006) pp. 315-355.

S. Blockmans, 'Role and Impact of the EU's Common Foreign and Security Policy towards the Western Balkans (2001-2006)', in 2 *Croatian Yearbook of European Law and Policy* (2006) pp. 209-264.

S. Blockmans, 'Reconciling Widening and Deepening: Enlargement as a Vehicle to Break the Union's Constitutional Deadlock', in A. Albi and J. Ziller, eds., *The European Constitution and National Constitutions: Ratification and Beyond* (The Hague, Kluwer Law International 2007) pp. 249-259.

S. Blockmans and A. Łazowski, 'Conclusions: Squaring the Ring of Friends', in S. Blockmans and A. Łazowski, eds., *The European Union and Its Neighbours: A Legal Appraisal of the EU's Policies of Stabilisation, Partnership and Integration* (The Hague, T.M.C. Asser Press 2006) pp. 613-639.

A. Bloed, 'The OSCE Main Political Bodies and Their Role in Conflict Prevention and Crisis Management', in M. Bothe, N. Ronzitti and A. Rosas, eds., *The OSCE in the Maintenance of Peace and Security: Conflict Prevention, Crisis Management, and Peaceful Settlement of Disputes* (The Hague, Kluwer Law International 1998) pp. 35-52.

N.M. Blokker, 'Is the Authorization Authorized? Powers and Practice of the UN Security Council to Authorize the Use of Force by "Coalitions of the Able and Willing"', 11 *EJIL* (2000) pp. 541-568.

N.M. Blokker, 'Internationale organisaties en hun leden. Van oude vragen, de dingen die voorbij gaan?', Inaugural Lecture, Leiden University, 2001.

N.M. Blokker, 'In Memoriam: Professor Henry G. Schermers (1928-2006)', 3 *IOLR* (2006) pp. 185-187.

Y. Blum, 'UN Membership of the "New" Yugoslavia: Continuity or Break?', 86 *AJIL* (1992) pp. 830-833.

A. Bodnar, 'Transitional Periods for Employment – "Second Class" EU Citizenship?', in O. Zetterquist, ed., *Law and Modernity* (Cracow, Polpress 2004) pp. 121-138.

S. Bohr, 'Sanctions by the United Nations Security Council and the European Community', 4 *EJIL* (1993) pp. 256-268.

V. Bojičić and D. Dyker, 'Sanctions on Serbia: Sledgehammer or Scalpel', *Sussex Working Papers in Contemporary European Studies*, No. 1, June 1993.

S. Bose, 'Mostar: International Intervention in a Divided Bosnian Town, 1994-2001', in P. Siani-Davies, ed., *International Intervention in the Balkans Since 1995* (London, Routledge 2003) pp. 68-87.

M. Bothe, 'Die Stellung der Europäischen Gemeinschaften im Völkerrecht', 37 *ZaöRv* (1977) pp. 122-137.

M. Bothe, 'Peace-keeping', in B. Simma, ed., *The Charter of the United Nations: A Commentary*, 2nd edn. (Oxford, Oxford University Press 2002) pp. 648-700.

M. Bothe and T. Marauhn, 'UN Administration of Kosovo and East Timor: Concept, Legality and Limitations of Security Council-Mandated Trusteeship Administration', in C. Tomuschat, ed., *Kosovo and the International Community: A Legal Assessment* (The Hague, Kluwer Law International 2002) pp. 217-325.

M. Bothe and C. Schmidt, 'Sur quelques questions de succession posées par la dissolution de l'URSS et celle de la Yougoslavie', 96 *RGDIP* (1992) pp. 811-842.

J. Boulois, 'Le droit des Communautés européennes dans ses rapports avec le droit international général', *Receuil des courts de l'Académie de droit international de la Haye*, vol. IV (1993) pp. 13-79.

B. Brandtner and A. Rosas, 'Trade Preferences and Human Rights', in P. Alston, ed., *The EU and Human Rights* (Oxford, Oxford University Press 1999) pp. 699-722.

S. Breitenmoser, 'Die Europäische Union zwischen Völkerrecht und Staatsrecht', 55 *ZaöRv* (1995) pp. 951-992.

O. Brenninkmeijer, 'The OSCE High Commissioner on National Minorities: Negotiating the 1992 Conflict Prevention Mandate', *PSIO Occasional Paper*, No. 5, 2005.

T. Buchsbaum, 'The OSCE and the Stability Pact for South Eastern Europe', 11 *Helsinki Monitor* (2000) pp. 62-79.

R. Bulajić, 'FR Yugoslavia and the European Union', XLVIII *Review of International Affairs* (1997) pp. 4-7.

M. Bulterman, 'European Union Membership and Political Conditionality', in M. Bulterman, A. Hendriks and J. Smith, eds., To Baehr in Our Minds: Essays on Human Rights from the Heart of the Netherlands, 21 *SIM* (1998) pp. 123-140.

M. Bulterman, 'Van wapenembargo tot luchtvaartverbod: het Europese sanctieregime voor Joegoslavië', *NTER* (1999) pp. 203-206.

M. Bulterman, 'Fundamental Rights and the United Nations Financial Sanction Regime: The *Kadi* and *Yusuf* Judgments of the Court of First Instance of the European Communities', 19 *LJIL* (2006) pp. 753-772.

B. Burgos, 'Breaking the Balkan Logjam by Applying the Burgos Principle' (Brussels, Spiritus 2006) pp. 1-10.

C

F. Cameron and A. Kintis, 'Southeastern Europe and the European Union', 2 *Journal of Southeast European and Black Sea Studies* (2001) pp. 94-112.

T. Ćapeta, D. Mihelin and S. Rodin, 'Croatia', in A.E. Kellermann, J. Czuczai, S. Blockmans, A. Albi and W.Th. Douma, eds., *The Impact of EU Accession on the Legal Orders of New EU Member States and (Pre-)Candidate Countries – Hopes and Fears* (The Hague, T.M.C. Asser Press 2006) pp. 69-112.

R. Caplan, 'International Authority and State Building: The Case of Bosnia and Herzegovina', 10 *Global Governance* (2004) pp. 53-66.

A. Cassese, 'Ex Iniuria Ius Oritur: Are We Moving towards International Legitimation of Forcible Humanitarian Countermeasures in the World Community?', 10 *EJIL* (1999) pp. 23-30.

J. Cerone, 'Minding the Gap: Outlining KFOR Accountability in post-conflict Kosovo', 12 *EJIL* (2001) pp. 469-488.

D. Chandler, 'The European Union and Governance in the Western Balkans: An Unequal Partnership', 1/2 *European Balkan Observer* (2003) pp. 5-9.

D. Chandler, 'From Dayton to Europe', 12 *International Peacekeeping* (2005) pp. 336-349.

J. Charpentier, 'Les declarations des Douze sur la reconnaissance des nouveaux Etats', 96 *RGDIP* (1992) pp. I-343-355.

E. Chevallier, 'L'ONU au Kosovo: leçons de la première MINUK', *35 EUISS Occasional Paper* (2002).

I. Cheyne, 'International Agreements and the European Community Legal System', 19 *EL Rev.* (1994) pp. 581-598.

S. Clément, 'Conflict Prevention in the Balkans: Case Studies of Kosovo and the FYR of Macedonia ', *EUISS Paper* (1997).

S. Clément, 'WEU and South-Eastern Europe', in G. Lenzi, ed., *WEU at Fifty* (Paris, ISS 1998) pp. 93-108.

S. Clément, 'Former Yugoslav Macedonia, the Regional Setting and European Security: Towards Balkan Stability?', in J. Pettifer, ed., *The New Macedonian Question* (Basingstoke, Palgrave 2001) pp. 285-302.

M. Craven, 'What's in a Name? The Former Yugoslav Republic of Macedonia and Issues of Statehood', 16 *Australian YIL* (1995) pp. 199-239.

M. Craven, 'The European Community Arbitration Commission on Yugoslavia', 66 *BYIL* (1996) pp. 333-413.

M. Craven, 'The Genocide Case, the Law of Treaties and State Succession', 68 *BYIL* (1998) pp. 127-163.

J. Crawford, 'State Practice and International Law in Relation to Secession', 69 *BYIL* (1999) pp. 85-117.

M. Cremona, 'Human Rights and Democracy Clauses in the EC's Trade Agreements', in N. Emiliou and D. O'Keeffe, eds., *The European Union and World Trade Law, After the GATT Uruguay Round 1996* (London, Wiley 1996) pp. 62-77.

M. Cremona, 'External Relations and External Competence: The Emergence of an Integrated Policy', in P. Craig and G. de Búrca, *The Evolution of EU Law* (Oxford, Oxford University Press 1999) pp. 137-176.

M. Cremona, 'Creating the New Europe: The Stability Pact for South Eastern Europe in the Context of EU-SEE Relations', in A. Dashwood and A. Ward, eds., *The Cambridge Yearbook of European Legal Studies – Volume 2, 1999* (Oxford, Hart Publishing 2000) pp. 463-506.

M. Cremona, 'External Policy and the European Economic Constitution', in G. de Búrca and J. Scott, eds., *Constitutional Change in the EU: From Uniformity to Flexibility* (Oxford, Hart Publishing 2000) pp. 64-65.

M. Cremona, 'Accession to the European Union: Membership Conditionality and Accession Criteria', 25 *Polish YIL* (2001) pp. 219-240.

M. Cremona, 'The Impact of Enlargement: External Policy and External Relations', in M. Cremona, ed., *The Enlargement of the European Union* (Oxford, Oxford University Press 2003) p. 161 et seq.

M. Cremona, 'The European Neighbourhood Policy: Legal and Institutional Issues', *CDDRL Working Papers*, No. 25, 2 November 2004.

M. Cremona, 'Enlargement: A Successful Instrument of Foreign Policy?', in T. Tridimas and P. Nebbia, eds., *European Union Law for the Twenty-First Century*, Vol. 1 (Oxford, Hart Publishing 2004) pp. 397-413.

M. Cremona, 'The Union as a Global Actor: Roles, Models and Identity', 41 *CML Rev.* (2004) pp. 553-574.

M. Cremona, 'EU Enlargement: Solidarity and Conditionality', 30 *EL Rev.* (2005) pp. 3-22.

M. Cremona, 'External Relations of the EU and the Member States: Competence, Mixed Agreements, International Responsibility, and Effects of International Law', *EUI Law Working Papers*, No. 22 (2006).

D. Curtin, 'The Constitutional Structure of the European Union: A Europe of Bits and Pieces', 30 *CML Rev.* (1993) pp. 17-69.

S. Cvijić, 'Self-determination as a Challenge to the Legitimacy of Humanitarian Intervention: The Case of Kosovo', 8 *German Law Journal* (2007) pp. 57-79.

W. Czaplinski, 'The Activities of the OSCE in Kosovo', in C. Tomuschat, ed., *Kosovo and the International Community: A Legal Assessment* (The Hague, Kluwer Law International 2002) pp. 37-44.

J. Czuczai, 'Practical Implementation by the Acceding Candidate Countries of the Constitutional Acquis of the EU. Problems and Challenges', in A.E. Kellermann, J.W. de Zwaan and J. Czuczai, eds., *EU Enlargement: The Constitutional Impact at EU and National Level* (The Hague, T.M.C. Asser Press 2001) pp. 411-422.

J. Czuczai, 'Constitutional Preparation for EU Accession in the New Central and Eastern European Member States: Is the Rule of Law Better than the Rule of Politics', in J.W. de Zwaan, J. Jans, F. Nelissen and S. Blockmans, eds., *The European Union: An Ongoing Process of Integration – Liber Amicorum Alfred E. Kellermann* (The Hague, T.M.C. Asser Press 2004) pp. 269-283.

J. Czuczai, 'Impact of EU Accession on the Role and Functioning of the National Judiciary', in A.E. Kellermann, J. Czuczai, S. Blockmans, A. Albi and W.Th. Douma, eds., *The Impact of EU Accession on the Legal Orders of New EU Member States and (Pre-)Candidate Countries – Hopes and Fears* (The Hague, T.M.C. Asser Press 2006) pp. 267-289.

D

L. Damrosch, 'Enforcing International Law through Non-forcible Measures', 269 *RdC* (1997) pp. 13-250.

A. Dashwood, 'External Relations Provisions of the Amsterdam Treaty', 35 *CML Rev.* (1998) pp. 1019-1045.

A. Dashwood, 'The Impact of Enlargement on the Union's Institutions', in C. Hillion, ed., *EU Enlargement: A Legal Perspective* (Oxford, Hart Publishing 2004) pp. 45-56.

E. Decaux, 'La Conférence de Rambouillet. Négociation de la dernière chance ou contrainte illicite?', in C. Tomuschat, ed., *Kosovo and the International Community: A Legal Assessment* (The Hague, Kluwer Law International 2002) pp. 45-64.

Z. Deen-Racsmány, 'A Redistribution of Authority between the UN and Regional Organizations in the Field of Maintenance of Peace and Security', 13 *LJIL* (2000) pp. 297-312.

A. Deighton, 'The European Security and Defence Policy', 40 *JCMS* (2002) pp. 719-741.

I. Dekker and R. Wessel, 'Van CVSE naar OVSE: de sluipende institutionalisering en onvermijdelijke juridisering van een internationale conferentie', 31 *Vrede en Veiligheid* (2002) pp. 425-438.

J. Devin and J. Dashti-Gibson, 'Sanctions in the Former Yugoslavia: Convoluted Goals and Complicated Consequences', in T. Weiss, et al., eds., *Political Gain and Civilian Pain: Humanitarian Impacts of Economic Sanctions* (Lanham, Rowman & Littlefield Publishers Inc. 1997) pp. 149-187.

M. Dougan, 'A Spectre is Haunting Europe… Free Movement of Persons and the Eastern Enlargement', in C. Hillion, ed., *EU Enlargement: A Legal Approach* (Oxford, Hart Publishing 2004) pp. 111-142.

W.Th. Douma, 'Russia and the Enlarged European Union: Mending Fences While Shaping a Wider Europe's Environment', in J.W. de Zwaan, J. Jans, F. Nelissen and S. Blockmans, eds., *The European Union: An Ongoing Process of Integration – Liber Amicorum Alfred E. Kellermann* (The Hague, T.M.C. Asser Press 2004) pp. 319-336.

W.Th. Douma, 'Israel and the Palestinian Authority', in S. Blockmans and A. Łazowski, eds., *The European Union and Its Neighbours: A Legal Appraisal of the EU's Policies of Stabilisation, Partnership and Integration* (The Hague, T.M.C. Asser Press 2006) pp. 433-461.

S. Duke, 'From Amsterdam to Kosovo: Lessons for the Future of CFSP', 2 *Eipascope* (1999) pp. 2-15.

S. Duke, 'The European Security Strategy in a Comparative Framework: Does it Make for Secure Alliances in a Better World?', 9 *EFA Rev.* (2004) pp. 459-481.

U. Dusjin, 'The Stability Pact for South-Eastern Europe: An Avenue to EU Membership', 53 *Zbornik PFZ* (2003) pp. 629-652.

E

Editorial Comments, 'The European Union – A New International Actor', 38 *CML Rev.* (2001) pp. 825-828.

G. Edwards, 'Reforming the Union's Institutional Framework: A New EU Obligation?', in C. Hillion, ed., *EU Enlargement: A Legal Approach* (Oxford, Hart Publishing 2004) pp. 23-43.

P. Eeckhout, 'External Relations of the EU and the Member States: Competence, Mixed Agreements, International Responsibility, and Effects of International Law – General Report', presented at FIDE 2006, available at: <http://www.fide2006.org>.

C.-D. Ehlermann, 'The Scope of Article 113 of the EEC Treaty', in P. Manin, et al., eds., *Mélanges offerts à Pierre-Henri Teitgen* (Paris, Editions Pédone 1984) pp. 145-169.

H.-G. Ehrhart, 'Prevention and Regional Security: The Royaumont Process and the Stabilisation of South-Eastern Europe', 4 *OSCE Yearbook* (1998) pp. 327-346.

K. Elliot, 'The Sanctions Glass: Half Full or Completely Empty?', 23 *International Security* (1998) pp. 50-65.

M. Emerson, 'Perspectives for the Balkans and a Wider European Order', paper presented at the WIIW/LSE Conference on 'Reconstruction and Integration in South-Eastern Europe: Economic Aspects', Vienna, 12-13 November 1999.

European Stability Initiative, 'The Helsinki Moment – European Member State Building in the Balkans' (2005).

European Stability Initiative, 'Breaking Out of the Balkan Ghetto: Why IPA Should Be Changed' (2005).

R. Everly, 'Reviewing Governmental Acts of the United Nations in Kosovo', 8 *German Law Journal* (2007) pp. 21-37.

F

R. Falk, 'Kosovo, World Order, and the Future of International Law', 93 *AJIL* (1999) pp. 847-857.

N. Figa-Talamanca, 'The Role of NATO in the Peace Agreement for Bosnia and Herzegovina', 7 *EJIL* (1996) pp. 164-175.

F. Fink-Hooijer, 'The Common Foreign and Security Policy of the European Union', 5 *EJIL* (1994) pp. 173-198.

E. Foster, 'Ad hoc in Albania: Did Europe Fail? A Rejoinder', 29 *Security Dialogue* (1998) pp. 213-219.

M. Fouwels, 'The European Union's Common Foreign and Security Policy and Human Rights', 15 *NQHR* (1997) pp. 291-324.

T. Franck, 'Lessons of Kosovo', 93 *AJIL* (1999) pp. 857-859.

L. Friis and A. Murphy, '"Turbo-charged negotiations": The EU and the Stability Pact for South Eastern Europe', 7 *Journal of European Public Policy* (2000) pp. 767-786.

L. Friis and A. Murphy, 'Enlargement of the European Union: Impacts on the EU, the Candidates and the "Next Neighbours"', 14 *ECSA Rev.* (2001) pp. 2-7.

J. Frowein, 'Die Europäische Union mit WEU als Sicherheitssystem', in O. Due, M. Lutter and J. Schwarze, eds., *Festschrift für Ulrich Everling* (Baden-Baden, Nomos 1995) pp. 315-326.

J. Frowein and N. Kirsch, 'Article 41', in B. Simma, ed., *The Charter of the United Nations: A Commentary*, 2nd edn. (Oxford, Oxford University Press 2002) pp. 735-749.

J. Frowein and N. Kirsch, 'Article 42', in B. Simma, ed., *The Charter of the United Nations: A Commentary*, 2nd edn. (Oxford, Oxford University Press 2002) pp. 749-759.

J. Frowein and N. Kirsch, 'Article 43', in B. Simma, ed., *The Charter of the United Nations: A Commentary*, 2nd edn. (Oxford, Oxford University Press 2002) pp. 760-763.

G

P. Gaeta, 'Is NATO Authorized or Obliged to Arrest Persons Indicted by the International Criminal Tribunal for the Former Yugoslavia', 9 *EJIL* (1998) pp. 174-181.

G. Gaja, 'Use of Force Made or Authorized by the United Nations', in C. Tomuschat, ed., *The United Nations at Age Fifty; A Legal Perspective* (The Hague, Kluwer Law International 1995) pp. 39-58.

G. Gaja, 'New Instruments and Institutions for Enhancing the Protection of Human Rights in Europe', in P. Alston, ed., *The EU and Human Rights* (Oxford, Oxford University Press 1999) pp. 781-800.

P. Gallis, 'NATO: Article V and Collective Defense', *CRS Report for Congress*, 17 July 1997.

W. Ganshof van der Meersch, 'L'ordre juridique des Communautés européennes et le droit international', *Receuil des courts de l'Académie de droit international de la Haye*, Vol. V (1975) pp. 1-389.

T. Garcia, 'La mission d'administration intérimaire des Nations Unies au Kosovo (MINUK)', 14 *RGDIP* (2000) pp. 61-71.

T. Gazzini, 'NATO's Role in the Collective Security System', 8 *Journal of Conflict and Security Law* (2003) pp. 231-263.

V. Gligorov, M. Kaldor and L. Tsoukalis, 'Balkan Reconstruction and European Integration', *WIIW Policy Paper*, October 1999.

M. Goodwin, 'From Province to Protectorate to State? Speculation on the Impact of Kosovo's Genesis upon the Doctrines of International Law', 8 *German Law Journal* (2007) pp. 1-20.

J. Gow, 'Nervous Bunnies – The International Community and the Yugoslav War of Dissolution', in L. Freedman, ed., *Military Intervention in European Conflicts* (Oxford, Blackwell Publishers 1994) pp. 14-33.

K. Grabar-Kitarović, 'Guest Editorial. The Stabilization and Association Process: The EU's Soft Power at Its Best', 12 *EFA Rev.* (2007) pp. 121-125.

H. Grabbe, 'A Partnership for Accession? The Implications of EU Conditionality for the Central and East European Applicants', Working Paper No. 99/12, EUI Robert Schuman Centre for Advanced Studies.

T. Grant, 'Internationally Guaranteed Constitutive Order: Cyprus and Bosnia as Predicates for a New Nontraditional Actor in the Society of States', 8 *Journal of Transnational Law and Policy* (1998) pp. 1-55.

J. Grussendorf, 'Conflict Prevention in the OSCE', in L. Nyholm, ed., *OSCE – A Need for Co-operation* (Copenhagen, The Danish United Nations Association 1998) pp. 43-56.

M. Guillaume, 'Le cadre juridique de l'action de la KFOR au Kosovo', in C. Tomuschat, ed., *Kosovo and the International Community: A Legal Assessment* (The Hague, Kluwer Law International 2002) pp. 243-286.

H

M. Hadzić, 'Kosovo and the Security Stabilization of South-East Europe', 7 *International Peacekeeping* (2000) pp. 83-94.

A. Heinemann-Grüder and I. Grebenschikov, 'Security Governance by Internationals: The Case of Kosovo', 13 *International Peacekeeping* (2006) pp. 43-59.

H.-J. Heintze, 'Minority Issues in Western Europe and the OSCE High Commissioner on National Minorities', 7 *International Journal on Minority and Group Rights* (2000) pp. 381-392.

L. Henkin, 'Kosovo and the Law of "Humanitarian Intervention"', 93 *AJIL* (1999) pp. 824-828.

C. Hill, 'The Capability-Expectations Gap, or Conceptualising Europe's International Role', 31 *JCMS* (1993) pp. 305-328.

C. Hill, 'Closing the Capabilities-Expectations Gap?', in J. Peterson and H. Sjursen, eds., *A Common Foreign Policy for Europe: Competing Visions of the CFSP* (London, Routledge 1998) pp. 18-38.

C. Hillion, 'The European Union is dead. Long live the European Union…', 29 *EL Rev.* (2004) pp. 583-612.

C. Hillion, 'Enlargement of the European Union – The Discrepancy between Membership Obligations and Accession Conditions as Regards the Protection of Minorities', 27 *Fordham International Law Journal* (2004) pp. 715-740.

C. Hillion, 'The Copenhagen Criteria and their Progeny', in C. Hillion, ed., *EU Enlargement: A Legal Approach* (Oxford, Hart Publishing 2004) pp. 1-22.

C. Hillion, 'You Cannot Have Your Cake and Eat It! The Limits to Member States' Discretion in EU Enlargement Negotiations', Inaugural lecture, Leiden University, 21 March 2006.

C. Hillion, 'Can "Widening" Serve as a Vehicle for "Deepening"? Potential and Limits of the Use of Accession Treaties to Achieve Institutional Reforms', in S. Blockmans, S. Prechal and W.Th. Douma, eds., *Reconciling 'Deepening' and 'Widening' of the European Union* (The Hague, T.M.C. Asser Press 2007).

P. Hilpold, 'Die Anerkennung der Neustaaten auf dem Balkan', 31 *Archiv des Völkerrechts* (1993) pp. 387-408.

F. Hoffmeister, 'Changing Requirements for Membership', in A. Ott and K. Inglis, eds., *Handbook on European Enlargement – A Commentary on the Enlargement Process* (The Hague, T.M.C. Asser Press 2002) pp. 90-102.

F. Hoffmeister, 'Die Beziehungen der Europäischen Union zu den Staaten des Westbalkans', in S. Kadelbach, ed., *Die Außenbeziehungen der Europäischen Union* (Baden-Baden, Nomos 2006) pp. 125-150 at pp. 132-138.

F. Hoffmeister, 'Outsider or Frontrunner? Recent Developments under International and European Law on the Status of the European Union in International Organizations and Treaty Bodies', 44 *CML Rev.* (2007) pp. 41-68.

B. Horvat, 'Towards the Balkan Union', XLVIII *Review of International Affairs* (1997) pp. 26-34.

W. Hummer and M. Schweitzer, 'Article 52', in B. Simma, ed., *The Charter of the United Nations: A Commentary*, 2nd edn. (Oxford, Oxford University Press 2002) pp. 807-853.

W. Hummer and M. Schweitzer, 'Article 54', in B. Simma, ed., *The Charter of the United Nations: A Commentary*, 2nd edn. (Oxford, Oxford University Press 2002) pp. 890-895.

B. Huszka, 'The Dispute over Montenegrin Independence', in F. Bieber, ed., *Montenegro in Transition: Problems of Identity and Statehood* (Baden-Baden, Nomos 2003) pp. 43-62.

B. Huszka, 'The Presevo Valley of Southern Serbia alongside Kosovo: The Case for Decentralisation and Minority Protection', *CEPS Policy Brief*, No. 120, January 2007.

I

A. Inder Singh, 'Minorities, Justice and Security in Post-Communist Europe', *Journal of Ethnopolitics and Minority Issues in Europe* (2002), available at: <http://ecmi.de/jemie>.

K. Inglis, 'The Europe Agreements Compared in the Light of Their Pre-accession Reorientation', 37 *CML Rev.* (2000) pp. 1173-1210.

K. Inglis, 'The Pre-Accession Strategy and the Accession Partnerships', in A. Ott and K. Inglis, eds., *Handbook on European Enlargement – A Commentary on the Enlargement Process* (The Hague, T.M.C. Asser Press 2002) pp. 103-111.

K. Inglis, 'The Union's Fifth Accession Treaty: New Means to Make Enlargement Possible', 41 *CML Rev.* (2004) pp. 937-973.

K. Inglis, 'The Accession Treaty and Its Transitional Arrangements: A Twilight zone for the New members of the Union', in C. Hillion, ed., *EU Enlargement: A Legal Approach* (Oxford, Hart Publishing 2004) pp. 77-109.

K. Inglis, 'EU Enlargement: Membership Conditions applied to Future and Potential Member States', in S. Blockmans and A. Łazowski, eds., *The European Union and Its Neighbours: A Legal Appraisal of the EU's Policies of Stabilisation, Partnership and Integration* (The Hague, T.M.C. Asser Press 2006) pp. 61-92.

International Crisis Group, 'Bosnia's Nationalist Governments: Paddy Ashdown and the Paradoxes of State Building', *Europe Report*, No. 146 (2003).

International Crisis Group, 'Pan-Albanianism: How Big a Threat to Balkan Stability?', *Europe Report*, No. 153 (2004).

International Crisis Group, 'Collapse in Kosovo', *Europe Report*, No. 155 (2004).

International Crisis Group, 'EUFOR: Changing Bosnia's Security Arrangements', *Europe Briefing*, No. 31 (2004).

International Crisis Group, 'Kosovo: Toward Final Status', *Europe Report*, No. 161 (2005).

International Crisis Group, 'Bosnia's Stalled Police Reform: No Progress, No EU', *Europe Report*, No. 164 (2005).

International Crisis Group, 'Bridging Kosovo's Mitrovica Divide', *Europe Report*, No. 165 (2005).

International Crisis Group, 'EU Visas and the Western Balkans', *Europe Report*, No. 168 (2005).

International Crisis Group, 'Montenegro's Independence Drive', *Europe Report*, No. 169 (2005).

International Crisis Group, 'Macedonia: Wobbling toward Europe', *Europe Briefing*, No. 41 (2006).

International Crisis Group, 'Kosovo: Challenge of Transition', *Europe Report*, No. 170 (2006).

International Crisis Group, 'Montenegro's Referendum', *Europe Briefing*, No. 42 (2006).

International Crisis Group, 'Serbia's New Constitution: Democracy Going Backwards', *Europe Briefing*, No. 44 (2006).

International Crisis Group, 'Kosovo Status: Delay is Risky', *Europe Report*, No. 177 (2006).

International Crisis Group, 'Kosovo's Status: Difficult Months Ahead', *Europe Briefing*, No. 45 (2006).

International Crisis Group, 'Ensuring Bosnia's Future: A New International Engagement Strategy', *Europe Report*, No. 180 (2007).

International Crisis Group, 'No Good Alternatives to the Ahtisaari Plan', *Europe Report*, No. 182 (2007).

J

C. Jaenicke, 'The OSCE Presence in Albania – Raison d'Etre and Future Plans', Institute for Peace Research and Security Policy at the University of Hamburg, ed., *OSCE Yearbook 2003* (Baden-Baden, Nomos 2004) pp. 125-138.

P. Jakobsen, 'The Emerging EU Civilian Crisis Management Capacity – A "Real Added Value" for the UN?', Background paper for the Copenhagen Seminar on Civilian Crisis Management arranged by the Royal Danish Ministry of Foreign Affairs, 8-9 June 2004.

D. Jović, 'Croatia and the European Union: A Long Delayed Journey', 8 *Journal of Southern Europe and the Balkans* (2006) pp. 85-103.

K

I. Kadare, 'The Balkans: Truths and Untruths', in D. Triantaphyllou, ed., 'The Southern Balkans: Perspectives from the Region', 46 *Chaillot Papers* (2001) pp. 5-16.

M. Kaldor, V. Bojičić and I. Vejvoda, 'Reconstruction in the Balkans: A Challenge for Europe?', 2 *EFA Rev.* (1997) pp. 329-350.

P. Kapteyn, 'Foreword', in V. Kronenberger, ed., *The European Union and the International Legal Order: Discord or Harmony?* (The Hague, T.M.C. Asser Press 2001) pp. V-VI.

S. Karagiannis, 'Sanctions internationales et droit communautaire. A propos du règlement 1901/98 sur l'interdiction de vol des transporteurs yougoslaves', 35 *RTDE* (1999) pp. 363-394.

M. Karnitschnig, 'The UN and the EU in Kosovo – The Challenges of Joint Nation-building', in J. Wouters, F. Hoffmeister and T. Ruys, eds., *The United Nations and the European Union: An Ever Stronger Partnership* (The Hague, T.M.C. Asser Press 2006) pp. 323-351.

R. Keane, 'The Case of the Solana Process in Serbia and Montenegro: Coherence in EU Foreign Policy', 11 *International Peacekeeping* (2004) pp. 1-17.

A.E. Kellermann, 'Institutional Problems of Enlargement of the European Union', in W.P. Heere, ed., *Contemporary International Law Issues: Conflicts and Convergence* (The Hague, T.M.C. Asser Instituut 1996) pp. 169-174.

A.E. Kellermann, 'Preparation of National Constitutions of Candidate Countries for Accession', 2 *Romanian Journal of European Affairs* (2002) pp. 74-81.

A.E. Kellermann, 'Direct Effect of Europe Agreements in the Pre-Accession Period', 2 *Revista Română de Drept Comunitar* (2004) pp. 90-108.

D. Kernohan, 'Reverse Balkanisation? Trade Integration in South-East Europe', *CEPS Working Document*, No. 249, August 2006.

T. King, 'The European Community and Human Rights in Eastern Europe', 23 *LIEI* (1996) pp. 93-125.

R. Kissack, 'The European Security Strategy: A First Appraisal', 2 *CFSP Forum* (2004) pp. 19-20.

J. Klabbers, 'Presumptive Personality: The European Union in International Law', in M. Koskenniemi, ed., *International Law Aspects of the European Union* (The Hague, Kluwer Law International 1998) pp. 231-253.

J. Klabbers, 'Re-inventing the Law of Treaties: The Contribution of the EC Courts', XXX *NYIL* (1999) pp. 45-74.

J. Klabbers and R. Lefeber, 'Africa: Lost between Self-Determination and Uti Possidetis', in C. Brölmann, R. Lefeber and M. Zieck, eds., *Peoples and Minorities in International Law* (Dordrecht, Martinus Nijhoff Publishers 1993) pp. 37-42.

J. Kleijssen, 'No Peace without Human Rights: The Council of Europe and Conflict Prevention', in V. Kronenberger and J. Wouters, eds., *The European Union and Conflict Prevention: Policy and Legal Aspects* (The Hague, T.M.C. Asser Press 2004) pp. 439-449.

G. Knaus and F. Martin, 'Travails of the European Raj', 14 *Journal of Democracy* (2003) pp. 60-74.

B. Knoll, 'From Benchmarking to Final status? Kosovo and the Problem of an International Administration's Open-ended Mandate', 16 *EJIL* (2005) pp. 637-660.

B. Knoll, 'Legitimacy and UN-Administration of Territory', 8 *German Law Journal* (2007) pp. 39-56.

M. Kohen, 'L'emploi de la force et la crise du Kosovo: vers un nouveau désordre juridique international', 32 *RBDI* (1999) pp. 122-148.

J. Kokott, 'The Development of the Human Rights Situation in Kosovo 1989-1999', in C. Tomuschat, ed., *Kosovo and the International Community: A Legal Assessment* (The Hague, Kluwer Law International 2002) pp. 1-35.

J. Kokott and F. Hoffmeister, 'ECJ, Case C-162/96, *A. Racke & Co.* v. *Hauptzollamt Mainz*', 93 *AJIL* (1999) pp. 205-209.

O. Korhonen, 'International Governance in Post-Conflict Situations', 14 *LJIL* (2001) pp. 495-526.

P. Kornfeld, 'CEFTA', 34 *ILM* (1995) pp. 3-7.

M. Koskenniemi, 'International Law Aspects of the Common Foreign and Security Policy', in M. Koskenniemi, ed., *International Law Aspects of the European Union* (The Hague, Kluwer Law International 1998) pp. 27-44.

G. Kostakos and D. Bourantonis, 'Innovations in Peace-keeping: The Case of Albania', 29 *Security Dialogue* (1998) pp. 49-58.

P. Koutrakos, 'Free Movement of Goods under the Europe Agreements', in A. Ott and K. Inglis, eds., *Handbook on European Enlargement – A Commentary on the Enlargement Process* (The Hague, T.M.C. Asser Press 2002) pp. 375-381.

P. Koutrakos, 'Security and Defence Policy within the Context of EU External Relations: Issues of Coherence, Consistency, and Effectiveness', in M. Trybus and N.D. White, eds., *European Security Law* (Oxford, Oxford University Press 2007) pp. 249-269.

O. Kovać, 'Regional Approach of the European Union to Cooperation among Countries of the Former Yugoslavia', XLVII *Review of International Affairs* (1996) pp. 1-5.

I. Krastev, 'The Balkans: Democracy without Choices', 13 *Journal of Democracy* (2002) pp. 39-53.

H.-G. Krenzler and H. Schneider, 'The Question of Consistency', in E. Regelsberger, P. de Schoutheete de Tervarent and W. Wessels, eds., *Foreign Policy of the European Union: From EPC to CFSP and Beyond* (Boulder, Lynne Rienner Publishers 1997) pp. 133-151.

V. Krivokhizha, 'The NATO Enlargement: Implications and Perspectives for Transatlantic Relations', in S. Trifunovska, ed., *The Transatlantic Alliance on the Eve of the New Millennium* (The Hague, Kluwer Law International 1996) pp. 57-67.

M. Kuijer, 'Het Europees Hof voor de Rechten van de Mens in de politieke arena', in T. Barkhuysen, M. Kuijer and R.A. Lawson, eds., *55 jaar EVRM* (Leiden, NJCM 2006) pp. 134-145.

P.J. Kuijper, 'Trade Sanctions, Security and Human Rights and Commercial Policy', in M. Maresceau, ed., *The European Community's Commercial Policy After 1992: The Legal Dimension* (Dordrecht, Martinus Nijhoff Publishers 1993) p. 387 et seq.

P.J. Kuijper and E. Paasivirta, 'Further Exploring International Responsibility: The European Community and the ILC's Project on Responsibility of International Organizations', 1 *IOLR* (2004) pp. 111-138.

L

E. Lannon, K. Inglis and T. Haenebalcke, 'The Many Faces of EU Conditionality in Pan-Euro-Mediterranean Relations', in M. Maresceau and E. Lannon, eds., *The EU's Enlargement and Mediterranean Strategies – A Comparative Analysis* (London, Palgrave 2001) pp. 97-138.

R.A. Lawson, 'Extending the European Family of Nations – The Response of the Council of Europe to Growing Membership', in N.M. Blokker and H.G. Schermers, eds., *Proliferation of International Organizations* (The Hague, Kluwer Law International 2001) pp. 415-432.

R.A. Lawson, 'Life After Banković: On the Extraterritorial Application of the European Convention on Human Rights', in F. Coomans and M. Kamminga, eds., *Extraterritorial Application of Human Rights Treaties* (Antwerp, Intersentia 2004) pp. 83-123.

A. Łazowski, 'Approximation of Laws', in A. Ott and K. Inglis, eds., *Handbook on European Enlargement – A Commentary on the Enlargement Process* (The Hague, T.M.C. Asser Press 2002) pp. 631-639.

A. Łazowski, 'EAA Countries (Iceland, Liechtenstein and Norway)', in S. Blockmans and A. Łazowski, eds., *The European Union and Its Neighbours: A Legal Appraisal of the EU's Policies of Stabilisation, Partnership and Integration* (The Hague, T.M.C. Asser Press 2006) pp. 95-146.

A. Łazowski, 'And Then They Were Twenty-Seven… A Legal Appraisal of the Sixth Accession Treaty', 44 *CML Rev.* (2007) pp. 401-430.

A. Łazowski, 'Box of Chocolates Integration: The European Economic Area and Swiss Model Revisited', in S. Blockmans, S. Prechal and W.Th. Douma, eds., *Reconciling 'Deepening' and 'Widening' of the European Union* (The Hague, T.M.C. Asser Press 2007).

A. Łazowski and S. Yosifova, 'Bulgaria', in S. Blockmans and A. Łazowski, eds., *The European Union and Its Neighbours: A Legal Appraisal of the EU's Policies of Stabilisation, Partnership and Integration* (The Hague, T.M.C. Asser Press 2006) pp. 207-246.

K. Lenaerts and E. De Smijter, 'The United Nations and the European Union: Living Apart Together', in K. Wellens, ed., *International Law: Theory and Practice. Essays in Honour of E. Suy* (The Hague, Kluwer Law International 1998) pp. 439-458.

K. Lenaerts and E. De Smijter, 'The European Union as an Actor Under International Law', 19 *YEL* (2000) pp. 95-138.

E. Lenski, 'Turkey (including Northern Cyprus)', in S. Blockmans and A. Łazowski, eds., *The European Union and Its Neighbours: A Legal Appraisal of the EU's Policies of Stabilisation, Partnership and Integration* (The Hague, T.M.C. Asser Press 2006) pp. 283-313.

G. Lenzi, 'WEU's Future: From Subcontractor to Conveyor Belt?', in G. Lenzi, ed., *WEU at Fifty* (Paris, ISS 1998) pp.109-124.

P. Liotta, 'The Geopolitics of the Balkans: Outcomes and Possibilities', 7/8 *New Balkan Politics* (2003).

O. Lissitzyn, 'Treaties and Changed Circumstances (*Rebus Sic Stantibus*)', 61 *AJIL* (1967) pp. 895-922.

D. Lopandić, 'Un exemple de sanctions économiques de la CEE: Suspension/dénonciation de l'accord de coopération entre la CEE et la Yougoslavie', *Revue des Affaires Européennes* (1992) pp. 67-72.

D. Lopandić, 'The European Community and the Yugoslav Crisis (1989-1992) – Some Issues of International Law', 41 *Jugoslovenska Revija za Medunarodno Pravo* (1994) pp. 311-349.

M

C. Mace, 'European Union Security and Defence Policy Comes of Age in the Balkans', *EPC Working Papers*, 2003, available at: <http://www.TheEPC.be>.

P. Manin, 'The EC and the Vienna Convention on the Law of Treaties between States and International Organisations or between International Organisations', 24 *CML Rev.* (1987) pp. 457-481.

M. Maresceau and E. Montaguti, 'The Relations between the European Union and Central and Eastern Europe: A Legal Appraisal', 32 *CML Rev.* (1995) pp. 1327-1367.

M. Maresceau, 'Pre-accession', in M. Cremona, ed., *The Enlargement of the European Union* (Oxford, Oxford University Press 2003) pp. 9-42.

M. Maresceau, 'Zuidoost-Europa en de Europese Unie', in R. Detrez, ed., *Ontmoeting met de Balkan* (Brussels, KVAB 2005) pp. 9-43.

J. Marko and J. Wilhelm, 'Stabilisation and Association Agreements', in A. Ott and K. Inglis, eds., *Handbook on European Enlargement – A Commentary on the Enlargement Process* (The Hague, T.M.C. Asser Press 2002) pp. 165-174.

S. Markotich, 'Pursuing Balkan Peace', 30 *OMRI Special Report* (1996).

S. Marquardt, 'The Conclusion of International Agreements under Article 24 of the Treaty on European Union', in V. Kronenberger, ed., *The EU and the International Legal Order: Discord or Harmony?* (The Hague, T.M.C. Asser Press 2001) pp. 333-349.

K. Meessen, 'The Application of Rules of Public International Law within Community Law', 13 *CML Rev.* (1976) pp. 485-501.

M. Merlingen and R. Ostrauskaite, 'ESDP Police Missions: Meaning, Context and Operational Challenges', 10 *EFA Rev.* (2005) pp. 215-235.

W. van Meurs, 'The Stability Pact Beyond EU Enlargement', in D. Lopandić, ed., *Regional Cooperation in South Eastern Europe – Conference Proceedings* (Belgrade, European Movement in Serbia 2002) pp. 39-45.

W. van Meurs, 'The Belgrade Agreement: Robust Mediation Between Serbia and Montenegro', in F. Bieber, ed., *Montenegro in Transition: Problems of Identity and Statehood* (Baden-Baden, Nomos 2003) pp. 63-79.

M. Milutinović, 'Promotion of Cooperation with All Neighbouring Countries – Participation in Integration Processes in Europe', XLVIII *Review of International Affairs* (1997) pp. 1-3.

J. Minić, 'Summary and Recommendations of the Conference', in D. Lopandić, ed., *Regional Cooperation in South Eastern Europe – Conference Proceedings* (Belgrade, European Movement in Serbia 2002) pp. 9-17.

A. Missiroli, 'European Security Policy: The Challenge of Coherence', 6 *EFA Rev.* (2001) pp. 177-196.

J. Monar, 'Mostar: Three Lessons for the European Union', 2 *EFA Rev.* (1997) pp. 1-5.

K. Mulaj, 'A Recurrent Tragedy: Ethnic Cleansing as a Tool of State Building in the Yugoslav Multinational Setting', 34 *Nationalities Papers* (2006) pp. 21-50.

R. Mullerson, 'The Continuity and Succession of States by Reference to the Former USSR and Yugoslavia', 42 *ICLQ* (1993) pp. 473-493.

N

F. Naert, 'European Security and Defence Policy in the EU Constitutional Treaty', 10 *Journal of Conflict and Security Law* (2005) pp. 187-207.

F. Naert, 'ESDP in Practice: Increasingly Varied and Ambitious EU Security and Defence Operations', in M. Trybus and N.D. White, eds., *European Security Law* (Oxford, Oxford University Press 2007) pp. 61-101.

V. Nanda, 'Tragedies in Northern Iraq, Liberia, Yugoslavia, and Haiti – Revisiting the Validity of Humanitarian Intervention under International Law – Part I', 20 *Denver Journal of International Law and Policy* (1992) pp. 305-334.

E. Neframi, 'International Responsibility of the European Community and of the Member States under Mixed Agreements', in E. Cannizaro, ed., *The European Union as an Actor in International Relations* (The Hague, Kluwer Law International 2002) pp. 193-206.

G. Nesi, 'The Relations between the European Union and the OSCE in Crisis Management', in E. Cannizaro, ed., *The European Union as an Actor in International Relations* (The Hague, Kluwer Law International 2002) pp. 271-278.

H. Neuhold, 'Collective Security After "Operation Allied Force"', in J. Frowein and R. Wolfrum, eds., *Max Planck Yearbook of United Nations Law* (2000) pp. 73-106.

H. Neuhold, 'The United Nations System for the Peaceful Settlement of International Disputes', in F. Cede and L. Sucharipa-Behrmann, eds., *The United Nations: Law and Practice* (The Hague, Kluwer Law International 2001) p. 59 et seq.

H. Neuhold, 'Terminological Ambiguity in the Field of International Security', in K. Dicke, et al., eds., *Weltinnenrecht: Liber Amicorum Jost Delbrück* (Berlin, Duncker & Humblot 2005) pp. 473-486.

N. Neuwahl, 'Foreign and Security Policy and the Implementation of the Requirement of 'Consistency' under the Treaty on European Union', in D. O'Keeffe and P. Twomey, eds., *Legal Issues of the Maastricht Treaty* (London, Chancery Law Publishing 1994) pp. 227-246.

N. Neuwahl, 'A Partner with a Troubled Personality: EU Treaty-Making in Matters of CFSP and JHA after Amsterdam', 3 *EFA Rev.* (1998) pp. 177-195.

N. Neuwahl, 'Legal Personality of the European Union – International and Institutional Aspects', in V. Kronenberger, ed., *The European Union and the International Legal Order: Discord or Harmony?* (The Hague, T.M.C. Asser Press 2001) pp. 3-22.

G. Niessen and J. te Velde, 'In Kosovo is geen plaats voor het Bosnisch model', 60 *Internationale Spectator* (2006) pp. 148-150.

J. Niño-Pérez, 'Conflict Indicators Developed by the Commission – the Checklist for Root Causes of Conflict/Early Warning Indicators', in V. Kronenberger and J. Wouters, eds., *The European Union and Conflict Prevention: Policy and Legal Aspects* (The Hague, T.M.C. Asser Press 2004) pp. 3-19.

G. Noutcheva, 'Negotiating a Viable State Union of Serbia and Montenegro', *CEPS Commentary* (2002).

A. Nowak, 'L'Union en action: la mission de police en Bosnie', *ISS Papers* (2003).

O

M.E. O'Connell, 'Debating the Law of Sanctions', 13 *EJIL* (2002) pp. 63-79.

S. Oeter, 'Selbstbestimmungsrecht im Wandel: Überlegungen zur Debatte um Selbstbestimmung, Sezessionsrecht und "vorzeitige" Anerkennung', 52 *ZaöRV* (1992) pp. 741-780.

R. van Ooik and R. Wessel, 'De Yusuf en Kadi-uitspraken in perspectief. Nieuwe verhoudingen in de interne en externe bevoegdheden van de Europese Unie', 54 *SEW* (2006) pp. 230-241.

S. Orucević, 'Mostar: Europe's Failure', 15 *Bosnia Report* (1996).

A. Ott, 'Thirty Years of Case-Law by the European Court of Justice on International Law: A Pragmatic Approach towards it Integration', in V. Kronenberger, ed., *The EU and the International Legal Order: Discord or Harmony?* (The Hague, T.M.C. Asser Press 2001) pp. 95-140.

A. Ott, 'The "Principle" of Differentiation in an Enlarged European Union: Unity in Diversity?', in K. Inglis and A. Ott, eds., *The Constitution for Europe and an Enlarging European Union: Unity in Diversity?* (Groningen, Europa Law Publishing 2005) pp. 105-133.

A. Ott and R. Wessel, 'The EU's External Relations Regime: Multi-level Complexity in an Expanding Union', in S. Blockmans and A. Łazowski, eds., *The European Union and Its Neighbours: A Legal Appraisal of the EU's Policies of Stabilisation, Partnership and Integration* (The Hague, T.M.C. Asser Press 2006) pp. 19-59.

P

E. Paasivirta and P.J. Kuijper, 'Does One Size Fit All? The European Community and the Responsibility of International Organizations', XXXVI *NYIL* (2007) pp. 169-226.

E. Paasivirta and A. Rosas, 'Sanctions, Countermeasures and Related Actions in the External Relations of the European Union: A Search for Legal Frameworks', in E. Cannizaro, ed., *The European Union as an Actor in International Relations* (The Hague, Kluwer Law International 2002) pp. 207-218.

F. Pagani, 'L'administration de Mostar par l'Union européenne', 42 *AFDI* (1996) pp. 234-254.

J.-F. Paganon, 'Western European Union's Pivotal Position Between the Atlantic Alliance and the European Union', in A. Deighton, ed., *Western European Union 1954-1997: Defence, Security, Integration* (Oxford, European Independent research Unit 1997) pp. 93-102.

P. Palchetti, 'Reactions by the European Union to Breaches of Erga Omnes Obligations', in E. Cannizzaro, ed., *The European Union as an Actor in International Relations* (The Hague, Kluwer Law International 2002) pp. 219-230.

P. Pantev, 'Security Risks and Instabilities in Southeastern Europe', in W. van Meurs, ed., *Beyond EU Enlargement, Volume 2: The Agenda of Stabilisation for Southeastern Europe* (Gütersloh, Bertelsmann Foundation Publishers 2001) pp. 118-138.

D. Papadimitriou, 'The EU's Strategy in the Post-Communist Balkans', 3 *Journal of Southeast European and Black Sea Studies* (2001) pp. 69-94.

D. Papadimitriou, P. Petrov and L. Greiçevci, 'To Build a State: Europeanization, EU Actorness and State-Building in Kosovo', 12 *EFA Rev.* (2007) pp. 219-238.

R. Pape, 'Why Economic Sanctions Do Not Work', 22 *International Security* (1997) pp. 90-136.

S. Peers, 'EC Frameworks of International Relations: Co-operation, Partnership and Association', in A. Dashwood and C. Hillion, eds., *The General Law of EC External Relations* (London, Sweet & Maxwell 2000) pp. 160-176.

A. Pellet, 'Note sur la Commission d'arbitrage de la Conférence européenne pour la Paix en Yougoslavie', 37 *Annuaire Français de Droit International* (1991) pp. 329-348.

A. Pellet, 'L'imputabilité d'éventuels actes illicites – Responsabilité de l'OTAN ou des Etats members', in C. Tomuschat, ed., *Kosovo and the International Community: A Legal Assessment* (The Hague, Kluwer Law International 2002) pp. 193-202.

S. Penksa, 'Policing Bosnia and Herzegovina 2003-2005: Issues of Mandates and Management in ESDP Missions', *CEPS Working Document*, No. 255, December 2006.

J. Pertek, 'Les sanctions politiques à objet économique prises par la CEE à l'encontre des Etats tiers', 26 *Revue du Marché Commun* (1983) p. 205.

P. Pescatore, 'Les Communautés en tant que des personnes de droit international', in W.J. Ganshof van der Meersch, ed., *Les Novelles: Droit des Communautés européennes* (Brussels, Larcier 1969) pp. 107-120.

E. Petersmann, 'Auswärtiges Gewalt, Völkerrechtspraxis und Völkerrechtsbindungen der Europäischen Wirtschaftsgemeinschaft', 35 *ZaöRv* (1975) pp. 213-281.

J. Peterson, 'The European Union as a Global Actor', in J. Peterson and H. Sjursen, eds., *A Common Foreign Policy for Europe? Competing Visions of the CFSP* (London, Routledge 1998) pp. 3-17.

A. Petričušić, 'Regional Cooperation in the Western Balkans – A Key to Integration into the European Union', 1 *Croatian Yearbook of European Law and Policy* (2005) pp. 213-233.

D. Phinnemore, 'Beyond 25 – The Changing Face of EU Enlargement: Commitment, Conditionality and the Constitutional Treaty', 8 *Journal of Southern Europe and the Balkans* (2006) pp. 7-26.

D. Phinnemore, 'Stabilisation and Association Agreements: Europe Agreements for the Western Balkans?', 8 *EFA Rev.* (2003) pp. 77-103.

D. Phinnemore and P. Siani-Davies, 'Beyond Intervention? The Balkans, the Stability Pact and the European Union', in P. Siani-Davies, ed., *International Intervention in the Balkans Since 1995* (London, Routledge 2003) pp. 172-193.

C. Piana, 'The EU's Decision-making Process in the Common Foreign and Security Policy: The Case of the Former Yugoslav Republic of Macedonia', 7 *EFA Rev.* (2002) pp. 209-226.

K. Pieters, 'The Mediterranean Countries', in S. Blockmans and A. Łazowski, eds., *The European Union and Its Neighbours: A Legal Appraisal of the EU's Policies of Stabilisation, Partnership and Integration* (The Hague, T.M.C. Asser Press 2006) pp. 391-432.

C. Pippan, 'The Rocky Road to Europe: The EU's Stabilisation and Association Process for the Western Balkans and the Principle of Conditionality', 9 *EFA Rev.* (2004) pp. 219-245 at pp. 229-238.

A. Pliakos, 'La nature juridique de l'Union européenne', 29 *RTDE* (1993) pp. 187-224.

M. Pugh, 'Postwar Political Economy in Bosnia and Herzegovina: The Spoils of Peace', 8 *Global Governance* (2002) pp. 467-482.

R

M. Ragazzi, 'Conference on Yugoslavia Arbitration Commission', 31 *ILM* (1992) pp. 1488-1493.

A. Randelzhofer, 'Article 51', in B. Simma, ed., *The Charter of the United Nations: A Commentary*, 2nd edn. (Oxford, Oxford University Press 2002) pp. 788-806.

S. Recchia, 'Beyond International Trusteeship: EU Peacebuilding in Bosnia and Herzegovina', *Occasional Papers*, No. 66, February 2007, EUISS, Paris.

O. Rehn, 'The European Community and the Challenge of a Wider Europe', *Sussex Working Papers in Contemporary European Studies*, No. 6, July 1994.

M. Reichard, 'Some Legal Issues Concerning the EU-NATO Berlin Plus Agreement', 73 *Nordic JIL* (2004) pp. 37-67.

E. Remacle, 'The Yugoslav Crisis as a Test Case for CSCE's Role in Conflict Prevention and Crisis Management', in M. Lucas, ed., *The CSCE in the 1990s: Constructing European Security and Cooperation* (Baden-Baden, Nomos 1993) pp. 109-123.

G. Ress and J. Bröhmer, 'Article 53', in B. Simma, ed., *The Charter of the United Nations: A Commentary*, 2nd edn. (Oxford, Oxford University Press 2002) pp. 854-890.

P. Reuter, 'Le droit international comme source de droit communautaire', in W.J. Ganshof van der Meersch, ed. *Les Novelles: Droit des Communautés européennes* (Brussels, Larcier 1969) pp. 437-440.

O. Ribbelink, 'State Succession and the Recognition of States and Governments', in J. Klabbers, M. Koskenniemi, O. Ribbelink and A. Zimmermann, eds., *State Practice Regarding State Succession and Issues of Recognition: The Pilot Project of the Council of Europe* (The Hague, Kluwer Law International 1999) pp. 32-79.

R. Rich, 'Recognition of States: The Collapse of Yugoslavia and the Soviet Union', 4 *EJIL* (1993) pp. 36-65.

E. Riedel and M. Will, 'Human Rights Clauses in External Agreements of the European Communities', in P. Alston, ed., *The EU and Human Rights* (Oxford, Oxford University Press 1999) pp. 723-754.

S. Rodin, 'Croatia', in Blockmans and Łazowski, S. Blockmans and A. Łazowski, eds., *The European Union and Its Neighbours: A Legal Appraisal of the EU's Policies of Stabilisation, Partnership and Integration* (The Hague, T.M.C. Asser Press 2006) pp. 357-389.

S. Rodin and I. Goldner, 'National Report for Croatia', presented at FIDE 2006, available at: <http://www.fide2006.org>.

J. Roper, 'Yugoslavia and European Security: EC, NATO, WEU, CSCE: Which Task for Whom?', XLIII *Review of International Affairs* (1992) pp. 2-5.

A. Rosas, 'Mixed Union – Mixed Agreements', in M. Koskenniemi, ed., *International Law Aspects of the European Union* (The Hague, Kluwer Law International 1998) pp. 125-148.

M. Ruffert, 'The Administration of Kosovo and East-Timor by the International Community', 50 *ICLQ* (2001) pp. 555-573.

S

D. Sandole, 'The Balkans Stability Pact as a Regional Conflict Management and Prevention "Space": An Evaluation', in P. Jureković, ed., *The Stability Pact for South East Europe – Dawn of an Era of Regional Co-operation* (Vienna, National Defence Academy 2002) pp. 20-36.

O. Schachter, et al., 'Symposium: State Succession in the Former Soviet Union and in Eastern Europe', 33 *Virginia JIL* (1993) pp. 253-350.

M. Scharf, 'Musical Chairs: The Dissolution of States and Membership in the United Nations', 28 *Cornell ILJ* (1995) pp. 29-69.

H.G. Schermers, 'Community Law and International Law', 12 *CML Rev.* (1975) pp. 77-90.

H.G. Schermers, 'A Typology of Mixed Agreements', in D. O'Keeffe and H.G. Schermers, eds., *Mixed Agreements* (Deventer, Kluwer 1983) pp. 23-33.

H.G. Schermers, 'Rights-giving Treaties: Higher Law?', in P. Manin, et al., eds., *Mélanges offerts à Pierre-Henri Teitgen* (Paris, Editions Pédone 1984) pp. 503-510.

H.G. Schermers, 'Liability of International Organizations', 1 *LJIL* (1988) pp. 3-14.

H.G. Schermers, 'The Obligation to Intervene in the Domestic Affairs of States', in A. Delissen and G. Tanja, eds., *Humanitarian Law of Armed Conflict – Challenges Ahead. Essays in Honour of Frits Kalshoven* (Dordrecht, Martinus Nijhoff Publishers 1991) pp. 583-593.

N.J. Schrijver, 'The Use of Economic Sanctions by the UN Security Council: An International Law Perspective', in H. Post, ed., *International Economic Law and Armed Conflict* (Dordrecht, Martinus Nijhoff 1994) pp. 123-161.

N.J. Schrijver, 'NATO in Kosovo: Humanitarian Intervention Turns into Von Clausewitz War', 1 *ILF* (1999) pp. 155-159.

N.J. Schrijver, 'UN Reform: A Once-in-a-Generation Opportunity', 2 *IOLR* (2005) pp. 271-275.

N.J. Schrijver, 'Reforming the UN Security Council in Pursuance of Collective Security', 12 *Journal of Conflict and Security Law* (2007) pp. 127-138.

G. Schusterschitz, 'European Agencies as Subjects of International Law', 1 *IOLR* (2004) pp. 163-188.

J. Schwarze, 'Das allgemeine Völkerrecht in den innergemeinschaftlichen Rechtsbeziehungen', 18 *EuR* (1983) pp. 1-39.

C. Schwegmann, 'The Contact Group and Its Impact on the European Institutional Structure', 16 *EUISS Occasional Papers* (2000).

T. Schweisfurth, 'Article 34', in B. Simma, ed., *The Charter of the United Nations: A Commentary*, 2nd edn. (Oxford, Oxford University Press 2002) pp. 594-608.

G. Seidel, 'A New Dimension of the Right of Self-Determination in Kosovo?', in C. Tomuschat, ed., *Kosovo and the International Community: A Legal Assessment* (The Hague, Kluwer Law International 2002) pp. 203-215.

I. Seidl-Hohenveldern, 'Internationale Organisationen aufgrund von soft law', in U. Beyerlin, et al., eds., *Recht zwischen Umbruch und Bewahrung – Festschrift für Rudolf Bernhardt* (Berlin, Springer Verlag 1995) pp. 229-239.
M. Shaw, 'State Succession Revisited', 5 *Finnish YIL* (1994) pp. 34-98.
M. Sica, 'The Role of the OSCE in the former Yugoslavia after the Dayton Peace Agreement', 7 *Helsinki Monitor* (1996) pp. 5-12.
P. Simić, 'Do the Balkans Exist?', in D. Triantaphyllou, ed., *The Southern Balkans: Perspectives from the Region* (Paris, ISS 2001).
B. Simma, 'NATO, the UN and the Use of Force', 10 *EJIL* (1999) pp. 1-22.
K. Smith, 'The Use of Political Conditionality in the EU's Relations with Third Countries: How Effective?', 3 *EFA Rev.* (1998) pp. 253-274.
K. Smith, 'Western Actors and the Promotion of Democracy', in J. Zielonka and A. Pravda, eds., *Democratic Consolidation in Eastern Europe, Vol. 2: International and Transnational Factors* (Oxford, Oxford University Press 2001) pp. 31-57.
K. Smith, 'The Evolution and Application of EU Membership Conditionality', in M. Cremona, ed., *The Enlargement of the European Union* (Oxford, Oxford University Press 2003) pp. 105-139.
M. Sornarajah, 'Internal Colonialism and Humanitarian Intervention', 11 *Georgia Journal of International and Comparative Law* (1981) pp. 45-77.
C. Stahn, 'International Territorial Administration in the Former Yugoslavia: Origins, Developments and Challenges Ahead', 61 *ZaöRV* (2001) p. 105 et seq.
C. Stahn, 'Constitution Without a State? Kosovo Under the United Nations Constitutional Framework for Self-Government', 14 *LJIL* (2001) pp. 531-561.
C. Stahn, 'Governance Beyond the State: Issues of Legitimacy in International Territorial Administration', 2 *IOLR* (2005) pp. 9-56.
C. Stahn, 'Institutionalizing Brahimi's "Light Footprint": A Comment on the Role and Mandate of the Peacebuilding Commission', 2 *IOLR* (2005) pp. 403-415.
T. Stein, 'Kosovo and the International Community. The Attribution of Possible Internationally Wrongful Acts: Responsibility of NATO or of Its Member States', in C. Tomuschat, ed., *Kosovo and the International Community: A Legal Assessment* (The Hague, Kluwer Law International 2002) at pp. 181-192.
J. Stilhoff Sörensen, 'Balkanism and the New Radical Interventionism: A Structural Critique', 9 *International Peacekeeping* (2002) pp. 1-22.
M. van der Stoel, 'The Role of the OSCE in Conflict Prevention', *Studia Diplomatica* (1996) pp. 33-39.
O. Stokke, 'Aid and Political Conditionality: Core Issues and State of the Art', in O. Stokke, ed., *Aid and Political Conditionality* (London, Frank Cass 1995) pp. 1-87.

E. Suy, 'The Development of Supervisory Mechanisms Within the CSCE Framework', in N.M. Blokker and S. Muller, eds., *Towards More Effective Supervision by International Organizations – Essays in Honour of Henry G. Schermers*, Vol. I (Dordrecht, Martinus Nijhoff Publishers 1994) pp. 83-92.

T

C. Timmermans, 'The EU and Public International Law', 4 *EFA Rev.* (1999) pp. 181-194.

G. Timmins and D. Jović, 'The Next Wave of Enlargement: The European Union and Southeast Europe After 2004', 8 *Journal of Southern Europe and the Balkans* (2006) pp. 1-5.

A. Tizzano, 'La personnalité internationale de l'Union européenne'. Paper given at the Jean Monnet Colloquium, Brussels, 4 April 2000, available at: <http://www.consuniv.orgcue.html>.

N. Tocci, 'EU Intervention in Ethno-political Conflicts: The Cases of Cyprus and Serbia-Montenegro', 9 *EFA Rev.* (2004) pp. 551-573.

A. Toje, 'The 2003 European Union Security Strategy: A Critical Appraisal', 10 *EFA Rev.* (2005) pp. 117-134.

C. Tomuschat, 'Yugoslavia's Damaged Sovereignty over the Province of Kosovo', in G. Kreijen, ed., *State, Sovereignty, and International Governance* (Oxford, Oxford University Press 2002) pp. 323-348.

C. Tomuschat, 'The International Responsibility of the European Union', in E. Cannizaro, ed., *The European Union as an Actor in International Relations* (The Hague, Kluwer Law International 2002) pp. 177-192.

F. Trauner, 'EU Justice and Home Affairs Strategy in the Western Balkans', *CEPS Working Document*, No. 259, February 2007.

D. Triantaphyllou, 'The Balkans between Stabilisation and Integration', in J. Blatt, et al., 'Partners and Neighbours: A CFSP for a Wider Europe', 64 *Chaillot Papers* (2003) pp. 60-76.

P. Tripodi, 'Operation *Alba*: A Necessary and Successful Preventive Deployment', 9 *International Peacekeeping* (2002) pp. 89-104.

M. Trivunovic, 'Police Reform – Introduction', 15 *Helsinki Monitor* (2004) p. 171.

M. Trivunovic, 'Status of Police Reform After Four Years of Democratic Transition in Serbia', 15 *Helsinki Monitor* (2004) pp. 172-186.

H. Tromp, 'NATO and the New World Order: Anarchy?', in S. Trifunovska, ed., *The Transatlantic Alliance on the Eve of the New Millenium* (The Hague, Kluwer Law International 1996) pp. 43-55.

N. Tsagourias, 'EU Peacekeeping Operations: Legal and Theoretical Issues', in M. Trybus and N.D. White, eds., *European Security Law* (Oxford, Oxford University Press 2007) pp. 102-133.

D. Türk, 'Recognition of States: A Comment', 4 *EJIL* (1993) pp. 66-71.

V

R. Väyrinen, 'Challenges to Preventive Action', in K. Spillmann, et al., eds., *Peace Support Operations: Lessons Learned and Future Perspectives* (Bern, Peter Lang 2001) at p. 59.

H. Vetschera, 'Ten Years of the Conflict Prevention Centre – Origins and Development', in Institute for Peace Research and Security Policy at the University of Hamburg, ed., *OSCE Yearbook 2001* (Baden-Baden, Nomos 2002) pp. 401-420.

H. Vetschera and M. Damian, 'Security Sector Reform in Bosnia and Herzegovina: The Role of the International Community', 13 *International Peacekeeping* (2006) pp. 28-42.

D. Vignes, 'The Stability Pact for South Eastern Europe', in C. Tomuschat, ed., *Kosovo and the International Community: A Legal Assessment* (The Hague, Kluwer Law International 2002) pp. 317-325.

L. Volmer, 'Crisis Prevention in Europe and the Strengthening of the OSCE: Lessons from the Kosovo Conflict', Institute for Peace Research and Security Policy at the University of Hamburg, ed., *OSCE Yearbook 1999* (Baden-Baden, Nomos 2000) pp. 41-48.

A. de Vries, 'European Union Sanctions Against the Federal Republic of Yugoslavia from 1998 to 2000: A Special Exercise in Targeting', in D. Cortright and G. Lopez, eds., *Smart Sanctions – Targeting Economic Statecraft* (Lanham, Rowman & Littlefield Publishers Inc. 2002) pp. 87-108.

D. Vučićević, 'FR Yugoslavia's Contribution to the Implementation of the Royaumont Initiative', XLVIII *Review of International Affairs* (1997) pp. 1-2.

R. Vukadinović, 'Former Yugoslavia: International Efforts to Link Peace, Stability, and Democracy', in J. Zielonka and A. Pravda, eds., *Democratic Consolidation in Eastern Europe, Vol. 2: International and Transnational Factors* (Oxford, Oxford University Press 2001) pp. 437-454.

W

C. Warbrick, 'Recognition of States (Current Developments)', 41 *ICLQ* (1992) pp. 473-482.

C. Warbrick, 'Recognition of States: Part 2', 42 *ICLQ* (1993) pp. 433-442.

R. Wedgwood, 'NATO's Campaign in Yugoslavia', 93 *AJIL* (1999) pp. 828-834.

P. Weil, 'Towards Relative Normativity in International Law?', 77 *AJIL* (1983) pp. 413-442.

J.H.H. Weiler, 'The External Relations of Non-unitary Actors: Mixity and the Federal Principle', in J.H.H. Weiler, ed., *The Constitution of Europe – 'Do the New Clothes have an Emperor?' and Other Essays on European Integration* (Cambridge, Cambridge University Press 1999) pp. 130-187.

J.H.H. Weiler and S. Fries, 'A Human Rights Policy for the European Community and Union: The Question of Competences', in P. Alston, ed., *The EU and Human Rights* (Oxford, Oxford University Press 1999) pp. 147-166.

M. Weller, 'The International Response to the Dissolution of the Socialist Federal Republic of Yugoslavia', 86 *AJIL* (1992) pp. 569-607.

M. Weller, 'The Rambouillet Conference on Kosovo', 75 *International Affairs* (1999) pp. 211-252.

R.A. Wessel, 'The International Legal Status of the European Union', 2 *EFA Rev.* (1997) pp. 109-129.

R.A. Wessel, 'The Legality of the New Functions of the Western European Union: The Attribution of Powers Reconsidered on the Occasion of the 50th Anniversary of the Brussels Treaty', in A. Deighton and E. Remacle, eds., *The Western European Union, 1948-1998: From the Brussels Treaty to the Treaty of Amsterdam*, published as 1-2 *Studia Diplomatica* (1998) pp. 15-28.

R.A. Wessel, 'Revisiting the International Legal Status of the European Union', 5 *EFA Rev.* (2000) pp. 507-537.

R.A. Wessel, 'The Inside Looking Out: Consistency and Delimitation in EU External Relations', 37 *CML Rev.* (2000) pp. 1135-1171.

R.A. Wessel, 'De Europese Unie in de internationale rechtsorde', in R.A. Wessel and B. de Witte, 'De plaats van de Europese Unie in het veranderende bestel van de volkenrechtelijke organisatie', 123 *Mededelingen van de Nederlandse Vereniging voor Internationaal Recht* (2001) pp. 1-77.

R.A. Wessel, 'The EU as a Black Widow: Devouring the WEU to Give Birth to a European Security and Defence Policy', in V. Kronenberger, ed., *The European Union and the International Legal Order: Discord or Harmony?* (The Hague, T.M.C. Asser Press 2001) pp. 405-434.

R.A. Wessel, 'The State of Affairs in European Security and Defence Policy: The Breakthrough in the Treaty of Nice', 8 *Journal of Conflict & Security Law* (2003) pp. 265-288.

R.A. Wessel, 'The Invasion by International Organizations. De toenemende samenhang tussen de mondiale, Europese en nationale rechtsorde', Inaugural Lecture, University of Twente, 2006.

R.A. Wessel, 'Editorial: The UN, the EU and *Jus Cogens*', 3 *IOLR* (2006) pp. 1-6.

R.A. Wessel, 'Differentiation in EU Foreign, Security, and Defence Policy: Between Coherence and Flexibility', in M. Trybus and N.D. White, eds., *European Security Law* (Oxford, Oxford University Press 2007) pp. 225-248.

N.D. White, 'The Will and Authority of the Security Council After Iraq', 17 *LJIL* (2004) pp. 645-672.

N.D. White, 'The EU as a Regional Security Actor within the International Legal Order', in M. Trybus and N.D. White, eds., *European Security Law* (Oxford, Oxford University Press 2007) pp. 329-350.

N. Whyte, N. Arbatova and D. Allin, 'The Macedonian Crisis and Balkan Security', *ESF Working Papers*, 2001.

D. Wibaux, 'A propos de quelques questions juridiques posées par l'interdiction des vols des compagnies yougoslaves', 44 *AFDI* (1998) p. 262.

A. Williams, 'Enlargement of the Union and Human Rights Conditionality: A Policy of Distinction', 25 *EL Rev.* (2000) pp. 601-617.

G. Wilson, 'WEU's Operational Capability – Delusion or Reality?', in G. Lenzi, ed., *WEU at Fifty* (Paris, ISS 1998) pp. 51-66.

B. de Witte, 'Internationale verdragen tussen lidstaten van de Europese Unie', in R.A. Wessel and B. de Witte, 'De plaats van de Europese Unie in het veranderende bestel van de volkenrechtelijke organisatie', 123 *Mededelingen van de Nederlandse Vereniging voor Internationaal Recht* (2001) pp. 79-131.

B. de Witte, 'The Process of Ratification and the Crisis Options: A Legal Perspective', D. Curtin, A. Kellermann and S. Blockmans, eds., *The EU Constitution: The Best Way Forward?* (The Hague, T.M.C. Asser Press 2005) pp. 21-38.

J. Wouters, 'De Europese Unie als internationale actor na het Verdrag van Nice', 8 *Nederlands Tijdschrift voor Europees Recht* (2002) pp. 62-70.

J. Wouters, 'The United Nations, the EU and Conflict Prevention: Interconnecting the Global and Regional Levels', in V. Kronenberger and J. Wouters, eds., *The European Union and Conflict Prevention: Policy and Legal Aspects* (The Hague, T.M.C. Asser Press 2004) pp. 369-392.

J. Wouters and F. Naert, 'EU, WEU, NAVO en OVSE – Welke veiligheidsarchitectuur voor Europa?', 52 *Studia Diplomatica* (1999) pp. 95-133.

J. Wouters and F. Naert, 'How Effective is the European Security Architecture? Lessons from Bosnia and Kosovo', 50 *ICLQ* (2001) pp. 540-576.

J. Wouters and T. Ruys, 'The European Security Strategy', in O. Horvath, ed., *European Cooperation Against Terrorism* (Nijmegen, Wolf Legal Publishers 2004) pp. 23-36.

J. Wouters and T. Ruys, 'UN-EU cooperation in Crisis Management', in J. Wouters, F. Hoffmeister and T. Ruys, eds., *The United Nations and the European Union: An Ever Stronger Partnership* (The Hague, T.M.C. Asser Press 2006) pp. 229-258.

Z

R. Zaagman, 'OSCE conflict prevention and the economic and environmental dimension', 10 *Helsinki Monitor* (1999) pp. 40-48.

K. Zemanek, 'Peace-keeping or Peace-making?', in N.M. Blokker and S. Muller, eds., *Towards More Effective Supervision by International Organizations – Essays in Honour of Henry G. Schermers*, Vol. I (Dordrecht, Martinus Nijhoff Publishers 1994) pp. 29-47.

J. Ziller, 'France: Revision of the Constitution and Popular Rejection', in A. Albi and J. Ziller, eds., *The European Constitution and National Constitutions: Ratification and Beyond* (The Hague, Kluwer Law International 2007) pp. 103-112.

A. Zimmermann and C. Stahn, 'Yugoslav Territory, United Nations Trusteeship or Sovereign State? Reflections on the current and Future Legal Status of Kosovo', 70 *Nordic JIL* (2001) pp. 423-433.

J.W. de Zwaan, 'Community Dimensions of the Second Pillar', in T. Heukels, N.M. Blokker and M. Brus, eds., *The European Union after Amsterdam: A legal Analysis* (The Hague, Kluwer Law International 1998) pp. 179-193.

J.W. de Zwaan, 'The legal personality of the European Communities and the European Union', XXX *NYIL* (1999) pp. 75-113.

J.W. de Zwaan, 'Het Verdrag van Amsterdam, Etappe in het proces van Europese Integratie', 74 *NJB* (1999) pp. 492-500.

J.W. de Zwaan, 'Het Verdrag van Nice, Een bescheiden stap in het proces van Europese Integratie', 49 *SEW* (2001) pp. 42-52.

M. Zwanenburg, 'Regional Organisations and Maintenance of International Peace and Security: Three Recent Regional African Peace Operations', 11 *Journal of Conflict and Security Law* (2006) pp. 483-508.

3. KEY DOCUMENTS

Directory of European Council Presidency Conclusions (1993-), Council documents, international agreements, texts adopted in the area of the CFSP and the ESDP
<http://www.consilium.europa.eu/docCenter.asp?lang=en&cmsid=245>

Directory of EU treaties, legislation, case law and legislative proposals
<http://eur-lex.europa.eu/en/index.htm>

Bulletin of the European Union (1996-)
<http://europa.eu/bulletin/en/welcome.htm>

Homepage of the SG/HR CFSP, including ESS, EU operations, Special Representatives
<http://www.consilium.europa.eu/cms3_applications/applications/solana/index.asp?lang=EN&cmsid=358>

Enlargement website of the European Commission
<http://ec.europa.eu/enlargement/index_en.htm>

European Parliament, Register of documents
<http://www.europarl.europa.eu/registre/recherche/RechercheSimplifiee.cfm>

European Court of Justice
<http://curia.europa.eu/>

UN Charter
<http://www.un.org/aboutun/charter/>

Official Document System of the United Nations (ODS)
<http://www.un.org/documents/>

NATO Basic Texts, including The Washington Treaty (1949)
<http://www.nato.int/docu/basics.htm>

WEU Modified Brussels Treaty (1954)
<http://www.weu.int/Treaty.htm>

CSCE/OSCE Documents Library
<http://www.osce.org/documents/>

Council of Europe treaties, judgments of the European Court of Human Rights, PACE documents, etc.
<http://www.coe.int/>

Venice Commission (CoE), documents by country
<http://www.venice.coe.int/site/dynamics/N_Country_ef.asp>

International Crisis Group, including reports on the Western Balkans
<http://www.crisisgroup.org/home/index.cfm?id=1162&l=1>

Media with a specific focus on the Western Balkans
<http://www.setimes.com/>
<http://www.seeurope.net/>
<http://www.dtt-net.com/en/>
<http://www.b92.net/eng/>
<http://www.euractiv.com/en/enlargement/>
<http://euobserver.com/15>

INDEX

FSC
www.fsc.org
MIX
Papier | Fördert gute Waldnutzung
FSC® C083411

Kolibri 360 GmbH
Ferdinand-Jühlke-Straße 7
99095 Erfurt, Deutschland
produktsicherheit@kolibri360.de